CONTENTS

The BOYS™

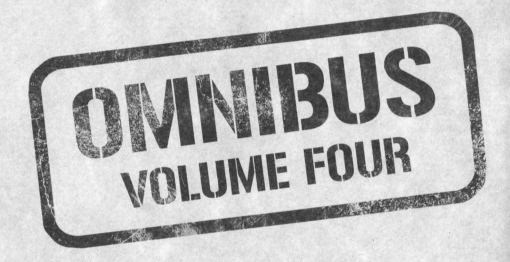

OMNIBUS
VOLUME FOUR

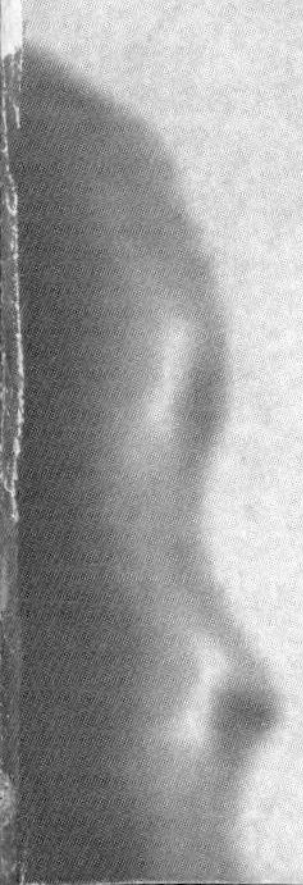

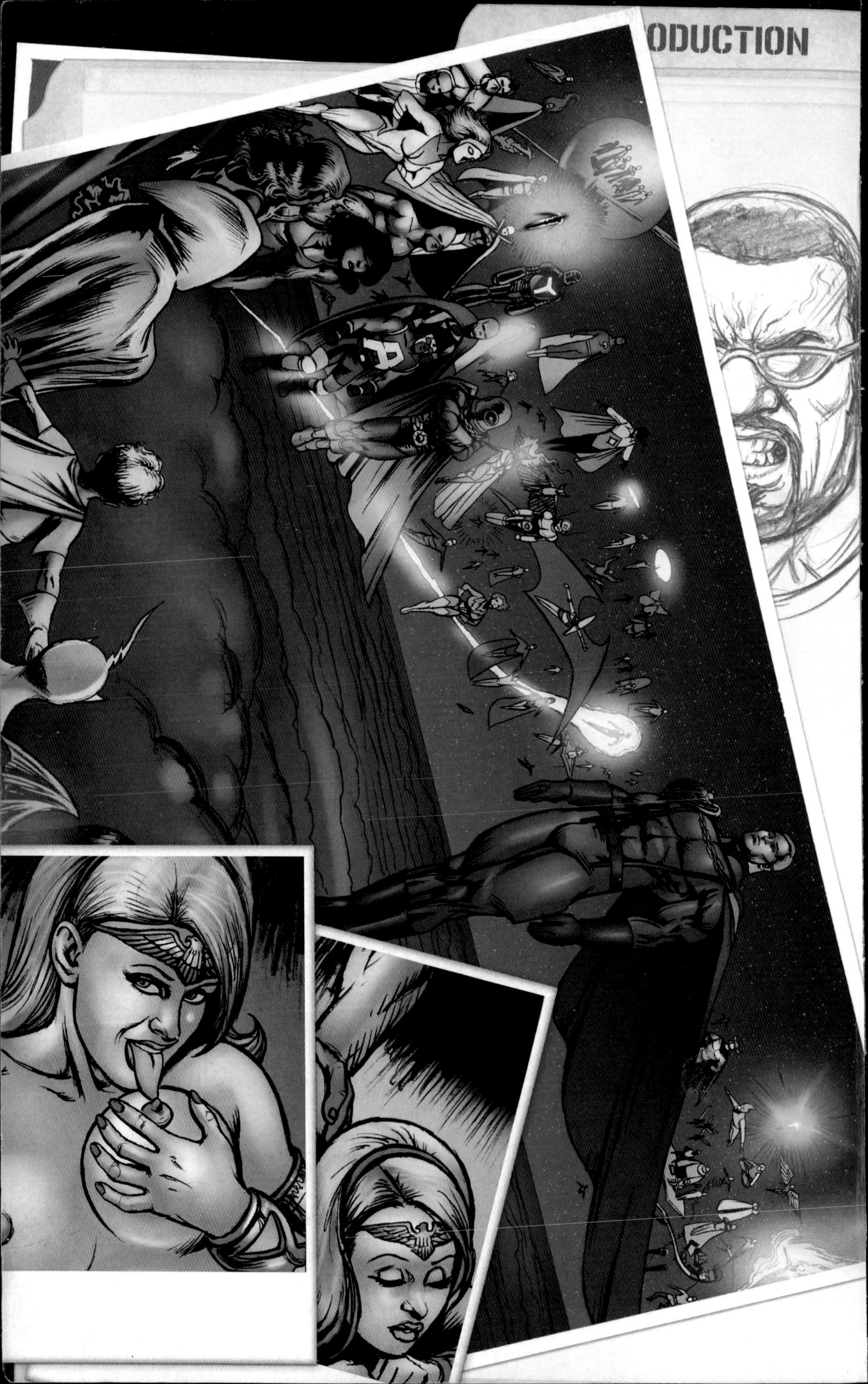
ODUCTION

CONTENTS

The BOYS

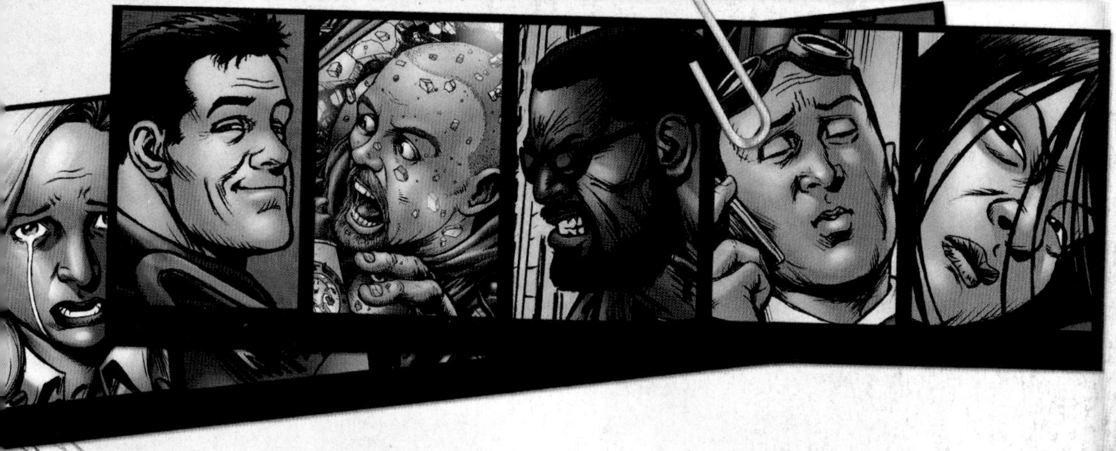

OMNIBUS VOLUME FOUR

The Boys created by: GARTH ENNIS & DARICK ROBERTSON

Written by:
GARTH ENNIS

Illustrated by:
JOHN McCREA w/ KEITH BURNS Highland Laddie #1-6
DARICK ROBERTSON The Boys #40-41
DARICK ROBERTSON w/ RICHARD P. CLARK The Boys #42-43
RUSS BRAUN The Boys #44-47

Additional inks by:
KEITH BURNS w/ JOHN McCREA Highland Laddie #1-6

Colored by:
TONY AVIÑA

Lettered by:
SIMON BOWLAND

Series covers by:
DARICK ROBERTSON & TONY AVIÑA

Book design by:
JASON ULLMEYER

Editor:
JOE RYBANDT

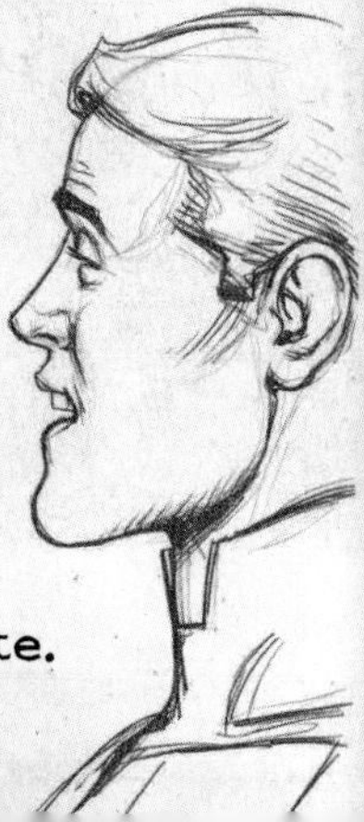

Collects issues one through six of The Boys: Highland Laddie and thirty-nine through fourty-seven of The Boys published by Dynamite.

DYNAMITE®

Nick Barrucci, CEO / Publisher

Juan Collado, President / COO

Brandon Dante Primavera, V.P. of IT and Operations

Joe Rybandt, Executive Editor

Matt Idelson, Senior Editor

Kevin Ketner, Editor

Cathleen Heard, Senior Graphic Designer

Rachel Kilbury, Digital Multimedia Assistant

Alexis Persson, Graphic Designer

Katie Hidalgo, Graphic Designer

Alan Payne, V.P. of Sales and Marketing

Rex Wang, Director of Consumer Sales

Pat O'Connell, Sales Manager

Vincent Faust, Marketing Coordinator

Jay Spence, Director of Product Development

Mariano Nicieza, Director of Research & Development

Amy Jackson, Administrative Coordinator

www.DYNAMITE.com

Facebook: /Dynamitecomics

Instagram: /Dynamitecomics

Twitter: @dynamitecomics

Standard ISBN: 978-1-5241-1140-3

Media Tie-In ISBN: 978-1-5241-1357-5

First Printing   10 9 8 7 6 5 4 3 2 1

Printed in Canada

For information regarding press, media rights, foreign rights, licensing, promotions, and advertising e-mail: marketing@dynamite.com

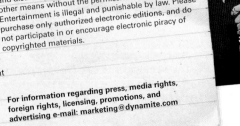

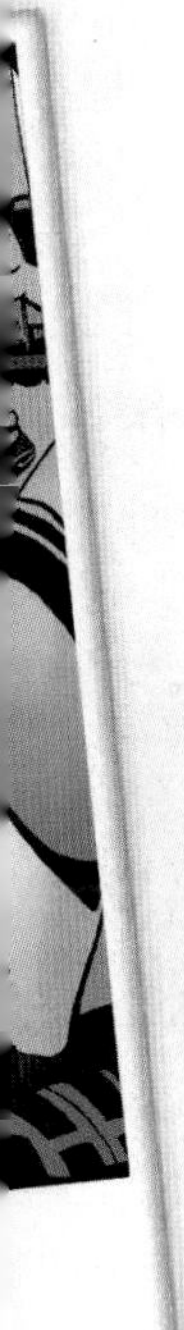

CONTENTS

BONUS MATERIALS

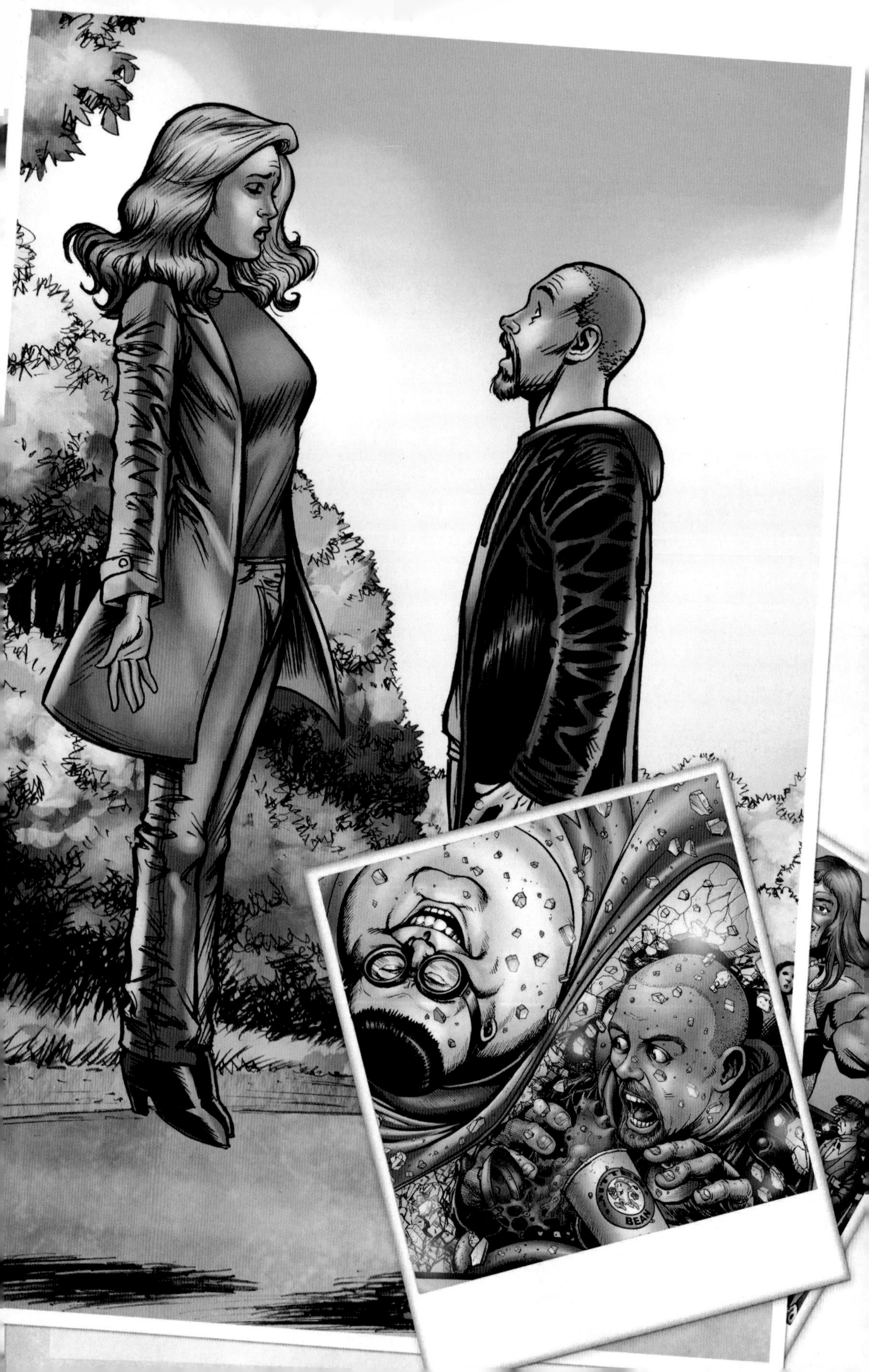
BEAN

CONTENTS

The BOYS

Before *The Boys*, and before my time here at Dynamite Entertainment, there was simply the work of a writer I liked. That writer was, of course, Garth Ennis. It started with his run on *Hellblazer*, flowed into his pitch-perfect collaboration with Steve Dillon on *Preacher* and continues to this day. Like so many of you, Garth joined the ranks of writers whose work I would always put to the front of the list. Writers like Neil Gaiman, Warren Ellis, Grant Morrison and Alan Moore. Writers who took the medium of comics, and used it in new and exciting ways. Writers who had something to say, and said it very, very well.

Coming into this position at Dynamite has afforded me the unique opportunity of working with both writers and artists I've always admired. Some from the comics of my youth and some from my current tastes. But more than just working with others, there's also all manner of relationships formed. When you're in the literal and metaphorical trenches of comic book production, you figure out pretty fast who you're hanging with. You figure out the guy that's gonna help make the time pass nice and easy while the shit is flying all around, up and down. Garth's one of those guys for sure and I think that's a big part of his popularity. His fans know he's one of those guys. It's just there, it comes out in the work, his appearances, etc. They just KNOW.

Now, I don't have a tremendous amount of insight into the volume you hold in your hand. The work certainly speaks for itself and the tedium of print production would not a sparkling introduction make. The work flowed like a tap from Garth and was put into the hands of his able artist collaborators: Darick Robertson, Russ Braun, John McCrea and Keith Burns, finished by colorist Tony Avina and letterer Simon Bowland. All ran like a finely tuned machine... albeit a machine that chews up chunks of bone and human spirit and puts out a dark, grisly mass... such is the world of *The Boys*, right? But underneath the blood and guts, there's real heart. Intact and pumping even. There's real meaning, real examination of the human goddamn condition, isn't there? It's a love story for fucks sake, who saw that coming? Granted, a love story written by a man who likes to explore the depths and well as the heights. Such is the world of *The Boys*...

The volume in your hand, and the stories it contains ("The Innocents", "Believe" and "Highland Laddie") cover the range of emotions expressed in the totality of the work itself - the sweetness and the light and the bitter and dark - but it's never mean spirited, even when it's taking the ultimate piss out of the four color world of super heroes. I mean, who can't find SOMEONE to love in SUPERDUPER, as pathetic and ridiculous as they are? Sure, it's HORRIBLE in large degrees, but there's a reason for that. And that's where Garth remains the master of his path in comics: there's a lot of horror, but there's always a point.

So, as we head into the tail end of the last year of regular production on the book, I look back on the last six years of *The Boys* and it's nothing but sweetness and light. Thanks to Garth and the team for all the good, hard work and patience and after all this time in the business it's nice to find a new guy for the trenches now and again.

Cheers.
Joe Rybandt
Mt. Laurel, NJ
June 25, 2012 (for *The Boys Definitive Edition Vol. 4*)

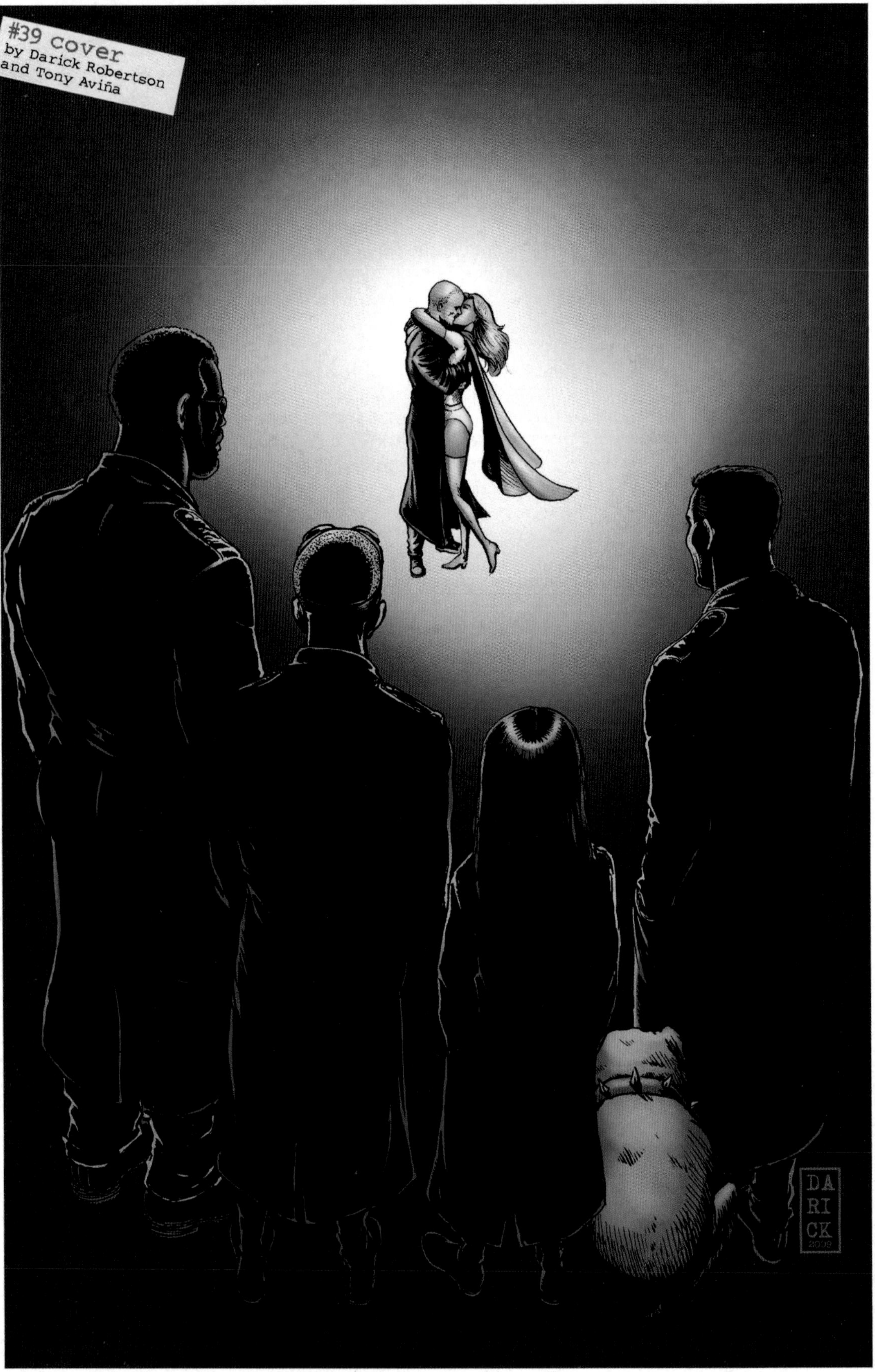
DA
RI
CK
2009

#39 cover
by Darick Robertson
and Tony Aviña

PROLOGUE

WHAT I KNOW

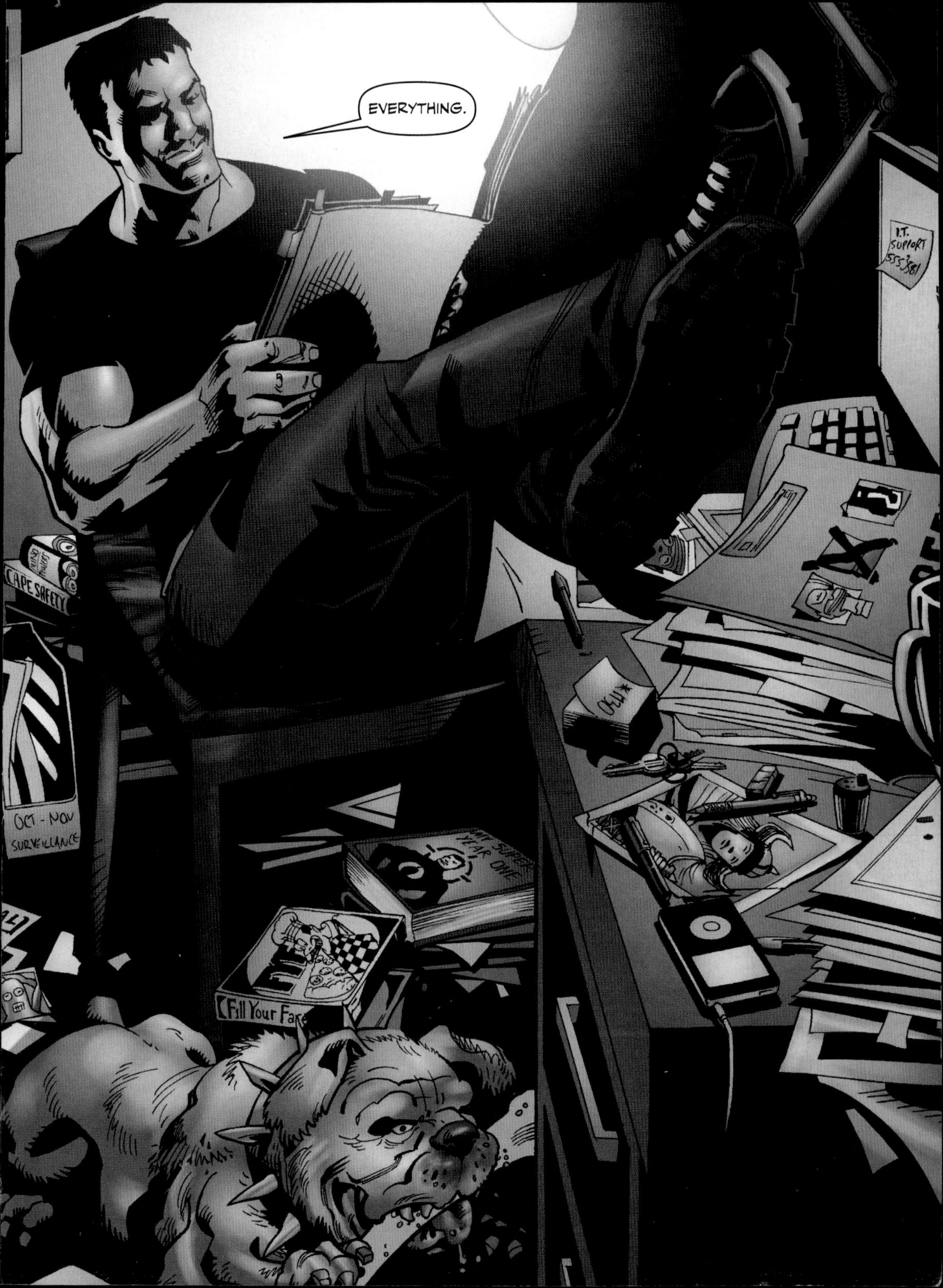
EVERYTHING.
I.T. SUPPORT
CAPE SAFETY
OCT - NOV
SURVEILLANCE
YEAR ONE
Fill Your Face

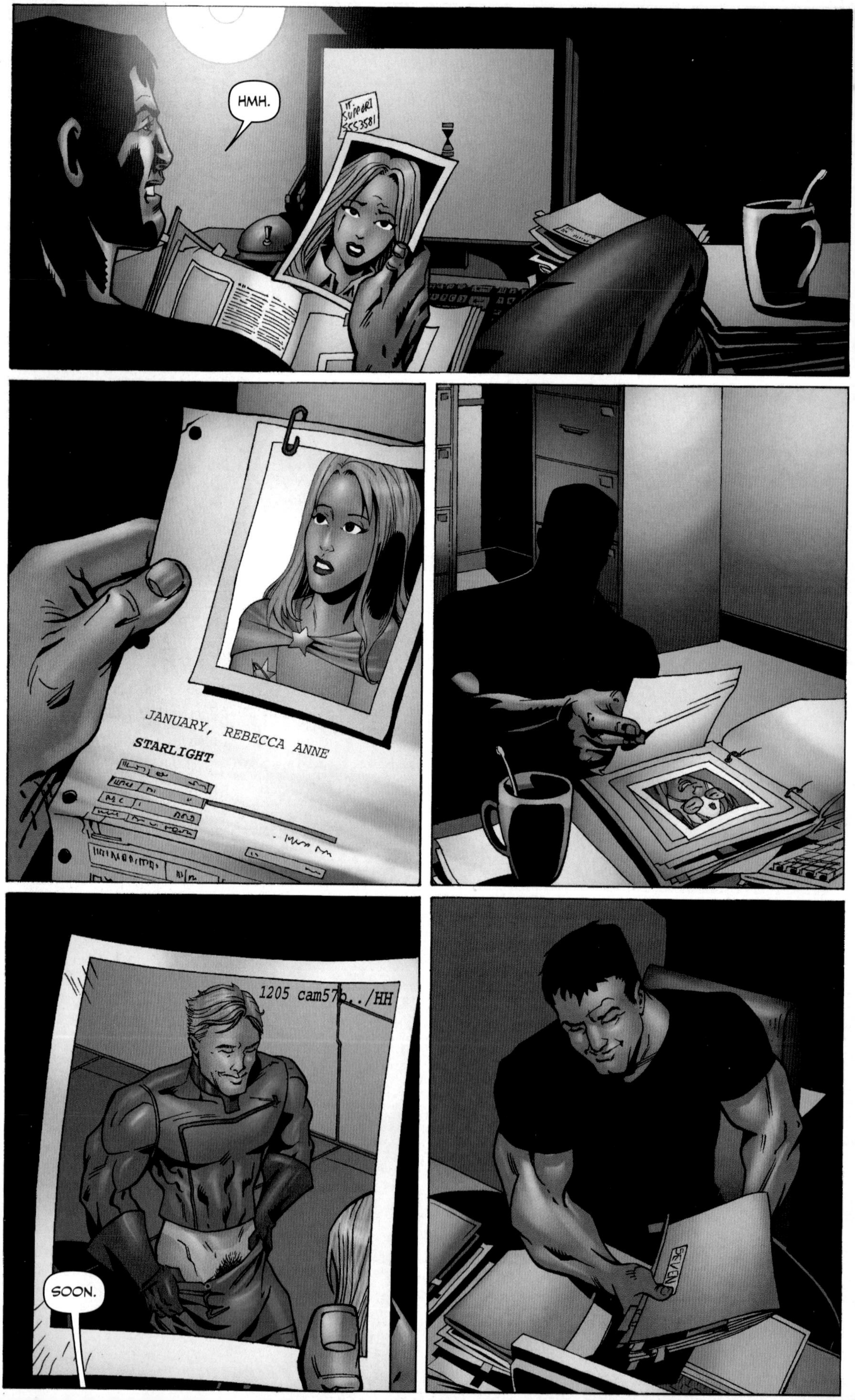
HMH.
JANUARY, REBECCA ANNE
STARLIGHT
1205 cam57b../HH
SOON.
SEVEN

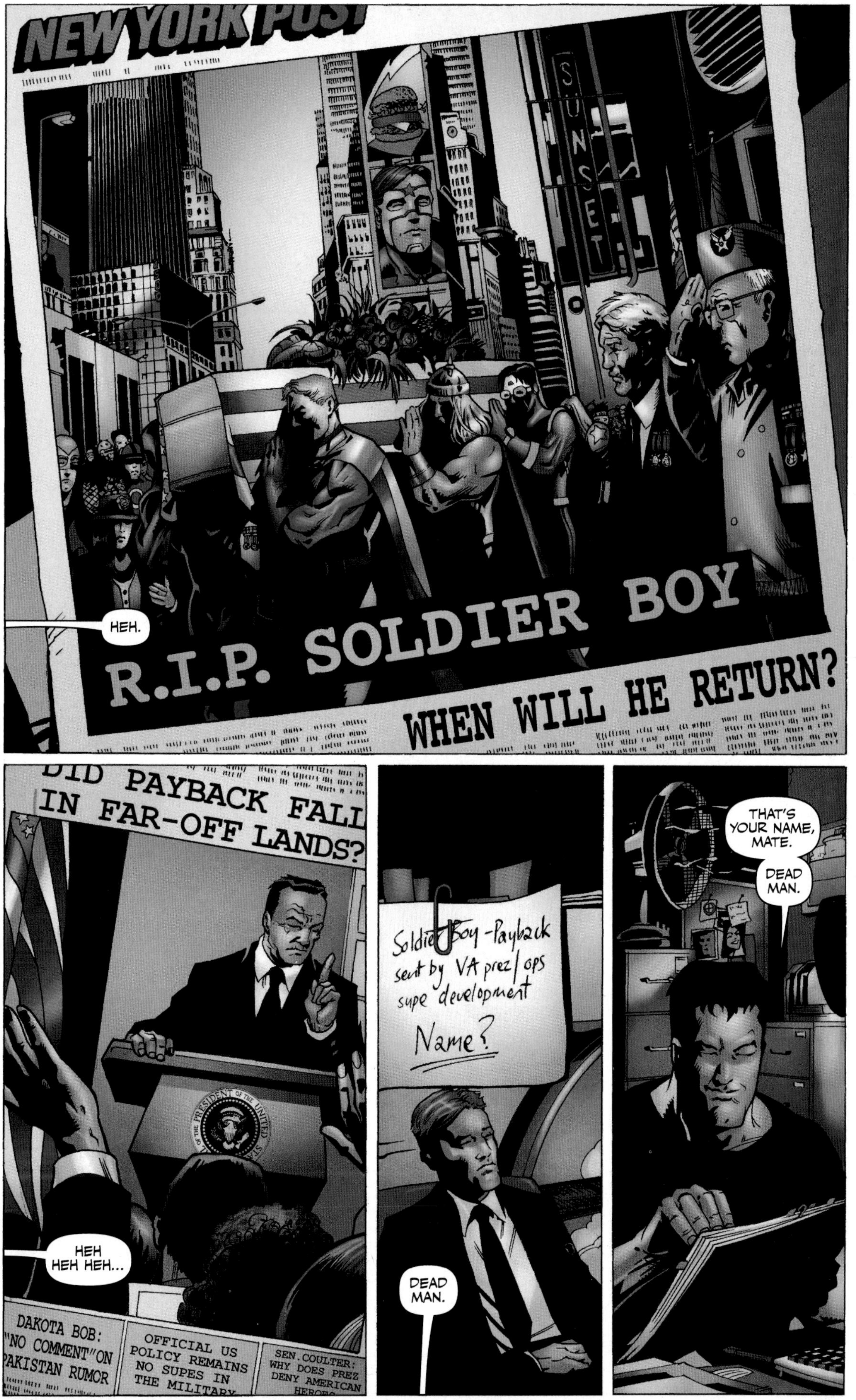

NEW YORK POST
HEH.
R.I.P. SOLDIER BOY
WHEN WILL HE RETURN?
DID PAYBACK FALL IN FAR-OFF LANDS?
HEH HEH HEH...
DAKOTA BOB: "NO COMMENT" ON PAKISTAN RUMOR
OFFICIAL US POLICY REMAINS NO SUPES IN THE MILITARY
SEN. COULTER: WHY DOES PREZ DENY AMERICAN
Soldier Boy - Payback sent by VA prez/ops supe development
Name?
DEAD MAN.
THAT'S YOUR NAME, MATE.
DEAD MAN.

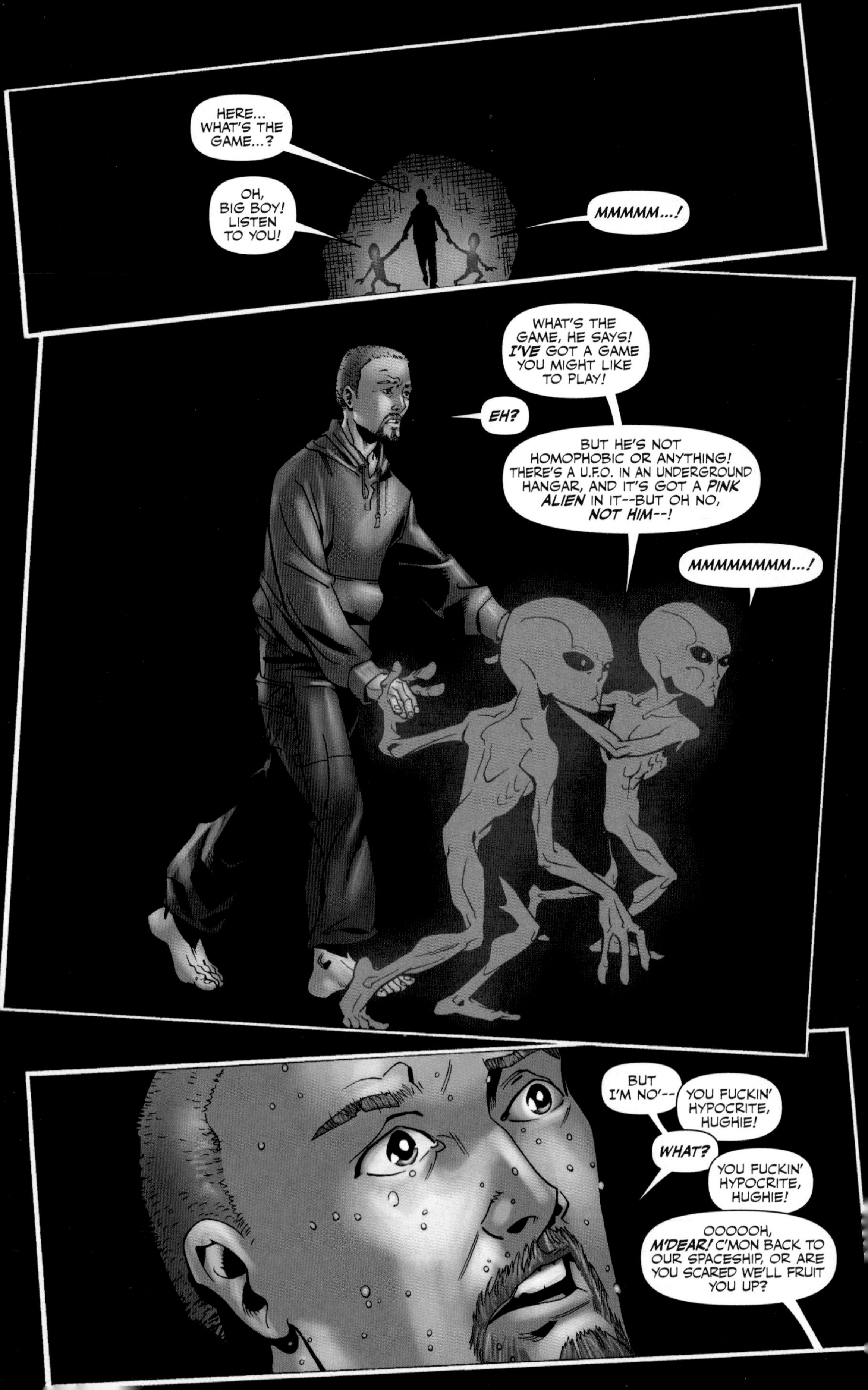
HERE... WHAT'S THE GAME...?
OH, BIG BOY! LISTEN TO YOU!
MMMMM...!
WHAT'S THE GAME, HE SAYS! I'VE GOT A GAME YOU MIGHT LIKE TO PLAY!
EH?
BUT HE'S NOT HOMOPHOBIC OR ANYTHING! THERE'S A U.F.O. IN AN UNDERGROUND HANGAR, AND IT'S GOT A PINK ALIEN IN IT--BUT OH NO, NOT HIM--!
MMMMMMMM...!
BUT I'M NO'--
YOU FUCKIN' HYPOCRITE, HUGHIE!
WHAT?
YOU FUCKIN' HYPOCRITE, HUGHIE!
OOOOOH, M'DEAR! C'MON BACK TO OUR SPACESHIP, OR ARE YOU SCARED WE'LL FRUIT YOU UP?

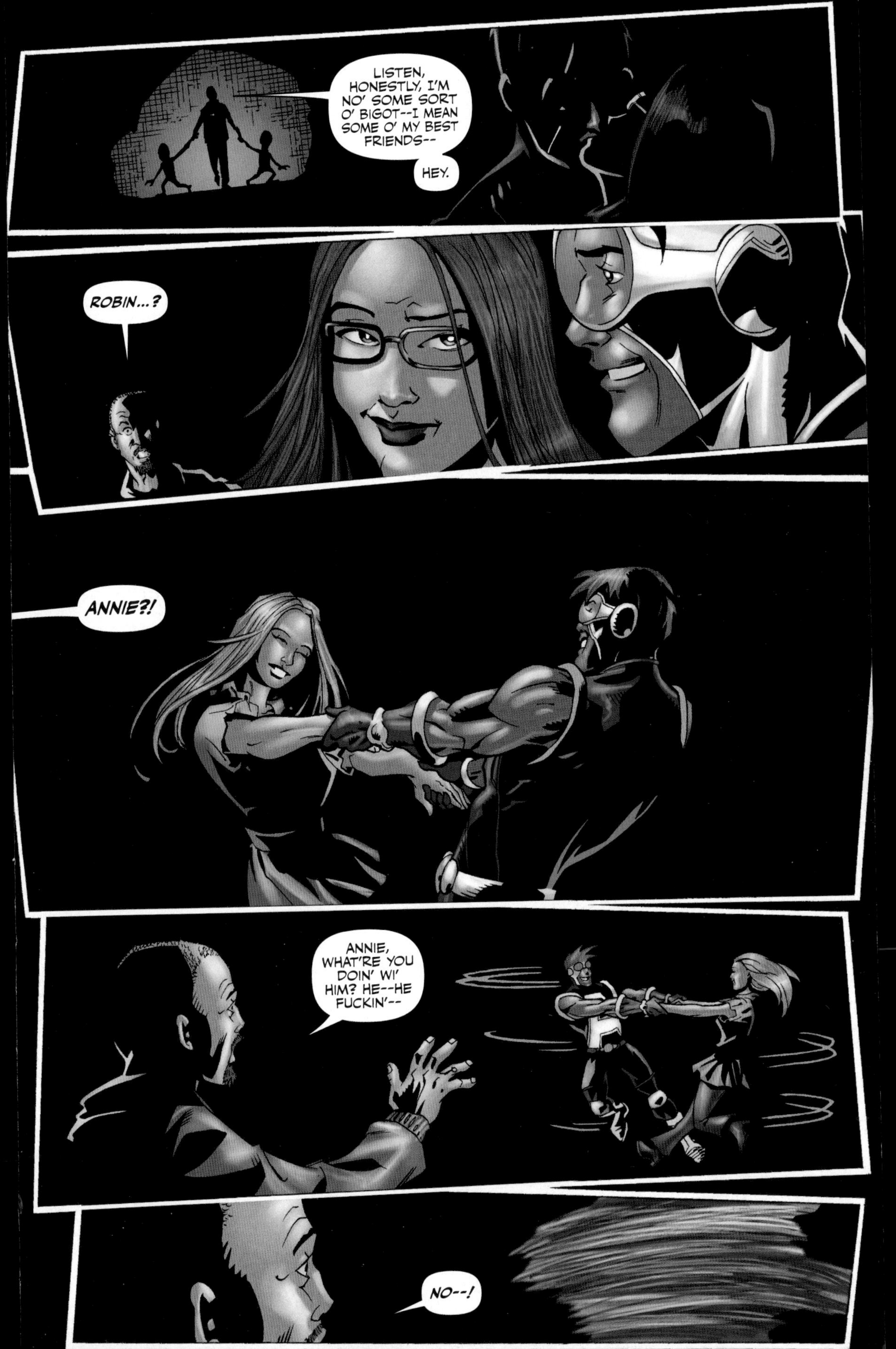
LISTEN, HONESTLY, I'M NO' SOME SORT O' BIGOT--I MEAN SOME O' MY BEST FRIENDS--
HEY.
ROBIN...?
ANNIE?!
ANNIE, WHAT'RE YOU DOIN' WI' HIM? HE--HE FUCKIN'--
NO--!

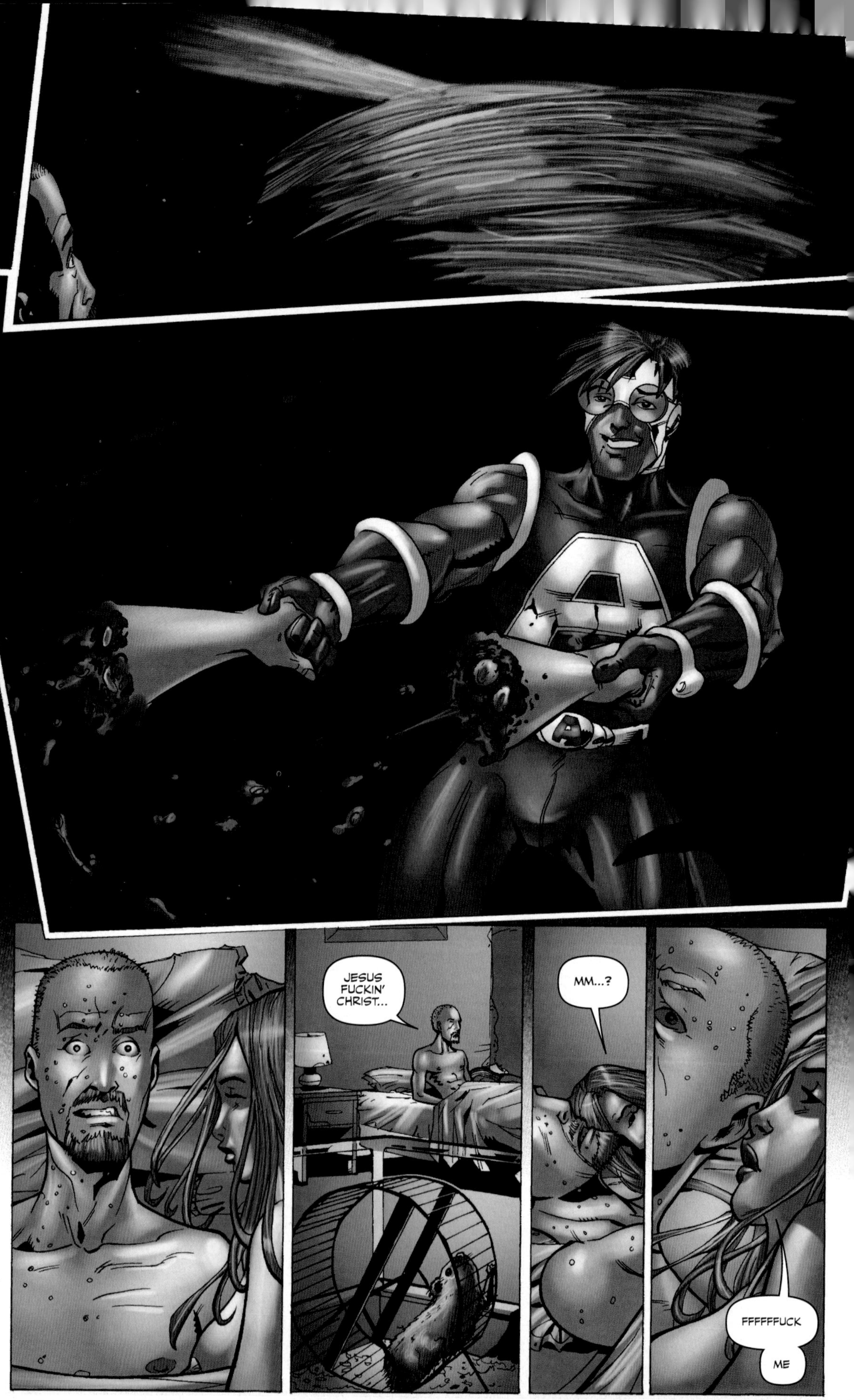
JESUS FUCKIN' CHRIST...
MM...?
FFFFFFUCK
ME

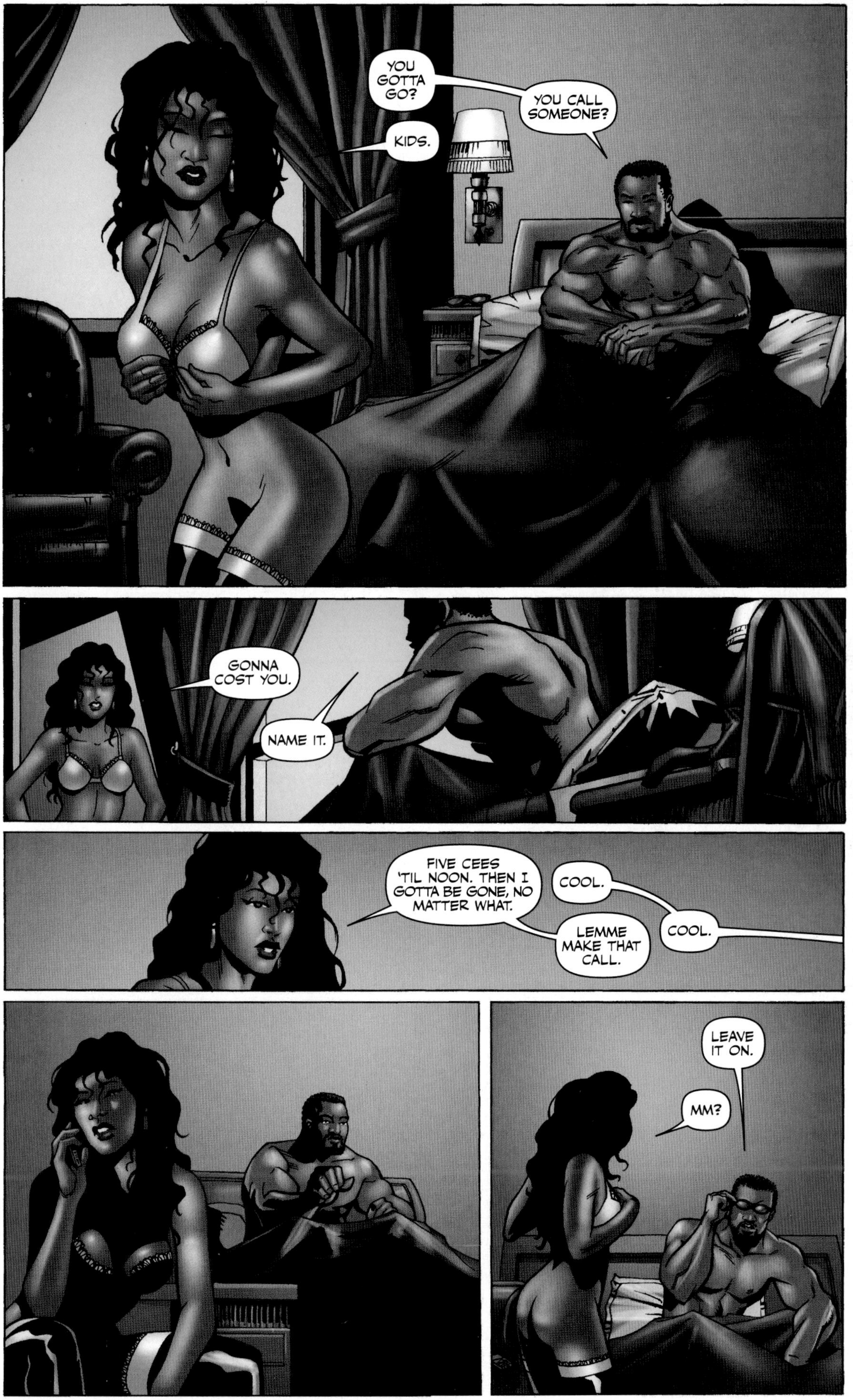
YOU GOTTA GO?
KIDS.
YOU CALL SOMEONE?
GONNA COST YOU.
NAME IT.
FIVE CEES 'TIL NOON. THEN I GOTTA BE GONE, NO MATTER WHAT.
COOL.
LEMME MAKE THAT CALL.
COOL.
LEAVE IT ON.
MM?

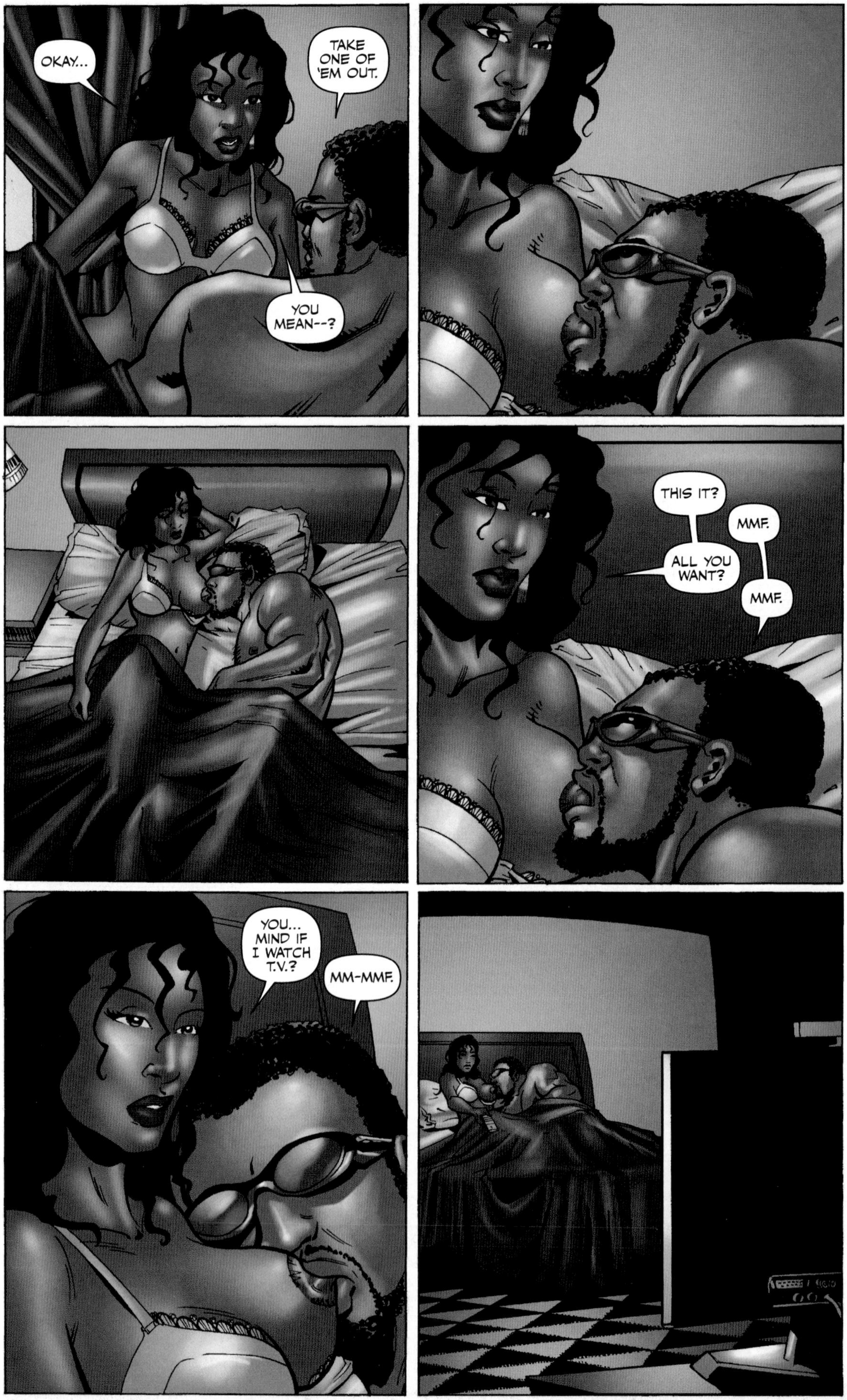
OKAY...
TAKE ONE OF 'EM OUT.
YOU MEAN--?
THIS IT?
ALL YOU WANT?
MMF.
MMF.
YOU... MIND IF I WATCH T.V.?
MM-MMF.

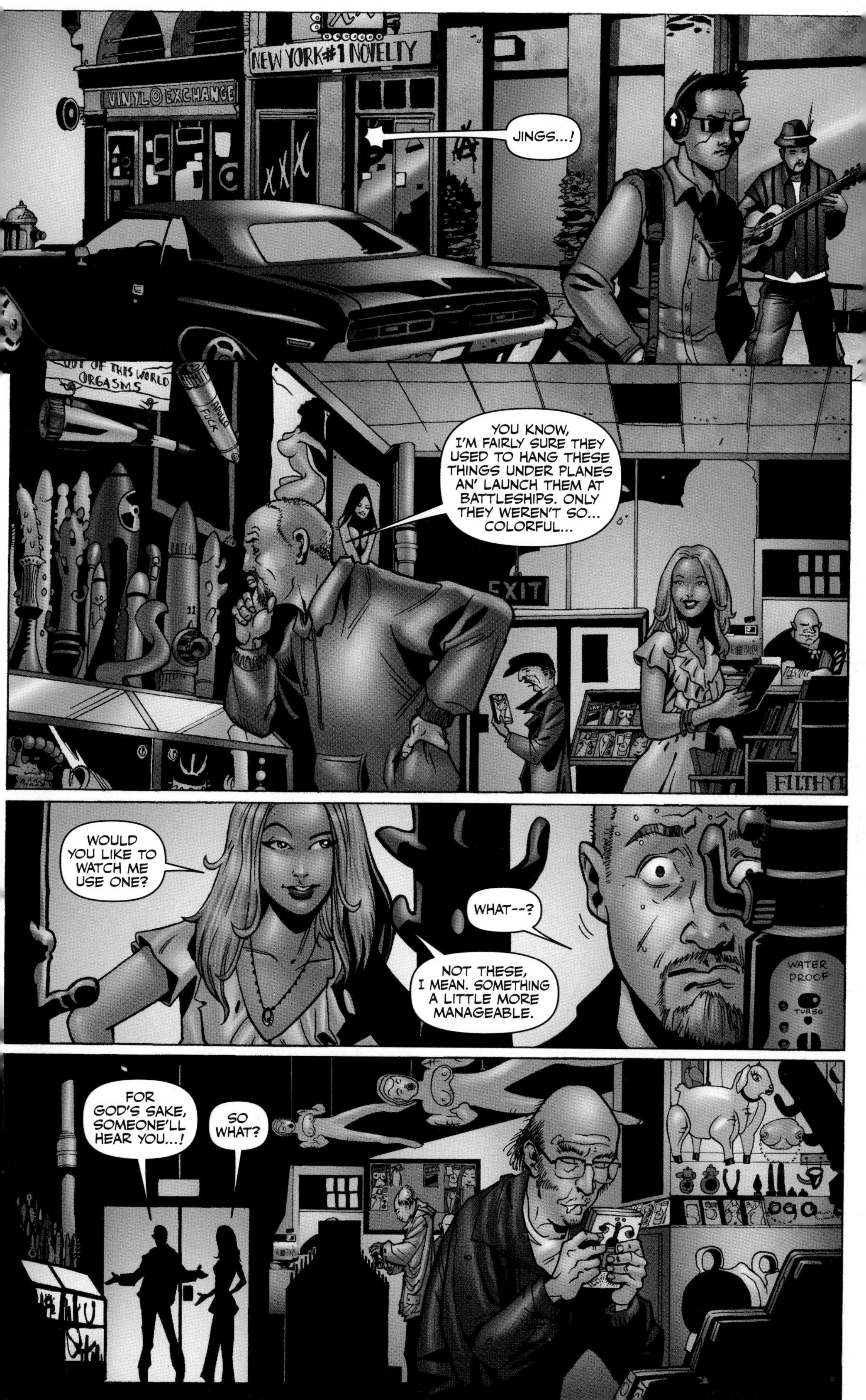
VINYL EXCHANGE
NEW YORK #1 NOVELTY
XXX
JINGS...!
OUT OF THIS WORLD ORGASMS
APOLLO FUCK
YOU KNOW, I'M FAIRLY SURE THEY USED TO HANG THESE THINGS UNDER PLANES AN' LAUNCH THEM AT BATTLESHIPS. ONLY THEY WEREN'T SO... COLORFUL...
EXIT
FILTHY
WOULD YOU LIKE TO WATCH ME USE ONE?
WHAT--?
NOT THESE, I MEAN. SOMETHING A LITTLE MORE MANAGEABLE.
WATER PROOF
TURBO
FOR GOD'S SAKE, SOMEONE'LL HEAR YOU...!
SO WHAT?

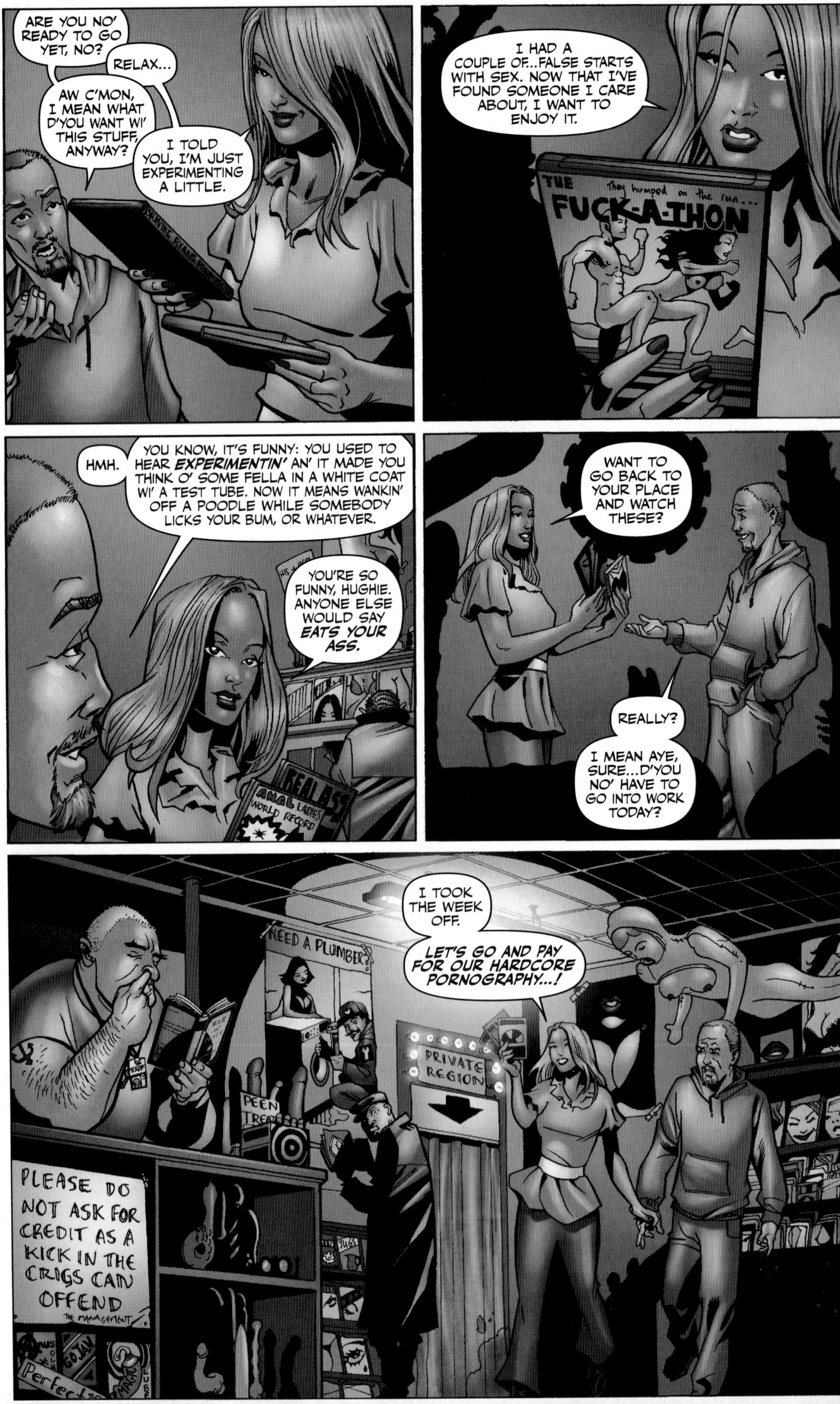
ARE YOU NO' READY TO GO YET, NO?
RELAX...
AW C'MON, I MEAN WHAT D'YOU WANT WI' THIS STUFF, ANYWAY?
I TOLD YOU, I'M JUST EXPERIMENTING A LITTLE.
I HAD A COUPLE OF...FALSE STARTS WITH SEX. NOW THAT I'VE FOUND SOMEONE I CARE ABOUT, I WANT TO ENJOY IT.
THE
They humped on the sun...
FUCK-A-THON
HMH.
YOU KNOW, IT'S FUNNY: YOU USED TO HEAR *EXPERIMENTIN'* AN' IT MADE YOU THINK O' SOME FELLA IN A WHITE COAT WI' A TEST TUBE. NOW IT MEANS WANKIN' OFF A POODLE WHILE SOMEBODY LICKS YOUR BUM, OR WHATEVER.
YOU'RE SO FUNNY, HUGHIE. ANYONE ELSE WOULD SAY *EATS YOUR ASS.*
REAL ASS
ANAL LADIES WORLD RECORD
WANT TO GO BACK TO YOUR PLACE AND WATCH THESE?
REALLY?
I MEAN AYE, SURE...D'YOU NO' HAVE TO GO INTO WORK TODAY?
I TOOK THE WEEK OFF.
LET'S GO AND PAY FOR OUR HARDCORE PORNOGRAPHY...!
NEED A PLUMBER
PRIVATE REGION
PEEN
PLEASE DO NOT ASK FOR CREDIT AS A KICK IN THE CRIGS CAN OFFEND
THE MANAGEMENT

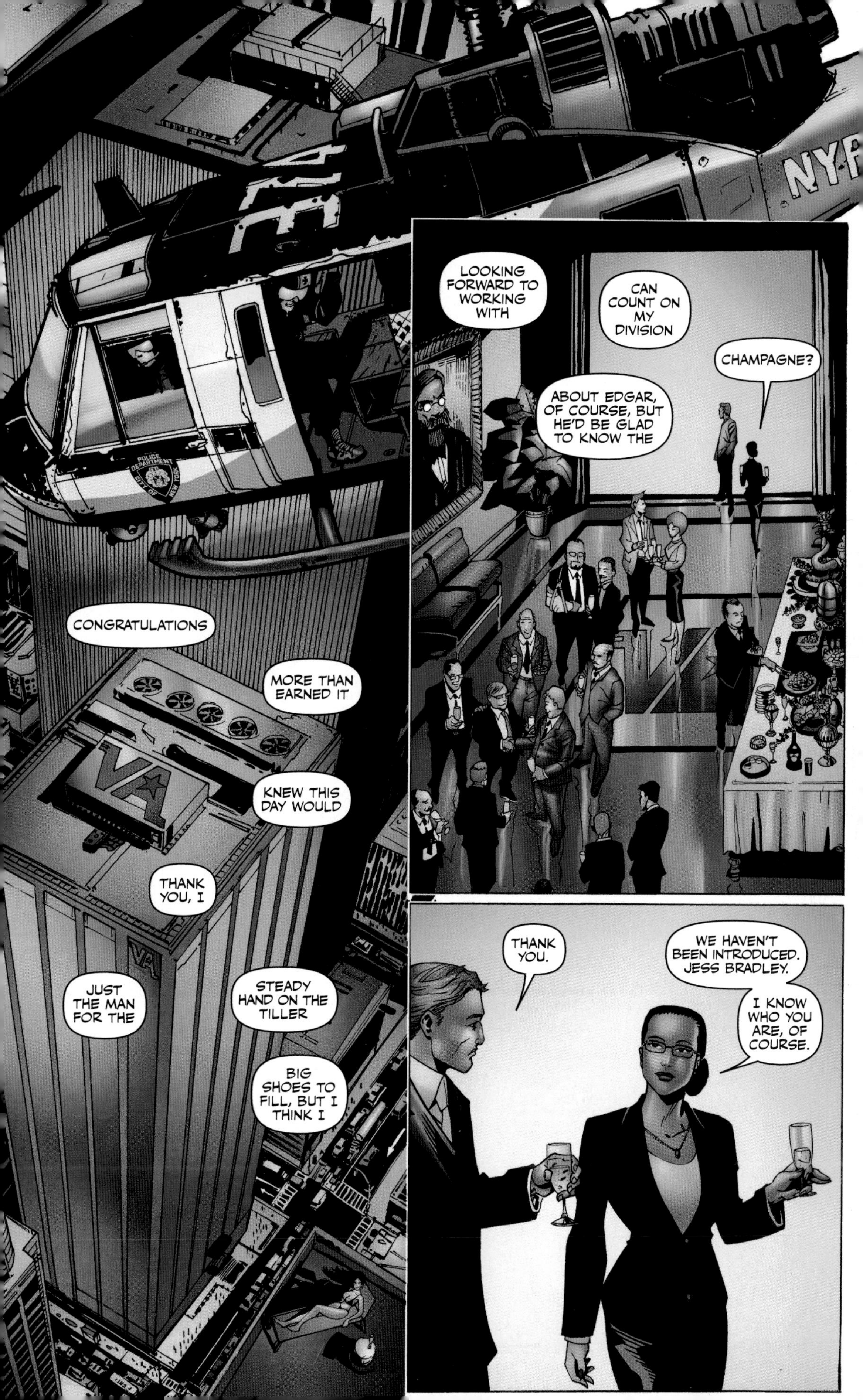
NYP
CONGRATULATIONS
MORE THAN EARNED IT
VA
KNEW THIS DAY WOULD
THANK YOU, I
JUST THE MAN FOR THE
STEADY HAND ON THE TILLER
BIG SHOES TO FILL, BUT I THINK I
LOOKING FORWARD TO WORKING WITH
CAN COUNT ON MY DIVISION
CHAMPAGNE?
ABOUT EDGAR, OF COURSE, BUT HE'D BE GLAD TO KNOW THE
THANK YOU.
WE HAVEN'T BEEN INTRODUCED. JESS BRADLEY.
I KNOW WHO YOU ARE, OF COURSE.

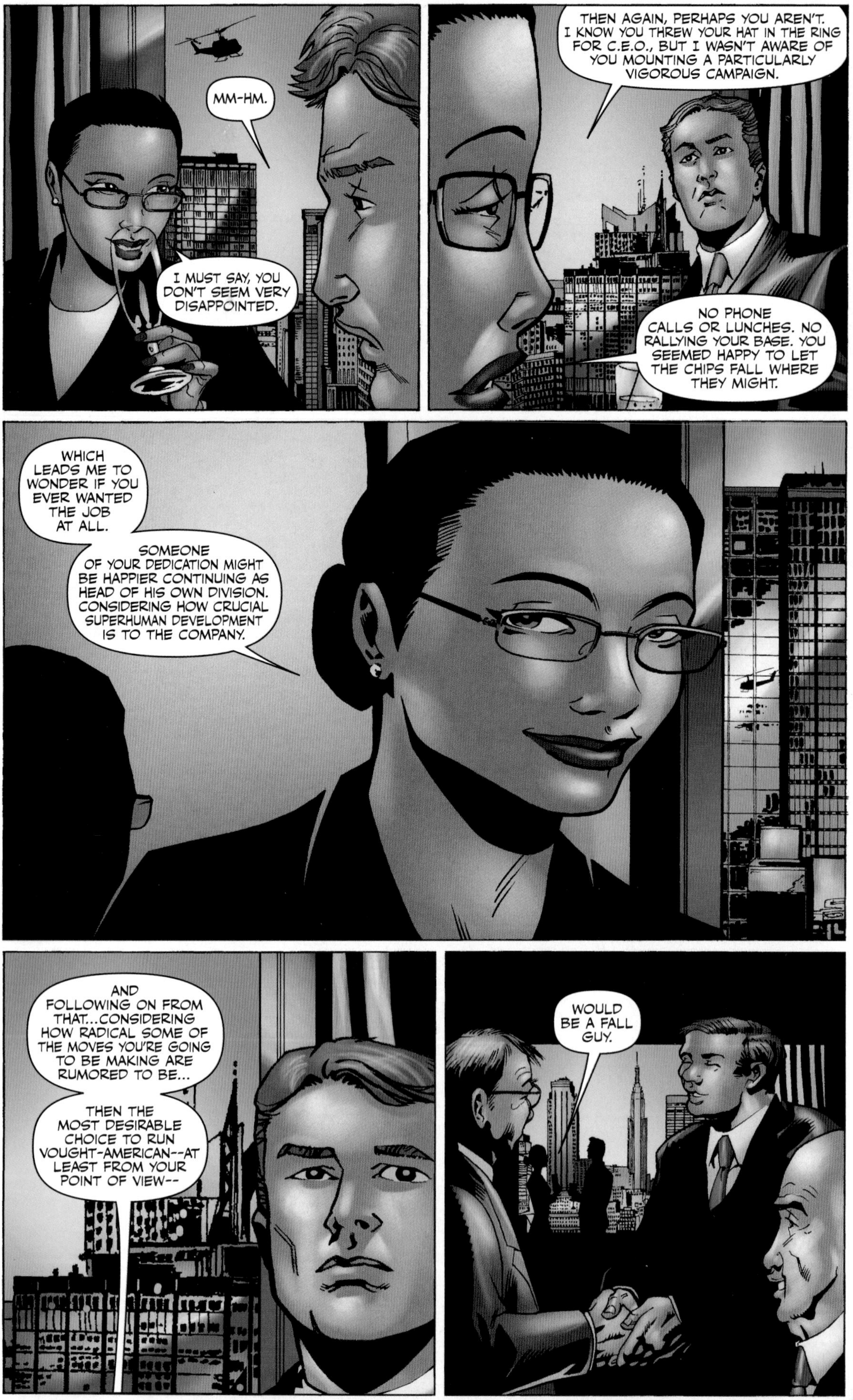
MM-HM.
I MUST SAY, YOU DON'T SEEM VERY DISAPPOINTED.
THEN AGAIN, PERHAPS YOU AREN'T. I KNOW YOU THREW YOUR HAT IN THE RING FOR C.E.O., BUT I WASN'T AWARE OF YOU MOUNTING A PARTICULARLY VIGOROUS CAMPAIGN.
NO PHONE CALLS OR LUNCHES. NO RALLYING YOUR BASE. YOU SEEMED HAPPY TO LET THE CHIPS FALL WHERE THEY MIGHT.
WHICH LEADS ME TO WONDER IF YOU EVER WANTED THE JOB AT ALL.
SOMEONE OF YOUR DEDICATION MIGHT BE HAPPIER CONTINUING AS HEAD OF HIS OWN DIVISION. CONSIDERING HOW CRUCIAL SUPERHUMAN DEVELOPMENT IS TO THE COMPANY.
AND FOLLOWING ON FROM THAT...CONSIDERING HOW RADICAL SOME OF THE MOVES YOU'RE GOING TO BE MAKING ARE RUMORED TO BE...
THEN THE MOST DESIRABLE CHOICE TO RUN VOUGHT-AMERICAN--AT LEAST FROM YOUR POINT OF VIEW--
WOULD BE A FALL GUY.

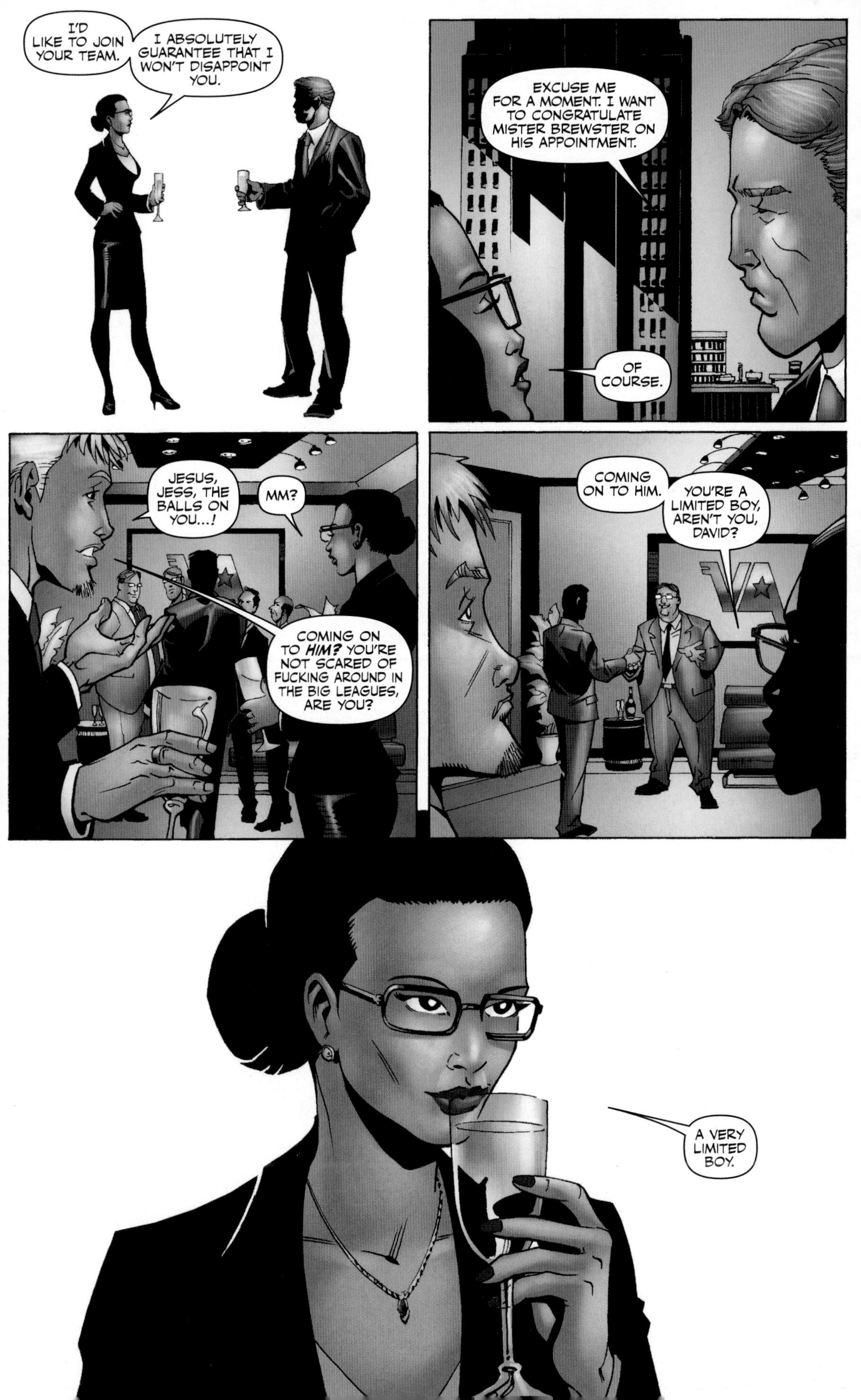
I'D LIKE TO JOIN YOUR TEAM.
I ABSOLUTELY GUARANTEE THAT I WON'T DISAPPOINT YOU.
EXCUSE ME FOR A MOMENT. I WANT TO CONGRATULATE MISTER BREWSTER ON HIS APPOINTMENT.
OF COURSE.
JESUS, JESS, THE BALLS ON YOU...!
MM?
COMING ON TO *HIM?* YOU'RE NOT SCARED OF FUCKING AROUND IN THE BIG LEAGUES, ARE YOU?
COMING ON TO HIM.
YOU'RE A LIMITED BOY, AREN'T YOU, DAVID?
A VERY LIMITED BOY.

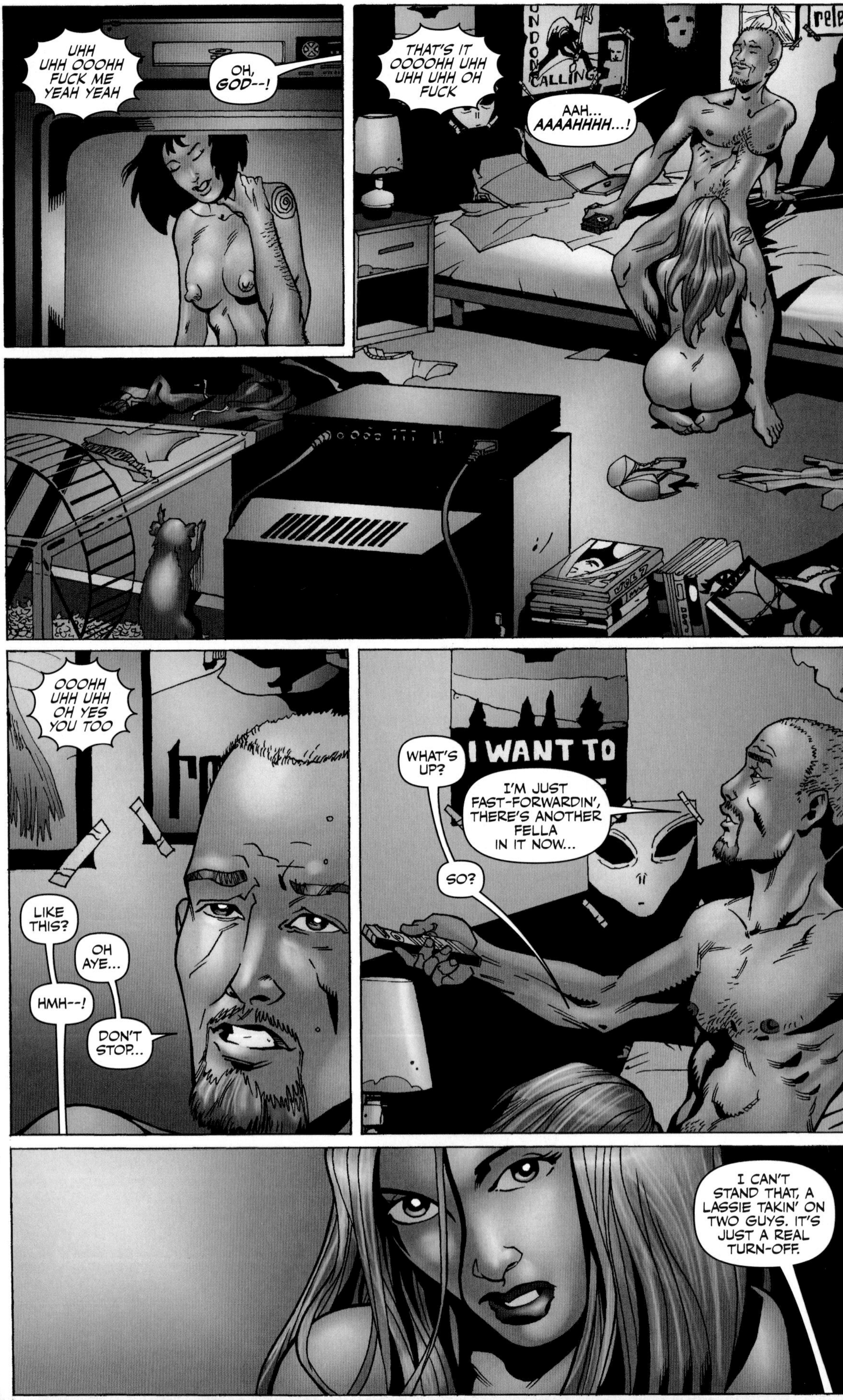
UHH UHH OOOHH FUCK ME YEAH YEAH
OH, GOD--!
THAT'S IT OOOOHH UHH UHH UHH OH FUCK
AAH... AAAAHHHH...!
OOOHH UHH UHH OH YES YOU TOO
LIKE THIS?
OH AYE...
HMH--!
DON'T STOP...
I WANT TO
WHAT'S UP?
I'M JUST FAST-FORWARDIN', THERE'S ANOTHER FELLA IN IT NOW...
SO?
I CAN'T STAND THAT, A LASSIE TAKIN' ON TWO GUYS. IT'S JUST A REAL TURN-OFF.

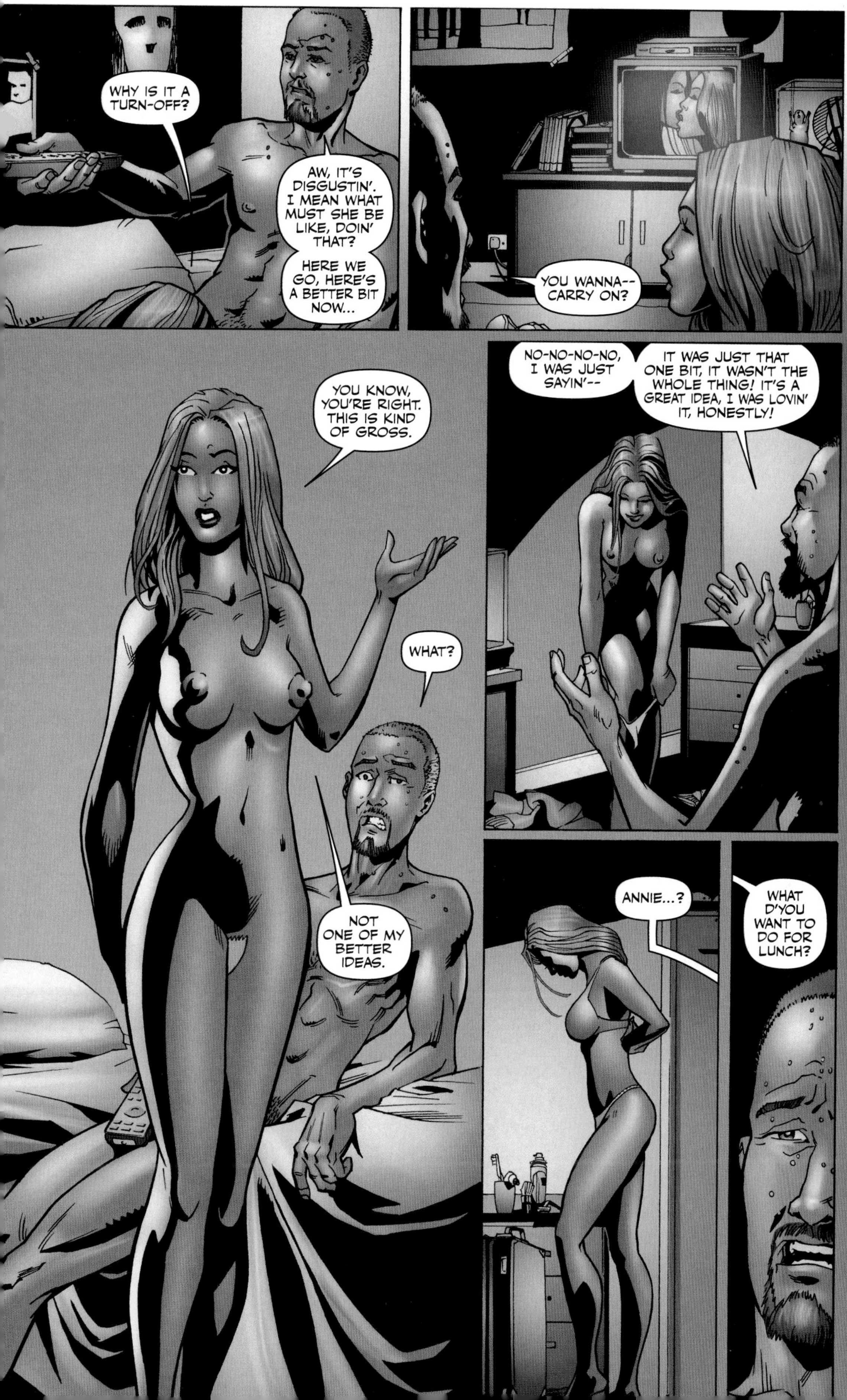
WHY IS IT A TURN-OFF?
AW, IT'S DISGUSTIN'. I MEAN WHAT MUST SHE BE LIKE, DOIN' THAT?
HERE WE GO, HERE'S A BETTER BIT NOW...
YOU WANNA-- CARRY ON?
YOU KNOW, YOU'RE RIGHT. THIS IS KIND OF GROSS.
WHAT?
NOT ONE OF MY BETTER IDEAS.
NO-NO-NO-NO, I WAS JUST SAYIN'--
IT WAS JUST THAT ONE BIT, IT WASN'T THE WHOLE THING! IT'S A GREAT IDEA, I WAS LOVIN' IT, HONESTLY!
ANNIE...?
WHAT D'YOU WANT TO DO FOR LUNCH?

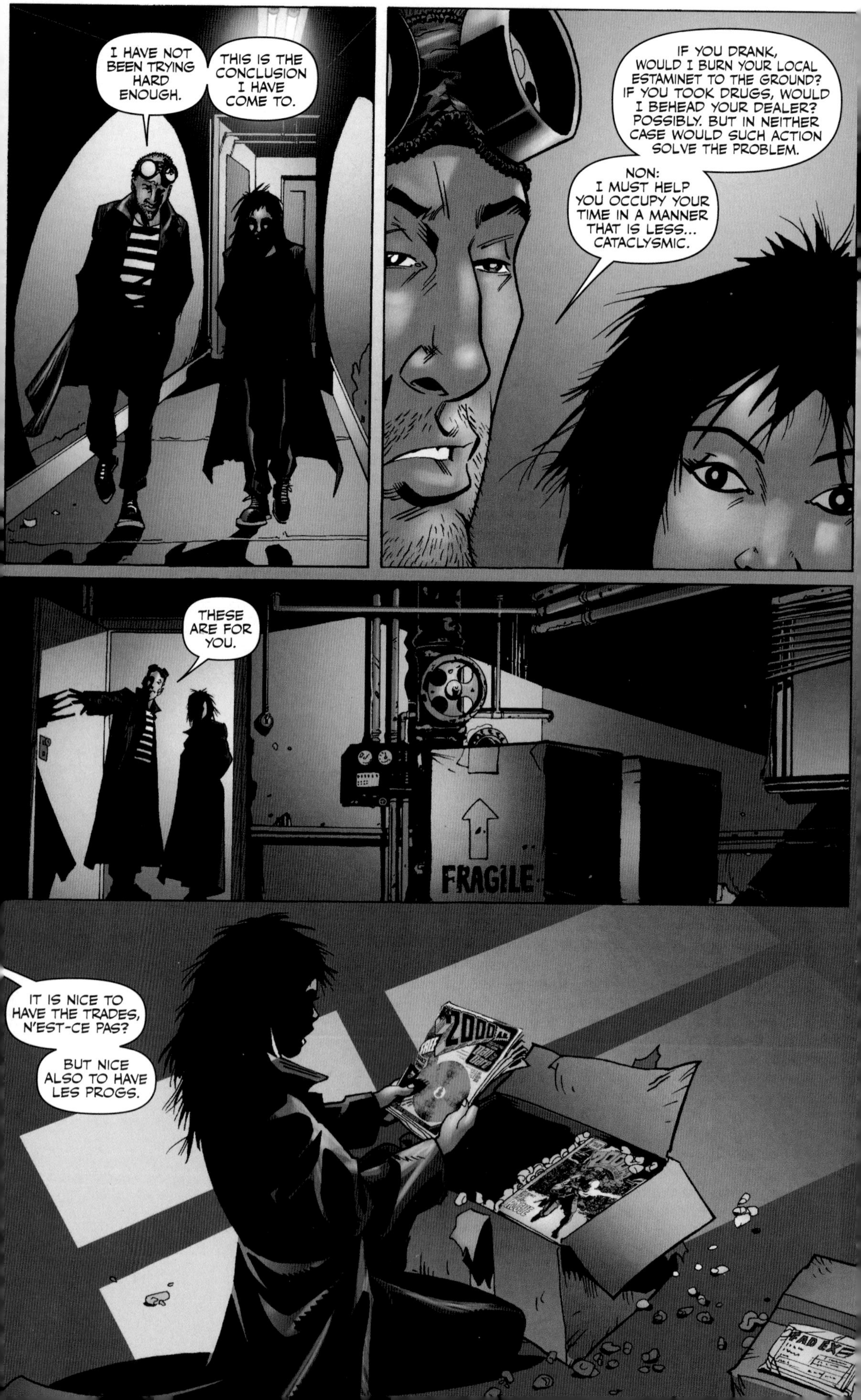
I HAVE NOT BEEN TRYING HARD ENOUGH.
THIS IS THE CONCLUSION I HAVE COME TO.
IF YOU DRANK, WOULD I BURN YOUR LOCAL ESTAMINET TO THE GROUND? IF YOU TOOK DRUGS, WOULD I BEHEAD YOUR DEALER? POSSIBLY. BUT IN NEITHER CASE WOULD SUCH ACTION SOLVE THE PROBLEM.
NON: I MUST HELP YOU OCCUPY YOUR TIME IN A MANNER THAT IS LESS... CATACLYSMIC.
THESE ARE FOR YOU.
FRAGILE
IT IS NICE TO HAVE THE TRADES, N'EST-CE PAS?
BUT NICE ALSO TO HAVE LES PROGS.
2000 AD

AFTER ALL, NO ONE WILL EVER REPRINT DEATH PLANET.

DE L'UN A CINQ-UN-NEUF. NEVER AGAIN SHALL I DOUBT THE POWER OF EBAY.

I WILL NOT GIVE UP ON YOU.

ENJOY.

SO WHAT'S THE SCORE?

SHE IS ENGROSSED.

ALAS, NOT PERMANENTLY.

MEANWHILE, THE WIRETAP ON HER PHONE COPIES ALL INCOMING MESSAGES TO MINE. THE BUG ENABLES ME TO MONITOR HER MOVEMENTS.

ALL YOU GOTTA DO IS BEAT HER TO IT, EH?

SHE WILL SEE NO NEED FOR URGENCY. SHOULD AN EMPLOYER REQUEST A MEETING, I WILL HAVE TIME TO REMONSTRATE WITH HIM.

SHOULD SHE BE REQUIRED TO MOVE DIRECTLY ON A TARGET, I CAN ENFORCE THEIR RAPID EMMIGRATION.

SIMPLE AS THAT...

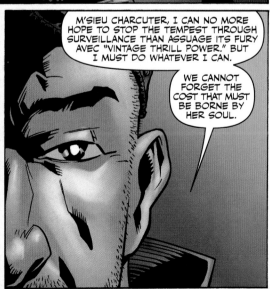

M'SIEU CHARCUTER, I CAN NO MORE HOPE TO STOP THE TEMPEST THROUGH SURVEILLANCE THAN ASSUAGE ITS FURY AVEC "VINTAGE THRILL POWER." BUT I MUST DO WHATEVER I CAN.

WE CANNOT FORGET THE COST THAT MUST BE BORNE BY HER SOUL.

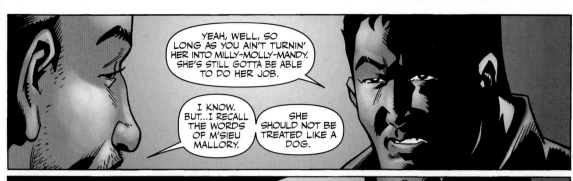

YEAH, WELL, SO LONG AS YOU AIN'T TURNIN' HER INTO MILLY-MOLLY-MANDY. SHE'S STILL GOTTA BE ABLE TO DO HER JOB.

I KNOW. BUT...I RECALL THE WORDS OF M'SIEU MALLORY.

SHE SHOULD NOT BE TREATED LIKE A DOG.

YEAH, D'YOU REMEMBER WHAT ELSE THE OL' MAN SAID? "THE LAMPLIGHTER'S A PUSSY, NO WAY HAS HE GOT THE BALLS FOR IT"? "DON'T WORRY, BOYS, A FORTY-FIVE HOLLOW POINT'LL STOP ANYONE"?

DON'T GO GETTIN' SENTIMENTAL ON ME, FRENCHIE.

RIGHT, I'VE RUN OUTTA TEABAGS, SO I'M NIPPIN' OUT FOR A BIT. YOU WANT ANYTHIN'?

NON. MERCI.

TERROR!

WUFF!

JE ME RAPPELE...IT'S NOT AN IT.

"SHE'S A SHE."

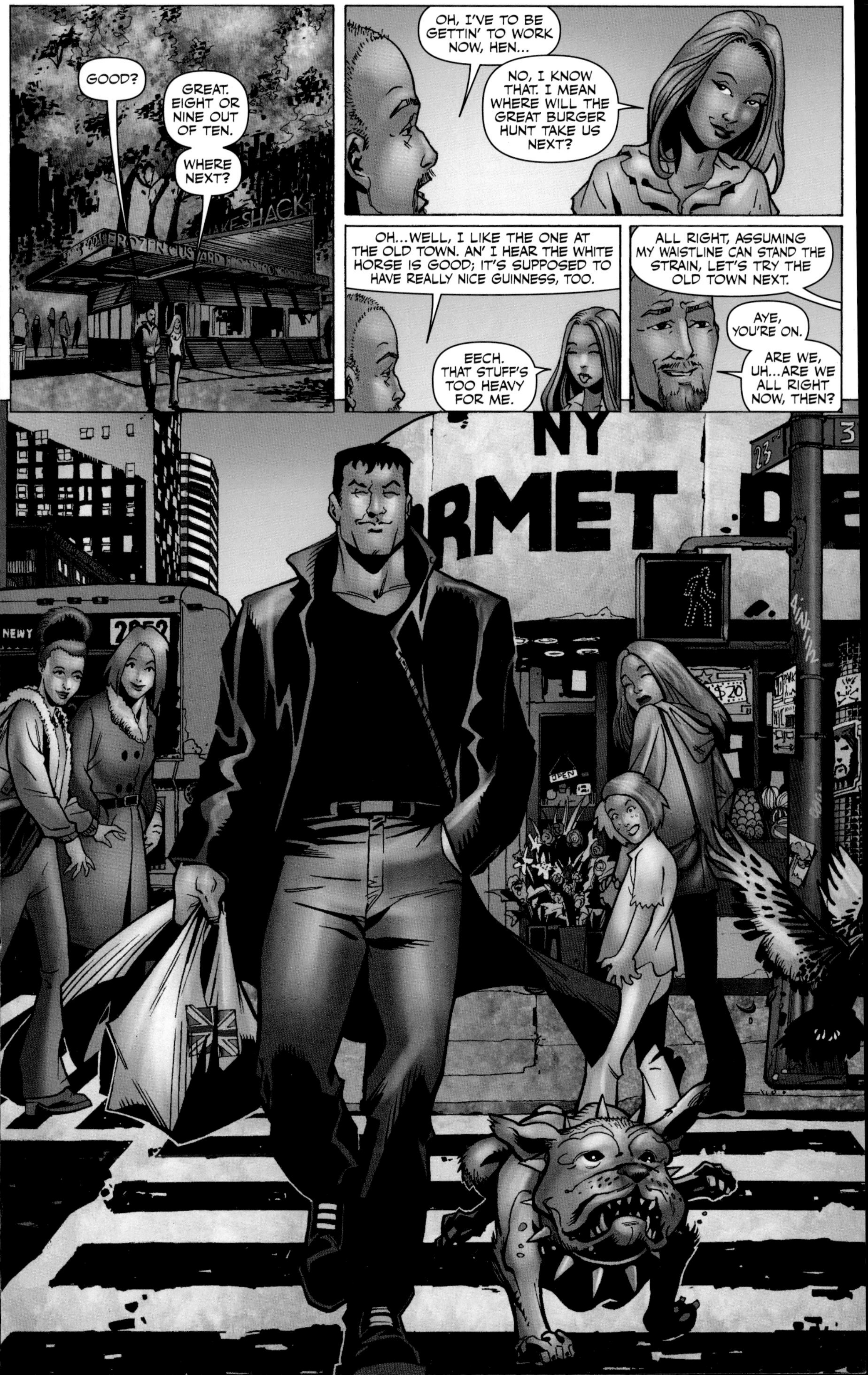
GOOD?
GREAT. EIGHT OR NINE OUT OF TEN.
WHERE NEXT?
OH, I'VE TO BE GETTIN' TO WORK NOW, HEN...
NO, I KNOW THAT. I MEAN WHERE WILL THE GREAT BURGER HUNT TAKE US NEXT?
OH...WELL, I LIKE THE ONE AT THE OLD TOWN. AN' I HEAR THE WHITE HORSE IS GOOD; IT'S SUPPOSED TO HAVE REALLY NICE GUINNESS, TOO.
EECH. THAT STUFF'S TOO HEAVY FOR ME.
ALL RIGHT, ASSUMING MY WAISTLINE CAN STAND THE STRAIN, LET'S TRY THE OLD TOWN NEXT.
AYE, YOU'RE ON.
ARE WE, UH...ARE WE ALL RIGHT NOW, THEN?
NY

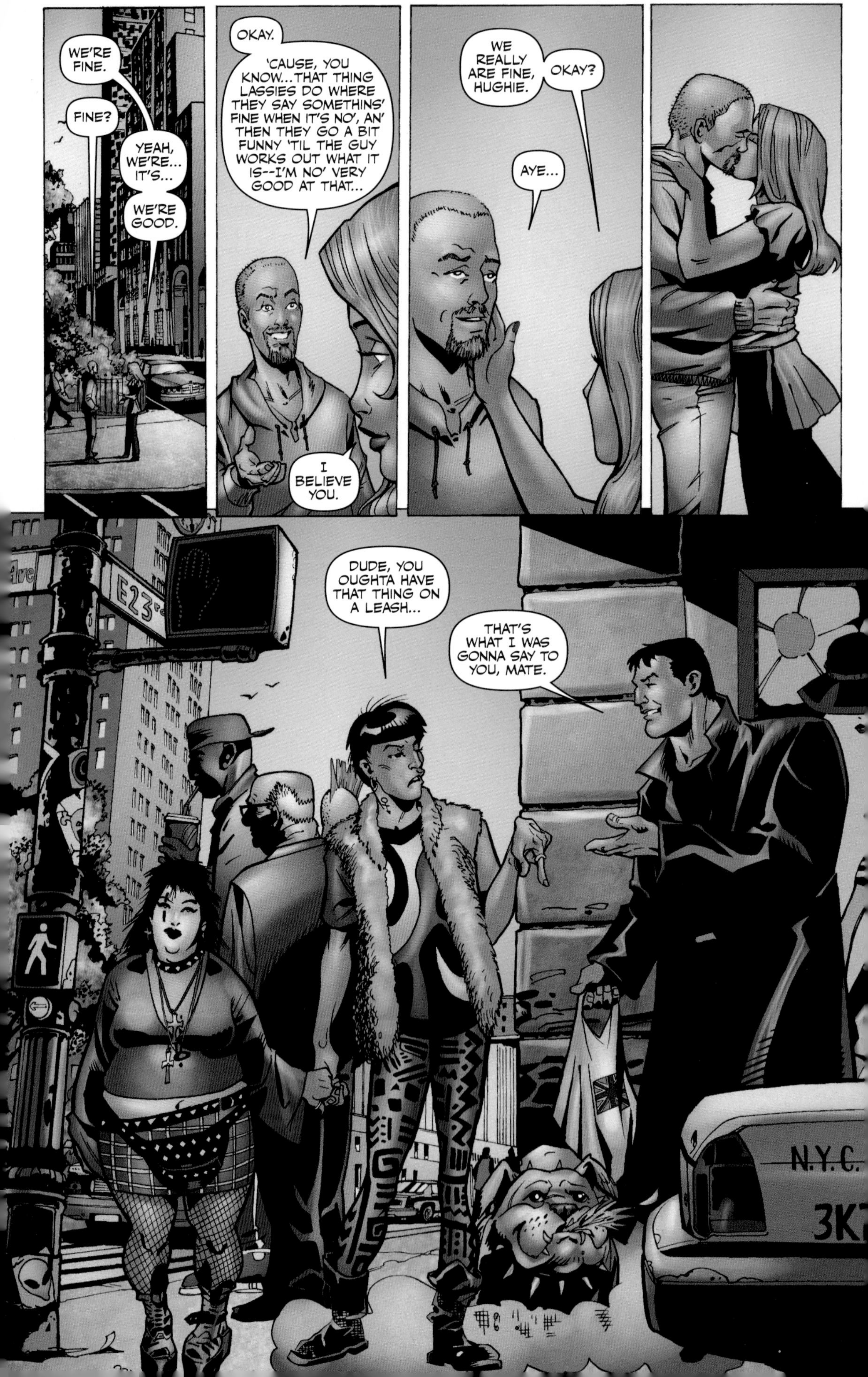

WE'RE FINE.
FINE?
YEAH, WE'RE... IT'S...
WE'RE GOOD.
OKAY.
'CAUSE, YOU KNOW...THAT THING LASSIES DO WHERE THEY SAY SOMETHINS' FINE WHEN IT'S NO', AN' THEN THEY GO A BIT FUNNY 'TIL THE GUY WORKS OUT WHAT IT IS--I'M NO' VERY GOOD AT THAT...
I BELIEVE YOU.
WE REALLY ARE FINE, HUGHIE.
OKAY?
AYE...
E 23 St
DUDE, YOU OUGHTA HAVE THAT THING ON A LEASH...
THAT'S WHAT I WAS GONNA SAY TO YOU, MATE.
N.Y.C.

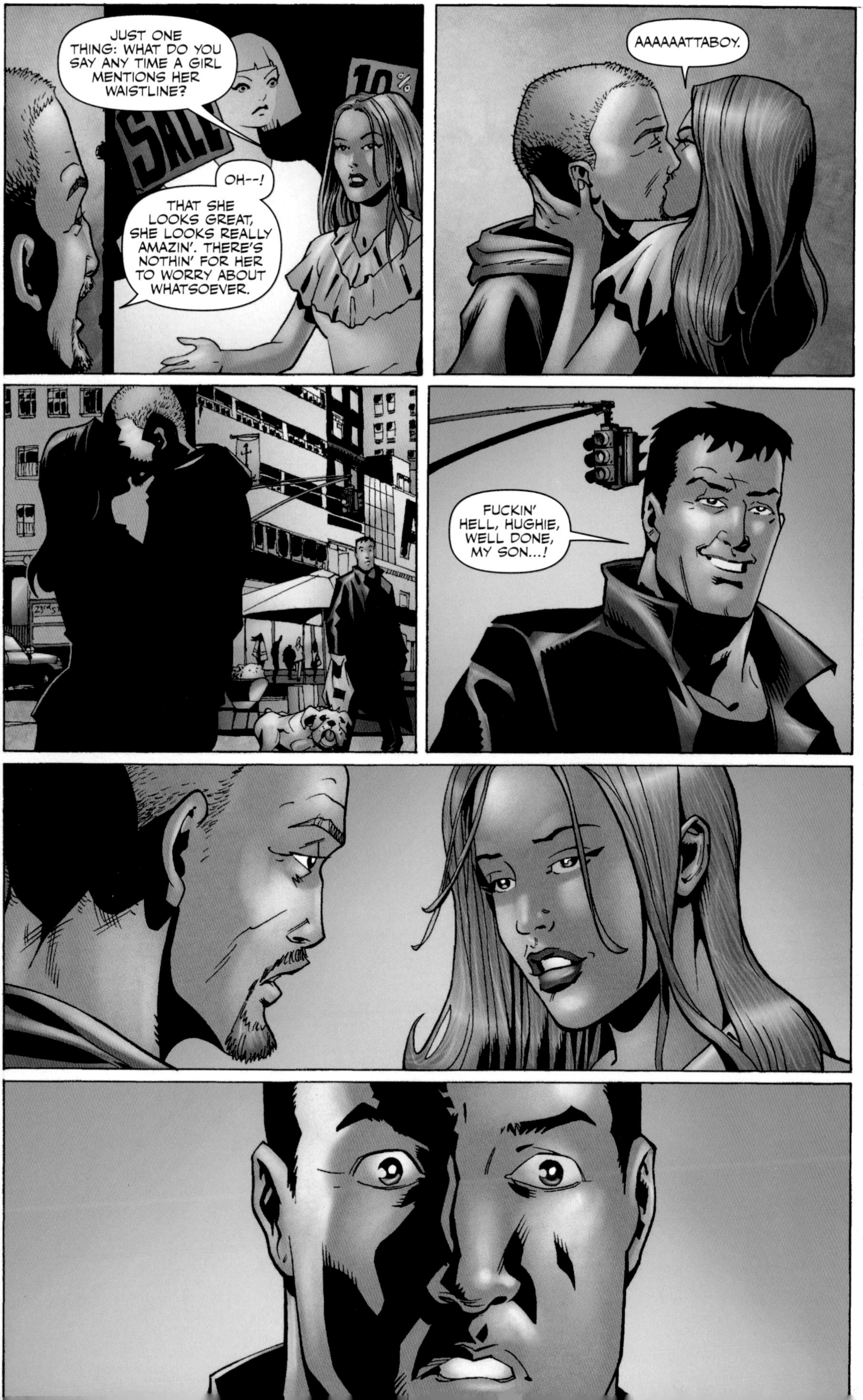
JUST ONE THING: WHAT DO YOU SAY ANY TIME A GIRL MENTIONS HER WAISTLINE?
SALE
10%
OH--!
THAT SHE LOOKS GREAT, SHE LOOKS REALLY AMAZIN'. THERE'S NOTHIN' FOR HER TO WORRY ABOUT WHATSOEVER.
AAAAAATTABOY.
FUCKIN' HELL, HUGHIE, WELL DONE, MY SON...!

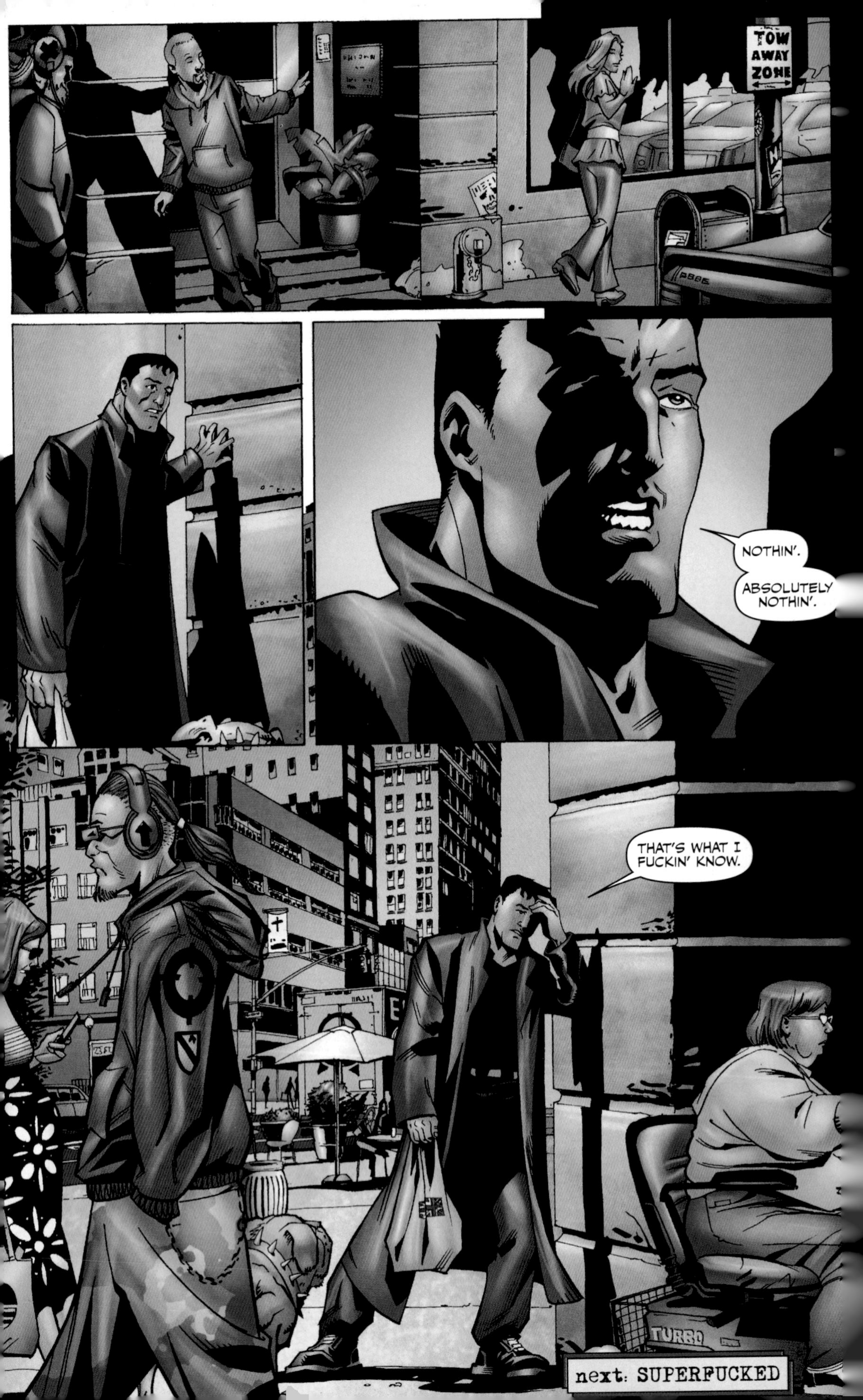
TOW AWAY ZONE
NOTHIN'.
ABSOLUTELY NOTHIN'.
THAT'S WHAT I FUCKIN' KNOW.
next: SUPERFUCKED

#40 cover
by Darick Robertson
and Tony Aviña

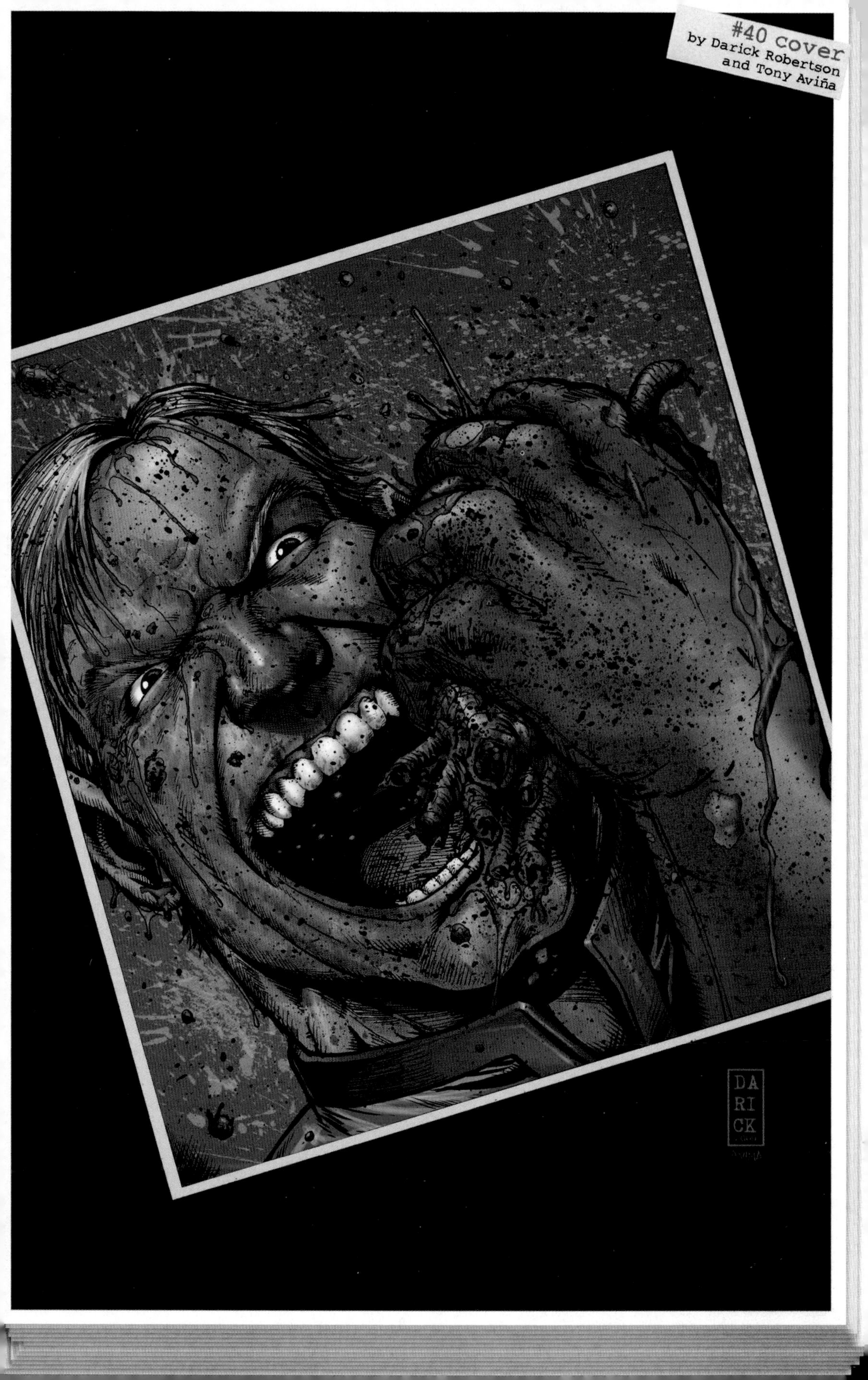
DA
RI
CK

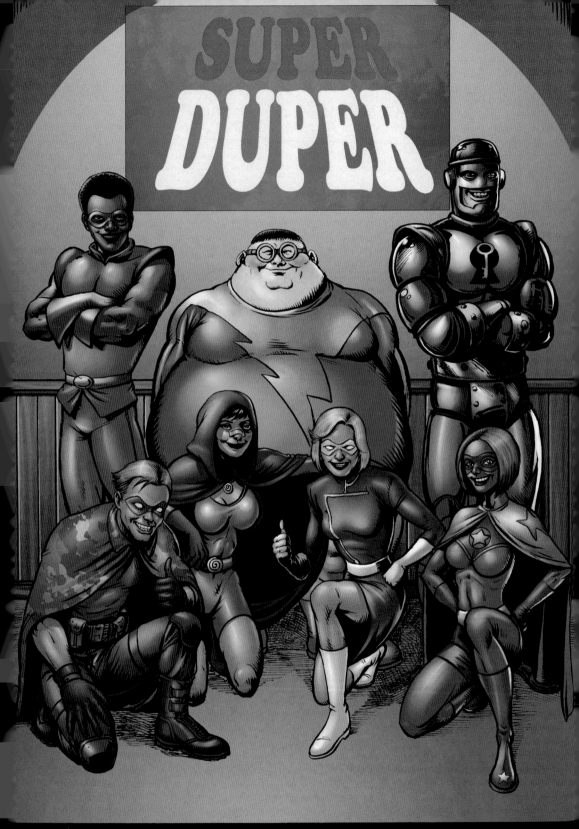

SUPER
DUPER

THE INNOCENTS

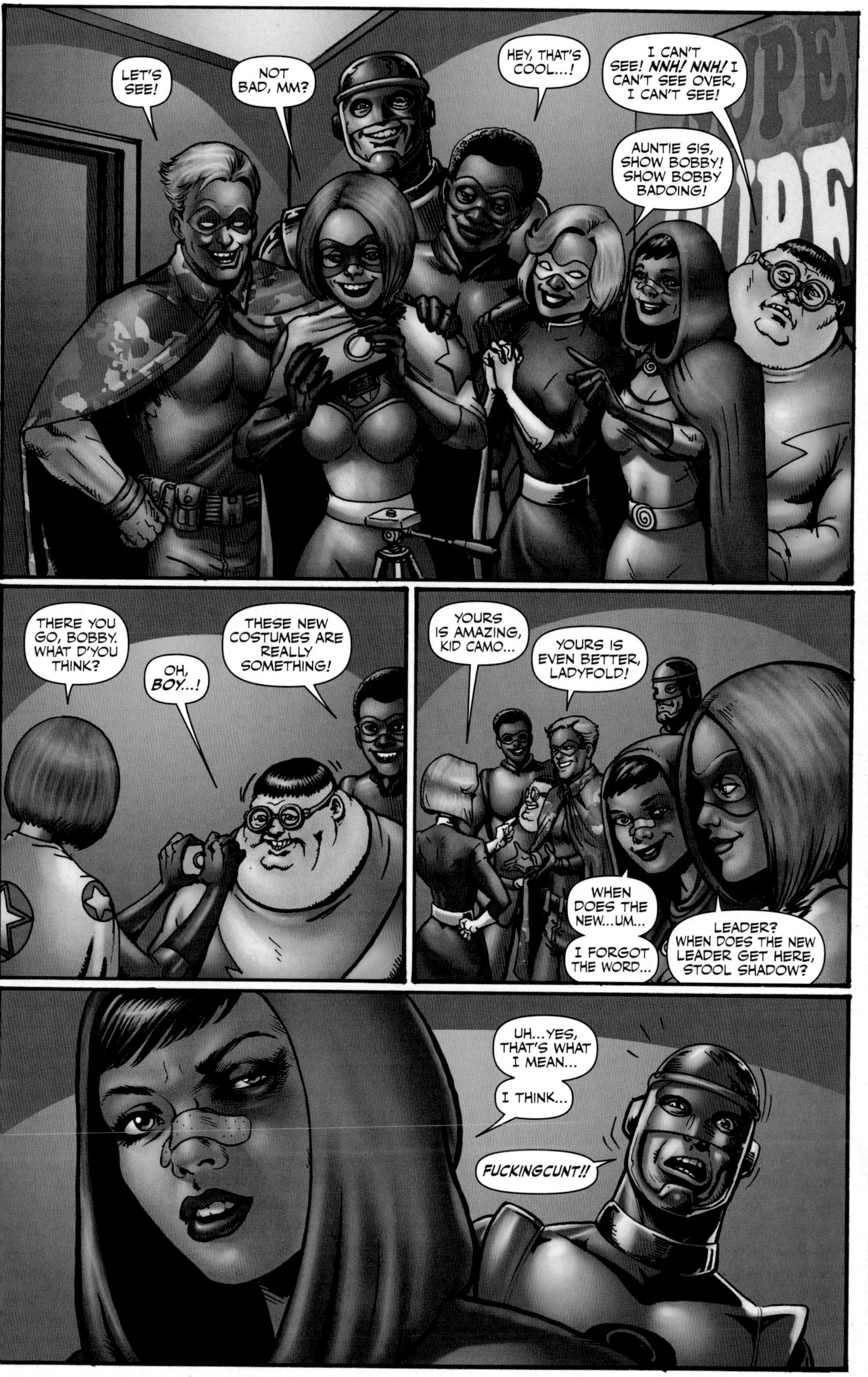
LET'S SEE!
NOT BAD, MM?
HEY, THAT'S COOL...!
I CAN'T SEE! NNH! NNH! I CAN'T SEE OVER, I CAN'T SEE!
AUNTIE SIS, SHOW BOBBY! SHOW BOBBY BADOING!
THERE YOU GO, BOBBY. WHAT D'YOU THINK?
OH, BOY...!
THESE NEW COSTUMES ARE REALLY SOMETHING!
YOURS IS AMAZING, KID CAMO...
YOURS IS EVEN BETTER, LADYFOLD!
WHEN DOES THE NEW...UM...
I FORGOT THE WORD...
LEADER? WHEN DOES THE NEW LEADER GET HERE, STOOL SHADOW?
UH...YES, THAT'S WHAT I MEAN...
I THINK...
FUCKINGCUNT!!

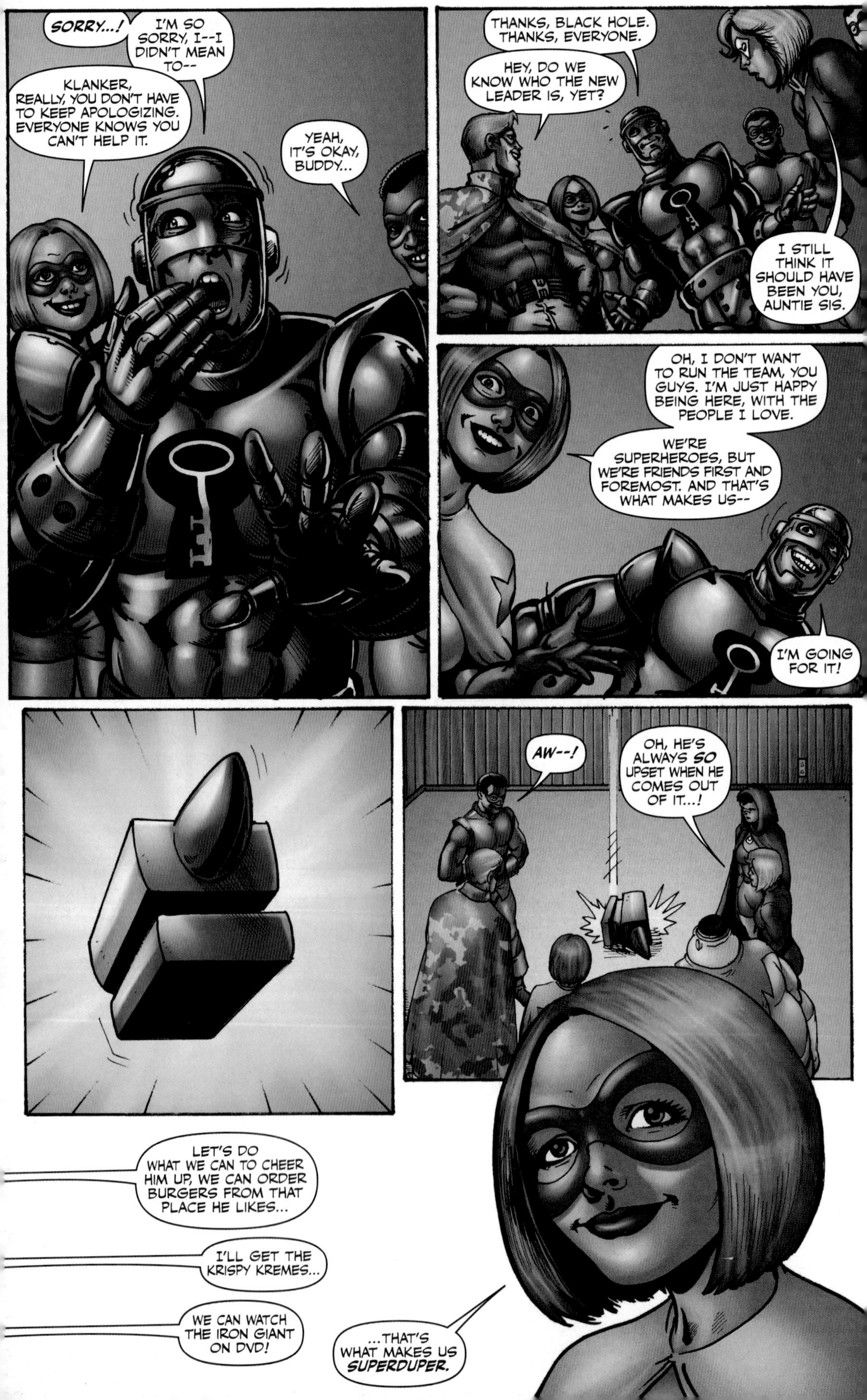
SORRY...!
I'M SO SORRY, I--I DIDN'T MEAN TO--
KLANKER, REALLY, YOU DON'T HAVE TO KEEP APOLOGIZING. EVERYONE KNOWS YOU CAN'T HELP IT.
YEAH, IT'S OKAY, BUDDY...
THANKS, BLACK HOLE. THANKS, EVERYONE.
HEY, DO WE KNOW WHO THE NEW LEADER IS, YET?
I STILL THINK IT SHOULD HAVE BEEN YOU, AUNTIE SIS.
OH, I DON'T WANT TO RUN THE TEAM, YOU GUYS. I'M JUST HAPPY BEING HERE, WITH THE PEOPLE I LOVE.
WE'RE SUPERHEROES, BUT WE'RE FRIENDS FIRST AND FOREMOST. AND THAT'S WHAT MAKES US--
I'M GOING FOR IT!
AW--!
OH, HE'S ALWAYS SO UPSET WHEN HE COMES OUT OF IT...!
LET'S DO WHAT WE CAN TO CHEER HIM UP, WE CAN ORDER BURGERS FROM THAT PLACE HE LIKES...
I'LL GET THE KRISPY KREMES...
WE CAN WATCH THE IRON GIANT ON DVD!
...THAT'S WHAT MAKES US SUPERDUPER.

WELL--*ACTUALLY*--IT'S CALLED *A NEW HOPE*, BECAUSE AAAAAAAAAAAAAAAAHHH!!!

HEY, BUTCHUH.

NNEEEEIIIIIIGGGHH...!

VINNIE'S COMICS
BASEBALL CARDS.
ACTION FIGURES

170

INFINITY WARS

OPEN

FUGLO

YA CAN GO ON DOWN, HE KNOWS YA COMIN'.

PRIVATE

PUNK

HERO 3RD

APE FIST

WEB ELF

FUCK YOU TOO...

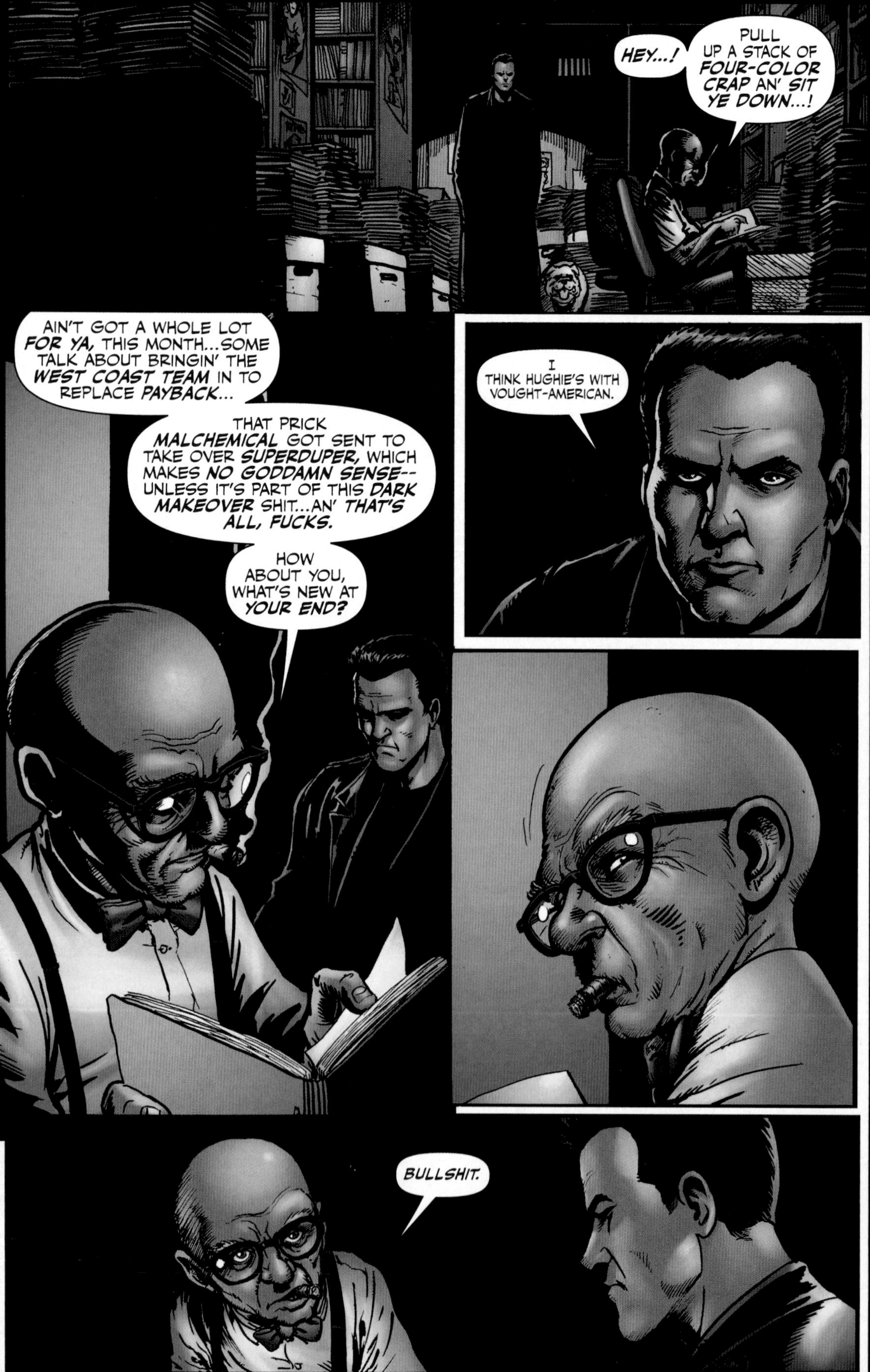
HEY...!
PULL UP A STACK OF FOUR-COLOR CRAP AN' SIT YE DOWN...!
AIN'T GOT A WHOLE LOT FOR YA, THIS MONTH...SOME TALK ABOUT BRINGIN' THE WEST COAST TEAM IN TO REPLACE PAYBACK...
THAT PRICK MALCHEMICAL GOT SENT TO TAKE OVER SUPERDUPER, WHICH MAKES NO GODDAMN SENSE-- UNLESS IT'S PART OF THIS DARK MAKEOVER SHIT...AN' THAT'S ALL, FUCKS.
HOW ABOUT YOU, WHAT'S NEW AT YOUR END?
I THINK HUGHIE'S WITH VOUGHT-AMERICAN.
BULLSHIT.

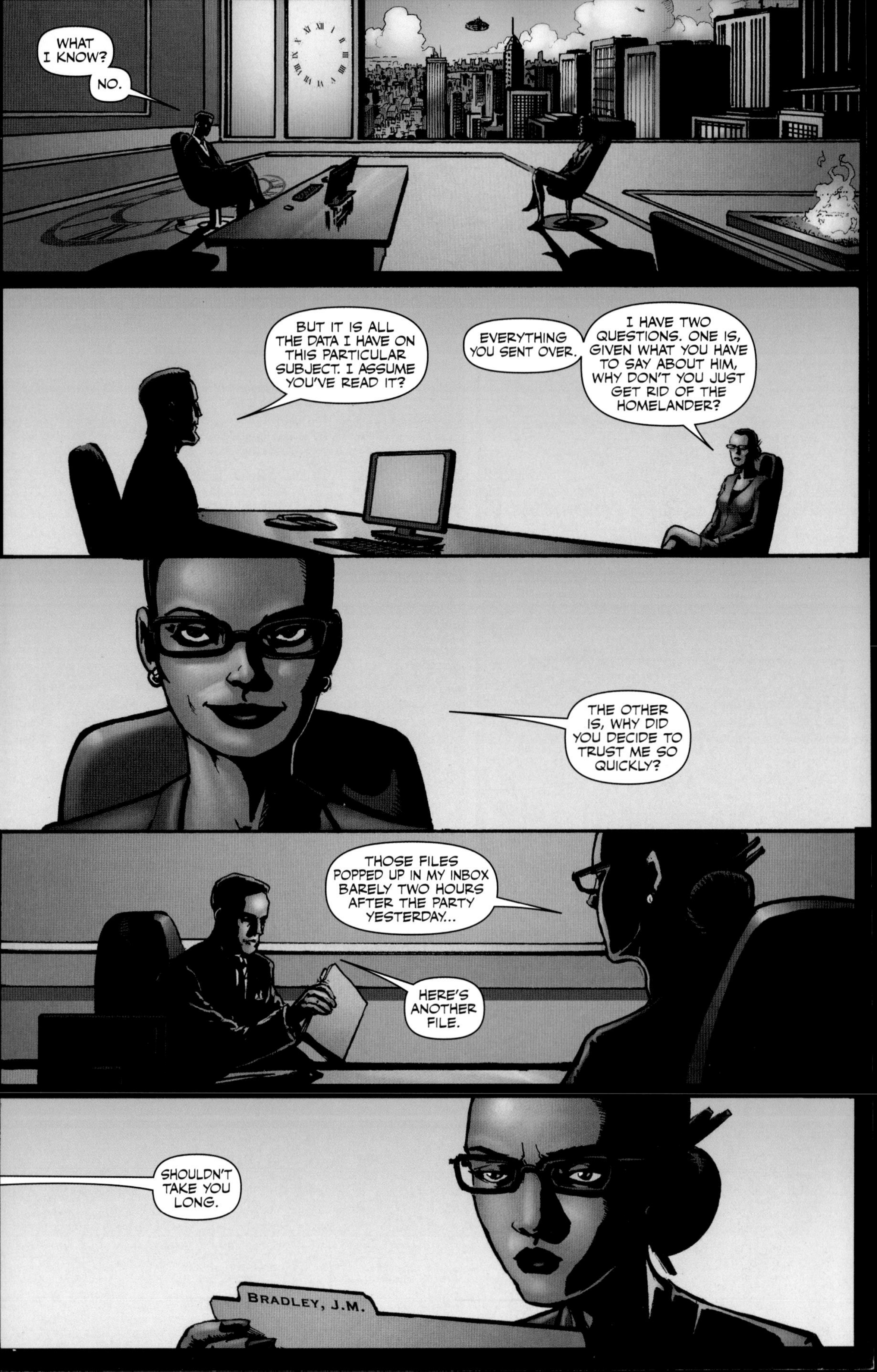
WHAT I KNOW?
NO.
BUT IT IS ALL THE DATA I HAVE ON THIS PARTICULAR SUBJECT. I ASSUME YOU'VE READ IT?
EVERYTHING YOU SENT OVER.
I HAVE TWO QUESTIONS. ONE IS, GIVEN WHAT YOU HAVE TO SAY ABOUT HIM, WHY DON'T YOU JUST GET RID OF THE HOMELANDER?
THE OTHER IS, WHY DID YOU DECIDE TO TRUST ME SO QUICKLY?
THOSE FILES POPPED UP IN MY INBOX BARELY TWO HOURS AFTER THE PARTY YESTERDAY...
HERE'S ANOTHER FILE.
SHOULDN'T TAKE YOU LONG.
BRADLEY, J.M.

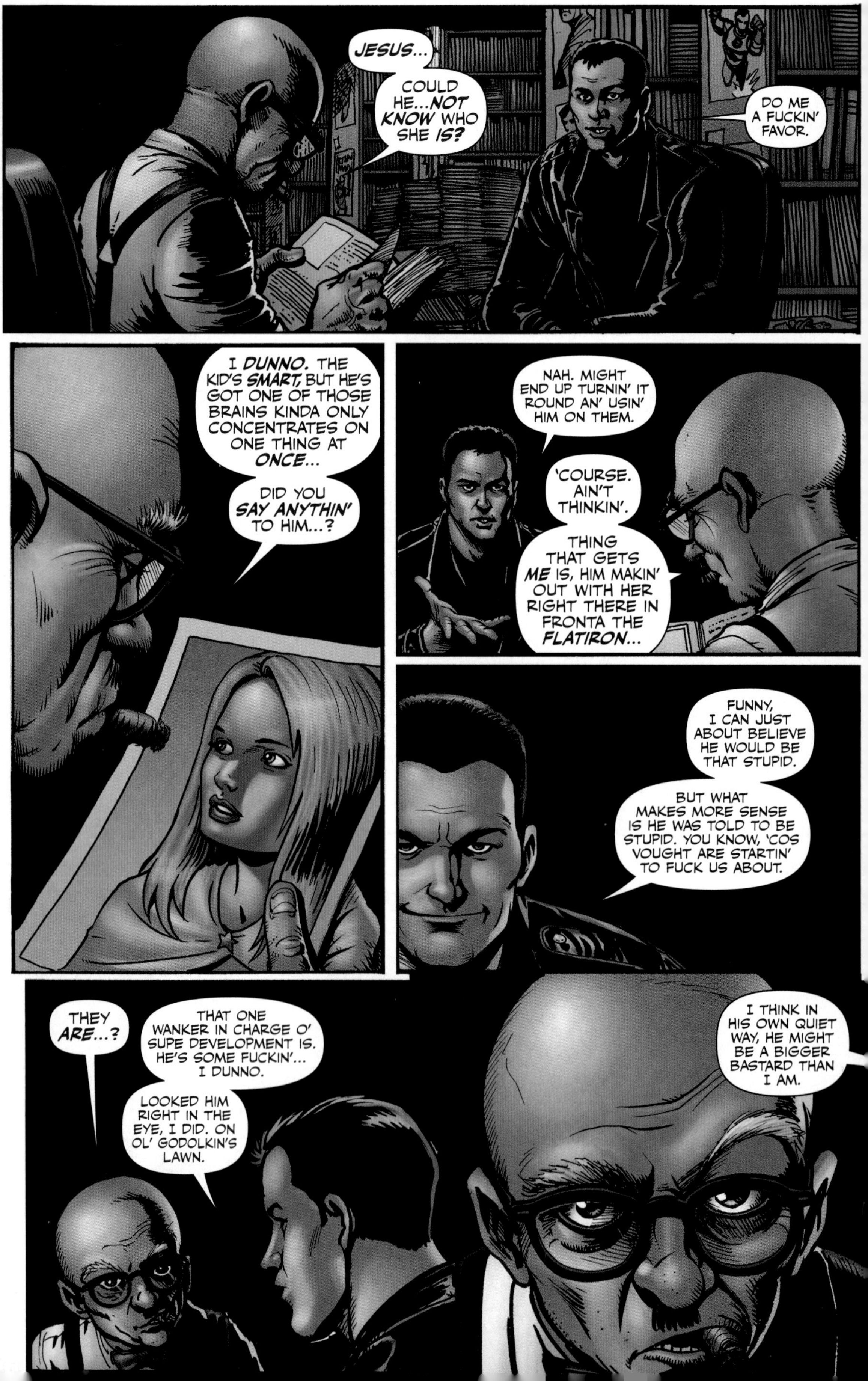
JESUS...
COULD HE...NOT KNOW WHO SHE IS?
DO ME A FUCKIN' FAVOR.
I DUNNO. THE KID'S SMART, BUT HE'S GOT ONE OF THOSE BRAINS KINDA ONLY CONCENTRATES ON ONE THING AT ONCE...
DID YOU SAY ANYTHIN' TO HIM...?
NAH. MIGHT END UP TURNIN' IT ROUND AN' USIN' HIM ON THEM.
'COURSE. AIN'T THINKIN'.
THING THAT GETS ME IS, HIM MAKIN' OUT WITH HER RIGHT THERE IN FRONTA THE FLATIRON...
FUNNY, I CAN JUST ABOUT BELIEVE HE WOULD BE THAT STUPID.
BUT WHAT MAKES MORE SENSE IS HE WAS TOLD TO BE STUPID. YOU KNOW, 'COS VOUGHT ARE STARTIN' TO FUCK US ABOUT.
THEY ARE...?
THAT ONE WANKER IN CHARGE O' SUPE DEVELOPMENT IS. HE'S SOME FUCKIN'... I DUNNO.
LOOKED HIM RIGHT IN THE EYE, I DID. ON OL' GODOLKIN'S LAWN.
I THINK IN HIS OWN QUIET WAY, HE MIGHT BE A BIGGER BASTARD THAN I AM.

HUH.

WELL.

HE'S GOT THE BOLLOCKS FOR THE GAME, I'LL TELL YOU THAT MUCH. HE SENT PAYBACK AFTER US AN' HE DIDN'T EVEN TRY TO KEEP HIMSELF OUT OF IT-- MADE THE DEAL WITH 'EM AT HEROGASM IN PERSON.

IT'S ALMOST LIKE HE'S DARIN' US TO HAVE A PROPER GO...

WHICH IS *CRAZY.* THE BOYS VERSUS THE SEVEN, IT'S A MUTUALLY ASSURED *BUTTFUCKIN'.*

BE THE ENDA THE HOMELANDER, FOR STARTERS. I JUST DON'T SEE HOW DOIN' AWAY WITH US'D EVER BE WORTH THAT.

YOU DONE A *LOTTA GODDAMN DAMAGE* IN YOUR TIME, MY FRIEND. THEY'RE DOWN *TWO OUTTA THEIR THREE TOP TEAMS* INSIDE THE PAST SIX MONTHS.

YEAH, EXCEPT HE DONE HIS BIT TO FINISH BOTH OF 'EM. 'CASE O' THE G-MEN, HE GAVE THE FUCKIN' ORDERS.

WHAT *IS IT* ABOUT THAT BLOKE...?

GOIN' BACK TO THE *KID...*

YOU FOUND *HIM.* SO WE'RE SAYIN' THEY GOT TO HIM *AFTER* HE CAME IN, AN' ALL THE *SHIT* HAPPENED TO HIM THEY *SET UP* TO MAKE HIM *LOOK GOOD...?*

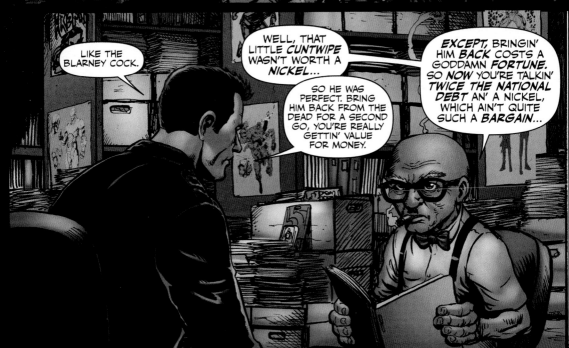

LIKE THE BLARNEY COCK.

WELL, THAT LITTLE *CUNTWIPE* WASN'T WORTH A *NICKEL...*

SO HE WAS PERFECT. BRING HIM BACK FROM THE DEAD FOR A SECOND GO, YOU'RE REALLY GETTIN' VALUE FOR MONEY.

EXCEPT, BRINGIN' HIM *BACK* COSTS A GODDAMN *FORTUNE.* SO *NOW* YOU'RE TALKIN' *TWICE THE NATIONAL DEBT* AN' A NICKEL, WHICH AIN'T QUITE SUCH A *BARGAIN...*

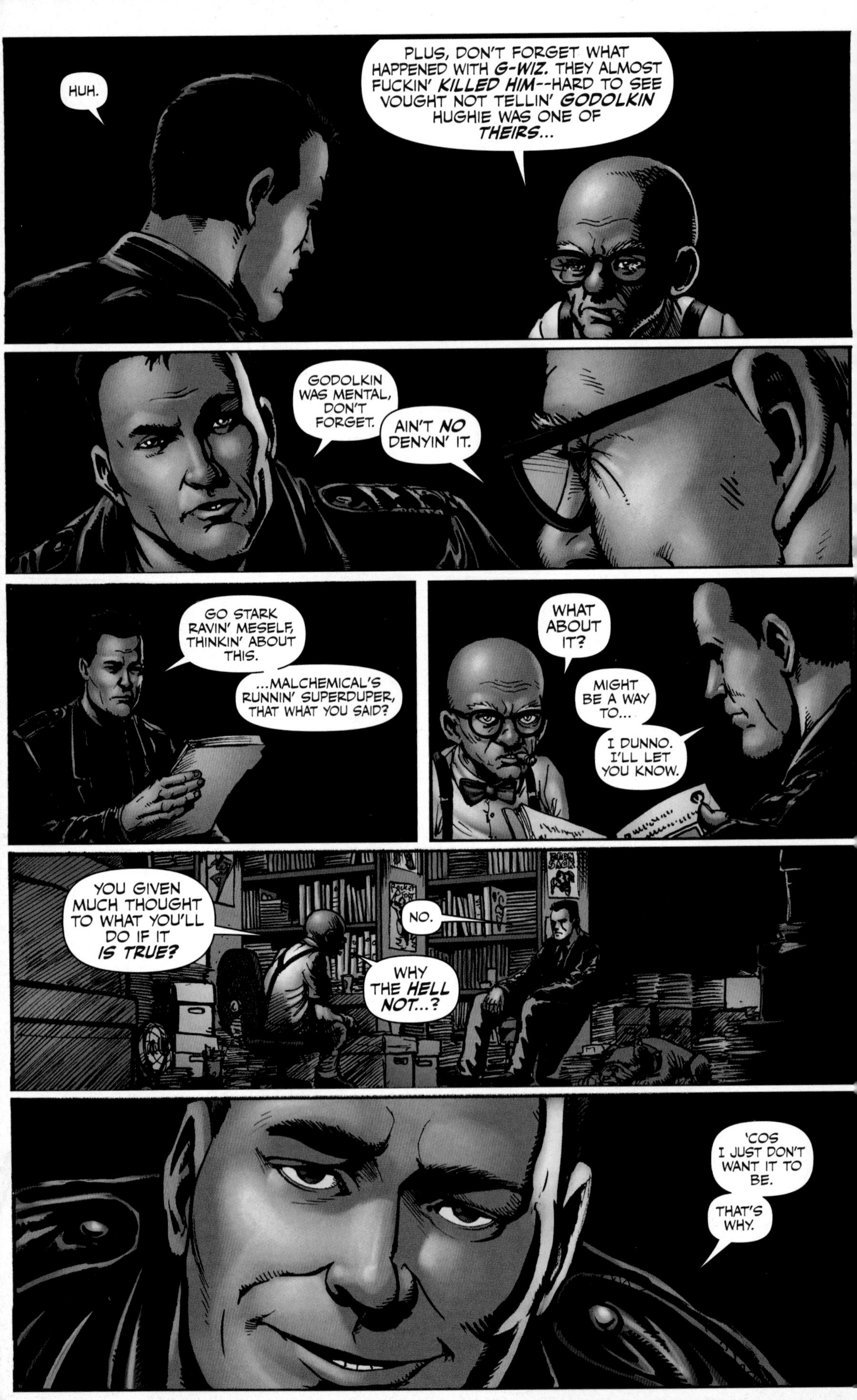
HUH.
PLUS, DON'T FORGET WHAT HAPPENED WITH G-WIZ. THEY ALMOST FUCKIN' KILLED HIM--HARD TO SEE VOUGHT NOT TELLIN' GODOLKIN HUGHIE WAS ONE OF THEIRS...
GODOLKIN WAS MENTAL, DON'T FORGET.
AIN'T NO DENYIN' IT.
GO STARK RAVIN' MESELF, THINKIN' ABOUT THIS.
...MALCHEMICAL'S RUNNIN' SUPERDUPER, THAT WHAT YOU SAID?
WHAT ABOUT IT?
MIGHT BE A WAY TO...
I DUNNO. I'LL LET YOU KNOW.
YOU GIVEN MUCH THOUGHT TO WHAT YOU'LL DO IF IT IS TRUE?
NO.
WHY THE HELL NOT...?
'COS I JUST DON'T WANT IT TO BE.
THAT'S WHY.

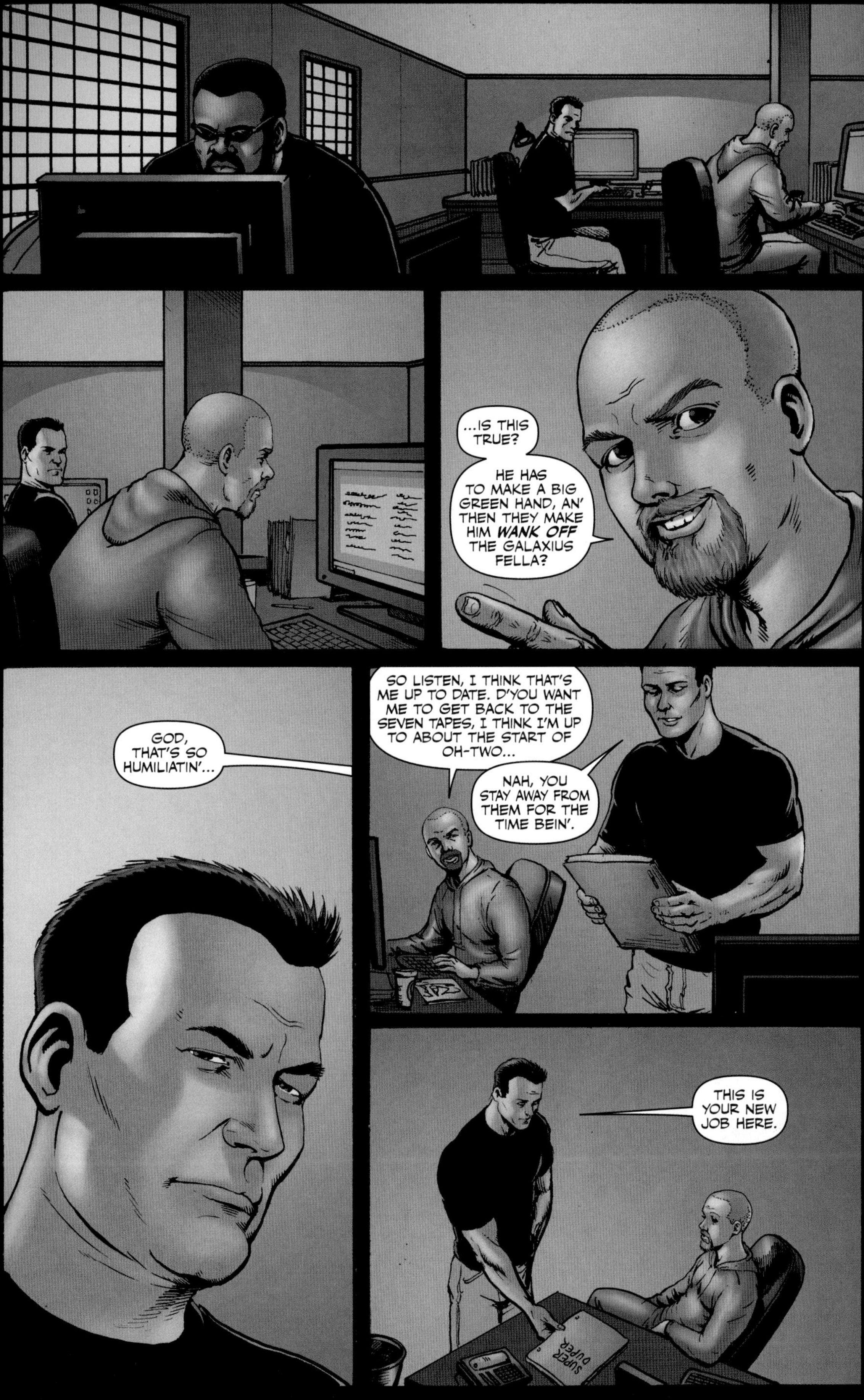
...IS THIS TRUE?
HE HAS TO MAKE A BIG GREEN HAND, AN' THEN THEY MAKE HIM WANK OFF THE GALAXIUS FELLA?
GOD, THAT'S SO HUMILIATIN'...
SO LISTEN, I THINK THAT'S ME UP TO DATE. D'YOU WANT ME TO GET BACK TO THE SEVEN TAPES, I THINK I'M UP TO ABOUT THE START OF OH-TWO...
NAH, YOU STAY AWAY FROM THEM FOR THE TIME BEIN'.
THIS IS YOUR NEW JOB HERE.
SUPER DUPER

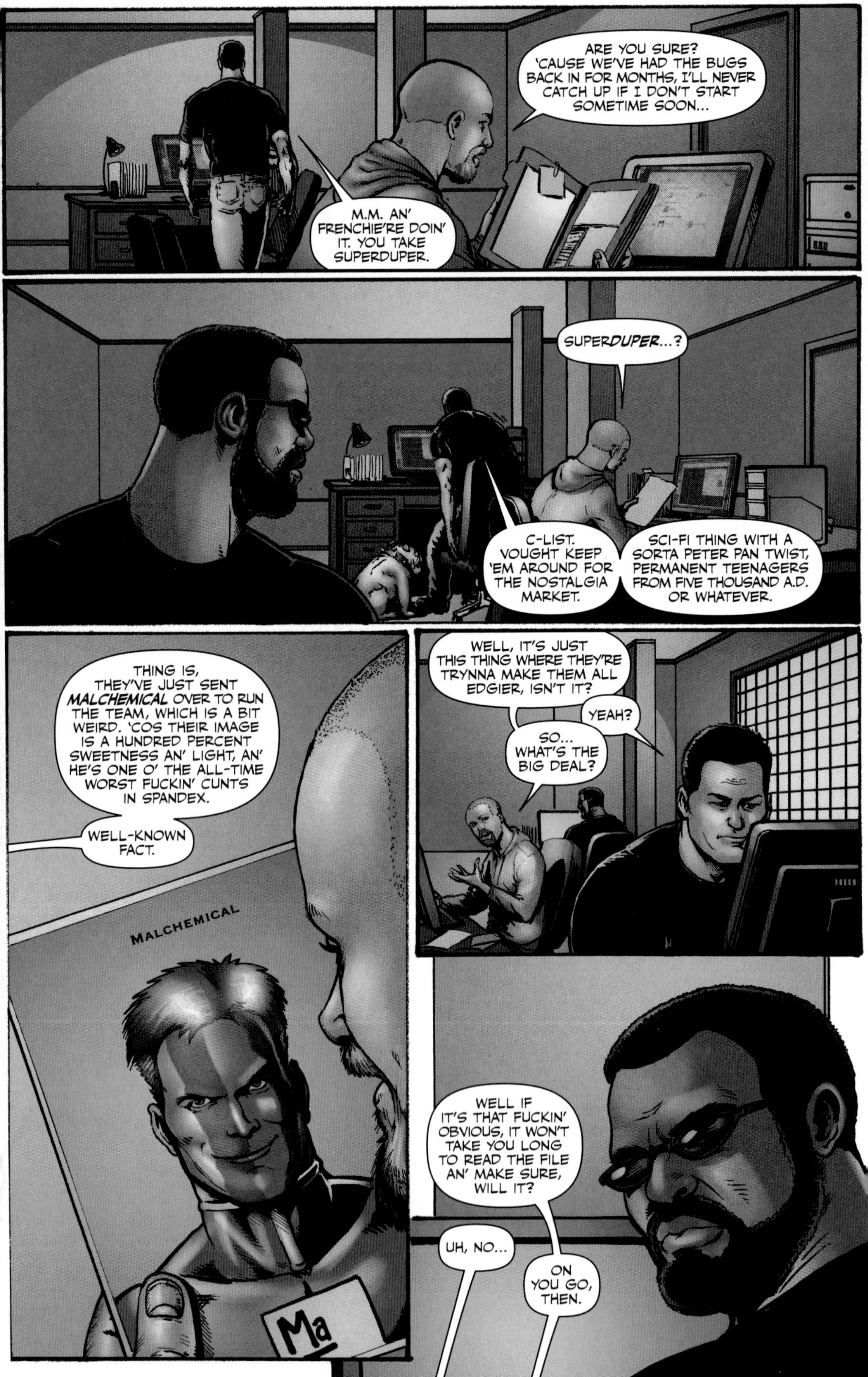
ARE YOU SURE? 'CAUSE WE'VE HAD THE BUGS BACK IN FOR MONTHS, I'LL NEVER CATCH UP IF I DON'T START SOMETIME SOON...
M.M. AN' FRENCHIE'RE DOIN' IT. YOU TAKE SUPERDUPER.
SUPERDUPER...?
C-LIST. VOUGHT KEEP 'EM AROUND FOR THE NOSTALGIA MARKET.
SCI-FI THING WITH A SORTA PETER PAN TWIST, PERMANENT TEENAGERS FROM FIVE THOUSAND A.D. OR WHATEVER.
THING IS, THEY'VE JUST SENT MALCHEMICAL OVER TO RUN THE TEAM, WHICH IS A BIT WEIRD. 'COS THEIR IMAGE IS A HUNDRED PERCENT SWEETNESS AN' LIGHT, AN' HE'S ONE O' THE ALL-TIME WORST FUCKIN' CUNTS IN SPANDEX.
WELL-KNOWN FACT.
MALCHEMICAL
Ma
WELL, IT'S JUST THIS THING WHERE THEY'RE TRYNNA MAKE THEM ALL EDGIER, ISN'T IT?
YEAH?
SO... WHAT'S THE BIG DEAL?
WELL IF IT'S THAT FUCKIN' OBVIOUS, IT WON'T TAKE YOU LONG TO READ THE FILE AN' MAKE SURE, WILL IT?
UH, NO...
ON YOU GO, THEN.

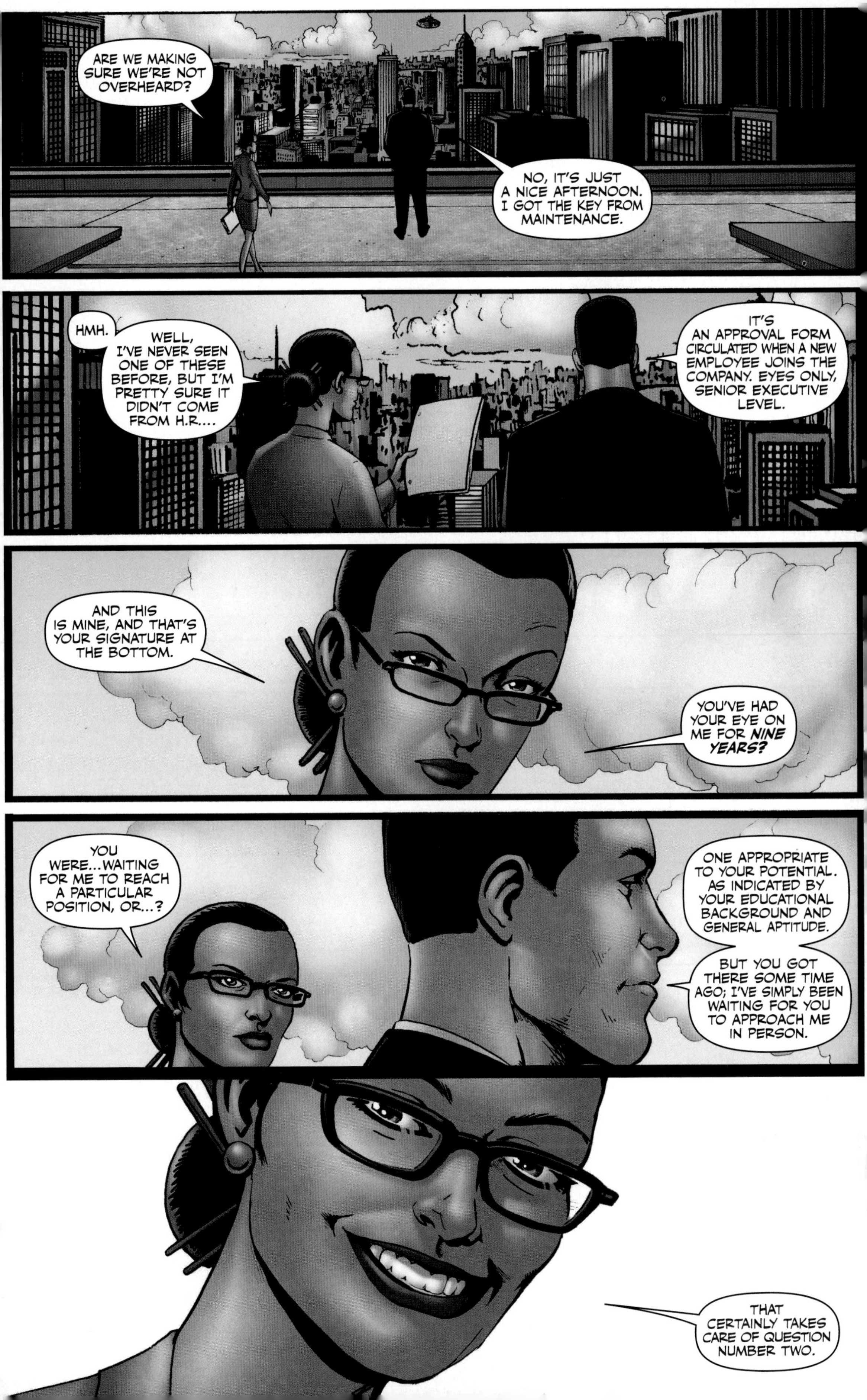
ARE WE MAKING SURE WE'RE NOT OVERHEARD?
NO, IT'S JUST A NICE AFTERNOON. I GOT THE KEY FROM MAINTENANCE.
HMH.
WELL, I'VE NEVER SEEN ONE OF THESE BEFORE, BUT I'M PRETTY SURE IT DIDN'T COME FROM H.R....
IT'S AN APPROVAL FORM CIRCULATED WHEN A NEW EMPLOYEE JOINS THE COMPANY. EYES ONLY, SENIOR EXECUTIVE LEVEL.
AND THIS IS MINE, AND THAT'S YOUR SIGNATURE AT THE BOTTOM.
YOU'VE HAD YOUR EYE ON ME FOR ***NINE YEARS?***
YOU WERE...WAITING FOR ME TO REACH A PARTICULAR POSITION, OR...?
ONE APPROPRIATE TO YOUR POTENTIAL. AS INDICATED BY YOUR EDUCATIONAL BACKGROUND AND GENERAL APTITUDE.
BUT YOU GOT THERE SOME TIME AGO; I'VE SIMPLY BEEN WAITING FOR YOU TO APPROACH ME IN PERSON.
THAT CERTAINLY TAKES CARE OF QUESTION NUMBER TWO.

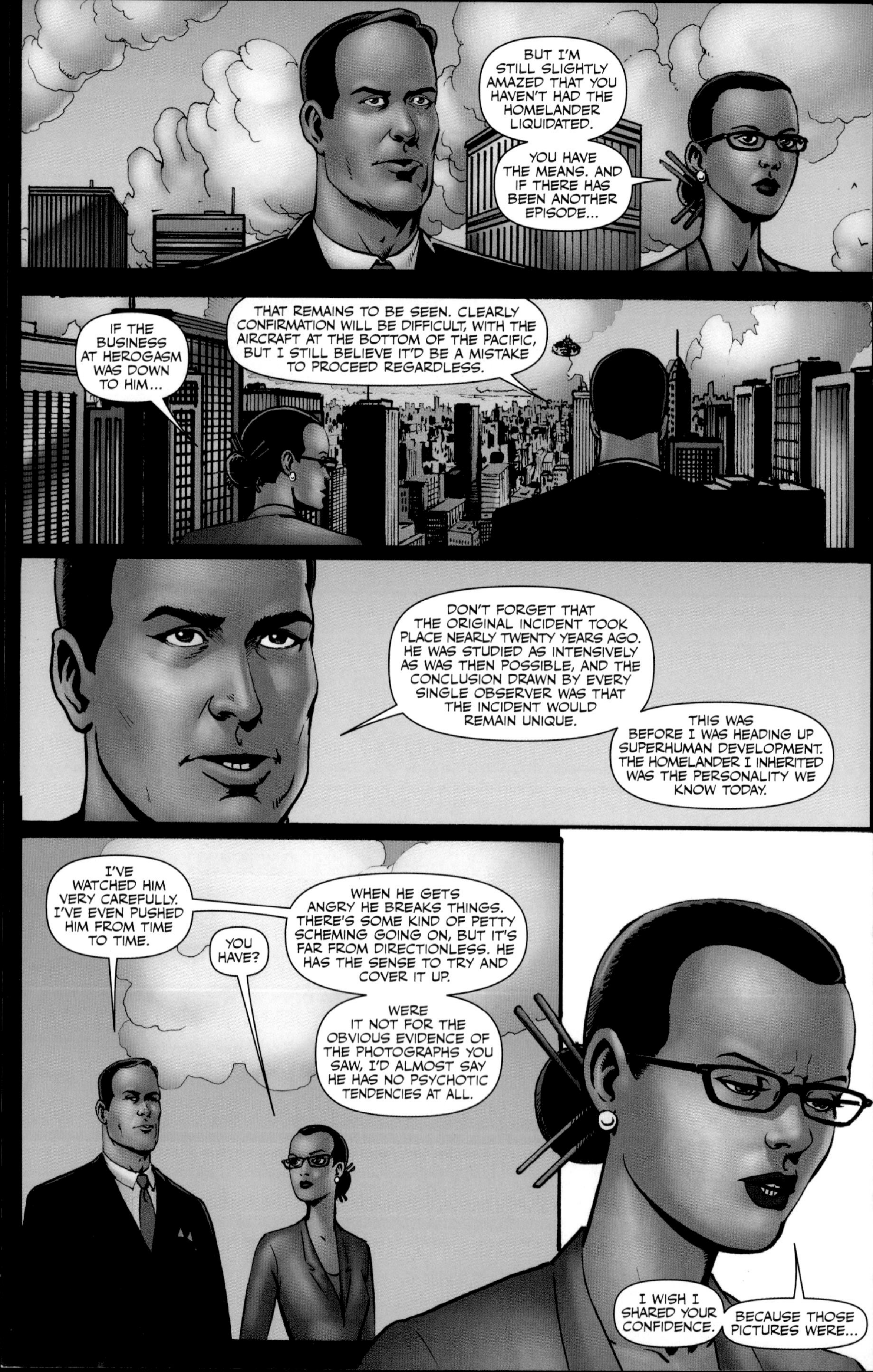
BUT I'M STILL SLIGHTLY AMAZED THAT YOU HAVEN'T HAD THE HOMELANDER LIQUIDATED.
YOU HAVE THE MEANS. AND IF THERE HAS BEEN ANOTHER EPISODE...
IF THE BUSINESS AT HEROGASM WAS DOWN TO HIM...
THAT REMAINS TO BE SEEN. CLEARLY CONFIRMATION WILL BE DIFFICULT, WITH THE AIRCRAFT AT THE BOTTOM OF THE PACIFIC, BUT I STILL BELIEVE IT'D BE A MISTAKE TO PROCEED REGARDLESS.
DON'T FORGET THAT THE ORIGINAL INCIDENT TOOK PLACE NEARLY TWENTY YEARS AGO. HE WAS STUDIED AS INTENSIVELY AS WAS THEN POSSIBLE, AND THE CONCLUSION DRAWN BY EVERY SINGLE OBSERVER WAS THAT THE INCIDENT WOULD REMAIN UNIQUE.
THIS WAS BEFORE I WAS HEADING UP SUPERHUMAN DEVELOPMENT. THE HOMELANDER I INHERITED WAS THE PERSONALITY WE KNOW TODAY.
I'VE WATCHED HIM VERY CAREFULLY. I'VE EVEN PUSHED HIM FROM TIME TO TIME.
YOU HAVE?
WHEN HE GETS ANGRY HE BREAKS THINGS. THERE'S SOME KIND OF PETTY SCHEMING GOING ON, BUT IT'S FAR FROM DIRECTIONLESS. HE HAS THE SENSE TO TRY AND COVER IT UP.
WERE IT NOT FOR THE OBVIOUS EVIDENCE OF THE PHOTOGRAPHS YOU SAW, I'D ALMOST SAY HE HAS NO PSYCHOTIC TENDENCIES AT ALL.
I WISH I SHARED YOUR CONFIDENCE.
BECAUSE THOSE PICTURES WERE...

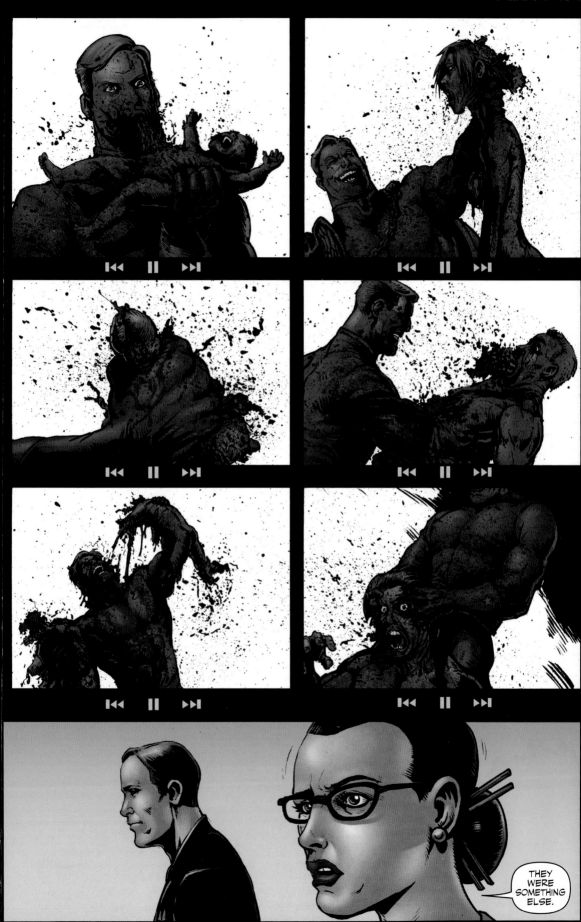

THEY
WERE
SOMETHING
ELSE.

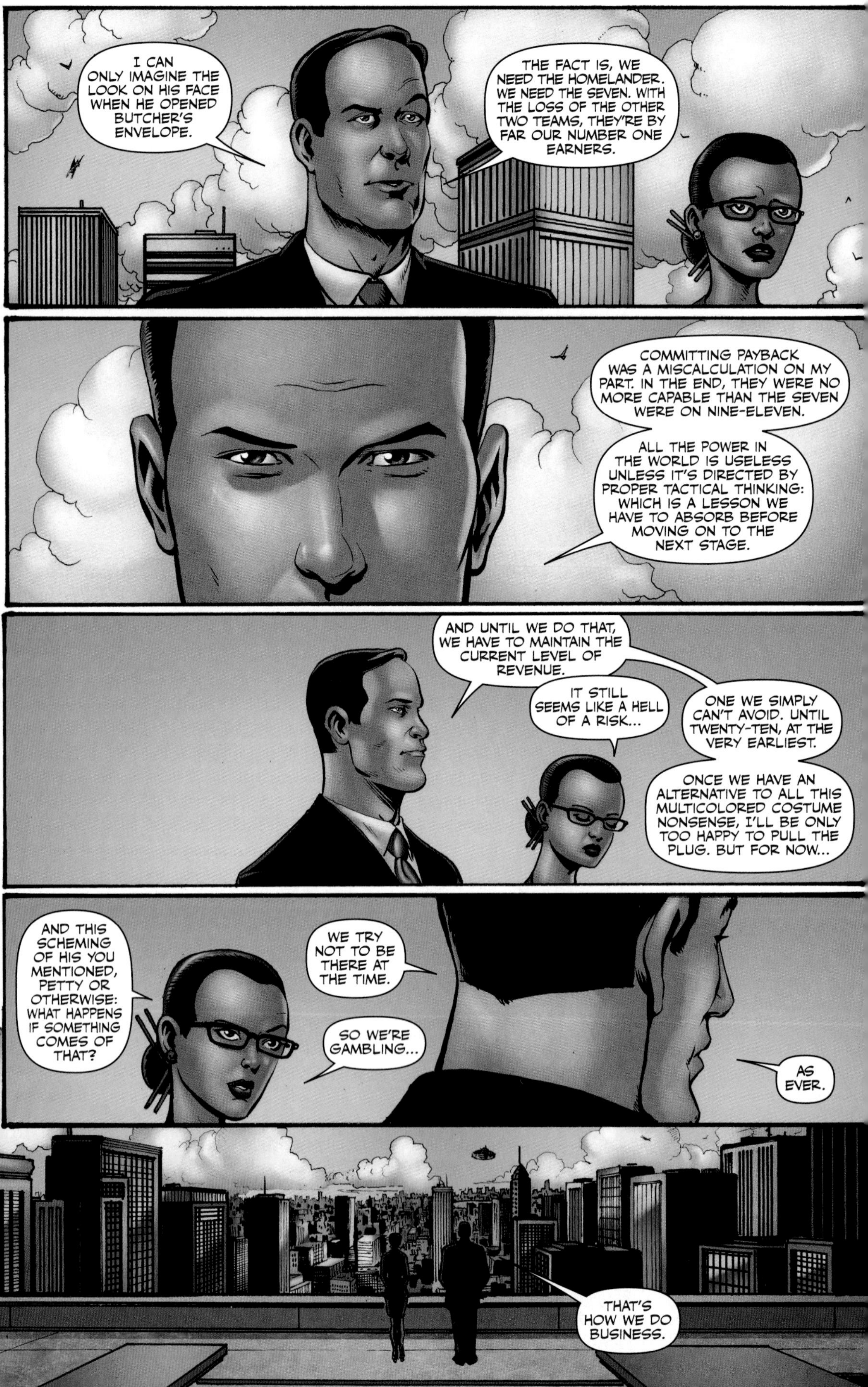
I CAN ONLY IMAGINE THE LOOK ON HIS FACE WHEN HE OPENED BUTCHER'S ENVELOPE.
THE FACT IS, WE NEED THE HOMELANDER. WE NEED THE SEVEN. WITH THE LOSS OF THE OTHER TWO TEAMS, THEY'RE BY FAR OUR NUMBER ONE EARNERS.
COMMITTING PAYBACK WAS A MISCALCULATION ON MY PART. IN THE END, THEY WERE NO MORE CAPABLE THAN THE SEVEN WERE ON NINE-ELEVEN.
ALL THE POWER IN THE WORLD IS USELESS UNLESS IT'S DIRECTED BY PROPER TACTICAL THINKING: WHICH IS A LESSON WE HAVE TO ABSORB BEFORE MOVING ON TO THE NEXT STAGE.
AND UNTIL WE DO THAT, WE HAVE TO MAINTAIN THE CURRENT LEVEL OF REVENUE.
IT STILL SEEMS LIKE A HELL OF A RISK...
ONE WE SIMPLY CAN'T AVOID. UNTIL TWENTY-TEN, AT THE VERY EARLIEST.
ONCE WE HAVE AN ALTERNATIVE TO ALL THIS MULTICOLORED COSTUME NONSENSE, I'LL BE ONLY TOO HAPPY TO PULL THE PLUG. BUT FOR NOW...
AND THIS SCHEMING OF HIS YOU MENTIONED, PETTY OR OTHERWISE: WHAT HAPPENS IF SOMETHING COMES OF THAT?
WE TRY NOT TO BE THERE AT THE TIME.
SO WE'RE GAMBLING...
AS EVER.
THAT'S HOW WE DO BUSINESS.

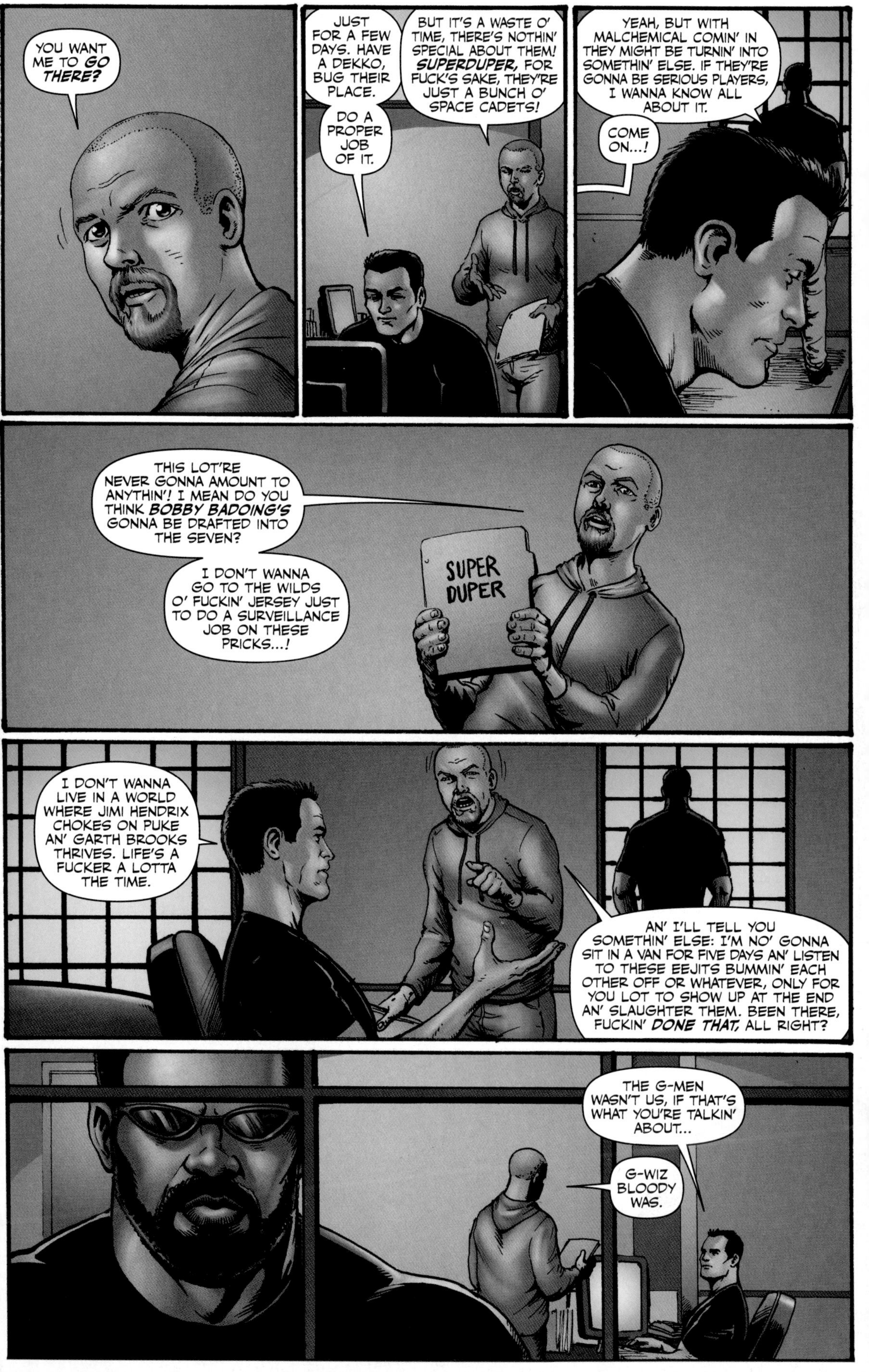
YOU WANT ME TO GO THERE?
JUST FOR A FEW DAYS. HAVE A DEKKO, BUG THEIR PLACE.
DO A PROPER JOB OF IT.
BUT IT'S A WASTE O' TIME, THERE'S NOTHIN' SPECIAL ABOUT THEM! SUPERDUPER, FOR FUCK'S SAKE, THEY'RE JUST A BUNCH O' SPACE CADETS!
YEAH, BUT WITH MALCHEMICAL COMIN' IN THEY MIGHT BE TURNIN' INTO SOMETHIN' ELSE. IF THEY'RE GONNA BE SERIOUS PLAYERS, I WANNA KNOW ALL ABOUT IT.
COME ON...!
THIS LOT'RE NEVER GONNA AMOUNT TO ANYTHIN'! I MEAN DO YOU THINK BOBBY BADOING'S GONNA BE DRAFTED INTO THE SEVEN?
I DON'T WANNA GO TO THE WILDS O' FUCKIN' JERSEY JUST TO DO A SURVEILLANCE JOB ON THESE PRICKS...!
SUPER DUPER
I DON'T WANNA LIVE IN A WORLD WHERE JIMI HENDRIX CHOKES ON PUKE AN' GARTH BROOKS THRIVES. LIFE'S A FUCKER A LOTTA THE TIME.
AN' I'LL TELL YOU SOMETHIN' ELSE: I'M NO' GONNA SIT IN A VAN FOR FIVE DAYS AN' LISTEN TO THESE EEJITS BUMMIN' EACH OTHER OFF OR WHATEVER, ONLY FOR YOU LOT TO SHOW UP AT THE END AN' SLAUGHTER THEM. BEEN THERE, FUCKIN' DONE THAT, ALL RIGHT?
THE G-MEN WASN'T US, IF THAT'S WHAT YOU'RE TALKIN' ABOUT...
G-WIZ BLOODY WAS.

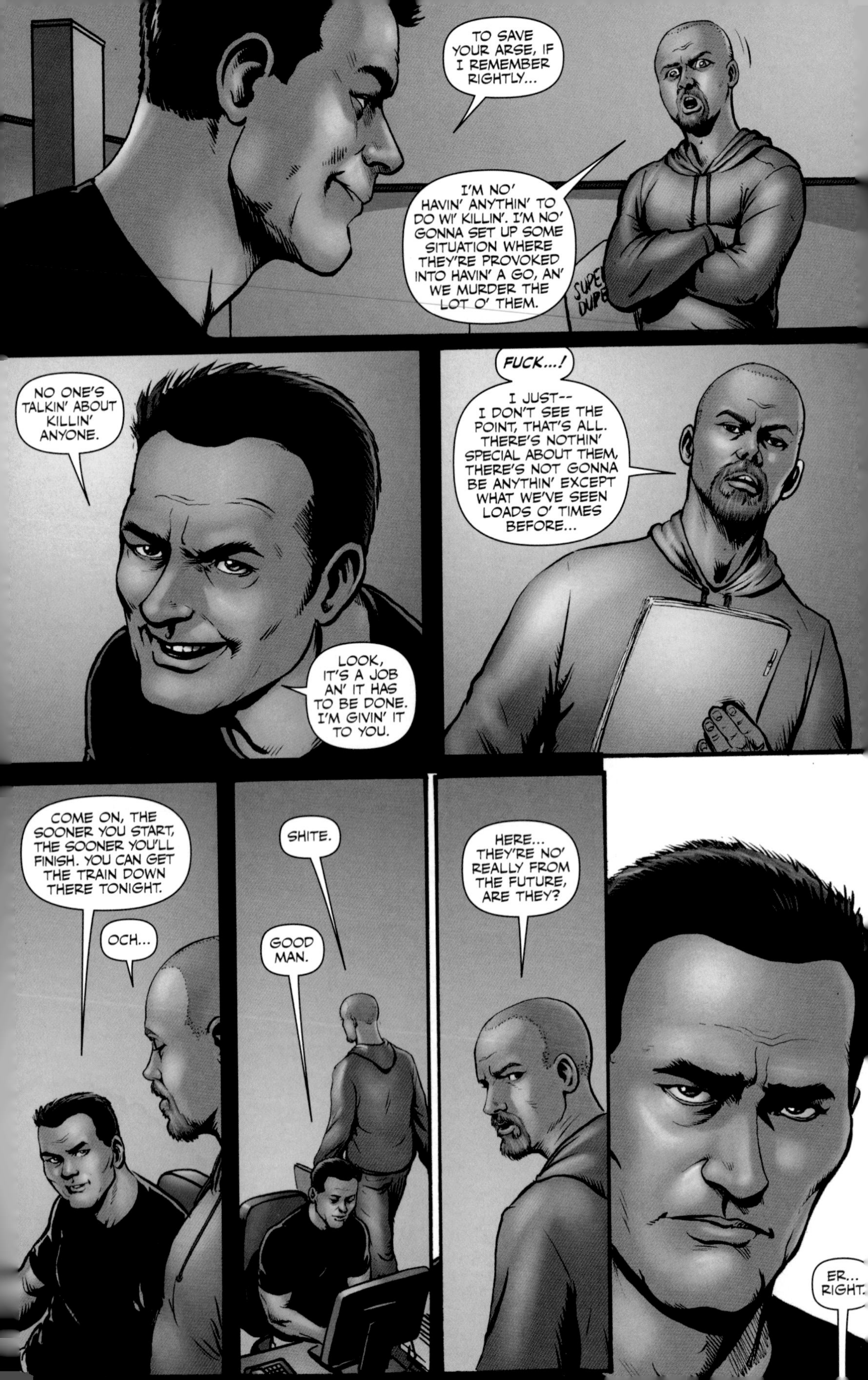
TO SAVE YOUR ARSE, IF I REMEMBER RIGHTLY...
I'M NO' HAVIN' ANYTHIN' TO DO WI' KILLIN'. I'M NO' GONNA SET UP SOME SITUATION WHERE THEY'RE PROVOKED INTO HAVIN' A GO, AN' WE MURDER THE LOT O' THEM.
NO ONE'S TALKIN' ABOUT KILLIN' ANYONE.
LOOK, IT'S A JOB AN' IT HAS TO BE DONE. I'M GIVIN' IT TO YOU.
FUCK...!
I JUST-- I DON'T SEE THE POINT, THAT'S ALL. THERE'S NOTHIN' SPECIAL ABOUT THEM, THERE'S NOT GONNA BE ANYTHIN' EXCEPT WHAT WE'VE SEEN LOADS O' TIMES BEFORE...
COME ON, THE SOONER YOU START, THE SOONER YOU'LL FINISH. YOU CAN GET THE TRAIN DOWN THERE TONIGHT.
OCH...
SHITE.
GOOD MAN.
HERE... THEY'RE NO' REALLY FROM THE FUTURE, ARE THEY?
ER... RIGHT.

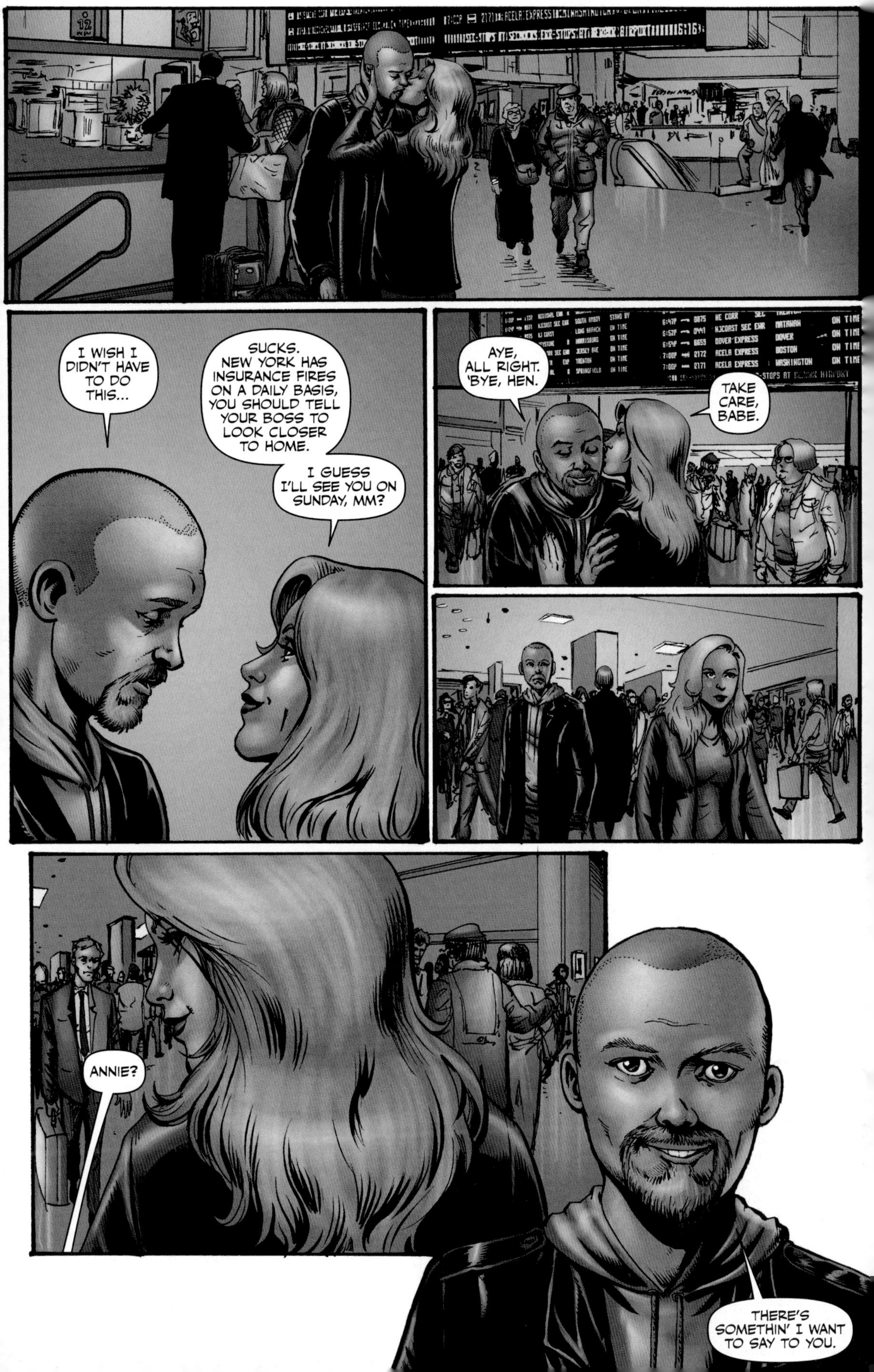

I WISH I DIDN'T HAVE TO DO THIS...
SUCKS. NEW YORK HAS INSURANCE FIRES ON A DAILY BASIS, YOU SHOULD TELL YOUR BOSS TO LOOK CLOSER TO HOME.
I GUESS I'LL SEE YOU ON SUNDAY, MM?
AYE, ALL RIGHT. 'BYE, HEN.
TAKE CARE, BABE.
ANNIE?
THERE'S SOMETHIN' I WANT TO SAY TO YOU.

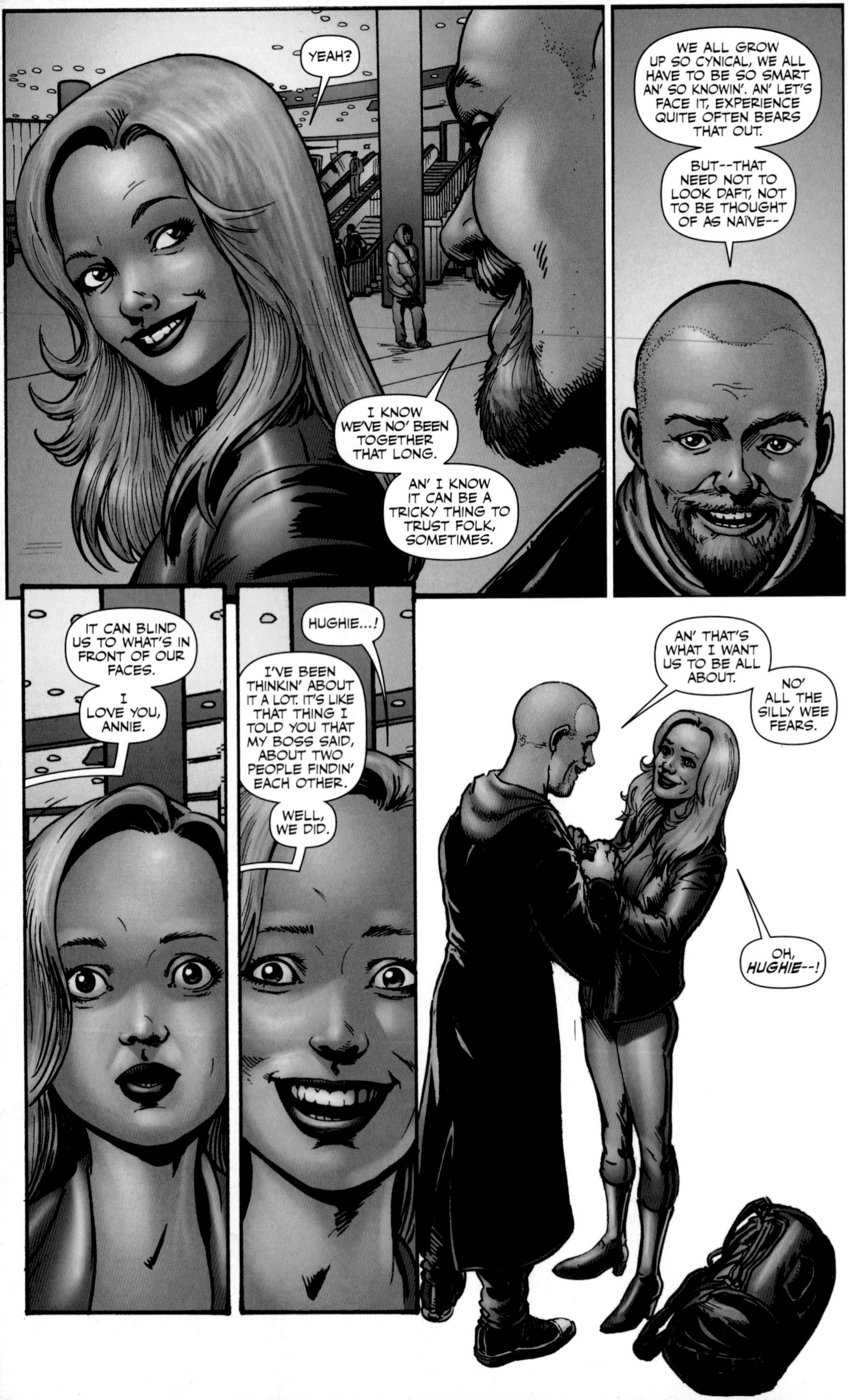
YEAH?
I KNOW WE'VE NO' BEEN TOGETHER THAT LONG.
AN' I KNOW IT CAN BE A TRICKY THING TO TRUST FOLK, SOMETIMES.
WE ALL GROW UP SO CYNICAL, WE ALL HAVE TO BE SO SMART AN' SO KNOWIN'. AN' LET'S FACE IT, EXPERIENCE QUITE OFTEN BEARS THAT OUT.
BUT--THAT NEED NOT TO LOOK DAFT, NOT TO BE THOUGHT OF AS NAÏVE--
IT CAN BLIND US TO WHAT'S IN FRONT OF OUR FACES.
I LOVE YOU, ANNIE.
HUGHIE...!
I'VE BEEN THINKIN' ABOUT IT A LOT. IT'S LIKE THAT THING I TOLD YOU THAT MY BOSS SAID, ABOUT TWO PEOPLE FINDIN' EACH OTHER.
WELL, WE DID.
AN' THAT'S WHAT I WANT US TO BE ALL ABOUT.
NO' ALL THE SILLY WEE FEARS.
OH, *HUGHIE*--!

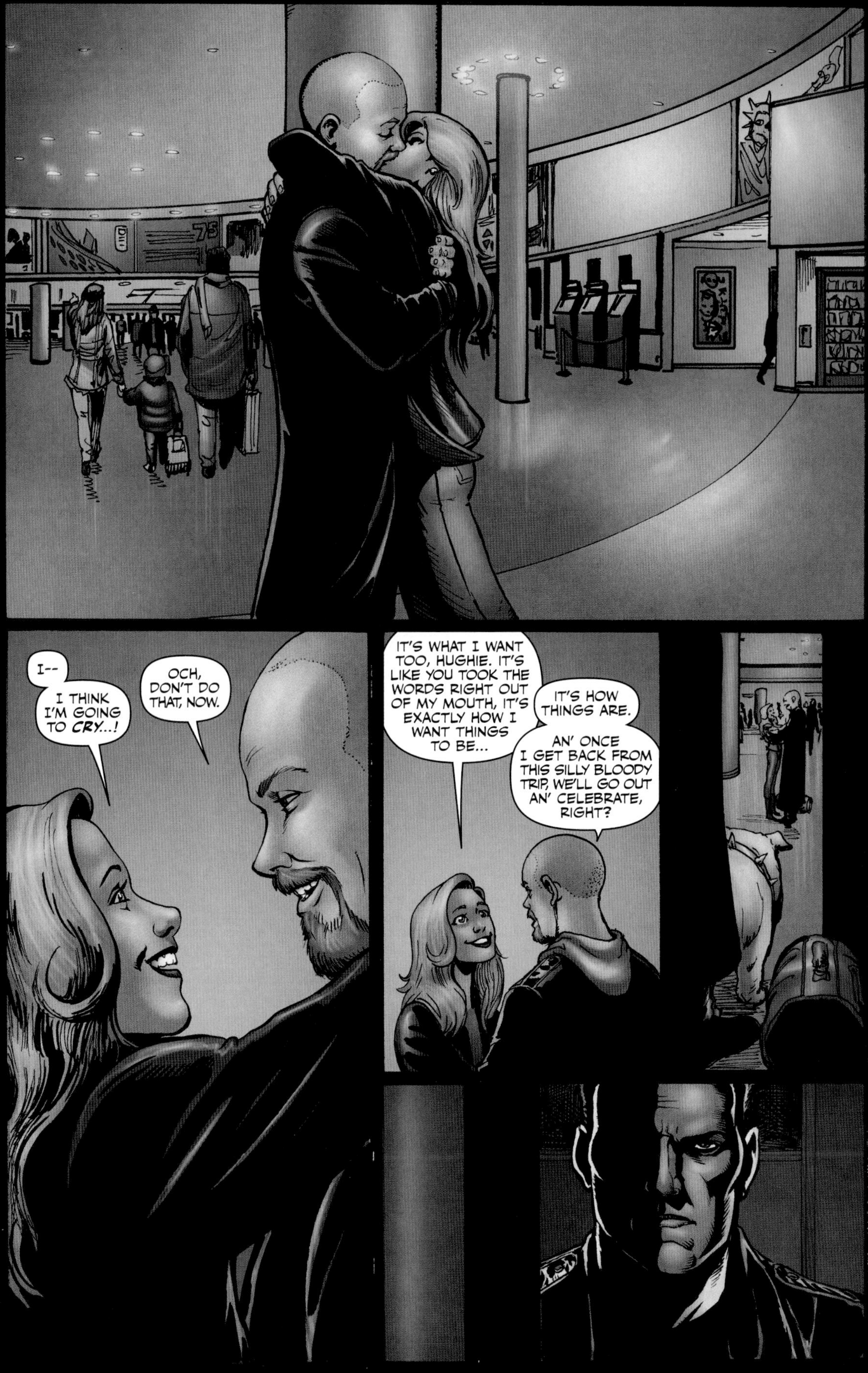
I--
I THINK I'M GOING TO *CRY*...!
OCH, DON'T DO THAT, NOW.
IT'S WHAT I WANT TOO, HUGHIE. IT'S LIKE YOU TOOK THE WORDS RIGHT OUT OF MY MOUTH, IT'S EXACTLY HOW I WANT THINGS TO BE...
IT'S HOW THINGS ARE.
AN' ONCE I GET BACK FROM THIS SILLY BLOODY TRIP, WE'LL GO OUT AN' CELEBRATE, RIGHT?

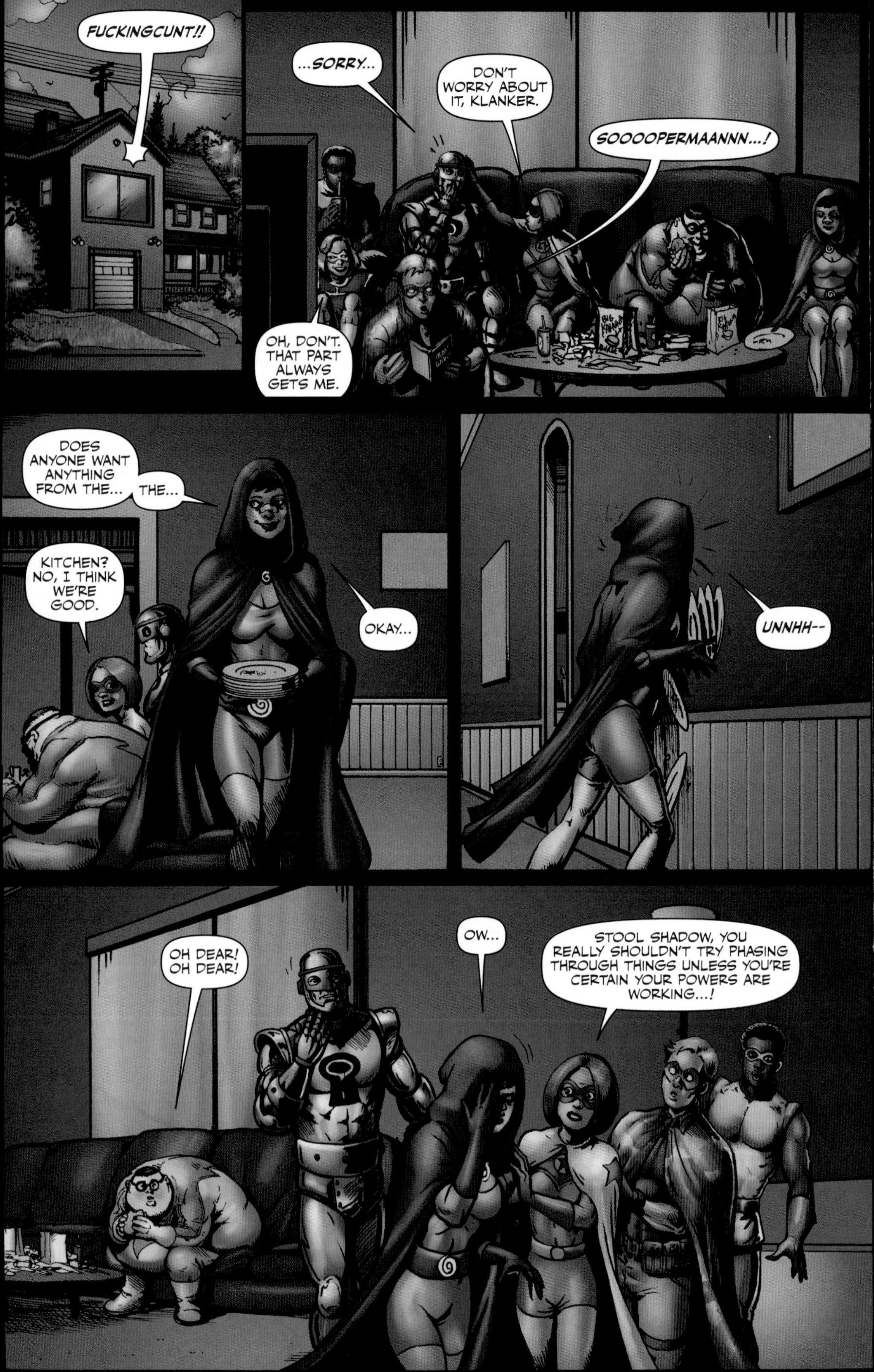
FUCKINGCUNT!!
...SORRY...
DON'T WORRY ABOUT IT, KLANKER.
SOOOOPERMAANNN...!
OH, DON'T. THAT PART ALWAYS GETS ME.
DOES ANYONE WANT ANYTHING FROM THE... THE...
KITCHEN? NO, I THINK WE'RE GOOD.
OKAY...
UNNHH--
OH DEAR! OH DEAR!
OW...
STOOL SHADOW, YOU REALLY SHOULDN'T TRY PHASING THROUGH THINGS UNLESS YOU'RE CERTAIN YOUR POWERS ARE WORKING...!

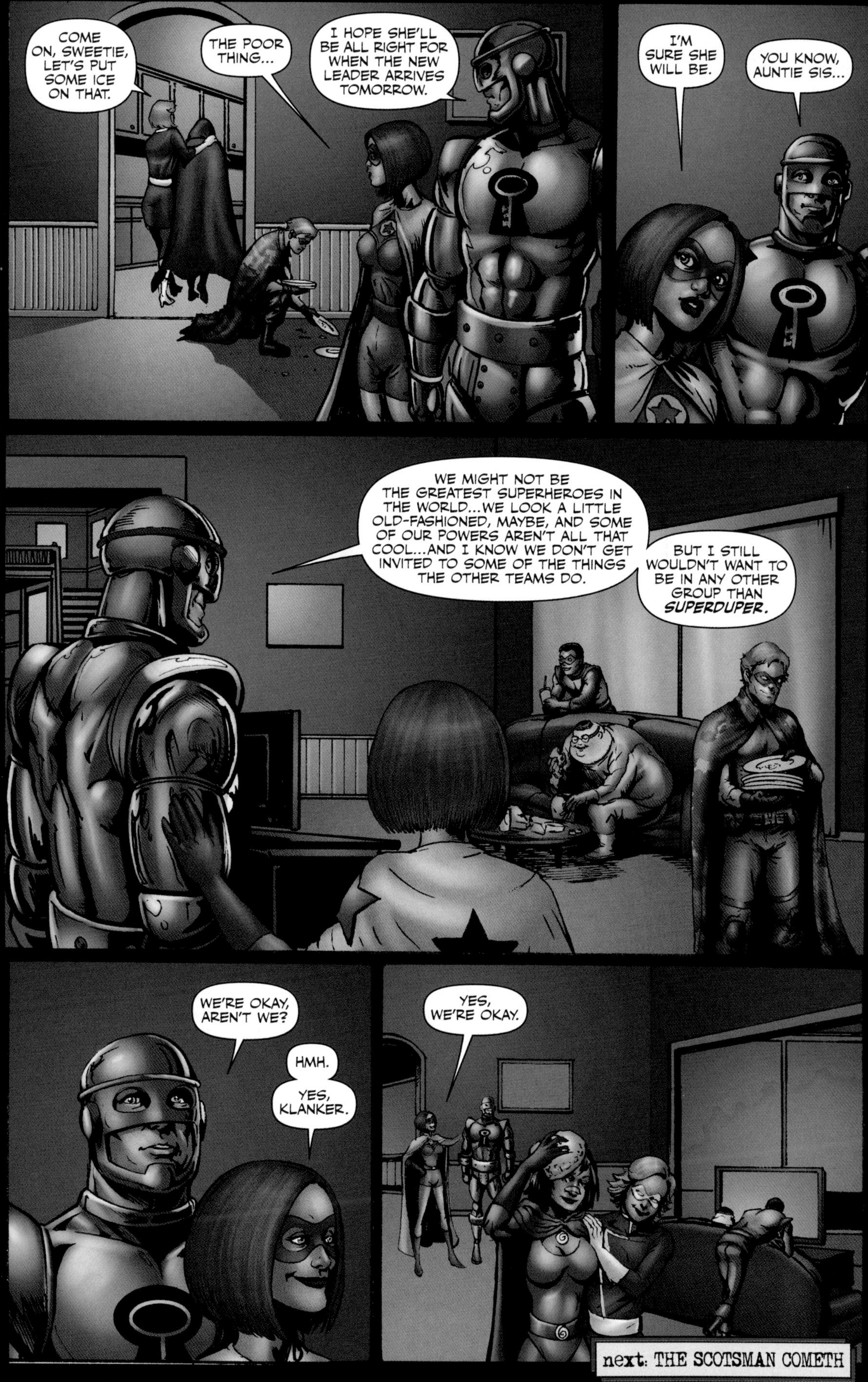
COME ON, SWEETIE, LET'S PUT SOME ICE ON THAT.
THE POOR THING...
I HOPE SHE'LL BE ALL RIGHT FOR WHEN THE NEW LEADER ARRIVES TOMORROW.
I'M SURE SHE WILL BE.
YOU KNOW, AUNTIE SIS...
WE MIGHT NOT BE THE GREATEST SUPERHEROES IN THE WORLD...WE LOOK A LITTLE OLD-FASHIONED, MAYBE, AND SOME OF OUR POWERS AREN'T ALL THAT COOL...AND I KNOW WE DON'T GET INVITED TO SOME OF THE THINGS THE OTHER TEAMS DO.
BUT I STILL WOULDN'T WANT TO BE IN ANY OTHER GROUP THAN *SUPERDUPER.*
WE'RE OKAY, AREN'T WE?
HMH.
YES, KLANKER.
YES, WE'RE OKAY.
next: THE SCOTSMAN COMETH

#41 cover
by Darick Robertson
and Tony Aviña

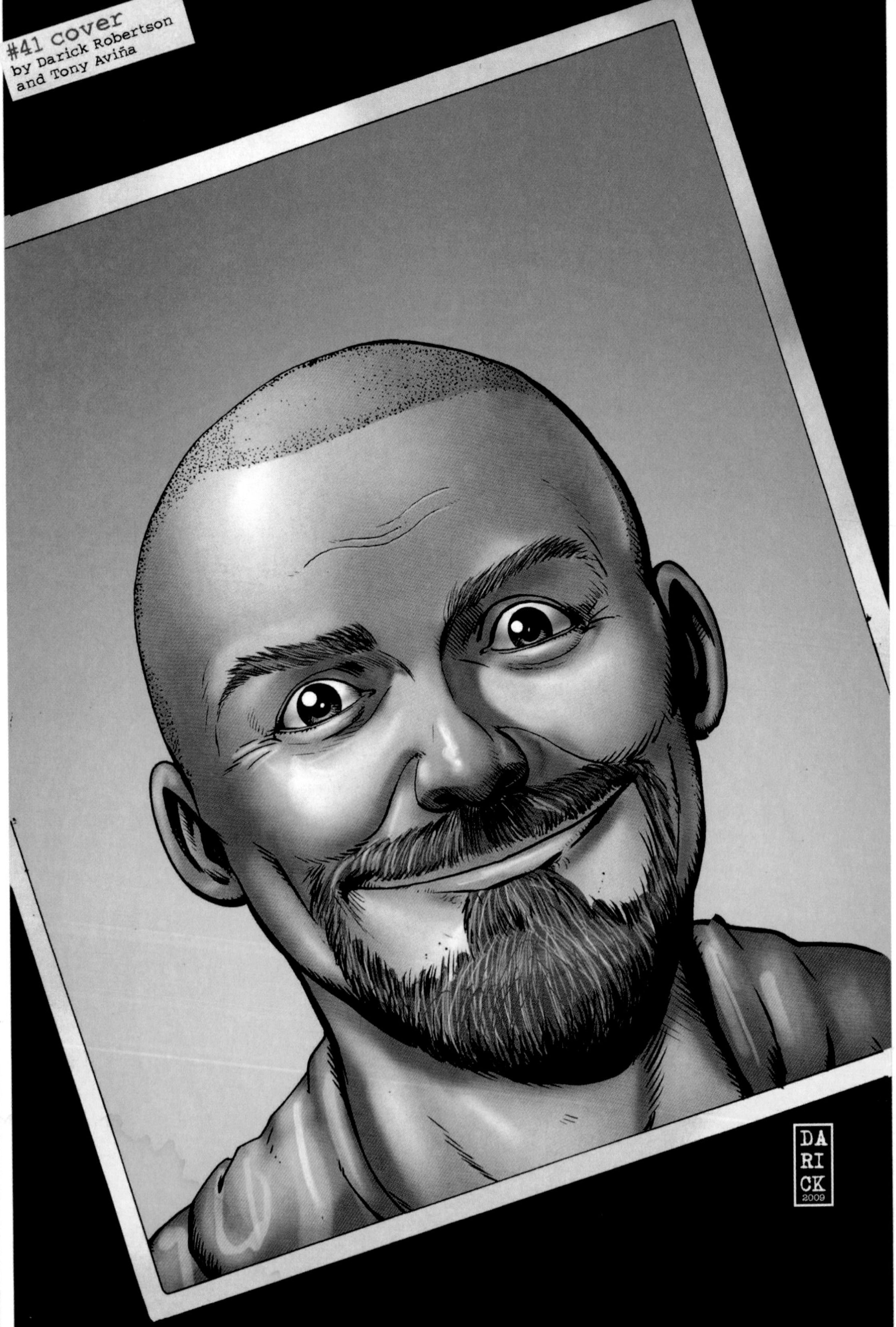
DA
RI
CK
2009

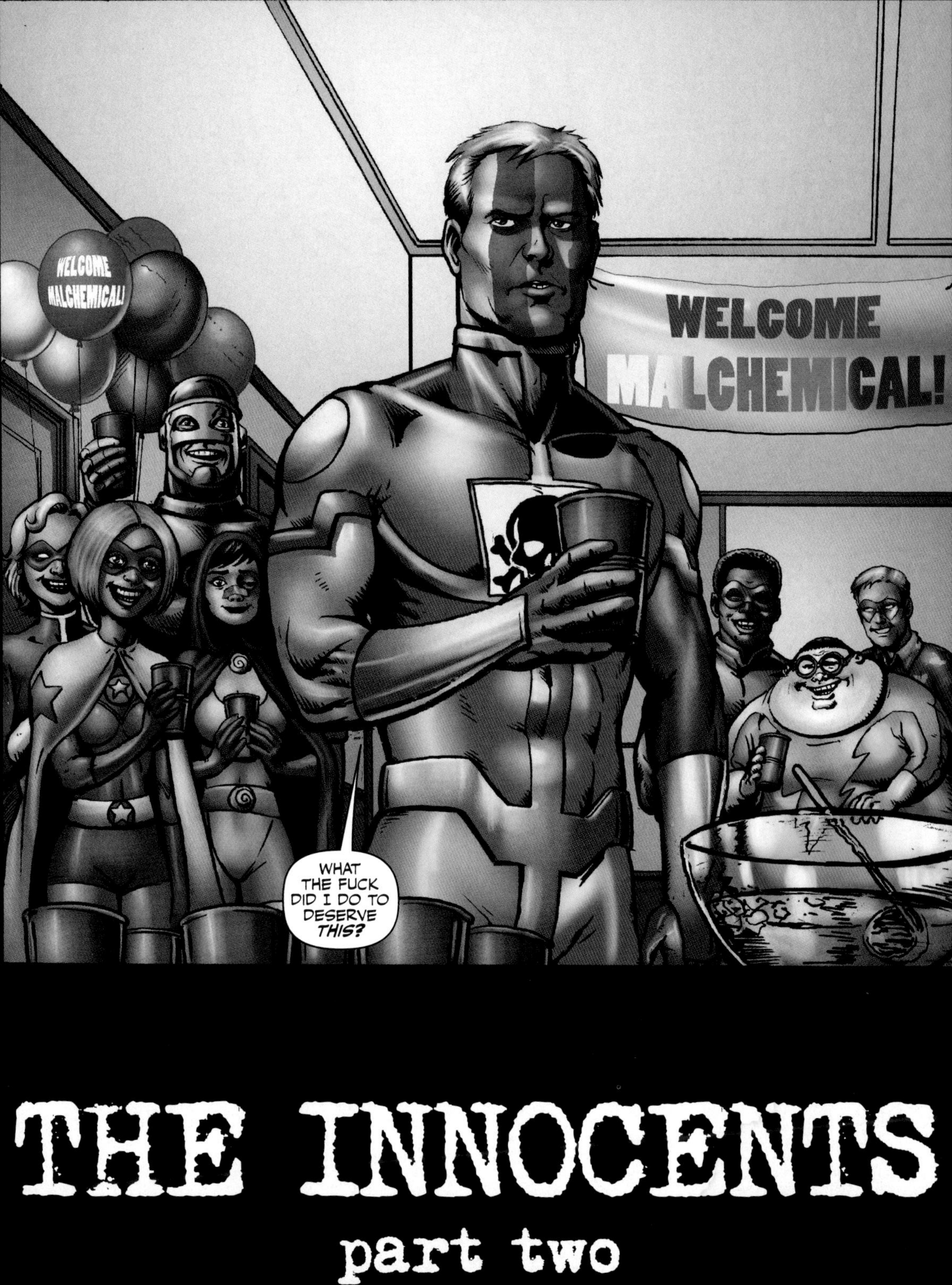
WELCOME MALCHEMICAL!
WELCOME MALCHEMICAL!
WHAT THE FUCK DID I DO TO DESERVE *THIS?*

THE INNOCENTS
part two

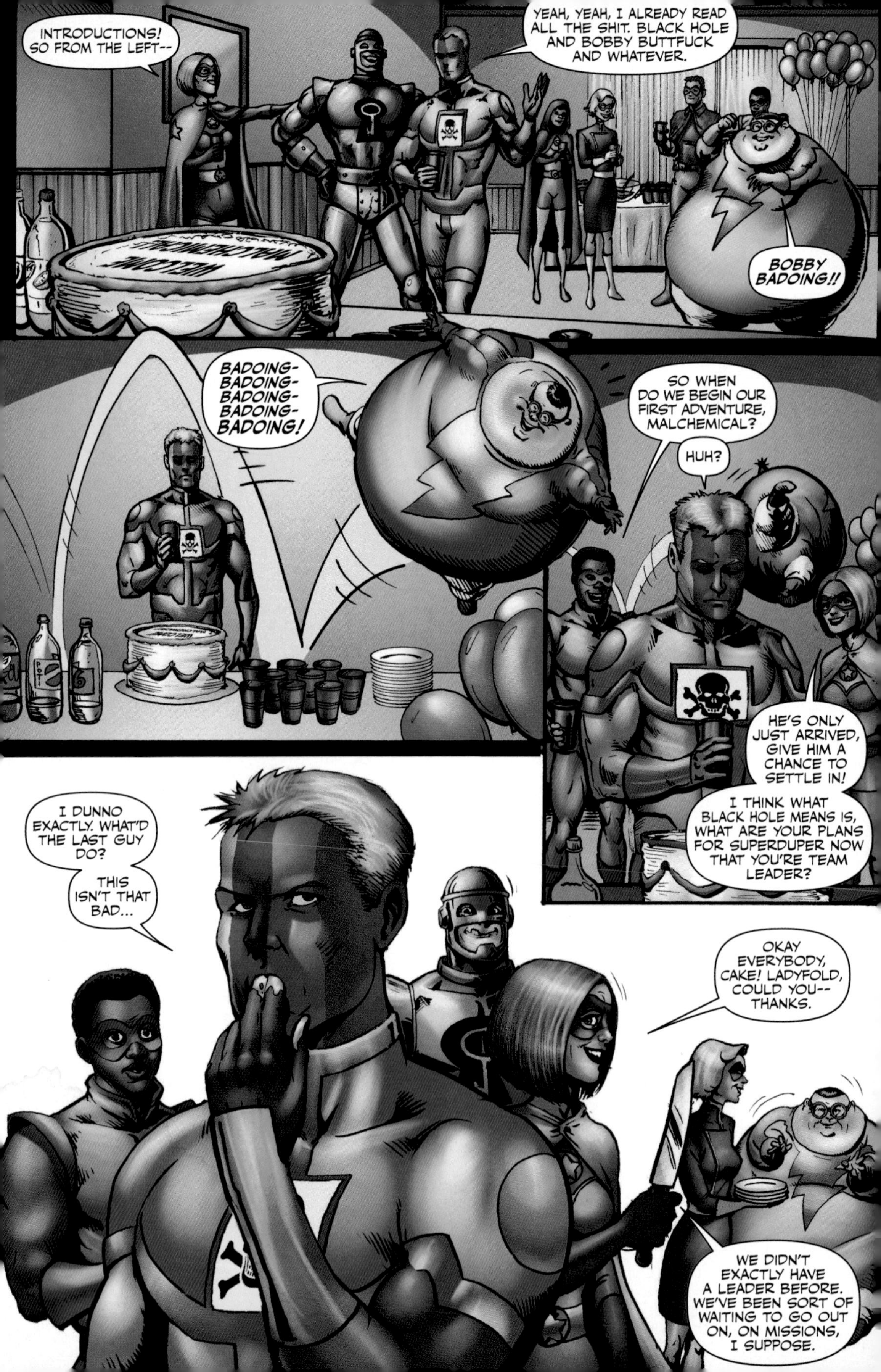
INTRODUCTIONS! SO FROM THE LEFT--
YEAH, YEAH, I ALREADY READ ALL THE SHIT. BLACK HOLE AND BOBBY BUTTFUCK AND WHATEVER.
BOBBY BADOING!!
BADOING-BADOING-BADOING-BADOING-BADOING!
SO WHEN DO WE BEGIN OUR FIRST ADVENTURE, MALCHEMICAL?
HUH?
HE'S ONLY JUST ARRIVED, GIVE HIM A CHANCE TO SETTLE IN!
I THINK WHAT BLACK HOLE MEANS IS, WHAT ARE YOUR PLANS FOR SUPERDUPER NOW THAT YOU'RE TEAM LEADER?
I DUNNO EXACTLY. WHAT'D THE LAST GUY DO?
THIS ISN'T THAT BAD...
OKAY EVERYBODY, CAKE! LADYFOLD, COULD YOU-- THANKS.
WE DIDN'T EXACTLY HAVE A LEADER BEFORE. WE'VE BEEN SORT OF WAITING TO GO OUT ON, ON MISSIONS, I SUPPOSE.

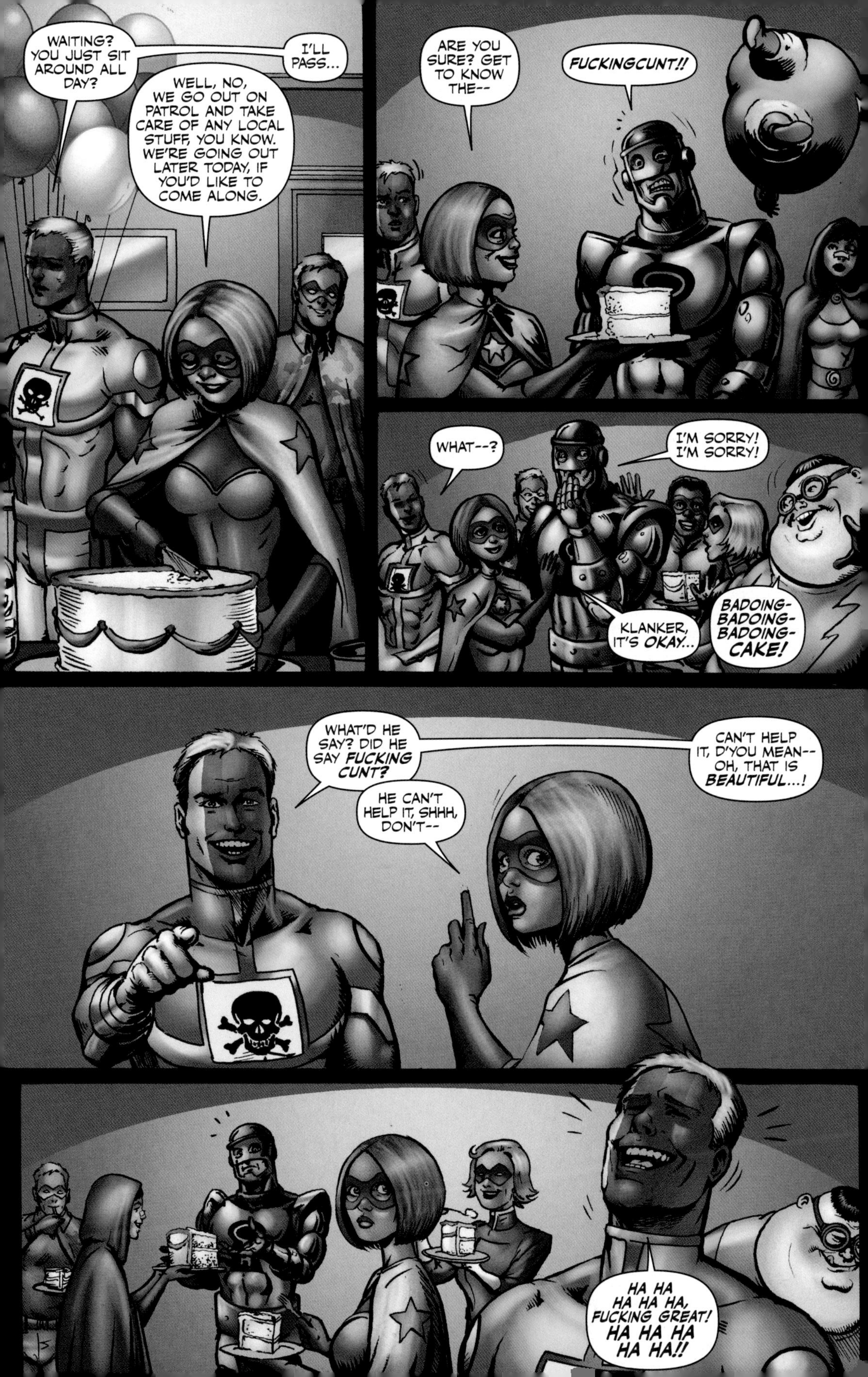

WAITING? YOU JUST SIT AROUND ALL DAY?
I'LL PASS...
WELL, NO, WE GO OUT ON PATROL AND TAKE CARE OF ANY LOCAL STUFF, YOU KNOW. WE'RE GOING OUT LATER TODAY, IF YOU'D LIKE TO COME ALONG.
ARE YOU SURE? GET TO KNOW THE--
FUCKINGCUNT!!
WHAT--?
I'M SORRY! I'M SORRY!
KLANKER, IT'S OKAY...
BADOING-BADOING-BADOING-CAKE!
WHAT'D HE SAY? DID HE SAY FUCKING CUNT?
HE CAN'T HELP IT, SHHH, DON'T--
CAN'T HELP IT, D'YOU MEAN--OH, THAT IS BEAUTIFUL...!
HA HA HA HA HA, FUCKING GREAT! HA HA HA HA HA!!

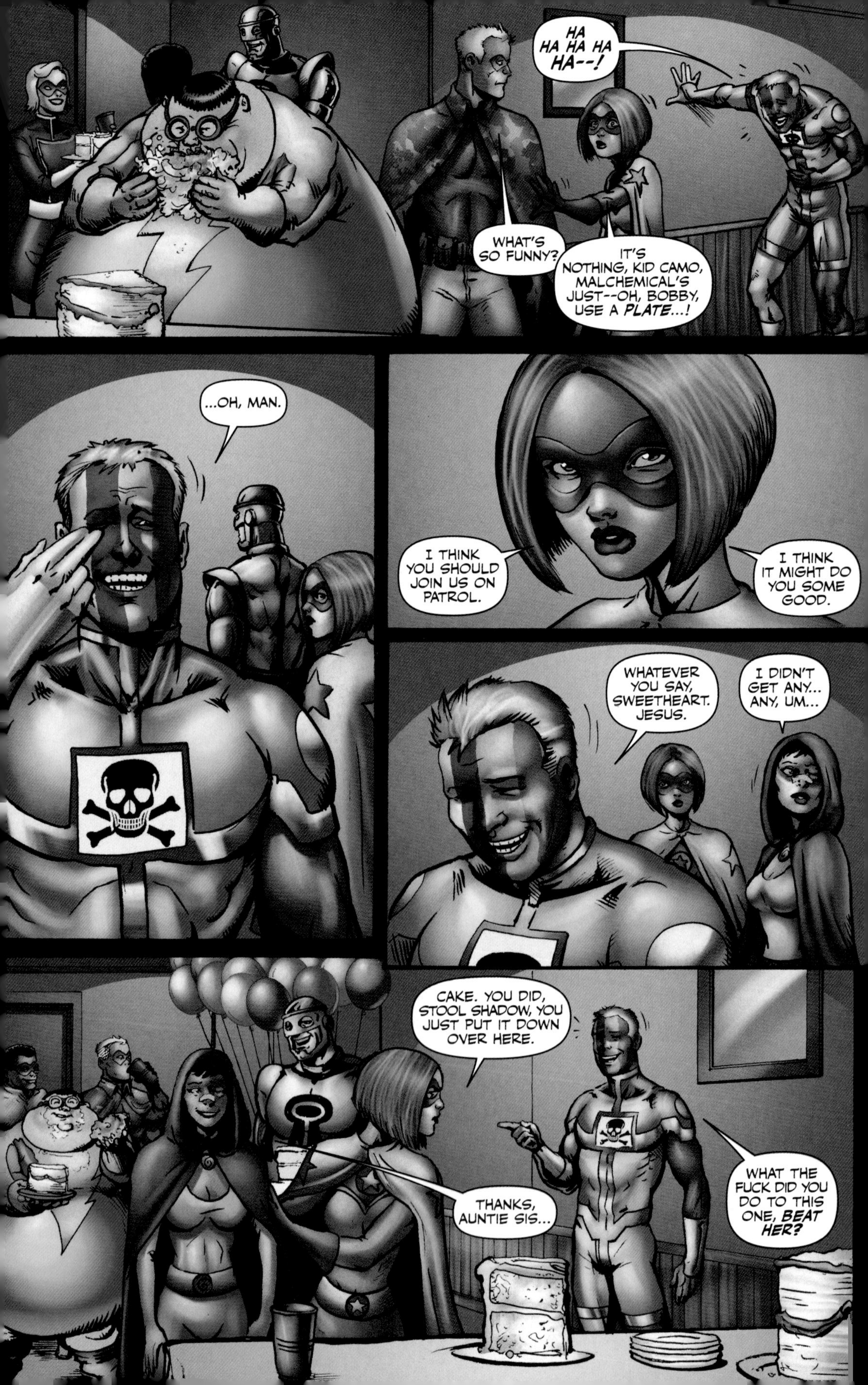
HA HA HA HA HA--!
WHAT'S SO FUNNY?
IT'S NOTHING, KID CAMO, MALCHEMICAL'S JUST--OH, BOBBY, USE A *PLATE*...!
...OH, MAN.
I THINK YOU SHOULD JOIN US ON PATROL.
I THINK IT MIGHT DO YOU SOME GOOD.
WHATEVER YOU SAY, SWEETHEART. JESUS.
I DIDN'T GET ANY... ANY, UM...
CAKE. YOU DID, STOOL SHADOW, YOU JUST PUT IT DOWN OVER HERE.
THANKS, AUNTIE SIS...
WHAT THE FUCK DID YOU DO TO THIS ONE, *BEAT HER?*

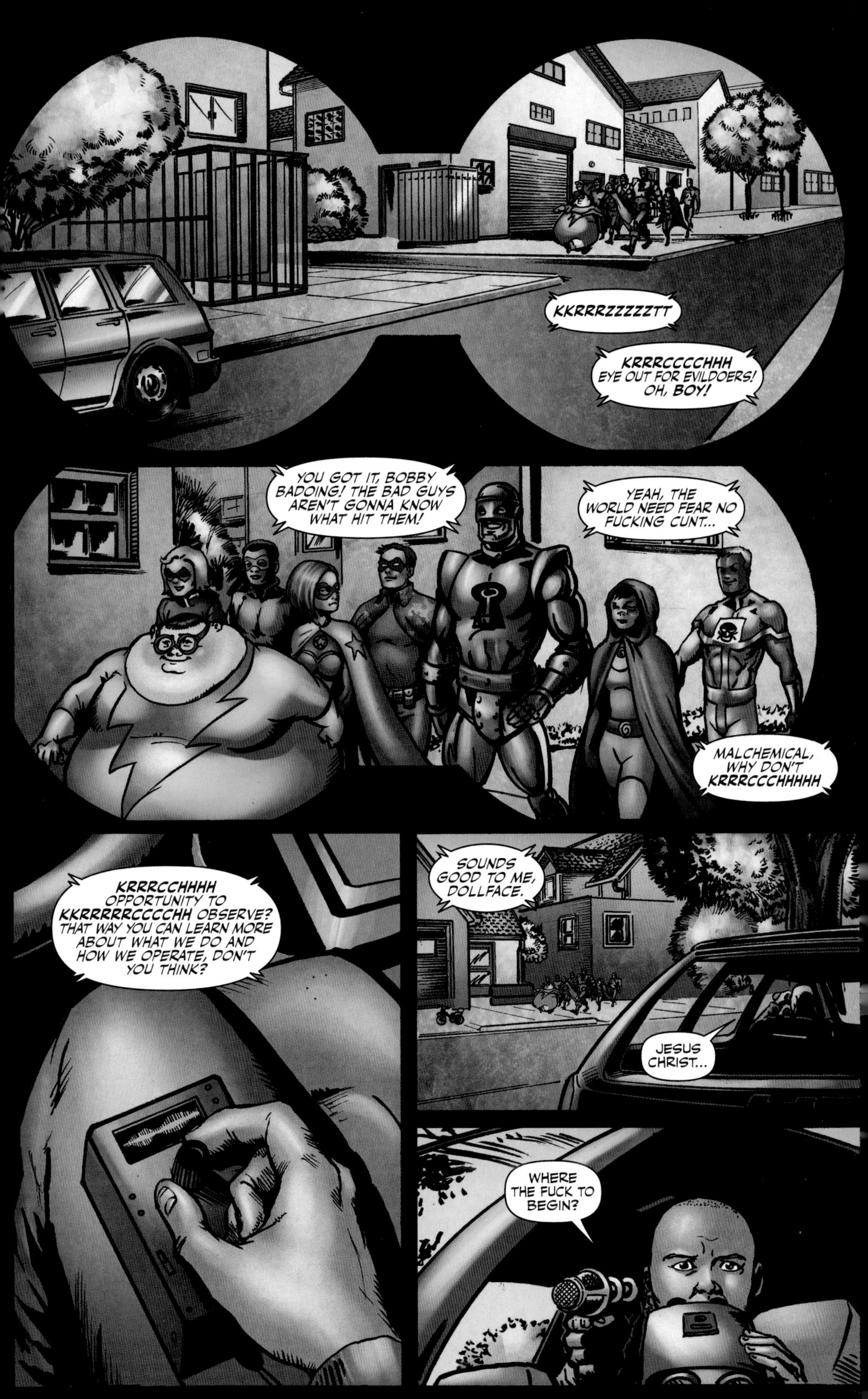
KKRRRZZZZZZTT
KRRRCCCCHHH
EYE OUT FOR EVILDOERS!
OH, BOY!
YOU GOT IT, BOBBY BADOING! THE BAD GUYS AREN'T GONNA KNOW WHAT HIT THEM!
YEAH, THE WORLD NEED FEAR NO FUCKING CUNT...
MALCHEMICAL, WHY DON'T KRRRCCCHHHHH
KRRRCCHHHH OPPORTUNITY TO KKRRRRRCCCCHH OBSERVE? THAT WAY YOU CAN LEARN MORE ABOUT WHAT WE DO AND HOW WE OPERATE, DON'T YOU THINK?
SOUNDS GOOD TO ME, DOLLFACE.
JESUS CHRIST...
WHERE THE FUCK TO BEGIN?

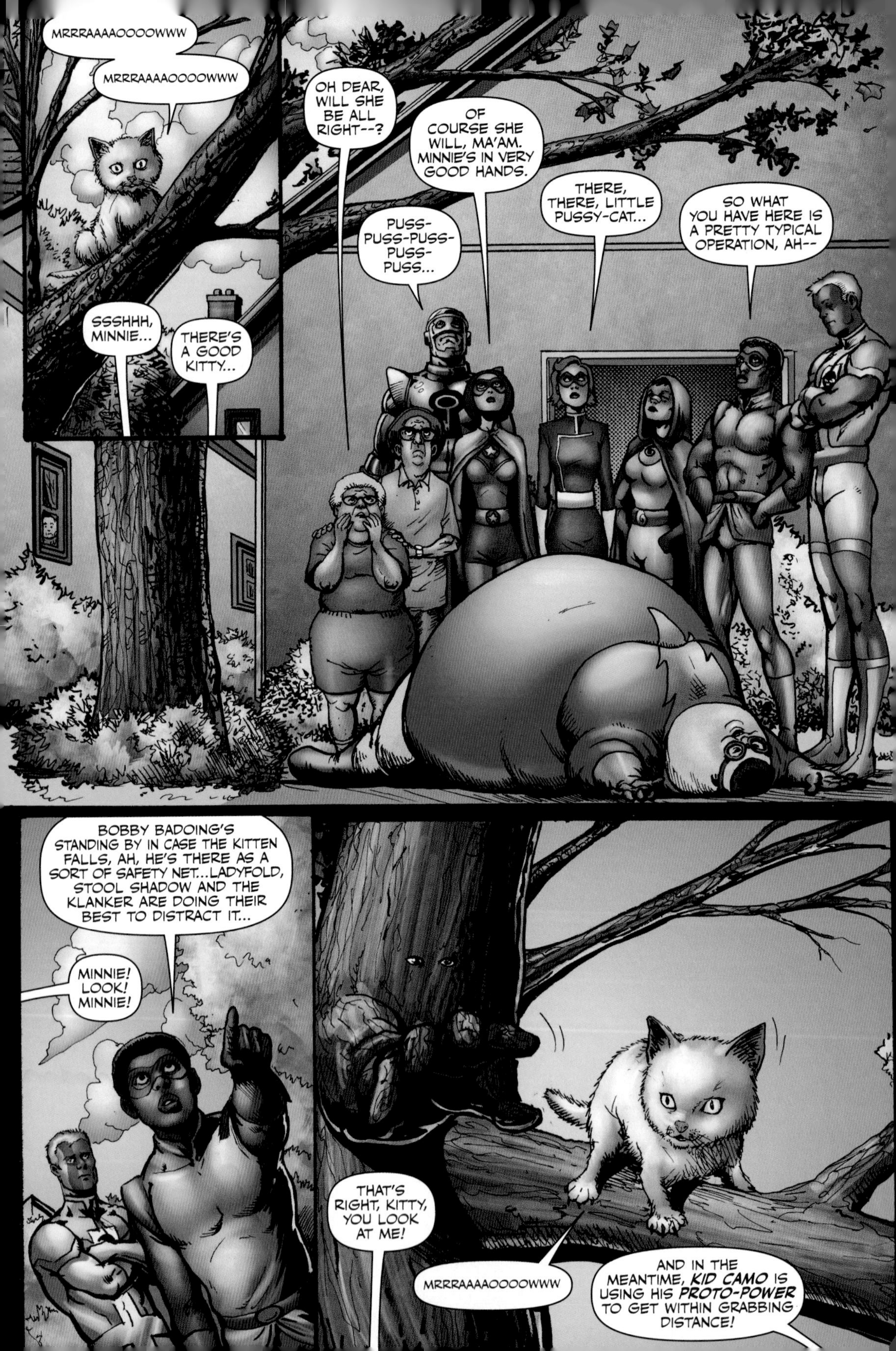
MRRRAAAAOOOOWWW
MRRRAAAAOOOOWWW
SSSHHH, MINNIE...
THERE'S A GOOD KITTY...
OH DEAR, WILL SHE BE ALL RIGHT--?
OF COURSE SHE WILL, MA'AM. MINNIE'S IN VERY GOOD HANDS.
PUSS-PUSS-PUSS-PUSS-PUSS...
THERE, THERE, LITTLE PUSSY-CAT...
SO WHAT YOU HAVE HERE IS A PRETTY TYPICAL OPERATION, AH--
BOBBY BADOING'S STANDING BY IN CASE THE KITTEN FALLS, AH, HE'S THERE AS A SORT OF SAFETY NET...LADYFOLD, STOOL SHADOW AND THE KLANKER ARE DOING THEIR BEST TO DISTRACT IT...
MINNIE! LOOK! MINNIE!
THAT'S RIGHT, KITTY, YOU LOOK AT ME!
MRRRAAAAOOOOWWW
AND IN THE MEANTIME, KID CAMO IS USING HIS PROTO-POWER TO GET WITHIN GRABBING DISTANCE!

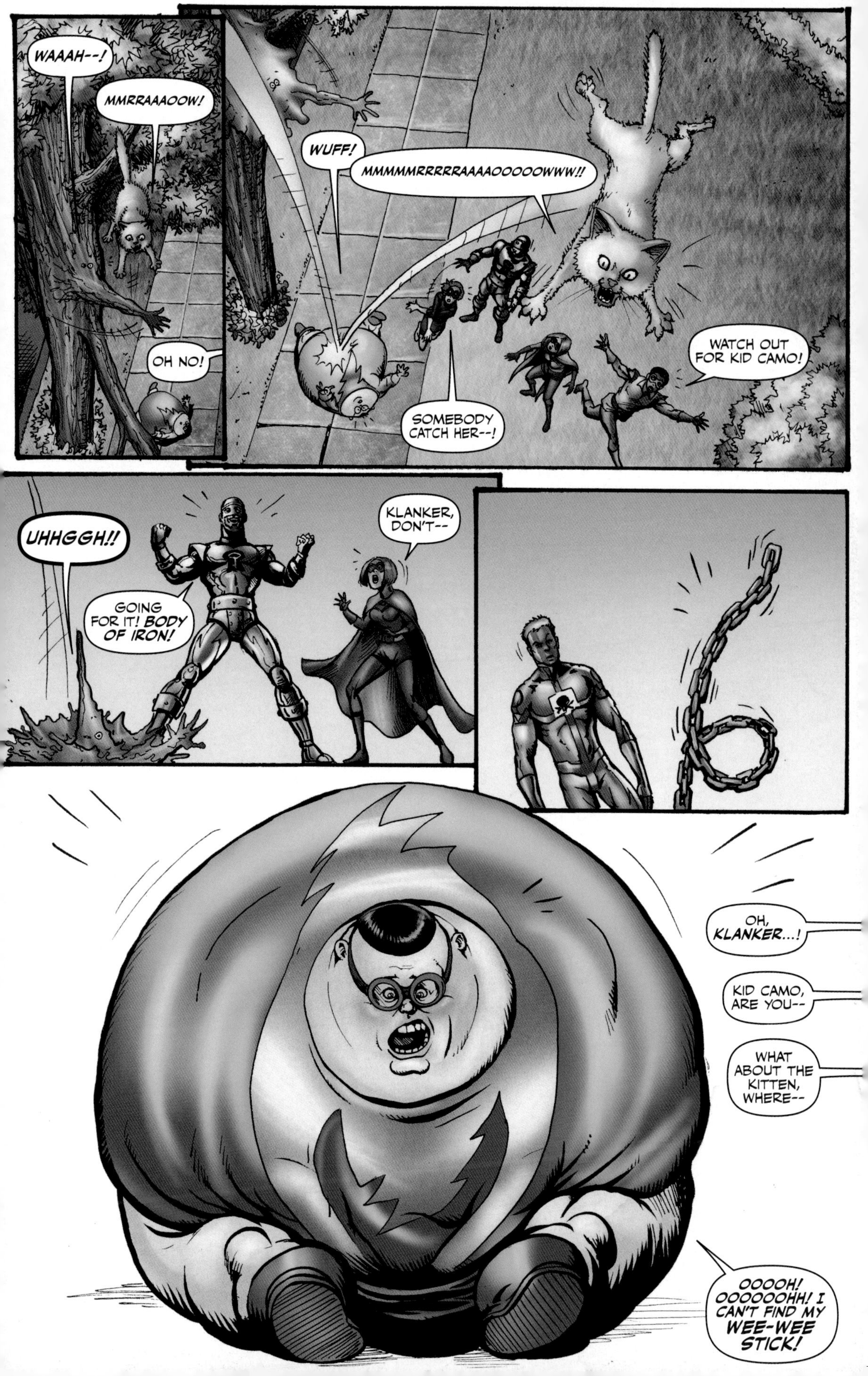
WAAAH--!
MMRRAAAOOW!
OH NO!
WUFF!
MMMMMRRRRRAAAAOOOOOWWW!!
SOMEBODY CATCH HER--!
WATCH OUT FOR KID CAMO!
UHHGGH!!
GOING FOR IT! BODY OF IRON!
KLANKER, DON'T--
OH, KLANKER...!
KID CAMO, ARE YOU--
WHAT ABOUT THE KITTEN, WHERE--
OOOOH! OOOOOOHH! I CAN'T FIND MY WEE-WEE STICK!

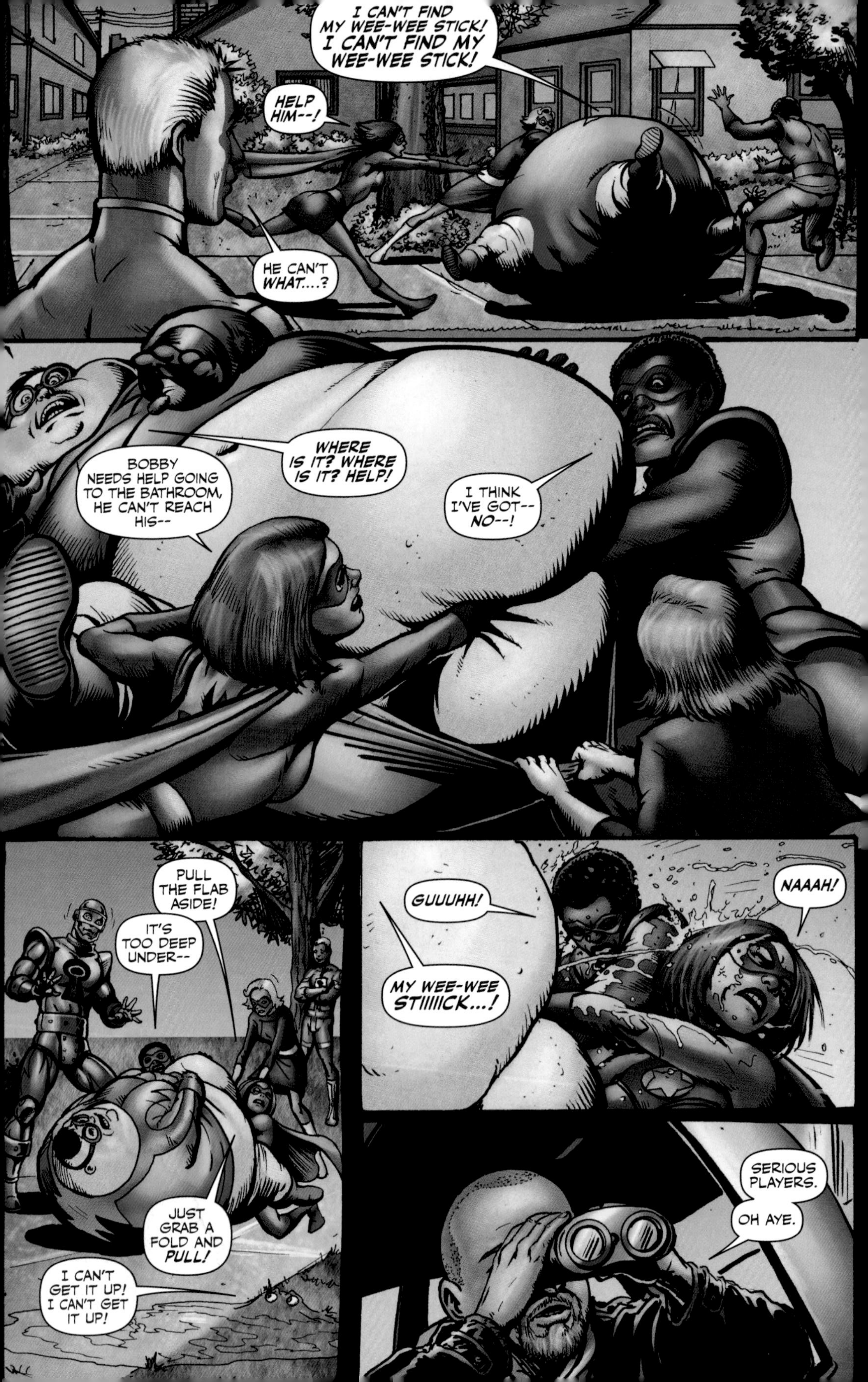
I CAN'T FIND MY WEE-WEE STICK! I CAN'T FIND MY WEE-WEE STICK!
HELP HIM--!
HE CAN'T WHAT....?
BOBBY NEEDS HELP GOING TO THE BATHROOM, HE CAN'T REACH HIS--
WHERE IS IT? WHERE IS IT? HELP!
I THINK I'VE GOT-- NO--!
PULL THE FLAB ASIDE!
IT'S TOO DEEP UNDER--
JUST GRAB A FOLD AND PULL!
I CAN'T GET IT UP! I CAN'T GET IT UP!
GUUUHH!
MY WEE-WEE STIIIICK...!
NAAAH!
SERIOUS PLAYERS.
OH AYE.

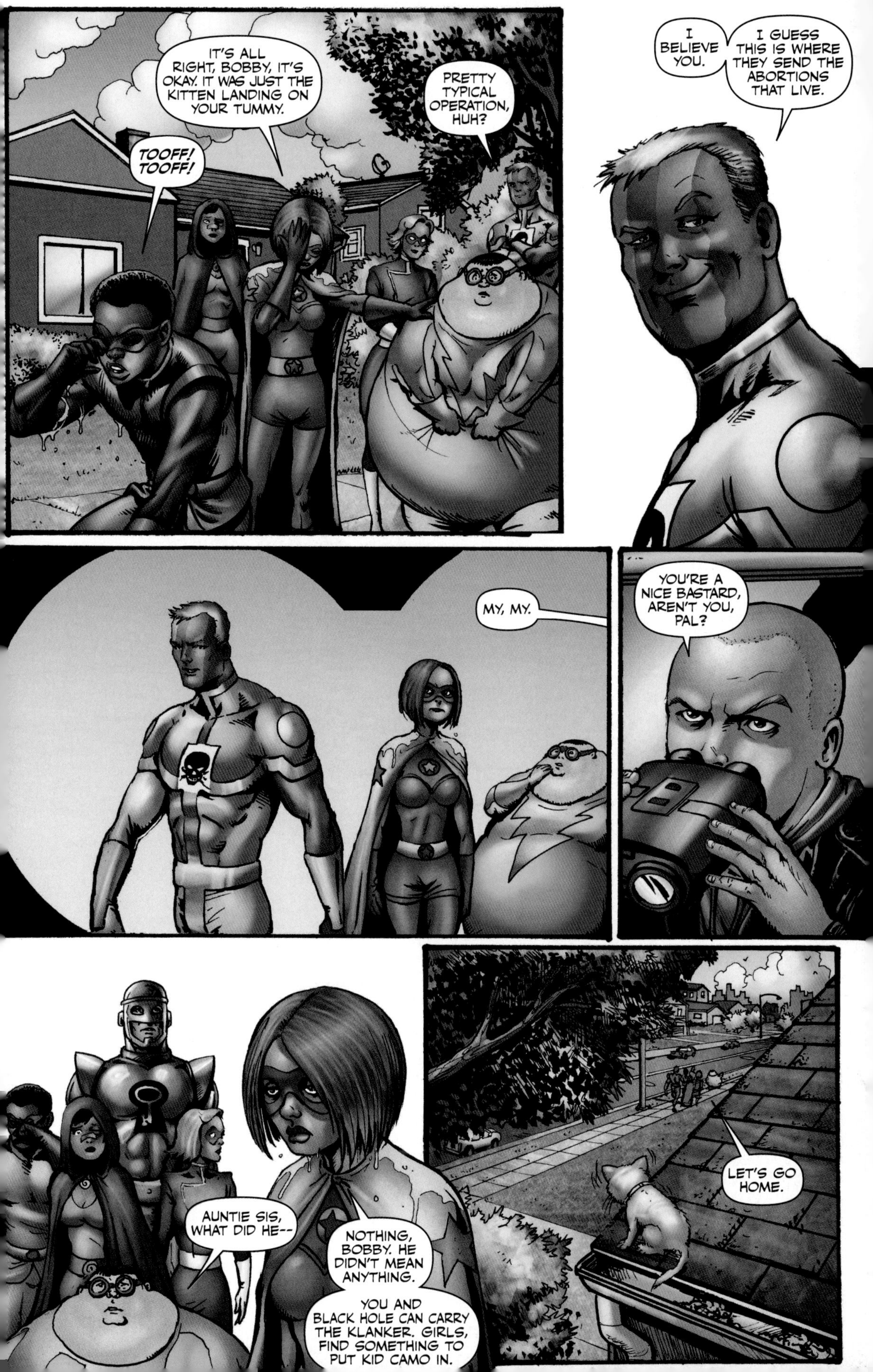
IT'S ALL RIGHT, BOBBY, IT'S OKAY. IT WAS JUST THE KITTEN LANDING ON YOUR TUMMY.
TOOFF! TOOFF!
PRETTY TYPICAL OPERATION, HUH?
I BELIEVE YOU.
I GUESS THIS IS WHERE THEY SEND THE ABORTIONS THAT LIVE.
MY, MY.
YOU'RE A NICE BASTARD, AREN'T YOU, PAL?
AUNTIE SIS, WHAT DID HE--
NOTHING, BOBBY. HE DIDN'T MEAN ANYTHING.
YOU AND BLACK HOLE CAN CARRY THE KLANKER. GIRLS, FIND SOMETHING TO PUT KID CAMO IN.
LET'S GO HOME.

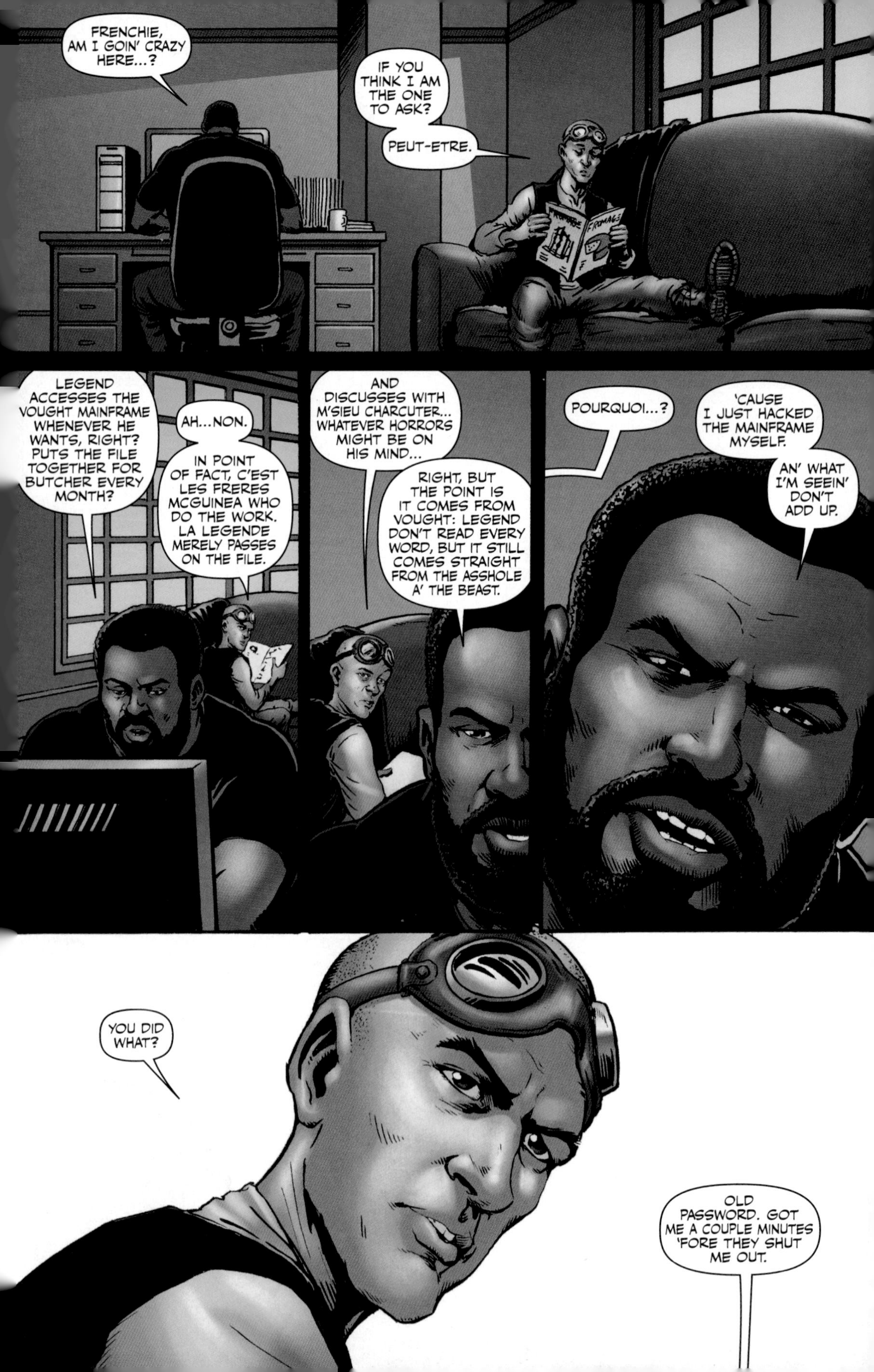
FRENCHIE, AM I GOIN' CRAZY HERE...?
IF YOU THINK I AM THE ONE TO ASK?
PEUT-ETRE.
LEGEND ACCESSES THE VOUGHT MAINFRAME WHENEVER HE WANTS, RIGHT? PUTS THE FILE TOGETHER FOR BUTCHER EVERY MONTH?
AH...NON.
IN POINT OF FACT, C'EST LES FRERES MCGUINEA WHO DO THE WORK. LA LEGENDE MERELY PASSES ON THE FILE.
AND DISCUSSES WITH M'SIEU CHARCUTER... WHATEVER HORRORS MIGHT BE ON HIS MIND...
RIGHT, BUT THE POINT IS IT COMES FROM VOUGHT: LEGEND DON'T READ EVERY WORD, BUT IT STILL COMES STRAIGHT FROM THE ASSHOLE A' THE BEAST.
POURQUOI...?
'CAUSE I JUST HACKED THE MAINFRAME MYSELF.
AN' WHAT I'M SEEIN' DON'T ADD UP.
YOU DID WHAT?
OLD PASSWORD. GOT ME A COUPLE MINUTES 'FORE THEY SHUT ME OUT.

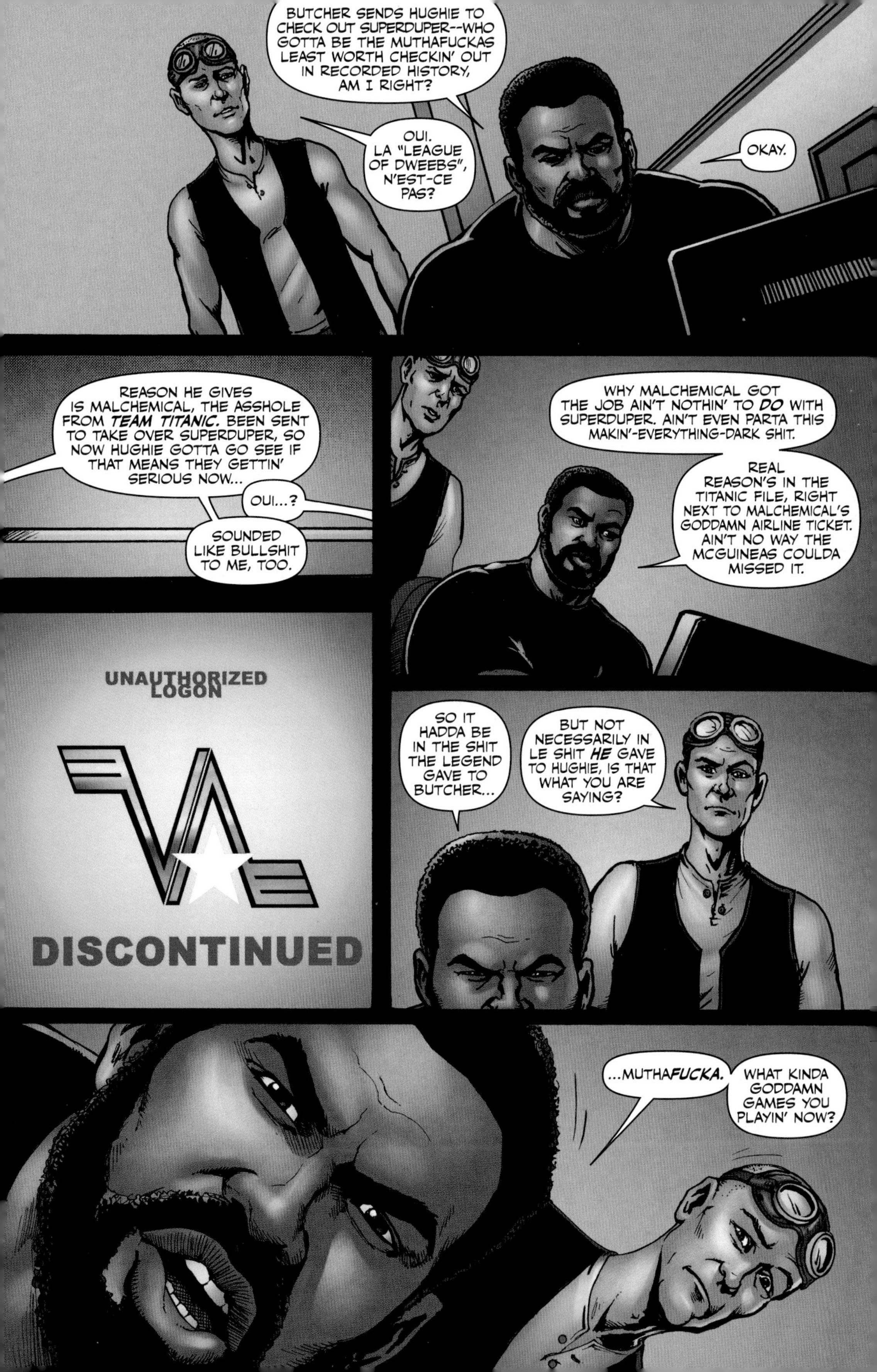
BUTCHER SENDS HUGHIE TO CHECK OUT SUPERDUPER--WHO GOTTA BE THE MUTHAFUCKAS LEAST WORTH CHECKIN' OUT IN RECORDED HISTORY, AM I RIGHT?
OUI. LA "LEAGUE OF DWEEBS", N'EST-CE PAS?
OKAY.
REASON HE GIVES IS MALCHEMICAL, THE ASSHOLE FROM TEAM TITANIC. BEEN SENT TO TAKE OVER SUPERDUPER, SO NOW HUGHIE GOTTA GO SEE IF THAT MEANS THEY GETTIN' SERIOUS NOW...
OUI...?
SOUNDED LIKE BULLSHIT TO ME, TOO.
WHY MALCHEMICAL GOT THE JOB AIN'T NOTHIN' TO DO WITH SUPERDUPER. AIN'T EVEN PARTA THIS MAKIN'-EVERYTHING-DARK SHIT.
REAL REASON'S IN THE TITANIC FILE, RIGHT NEXT TO MALCHEMICAL'S GODDAMN AIRLINE TICKET. AIN'T NO WAY THE MCGUINEAS COULDA MISSED IT.
UNAUTHORIZED LOGON
DISCONTINUED
SO IT HADDA BE IN THE SHIT THE LEGEND GAVE TO BUTCHER...
BUT NOT NECESSARILY IN LE SHIT HE GAVE TO HUGHIE, IS THAT WHAT YOU ARE SAYING?
...MUTHAFUCKA.
WHAT KINDA GODDAMN GAMES YOU PLAYIN' NOW?

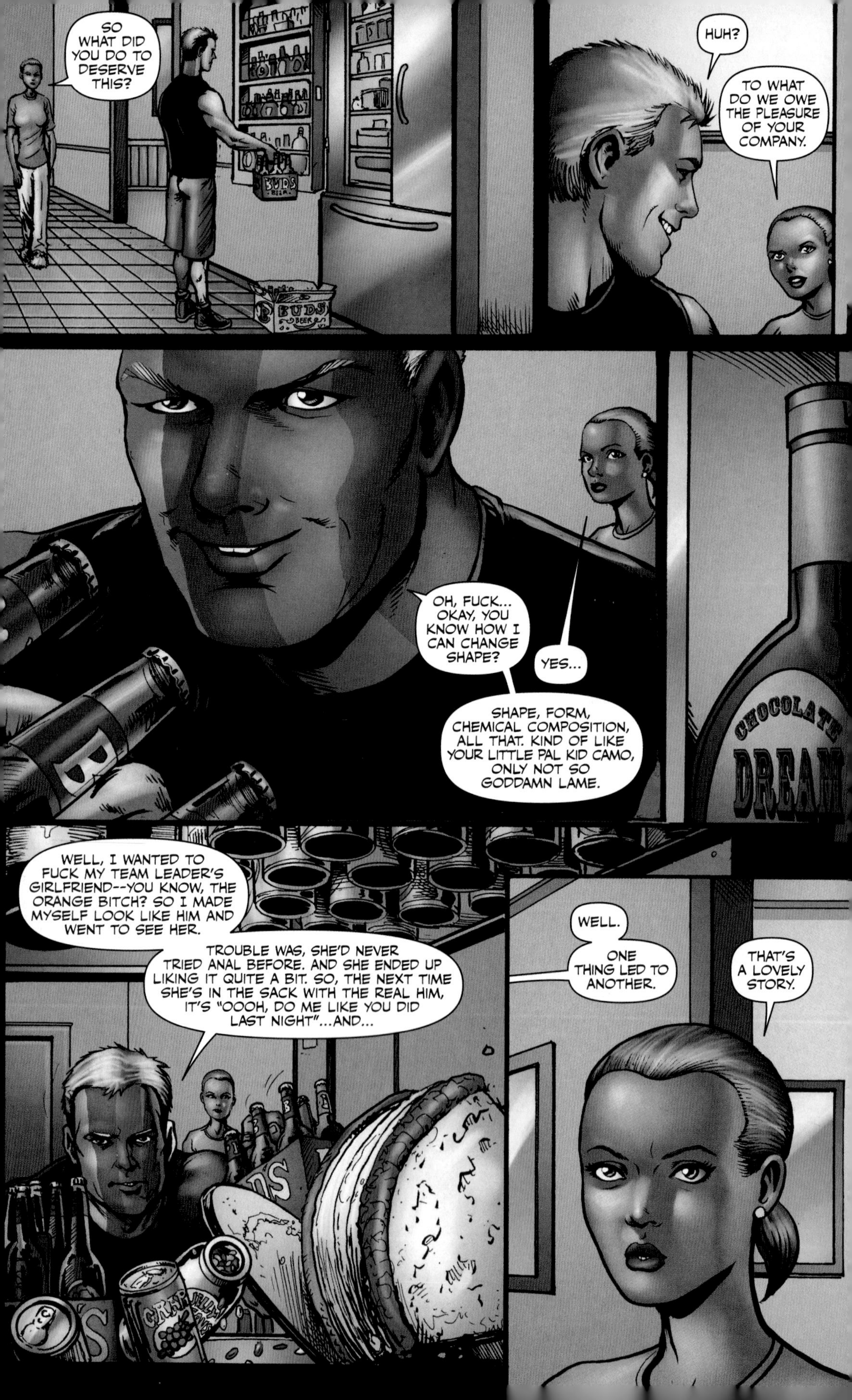
SO WHAT DID YOU DO TO DESERVE THIS?
BUDS BEER
HUH?
TO WHAT DO WE OWE THE PLEASURE OF YOUR COMPANY.
OH, FUCK... OKAY, YOU KNOW HOW I CAN CHANGE SHAPE?
YES...
SHAPE, FORM, CHEMICAL COMPOSITION, ALL THAT. KIND OF LIKE YOUR LITTLE PAL KID CAMO, ONLY NOT SO GODDAMN LAME.
CHOCOLATE DREAM
WELL, I WANTED TO FUCK MY TEAM LEADER'S GIRLFRIEND--YOU KNOW, THE ORANGE BITCH? SO I MADE MYSELF LOOK LIKE HIM AND WENT TO SEE HER.
TROUBLE WAS, SHE'D NEVER TRIED ANAL BEFORE. AND SHE ENDED UP LIKING IT QUITE A BIT. SO, THE NEXT TIME SHE'S IN THE SACK WITH THE REAL HIM, IT'S "OOOH, DO ME LIKE YOU DID LAST NIGHT"...AND...
WELL.
ONE THING LED TO ANOTHER.
THAT'S A LOVELY STORY.

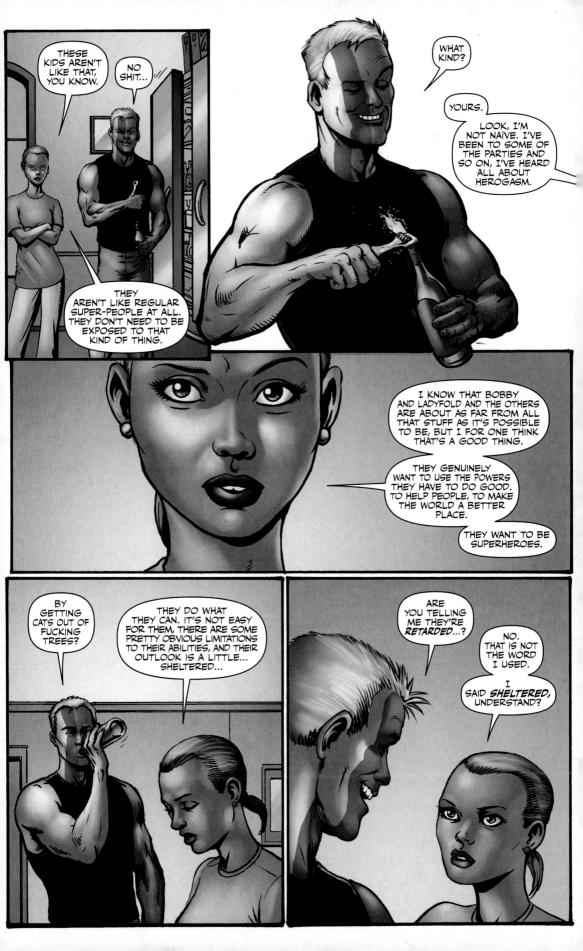

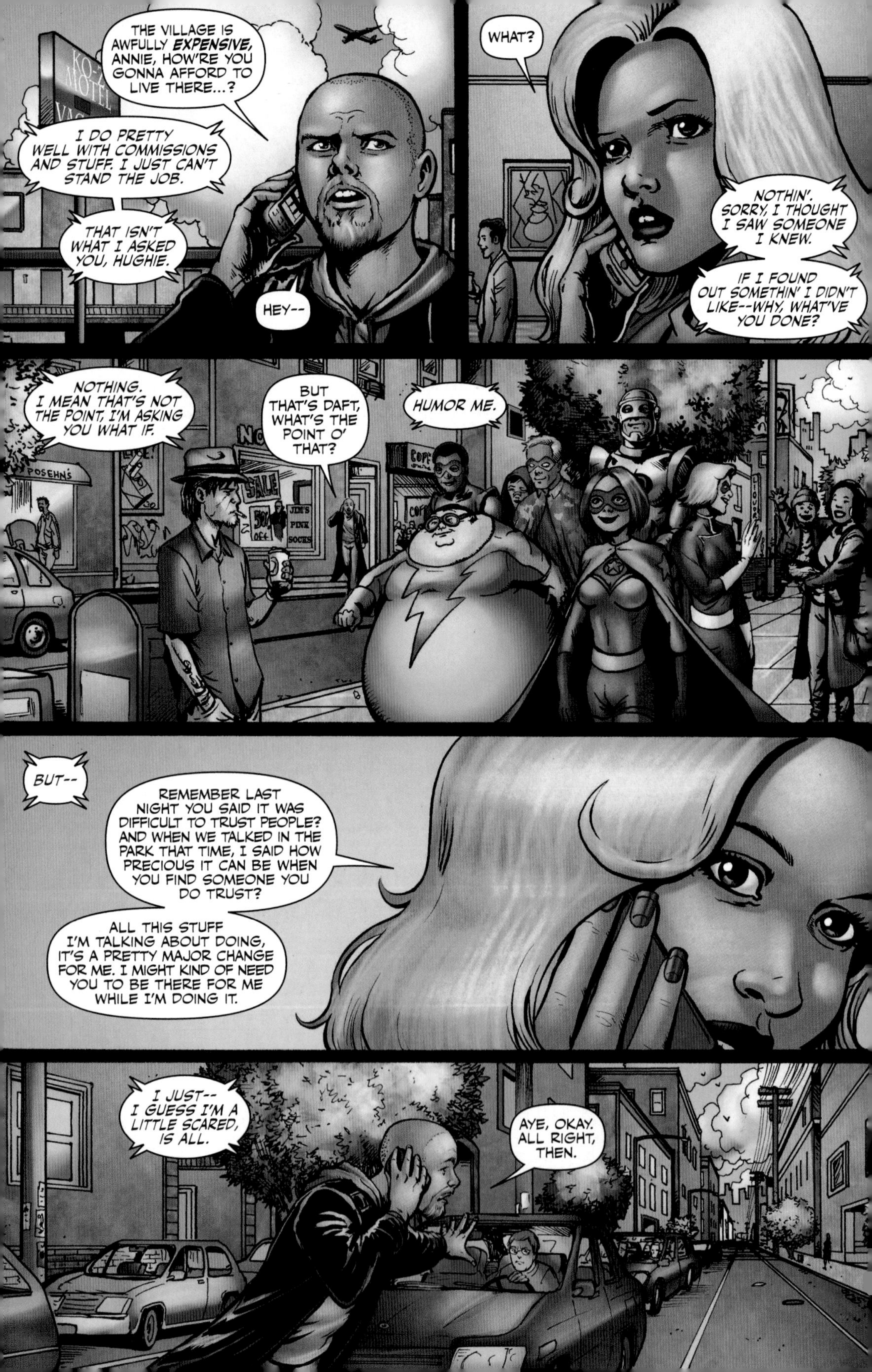
THE VILLAGE IS AWFULLY EXPENSIVE, ANNIE, HOW'RE YOU GONNA AFFORD TO LIVE THERE...?
I DO PRETTY WELL WITH COMMISSIONS AND STUFF. I JUST CAN'T STAND THE JOB.
THAT ISN'T WHAT I ASKED YOU, HUGHIE.
HEY--
WHAT?
NOTHIN'. SORRY, I THOUGHT I SAW SOMEONE I KNEW.
IF I FOUND OUT SOMETHIN' I DIDN'T LIKE--WHY, WHAT'VE YOU DONE?
NOTHING. I MEAN THAT'S NOT THE POINT, I'M ASKING YOU WHAT IF.
BUT THAT'S DAFT, WHAT'S THE POINT O' THAT?
HUMOR ME.
POSEHN'S
SALE
JIM'S PINK SOCKS
BUT--
REMEMBER LAST NIGHT YOU SAID IT WAS DIFFICULT TO TRUST PEOPLE? AND WHEN WE TALKED IN THE PARK THAT TIME, I SAID HOW PRECIOUS IT CAN BE WHEN YOU FIND SOMEONE YOU DO TRUST?
ALL THIS STUFF I'M TALKING ABOUT DOING, IT'S A PRETTY MAJOR CHANGE FOR ME. I MIGHT KIND OF NEED YOU TO BE THERE FOR ME WHILE I'M DOING IT.
I JUST-- I GUESS I'M A LITTLE SCARED, IS ALL.
AYE, OKAY. ALL RIGHT, THEN.

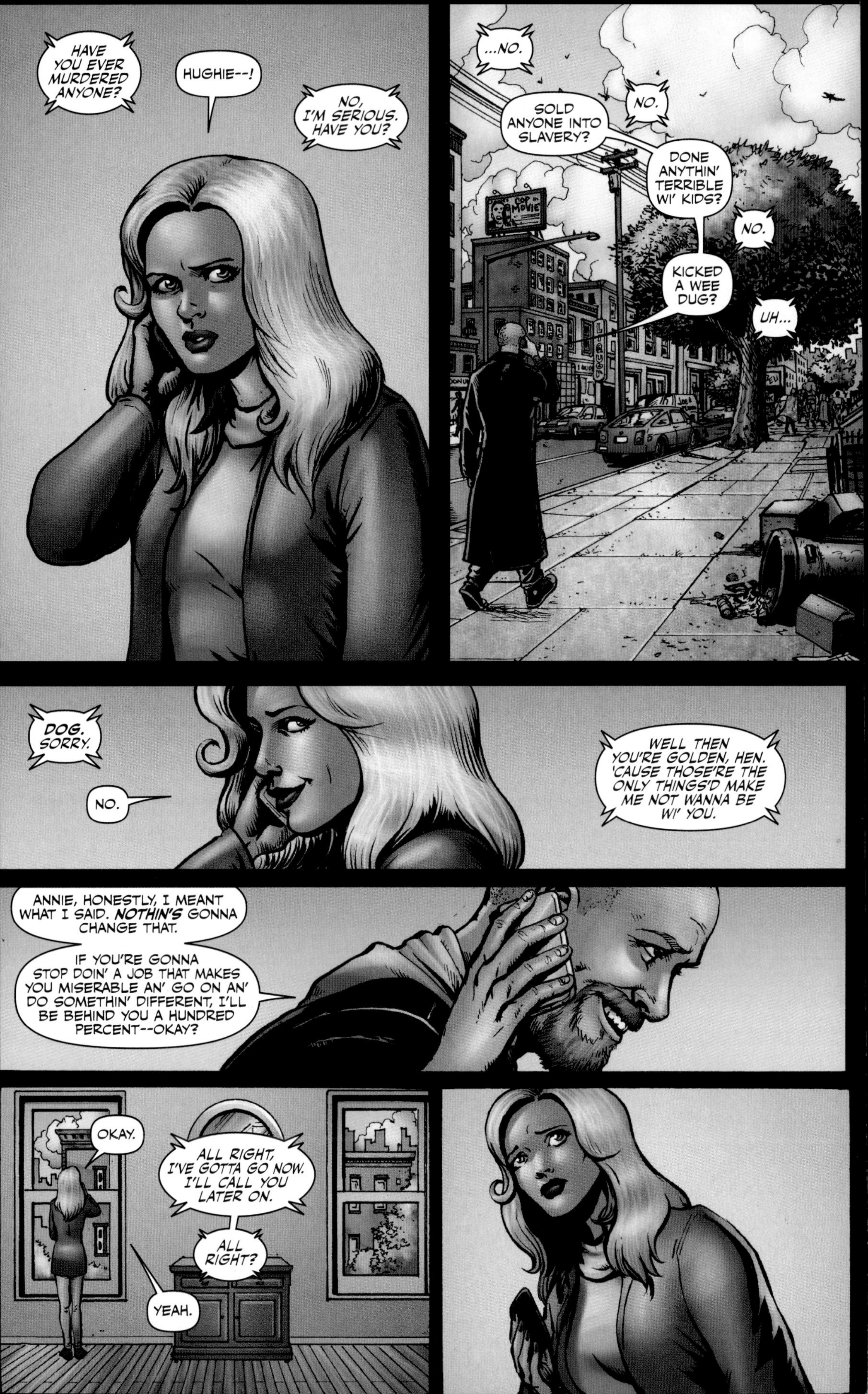
HAVE YOU EVER MURDERED ANYONE?
HUGHIE--!
NO, I'M SERIOUS. HAVE YOU?
...NO.
SOLD ANYONE INTO SLAVERY?
NO.
DONE ANYTHIN' TERRIBLE WI' KIDS?
NO.
KICKED A WEE DUG?
UH...
DOG. SORRY.
NO.
WELL THEN YOU'RE GOLDEN, HEN. 'CAUSE THOSE'RE THE ONLY THINGS'D MAKE ME NOT WANNA BE WI' YOU.
ANNIE, HONESTLY, I MEANT WHAT I SAID. NOTHIN'S GONNA CHANGE THAT.
IF YOU'RE GONNA STOP DOIN' A JOB THAT MAKES YOU MISERABLE AN' GO ON AN' DO SOMETHIN' DIFFERENT, I'LL BE BEHIND YOU A HUNDRED PERCENT--OKAY?
OKAY.
ALL RIGHT, I'VE GOTTA GO NOW. I'LL CALL YOU LATER ON.
ALL RIGHT?
YEAH.

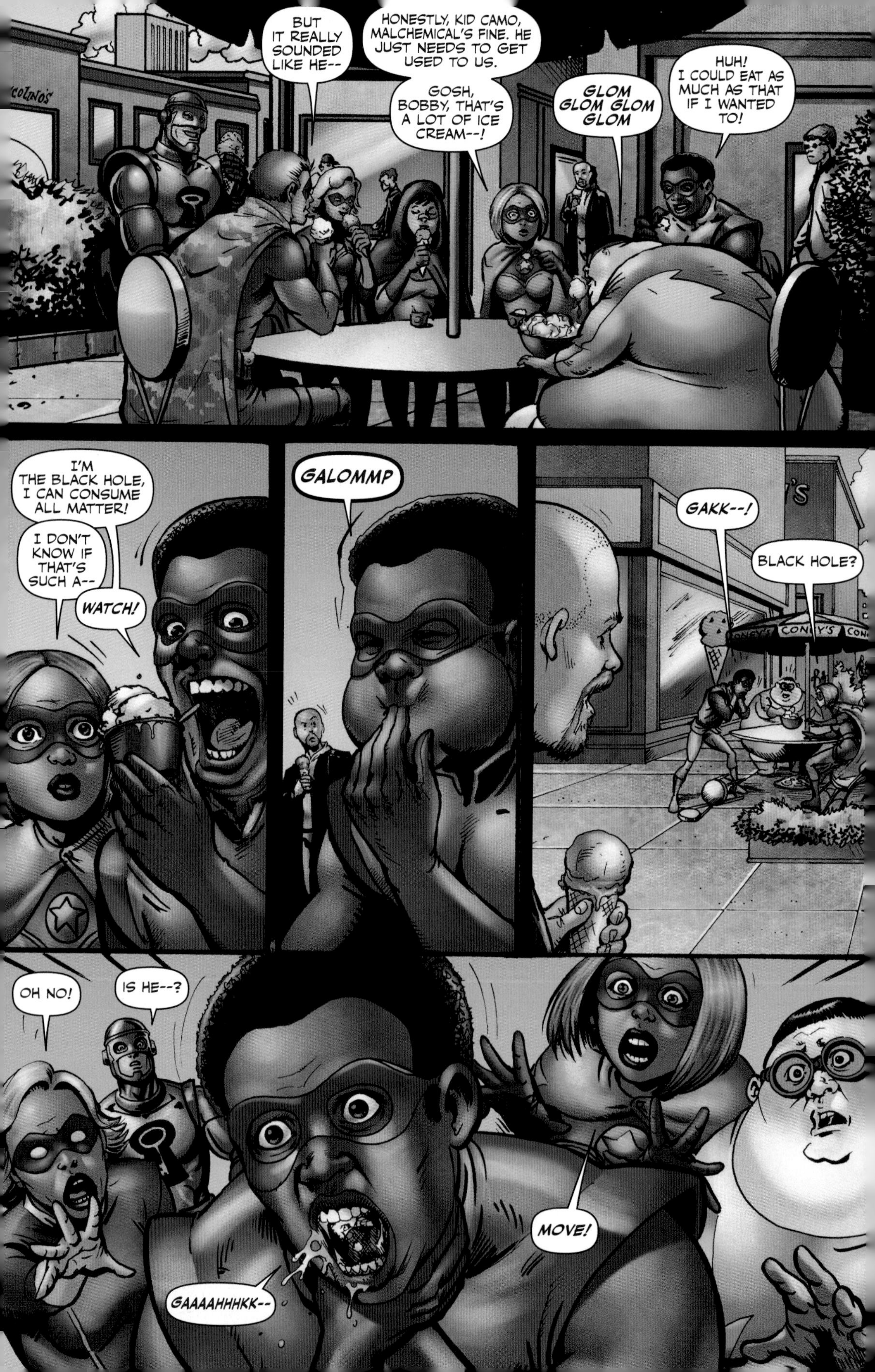

BUT IT REALLY SOUNDED LIKE HE--
HONESTLY, KID CAMO, MALCHEMICAL'S FINE. HE JUST NEEDS TO GET USED TO US.
GOSH, BOBBY, THAT'S A LOT OF ICE CREAM--!
GLOM GLOM GLOM GLOM
HUH! I COULD EAT AS MUCH AS THAT IF I WANTED TO!
I'M THE BLACK HOLE, I CAN CONSUME ALL MATTER!
I DON'T KNOW IF THAT'S SUCH A--
WATCH!
GALOMMP
GAKK--!
BLACK HOLE?
CONEY'S
OH NO!
IS HE--?
MOVE!
GAAAAHHHKK--

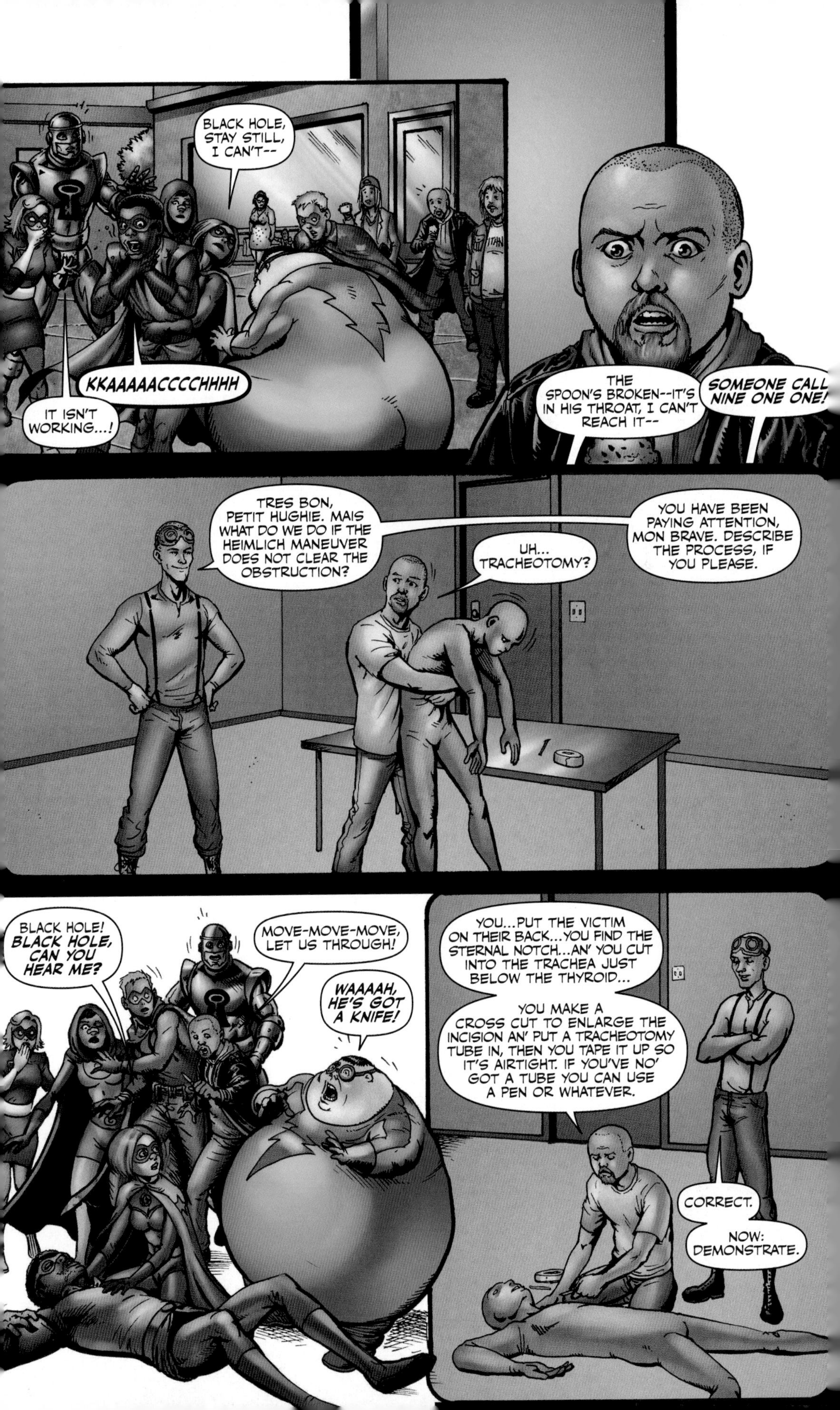

BLACK HOLE, STAY STILL, I CAN'T--
KKAAAAACCCCHHHH
IT ISN'T WORKING...!
THE SPOON'S BROKEN--IT'S IN HIS THROAT, I CAN'T REACH IT--
SOMEONE CALL NINE ONE ONE!
TRES BON, PETIT HUGHIE. MAIS WHAT DO WE DO IF THE HEIMLICH MANEUVER DOES NOT CLEAR THE OBSTRUCTION?
UH... TRACHEOTOMY?
YOU HAVE BEEN PAYING ATTENTION, MON BRAVE. DESCRIBE THE PROCESS, IF YOU PLEASE.
BLACK HOLE! BLACK HOLE, CAN YOU HEAR ME?
MOVE-MOVE-MOVE, LET US THROUGH!
WAAAAH, HE'S GOT A KNIFE!
YOU...PUT THE VICTIM ON THEIR BACK...YOU FIND THE STERNAL NOTCH...AN' YOU CUT INTO THE TRACHEA JUST BELOW THE THYROID...
YOU MAKE A CROSS CUT TO ENLARGE THE INCISION AN' PUT A TRACHEOTOMY TUBE IN, THEN YOU TAPE IT UP SO IT'S AIRTIGHT. IF YOU'VE NO' GOT A TUBE YOU CAN USE A PEN OR WHATEVER.
CORRECT.
NOW: DEMONSTRATE.

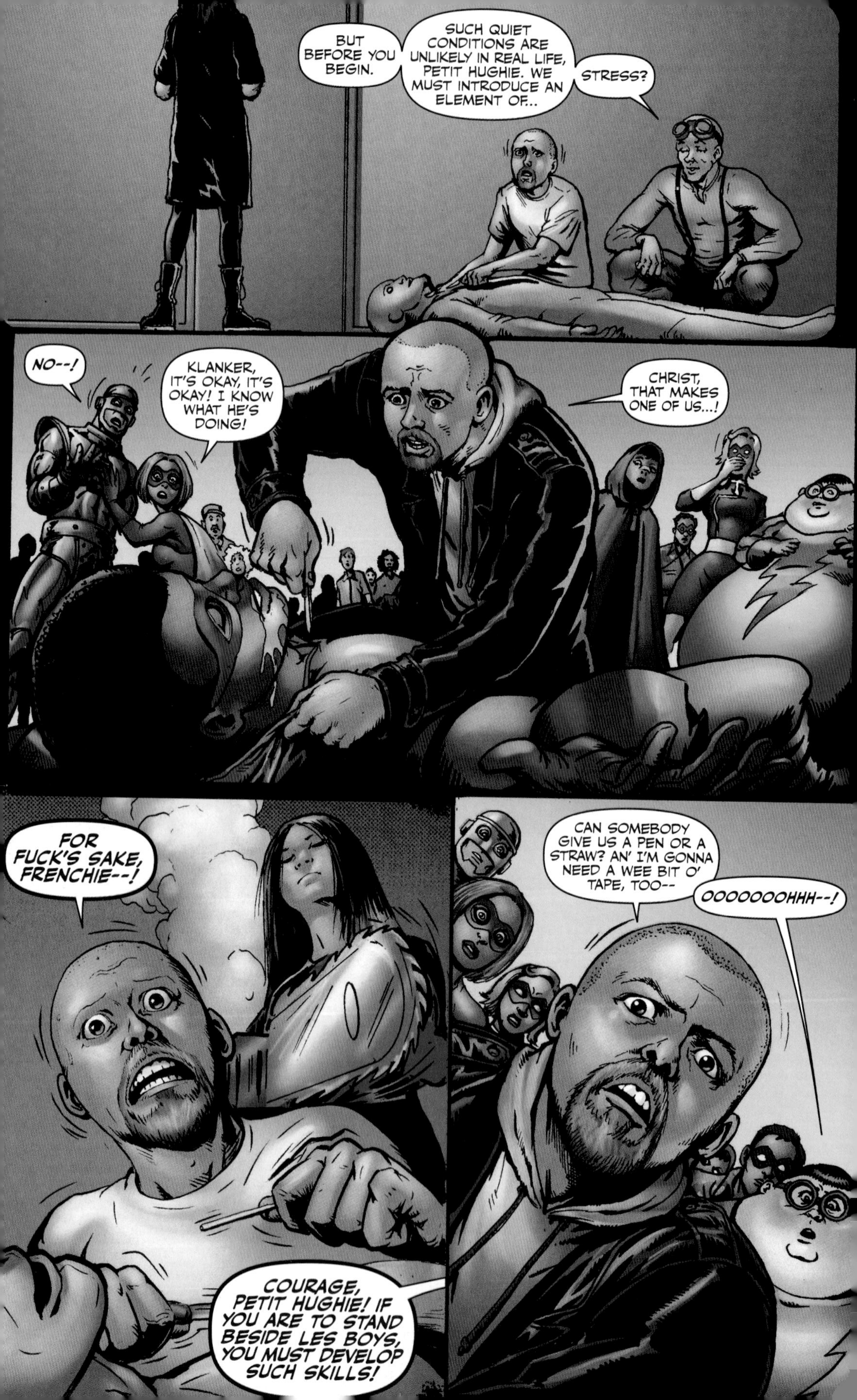
BUT BEFORE YOU BEGIN.
SUCH QUIET CONDITIONS ARE UNLIKELY IN REAL LIFE, PETIT HUGHIE. WE MUST INTRODUCE AN ELEMENT OF...
STRESS?
NO--!
KLANKER, IT'S OKAY, IT'S OKAY! I KNOW WHAT HE'S DOING!
CHRIST, THAT MAKES ONE OF US...!
FOR FUCK'S SAKE, FRENCHIE--!
COURAGE, PETIT HUGHIE! IF YOU ARE TO STAND BESIDE LES BOYS, YOU MUST DEVELOP SUCH SKILLS!
CAN SOMEBODY GIVE US A PEN OR A STRAW? AN' I'M GONNA NEED A WEE BIT O' TAPE, TOO--
OOOOOOOHHH--!

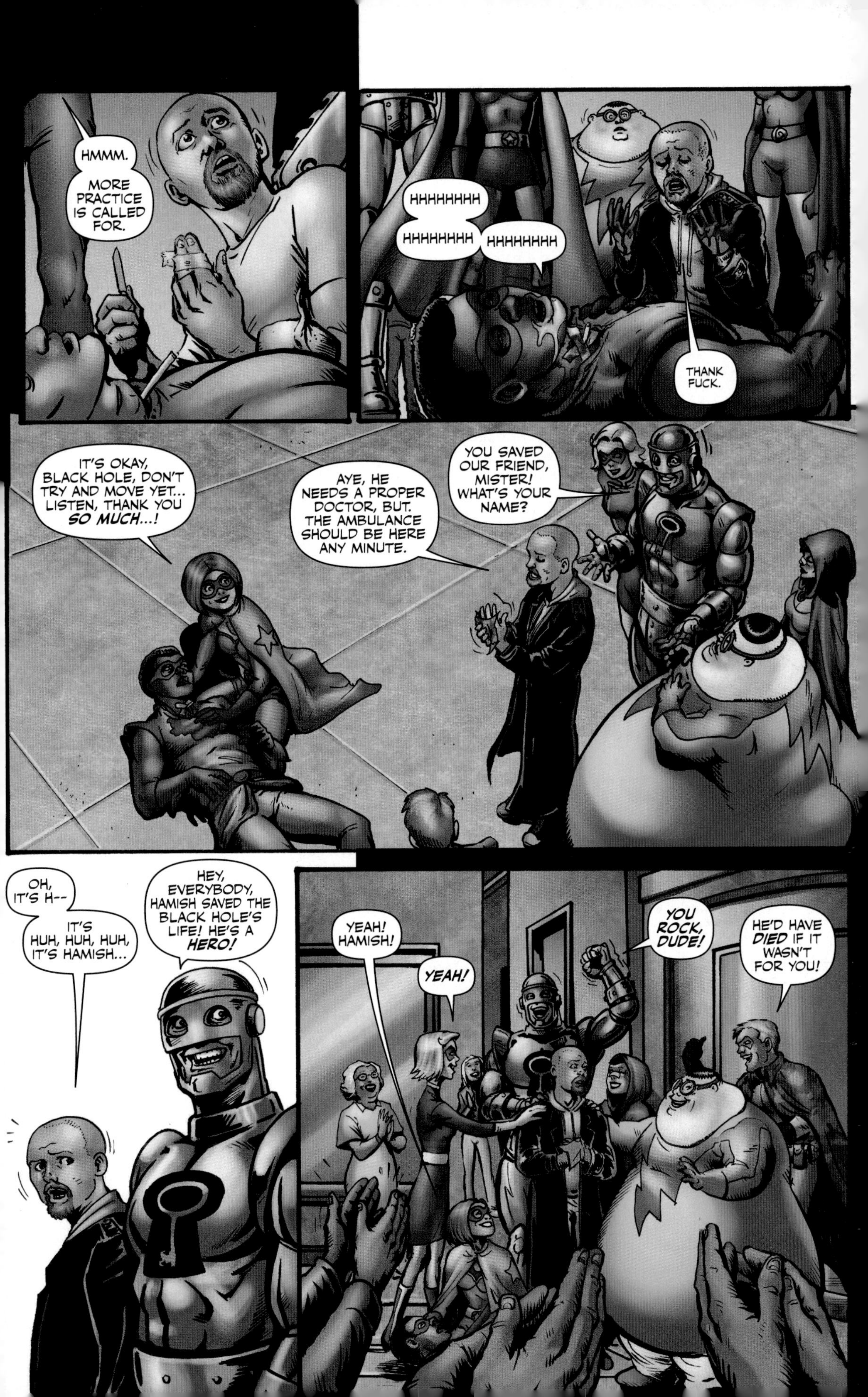

HMMM.
MORE PRACTICE IS CALLED FOR.
HHHHHHHH
HHHHHHHH
HHHHHHHH
THANK FUCK.
IT'S OKAY, BLACK HOLE, DON'T TRY AND MOVE YET... LISTEN, THANK YOU SO MUCH...!
AYE, HE NEEDS A PROPER DOCTOR, BUT. THE AMBULANCE SHOULD BE HERE ANY MINUTE.
YOU SAVED OUR FRIEND, MISTER! WHAT'S YOUR NAME?
OH, IT'S H--
IT'S HUH, HUH, HUH, IT'S HAMISH...
HEY, EVERYBODY, HAMISH SAVED THE BLACK HOLE'S LIFE! HE'S A HERO!
YEAH! HAMISH!
YEAH!
YOU ROCK, DUDE!
HE'D HAVE DIED IF IT WASN'T FOR YOU!

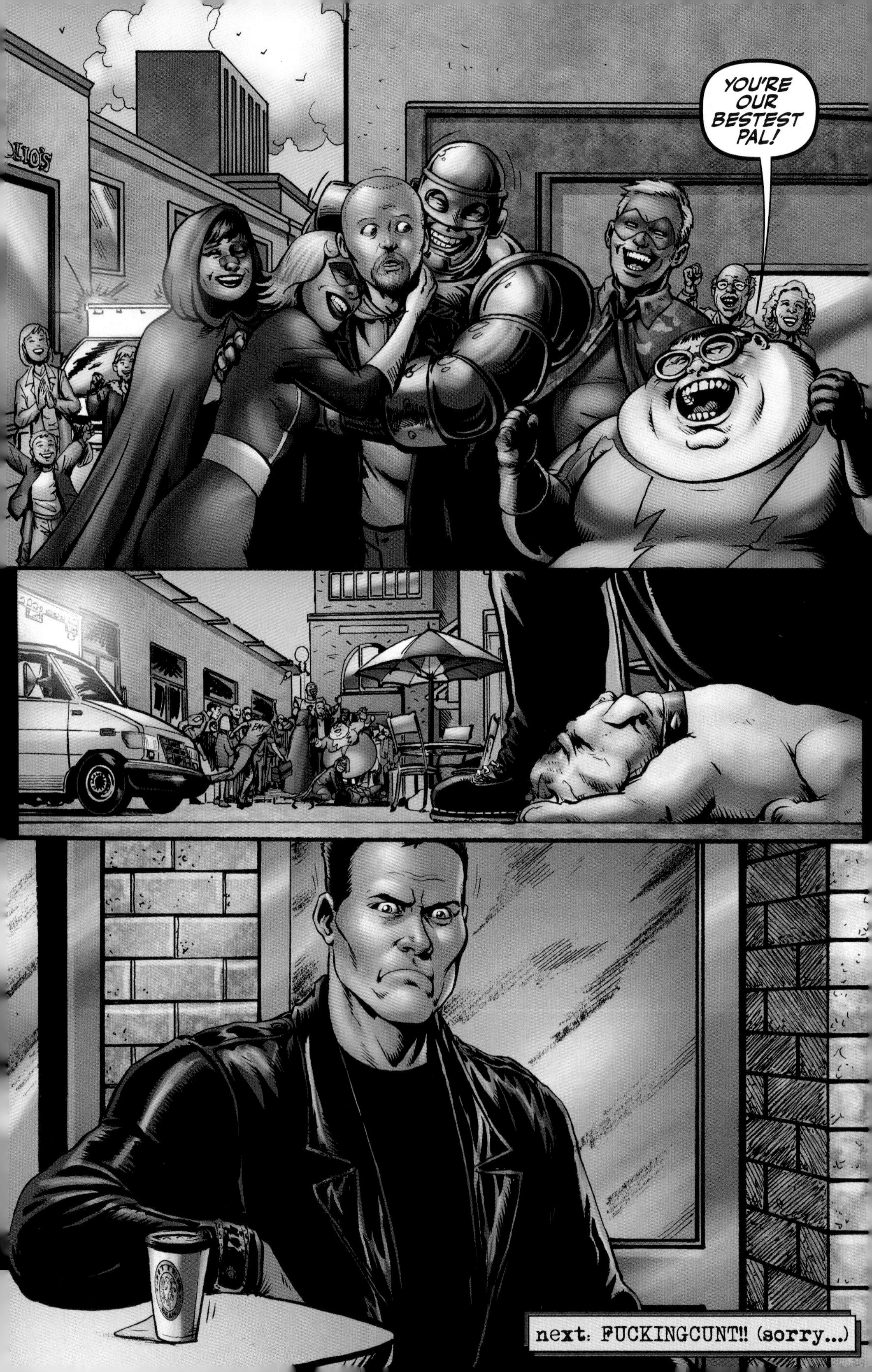
YOU'RE OUR BESTEST PAL!
next: FUCKINGCUNT!! (sorry...)

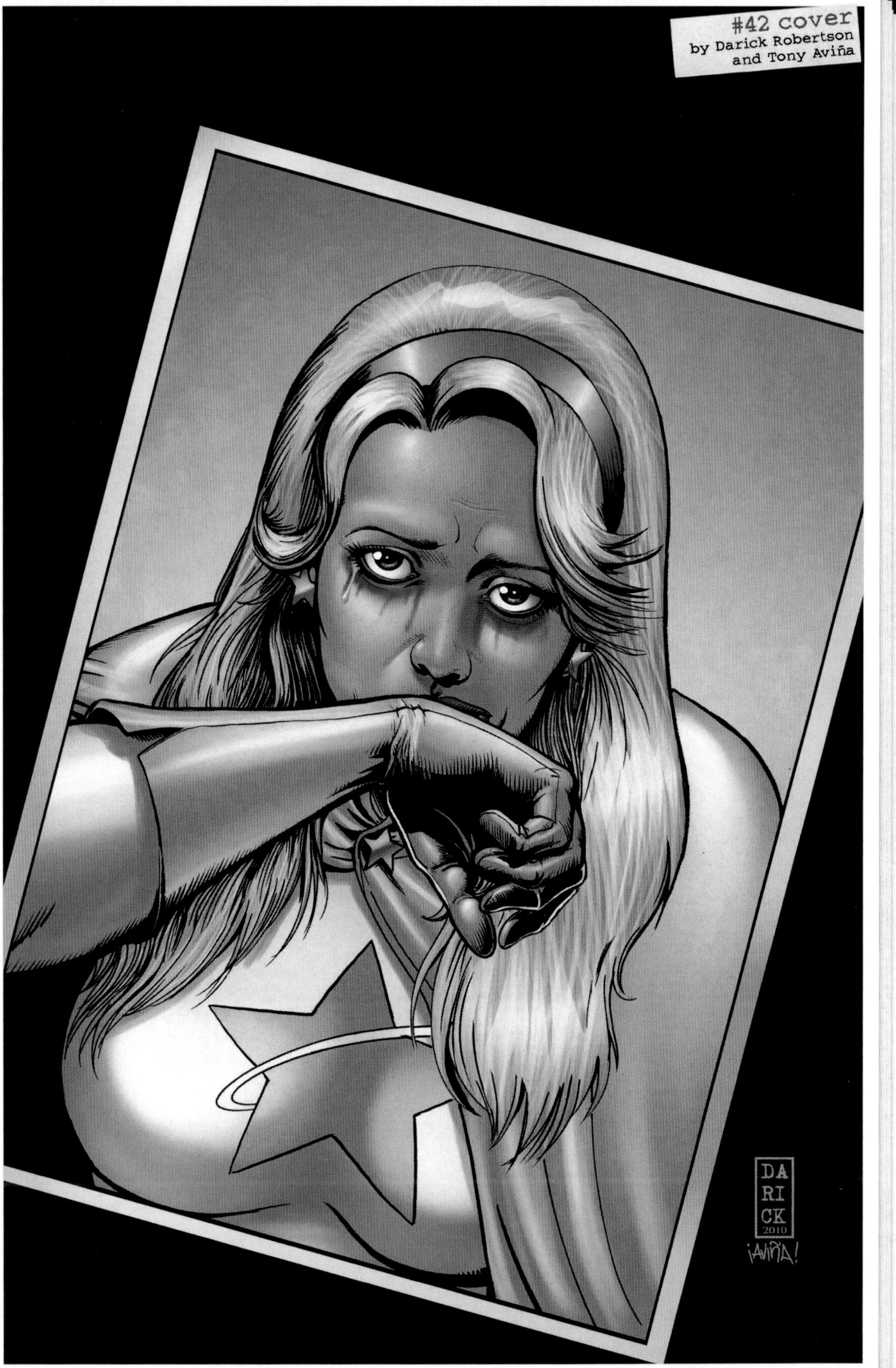

#42 cover
by Darick Robertson
and Tony Aviña

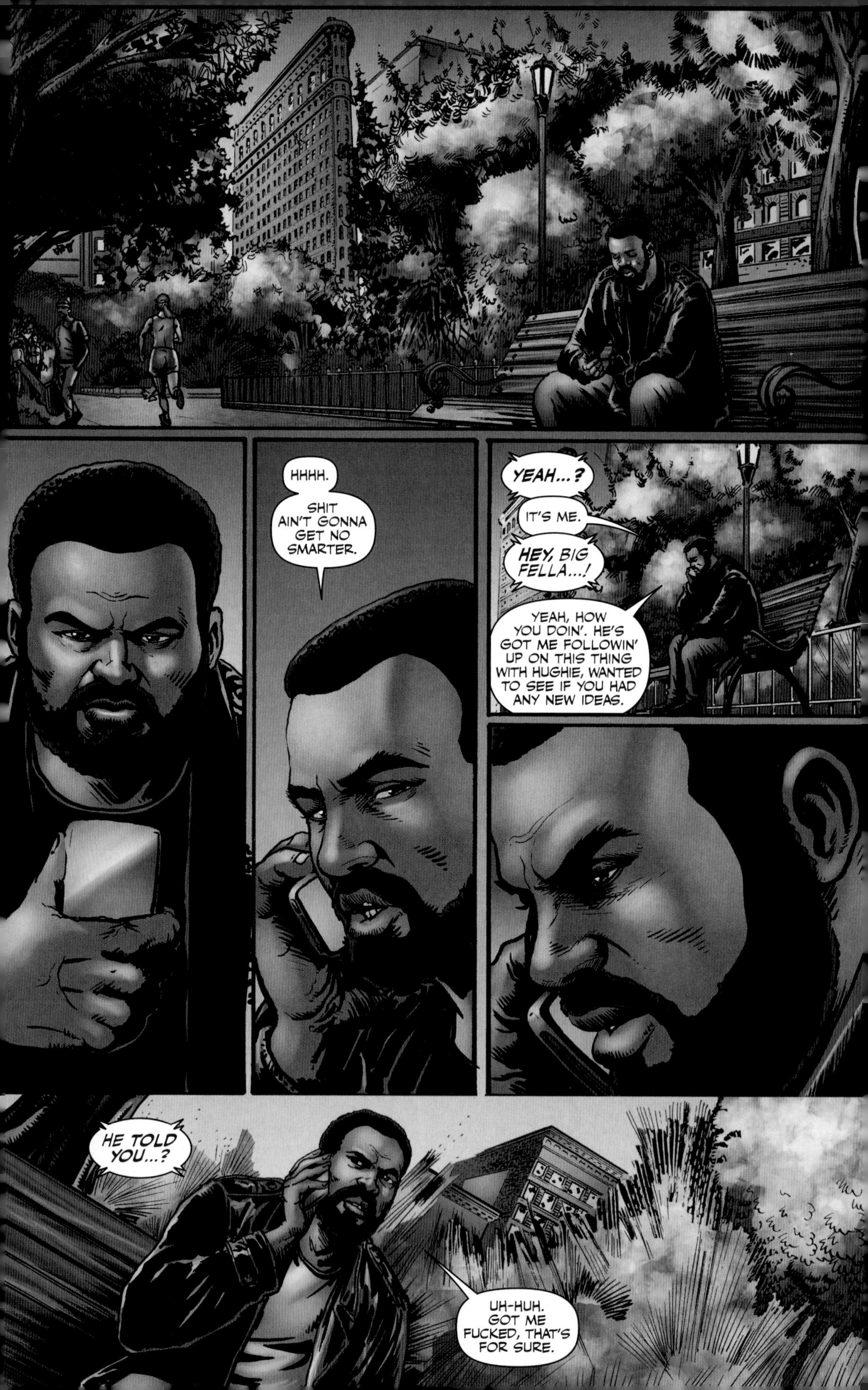
HHHH.
SHIT AIN'T GONNA GET NO SMARTER.
YEAH...?
IT'S ME.
HEY, BIG FELLA...!
YEAH, HOW YOU DOIN'. HE'S GOT ME FOLLOWIN' UP ON THIS THING WITH HUGHIE, WANTED TO SEE IF YOU HAD ANY NEW IDEAS.
HE TOLD YOU...?
UH-HUH. GOT ME FUCKED, THAT'S FOR SURE.

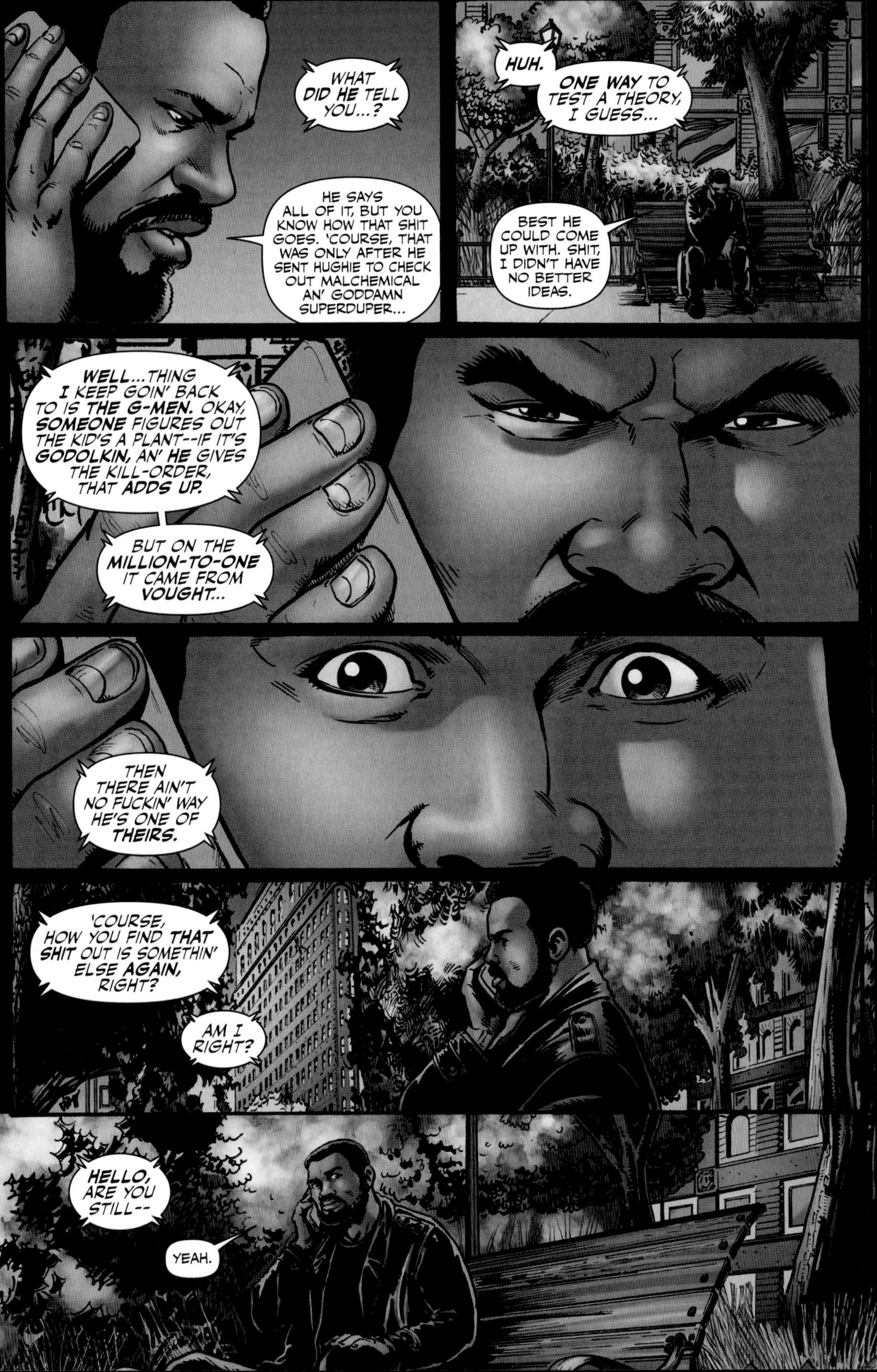
WHAT DID HE TELL YOU...?
HE SAYS ALL OF IT, BUT YOU KNOW HOW THAT SHIT GOES. 'COURSE, THAT WAS ONLY AFTER HE SENT HUGHIE TO CHECK OUT MALCHEMICAL AN' GODDAMN SUPERDUPER...
HUH.
ONE WAY TO TEST A THEORY, I GUESS...
BEST HE COULD COME UP WITH. SHIT, I DIDN'T HAVE NO BETTER IDEAS.
WELL...THING I KEEP GOIN' BACK TO IS THE G-MEN. OKAY, SOMEONE FIGURES OUT THE KID'S A PLANT--IF IT'S GODOLKIN, AN' HE GIVES THE KILL-ORDER, THAT ADDS UP.
BUT ON THE MILLION-TO-ONE IT CAME FROM VOUGHT...
THEN THERE AIN'T NO FUCKIN' WAY HE'S ONE OF THEIRS.
'COURSE, HOW YOU FIND THAT SHIT OUT IS SOMETHIN' ELSE AGAIN, RIGHT?
AM I RIGHT?
HELLO, ARE YOU STILL--
YEAH.

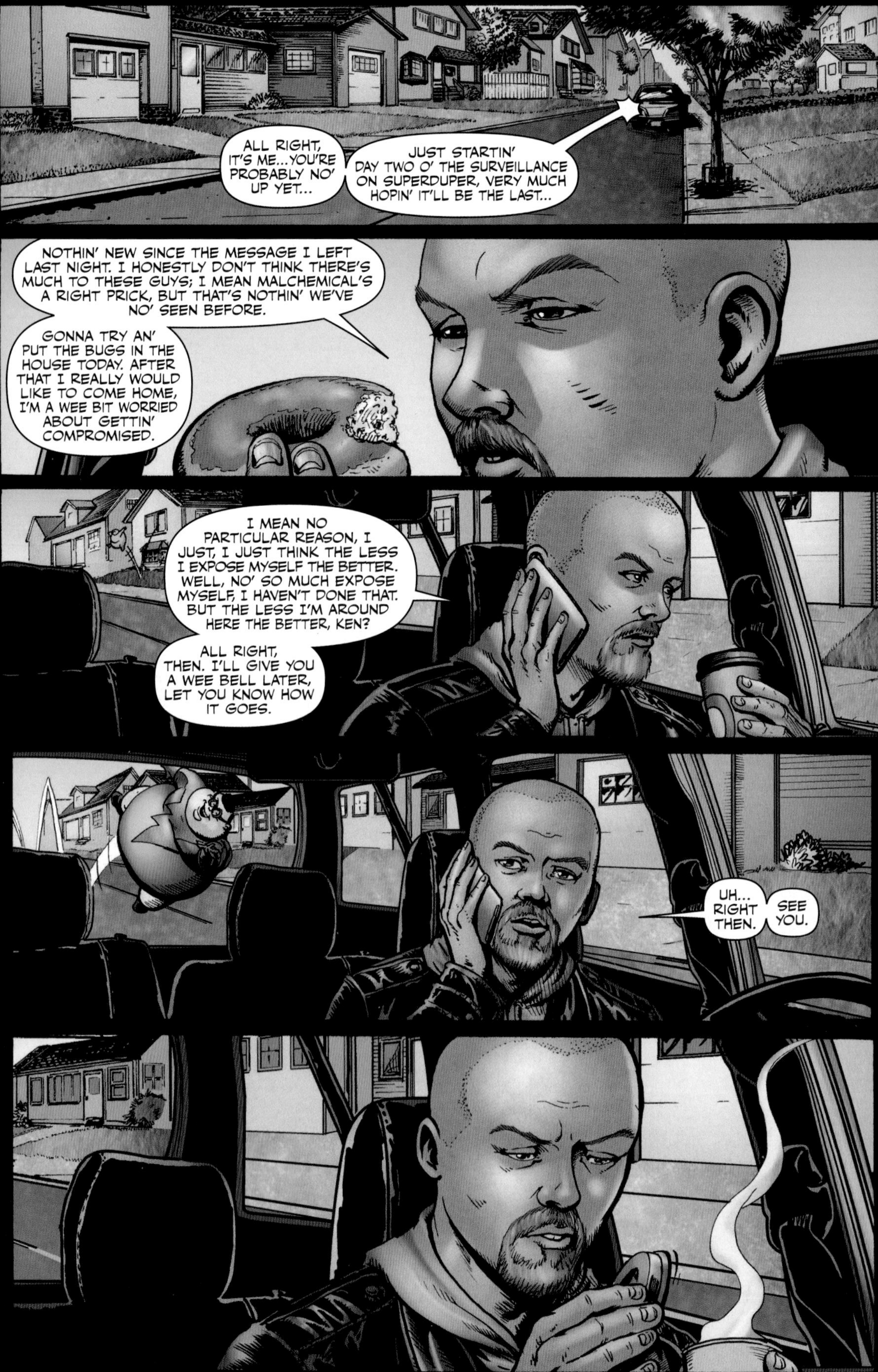
ALL RIGHT, IT'S ME...YOU'RE PROBABLY NO' UP YET...
JUST STARTIN' DAY TWO O' THE SURVEILLANCE ON SUPERDUPER, VERY MUCH HOPIN' IT'LL BE THE LAST...
NOTHIN' NEW SINCE THE MESSAGE I LEFT LAST NIGHT. I HONESTLY DON'T THINK THERE'S MUCH TO THESE GUYS; I MEAN MALCHEMICAL'S A RIGHT PRICK, BUT THAT'S NOTHIN' WE'VE NO' SEEN BEFORE.
GONNA TRY AN' PUT THE BUGS IN THE HOUSE TODAY. AFTER THAT I REALLY WOULD LIKE TO COME HOME, I'M A WEE BIT WORRIED ABOUT GETTIN' COMPROMISED.
I MEAN NO PARTICULAR REASON, I JUST, I JUST THINK THE LESS I EXPOSE MYSELF THE BETTER. WELL, NO' SO MUCH EXPOSE MYSELF, I HAVEN'T DONE THAT. BUT THE LESS I'M AROUND HERE THE BETTER, KEN?
ALL RIGHT, THEN. I'LL GIVE YOU A WEE BELL LATER, LET YOU KNOW HOW IT GOES.
UH... RIGHT THEN.
SEE YOU.

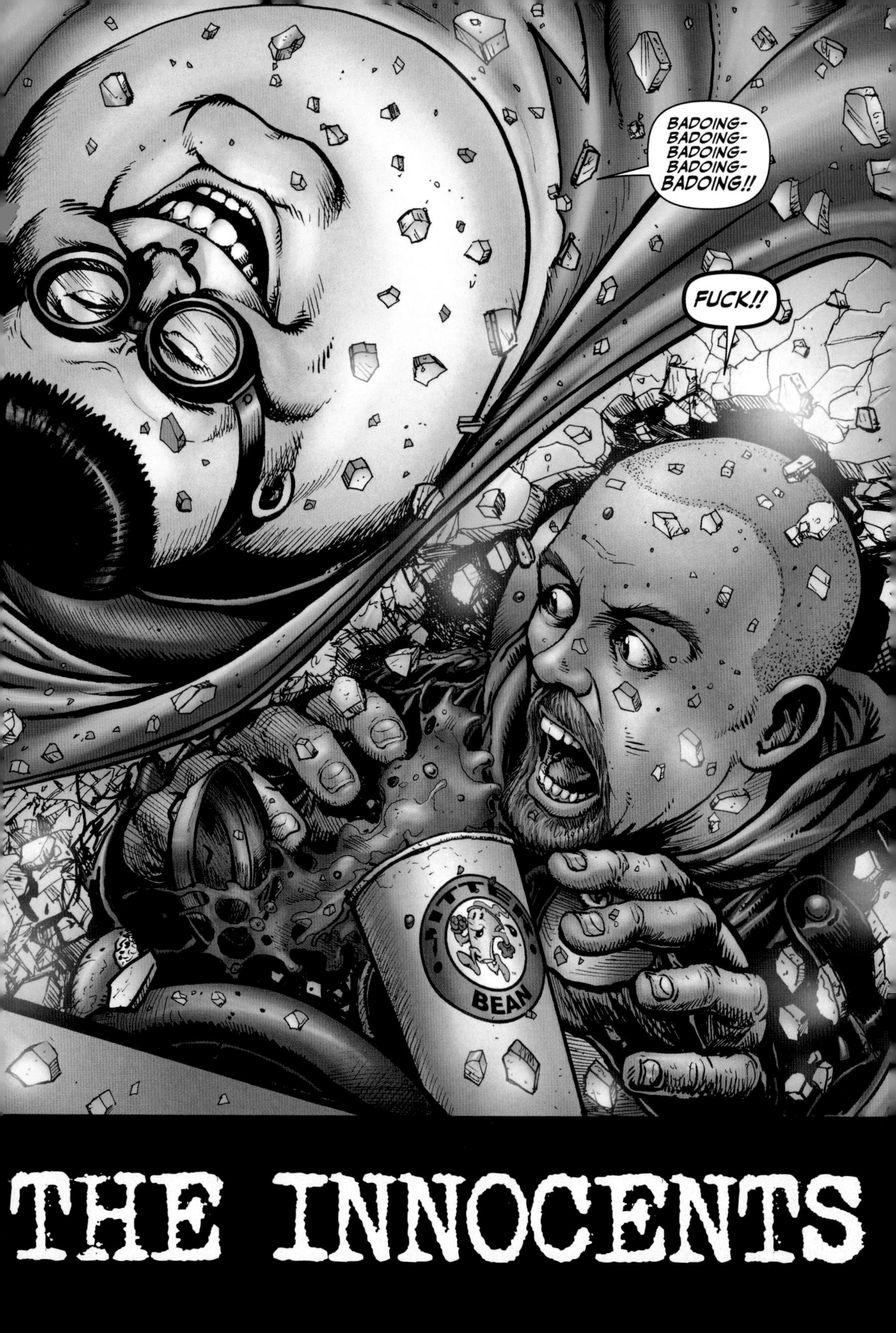
BADOING-BADOING-BADOING-BADOING-BADOING!!
FUCK!!

THE INNOCENTS

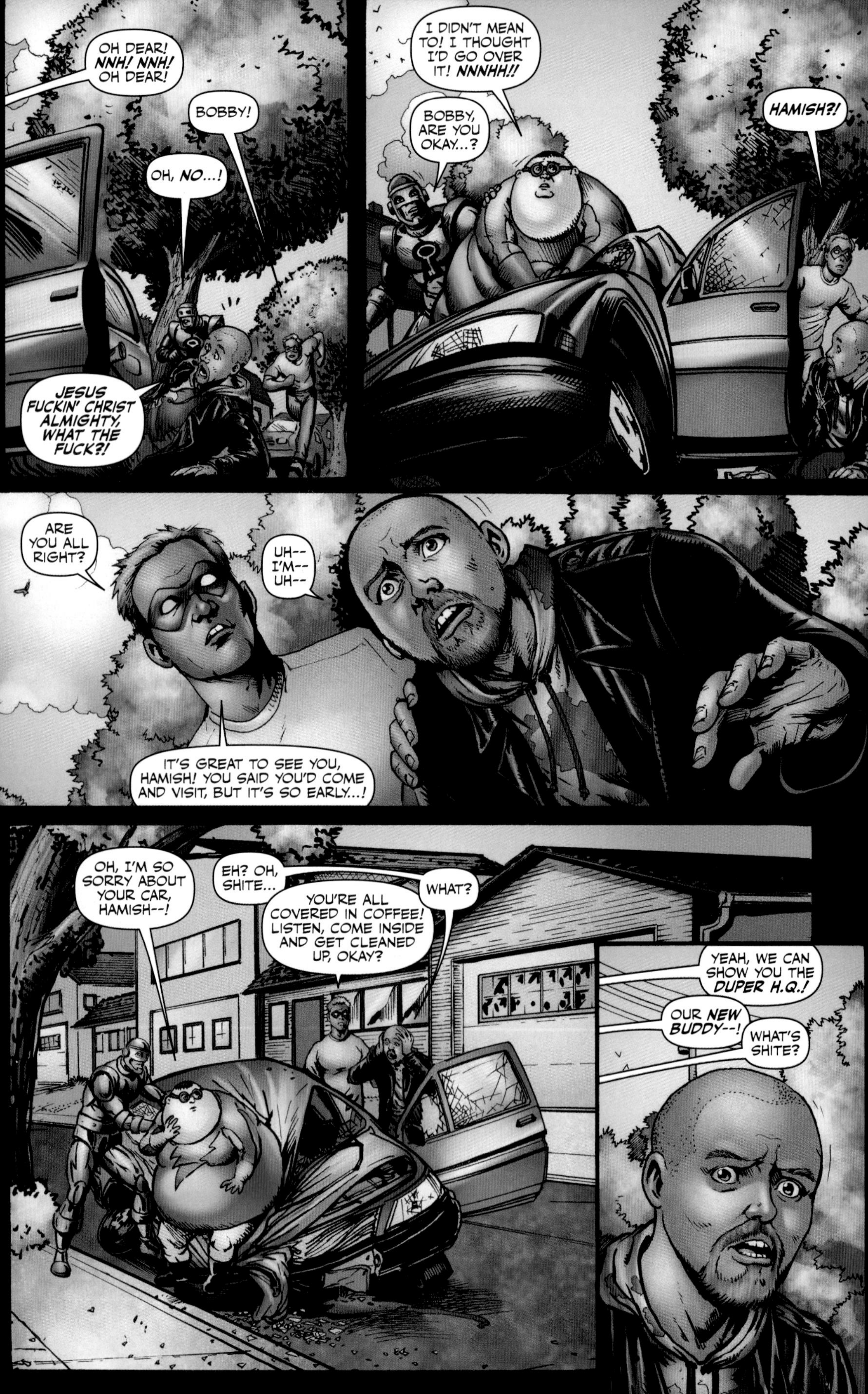
OH DEAR! NNH! NNH! OH DEAR!
BOBBY!
OH, NO...!
JESUS FUCKIN' CHRIST ALMIGHTY, WHAT THE FUCK?!
I DIDN'T MEAN TO! I THOUGHT I'D GO OVER IT! NNNHH!!
BOBBY, ARE YOU OKAY...?
HAMISH?!
ARE YOU ALL RIGHT?
UH-- I'M-- UH--
IT'S GREAT TO SEE YOU, HAMISH! YOU SAID YOU'D COME AND VISIT, BUT IT'S SO EARLY...!
OH, I'M SO SORRY ABOUT YOUR CAR, HAMISH--!
EH? OH, SHITE...
YOU'RE ALL COVERED IN COFFEE! LISTEN, COME INSIDE AND GET CLEANED UP, OKAY?
WHAT?
YEAH, WE CAN SHOW YOU THE DUPER H.Q.!
OUR NEW BUDDY--!
WHAT'S SHITE?

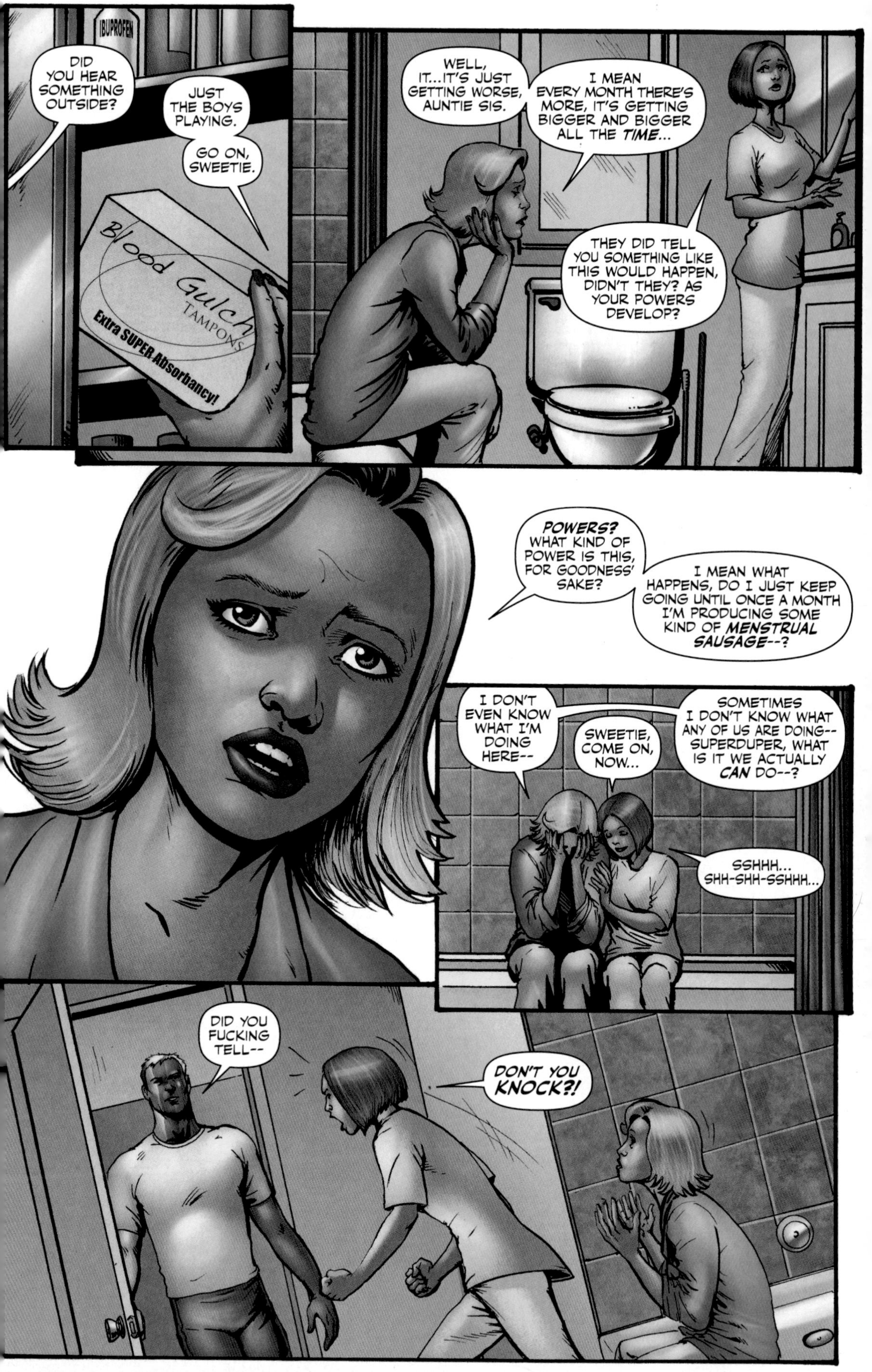
IBUPROFEN
DID YOU HEAR SOMETHING OUTSIDE?
JUST THE BOYS PLAYING.
GO ON, SWEETIE.
Blood Gulch TAMPONS Extra SUPER Absorbancy!
WELL, IT...IT'S JUST GETTING WORSE, AUNTIE SIS.
I MEAN EVERY MONTH THERE'S MORE, IT'S GETTING BIGGER AND BIGGER ALL THE TIME...
THEY DID TELL YOU SOMETHING LIKE THIS WOULD HAPPEN, DIDN'T THEY? AS YOUR POWERS DEVELOP?
POWERS? WHAT KIND OF POWER IS THIS, FOR GOODNESS' SAKE?
I MEAN WHAT HAPPENS, DO I JUST KEEP GOING UNTIL ONCE A MONTH I'M PRODUCING SOME KIND OF MENSTRUAL SAUSAGE--?
I DON'T EVEN KNOW WHAT I'M DOING HERE--
SOMETIMES I DON'T KNOW WHAT ANY OF US ARE DOING--SUPERDUPER, WHAT IS IT WE ACTUALLY CAN DO--?
SWEETIE, COME ON, NOW...
SSHHH... SHH-SHH-SSHHH...
DID YOU FUCKING TELL--
DON'T YOU KNOCK?!

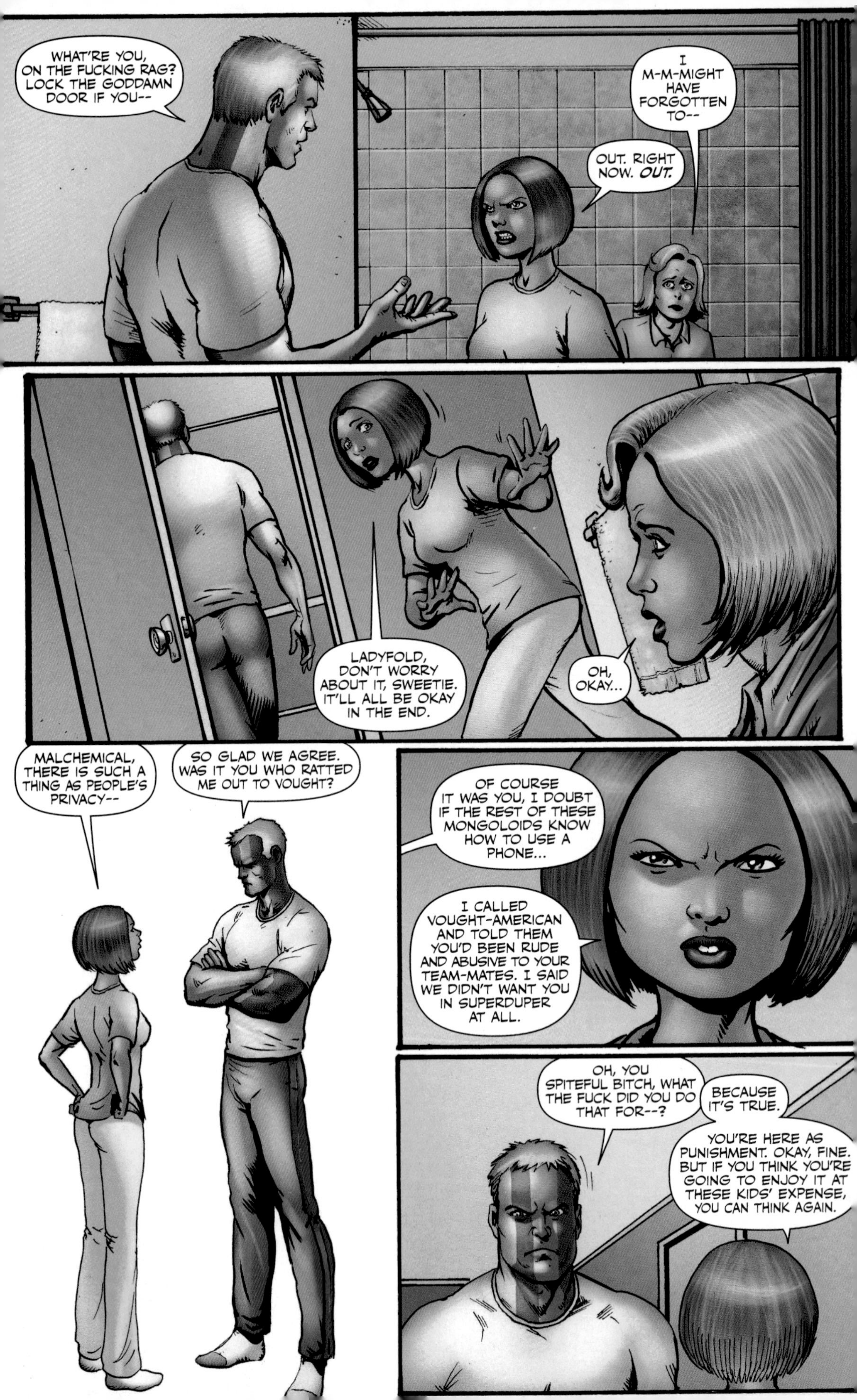
WHAT'RE YOU, ON THE FUCKING RAG? LOCK THE GODDAMN DOOR IF YOU--
I M-M-MIGHT HAVE FORGOTTEN TO--
OUT. RIGHT NOW. OUT.
LADYFOLD, DON'T WORRY ABOUT IT, SWEETIE. IT'LL ALL BE OKAY IN THE END.
OH, OKAY...
MALCHEMICAL, THERE IS SUCH A THING AS PEOPLE'S PRIVACY--
SO GLAD WE AGREE. WAS IT YOU WHO RATTED ME OUT TO VOUGHT?
OF COURSE IT WAS YOU, I DOUBT IF THE REST OF THESE MONGOLOIDS KNOW HOW TO USE A PHONE...
I CALLED VOUGHT-AMERICAN AND TOLD THEM YOU'D BEEN RUDE AND ABUSIVE TO YOUR TEAM-MATES. I SAID WE DIDN'T WANT YOU IN SUPERDUPER AT ALL.
OH, YOU SPITEFUL BITCH, WHAT THE FUCK DID YOU DO THAT FOR--?
BECAUSE IT'S TRUE.
YOU'RE HERE AS PUNISHMENT. OKAY, FINE. BUT IF YOU THINK YOU'RE GOING TO ENJOY IT AT THESE KIDS' EXPENSE, YOU CAN THINK AGAIN.

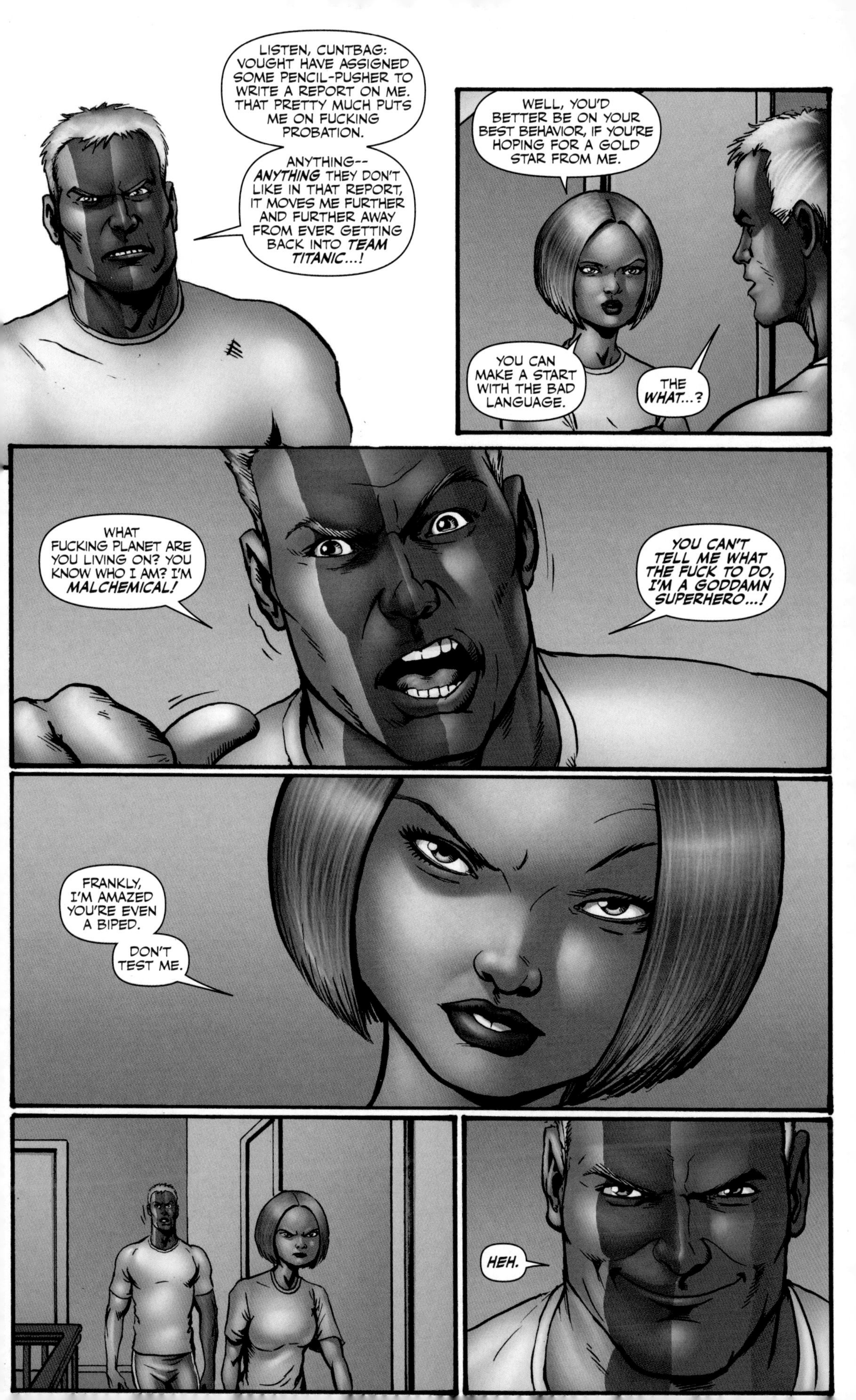
LISTEN, CUNTBAG: VOUGHT HAVE ASSIGNED SOME PENCIL-PUSHER TO WRITE A REPORT ON ME. THAT PRETTY MUCH PUTS ME ON FUCKING PROBATION.
ANYTHING-- *ANYTHING* THEY DON'T LIKE IN THAT REPORT, IT MOVES ME FURTHER AND FURTHER AWAY FROM EVER GETTING BACK INTO *TEAM TITANIC*...!
WELL, YOU'D BETTER BE ON YOUR BEST BEHAVIOR, IF YOU'RE HOPING FOR A GOLD STAR FROM ME.
YOU CAN MAKE A START WITH THE BAD LANGUAGE.
THE *WHAT*...?
WHAT FUCKING PLANET ARE YOU LIVING ON? YOU KNOW WHO I AM? I'M *MALCHEMICAL!*
YOU CAN'T TELL ME WHAT THE FUCK TO DO, I'M A GODDAMN SUPERHERO...!
FRANKLY, I'M AMAZED YOU'RE EVEN A BIPED.
DON'T TEST ME.
HEH.

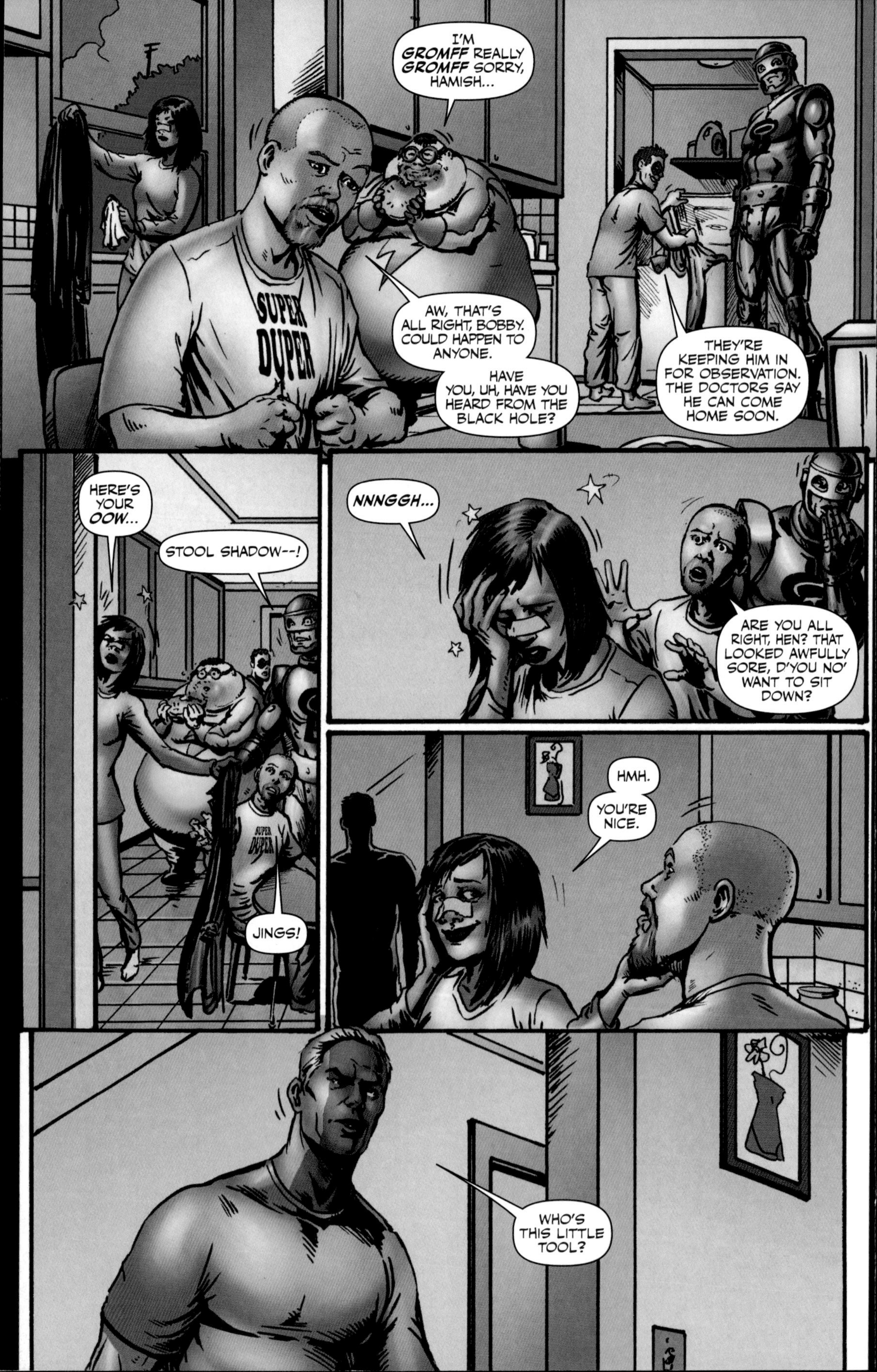
I'M GROMFF REALLY GROMFF SORRY, HAMISH...
AW, THAT'S ALL RIGHT, BOBBY. COULD HAPPEN TO ANYONE.
HAVE YOU, UH, HAVE YOU HEARD FROM THE BLACK HOLE?
THEY'RE KEEPING HIM IN FOR OBSERVATION. THE DOCTORS SAY HE CAN COME HOME SOON.
HERE'S YOUR OOW...
STOOL SHADOW--!
JINGS!
NNNGGH...
ARE YOU ALL RIGHT, HEN? THAT LOOKED AWFULLY SORE, D'YOU NO' WANT TO SIT DOWN?
HMH.
YOU'RE NICE.
WHO'S THIS LITTLE TOOL?

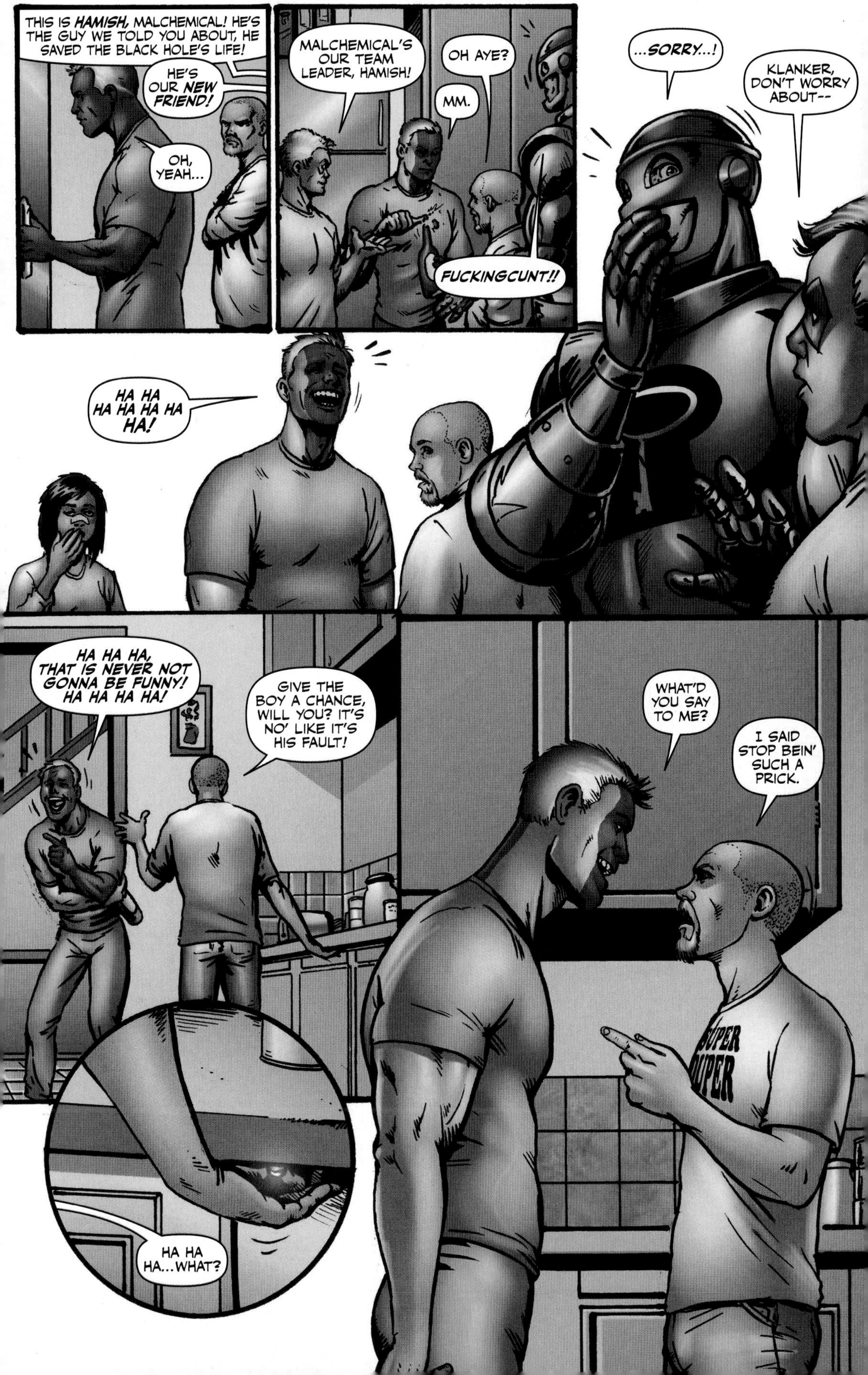
THIS IS HAMISH, MALCHEMICAL! HE'S THE GUY WE TOLD YOU ABOUT, HE SAVED THE BLACK HOLE'S LIFE!
HE'S OUR NEW FRIEND!
OH, YEAH...
MALCHEMICAL'S OUR TEAM LEADER, HAMISH!
OH AYE?
MM.
FUCKINGCUNT!!
...SORRY...!
KLANKER, DON'T WORRY ABOUT--
HA HA HA HA HA HA HA!
HA HA HA, THAT IS NEVER NOT GONNA BE FUNNY! HA HA HA HA!
GIVE THE BOY A CHANCE, WILL YOU? IT'S NO' LIKE IT'S HIS FAULT!
HA HA HA...WHAT?
WHAT'D YOU SAY TO ME?
I SAID STOP BEIN' SUCH A PRICK.
SUPER DUPER

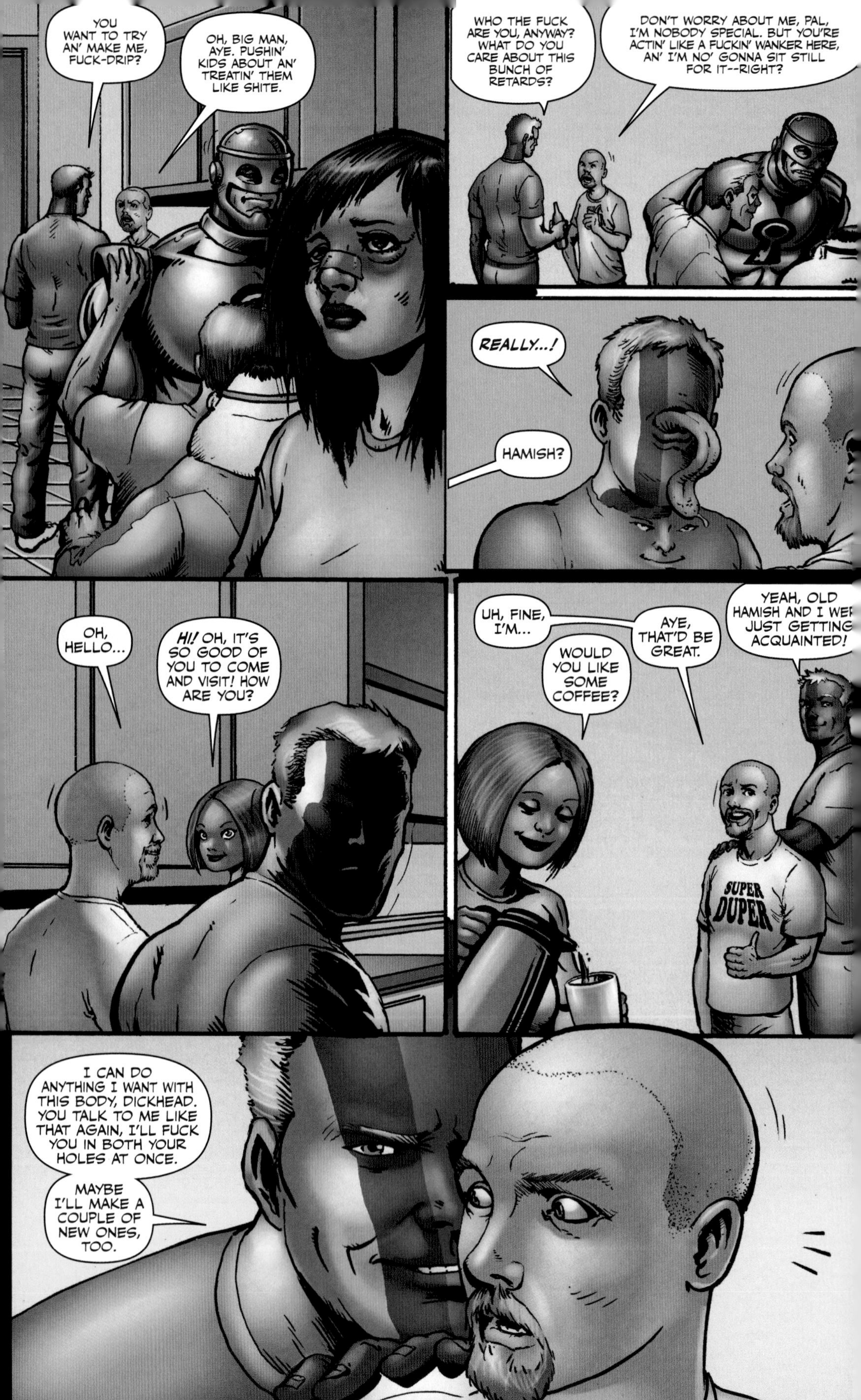
YOU WANT TO TRY AN' MAKE ME, FUCK-DRIP?
OH, BIG MAN, AYE. PUSHIN' KIDS ABOUT AN' TREATIN' THEM LIKE SHITE.
WHO THE FUCK ARE YOU, ANYWAY? WHAT DO YOU CARE ABOUT THIS BUNCH OF RETARDS?
DON'T WORRY ABOUT ME, PAL, I'M NOBODY SPECIAL. BUT YOU'RE ACTIN' LIKE A FUCKIN' WANKER HERE, AN' I'M NO' GONNA SIT STILL FOR IT--RIGHT?
REALLY...!
HAMISH?
OH, HELLO...
HI! OH, IT'S SO GOOD OF YOU TO COME AND VISIT! HOW ARE YOU?
UH, FINE, I'M...
WOULD YOU LIKE SOME COFFEE?
AYE, THAT'D BE GREAT.
YEAH, OLD HAMISH AND I WEF JUST GETTING ACQUAINTED!
SUPER DUPER
I CAN DO ANYTHING I WANT WITH THIS BODY, DICKHEAD. YOU TALK TO ME LIKE THAT AGAIN, I'LL FUCK YOU IN BOTH YOUR HOLES AT ONCE.
MAYBE I'LL MAKE A COUPLE OF NEW ONES, TOO.

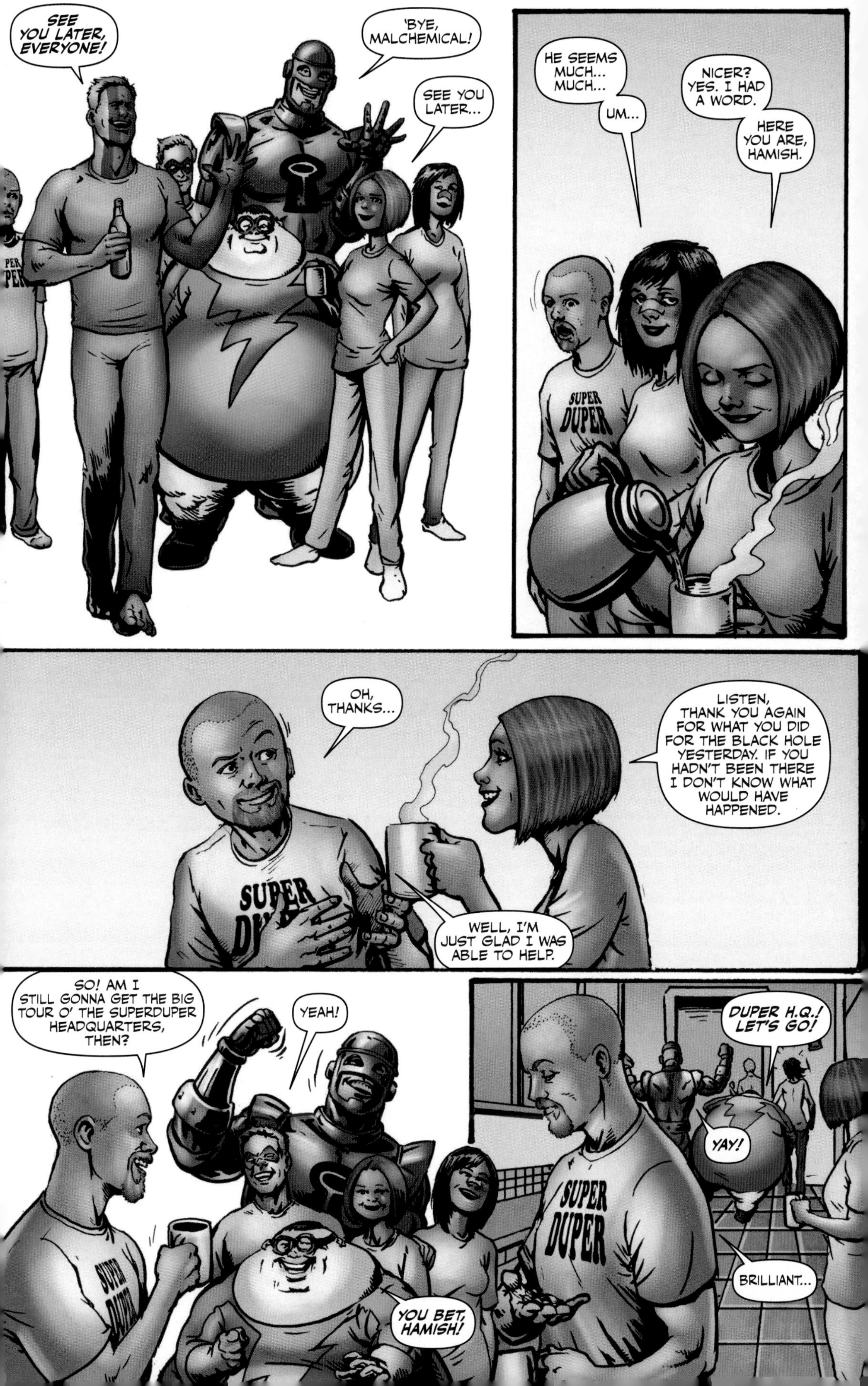
SEE YOU LATER, EVERYONE!
'BYE, MALCHEMICAL!
SEE YOU LATER...
SUPER DUPER
HE SEEMS MUCH... MUCH...
UM...
NICER? YES. I HAD A WORD.
HERE YOU ARE, HAMISH.
SUPER DUPER
OH, THANKS...
LISTEN, THANK YOU AGAIN FOR WHAT YOU DID FOR THE BLACK HOLE YESTERDAY. IF YOU HADN'T BEEN THERE I DON'T KNOW WHAT WOULD HAVE HAPPENED.
WELL, I'M JUST GLAD I WAS ABLE TO HELP.
SO! AM I STILL GONNA GET THE BIG TOUR O' THE SUPERDUPER HEADQUARTERS, THEN?
YEAH!
YOU BET, HAMISH!
DUPER H.Q.! LET'S GO!
YAY!
SUPER DUPER
BRILLIANT...

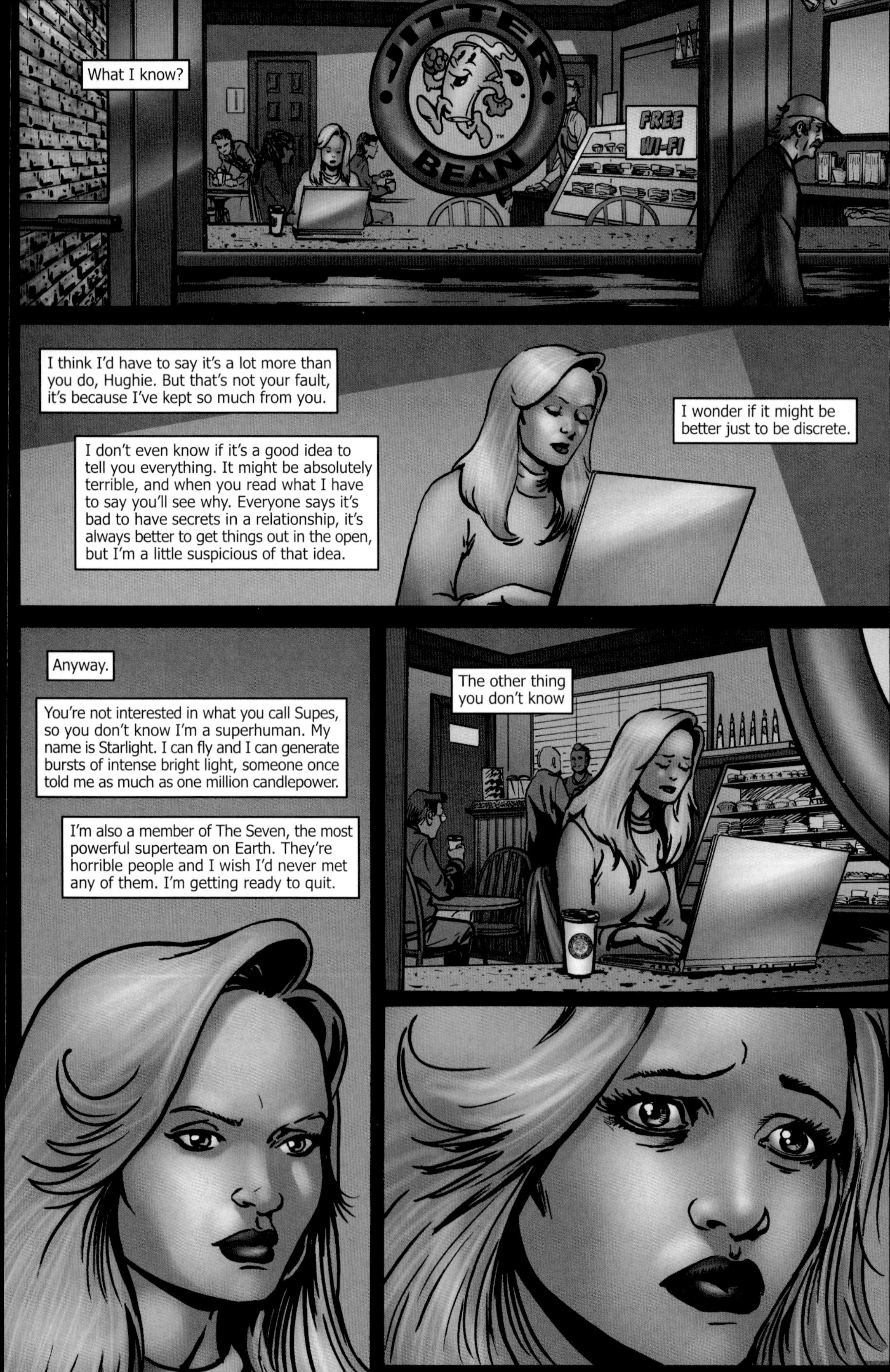
JITTER BEAN
FREE WI-FI
What I know?
I think I'd have to say it's a lot more than you do, Hughie. But that's not your fault, it's because I've kept so much from you.
I don't even know if it's a good idea to tell you everything. It might be absolutely terrible, and when you read what I have to say you'll see why. Everyone says it's bad to have secrets in a relationship, it's always better to get things out in the open, but I'm a little suspicious of that idea.
I wonder if it might be better just to be discrete.
Anyway.
You're not interested in what you call Supes, so you don't know I'm a superhuman. My name is Starlight. I can fly and I can generate bursts of intense bright light, someone once told me as much as one million candlepower.
I'm also a member of The Seven, the most powerful superteam on Earth. They're horrible people and I wish I'd never met any of them. I'm getting ready to quit.
The other thing you don't know

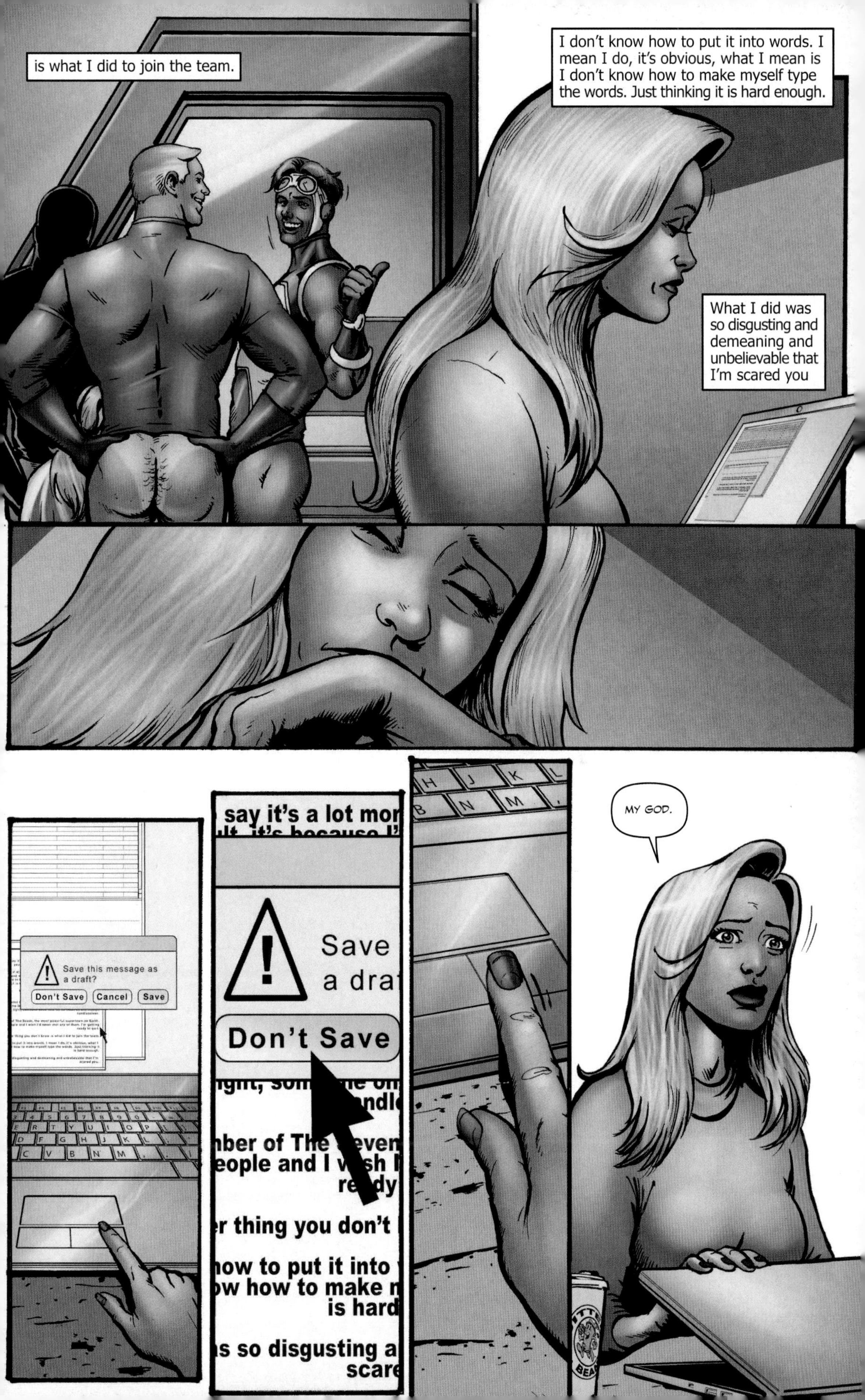
is what I did to join the team.
I don't know how to put it into words. I mean I do, it's obvious, what I mean is I don't know how to make myself type the words. Just thinking it is hard enough.
What I did was so disgusting and demeaning and unbelievable that I'm scared you
Save this message as a draft?
Don't Save
Cancel
Save
Don't Save
MY GOD.

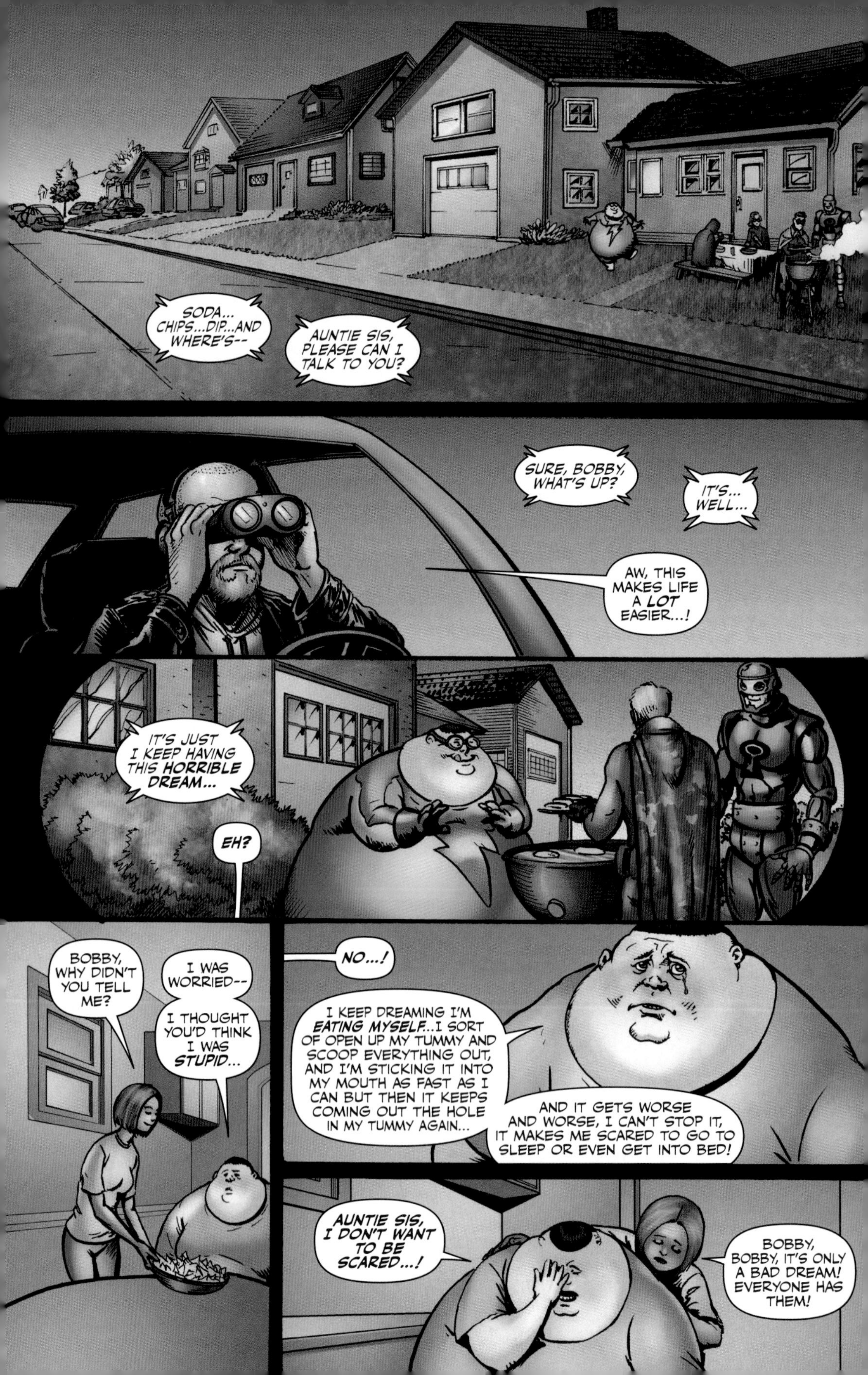
SODA... CHIPS...DIP...AND WHERE'S--
AUNTIE SIS, PLEASE CAN I TALK TO YOU?
SURE, BOBBY, WHAT'S UP?
IT'S... WELL...
AW, THIS MAKES LIFE A LOT EASIER...!
IT'S JUST I KEEP HAVING THIS HORRIBLE DREAM...
EH?
BOBBY, WHY DIDN'T YOU TELL ME?
I WAS WORRIED--
I THOUGHT YOU'D THINK I WAS STUPID...
NO...!
I KEEP DREAMING I'M EATING MYSELF...I SORT OF OPEN UP MY TUMMY AND SCOOP EVERYTHING OUT, AND I'M STICKING IT INTO MY MOUTH AS FAST AS I CAN BUT THEN IT KEEPS COMING OUT THE HOLE IN MY TUMMY AGAIN...
AND IT GETS WORSE AND WORSE, I CAN'T STOP IT, IT MAKES ME SCARED TO GO TO SLEEP OR EVEN GET INTO BED!
AUNTIE SIS, I DON'T WANT TO BE SCARED...!
BOBBY, BOBBY, IT'S ONLY A BAD DREAM! EVERYONE HAS THEM!

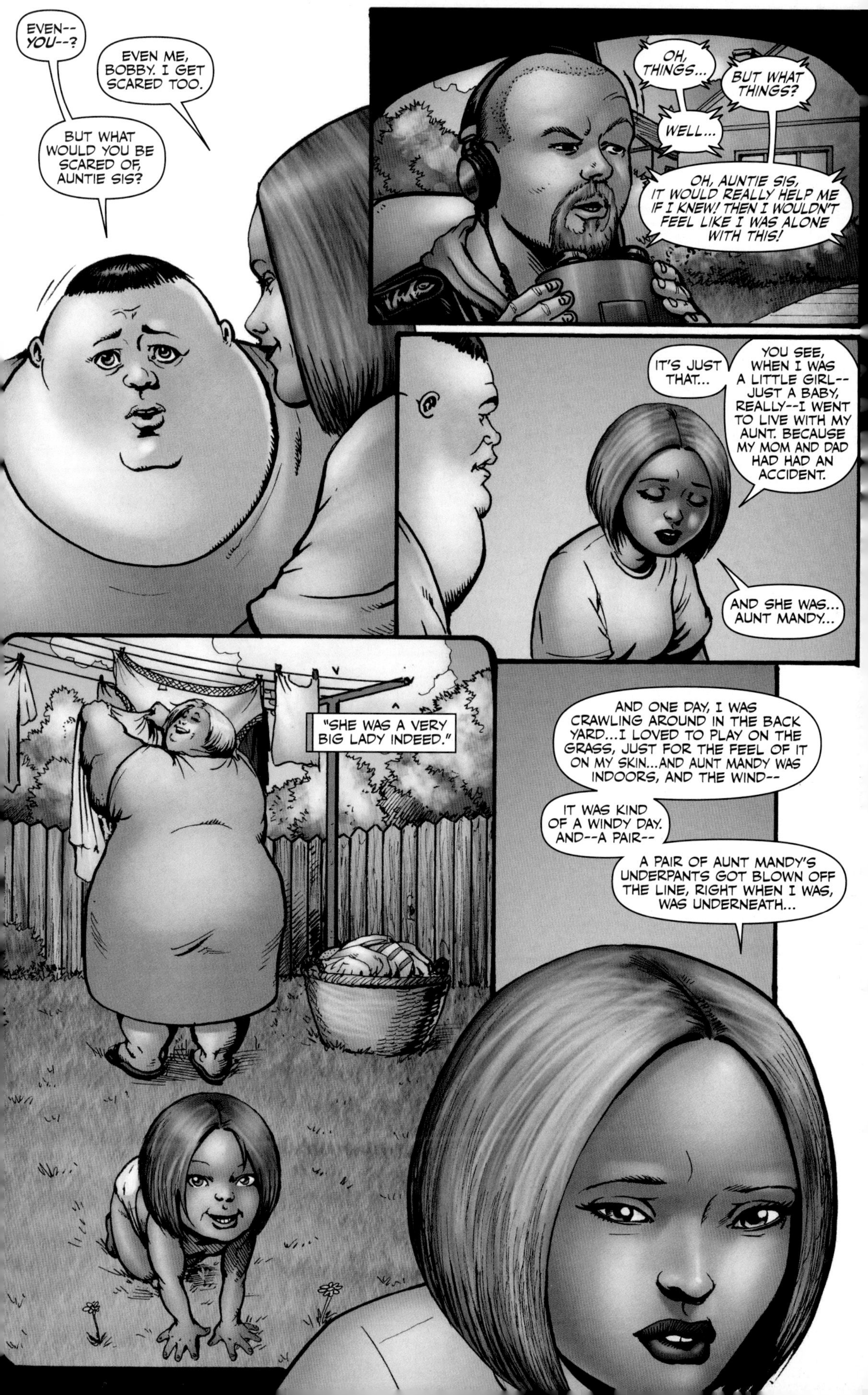
EVEN--
YOU--?
EVEN ME, BOBBY. I GET SCARED TOO.
BUT WHAT WOULD YOU BE SCARED OF, AUNTIE SIS?
OH, THINGS...
BUT WHAT THINGS?
WELL...
OH, AUNTIE SIS, IT WOULD REALLY HELP ME IF I KNEW! THEN I WOULDN'T FEEL LIKE I WAS ALONE WITH THIS!
IT'S JUST THAT...
YOU SEE, WHEN I WAS A LITTLE GIRL--JUST A BABY, REALLY--I WENT TO LIVE WITH MY AUNT. BECAUSE MY MOM AND DAD HAD HAD AN ACCIDENT.
AND SHE WAS... AUNT MANDY...
"SHE WAS A VERY BIG LADY INDEED."
AND ONE DAY, I WAS CRAWLING AROUND IN THE BACK YARD...I LOVED TO PLAY ON THE GRASS, JUST FOR THE FEEL OF IT ON MY SKIN...AND AUNT MANDY WAS INDOORS, AND THE WIND--
IT WAS KIND OF A WINDY DAY. AND--A PAIR--
A PAIR OF AUNT MANDY'S UNDERPANTS GOT BLOWN OFF THE LINE, RIGHT WHEN I WAS, WAS UNDERNEATH...

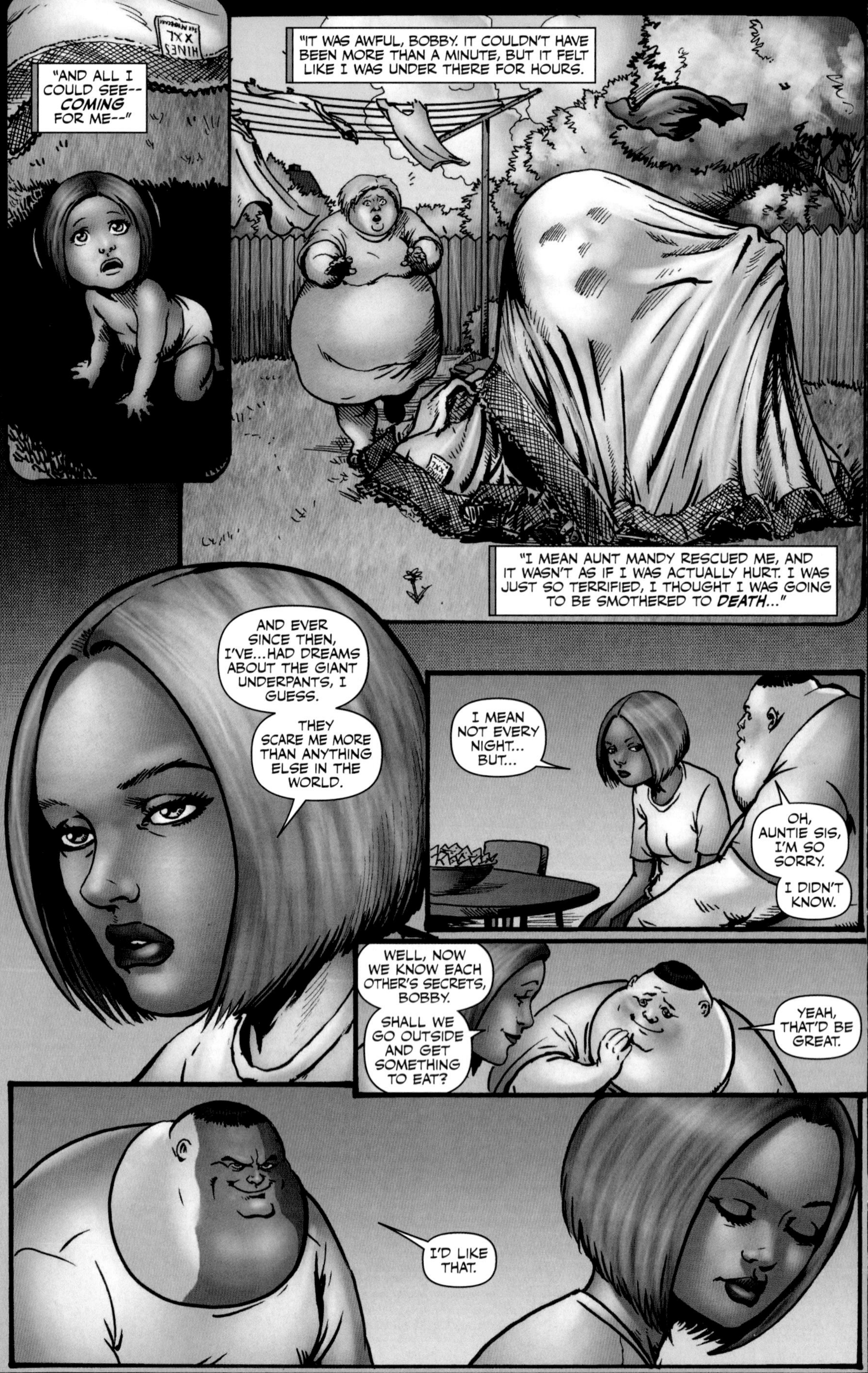

"AND ALL I COULD SEE-- COMING FOR ME--"
"IT WAS AWFUL, BOBBY. IT COULDN'T HAVE BEEN MORE THAN A MINUTE, BUT IT FELT LIKE I WAS UNDER THERE FOR HOURS.
"I MEAN AUNT MANDY RESCUED ME, AND IT WASN'T AS IF I WAS ACTUALLY HURT. I WAS JUST SO TERRIFIED, I THOUGHT I WAS GOING TO BE SMOTHERED TO DEATH..."
AND EVER SINCE THEN, I'VE...HAD DREAMS ABOUT THE GIANT UNDERPANTS, I GUESS.
THEY SCARE ME MORE THAN ANYTHING ELSE IN THE WORLD.
I MEAN NOT EVERY NIGHT... BUT...
OH, AUNTIE SIS, I'M SO SORRY.
I DIDN'T KNOW.
WELL, NOW WE KNOW EACH OTHER'S SECRETS, BOBBY.
SHALL WE GO OUTSIDE AND GET SOMETHING TO EAT?
YEAH, THAT'D BE GREAT.
I'D LIKE THAT.

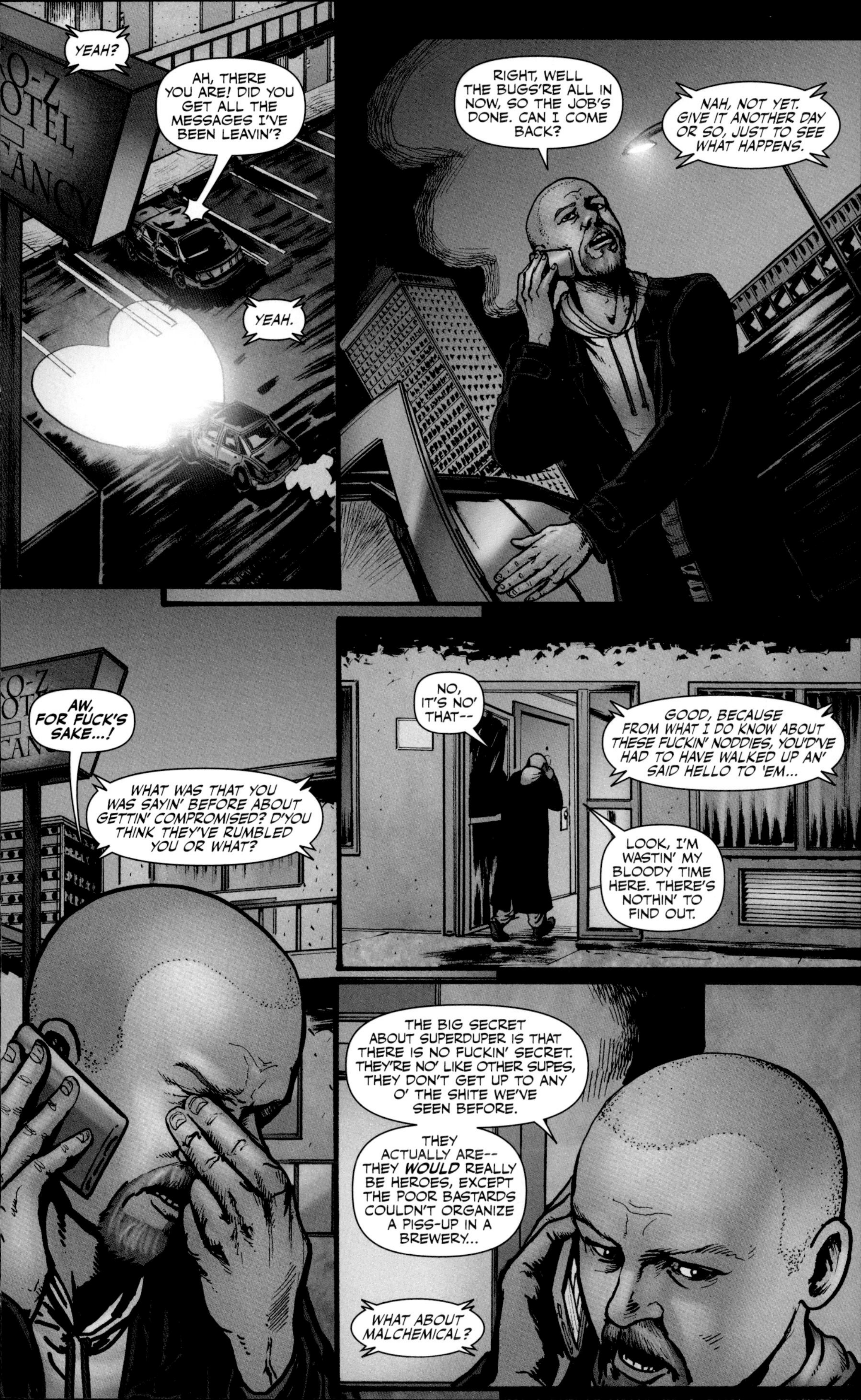
YEAH?
AH, THERE YOU ARE! DID YOU GET ALL THE MESSAGES I'VE BEEN LEAVIN'?
YEAH.
RIGHT, WELL THE BUGS'RE ALL IN NOW, SO THE JOB'S DONE. CAN I COME BACK?
NAH, NOT YET. GIVE IT ANOTHER DAY OR SO, JUST TO SEE WHAT HAPPENS.
AW, FOR FUCK'S SAKE...!
WHAT WAS THAT YOU WAS SAYIN' BEFORE ABOUT GETTIN' COMPROMISED? D'YOU THINK THEY'VE RUMBLED YOU OR WHAT?
NO, IT'S NO' THAT--
GOOD, BECAUSE FROM WHAT I DO KNOW ABOUT THESE FUCKIN' NODDIES, YOU'D'VE HAD TO HAVE WALKED UP AN' SAID HELLO TO 'EM...
LOOK, I'M WASTIN' MY BLOODY TIME HERE. THERE'S NOTHIN' TO FIND OUT.
THE BIG SECRET ABOUT SUPERDUPER IS THAT THERE IS NO FUCKIN' SECRET. THEY'RE NO' LIKE OTHER SUPES, THEY DON'T GET UP TO ANY O' THE SHITE WE'VE SEEN BEFORE.
THEY ACTUALLY ARE-- THEY WOULD REALLY BE HEROES, EXCEPT THE POOR BASTARDS COULDN'T ORGANIZE A PISS-UP IN A BREWERY...
WHAT ABOUT MALCHEMICAL?

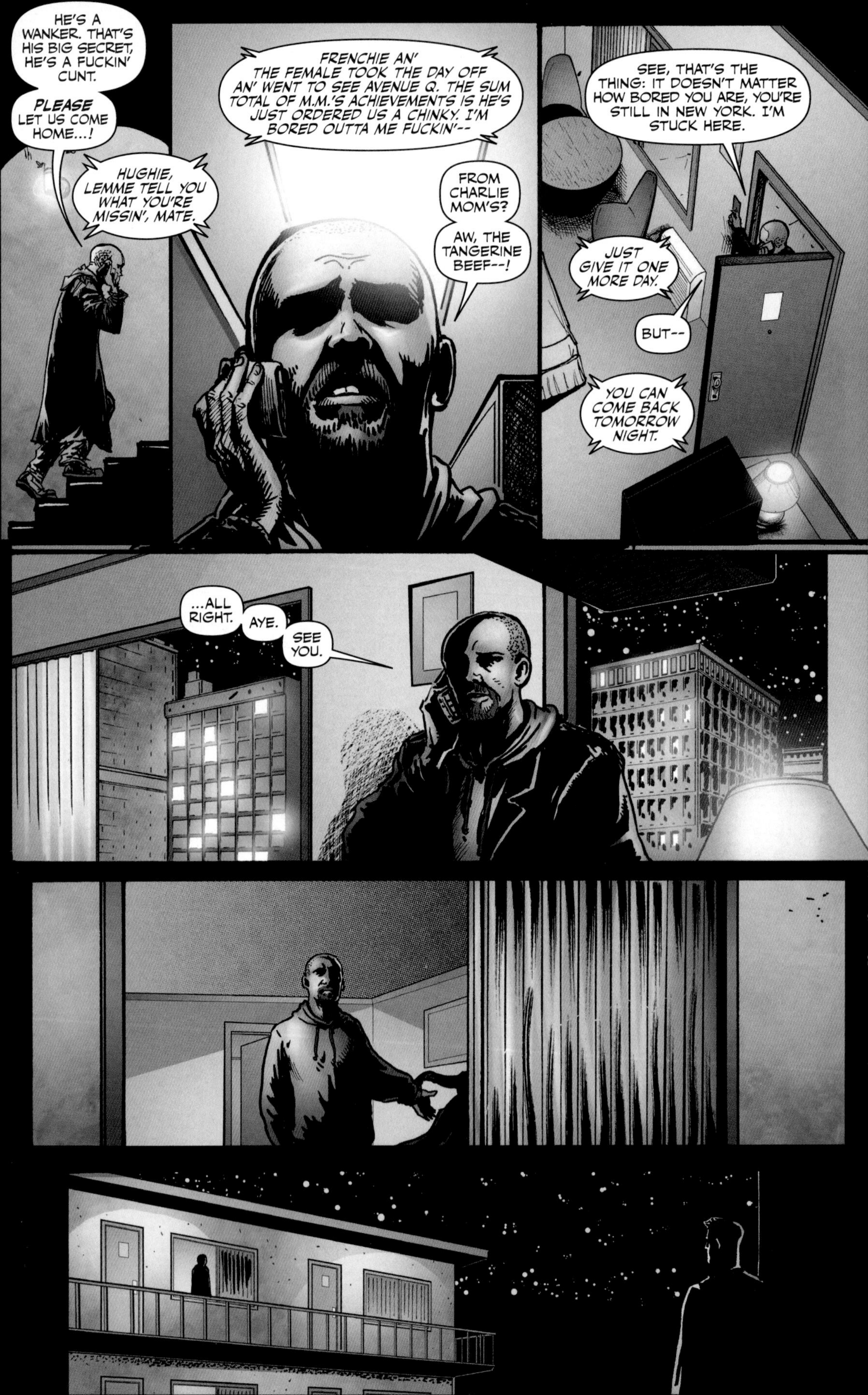
HE'S A WANKER. THAT'S HIS BIG SECRET, HE'S A FUCKIN' CUNT.
PLEASE LET US COME HOME...!
HUGHIE, LEMME TELL YOU WHAT YOU'RE MISSIN', MATE.
FRENCHIE AN' THE FEMALE TOOK THE DAY OFF AN' WENT TO SEE AVENUE Q. THE SUM TOTAL OF M.M.'S ACHIEVEMENTS IS HE'S JUST ORDERED US A CHINKY. I'M BORED OUTTA ME FUCKIN'--
FROM CHARLIE MOM'S?
AW, THE TANGERINE BEEF--!
SEE, THAT'S THE THING: IT DOESN'T MATTER HOW BORED YOU ARE, YOU'RE STILL IN NEW YORK. I'M STUCK HERE.
JUST GIVE IT ONE MORE DAY.
BUT--
YOU CAN COME BACK TOMORROW NIGHT.
...ALL RIGHT.
AYE.
SEE YOU.

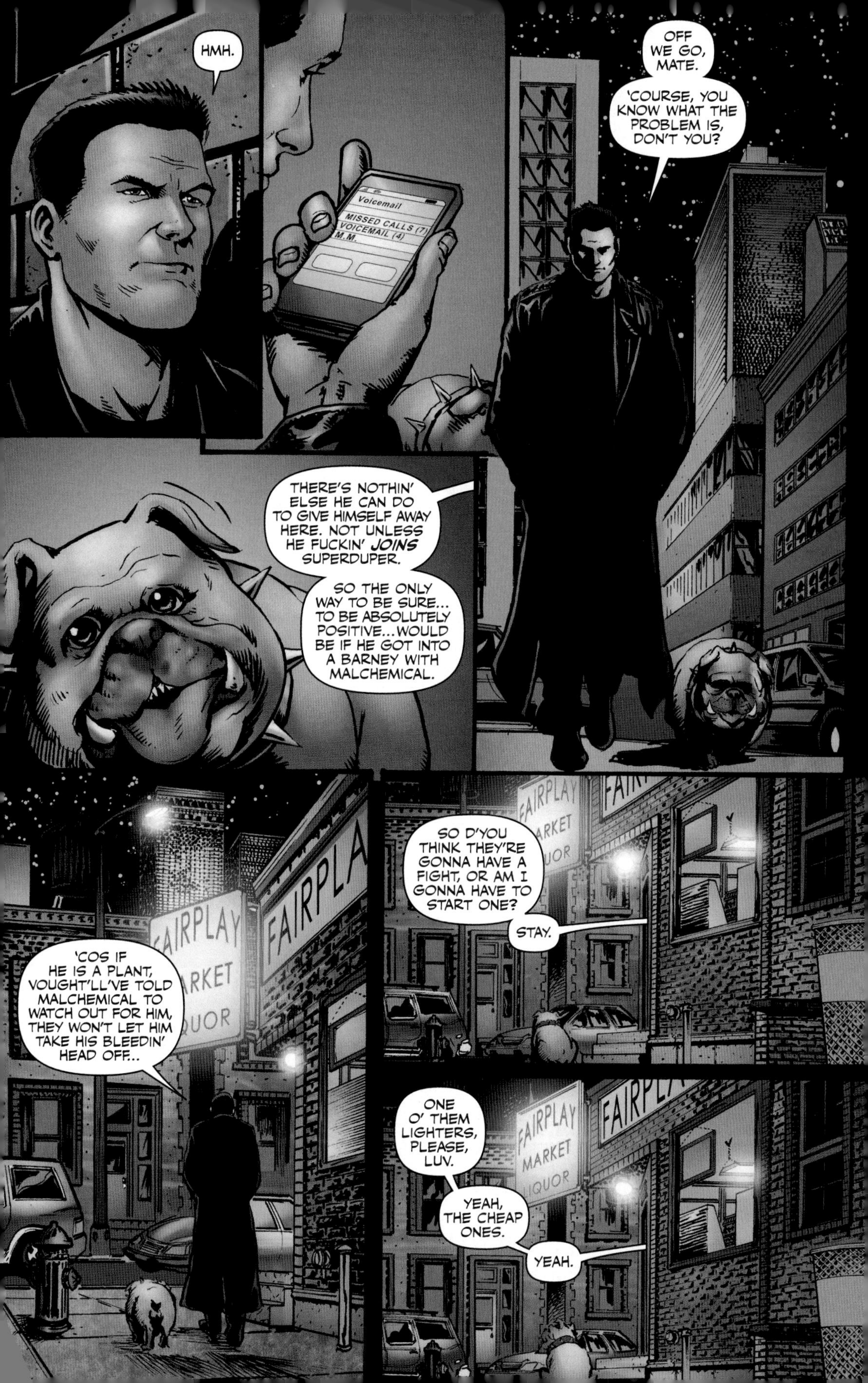
HMH.
Voicemail
MISSED CALLS (7)
VOICEMAIL (4)
M.M.
OFF WE GO, MATE.
'COURSE, YOU KNOW WHAT THE PROBLEM IS, DON'T YOU?
THERE'S NOTHIN' ELSE HE CAN DO TO GIVE HIMSELF AWAY HERE. NOT UNLESS HE FUCKIN' *JOINS* SUPERDUPER.
SO THE ONLY WAY TO BE SURE... TO BE ABSOLUTELY POSITIVE...WOULD BE IF HE GOT INTO A BARNEY WITH MALCHEMICAL.
FAIRPLAY
FAIRPLAY MARKET LIQUOR
'COS IF HE IS A PLANT, VOUGHT'LL'VE TOLD MALCHEMICAL TO WATCH OUT FOR HIM, THEY WON'T LET HIM TAKE HIS BLEEDIN' HEAD OFF...
SO D'YOU THINK THEY'RE GONNA HAVE A FIGHT, OR AM I GONNA HAVE TO START ONE?
STAY.
ONE O' THEM LIGHTERS, PLEASE, LUV.
YEAH, THE CHEAP ONES.
YEAH.

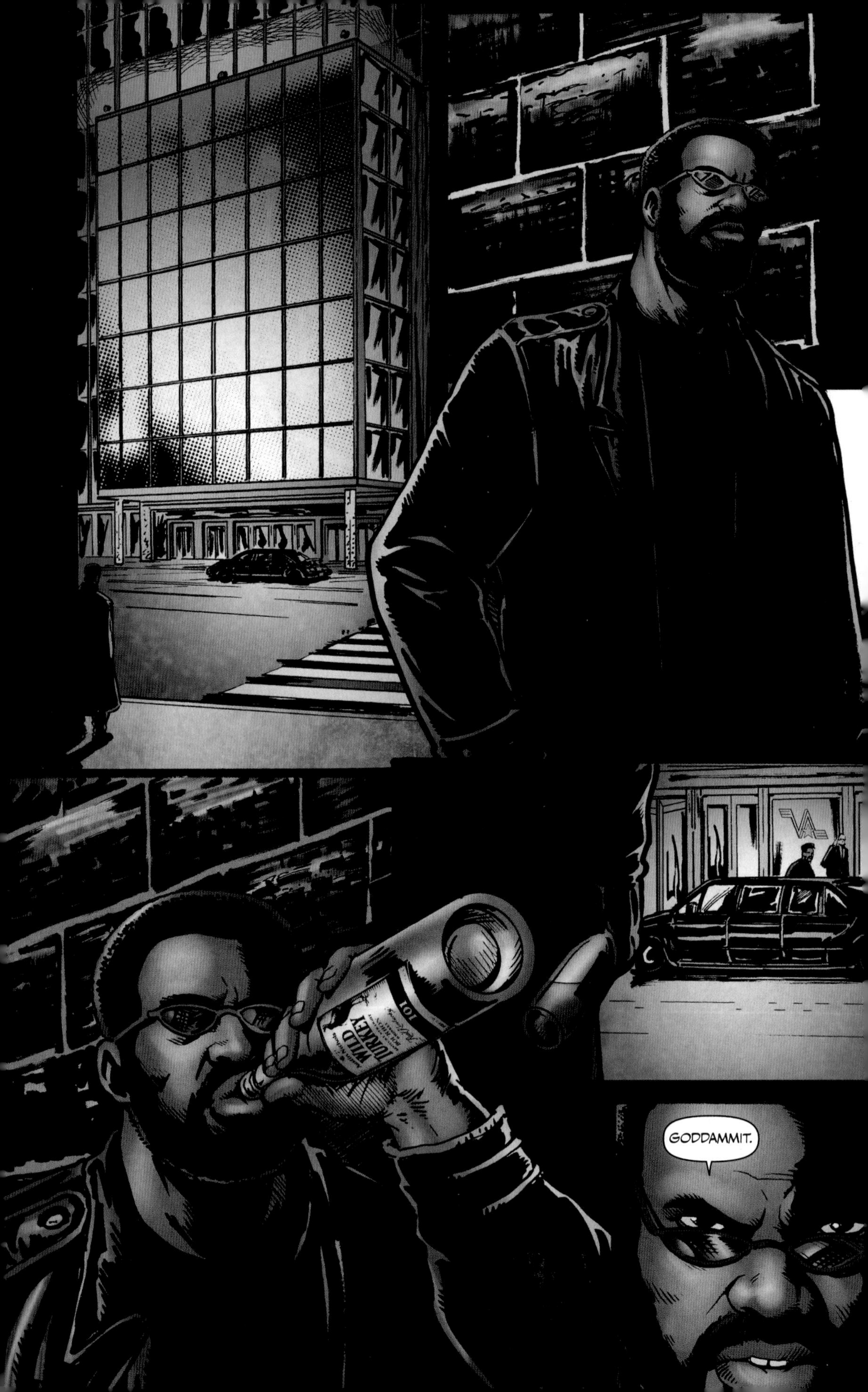
GODDAMMIT.

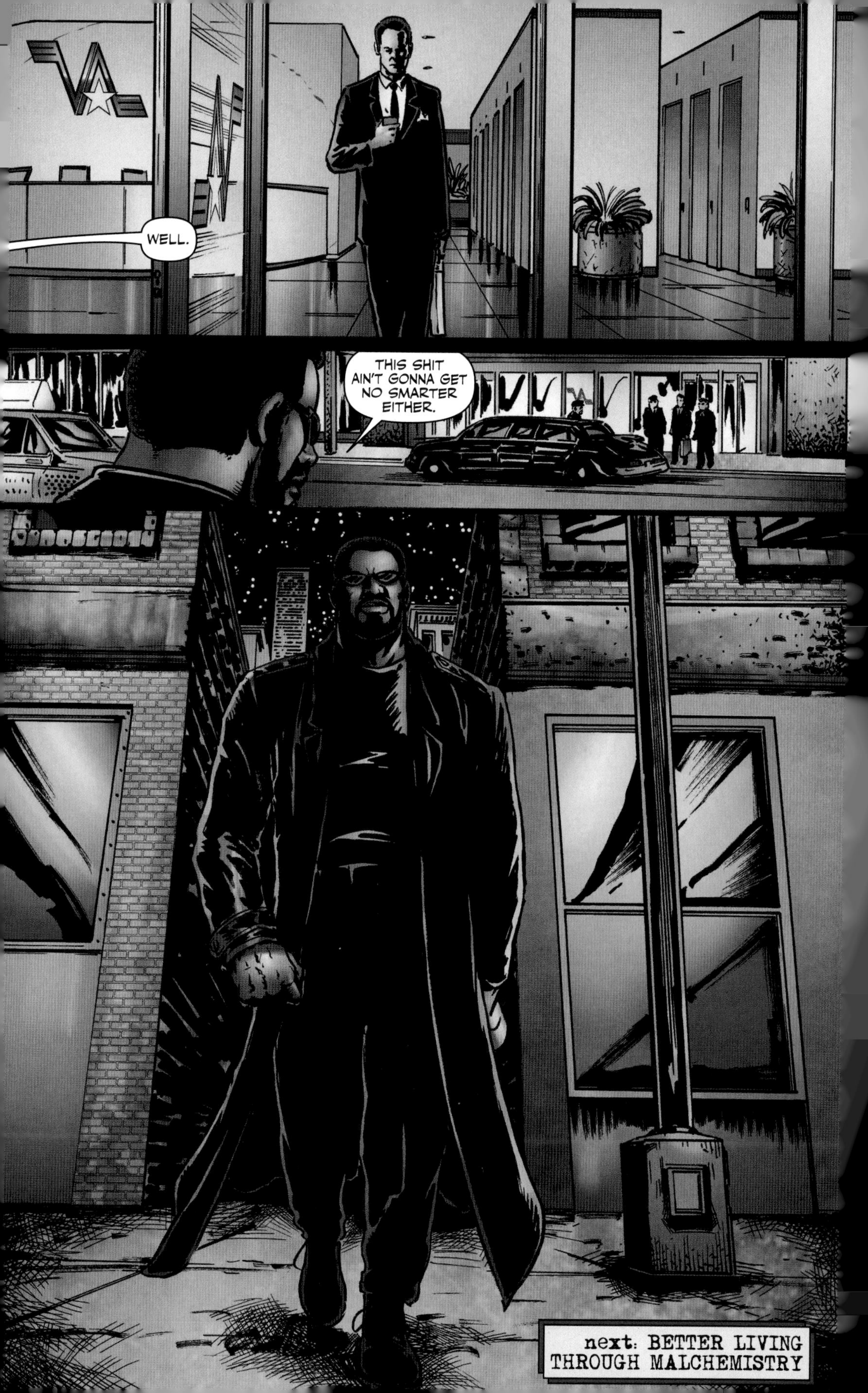
WELL.
THIS SHIT AIN'T GONNA GET NO SMARTER EITHER.
next: BETTER LIVING THROUGH MALCHEMISTRY

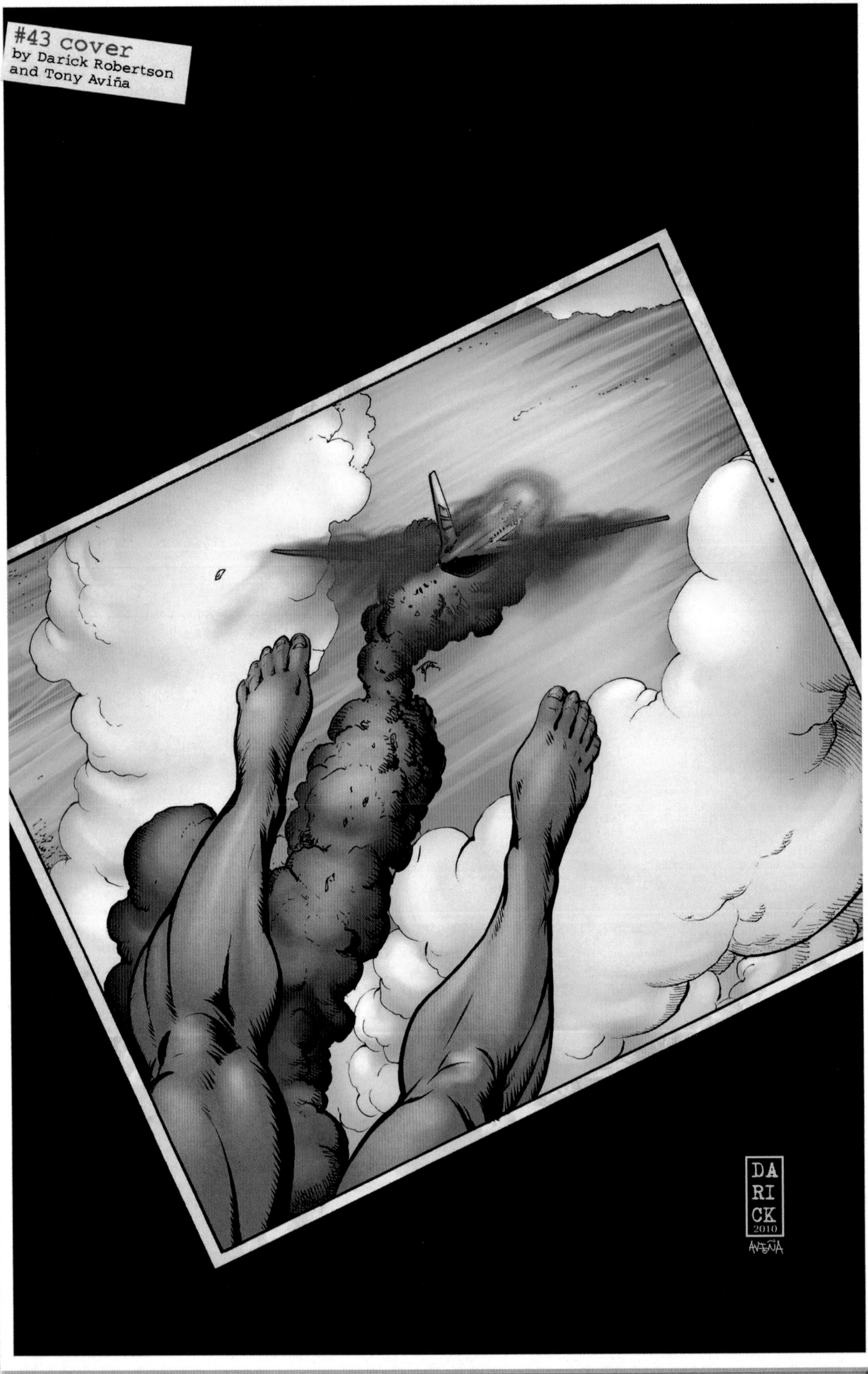

#43 cover
by Darick Robertson
and Tony Aviña

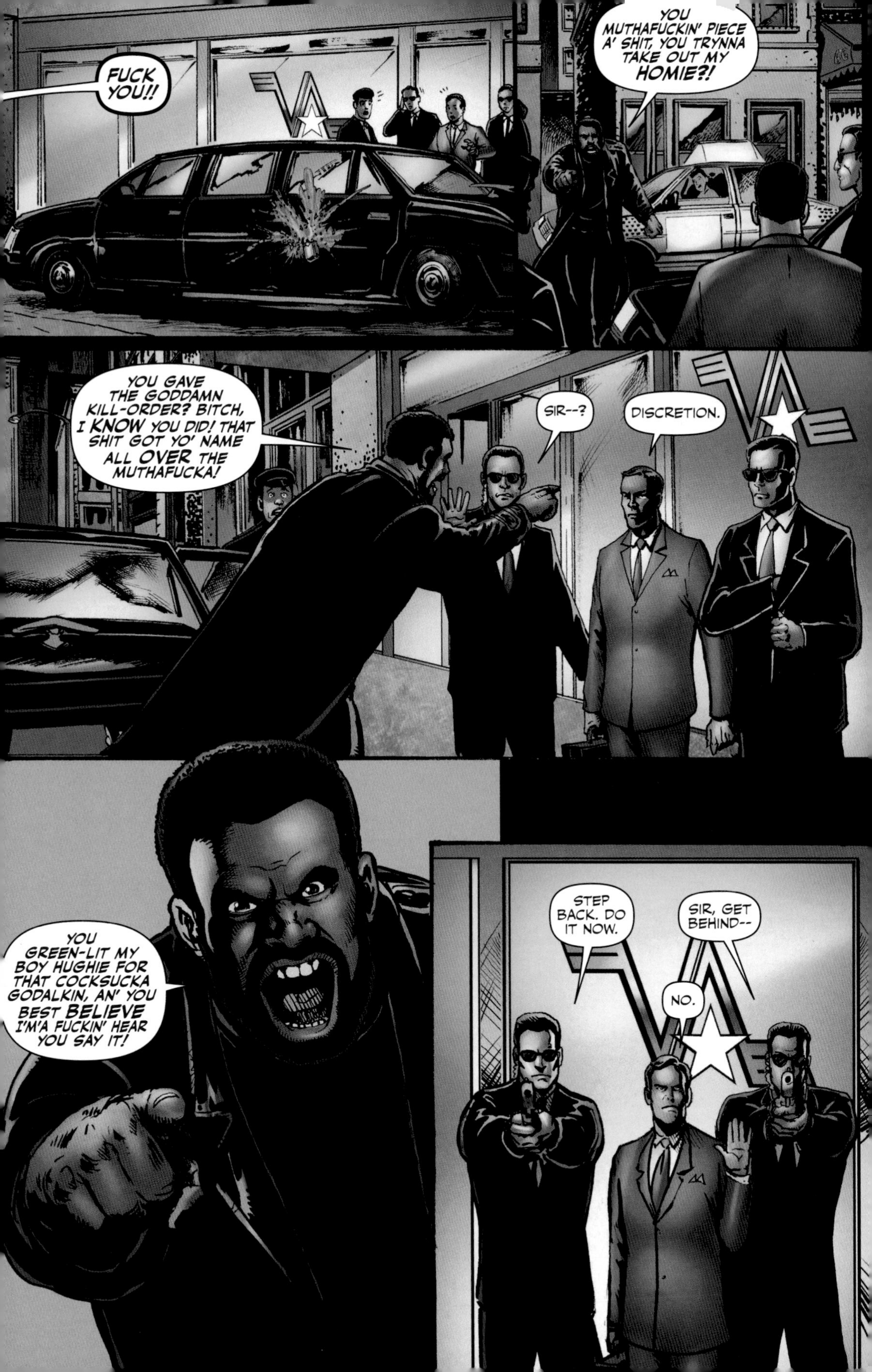
FUCK YOU!!
YOU MUTHAFUCKIN' PIECE A' SHIT, YOU TRYNNA TAKE OUT MY HOMIE?!
YOU GAVE THE GODDAMN KILL-ORDER? BITCH, I KNOW YOU DID! THAT SHIT GOT YO' NAME ALL OVER THE MUTHAFUCKA!
SIR--?
DISCRETION.
YOU GREEN-LIT MY BOY HUGHIE FOR THAT COCKSUCKA GODALKIN, AN' YOU BEST BELIEVE I'M'A FUCKIN' HEAR YOU SAY IT!
STEP BACK. DO IT NOW.
SIR, GET BEHIND--
NO.

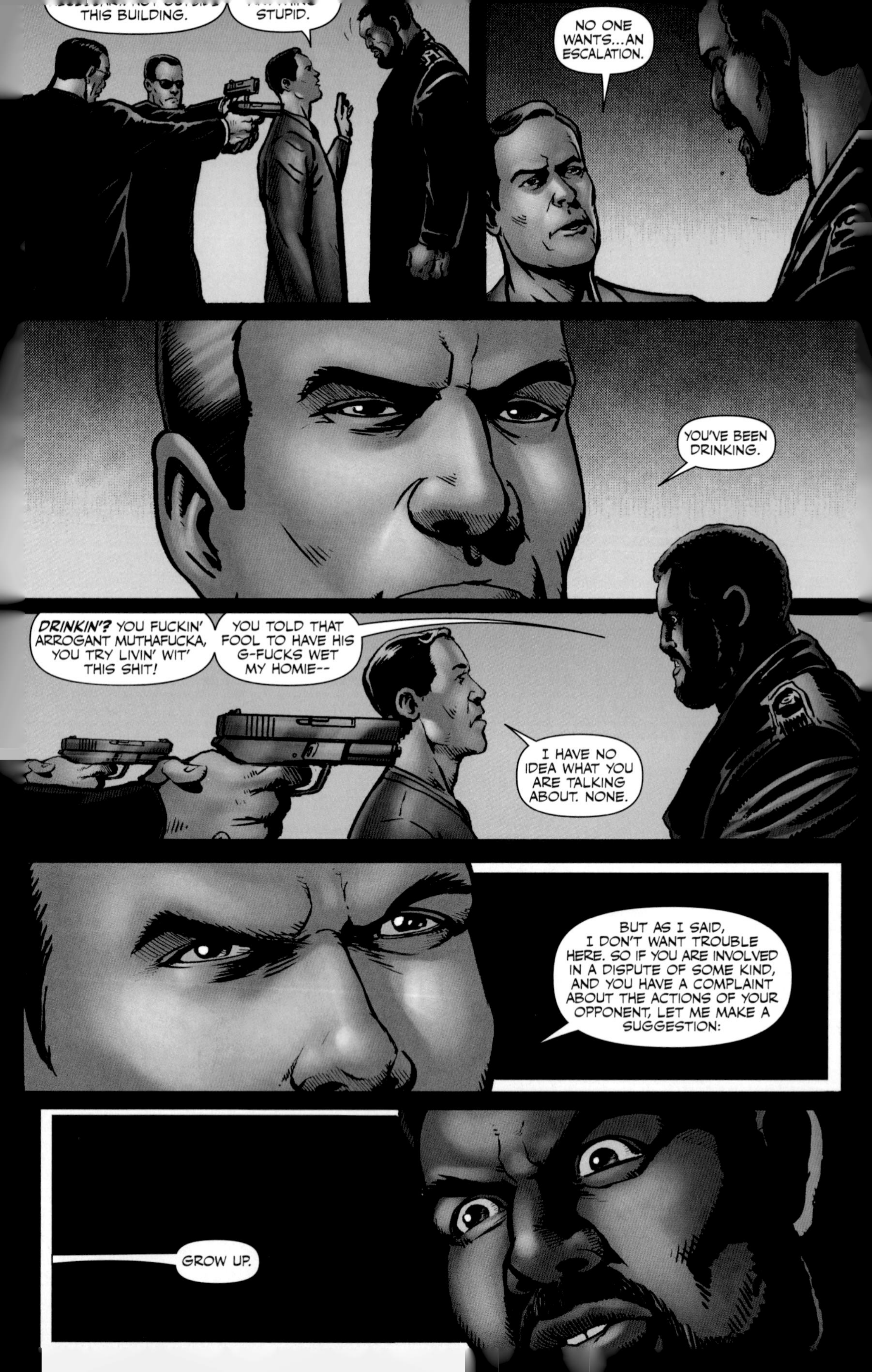
THIS BUILDING.
STUPID.
NO ONE WANTS...AN ESCALATION.
YOU'VE BEEN DRINKING.
DRINKIN'? YOU FUCKIN' ARROGANT MUTHAFUCKA, YOU TRY LIVIN' WIT' THIS SHIT!
YOU TOLD THAT FOOL TO HAVE HIS G-FUCKS WET MY HOMIE--
I HAVE NO IDEA WHAT YOU ARE TALKING ABOUT. NONE.
BUT AS I SAID, I DON'T WANT TROUBLE HERE. SO IF YOU ARE INVOLVED IN A DISPUTE OF SOME KIND, AND YOU HAVE A COMPLAINT ABOUT THE ACTIONS OF YOUR OPPONENT, LET ME MAKE A SUGGESTION:
GROW UP.

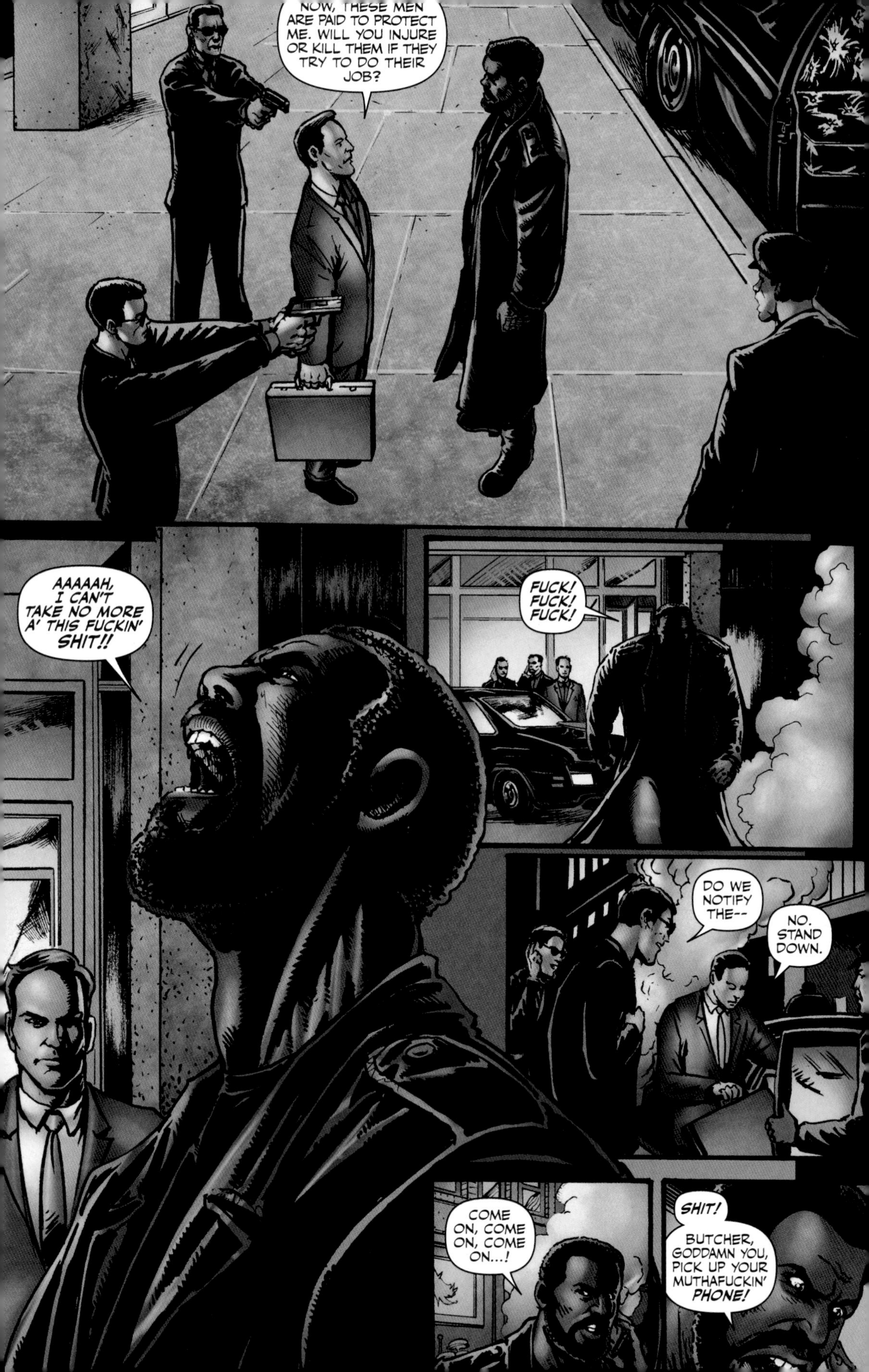
NOW, THESE MEN ARE PAID TO PROTECT ME. WILL YOU INJURE OR KILL THEM IF THEY TRY TO DO THEIR JOB?
AAAAAH, I CAN'T TAKE NO MORE A' THIS FUCKIN' SHIT!!
FUCK! FUCK! FUCK!
DO WE NOTIFY THE--
NO. STAND DOWN.
COME ON, COME ON, COME ON...!
SHIT!
BUTCHER, GODDAMN YOU, PICK UP YOUR MUTHAFUCKIN' PHONE!

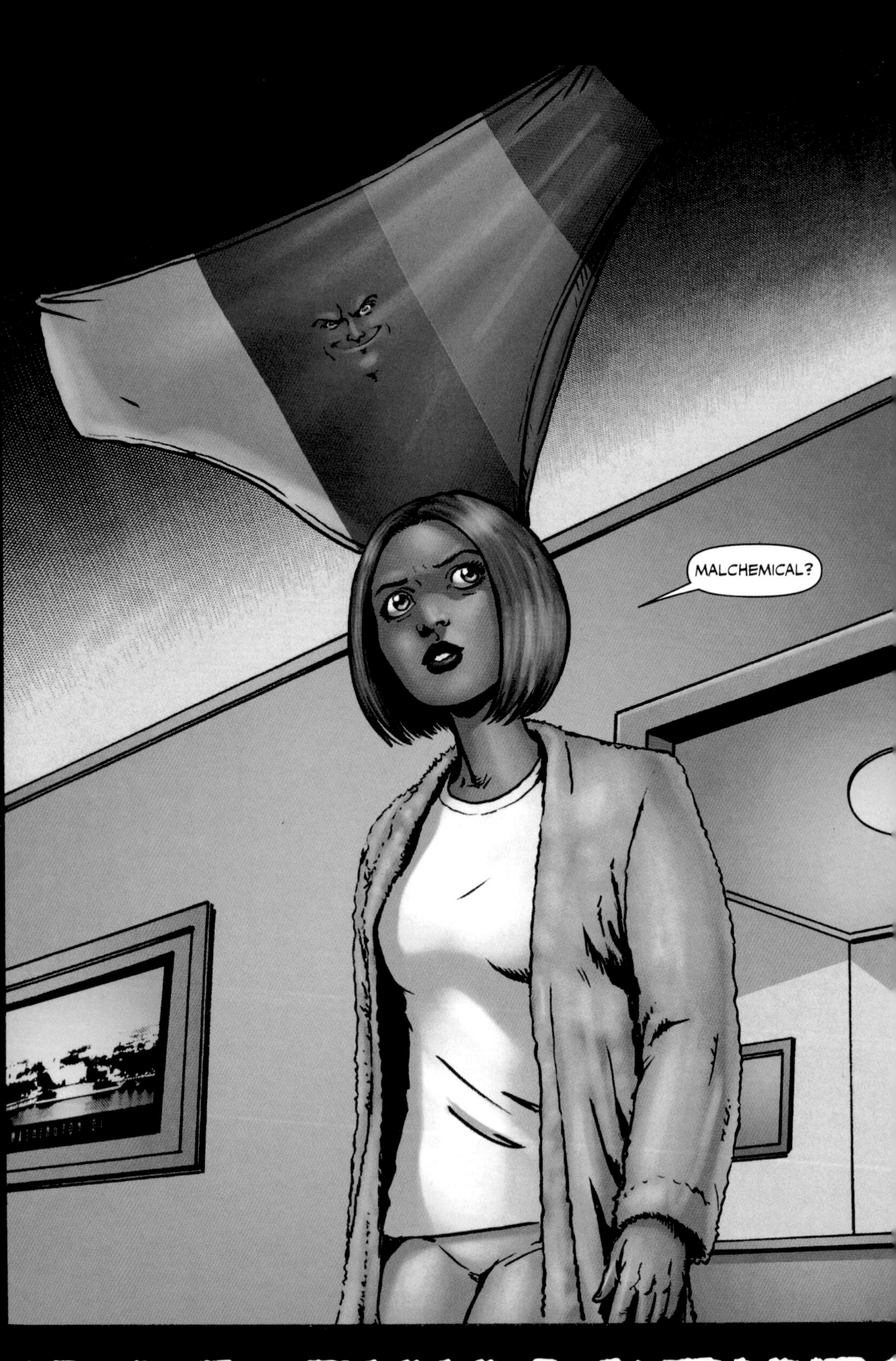
MALCHEMICAL?

THE INNOCENTS
conclusion

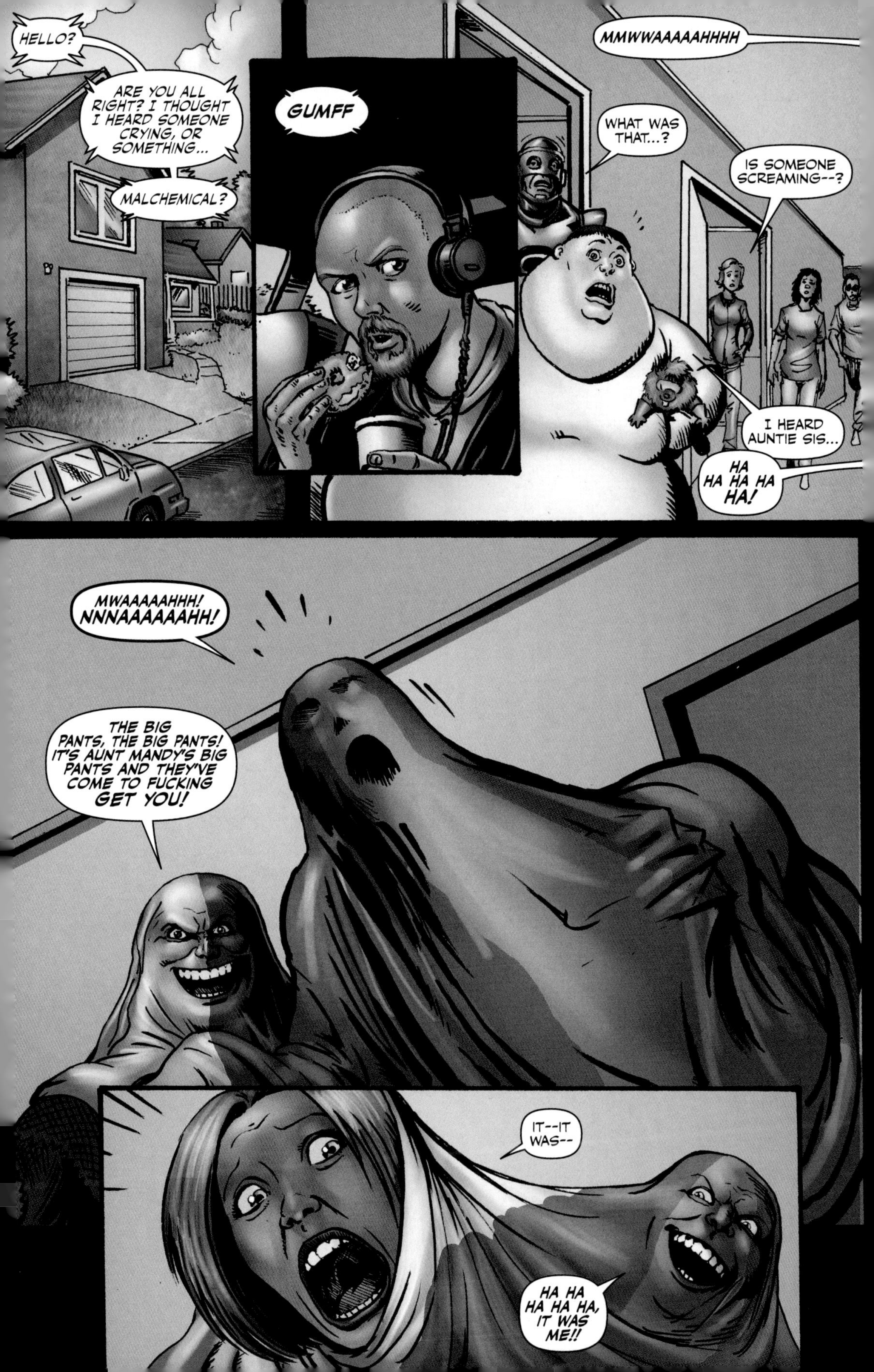
HELLO?
ARE YOU ALL RIGHT? I THOUGHT I HEARD SOMEONE CRYING, OR SOMETHING...
MALCHEMICAL?
GUMFF
MMWWAAAAAHHHH
WHAT WAS THAT...?
IS SOMEONE SCREAMING--?
I HEARD AUNTIE SIS...
HA HA HA HA HA HA!
MWAAAAAHHH! NNNAAAAAAAHH!
THE BIG PANTS, THE BIG PANTS! IT'S AUNT MANDY'S BIG PANTS AND THEY'VE COME TO FUCKING GET YOU!
IT--IT WAS--
HA HA HA HA HA, IT WAS ME!!

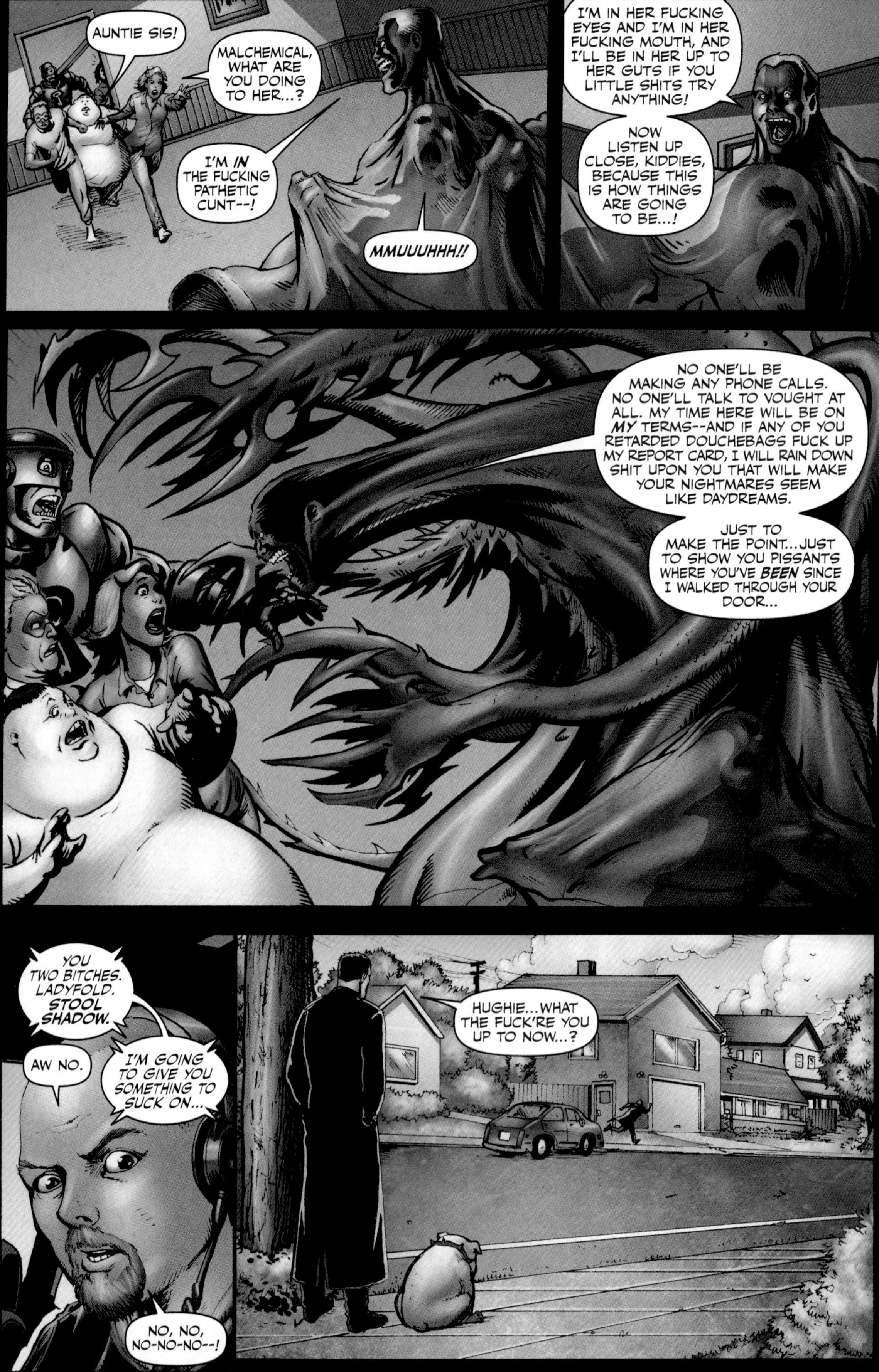
AUNTIE SIS!
MALCHEMICAL, WHAT ARE YOU DOING TO HER...?
I'M *IN* THE FUCKING PATHETIC CUNT--!
MMUUUHHH!!
I'M IN HER FUCKING EYES AND I'M IN HER FUCKING MOUTH, AND I'LL BE IN HER UP TO HER GUTS IF YOU LITTLE SHITS TRY ANYTHING!
NOW LISTEN UP CLOSE, KIDDIES, BECAUSE THIS IS HOW THINGS ARE GOING TO BE...!
NO ONE'LL BE MAKING ANY PHONE CALLS. NO ONE'LL TALK TO VOUGHT AT ALL. MY TIME HERE WILL BE ON *MY* TERMS--AND IF ANY OF YOU RETARDED DOUCHEBAGS FUCK UP MY REPORT CARD, I WILL RAIN DOWN SHIT UPON YOU THAT WILL MAKE YOUR NIGHTMARES SEEM LIKE DAYDREAMS.
JUST TO MAKE THE POINT...JUST TO SHOW YOU PISSANTS WHERE YOU'VE *BEEN* SINCE I WALKED THROUGH YOUR DOOR...
YOU TWO BITCHES. LADYFOLD. **STOOL SHADOW.**
I'M GOING TO GIVE YOU SOMETHING TO SUCK ON...
AW NO.
NO, NO, NO-NO-NO--!
HUGHIE...WHAT THE FUCK'RE YOU UP TO NOW...?

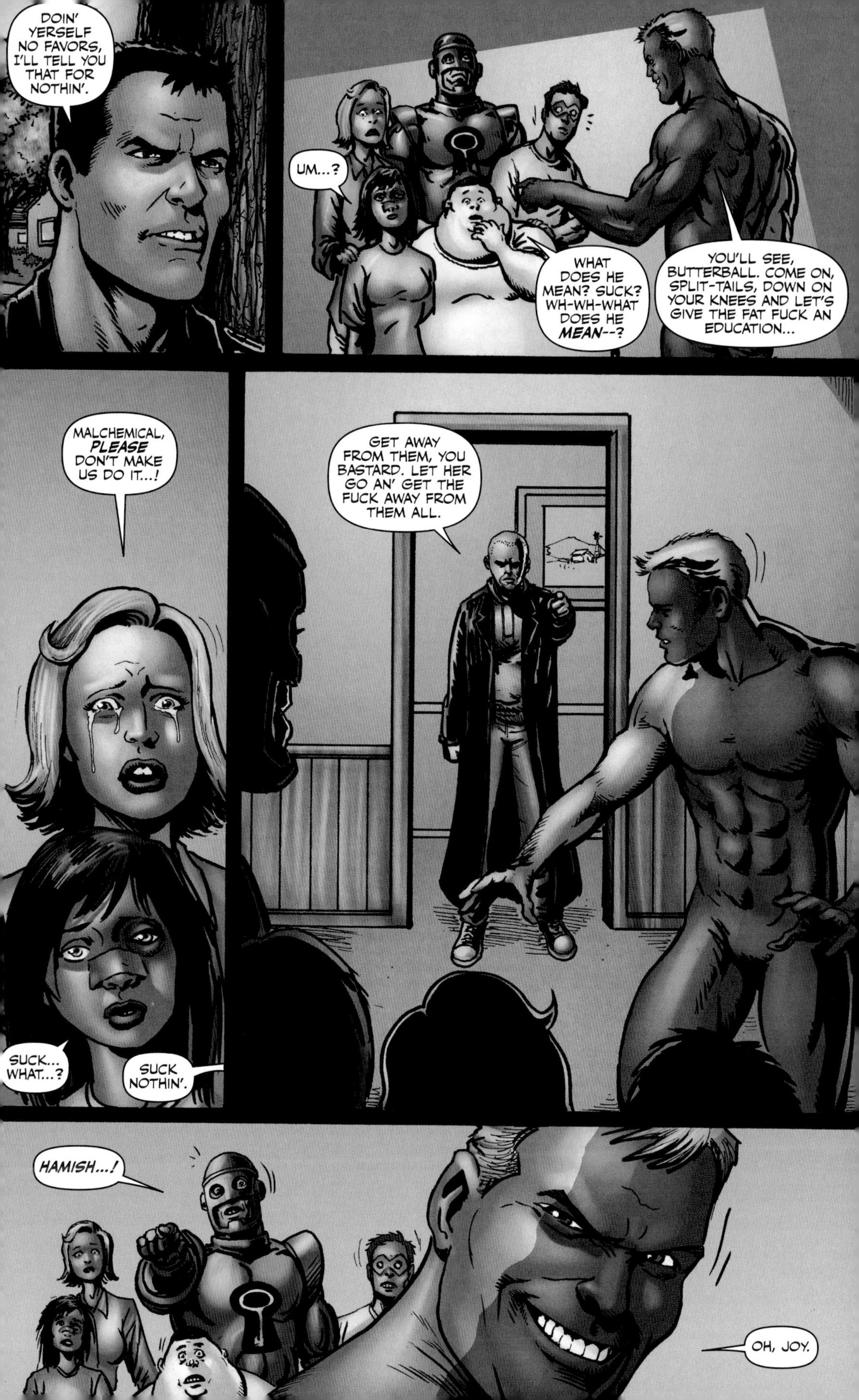
DOIN' YERSELF NO FAVORS, I'LL TELL YOU THAT FOR NOTHIN'.
UM...?
WHAT DOES HE MEAN? SUCK? WH-WH-WHAT DOES HE *MEAN*--?
YOU'LL SEE, BUTTERBALL. COME ON, SPLIT-TAILS, DOWN ON YOUR KNEES AND LET'S GIVE THE FAT FUCK AN EDUCATION...
MALCHEMICAL, *PLEASE* DON'T MAKE US DO IT...!
SUCK... WHAT...?
SUCK NOTHIN'.
GET AWAY FROM THEM, YOU BASTARD. LET HER GO AN' GET THE FUCK AWAY FROM THEM ALL.
HAMISH...!
OH, JOY.

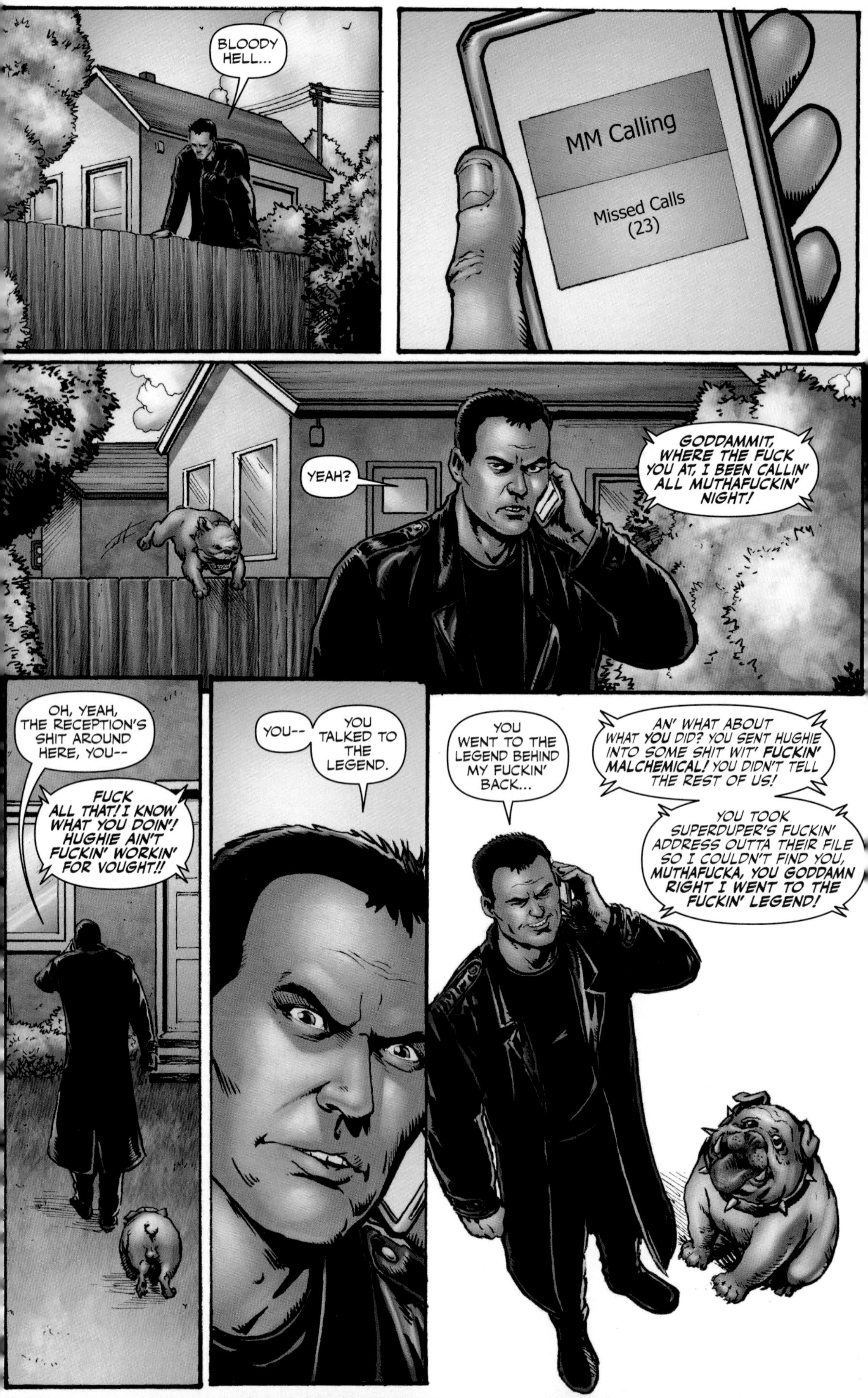
BLOODY HELL...
MM Calling
Missed Calls (23)
YEAH?
GODDAMMIT, WHERE THE FUCK YOU AT, I BEEN CALLIN' ALL MUTHAFUCKIN' NIGHT!
OH, YEAH, THE RECEPTION'S SHIT AROUND HERE, YOU--
FUCK ALL THAT! I KNOW WHAT YOU DOIN'! HUGHIE AIN'T FUCKIN' WORKIN' FOR VOUGHT!!
YOU--
YOU TALKED TO THE LEGEND.
YOU WENT TO THE LEGEND BEHIND MY FUCKIN' BACK...
AN' WHAT ABOUT WHAT YOU DID? YOU SENT HUGHIE INTO SOME SHIT WIT' FUCKIN' MALCHEMICAL! YOU DIDN'T TELL THE REST OF US!
YOU TOOK SUPERDUPER'S FUCKIN' ADDRESS OUTTA THEIR FILE SO I COULDN'T FIND YOU, MUTHAFUCKA, YOU GODDAMN RIGHT I WENT TO THE FUCKIN' LEGEND!

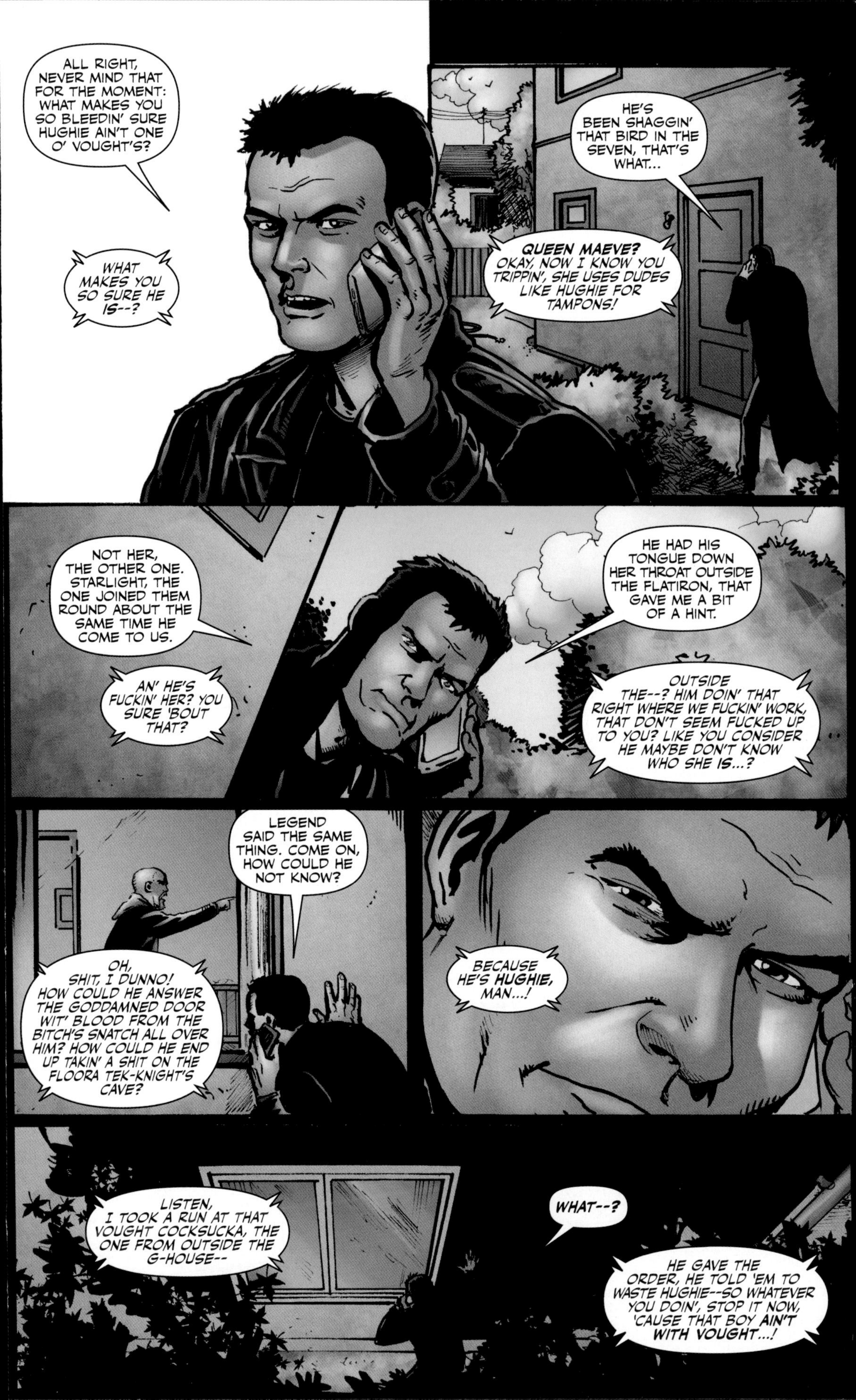
ALL RIGHT, NEVER MIND THAT FOR THE MOMENT: WHAT MAKES YOU SO BLEEDIN' SURE HUGHIE AIN'T ONE O' VOUGHT'S?
WHAT MAKES YOU SO SURE HE IS--?
HE'S BEEN SHAGGIN' THAT BIRD IN THE SEVEN, THAT'S WHAT...
QUEEN MAEVE? OKAY, NOW I KNOW YOU TRIPPIN', SHE USES DUDES LIKE HUGHIE FOR TAMPONS!
NOT HER, THE OTHER ONE. STARLIGHT, THE ONE JOINED THEM ROUND ABOUT THE SAME TIME HE COME TO US.
AN' HE'S FUCKIN' HER? YOU SURE 'BOUT THAT?
HE HAD HIS TONGUE DOWN HER THROAT OUTSIDE THE FLATIRON, THAT GAVE ME A BIT OF A HINT.
OUTSIDE THE--? HIM DOIN' THAT RIGHT WHERE WE FUCKIN' WORK, THAT DON'T SEEM FUCKED UP TO YOU? LIKE YOU CONSIDER HE MAYBE DON'T KNOW WHO SHE IS...?
LEGEND SAID THE SAME THING. COME ON, HOW COULD HE NOT KNOW?
OH, SHIT, I DUNNO! HOW COULD HE ANSWER THE GODDAMNED DOOR WIT' BLOOD FROM THE BITCH'S SNATCH ALL OVER HIM? HOW COULD HE END UP TAKIN' A SHIT ON THE FLOORA TEK-KNIGHT'S CAVE?
BECAUSE HE'S HUGHIE, MAN...!
LISTEN, I TOOK A RUN AT THAT VOUGHT COCKSUCKA, THE ONE FROM OUTSIDE THE G-HOUSE--
WHAT--?
HE GAVE THE ORDER, HE TOLD 'EM TO WASTE HUGHIE--SO WHATEVER YOU DOIN', STOP IT NOW, 'CAUSE THAT BOY AIN'T WITH VOUGHT...!

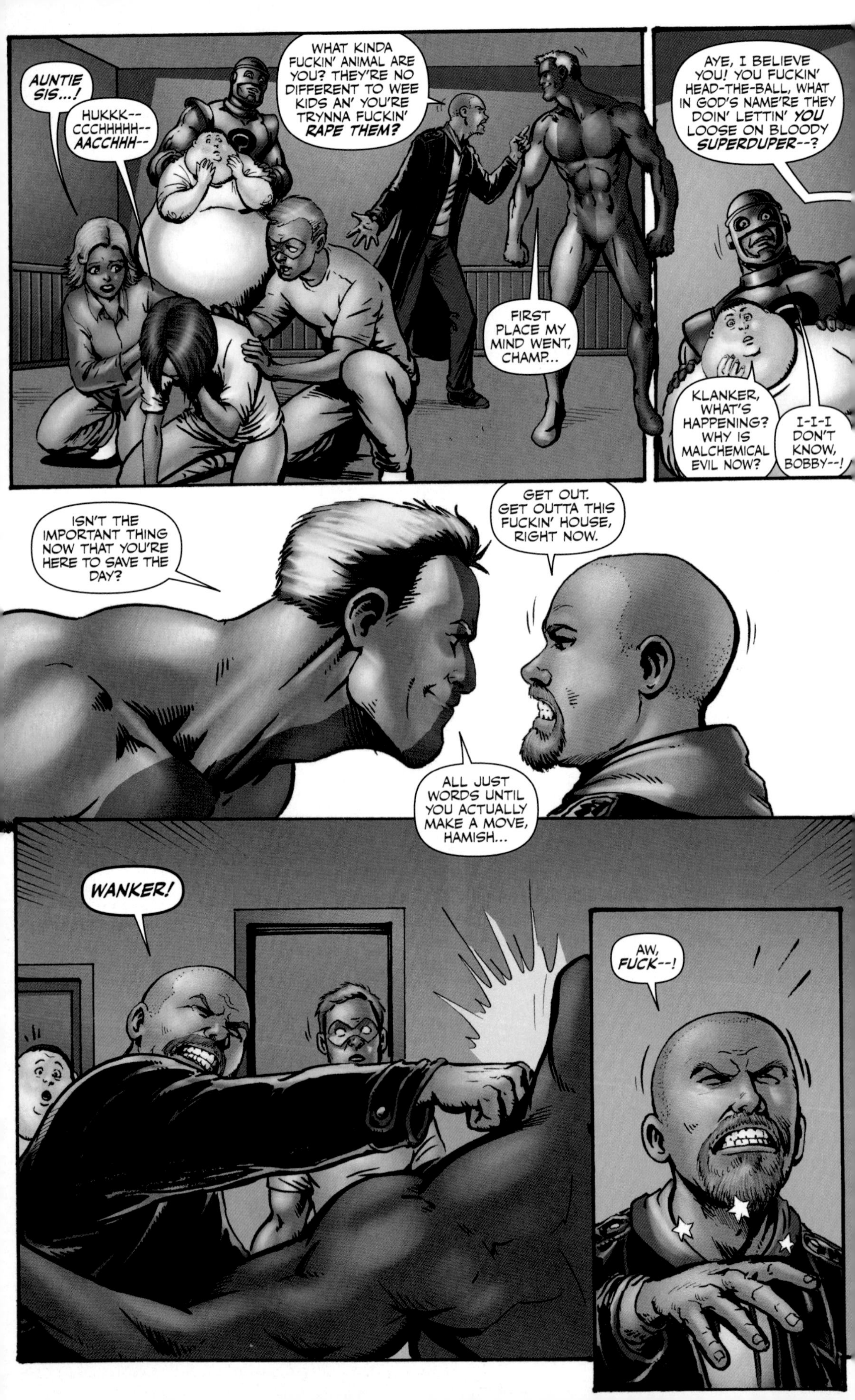
AUNTIE SIS...!
HUKKK-- CCCHHHHH-- AACCHHH--
WHAT KINDA FUCKIN' ANIMAL ARE YOU? THEY'RE NO DIFFERENT TO WEE KIDS AN' YOU'RE TRYNNA FUCKIN' RAPE THEM?
FIRST PLACE MY MIND WENT, CHAMP...
AYE, I BELIEVE YOU! YOU FUCKIN' HEAD-THE-BALL, WHAT IN GOD'S NAME'RE THEY DOIN' LETTIN' YOU LOOSE ON BLOODY SUPERDUPER--?
KLANKER, WHAT'S HAPPENING? WHY IS MALCHEMICAL EVIL NOW?
I-I-I DON'T KNOW, BOBBY--!
ISN'T THE IMPORTANT THING NOW THAT YOU'RE HERE TO SAVE THE DAY?
GET OUT. GET OUTTA THIS FUCKIN' HOUSE, RIGHT NOW.
ALL JUST WORDS UNTIL YOU ACTUALLY MAKE A MOVE, HAMISH...
WANKER!
AW, FUCK--!

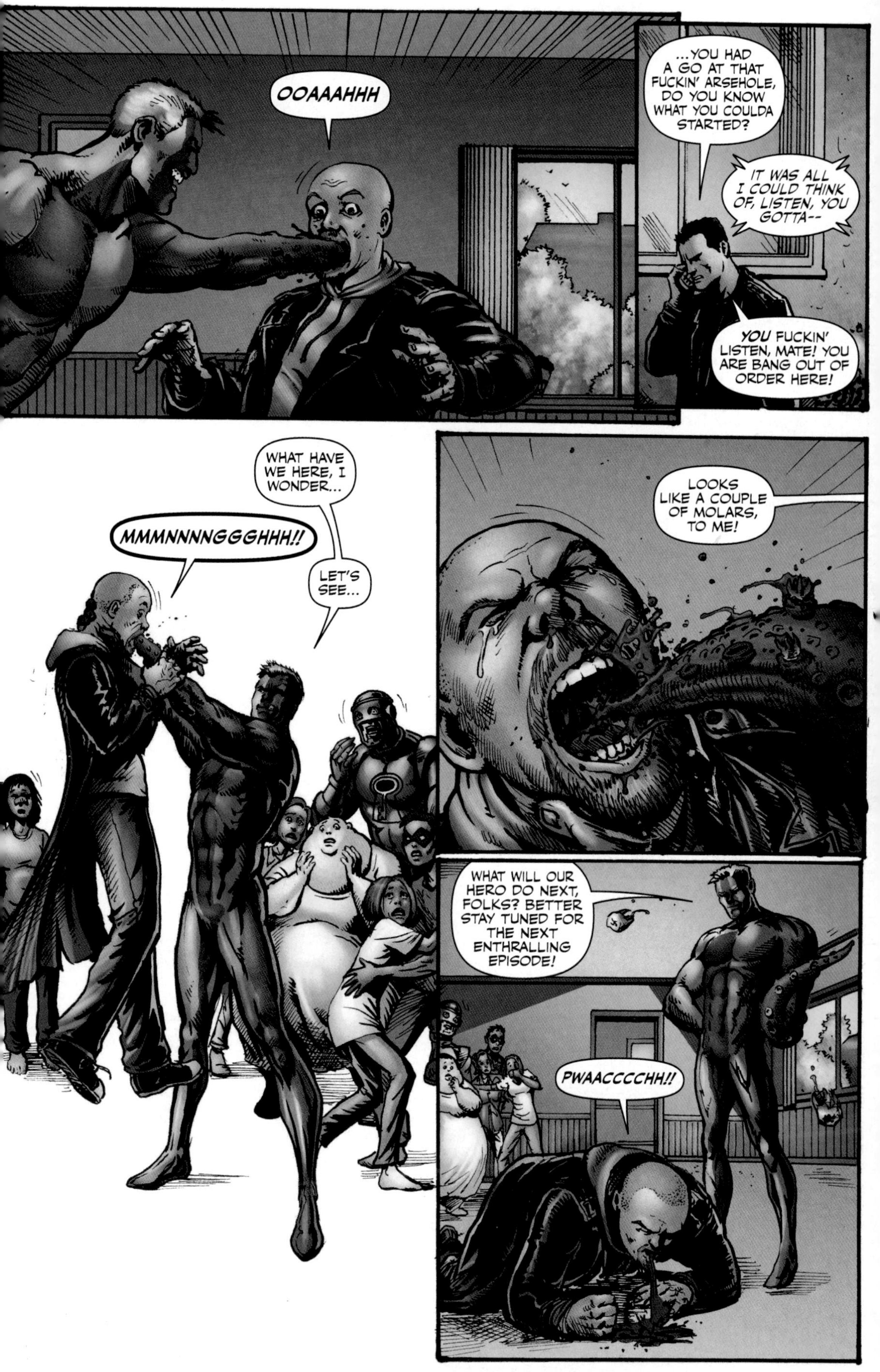
OOAAAHHH
...YOU HAD A GO AT THAT FUCKIN' ARSEHOLE, DO YOU KNOW WHAT YOU COULDA STARTED?
IT WAS ALL I COULD THINK OF, LISTEN, YOU GOTTA--
YOU FUCKIN' LISTEN, MATE! YOU ARE BANG OUT OF ORDER HERE!
WHAT HAVE WE HERE, I WONDER...
MMMNNNNGGGHHH!!
LET'S SEE...
LOOKS LIKE A COUPLE OF MOLARS, TO ME!
WHAT WILL OUR HERO DO NEXT, FOLKS? BETTER STAY TUNED FOR THE NEXT ENTHRALLING EPISODE!
PWAACCCCHH!!

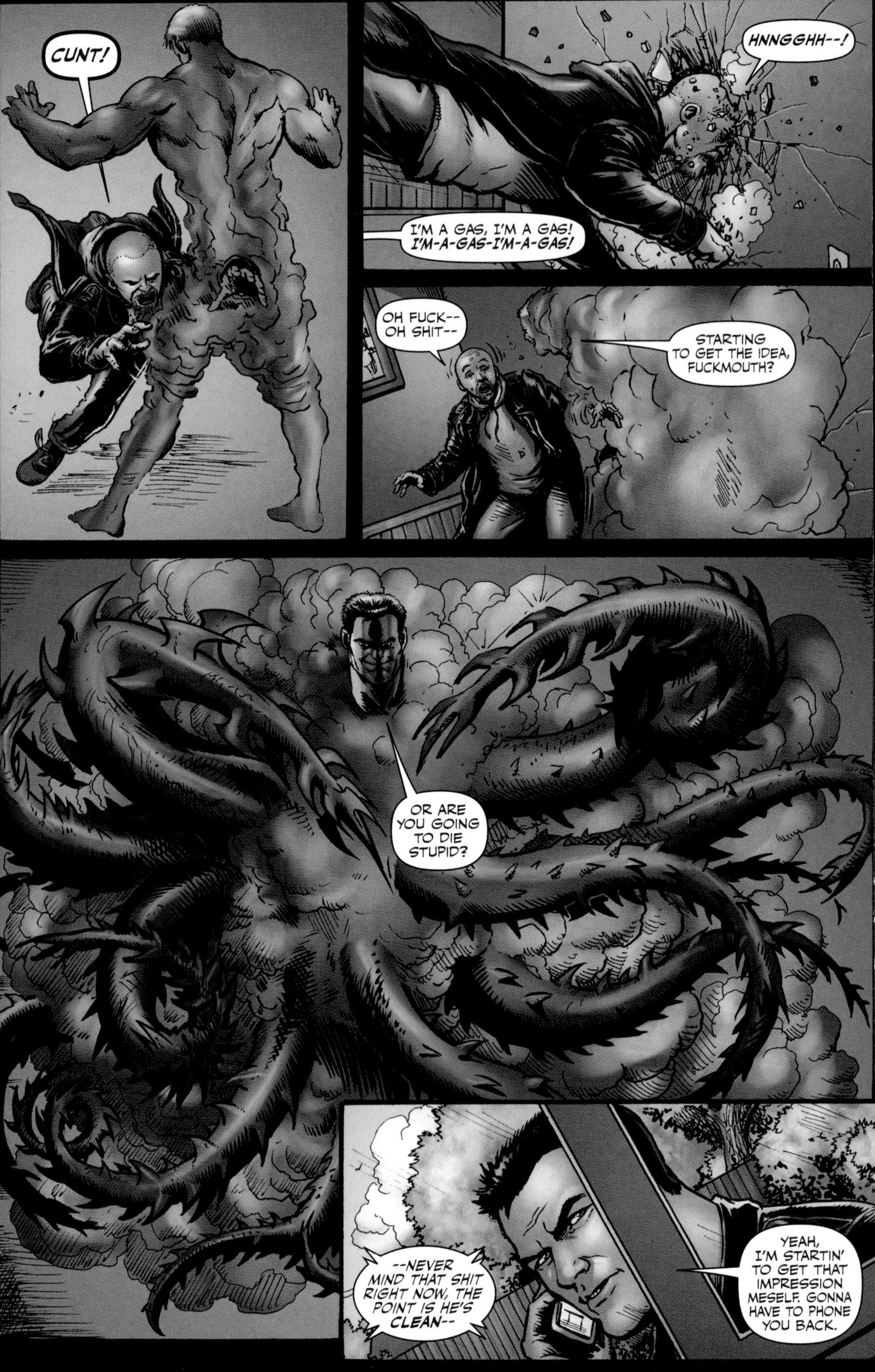
CUNT!
HNNGGHH--!
I'M A GAS, I'M A GAS! I'M-A-GAS-I'M-A-GAS!
OH FUCK-- OH SHIT--
STARTING TO GET THE IDEA, FUCKMOUTH?
OR ARE YOU GOING TO DIE STUPID?
--NEVER MIND THAT SHIT RIGHT NOW, THE POINT IS HE'S CLEAN--
YEAH, I'M STARTIN' TO GET THAT IMPRESSION MESELF. GONNA HAVE TO PHONE YOU BACK.

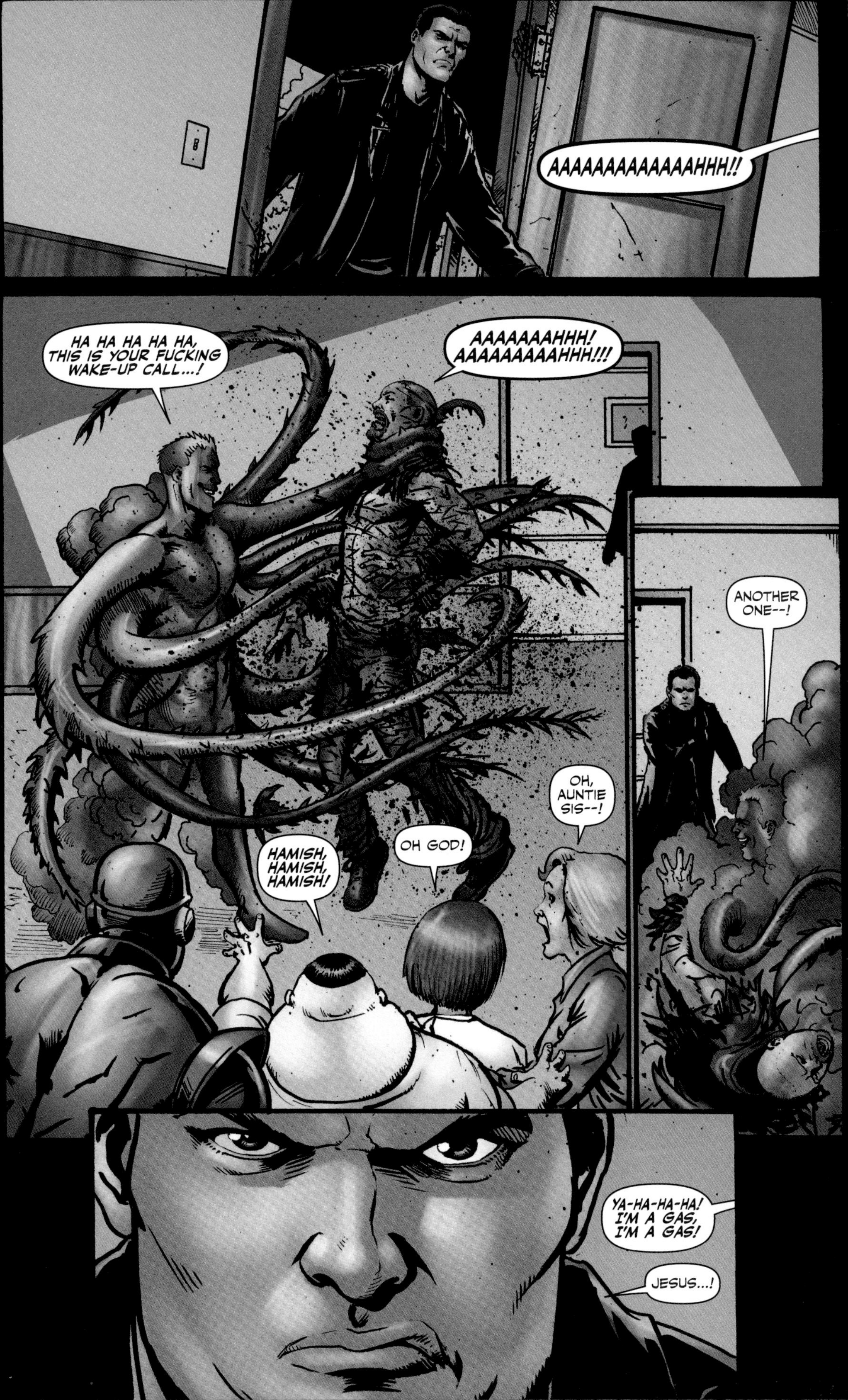
AAAAAAAAAAAAAAHHH!!
HA HA HA HA HA, THIS IS YOUR FUCKING WAKE-UP CALL...!
AAAAAAAAHHH! AAAAAAAAAAHHH!!!
ANOTHER ONE--!
OH, AUNTIE SIS--!
OH GOD!
HAMISH, HAMISH, HAMISH!
YA-HA-HA-HA! I'M A GAS, I'M A GAS!
JESUS...!

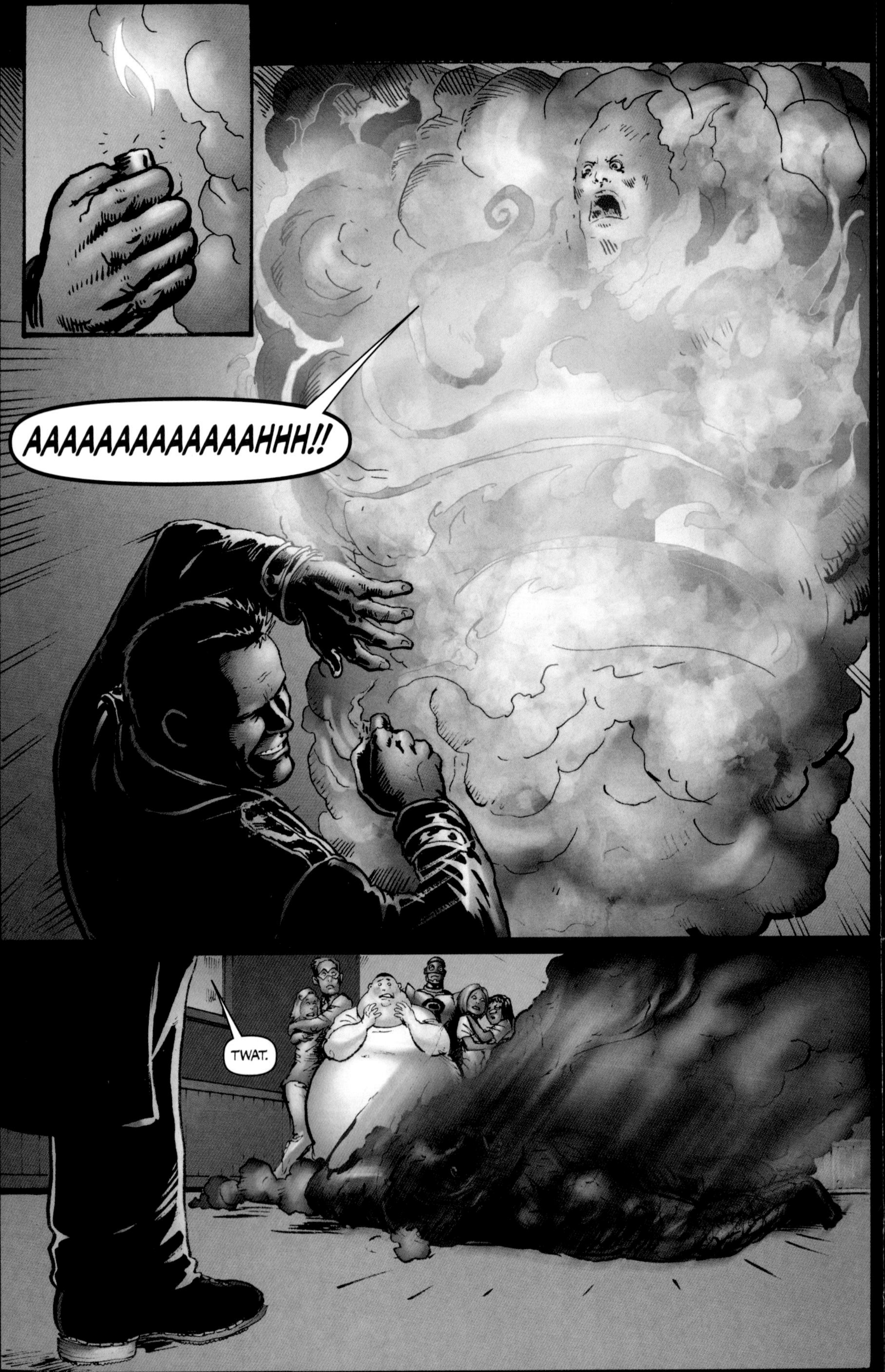
AAAAAAAAAAAAAHHH!!
TWAT.

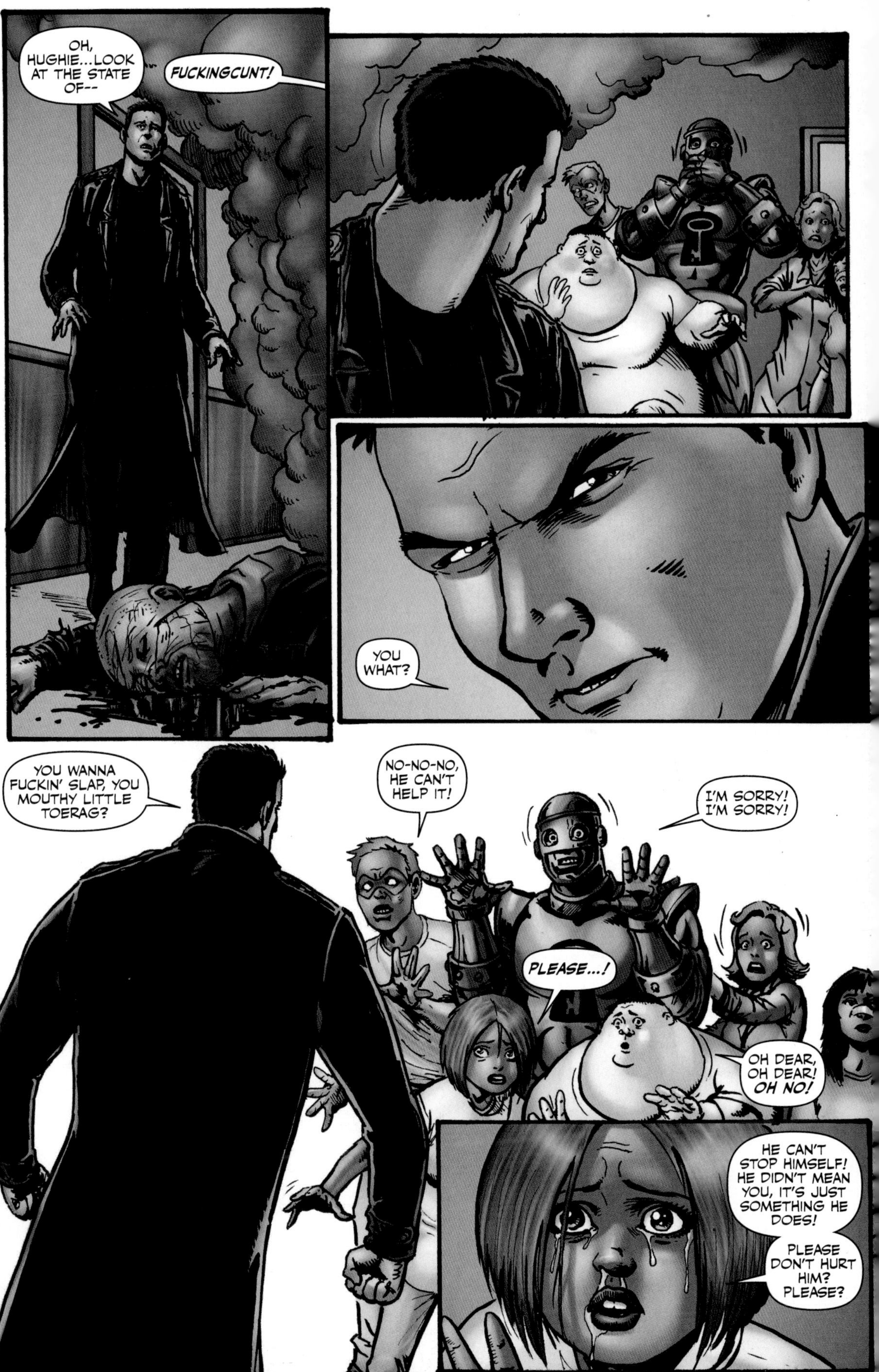
OH, HUGHIE...LOOK AT THE STATE OF--
FUCKINGCUNT!
YOU WHAT?
YOU WANNA FUCKIN' SLAP, YOU MOUTHY LITTLE TOERAG?
NO-NO-NO, HE CAN'T HELP IT!
I'M SORRY! I'M SORRY!
PLEASE...!
OH DEAR, OH DEAR! OH NO!
HE CAN'T STOP HIMSELF! HE DIDN'T MEAN YOU, IT'S JUST SOMETHING HE DOES!
PLEASE DON'T HURT HIM? PLEASE?

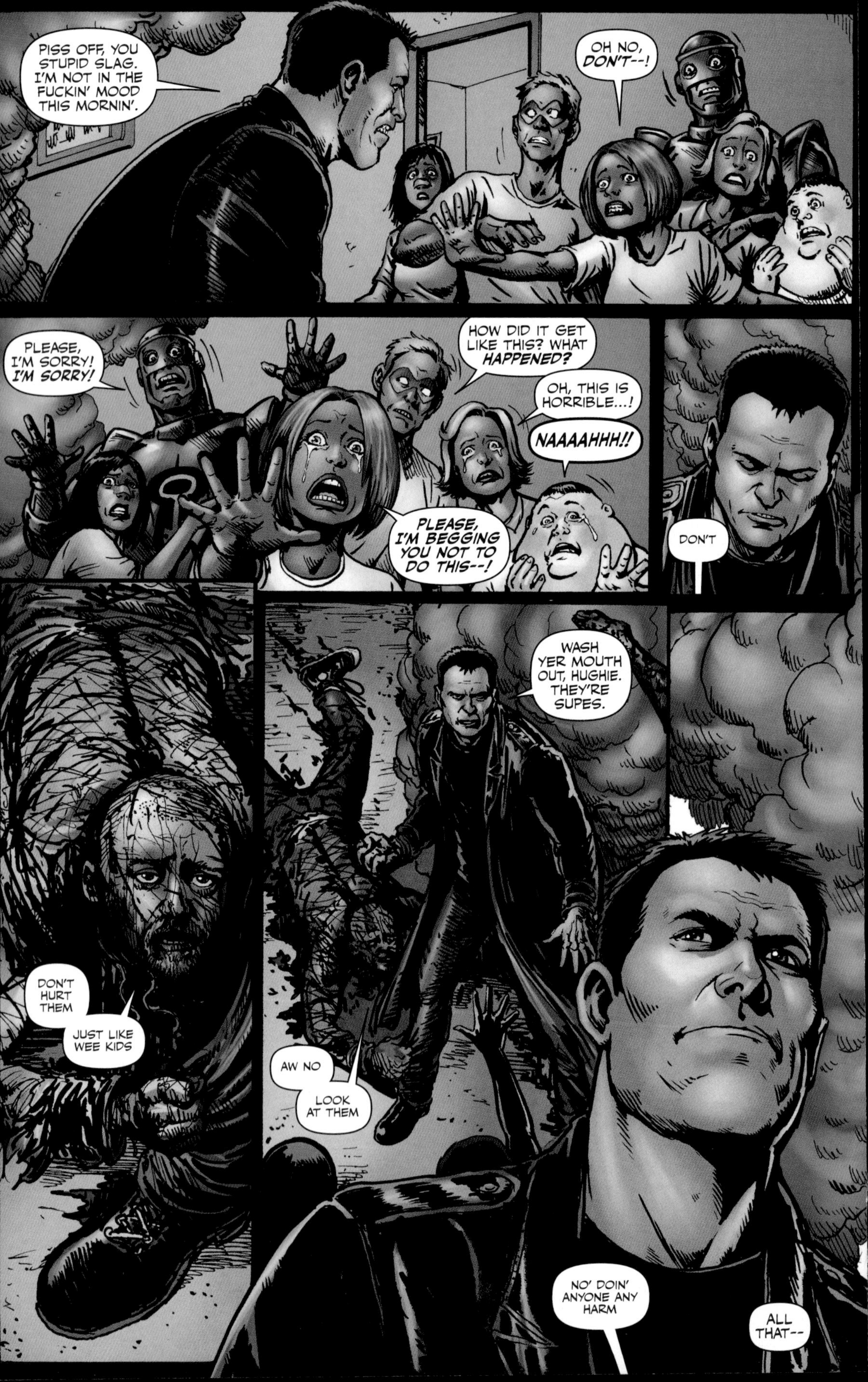
PISS OFF, YOU STUPID SLAG. I'M NOT IN THE FUCKIN' MOOD THIS MORNIN'.
OH NO, *DON'T*--!
PLEASE, I'M SORRY! *I'M SORRY!*
HOW DID IT GET LIKE THIS? WHAT *HAPPENED?*
OH, THIS IS HORRIBLE...!
NAAAAHHH!!
PLEASE, I'M BEGGING YOU NOT TO DO THIS--!
DON'T
WASH YER MOUTH OUT, HUGHIE. THEY'RE SUPES.
DON'T HURT THEM
JUST LIKE WEE KIDS
AW NO
LOOK AT THEM
NO' DOIN' ANYONE ANY HARM
ALL THAT--

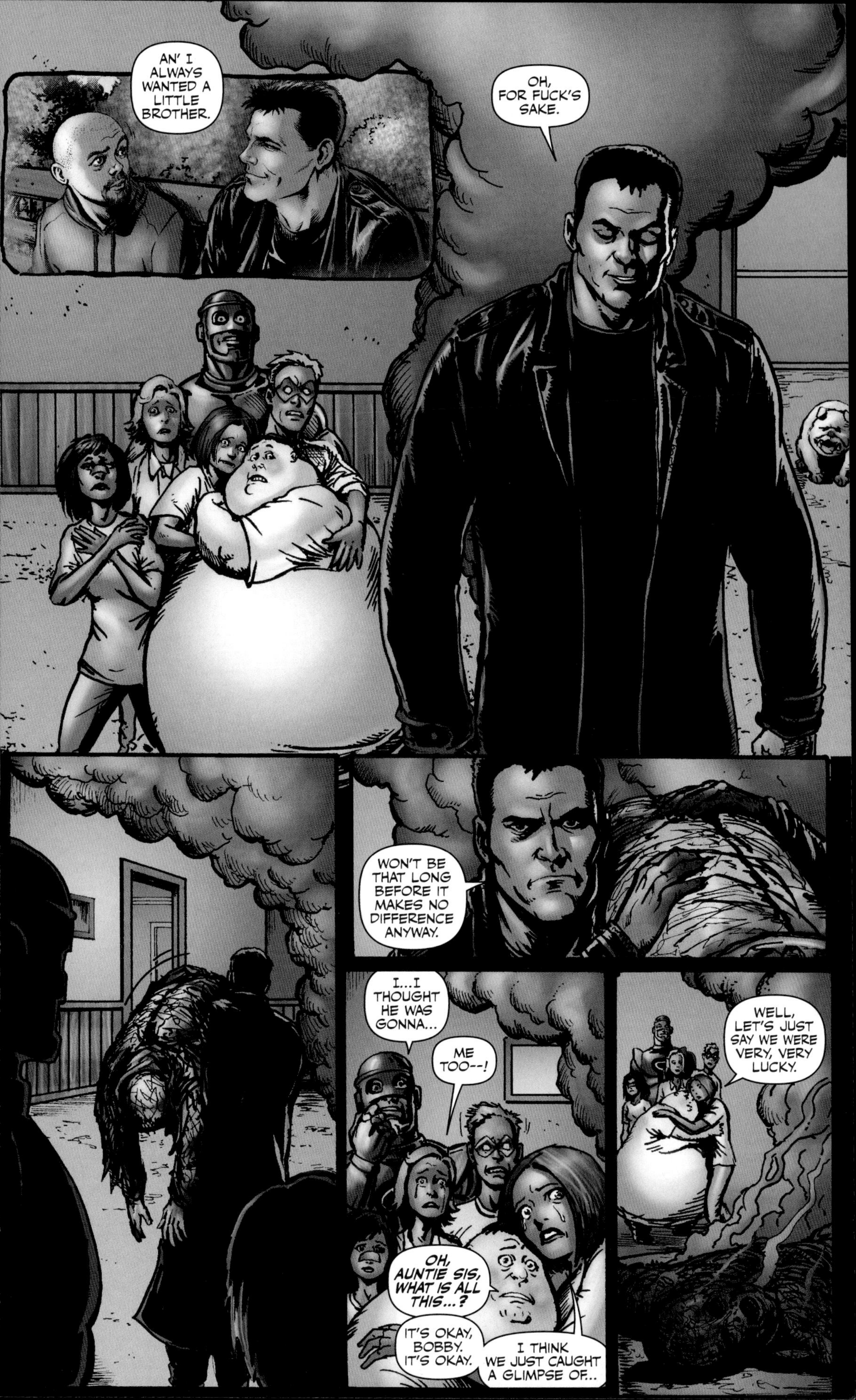
AN' I ALWAYS WANTED A LITTLE BROTHER.
OH, FOR FUCK'S SAKE.
WON'T BE THAT LONG BEFORE IT MAKES NO DIFFERENCE ANYWAY.
I...I THOUGHT HE WAS GONNA...
ME TOO--!
OH, AUNTIE SIS, WHAT IS ALL THIS...?
IT'S OKAY, BOBBY. IT'S OKAY.
I THINK WE JUST CAUGHT A GLIMPSE OF...
WELL, LET'S JUST SAY WE WERE VERY, VERY LUCKY.

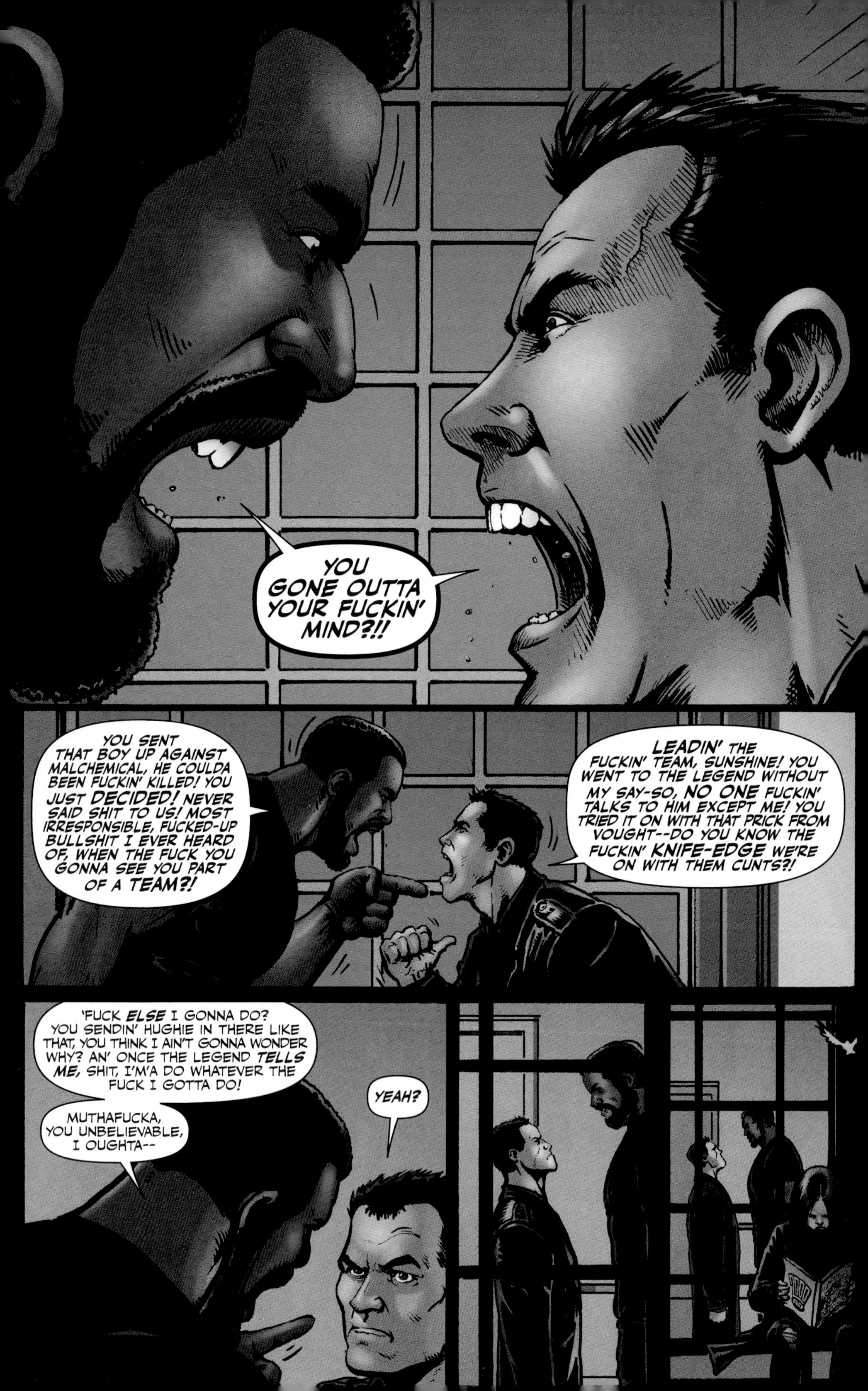
YOU GONE OUTTA YOUR FUCKIN' MIND?!!
YOU SENT THAT BOY UP AGAINST MALCHEMICAL, HE COULDA BEEN FUCKIN' KILLED! YOU JUST DECIDED! NEVER SAID SHIT TO US! MOST IRRESPONSIBLE, FUCKED-UP BULLSHIT I EVER HEARD OF, WHEN THE FUCK YOU GONNA SEE YOU PART OF A TEAM?!
LEADIN' THE FUCKIN' TEAM, SUNSHINE! YOU WENT TO THE LEGEND WITHOUT MY SAY-SO, NO ONE FUCKIN' TALKS TO HIM EXCEPT ME! YOU TRIED IT ON WITH THAT PRICK FROM VOUGHT--DO YOU KNOW THE FUCKIN' KNIFE-EDGE WE'RE ON WITH THEM CUNTS?!
'FUCK ELSE I GONNA DO? YOU SENDIN' HUGHIE IN THERE LIKE THAT, YOU THINK I AIN'T GONNA WONDER WHY? AN' ONCE THE LEGEND TELLS ME, SHIT, I'M'A DO WHATEVER THE FUCK I GOTTA DO!
MUTHAFUCKA, YOU UNBELIEVABLE, I OUGHTA--
YEAH?

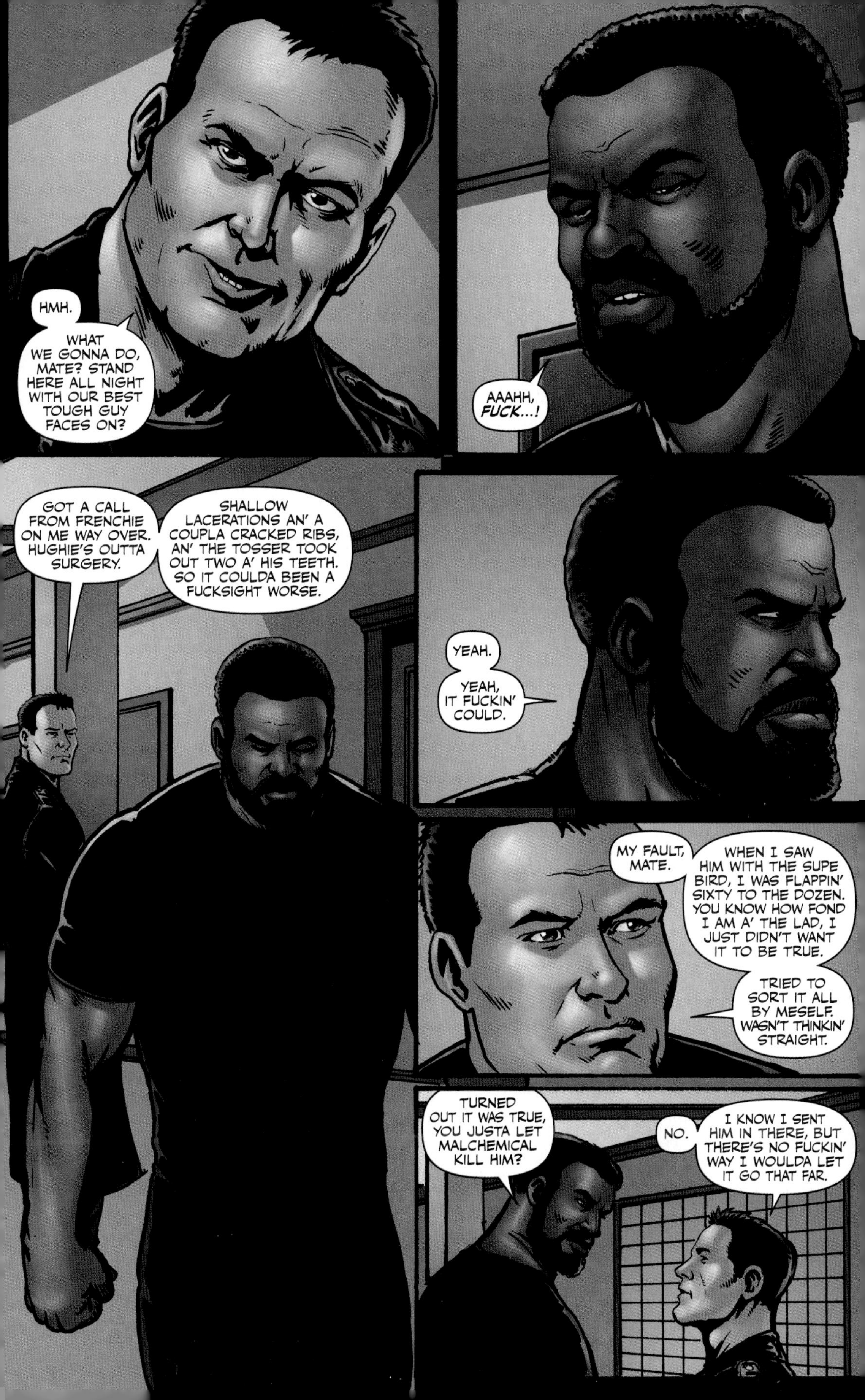
HMH.
WHAT WE GONNA DO, MATE? STAND HERE ALL NIGHT WITH OUR BEST TOUGH GUY FACES ON?
AAAHH, *FUCK*...!
GOT A CALL FROM FRENCHIE ON ME WAY OVER. HUGHIE'S OUTTA SURGERY.
SHALLOW LACERATIONS AN' A COUPLA CRACKED RIBS, AN' THE TOSSER TOOK OUT TWO A' HIS TEETH. SO IT COULDA BEEN A FUCKSIGHT WORSE.
YEAH.
YEAH, IT FUCKIN' COULD.
MY FAULT, MATE.
WHEN I SAW HIM WITH THE SUPE BIRD, I WAS FLAPPIN' SIXTY TO THE DOZEN. YOU KNOW HOW FOND I AM A' THE LAD, I JUST DIDN'T WANT IT TO BE TRUE.
TRIED TO SORT IT ALL BY MESELF. WASN'T THINKIN' STRAIGHT.
TURNED OUT IT WAS TRUE, YOU JUSTA LET MALCHEMICAL KILL HIM?
NO.
I KNOW I SENT HIM IN THERE, BUT THERE'S NO FUCKIN' WAY I WOULDA LET IT GO THAT FAR.

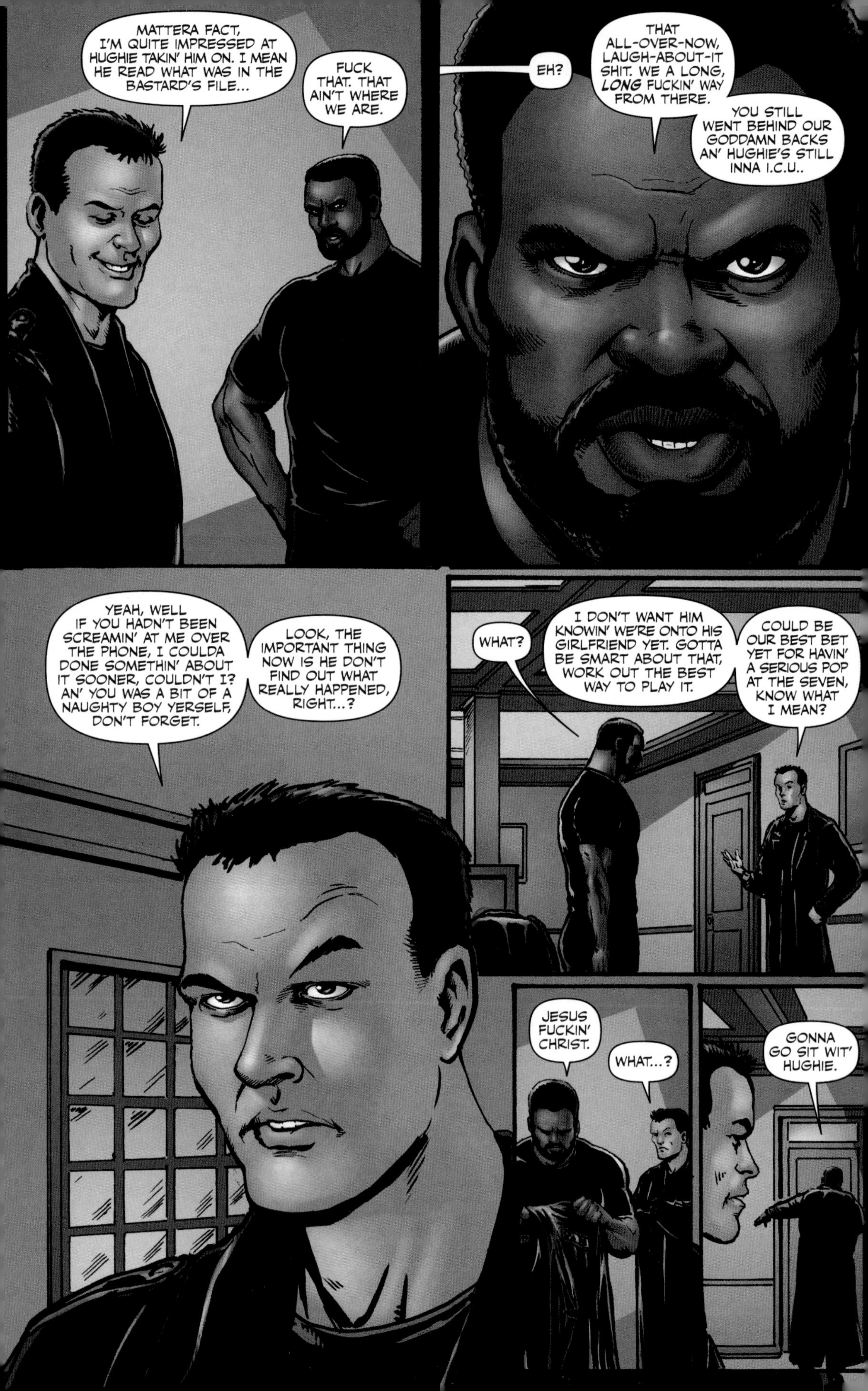

MATTERA FACT, I'M QUITE IMPRESSED AT HUGHIE TAKIN' HIM ON. I MEAN HE READ WHAT WAS IN THE BASTARD'S FILE...
FUCK THAT. THAT AIN'T WHERE WE ARE.
EH?
THAT ALL-OVER-NOW, LAUGH-ABOUT-IT SHIT. WE A LONG, *LONG* FUCKIN' WAY FROM THERE.
YOU STILL WENT BEHIND OUR GODDAMN BACKS AN' HUGHIE'S STILL INNA I.C.U..
YEAH, WELL IF YOU HADN'T BEEN SCREAMIN' AT ME OVER THE PHONE, I COULDA DONE SOMETHIN' ABOUT IT SOONER, COULDN'T I? AN' YOU WAS A BIT OF A NAUGHTY BOY YERSELF, DON'T FORGET.
LOOK, THE IMPORTANT THING NOW IS HE DON'T FIND OUT WHAT REALLY HAPPENED, RIGHT...?
WHAT?
I DON'T WANT HIM KNOWIN' WE'RE ONTO HIS GIRLFRIEND YET. GOTTA BE SMART ABOUT THAT, WORK OUT THE BEST WAY TO PLAY IT.
COULD BE OUR BEST BET YET FOR HAVIN' A SERIOUS POP AT THE SEVEN, KNOW WHAT I MEAN?
JESUS FUCKIN' CHRIST.
WHAT...?
GONNA GO SIT WIT' HUGHIE.

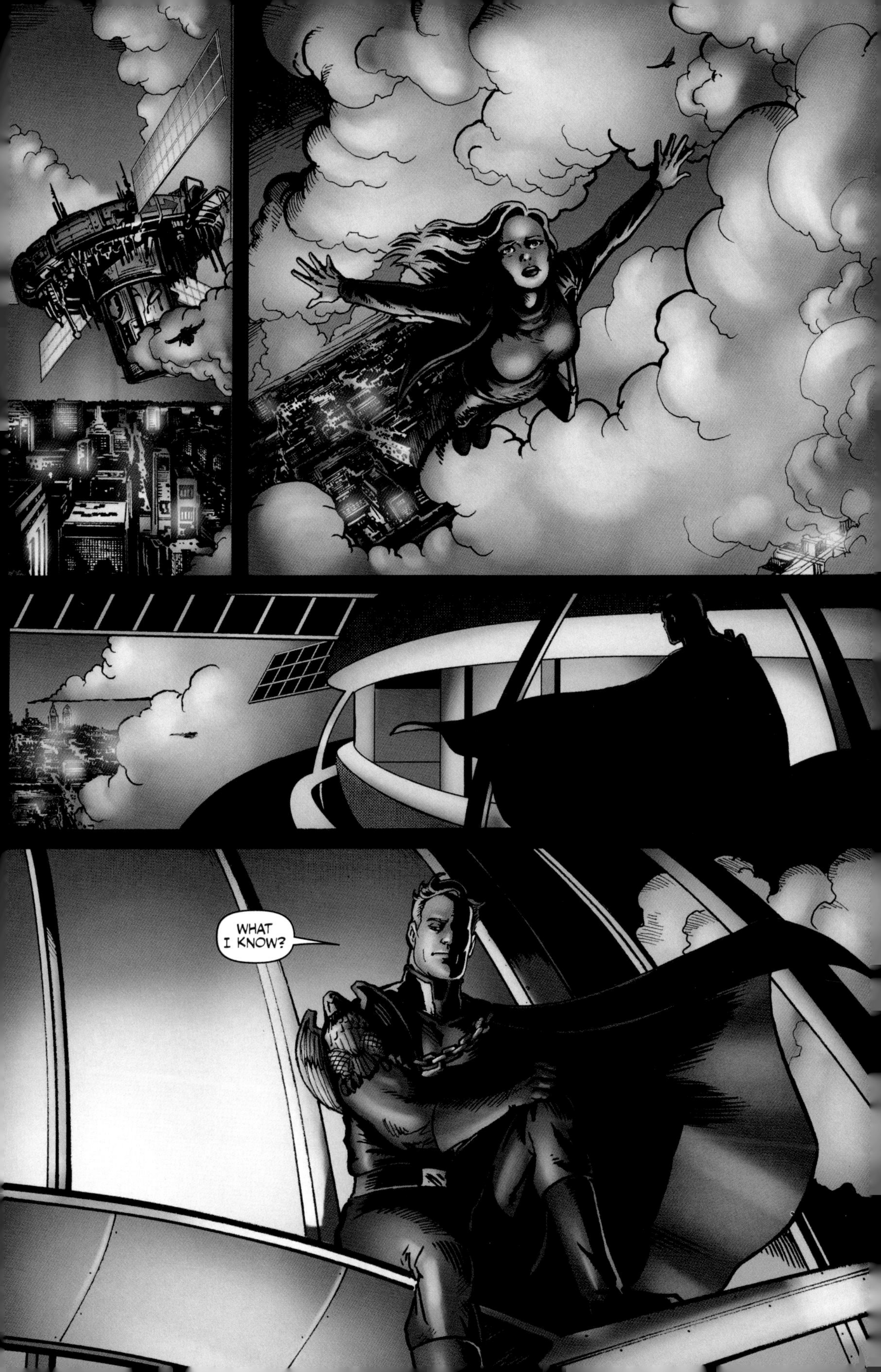
WHAT I KNOW?

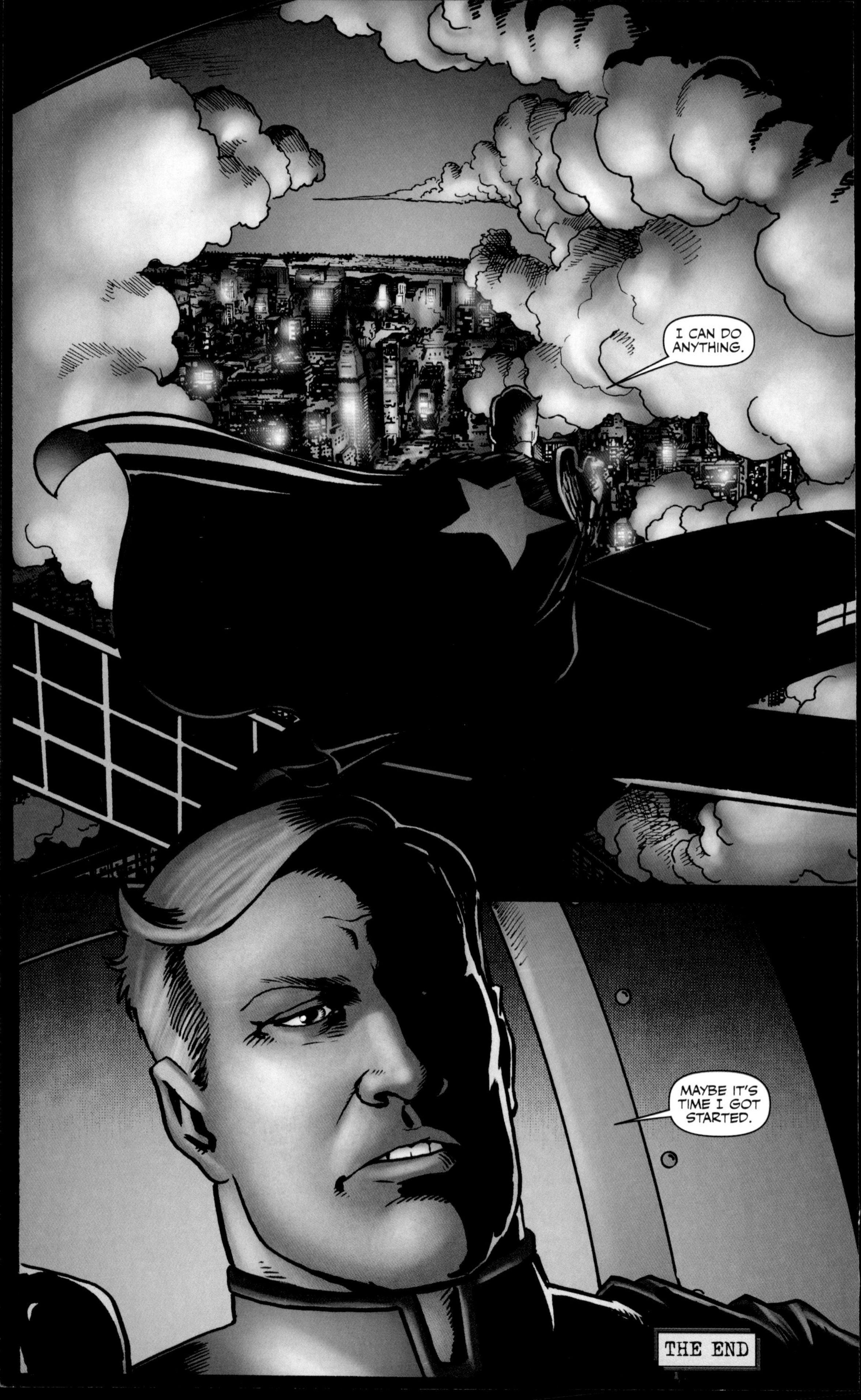
I CAN DO ANYTHING.
MAYBE IT'S TIME I GOT STARTED.
THE END

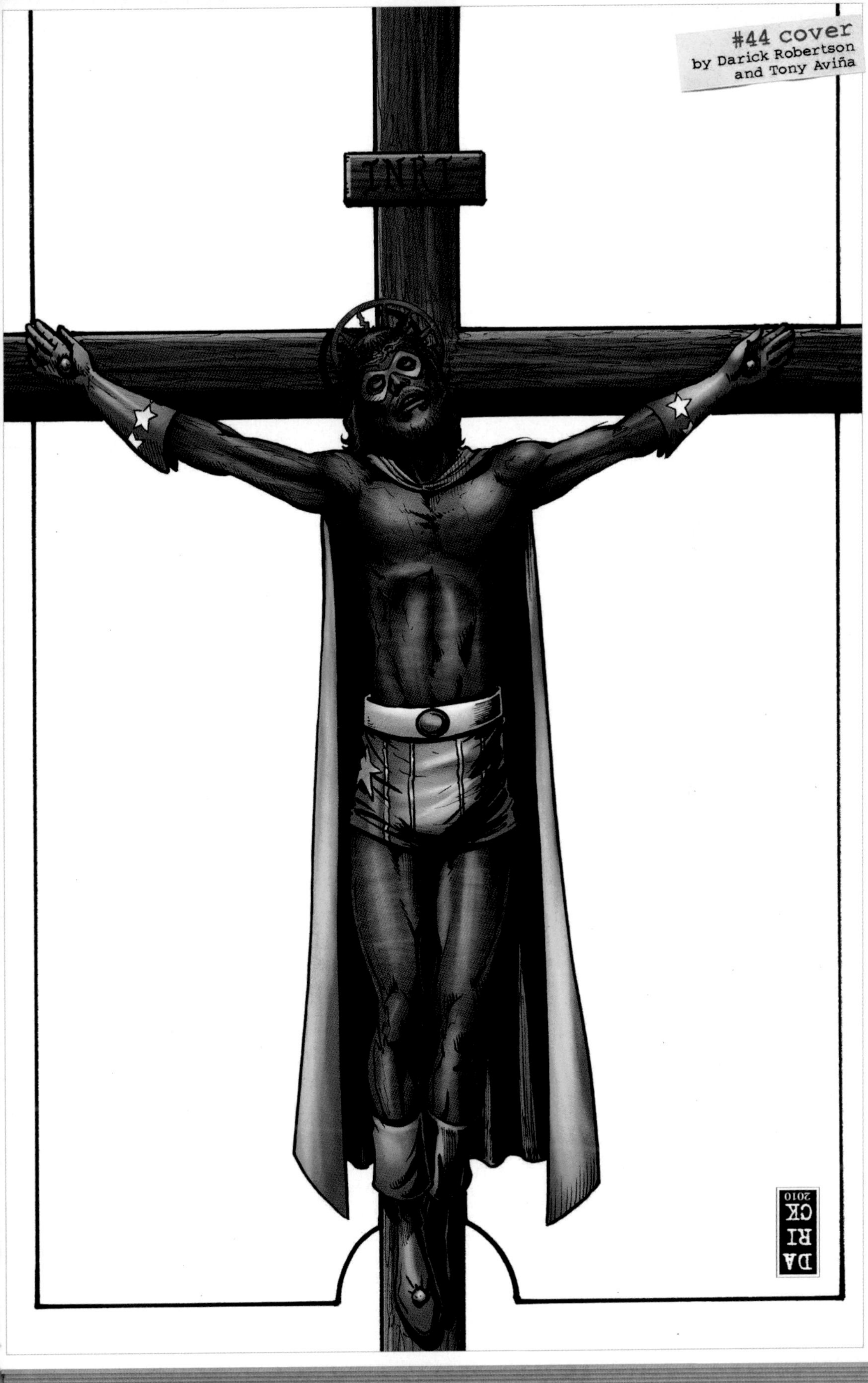
INRI

#44 cover
by Darick Robertson
and Tony Aviña

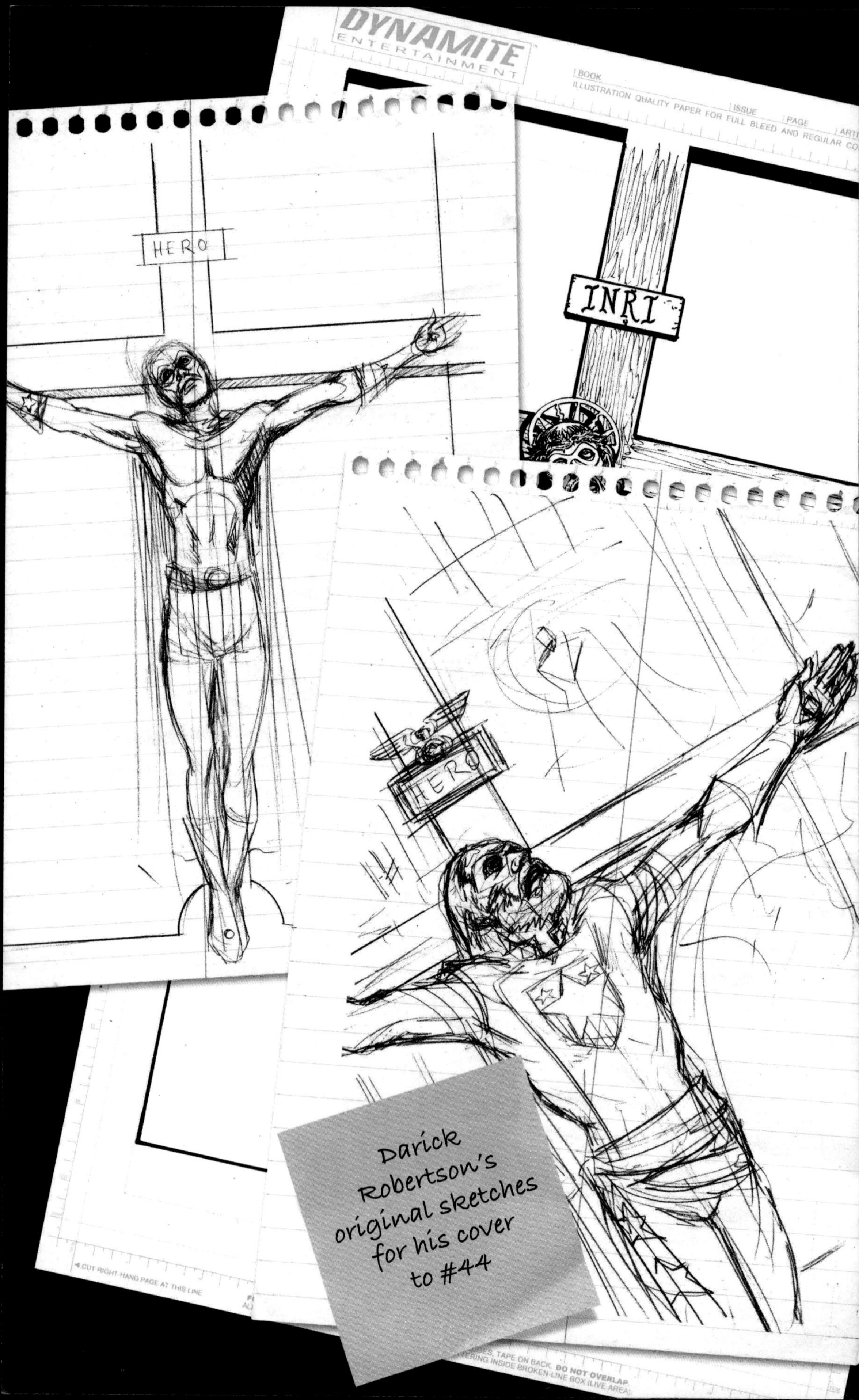
DYNAMITE
ENTERTAINMENT
BOOK
ILLUSTRATION QUALITY PAPER FOR FULL BLEED AND REGULAR
ISSUE
PAGE
HERO
INRI
HERO
CUT RIGHT-HAND PAGE AT THIS LINE
TAPE ON BACK. DO NOT OVERLAP
LETTERING INSIDE BROKEN-LINE BOX (LIVE AREA)

Darick Robertson's original sketches for his cover to #44

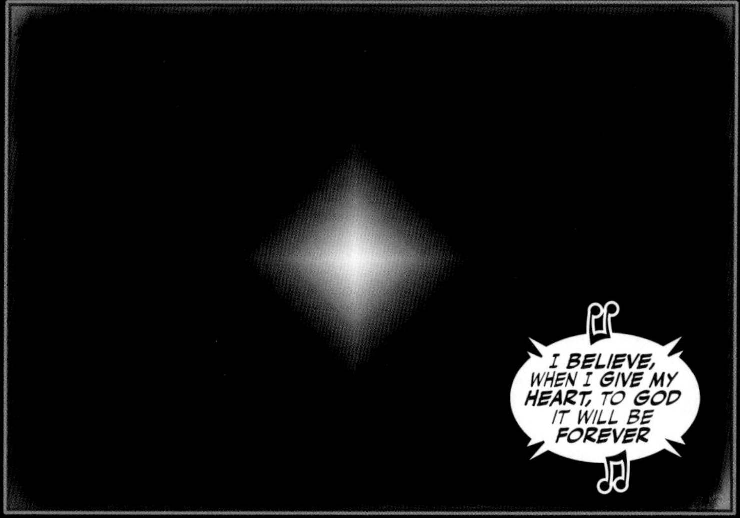
I BELIEVE, WHEN I GIVE MY HEART, TO GOD IT WILL BE FOREVER

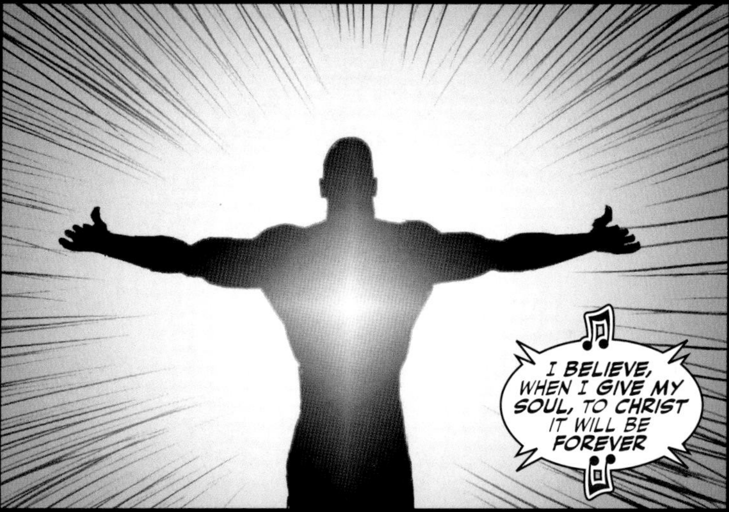
I BELIEVE, WHEN I GIVE MY SOUL, TO CHRIST IT WILL BE FOREVER

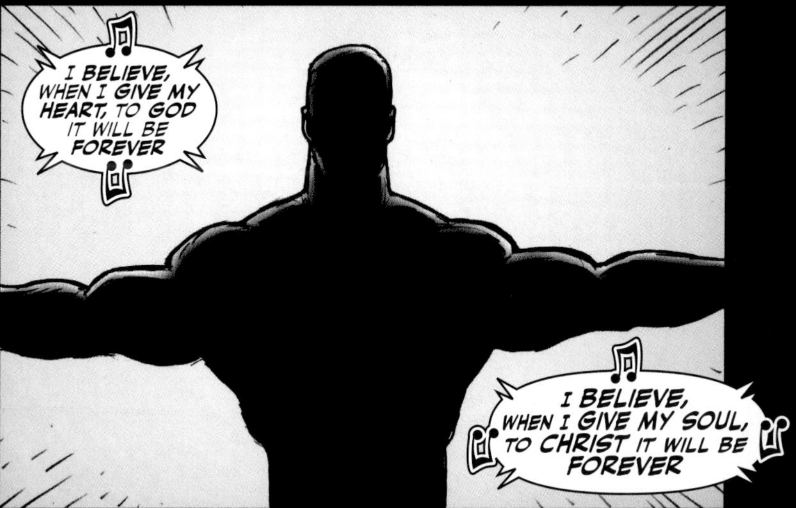
I BELIEVE, WHEN I GIVE MY HEART, TO GOD IT WILL BE FOREVER
I BELIEVE, WHEN I GIVE MY SOUL, TO CHRIST IT WILL BE FOREVER

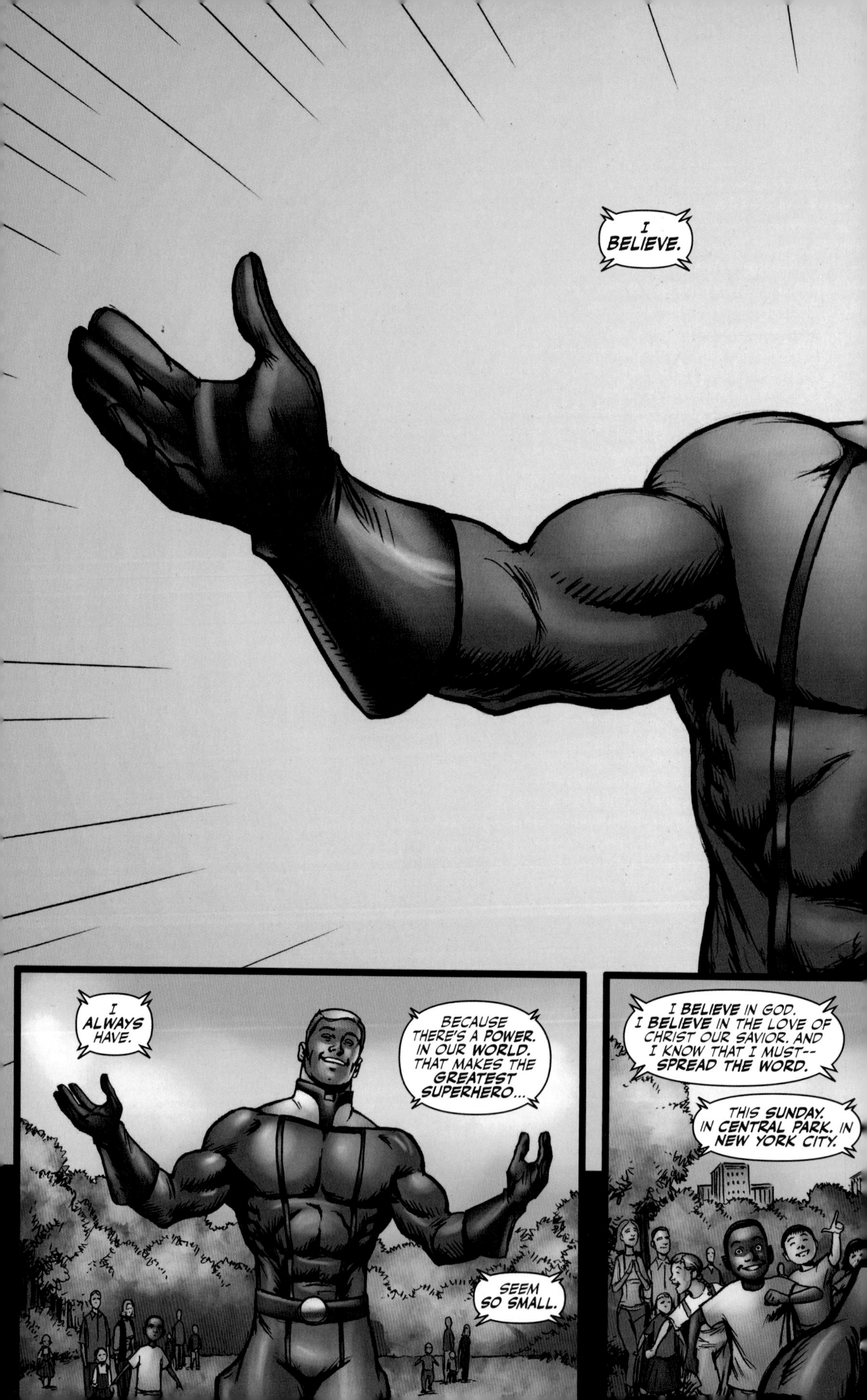
I BELIEVE.
I ALWAYS HAVE.
BECAUSE THERE'S A POWER. IN OUR WORLD. THAT MAKES THE GREATEST SUPERHERO...
SEEM SO SMALL.
I BELIEVE IN GOD. I BELIEVE IN THE LOVE OF CHRIST OUR SAVIOR. AND I KNOW THAT I MUST-- SPREAD THE WORD.
THIS SUNDAY. IN CENTRAL PARK. IN NEW YORK CITY.

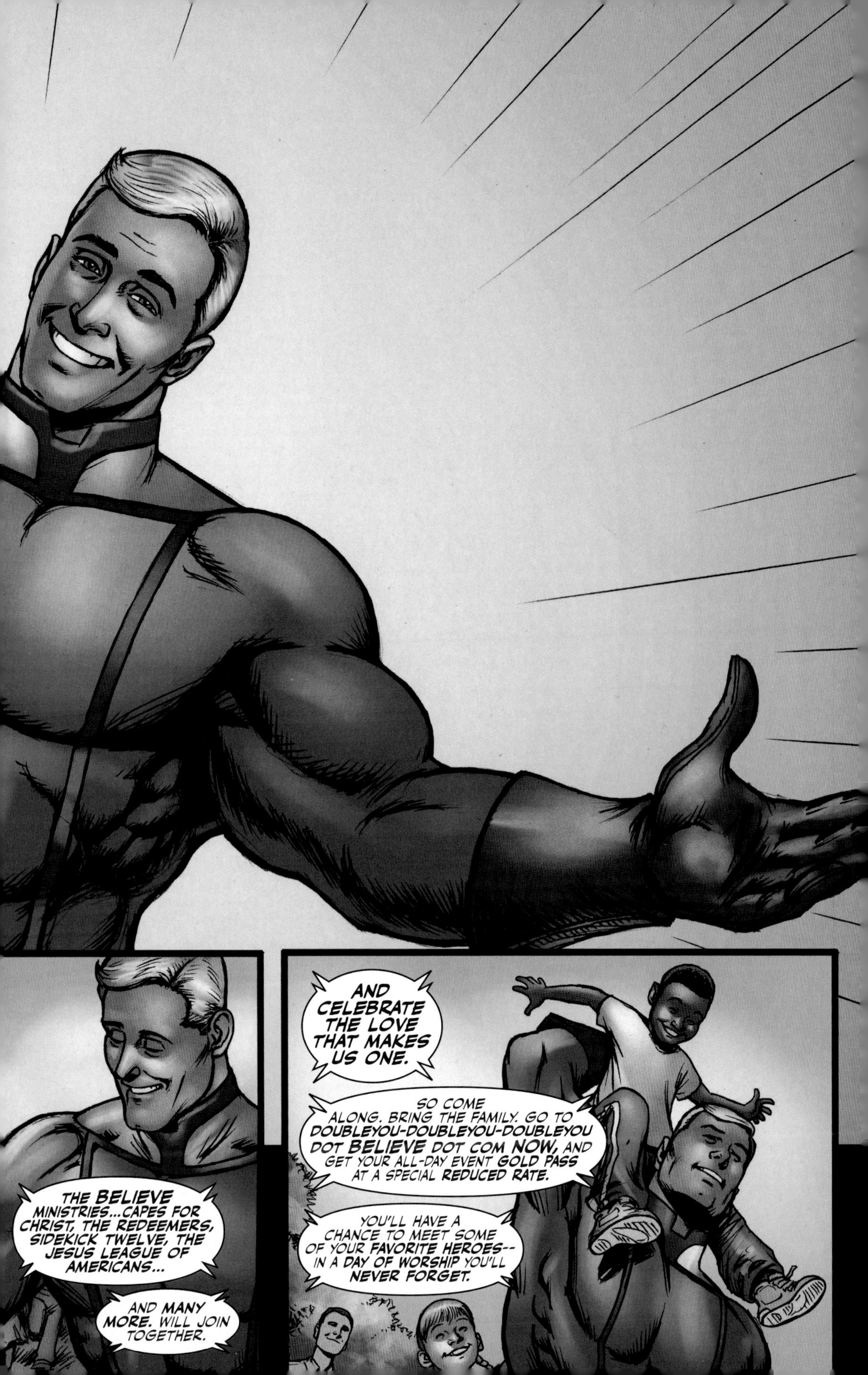
THE BELIEVE MINISTRIES...CAPES FOR CHRIST, THE REDEEMERS, SIDEKICK TWELVE, THE JESUS LEAGUE OF AMERICANS...
AND MANY MORE. WILL JOIN TOGETHER.
AND CELEBRATE THE LOVE THAT MAKES US ONE.
SO COME ALONG. BRING THE FAMILY. GO TO DOUBLEYOU-DOUBLEYOU-DOUBLEYOU DOT BELIEVE DOT COM NOW, AND GET YOUR ALL-DAY EVENT GOLD PASS AT A SPECIAL REDUCED RATE.
YOU'LL HAVE A CHANCE TO MEET SOME OF YOUR FAVORITE HEROES-- IN A DAY OF WORSHIP YOU'LL NEVER FORGET.

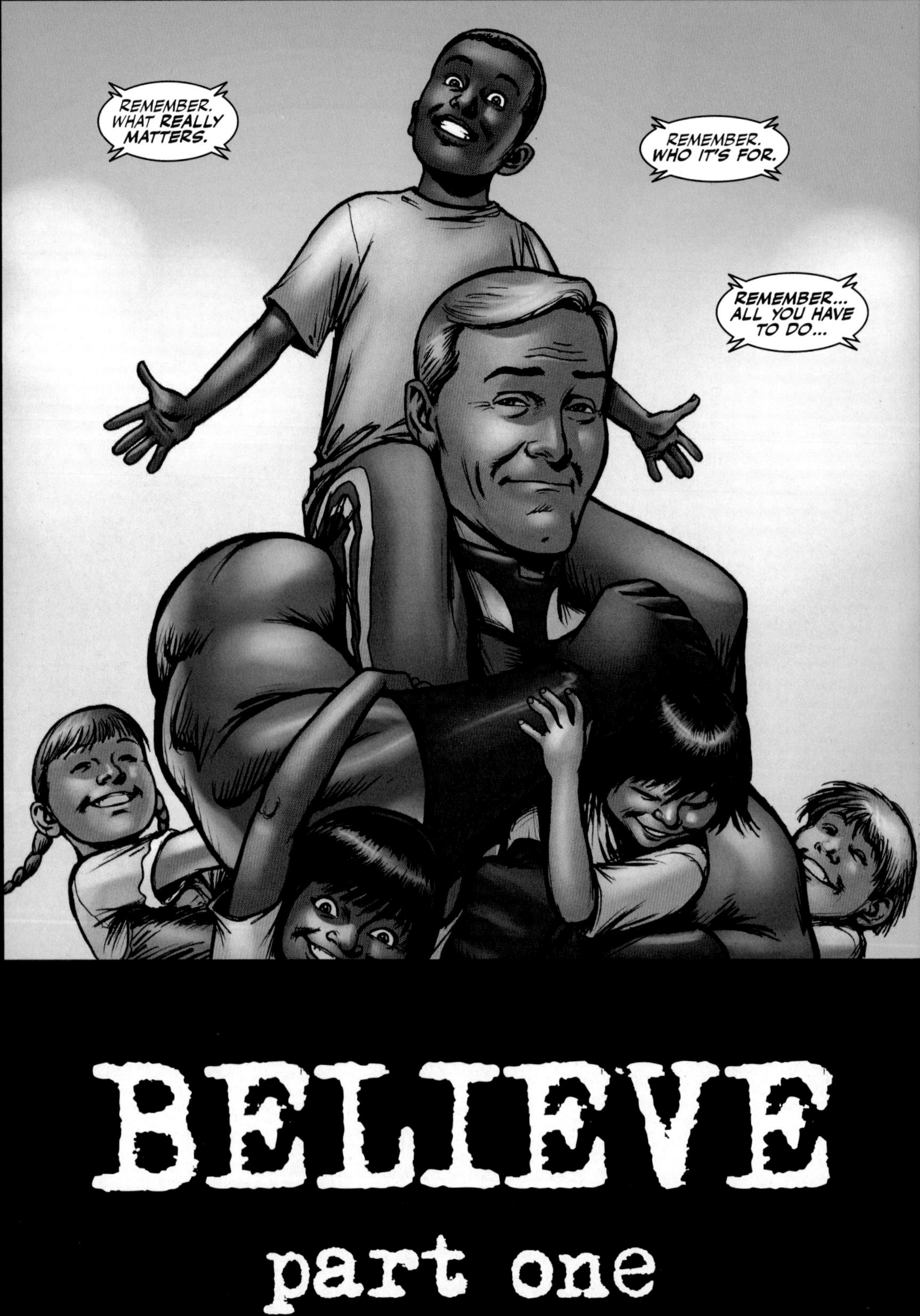
REMEMBER. WHAT REALLY MATTERS.
REMEMBER. WHO IT'S FOR.
REMEMBER... ALL YOU HAVE TO DO...

BELIEVE

part one

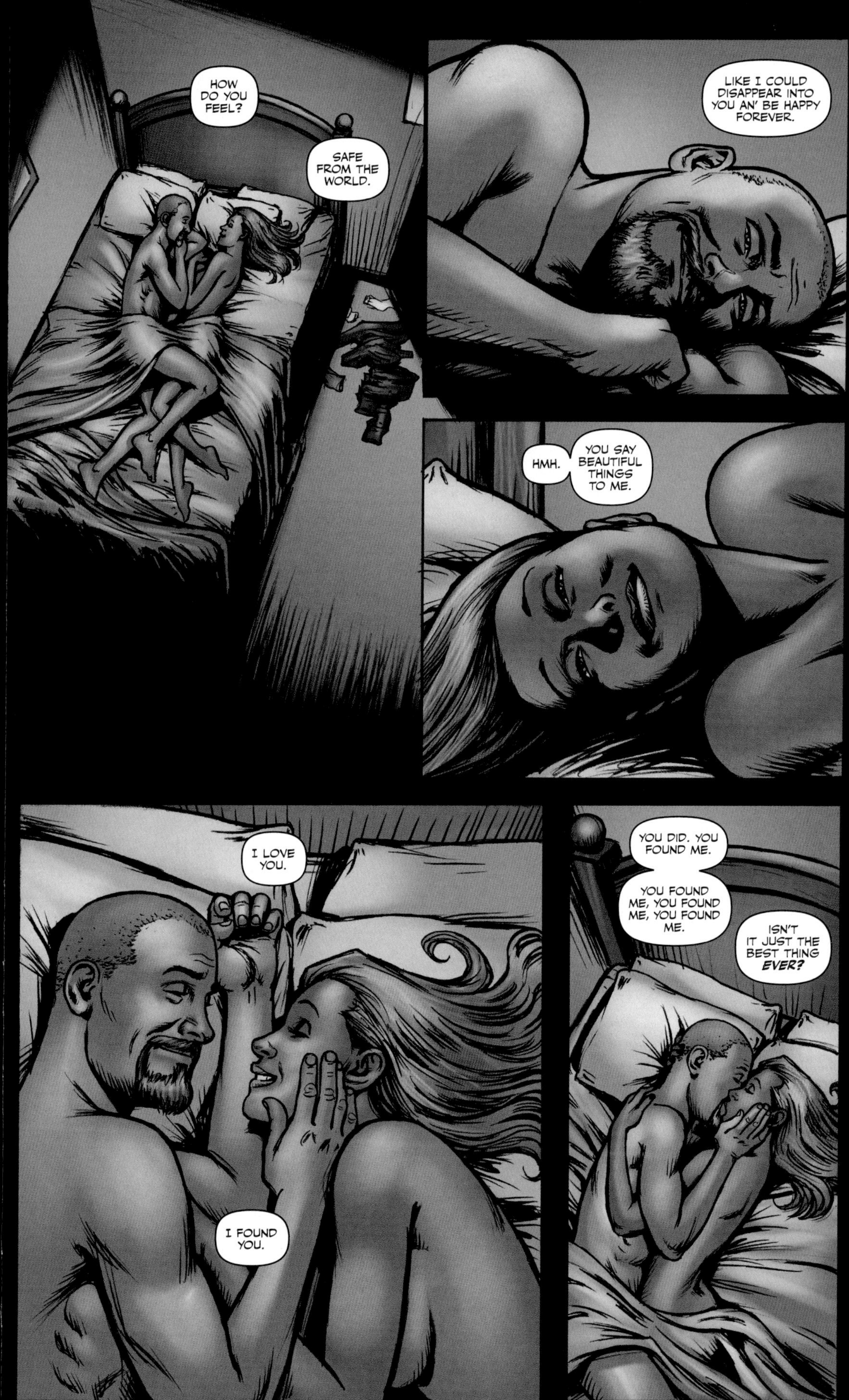
HOW DO YOU FEEL?
SAFE FROM THE WORLD.
LIKE I COULD DISAPPEAR INTO YOU AN' BE HAPPY FOREVER.
HMH.
YOU SAY BEAUTIFUL THINGS TO ME.
I LOVE YOU.
I FOUND YOU.
YOU DID. YOU FOUND ME.
YOU FOUND ME, YOU FOUND ME, YOU FOUND ME.
ISN'T IT JUST THE BEST THING *EVER?*

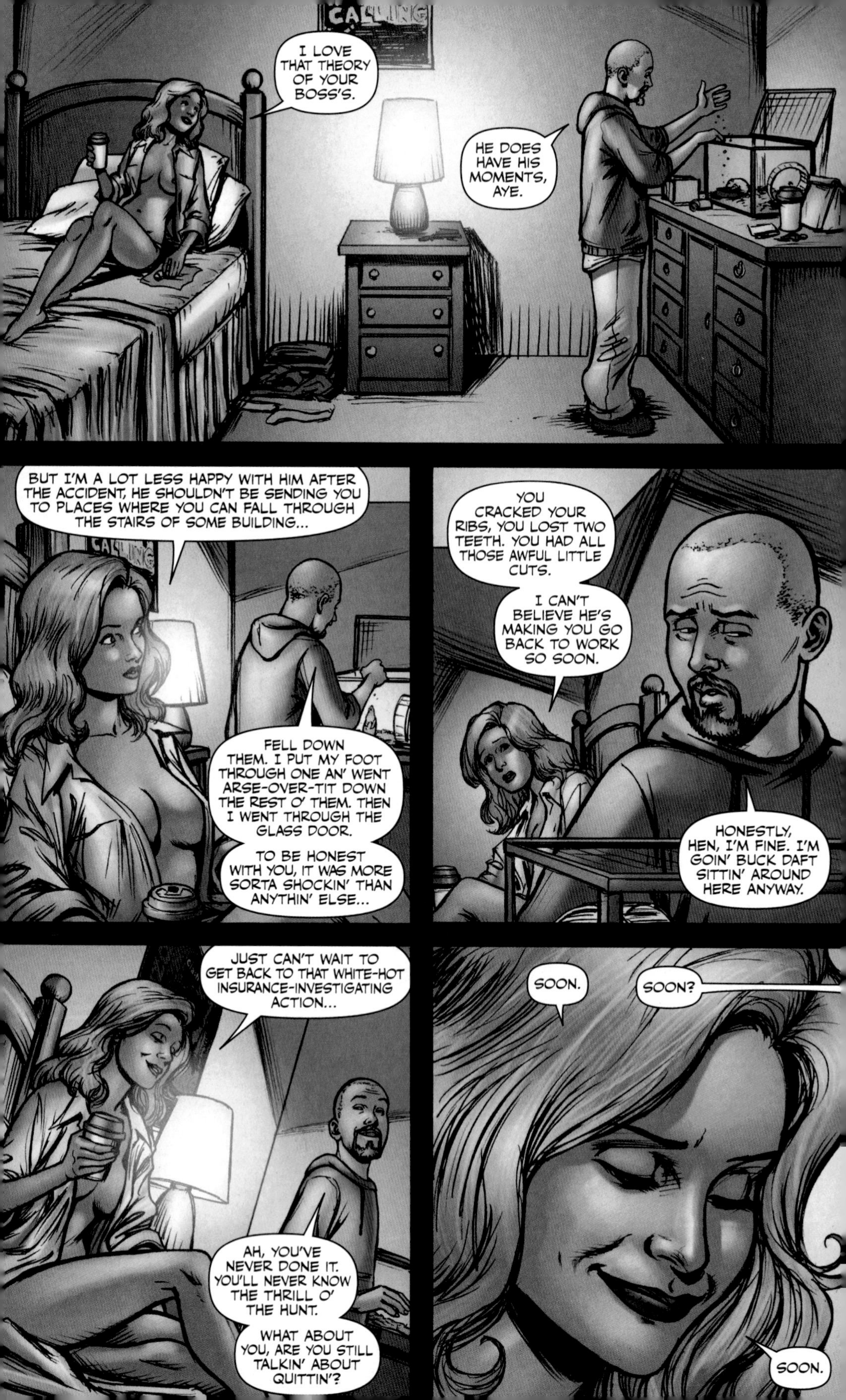
CALLING
I LOVE THAT THEORY OF YOUR BOSS'S.
HE DOES HAVE HIS MOMENTS, AYE.
BUT I'M A LOT LESS HAPPY WITH HIM AFTER THE ACCIDENT, HE SHOULDN'T BE SENDING YOU TO PLACES WHERE YOU CAN FALL THROUGH THE STAIRS OF SOME BUILDING...
FELL DOWN THEM. I PUT MY FOOT THROUGH ONE AN' WENT ARSE-OVER-TIT DOWN THE REST O' THEM. THEN I WENT THROUGH THE GLASS DOOR.
TO BE HONEST WITH YOU, IT WAS MORE SORTA SHOCKIN' THAN ANYTHIN' ELSE...
YOU CRACKED YOUR RIBS, YOU LOST TWO TEETH. YOU HAD ALL THOSE AWFUL LITTLE CUTS.
I CAN'T BELIEVE HE'S MAKING YOU GO BACK TO WORK SO SOON.
HONESTLY, HEN, I'M FINE. I'M GOIN' BUCK DAFT SITTIN' AROUND HERE ANYWAY.
JUST CAN'T WAIT TO GET BACK TO THAT WHITE-HOT INSURANCE-INVESTIGATING ACTION...
AH, YOU'VE NEVER DONE IT. YOU'LL NEVER KNOW THE THRILL O' THE HUNT.
WHAT ABOUT YOU, ARE YOU STILL TALKIN' ABOUT QUITTIN'?
SOON.
SOON?
SOON.

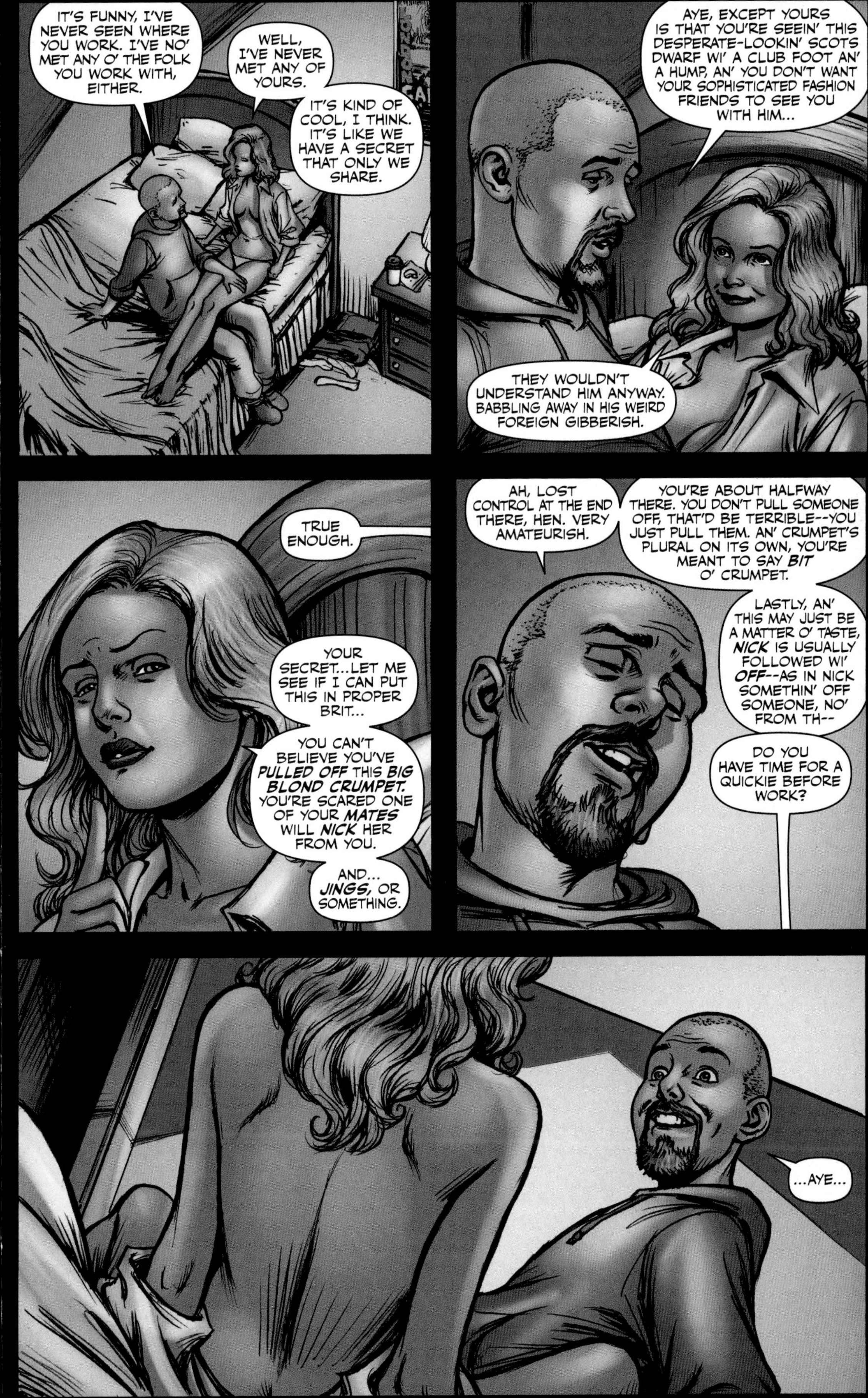
IT'S FUNNY, I'VE NEVER SEEN WHERE YOU WORK. I'VE NO' MET ANY O' THE FOLK YOU WORK WITH, EITHER.
WELL, I'VE NEVER MET ANY OF YOURS.
IT'S KIND OF COOL, I THINK. IT'S LIKE WE HAVE A SECRET THAT ONLY WE SHARE.
AYE, EXCEPT YOURS IS THAT YOU'RE SEEIN' THIS DESPERATE-LOOKIN' SCOTS DWARF WI' A CLUB FOOT AN' A HUMP, AN' YOU DON'T WANT YOUR SOPHISTICATED FASHION FRIENDS TO SEE YOU WITH HIM...
THEY WOULDN'T UNDERSTAND HIM ANYWAY. BABBLING AWAY IN HIS WEIRD FOREIGN GIBBERISH.
TRUE ENOUGH.
YOUR SECRET...LET ME SEE IF I CAN PUT THIS IN PROPER BRIT...
YOU CAN'T BELIEVE YOU'VE *PULLED OFF* THIS *BIG BLOND CRUMPET.* YOU'RE SCARED ONE OF YOUR *MATES* WILL *NICK* HER FROM YOU.
AND... *JINGS,* OR SOMETHING.
AH, LOST CONTROL AT THE END THERE, HEN. VERY AMATEURISH.
YOU'RE ABOUT HALFWAY THERE. YOU DON'T PULL SOMEONE OFF, THAT'D BE TERRIBLE--YOU JUST PULL THEM. AN' CRUMPET'S PLURAL ON ITS OWN, YOU'RE MEANT TO SAY *BIT* O' CRUMPET.
LASTLY, AN' THIS MAY JUST BE A MATTER O' TASTE, *NICK* IS USUALLY FOLLOWED WI' *OFF*--AS IN NICK SOMETHIN' OFF SOMEONE, NO' FROM TH--
DO YOU HAVE TIME FOR A QUICKIE BEFORE WORK?
...AYE...

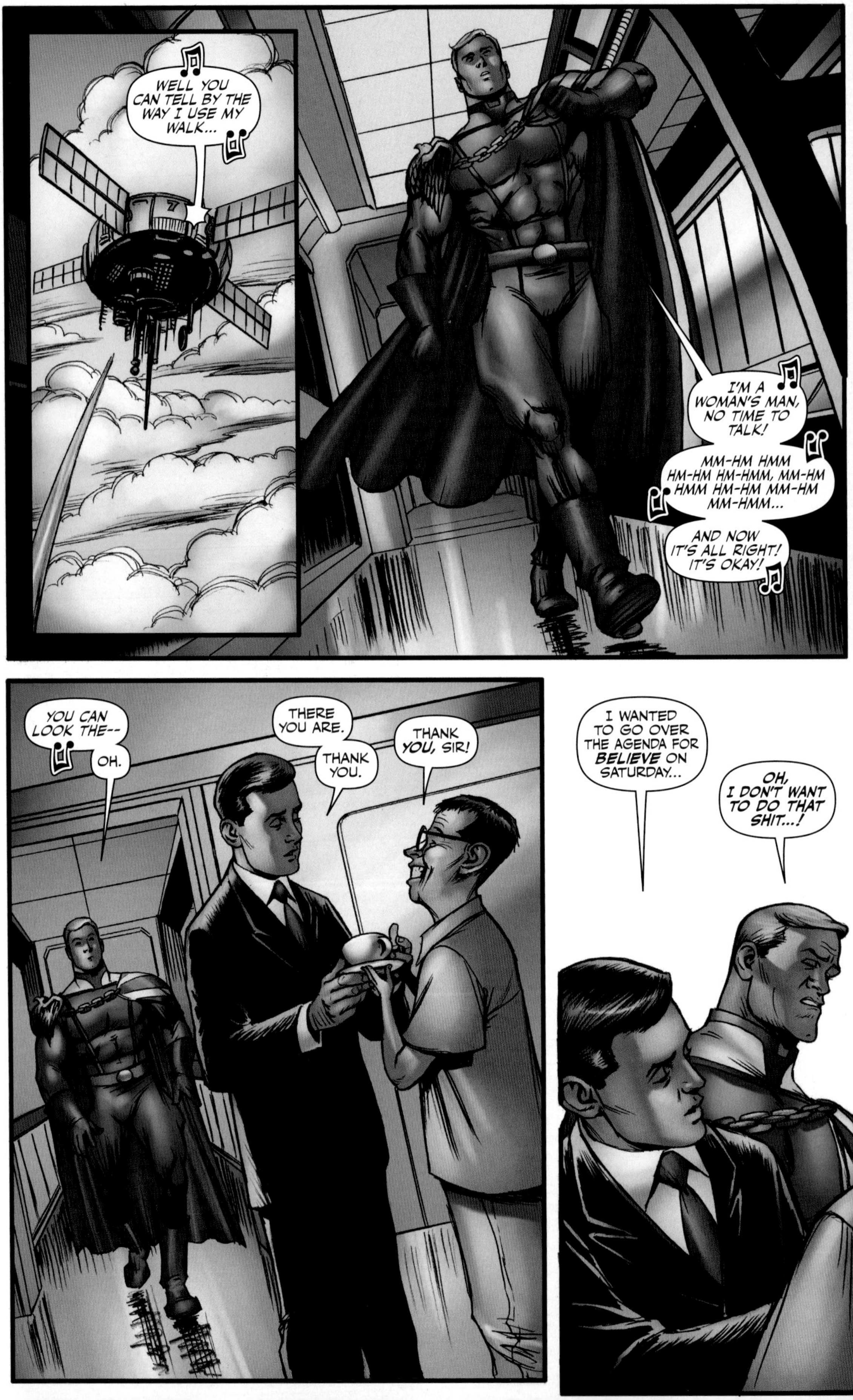
WELL YOU CAN TELL BY THE WAY I USE MY WALK...
I'M A WOMAN'S MAN, NO TIME TO TALK!
MM-HM HMM HM-HM HM-HMM, MM-HM HMM HM-HM MM-HM MM-HMM...
AND NOW IT'S ALL RIGHT! IT'S OKAY!
YOU CAN LOOK THE--
OH.
THERE YOU ARE.
THANK YOU.
THANK YOU, SIR!
I WANTED TO GO OVER THE AGENDA FOR BELIEVE ON SATURDAY...
OH, I DON'T WANT TO DO THAT SHIT...!

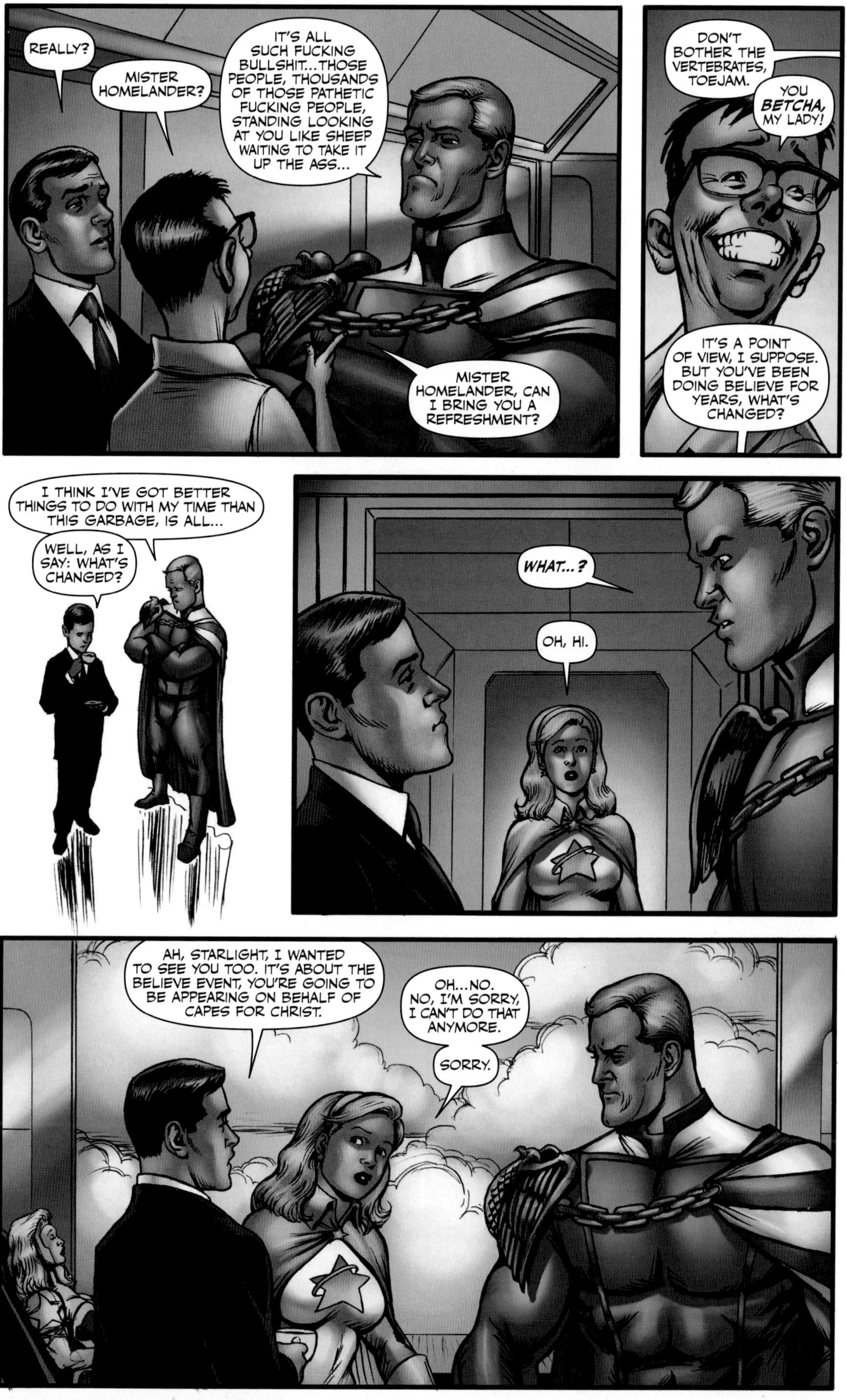
REALLY?
MISTER HOMELANDER?
IT'S ALL SUCH FUCKING BULLSHIT...THOSE PEOPLE, THOUSANDS OF THOSE PATHETIC FUCKING PEOPLE, STANDING LOOKING AT YOU LIKE SHEEP WAITING TO TAKE IT UP THE ASS...
MISTER HOMELANDER, CAN I BRING YOU A REFRESHMENT?
DON'T BOTHER THE VERTEBRATES, TOEJAM.
YOU *BETCHA,* MY LADY!
IT'S A POINT OF VIEW, I SUPPOSE. BUT YOU'VE BEEN DOING BELIEVE FOR YEARS, WHAT'S CHANGED?
I THINK I'VE GOT BETTER THINGS TO DO WITH MY TIME THAN THIS GARBAGE, IS ALL...
WELL, AS I SAY: WHAT'S CHANGED?
WHAT...?
OH, HI.
AH, STARLIGHT, I WANTED TO SEE YOU TOO. IT'S ABOUT THE BELIEVE EVENT, YOU'RE GOING TO BE APPEARING ON BEHALF OF CAPES FOR CHRIST.
OH...NO. NO, I'M SORRY, I CAN'T DO THAT ANYMORE.
SORRY.

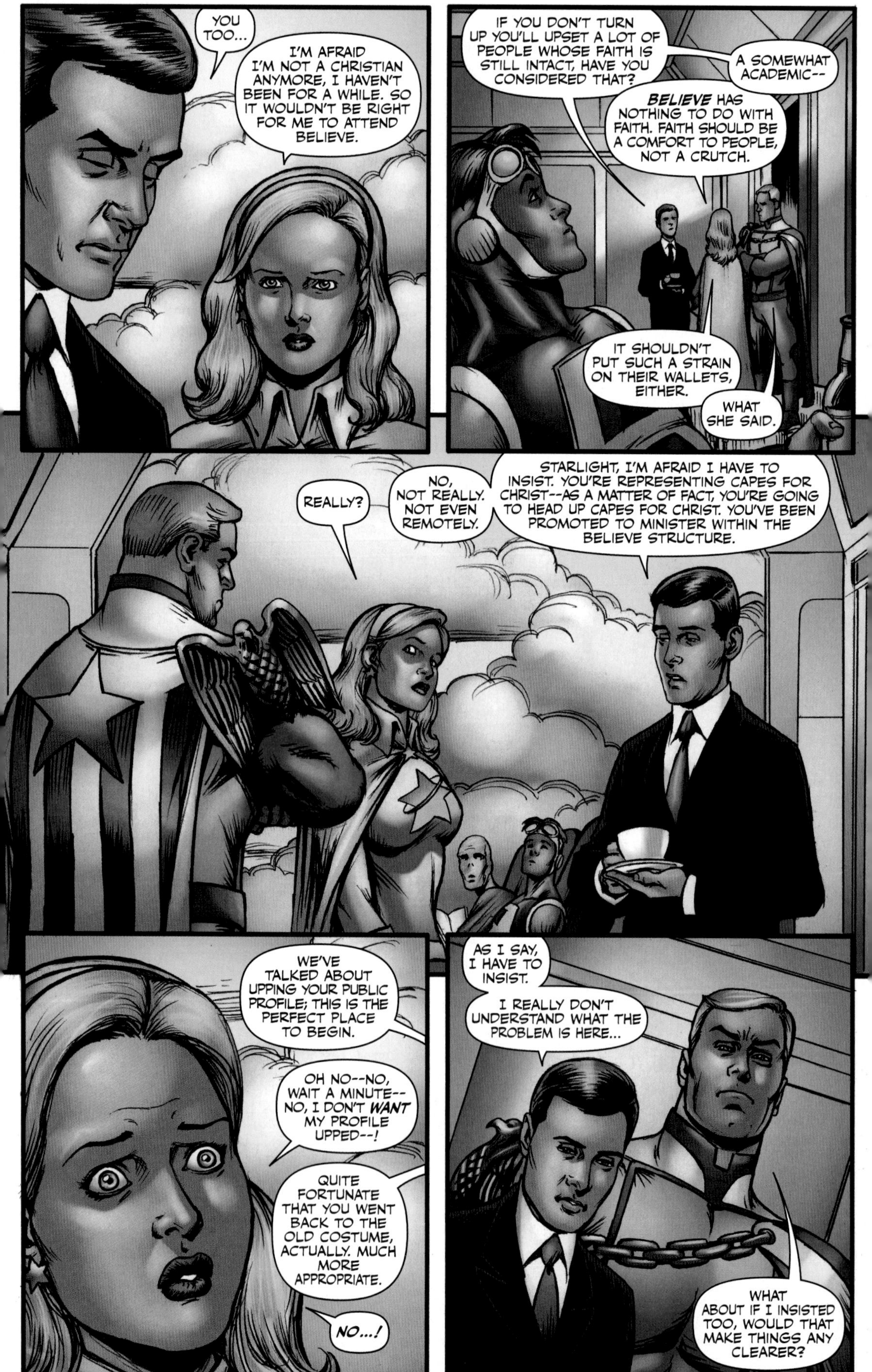
YOU TOO...
I'M AFRAID I'M NOT A CHRISTIAN ANYMORE, I HAVEN'T BEEN FOR A WHILE. SO IT WOULDN'T BE RIGHT FOR ME TO ATTEND BELIEVE.
IF YOU DON'T TURN UP YOU'LL UPSET A LOT OF PEOPLE WHOSE FAITH IS STILL INTACT, HAVE YOU CONSIDERED THAT?
A SOMEWHAT ACADEMIC--
BELIEVE HAS NOTHING TO DO WITH FAITH. FAITH SHOULD BE A COMFORT TO PEOPLE, NOT A CRUTCH.
IT SHOULDN'T PUT SUCH A STRAIN ON THEIR WALLETS, EITHER.
WHAT SHE SAID.
REALLY?
NO, NOT REALLY. NOT EVEN REMOTELY.
STARLIGHT, I'M AFRAID I HAVE TO INSIST. YOU'RE REPRESENTING CAPES FOR CHRIST--AS A MATTER OF FACT, YOU'RE GOING TO HEAD UP CAPES FOR CHRIST. YOU'VE BEEN PROMOTED TO MINISTER WITHIN THE BELIEVE STRUCTURE.
WE'VE TALKED ABOUT UPPING YOUR PUBLIC PROFILE; THIS IS THE PERFECT PLACE TO BEGIN.
OH NO--NO, WAIT A MINUTE--NO, I DON'T WANT MY PROFILE UPPED--!
QUITE FORTUNATE THAT YOU WENT BACK TO THE OLD COSTUME, ACTUALLY. MUCH MORE APPROPRIATE.
NO...!
AS I SAY, I HAVE TO INSIST.
I REALLY DON'T UNDERSTAND WHAT THE PROBLEM IS HERE...
WHAT ABOUT IF I INSISTED TOO, WOULD THAT MAKE THINGS ANY CLEARER?

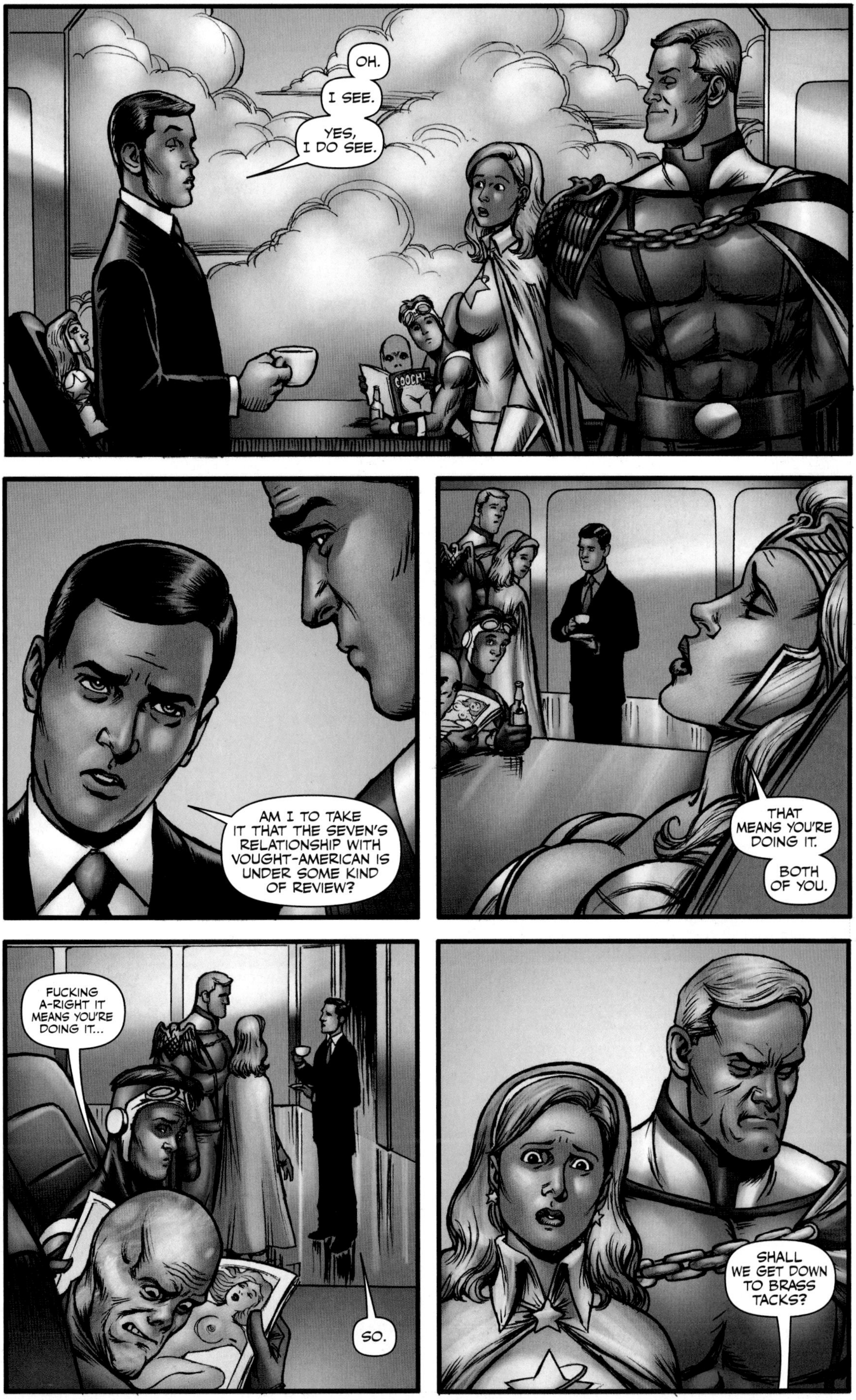
OH.
I SEE.
YES, I DO SEE.
COOCH!
AM I TO TAKE IT THAT THE SEVEN'S RELATIONSHIP WITH VOUGHT-AMERICAN IS UNDER SOME KIND OF REVIEW?
THAT MEANS YOU'RE DOING IT.
BOTH OF YOU.
FUCKING A-RIGHT IT MEANS YOU'RE DOING IT...
SO.
SHALL WE GET DOWN TO BRASS TACKS?

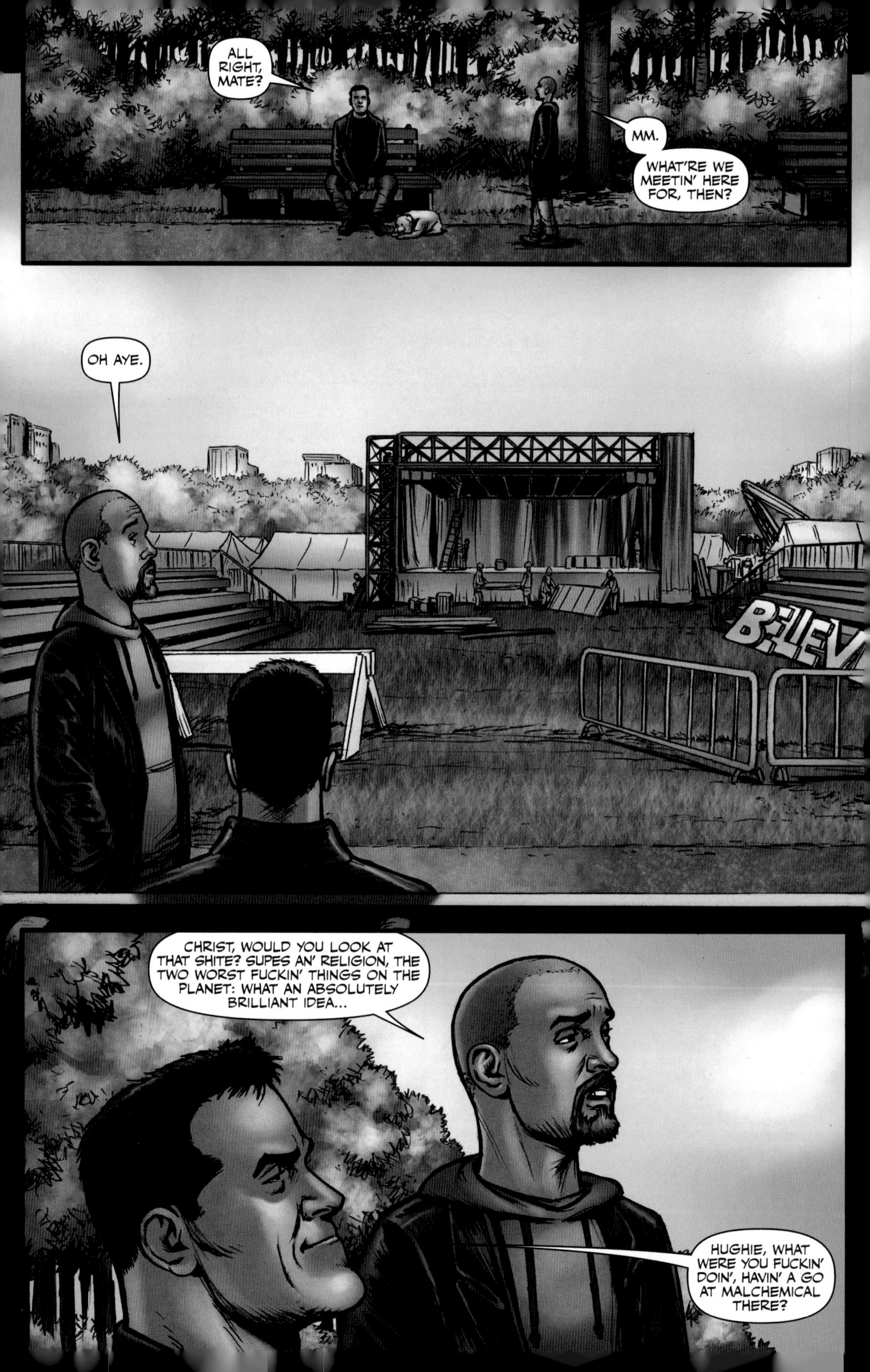
ALL RIGHT, MATE?
MM.
WHAT'RE WE MEETIN' HERE FOR, THEN?
OH AYE.
CHRIST, WOULD YOU LOOK AT THAT SHITE? SUPES AN' RELIGION, THE TWO WORST FUCKIN' THINGS ON THE PLANET: WHAT AN ABSOLUTELY BRILLIANT IDEA...
HUGHIE, WHAT WERE YOU FUCKIN' DOIN', HAVIN' A GO AT MALCHEMICAL THERE?

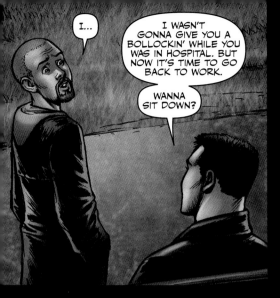

I...

I WASN'T GONNA GIVE YOU A BOLLOCKIN' WHILE YOU WAS IN HOSPITAL. BUT NOW IT'S TIME TO GO BACK TO WORK.

WANNA SIT DOWN?

I JUST--LOOK, FOR CHRIST'S SAKE, HE WAS GONNA RAPE THEM. MALCHEMICAL, HE WAS GONNA MAKE THOSE TWO WEE LASSIES SUCK HIM OFF, THE FUCKIN' DISGUSTIN' PRICK...

DONE A FUCKSIGHT WORSE'N THAT IN HIS TIME. YOU READ THE FILE.

AYE, BUT NO' IN FRONTA ME--!

YOU KNOW AS WELL AS I DO, THEY WERE NO DIFFERENT TO KIDS! AN' HE WAS GONNA DO THAT TO THEM WI' THE REST WATCHIN'--HE WAS GONNA *RAPE THEM*, I MEAN DO YOU EVEN KNOW WHAT THAT MEANS...?

YEAH, I THINK I MIGHT HAVE AN INKLIN'.

AW FUCK.

SORRY.

SIT DOWN, WILL YOU? YOU'RE GIVIN' ME A FUCKIN' CRICK IN ME NECK.

I REALLY AM SORRY...

DIDN'T YOU LEARN ANYTHIN' AFTER G-WIZ? I'M NOT TALKIN' ABOUT RISKIN' YOUR FUCKIN' LIFE, I'M TALKIN' ABOUT NOT GETTIN' *INVOLVED* WITH THESE NOBBERS...!

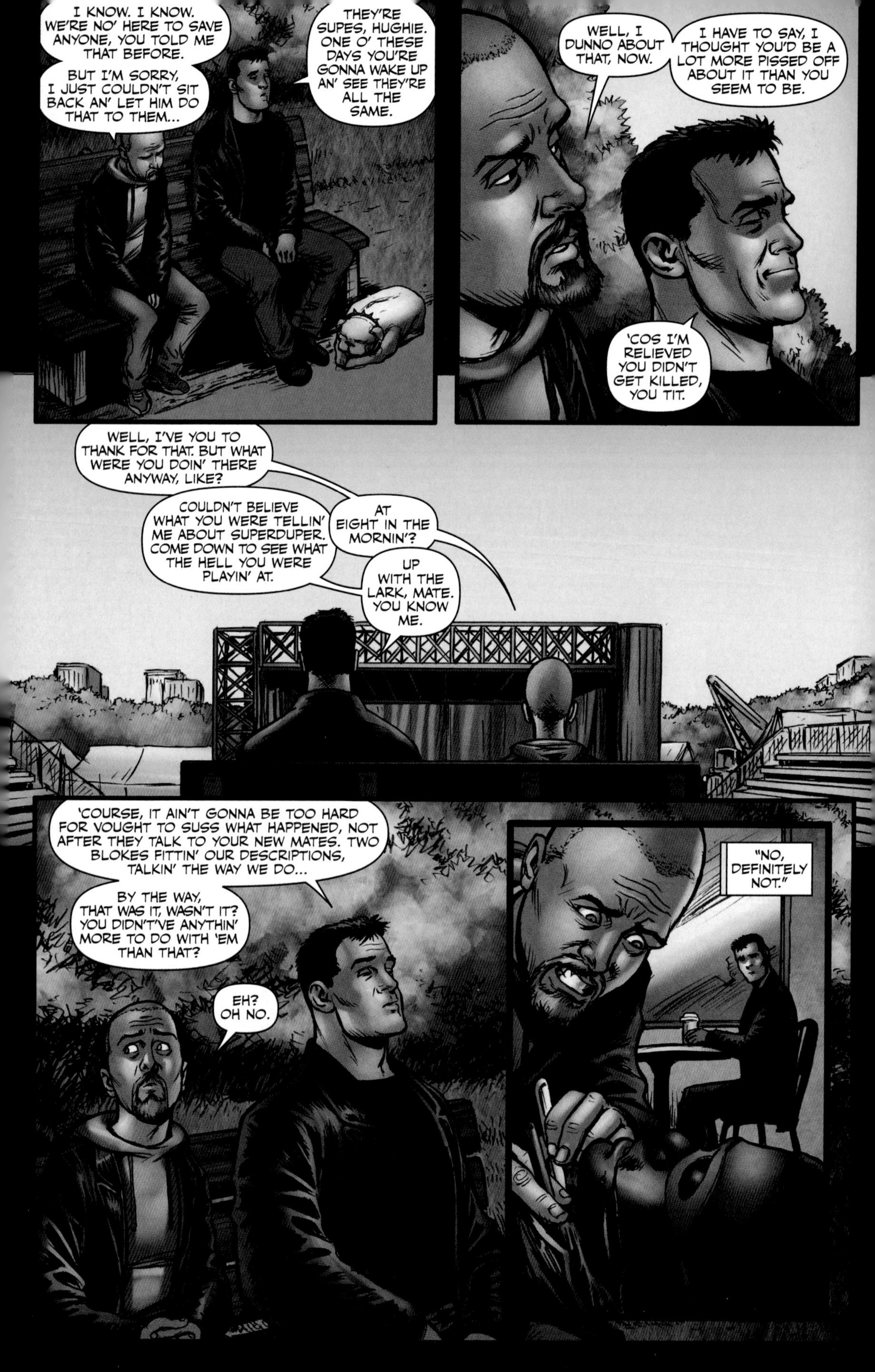
I KNOW. I KNOW. WE'RE NO' HERE TO SAVE ANYONE, YOU TOLD ME THAT BEFORE.
BUT I'M SORRY, I JUST COULDN'T SIT BACK AN' LET HIM DO THAT TO THEM...
THEY'RE SUPES, HUGHIE. ONE O' THESE DAYS YOU'RE GONNA WAKE UP AN' SEE THEY'RE ALL THE SAME.
WELL, I DUNNO ABOUT THAT, NOW.
I HAVE TO SAY, I THOUGHT YOU'D BE A LOT MORE PISSED OFF ABOUT IT THAN YOU SEEM TO BE.
'COS I'M RELIEVED YOU DIDN'T GET KILLED, YOU TIT.
WELL, I'VE YOU TO THANK FOR THAT. BUT WHAT WERE YOU DOIN' THERE ANYWAY, LIKE?
COULDN'T BELIEVE WHAT YOU WERE TELLIN' ME ABOUT SUPERDUPER. COME DOWN TO SEE WHAT THE HELL YOU WERE PLAYIN' AT.
AT EIGHT IN THE MORNIN'?
UP WITH THE LARK, MATE. YOU KNOW ME.
'COURSE, IT AIN'T GONNA BE TOO HARD FOR VOUGHT TO SUSS WHAT HAPPENED, NOT AFTER THEY TALK TO YOUR NEW MATES. TWO BLOKES FITTIN' OUR DESCRIPTIONS, TALKIN' THE WAY WE DO...
BY THE WAY, THAT WAS IT, WASN'T IT? YOU DIDN'T'VE ANYTHIN' MORE TO DO WITH 'EM THAN THAT?
EH? OH NO.
"NO, DEFINITELY NOT."

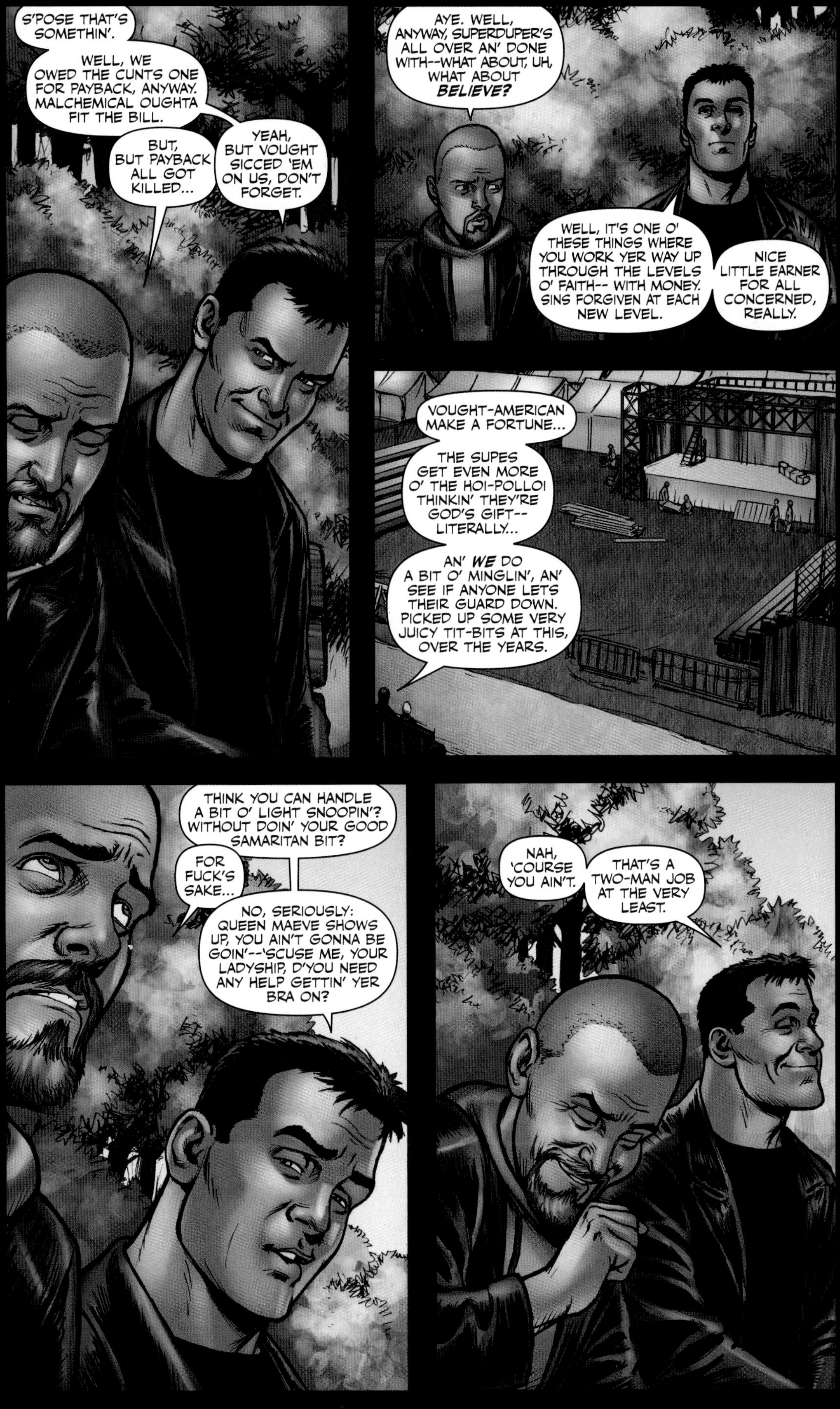
S'POSE THAT'S SOMETHIN'.
WELL, WE OWED THE CUNTS ONE FOR PAYBACK, ANYWAY. MALCHEMICAL OUGHTA FIT THE BILL.
BUT, BUT PAYBACK ALL GOT KILLED...
YEAH, BUT VOUGHT SICCED 'EM ON US, DON'T FORGET.
AYE. WELL, ANYWAY, SUPERDUPER'S ALL OVER AN' DONE WITH--WHAT ABOUT, UH, WHAT ABOUT BELIEVE?
WELL, IT'S ONE O' THESE THINGS WHERE YOU WORK YER WAY UP THROUGH THE LEVELS O' FAITH-- WITH MONEY. SINS FORGIVEN AT EACH NEW LEVEL.
NICE LITTLE EARNER FOR ALL CONCERNED, REALLY.
VOUGHT-AMERICAN MAKE A FORTUNE...
THE SUPES GET EVEN MORE O' THE HOI-POLLOI THINKIN' THEY'RE GOD'S GIFT-- LITERALLY...
AN' WE DO A BIT O' MINGLIN', AN' SEE IF ANYONE LETS THEIR GUARD DOWN. PICKED UP SOME VERY JUICY TIT-BITS AT THIS, OVER THE YEARS.
THINK YOU CAN HANDLE A BIT O' LIGHT SNOOPIN'? WITHOUT DOIN' YOUR GOOD SAMARITAN BIT?
FOR FUCK'S SAKE...
NO, SERIOUSLY: QUEEN MAEVE SHOWS UP, YOU AIN'T GONNA BE GOIN'--'SCUSE ME, YOUR LADYSHIP, D'YOU NEED ANY HELP GETTIN' YER BRA ON?
NAH, 'COURSE YOU AIN'T.
THAT'S A TWO-MAN JOB AT THE VERY LEAST.

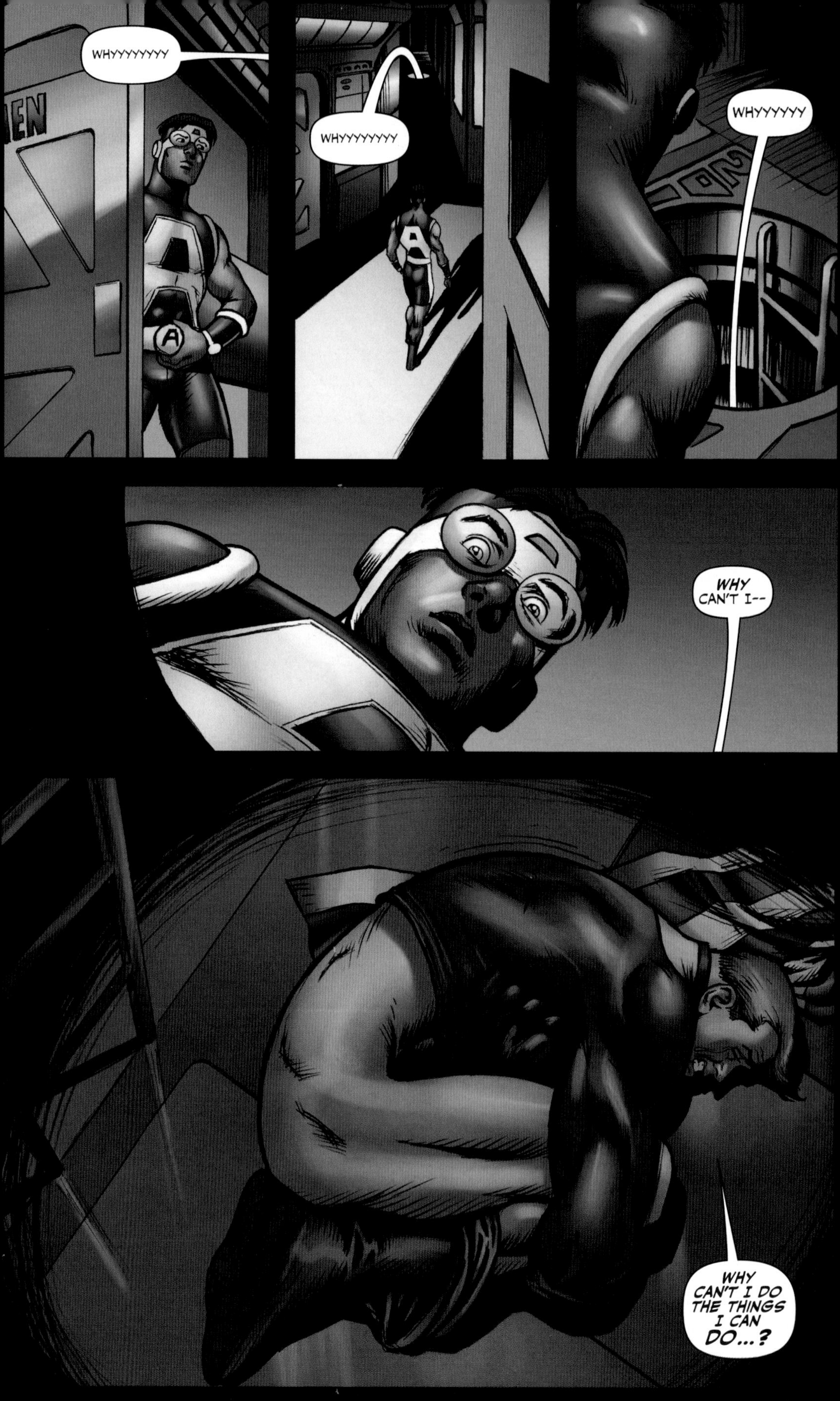

WHYYYYYYYY
WHYYYYYYYYY
WHYYYYYY
WHY CAN'T I--
WHY CAN'T I DO THE THINGS I CAN DO...?

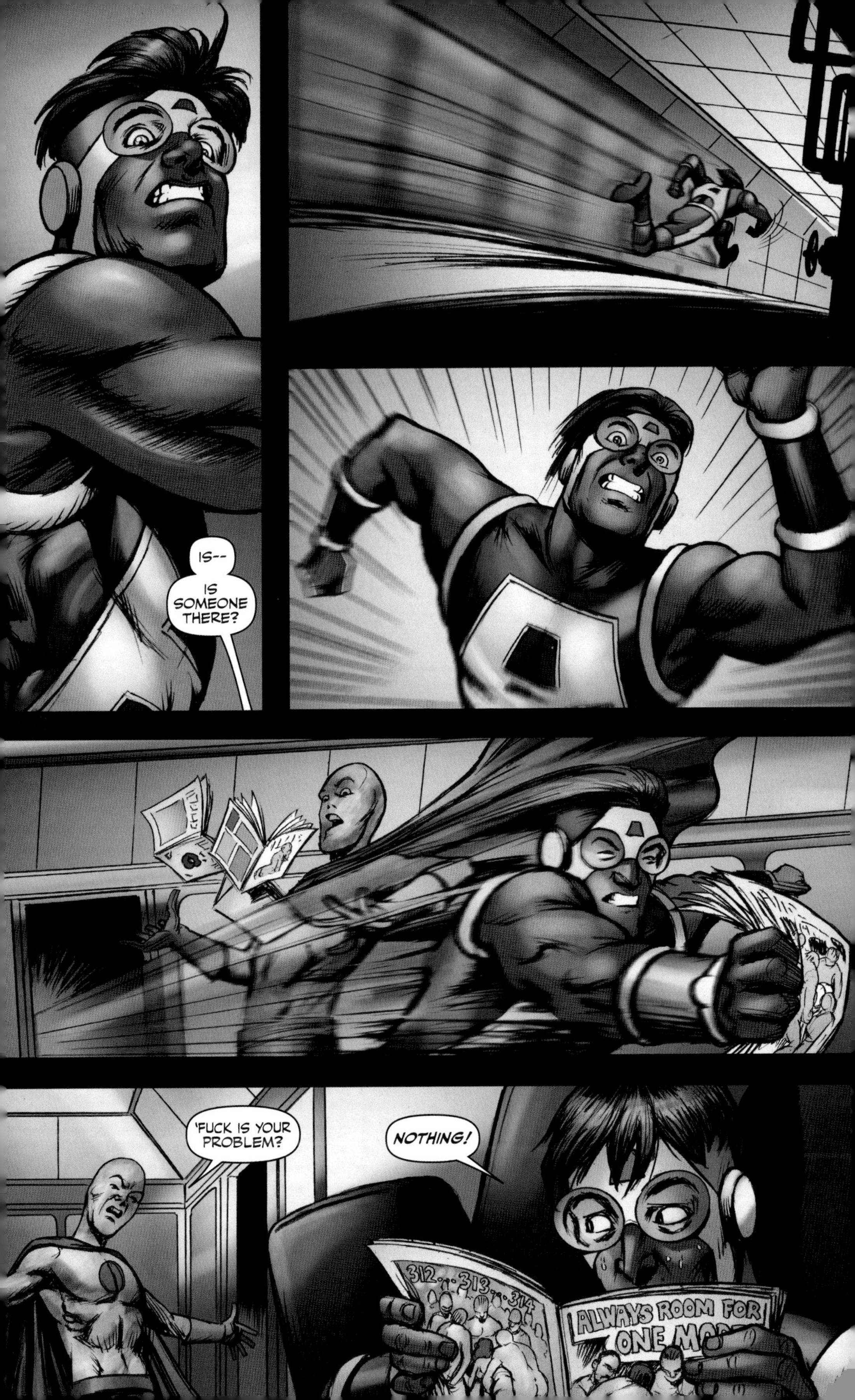
IS--
IS SOMEONE THERE?
'FUCK IS YOUR PROBLEM?
NOTHING!
312...313...314
ALWAYS ROOM FOR

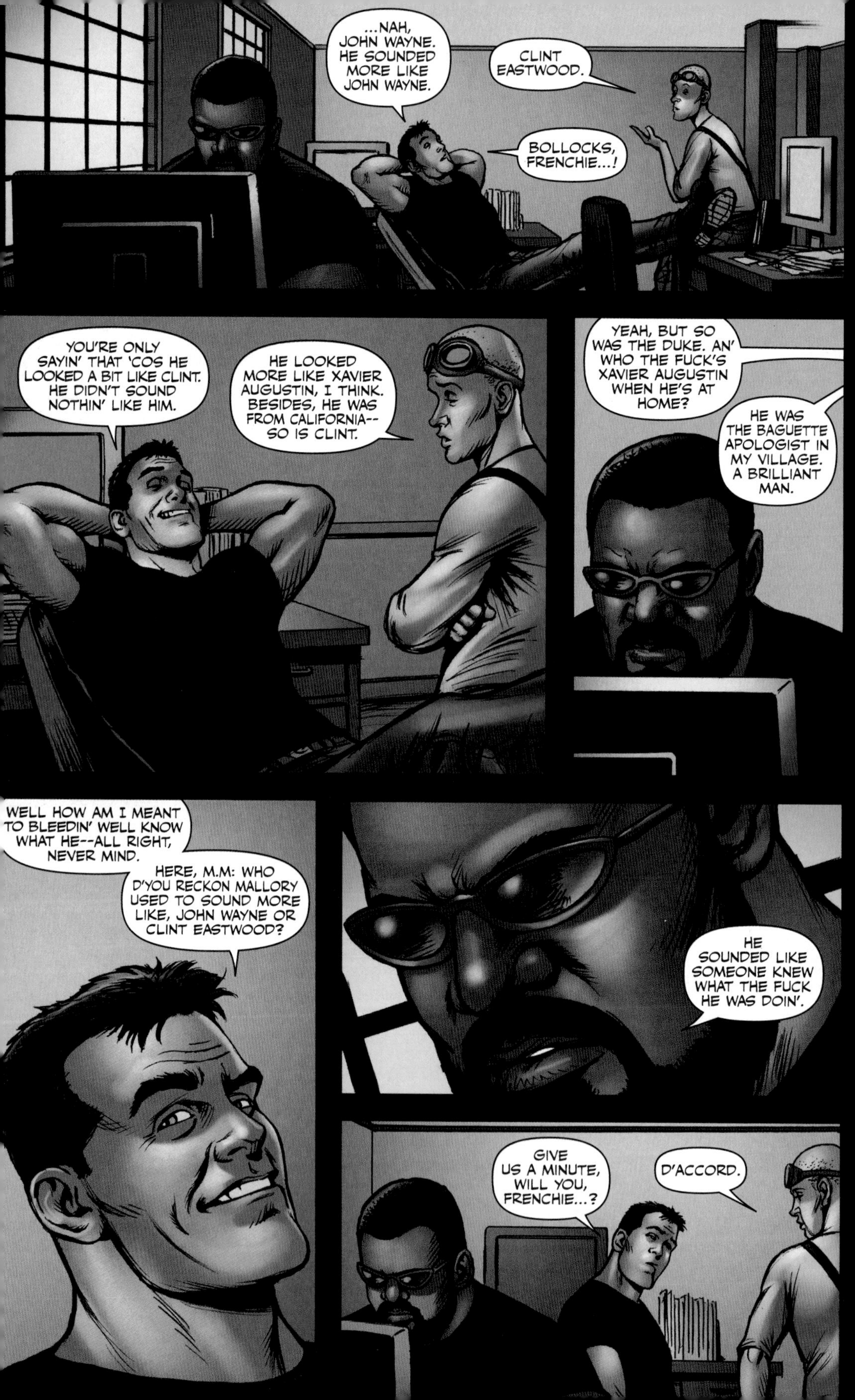
...NAH, JOHN WAYNE. HE SOUNDED MORE LIKE JOHN WAYNE.
CLINT EASTWOOD.
BOLLOCKS, FRENCHIE...!
YOU'RE ONLY SAYIN' THAT 'COS HE LOOKED A BIT LIKE CLINT. HE DIDN'T SOUND NOTHIN' LIKE HIM.
HE LOOKED MORE LIKE XAVIER AUGUSTIN, I THINK. BESIDES, HE WAS FROM CALIFORNIA-- SO IS CLINT.
YEAH, BUT SO WAS THE DUKE. AN' WHO THE FUCK'S XAVIER AUGUSTIN WHEN HE'S AT HOME?
HE WAS THE BAGUETTE APOLOGIST IN MY VILLAGE. A BRILLIANT MAN.
WELL HOW AM I MEANT TO BLEEDIN' WELL KNOW WHAT HE--ALL RIGHT, NEVER MIND.
HERE, M.M: WHO D'YOU RECKON MALLORY USED TO SOUND MORE LIKE, JOHN WAYNE OR CLINT EASTWOOD?
HE SOUNDED LIKE SOMEONE KNEW WHAT THE FUCK HE WAS DOIN'.
GIVE US A MINUTE, WILL YOU, FRENCHIE...?
D'ACCORD.

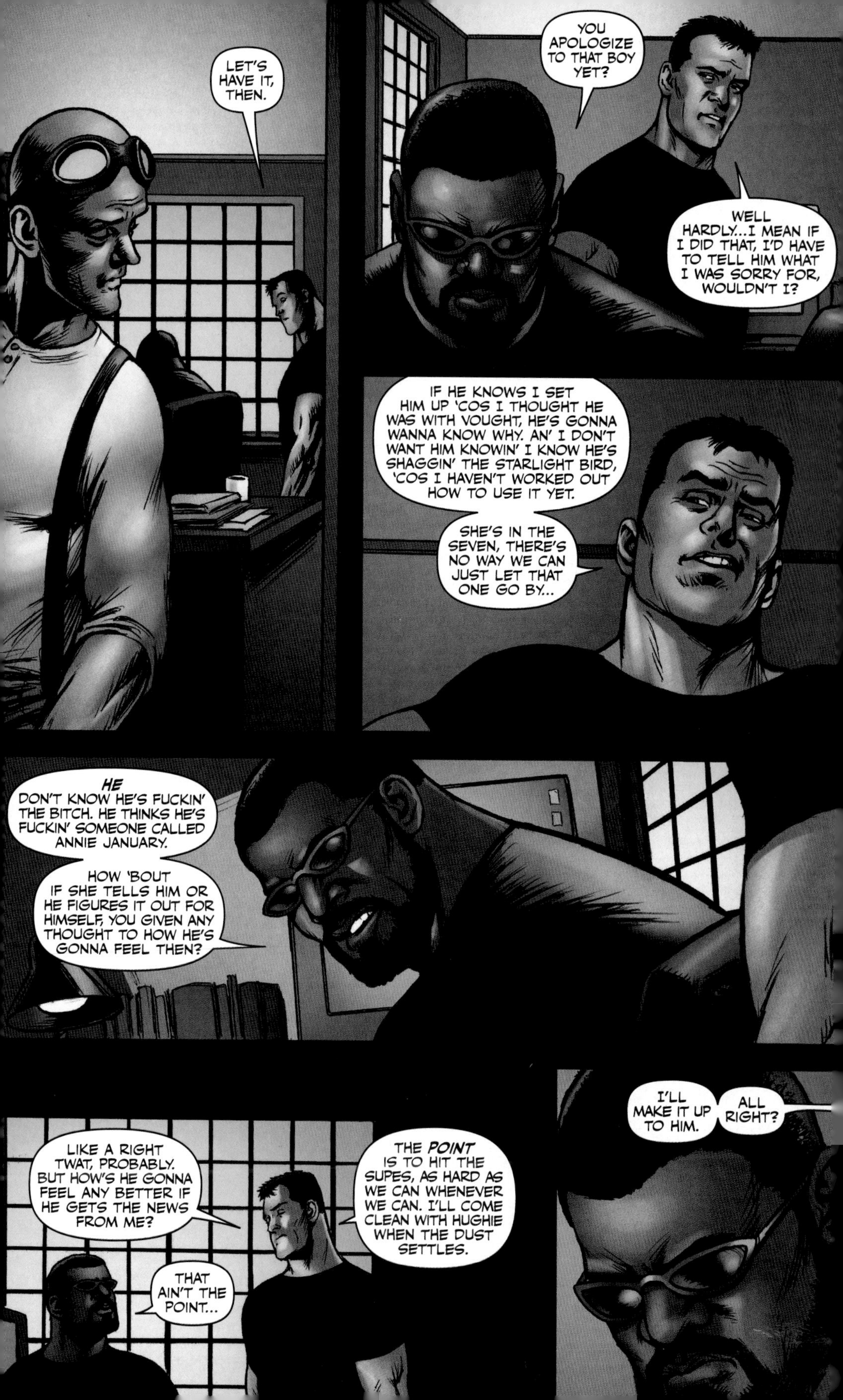
LET'S HAVE IT, THEN.
YOU APOLOGIZE TO THAT BOY YET?
WELL HARDLY...I MEAN IF I DID THAT, I'D HAVE TO TELL HIM WHAT I WAS SORRY FOR, WOULDN'T I?
IF HE KNOWS I SET HIM UP 'COS I THOUGHT HE WAS WITH VOUGHT, HE'S GONNA WANNA KNOW WHY. AN' I DON'T WANT HIM KNOWIN' I KNOW HE'S SHAGGIN' THE STARLIGHT BIRD, 'COS I HAVEN'T WORKED OUT HOW TO USE IT YET.
SHE'S IN THE SEVEN, THERE'S NO WAY WE CAN JUST LET THAT ONE GO BY...
HE DON'T KNOW HE'S FUCKIN' THE BITCH. HE THINKS HE'S FUCKIN' SOMEONE CALLED ANNIE JANUARY.
HOW 'BOUT IF SHE TELLS HIM OR HE FIGURES IT OUT FOR HIMSELF, YOU GIVEN ANY THOUGHT TO HOW HE'S GONNA FEEL THEN?
LIKE A RIGHT TWAT, PROBABLY. BUT HOW'S HE GONNA FEEL ANY BETTER IF HE GETS THE NEWS FROM ME?
THAT AIN'T THE POINT...
THE *POINT* IS TO HIT THE SUPES, AS HARD AS WE CAN WHENEVER WE CAN. I'LL COME CLEAN WITH HUGHIE WHEN THE DUST SETTLES.
I'LL MAKE IT UP TO HIM.
ALL RIGHT?

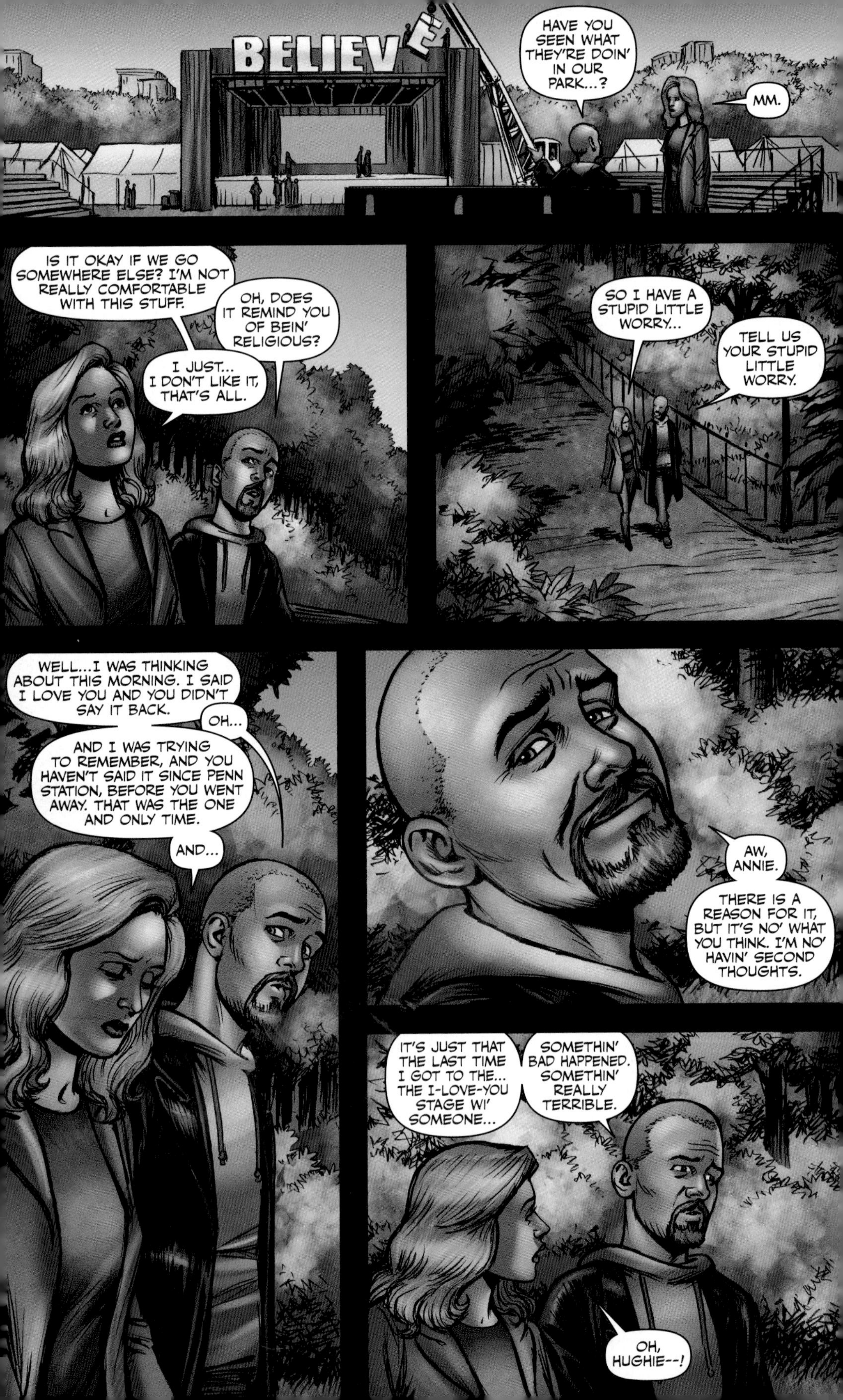
BELIEVE
HAVE YOU SEEN WHAT THEY'RE DOIN' IN OUR PARK...?
MM.
IS IT OKAY IF WE GO SOMEWHERE ELSE? I'M NOT REALLY COMFORTABLE WITH THIS STUFF.
OH, DOES IT REMIND YOU OF BEIN' RELIGIOUS?
I JUST... I DON'T LIKE IT, THAT'S ALL.
SO I HAVE A STUPID LITTLE WORRY...
TELL US YOUR STUPID LITTLE WORRY.
WELL...I WAS THINKING ABOUT THIS MORNING. I SAID I LOVE YOU AND YOU DIDN'T SAY IT BACK.
OH...
AND I WAS TRYING TO REMEMBER, AND YOU HAVEN'T SAID IT SINCE PENN STATION, BEFORE YOU WENT AWAY. THAT WAS THE ONE AND ONLY TIME.
AND...
AW, ANNIE.
THERE IS A REASON FOR IT, BUT IT'S NO' WHAT YOU THINK. I'M NO' HAVIN' SECOND THOUGHTS.
IT'S JUST THAT THE LAST TIME I GOT TO THE... THE I-LOVE-YOU STAGE WI' SOMEONE...
SOMETHIN' BAD HAPPENED. SOMETHIN' REALLY TERRIBLE.
OH, HUGHIE--!

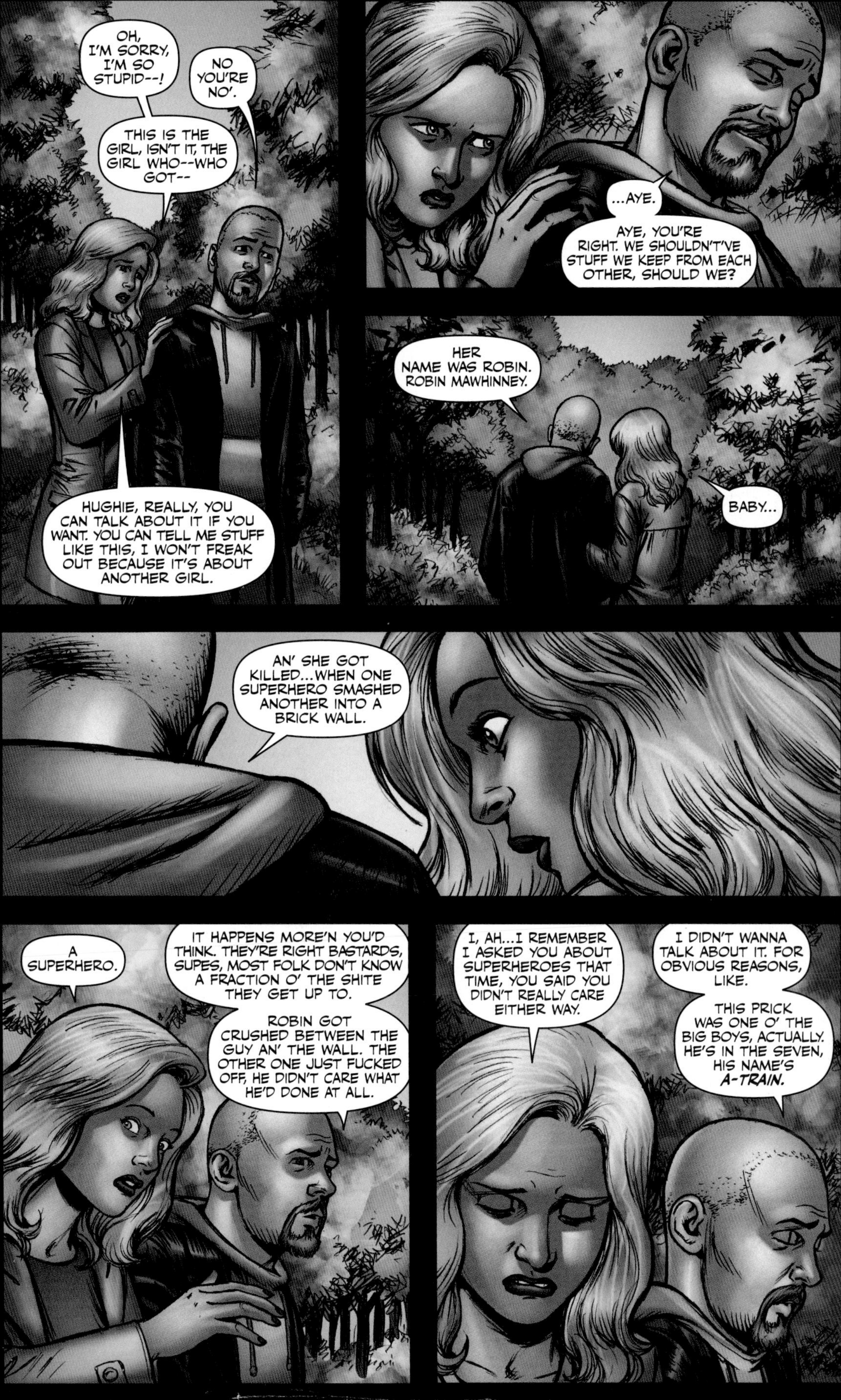

OH, I'M SORRY, I'M SO STUPID--!
NO YOU'RE NO'.
THIS IS THE GIRL, ISN'T IT, THE GIRL WHO--WHO GOT--
HUGHIE, REALLY, YOU CAN TALK ABOUT IT IF YOU WANT. YOU CAN TELL ME STUFF LIKE THIS, I WON'T FREAK OUT BECAUSE IT'S ABOUT ANOTHER GIRL.
...AYE.
AYE, YOU'RE RIGHT. WE SHOULDN'T'VE STUFF WE KEEP FROM EACH OTHER, SHOULD WE?
HER NAME WAS ROBIN. ROBIN MAWHINNEY.
BABY...
AN' SHE GOT KILLED...WHEN ONE SUPERHERO SMASHED ANOTHER INTO A BRICK WALL.
A SUPERHERO.
IT HAPPENS MORE'N YOU'D THINK. THEY'RE RIGHT BASTARDS, SUPES, MOST FOLK DON'T KNOW A FRACTION O' THE SHITE THEY GET UP TO.
ROBIN GOT CRUSHED BETWEEN THE GUY AN' THE WALL. THE OTHER ONE JUST FUCKED OFF, HE DIDN'T CARE WHAT HE'D DONE AT ALL.
I, AH...I REMEMBER I ASKED YOU ABOUT SUPERHEROES THAT TIME, YOU SAID YOU DIDN'T REALLY CARE EITHER WAY.
I DIDN'T WANNA TALK ABOUT IT. FOR OBVIOUS REASONS, LIKE.
THIS PRICK WAS ONE O' THE BIG BOYS, ACTUALLY. HE'S IN THE SEVEN, HIS NAME'S *A-TRAIN.*

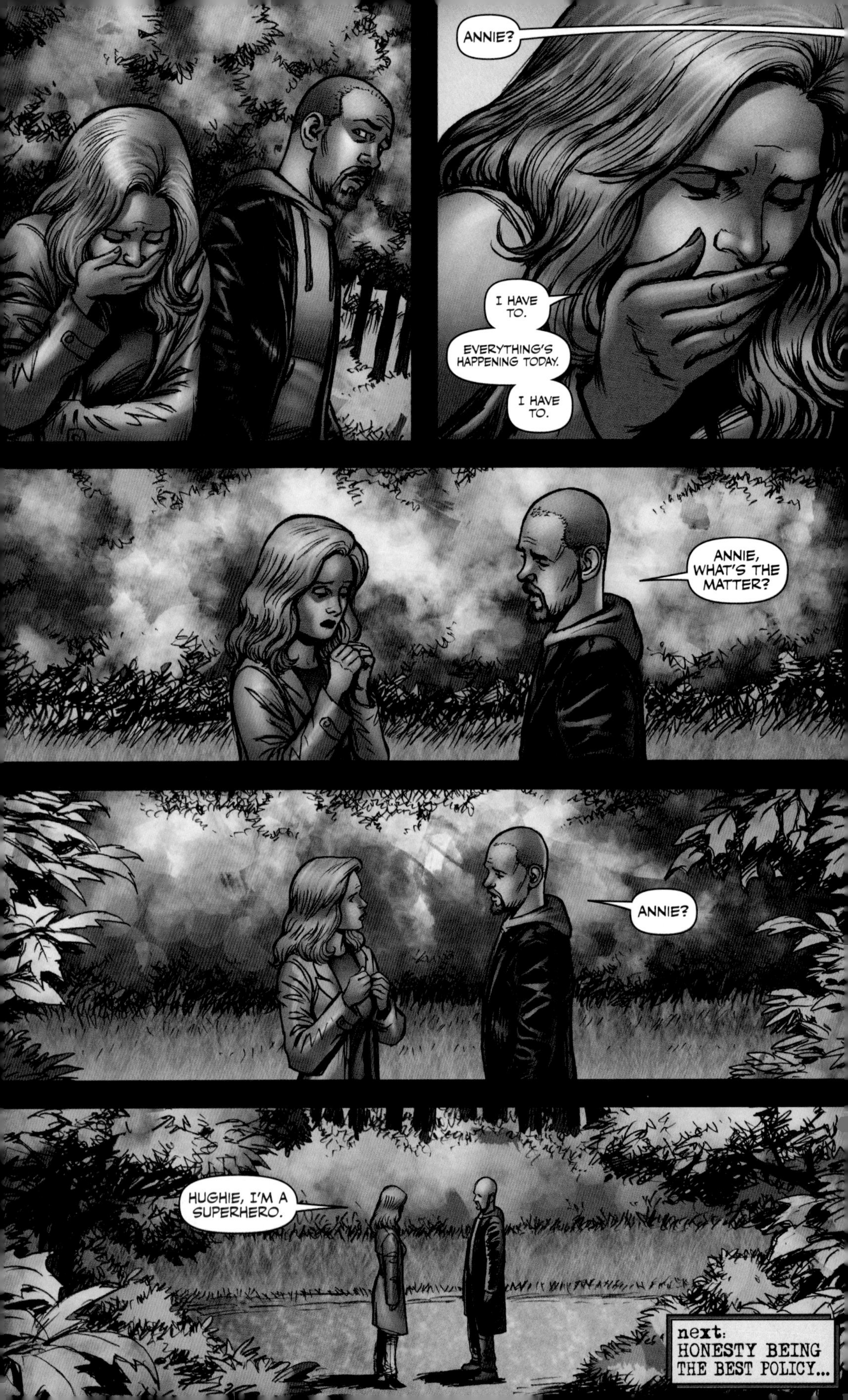
ANNIE?
I HAVE TO.
EVERYTHING'S HAPPENING TODAY.
I HAVE TO.
ANNIE, WHAT'S THE MATTER?
ANNIE?
HUGHIE, I'M A SUPERHERO.
next: HONESTY BEING THE BEST POLICY...

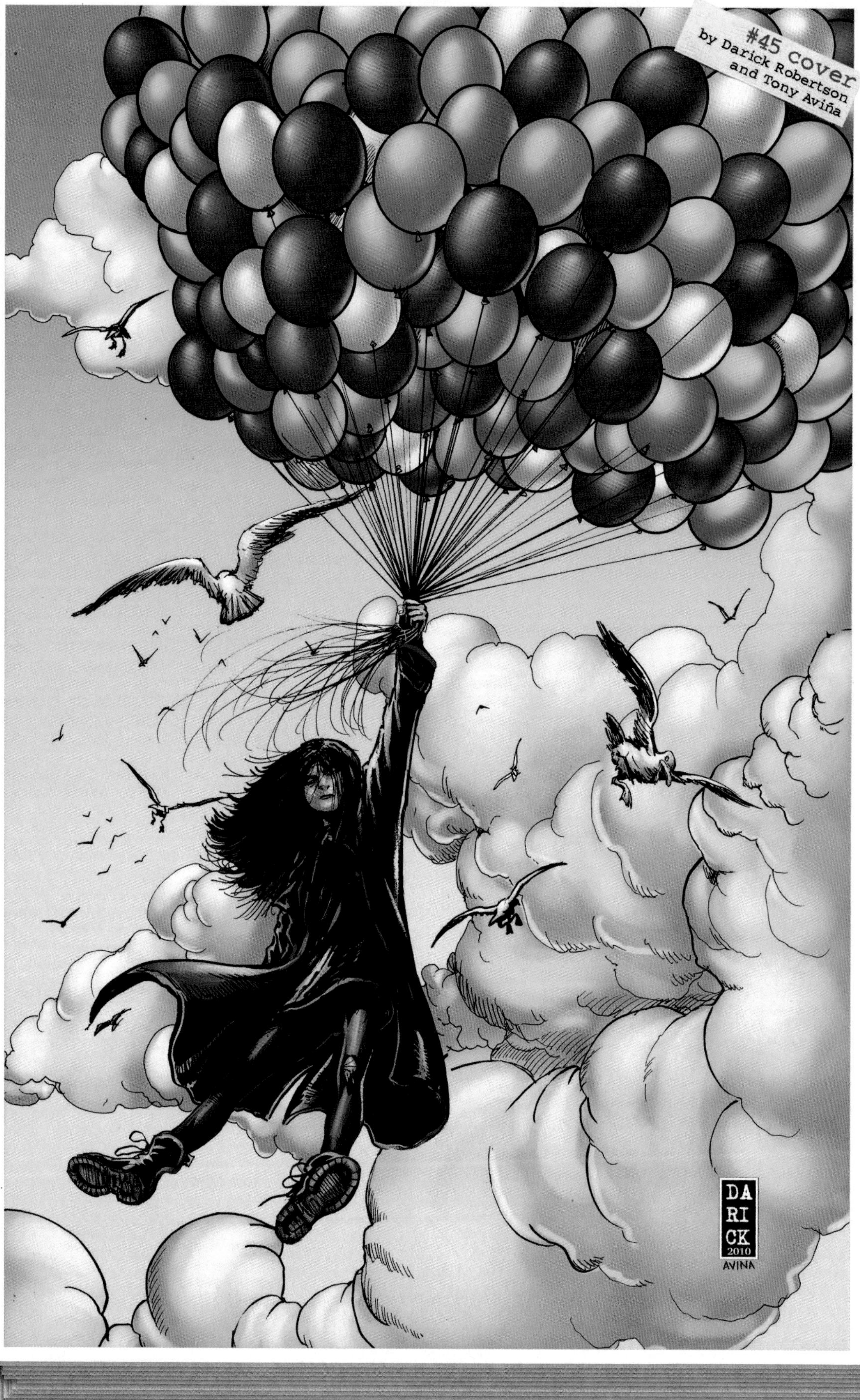
DA
RI
CK
2010
AVINA

#45 cover
by Darick Robertson
and Tony Aviña

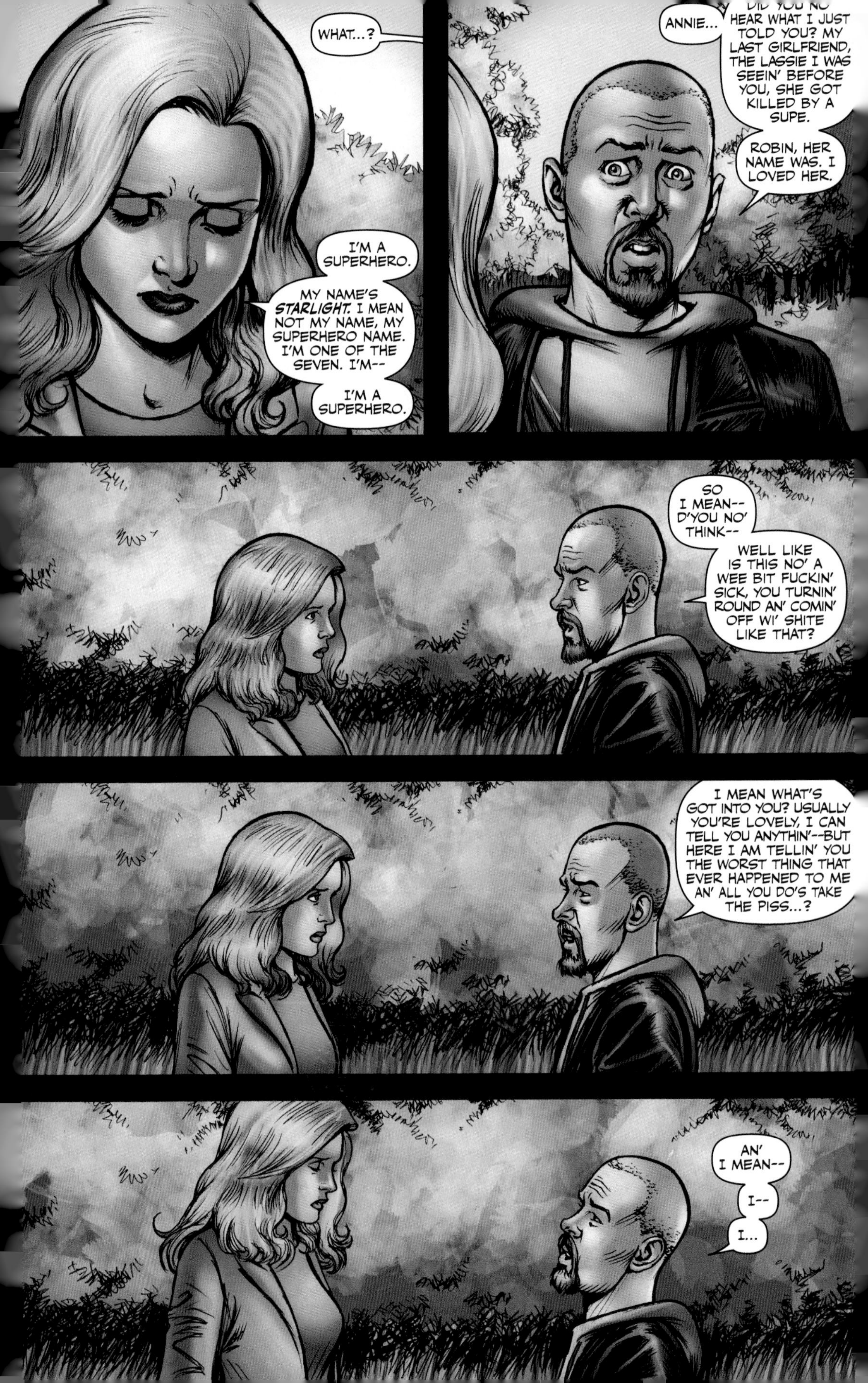
WHAT...?
I'M A SUPERHERO.
MY NAME'S STARLIGHT. I MEAN NOT MY NAME, MY SUPERHERO NAME. I'M ONE OF THE SEVEN. I'M--
I'M A SUPERHERO.
ANNIE...
DID YOU NO HEAR WHAT I JUST TOLD YOU? MY LAST GIRLFRIEND, THE LASSIE I WAS SEEIN' BEFORE YOU, SHE GOT KILLED BY A SUPE.
ROBIN, HER NAME WAS. I LOVED HER.
SO I MEAN-- D'YOU NO' THINK--
WELL LIKE IS THIS NO' A WEE BIT FUCKIN' SICK, YOU TURNIN' ROUND AN' COMIN' OFF WI' SHITE LIKE THAT?
I MEAN WHAT'S GOT INTO YOU? USUALLY YOU'RE LOVELY, I CAN TELL YOU ANYTHIN'--BUT HERE I AM TELLIN' YOU THE WORST THING THAT EVER HAPPENED TO ME AN' ALL YOU DO'S TAKE THE PISS...?
AN' I MEAN--
I--
I...

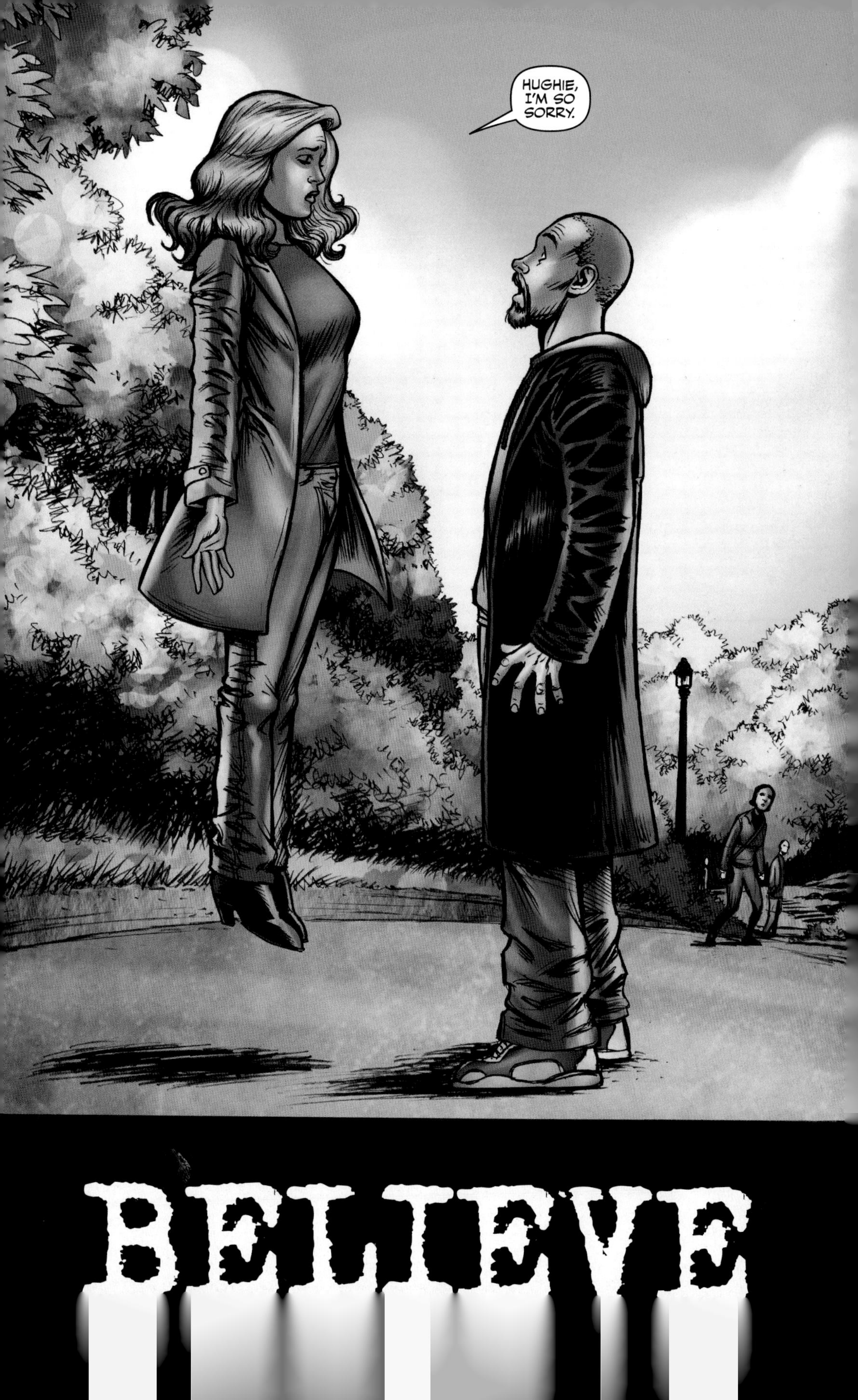
HUGHIE, I'M SO SORRY.

BELIEVE

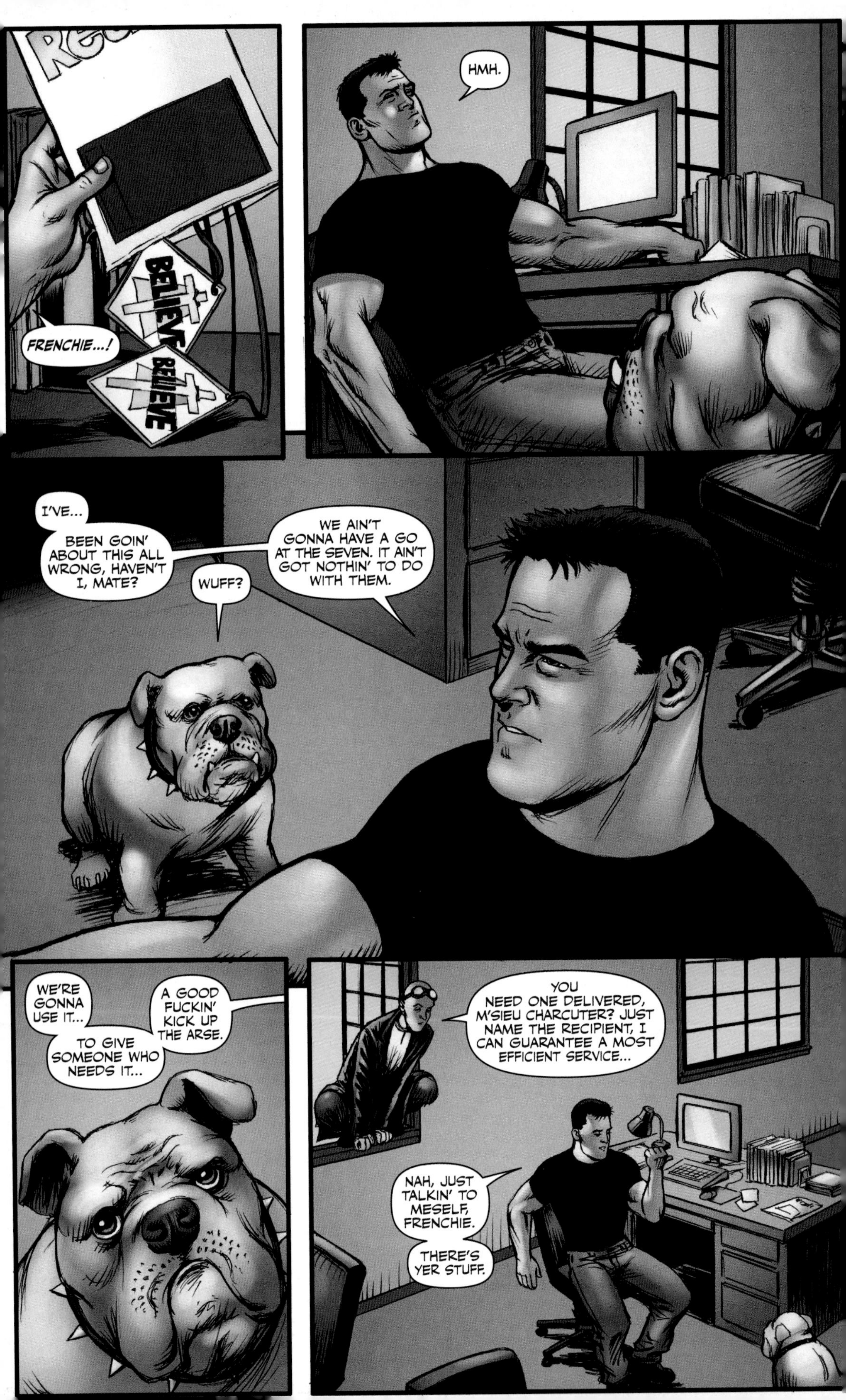

FRENCHIE...!
BELIEVE
BELIEVE
HMH.
I'VE...
BEEN GOIN' ABOUT THIS ALL WRONG, HAVEN'T I, MATE?
WUFF?
WE AIN'T GONNA HAVE A GO AT THE SEVEN. IT AIN'T GOT NOTHIN' TO DO WITH THEM.
WE'RE GONNA USE IT...
TO GIVE SOMEONE WHO NEEDS IT...
A GOOD FUCKIN' KICK UP THE ARSE.
YOU NEED ONE DELIVERED, M'SIEU CHARCUTER? JUST NAME THE RECIPIENT, I CAN GUARANTEE A MOST EFFICIENT SERVICE...
NAH, JUST TALKIN' TO MESELF, FRENCHIE.
THERE'S YER STUFF.

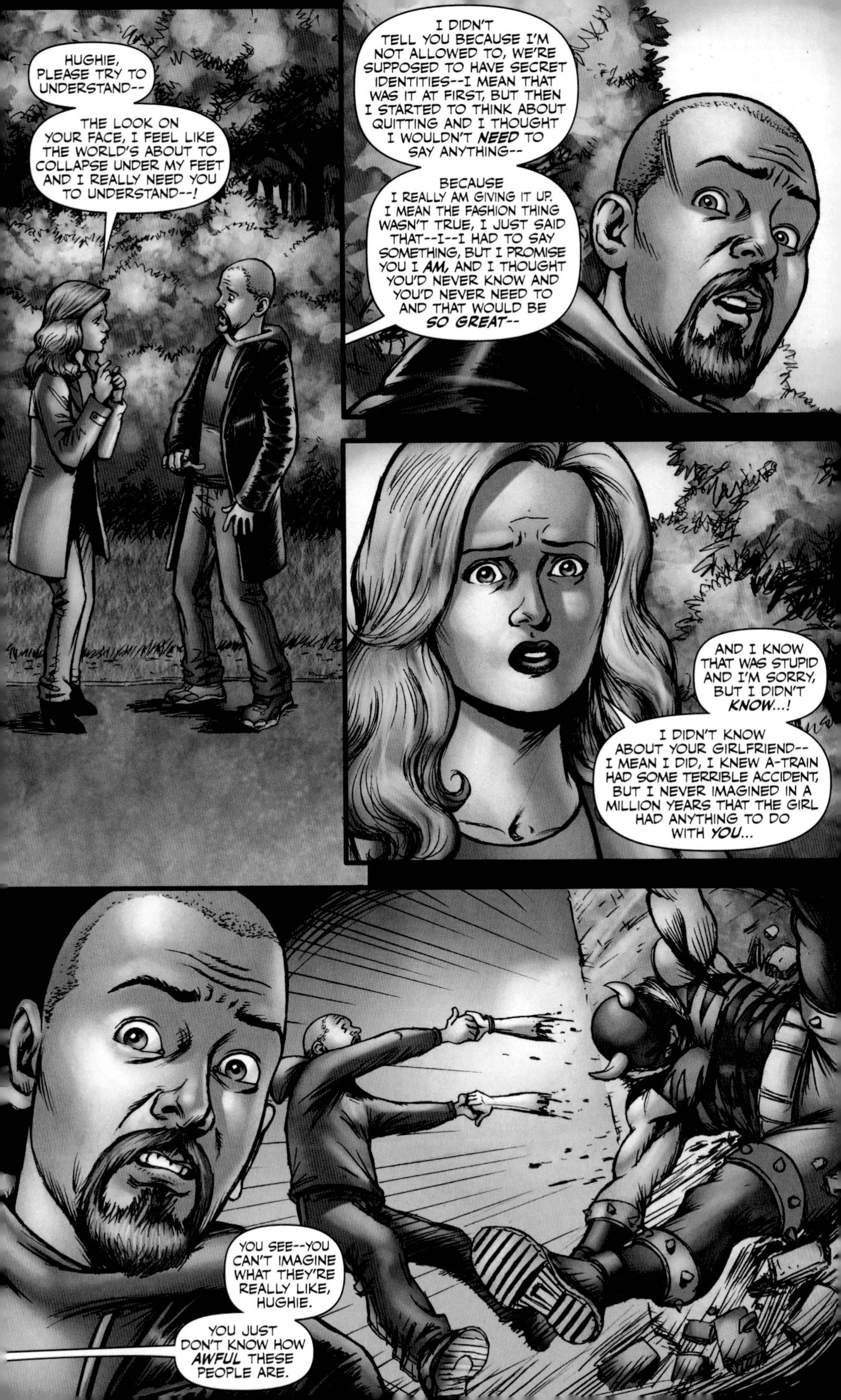

HUGHIE, PLEASE TRY TO UNDERSTAND--
THE LOOK ON YOUR FACE, I FEEL LIKE THE WORLD'S ABOUT TO COLLAPSE UNDER MY FEET AND I REALLY NEED YOU TO UNDERSTAND--!
I DIDN'T TELL YOU BECAUSE I'M NOT ALLOWED TO, WE'RE SUPPOSED TO HAVE SECRET IDENTITIES--I MEAN THAT WAS IT AT FIRST, BUT THEN I STARTED TO THINK ABOUT QUITTING AND I THOUGHT I WOULDN'T NEED TO SAY ANYTHING--
BECAUSE I REALLY AM GIVING IT UP. I MEAN THE FASHION THING WASN'T TRUE, I JUST SAID THAT--I--I HAD TO SAY SOMETHING, BUT I PROMISE YOU I AM, AND I THOUGHT YOU'D NEVER KNOW AND YOU'D NEVER NEED TO AND THAT WOULD BE SO GREAT--
AND I KNOW THAT WAS STUPID AND I'M SORRY, BUT I DIDN'T KNOW...!
I DIDN'T KNOW ABOUT YOUR GIRLFRIEND-- I MEAN I DID, I KNEW A-TRAIN HAD SOME TERRIBLE ACCIDENT, BUT I NEVER IMAGINED IN A MILLION YEARS THAT THE GIRL HAD ANYTHING TO DO WITH YOU...
YOU SEE--YOU CAN'T IMAGINE WHAT THEY'RE REALLY LIKE, HUGHIE.
YOU JUST DON'T KNOW HOW AWFUL THESE PEOPLE ARE.

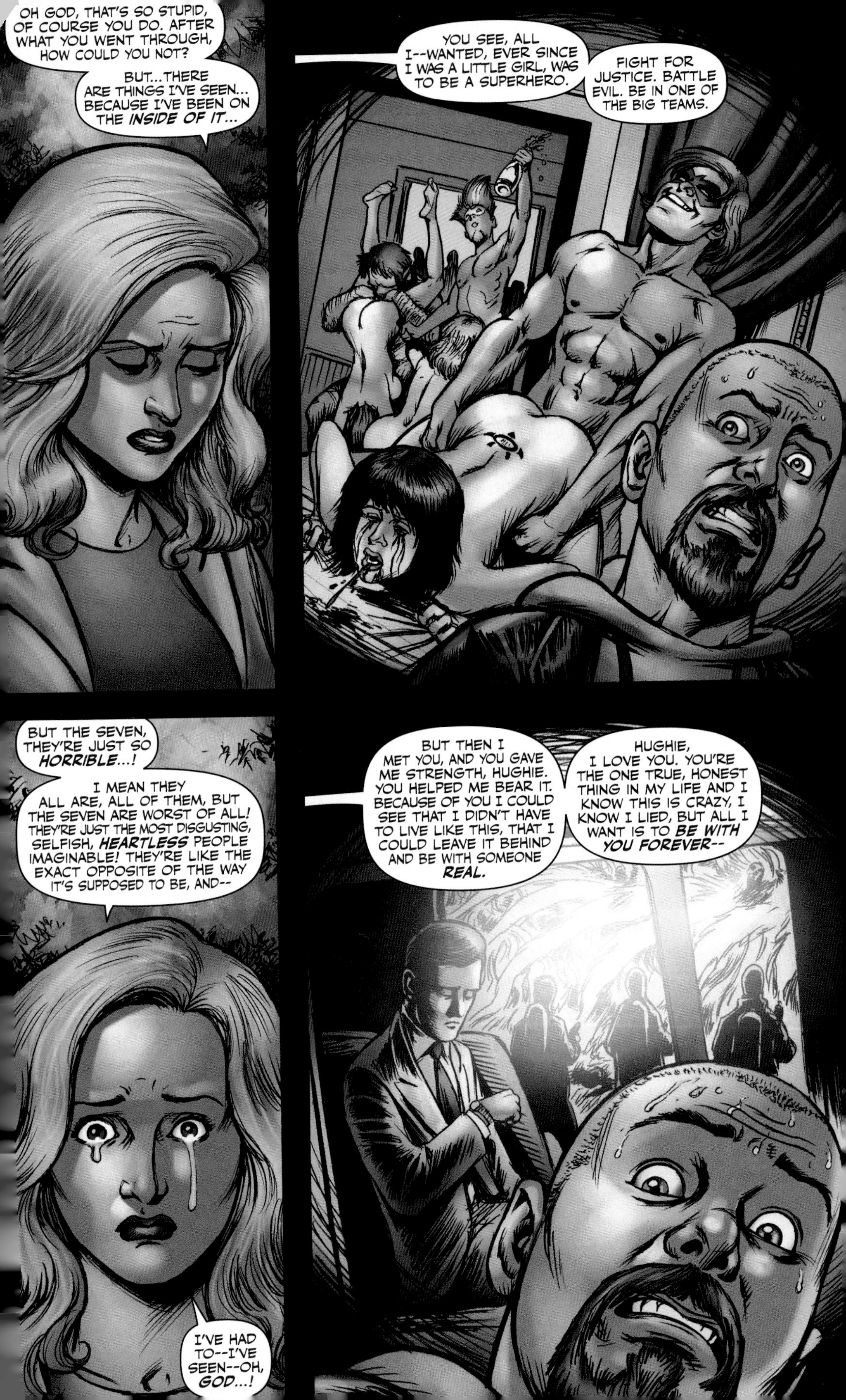
OH GOD, THAT'S SO STUPID, OF COURSE YOU DO. AFTER WHAT YOU WENT THROUGH, HOW COULD YOU NOT?
BUT...THERE ARE THINGS I'VE SEEN... BECAUSE I'VE BEEN ON THE *INSIDE OF IT*...
YOU SEE, ALL I--WANTED, EVER SINCE I WAS A LITTLE GIRL, WAS TO BE A SUPERHERO.
FIGHT FOR JUSTICE. BATTLE EVIL. BE IN ONE OF THE BIG TEAMS.
BUT THE SEVEN, THEY'RE JUST SO *HORRIBLE*...!
I MEAN THEY ALL ARE, ALL OF THEM, BUT THE SEVEN ARE WORST OF ALL! THEY'RE JUST THE MOST DISGUSTING, SELFISH, *HEARTLESS* PEOPLE IMAGINABLE! THEY'RE LIKE THE EXACT OPPOSITE OF THE WAY IT'S SUPPOSED TO BE, AND--
I'VE HAD TO--I'VE SEEN--OH, *GOD*...!
BUT THEN I MET YOU, AND YOU GAVE ME STRENGTH, HUGHIE. YOU HELPED ME BEAR IT. BECAUSE OF YOU I COULD SEE THAT I DIDN'T HAVE TO LIVE LIKE THIS, THAT I COULD LEAVE IT BEHIND AND BE WITH SOMEONE *REAL*.
HUGHIE, I LOVE YOU. YOU'RE THE ONE TRUE, HONEST THING IN MY LIFE AND I KNOW THIS IS CRAZY, I KNOW I LIED, BUT ALL I WANT IS TO *BE WITH YOU FOREVER*--

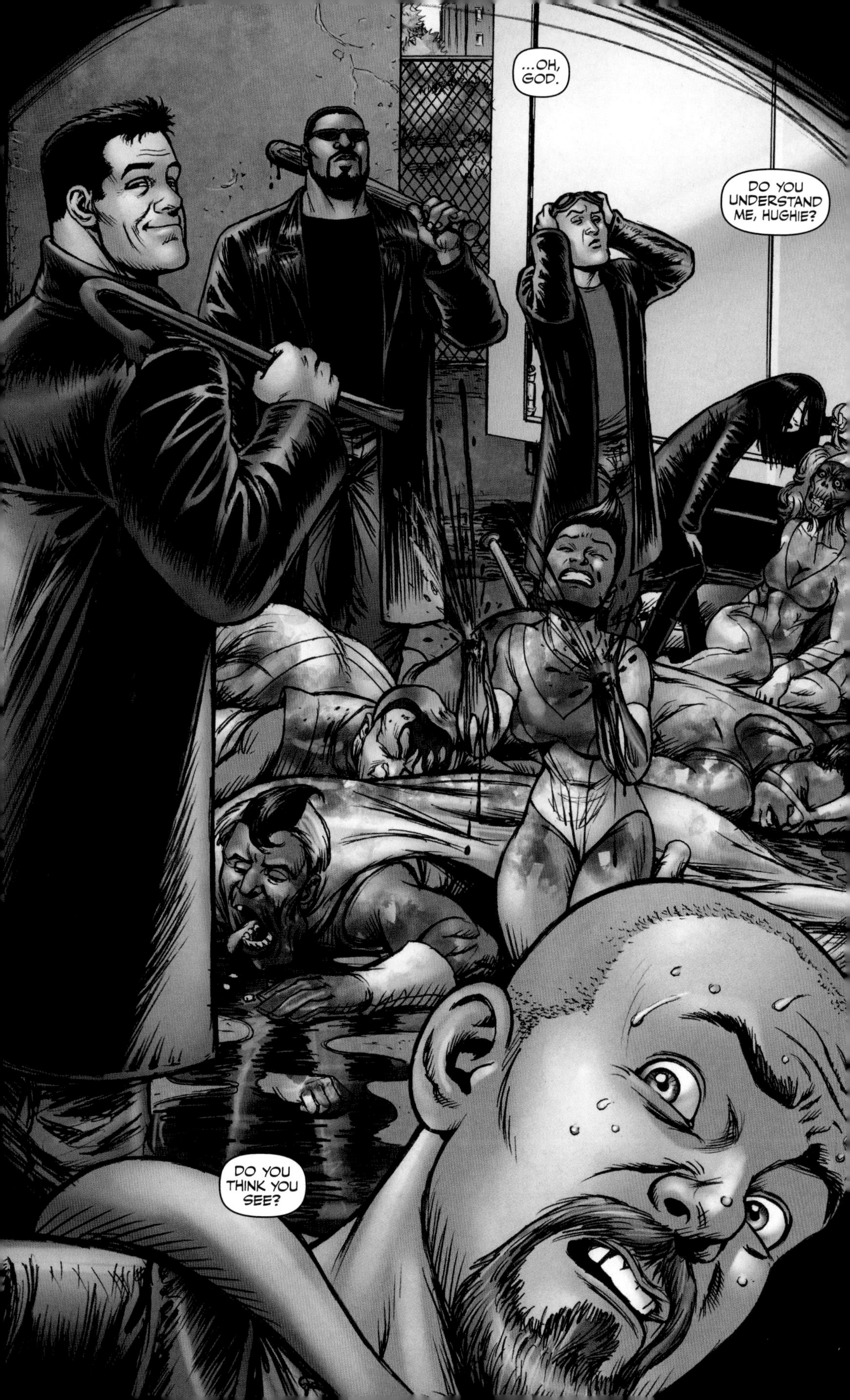
...OH, GOD.
DO YOU UNDERSTAND ME, HUGHIE?
DO YOU THINK YOU SEE?

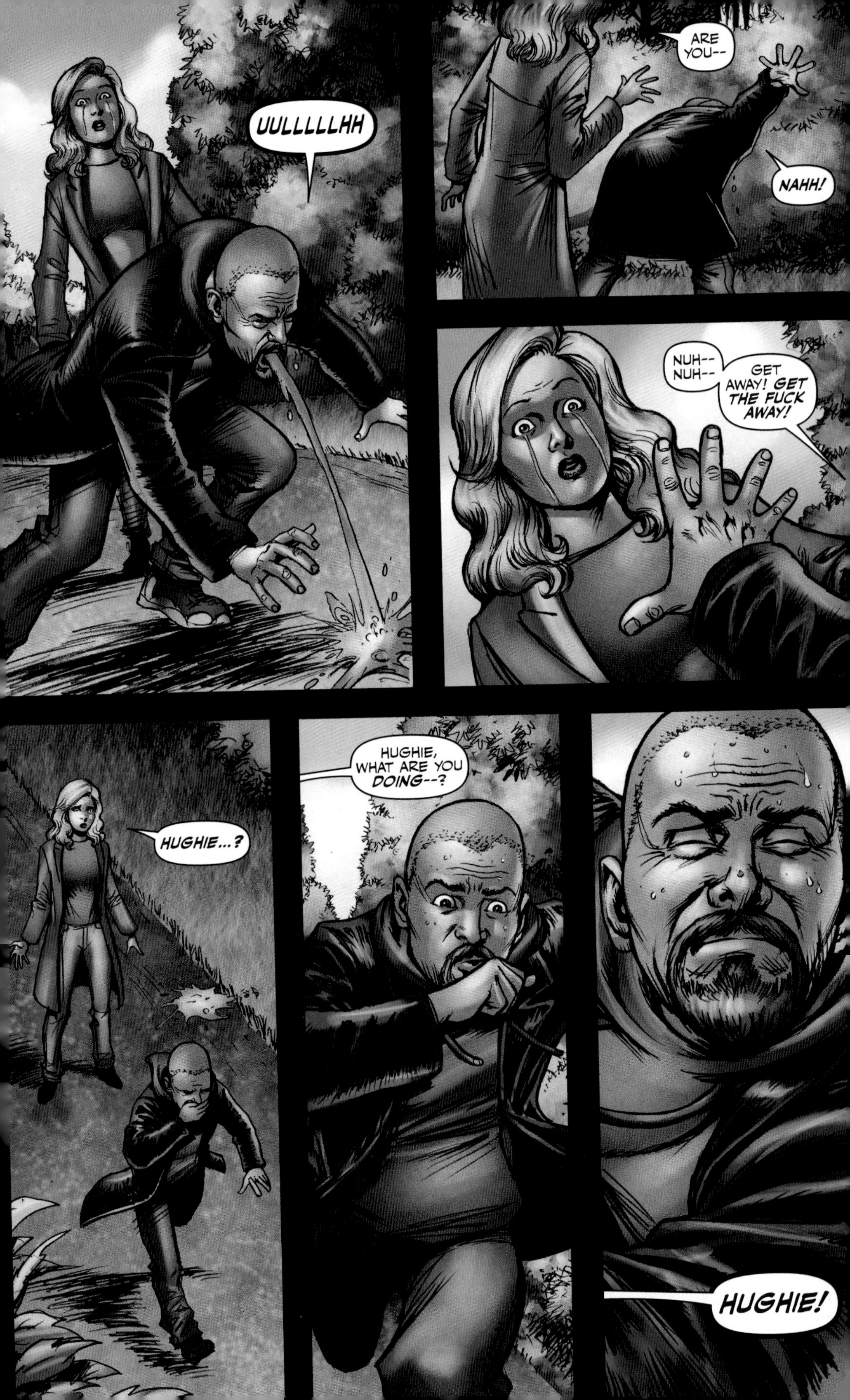
UULLLLLLH
ARE YOU--
NAHH!
NUH-- NUH--
GET AWAY! GET THE FUCK AWAY!
HUGHIE...?
HUGHIE, WHAT ARE YOU DOING--?
HUGHIE!

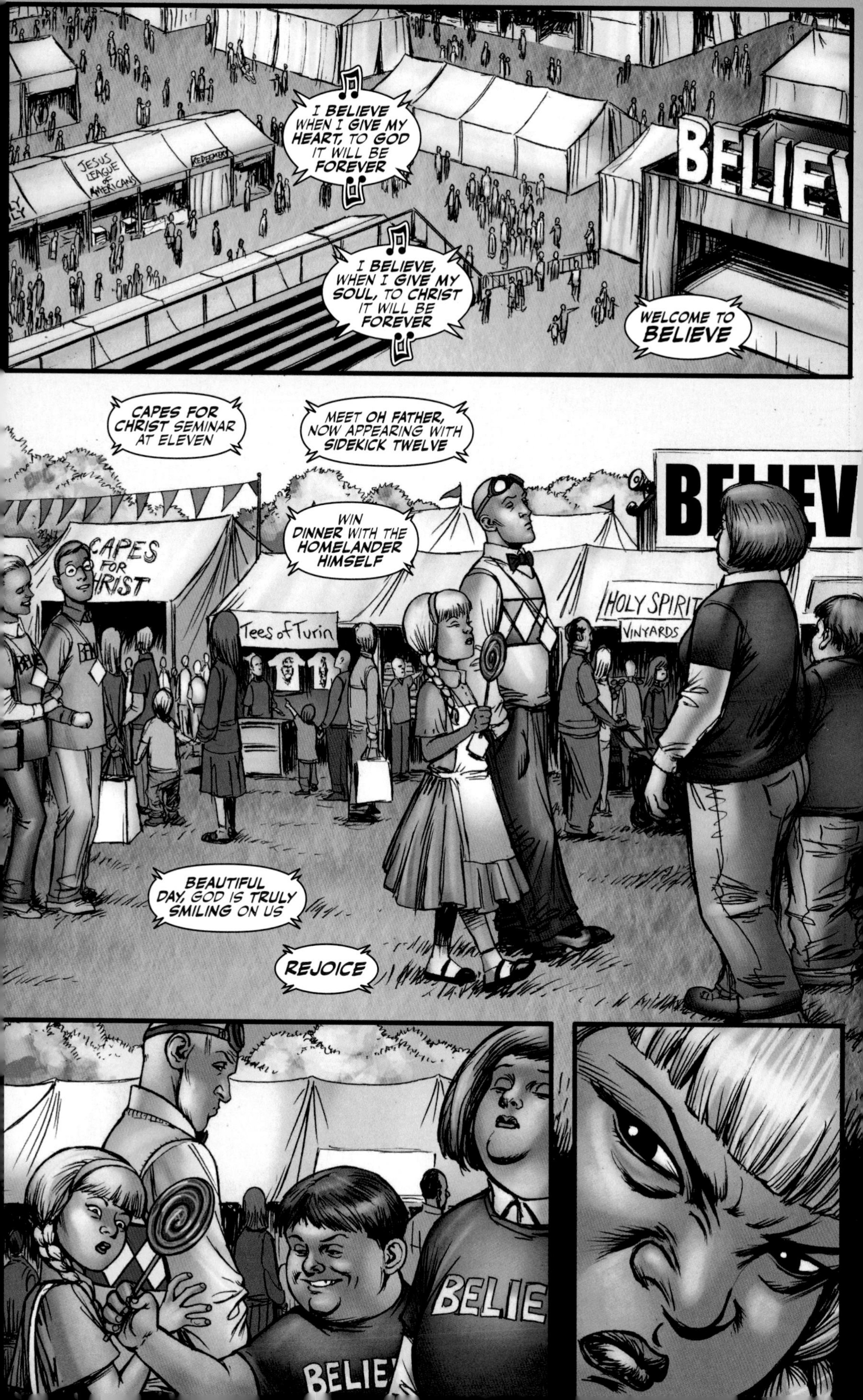
JESUS LEAGUE OF AMERICANS
REDEEMERS
I BELIEVE WHEN I GIVE MY HEART, TO GOD IT WILL BE FOREVER
I BELIEVE, WHEN I GIVE MY SOUL, TO CHRIST IT WILL BE FOREVER
WELCOME TO BELIEVE
CAPES FOR CHRIST SEMINAR AT ELEVEN
MEET OH FATHER, NOW APPEARING WITH SIDEKICK TWELVE
WIN DINNER WITH THE HOMELANDER HIMSELF
Tees of Turin
HOLY SPIRIT
VINYARDS
BEAUTIFUL DAY, GOD IS TRULY SMILING ON US
REJOICE

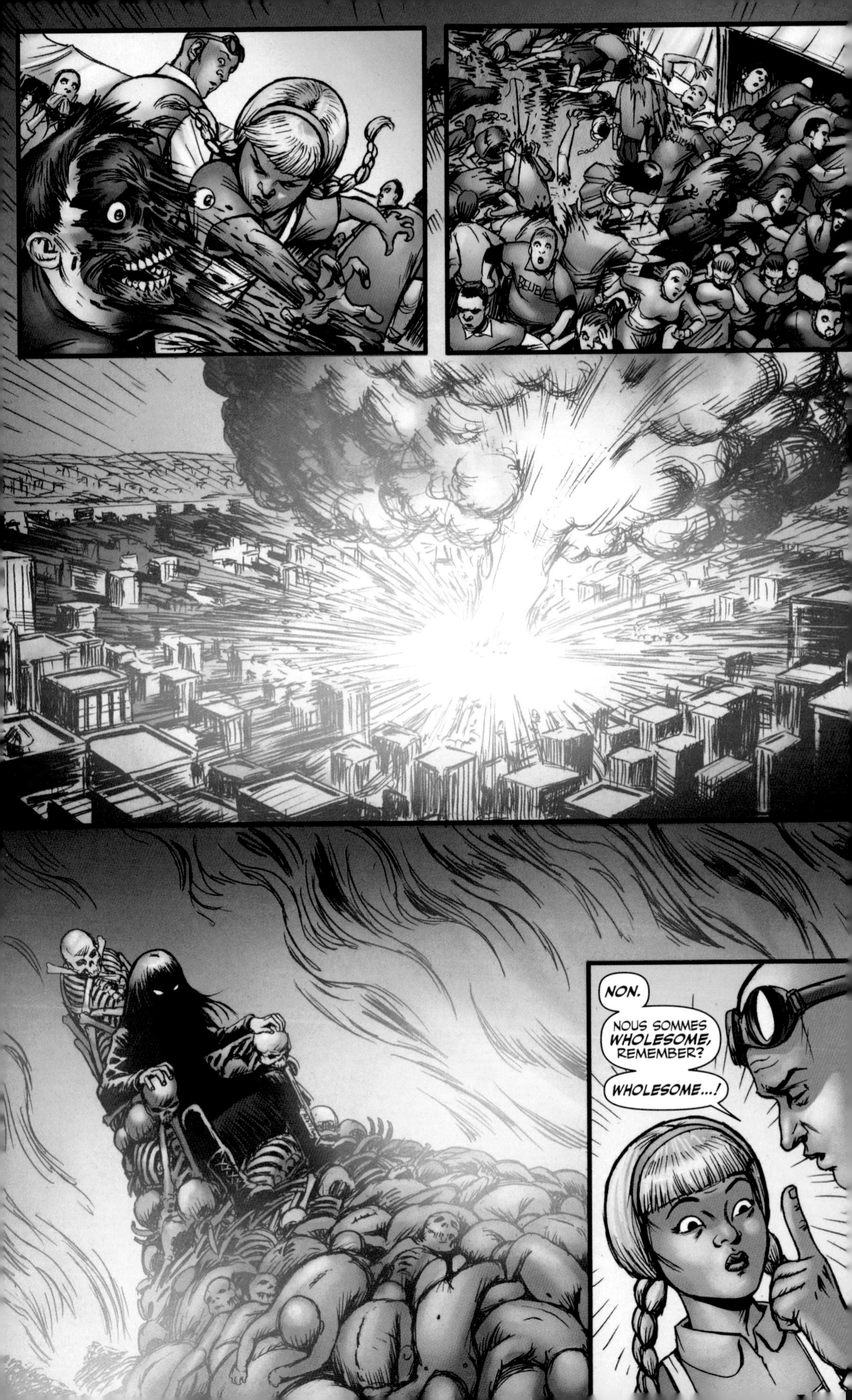
BELIEVE
NON.
NOUS SOMMES WHOLESOME, REMEMBER?
WHOLESOME...!

...MERDE.

CLAIREMENT, IF WE ARE TO REMAIN UNDERCOVER, *MEASURES* WILL HAVE TO BE TAKEN.

LITE UP MY LIFE

BELIEV

BELIEVE

ALL OF THEM?

OUI.

LIB

BELIEVE

BELIEVE

BELIEVE

BE

BEL

Sidekick Twelve

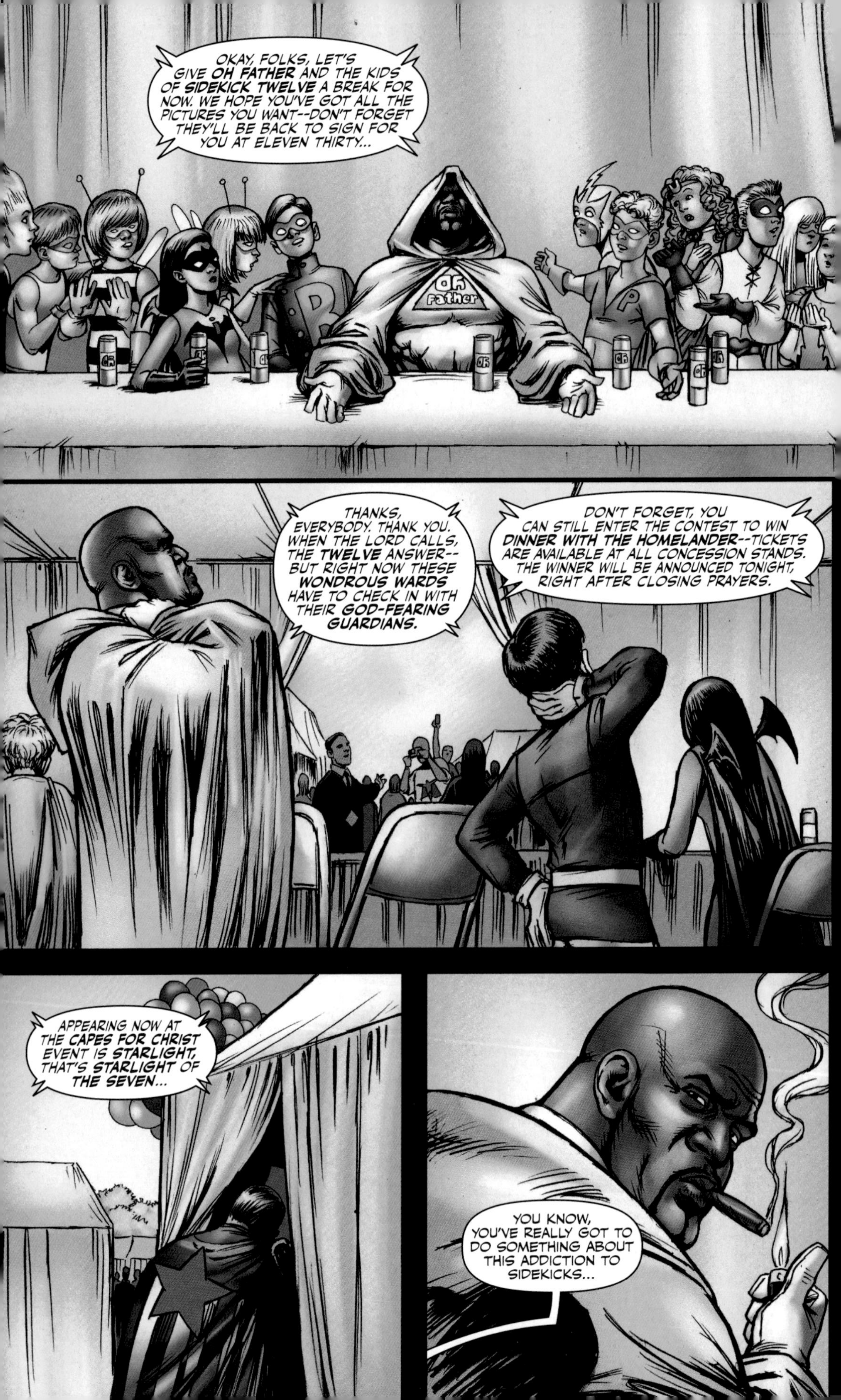
OKAY, FOLKS, LET'S GIVE **OH FATHER** AND THE KIDS OF **SIDEKICK TWELVE** A BREAK FOR NOW. WE HOPE YOU'VE GOT ALL THE PICTURES YOU WANT--DON'T FORGET THEY'LL BE BACK TO SIGN FOR YOU AT ELEVEN THIRTY...
THANKS, EVERYBODY. THANK YOU. WHEN THE LORD CALLS, THE **TWELVE** ANSWER-- BUT RIGHT NOW THESE **WONDROUS WARDS** HAVE TO CHECK IN WITH THEIR **GOD-FEARING GUARDIANS.**
DON'T FORGET, YOU CAN STILL ENTER THE CONTEST TO WIN **DINNER WITH THE HOMELANDER**--TICKETS ARE AVAILABLE AT ALL CONCESSION STANDS. THE WINNER WILL BE ANNOUNCED TONIGHT, RIGHT AFTER CLOSING PRAYERS.
APPEARING NOW AT THE **CAPES FOR CHRIST** EVENT IS **STARLIGHT,** THAT'S **STARLIGHT** OF **THE SEVEN...**
YOU KNOW, YOU'VE REALLY GOT TO DO SOMETHING ABOUT THIS ADDICTION TO SIDEKICKS...

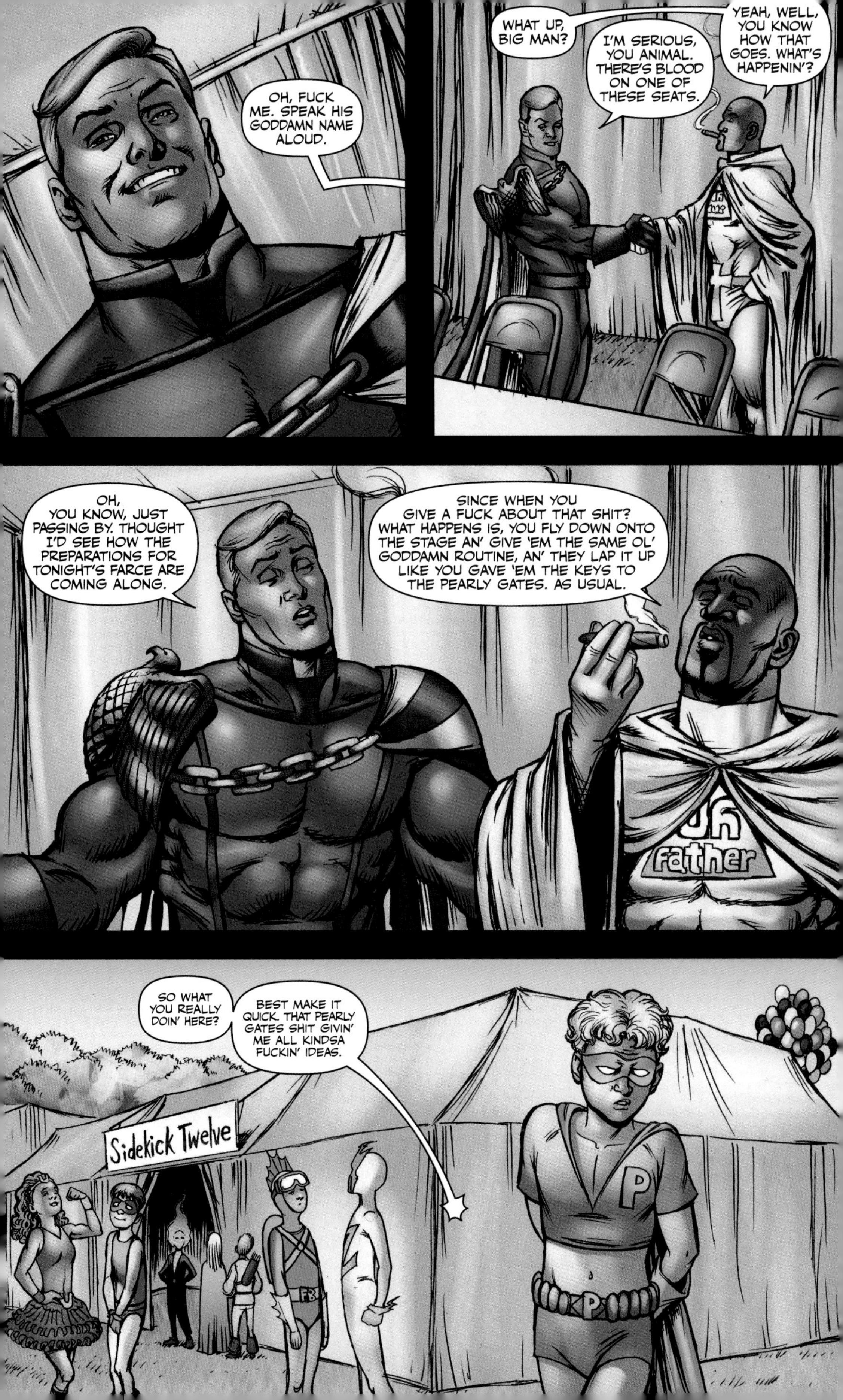
OH, FUCK ME. SPEAK HIS GODDAMN NAME ALOUD.
WHAT UP, BIG MAN?
YEAH, WELL, YOU KNOW HOW THAT GOES. WHAT'S HAPPENIN'?
I'M SERIOUS, YOU ANIMAL. THERE'S BLOOD ON ONE OF THESE SEATS.
OH, YOU KNOW, JUST PASSING BY. THOUGHT I'D SEE HOW THE PREPARATIONS FOR TONIGHT'S FARCE ARE COMING ALONG.
SINCE WHEN YOU GIVE A FUCK ABOUT THAT SHIT? WHAT HAPPENS IS, YOU FLY DOWN ONTO THE STAGE AN' GIVE 'EM THE SAME OL' GODDAMN ROUTINE, AN' THEY LAP IT UP LIKE YOU GAVE 'EM THE KEYS TO THE PEARLY GATES. AS USUAL.
Father
SO WHAT YOU REALLY DOIN' HERE?
BEST MAKE IT QUICK. THAT PEARLY GATES SHIT GIVIN' ME ALL KINDSA FUCKIN' IDEAS.
Sidekick Twelve

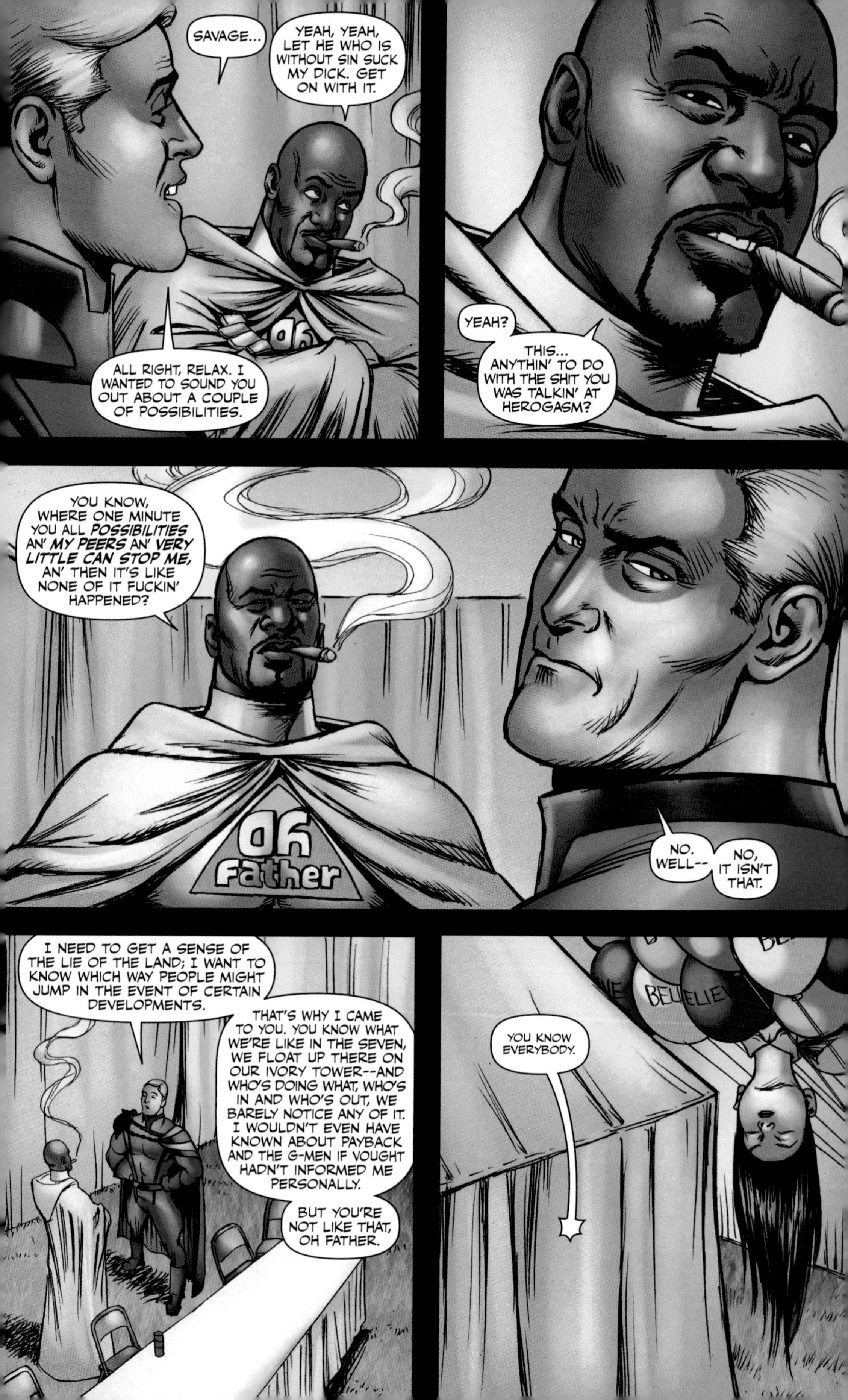
SAVAGE...
YEAH, YEAH, LET HE WHO IS WITHOUT SIN SUCK MY DICK. GET ON WITH IT.
ALL RIGHT, RELAX. I WANTED TO SOUND YOU OUT ABOUT A COUPLE OF POSSIBILITIES.
YEAH?
THIS... ANYTHIN' TO DO WITH THE SHIT YOU WAS TALKIN' AT HEROGASM?
YOU KNOW, WHERE ONE MINUTE YOU ALL POSSIBILITIES AN' MY PEERS AN' VERY LITTLE CAN STOP ME, AN' THEN IT'S LIKE NONE OF IT FUCKIN' HAPPENED?
OF Father
NO. WELL--
NO, IT ISN'T THAT.
I NEED TO GET A SENSE OF THE LIE OF THE LAND; I WANT TO KNOW WHICH WAY PEOPLE MIGHT JUMP IN THE EVENT OF CERTAIN DEVELOPMENTS.
THAT'S WHY I CAME TO YOU. YOU KNOW WHAT WE'RE LIKE IN THE SEVEN, WE FLOAT UP THERE ON OUR IVORY TOWER--AND WHO'S DOING WHAT, WHO'S IN AND WHO'S OUT, WE BARELY NOTICE ANY OF IT. I WOULDN'T EVEN HAVE KNOWN ABOUT PAYBACK AND THE G-MEN IF VOUGHT HADN'T INFORMED ME PERSONALLY.
BUT YOU'RE NOT LIKE THAT, OH FATHER.
YOU KNOW EVERYBODY.

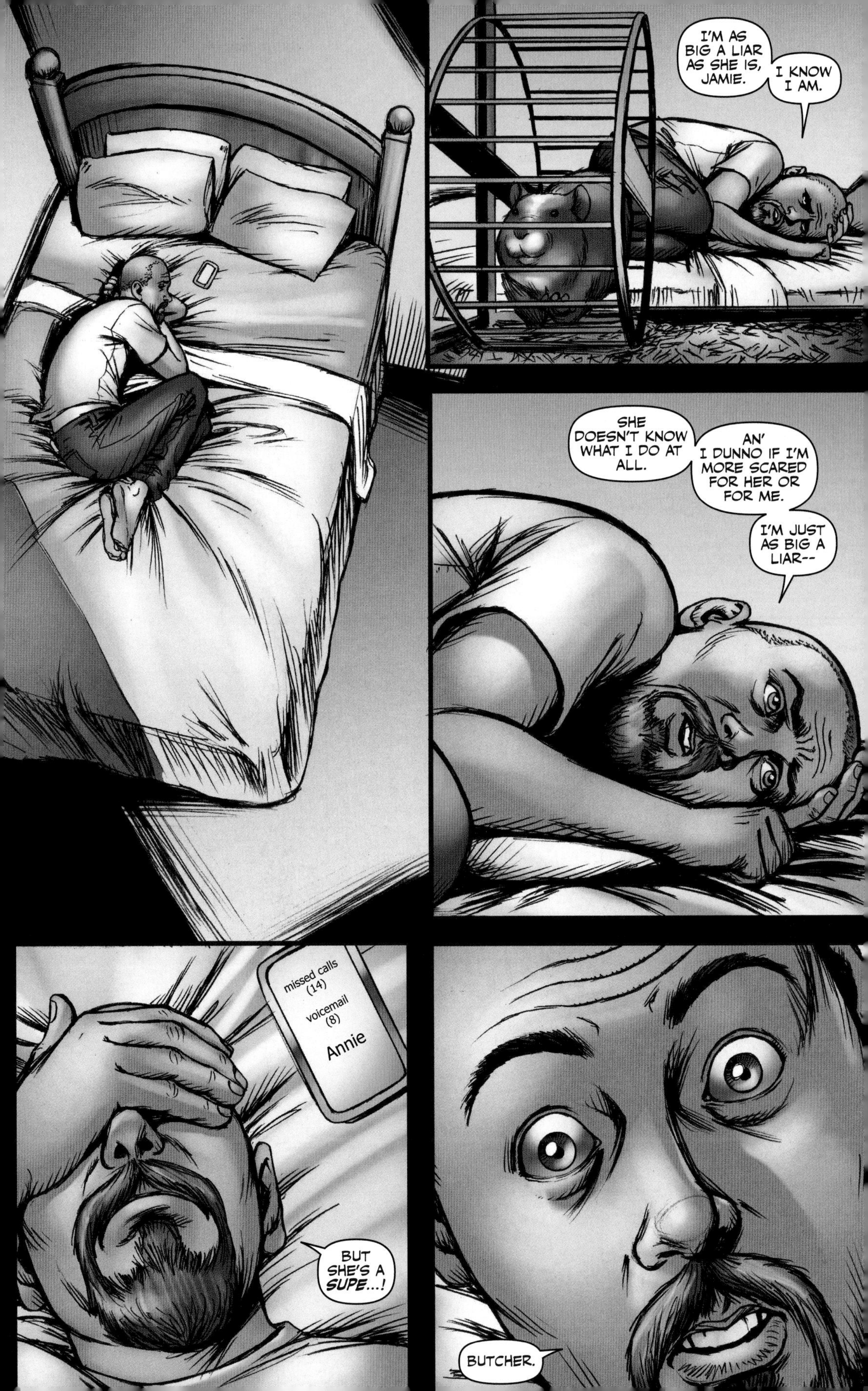
I'M AS BIG A LIAR AS SHE IS, JAMIE.
I KNOW I AM.
SHE DOESN'T KNOW WHAT I DO AT ALL.
AN' I DUNNO IF I'M MORE SCARED FOR HER OR FOR ME.
I'M JUST AS BIG A LIAR--
missed calls (14)
voicemail (8)
Annie
BUT SHE'S A *SUPE*...!
BUTCHER.

...ANNIE, PICK UP, JUST PICK UP--OR CALL ME, ALL RIGHT? CALL ME AS SOON AS YOU GET THIS!

OH FUCK, WHERE *ARE* YOU...?

SORRY, MISTER POTAMUS! CAN'T STOP!

UH-HUH.

CHOCOLATE FIS

TAXI--!

AMERICAN DOUCHE BAG

RB67

FUCK!

AW, *FUCK*...!

RB67

JF29

ALL RIGHT, MATE?

AAAAAAHH!

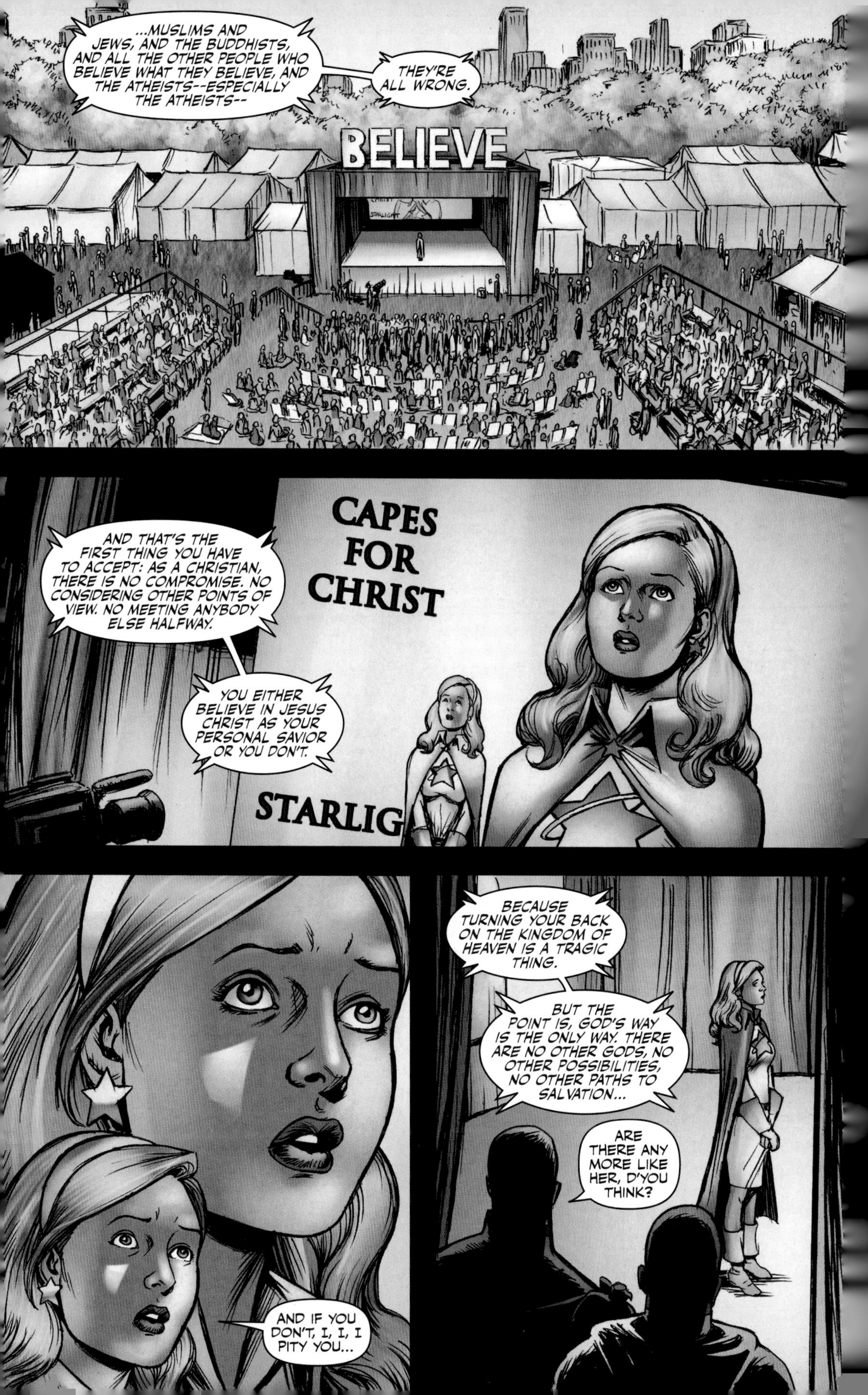
...MUSLIMS AND JEWS, AND THE BUDDHISTS, AND ALL THE OTHER PEOPLE WHO BELIEVE WHAT THEY BELIEVE, AND THE ATHEISTS--ESPECIALLY THE ATHEISTS--
THEY'RE ALL WRONG.
BELIEVE
AND THAT'S THE FIRST THING YOU HAVE TO ACCEPT: AS A CHRISTIAN, THERE IS NO COMPROMISE. NO CONSIDERING OTHER POINTS OF VIEW. NO MEETING ANYBODY ELSE HALFWAY.
CAPES FOR CHRIST
YOU EITHER BELIEVE IN JESUS CHRIST AS YOUR PERSONAL SAVIOR OR YOU DON'T.
STARLIG
AND IF YOU DON'T, I, I, I PITY YOU...
BECAUSE TURNING YOUR BACK ON THE KINGDOM OF HEAVEN IS A TRAGIC THING.
BUT THE POINT IS, GOD'S WAY IS THE ONLY WAY. THERE ARE NO OTHER GODS, NO OTHER POSSIBILITIES, NO OTHER PATHS TO SALVATION...
ARE THERE ANY MORE LIKE HER, D'YOU THINK?

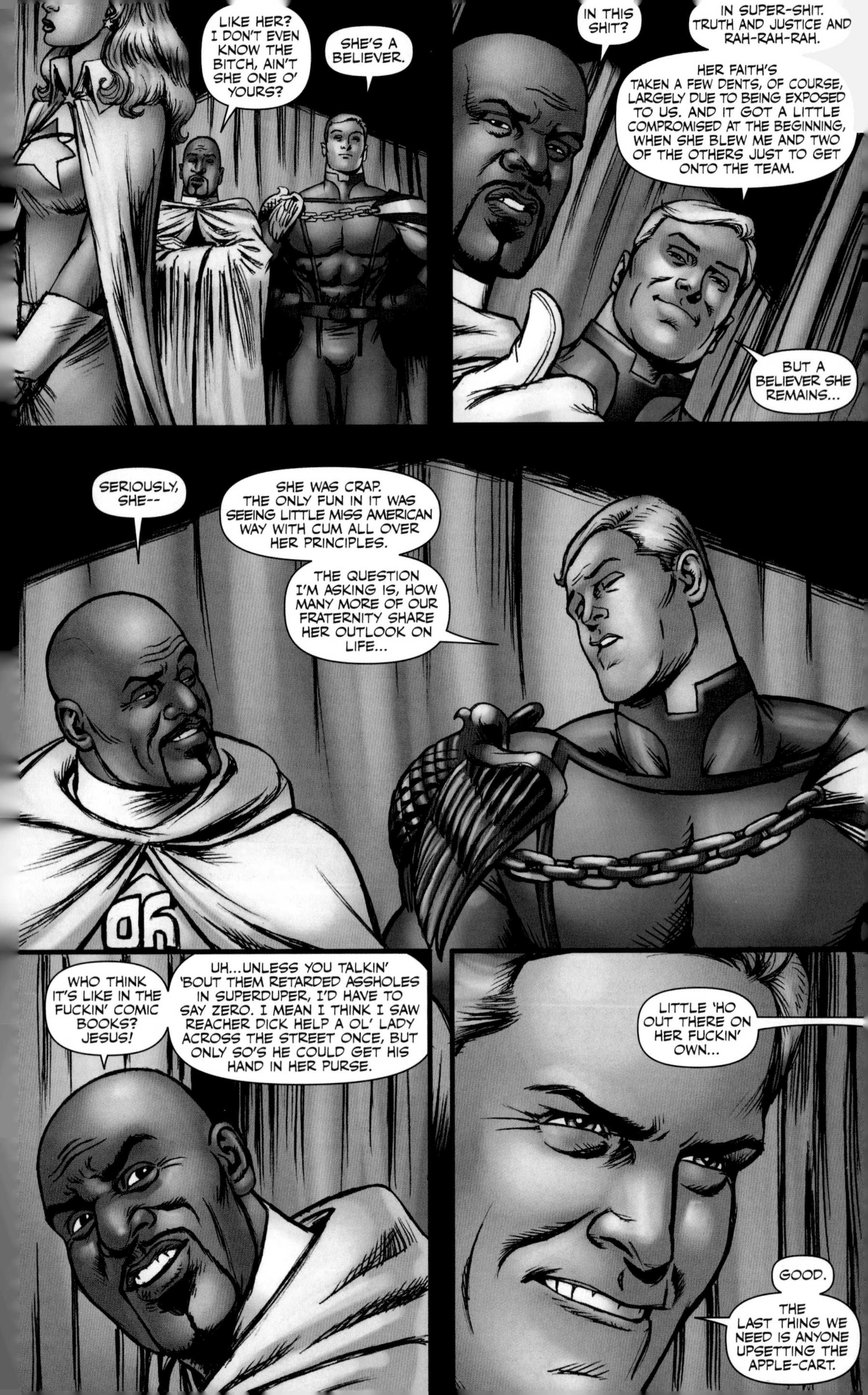
LIKE HER? I DON'T EVEN KNOW THE BITCH, AIN'T SHE ONE O' YOURS?
SHE'S A BELIEVER.
IN THIS SHIT?
IN SUPER-SHIT. TRUTH AND JUSTICE AND RAH-RAH-RAH.
HER FAITH'S TAKEN A FEW DENTS, OF COURSE, LARGELY DUE TO BEING EXPOSED TO US. AND IT GOT A LITTLE COMPROMISED AT THE BEGINNING, WHEN SHE BLEW ME AND TWO OF THE OTHERS JUST TO GET ONTO THE TEAM.
BUT A BELIEVER SHE REMAINS...
SERIOUSLY, SHE--
SHE WAS CRAP. THE ONLY FUN IN IT WAS SEEING LITTLE MISS AMERICAN WAY WITH CUM ALL OVER HER PRINCIPLES.
THE QUESTION I'M ASKING IS, HOW MANY MORE OF OUR FRATERNITY SHARE HER OUTLOOK ON LIFE...
WHO THINK IT'S LIKE IN THE FUCKIN' COMIC BOOKS? JESUS!
UH...UNLESS YOU TALKIN' 'BOUT THEM RETARDED ASSHOLES IN SUPERDUPER, I'D HAVE TO SAY ZERO. I MEAN I THINK I SAW REACHER DICK HELP A OL' LADY ACROSS THE STREET ONCE, BUT ONLY SO'S HE COULD GET HIS HAND IN HER PURSE.
LITTLE 'HO OUT THERE ON HER FUCKIN' OWN...
GOOD.
THE LAST THING WE NEED IS ANYONE UPSETTING THE APPLE-CART.

YOU KNOW HOW VOUGHT ARE PUSHING THIS AGENDA OF THEIRS, THIS SUPERPOWER FOR NATIONAL DEFENSE THING?

OH FUCK, AIN'T THEY GIVEN UP ON THAT YET? SHIT AIN'T NEVER GONNA WORK, A GODDAMN BLIND MAN CAN SEE IT...

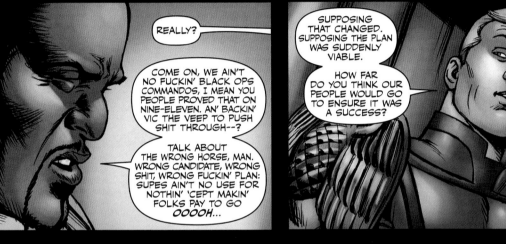

REALLY?

COME ON, WE AIN'T NO FUCKIN' BLACK OPS COMMANDOS, I MEAN YOU PEOPLE PROVED THAT ON NINE-ELEVEN. AN' BACKIN' VIC THE VEEP TO PUSH SHIT THROUGH--?

TALK ABOUT THE WRONG HORSE, MAN. WRONG CANDIDATE, WRONG SHIT, WRONG FUCKIN' PLAN: SUPES AIN'T NO USE FOR NOTHIN' 'CEPT MAKIN' FOLKS PAY TO GO *OOOOH*...

SUPPOSING THAT CHANGED. SUPPOSING THE PLAN WAS SUDDENLY VIABLE.

HOW FAR DO YOU THINK OUR PEOPLE WOULD GO TO ENSURE IT WAS A SUCCESS?

YOU MEAN HOW THEY GONNA FEEL ABOUT GETTIN' FUCKIN' DRAFTED?

NO: ABOUT GETTING THE PLAN ITSELF IMPLEMENTED.

IF VOUGHT WANTED THEIR HELP IN FORCING THE ISSUE.

YOU TALKIN' 'BOUT... WHAT I THINK YOU TALKIN' 'BOUT...?

GIVING VIC WHATEVER SUPPORT HE NEEDS IN WHATEVER CIRCUMSTANCES ARISE.

IF IT REALLY COMES TO IT.

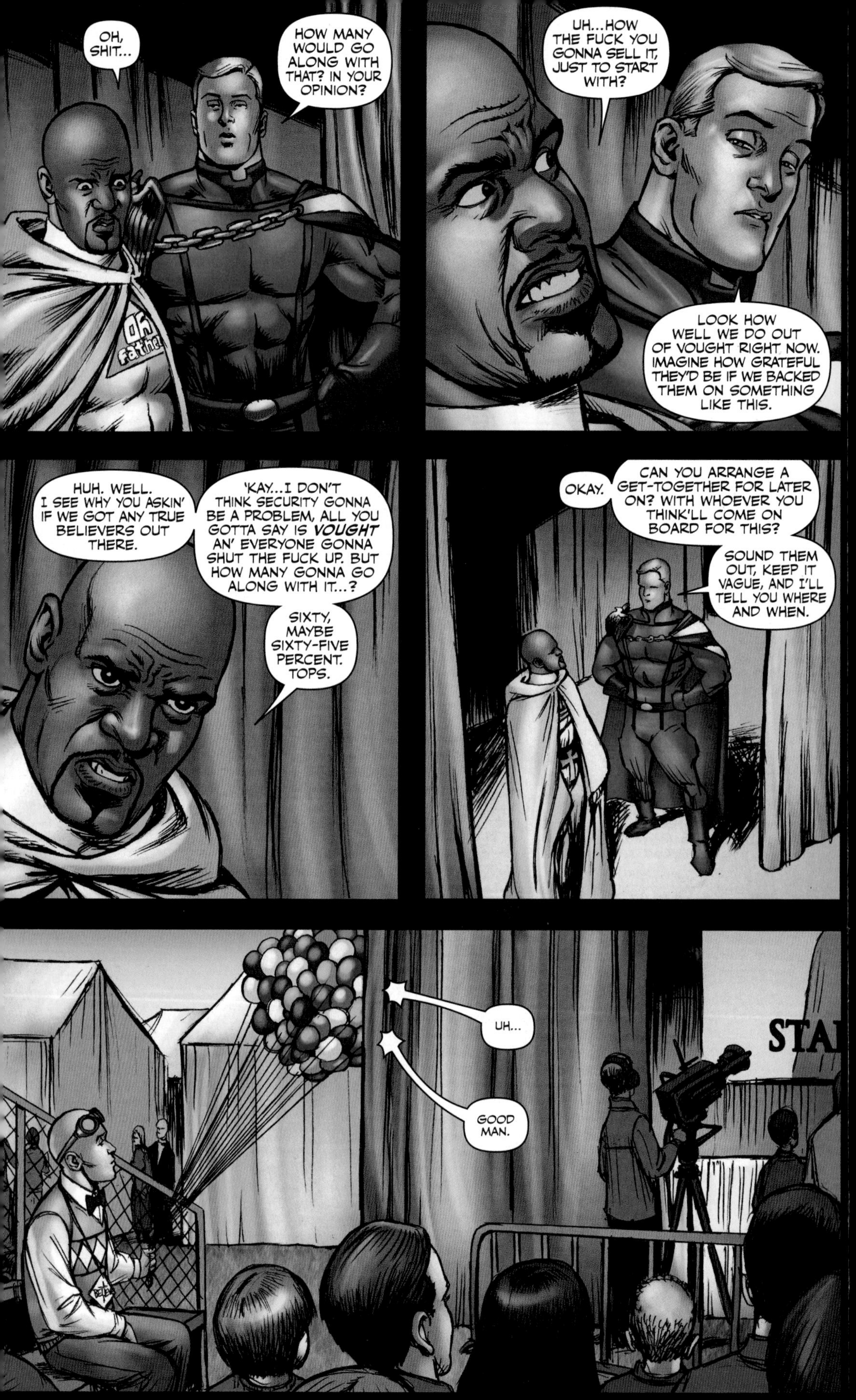
OH, SHIT...
HOW MANY WOULD GO ALONG WITH THAT? IN YOUR OPINION?
UH...HOW THE FUCK YOU GONNA SELL IT, JUST TO START WITH?
LOOK HOW WELL WE DO OUT OF VOUGHT RIGHT NOW. IMAGINE HOW GRATEFUL THEY'D BE IF WE BACKED THEM ON SOMETHING LIKE THIS.
HUH. WELL. I SEE WHY YOU ASKIN' IF WE GOT ANY TRUE BELIEVERS OUT THERE.
'KAY...I DON'T THINK SECURITY GONNA BE A PROBLEM, ALL YOU GOTTA SAY IS *VOUGHT* AN' EVERYONE GONNA SHUT THE FUCK UP. BUT HOW MANY GONNA GO ALONG WITH IT...?
SIXTY, MAYBE SIXTY-FIVE PERCENT. TOPS.
OKAY.
CAN YOU ARRANGE A GET-TOGETHER FOR LATER ON? WITH WHOEVER YOU THINK'LL COME ON BOARD FOR THIS?
SOUND THEM OUT, KEEP IT VAGUE, AND I'LL TELL YOU WHERE AND WHEN.
UH...
GOOD MAN.
STA

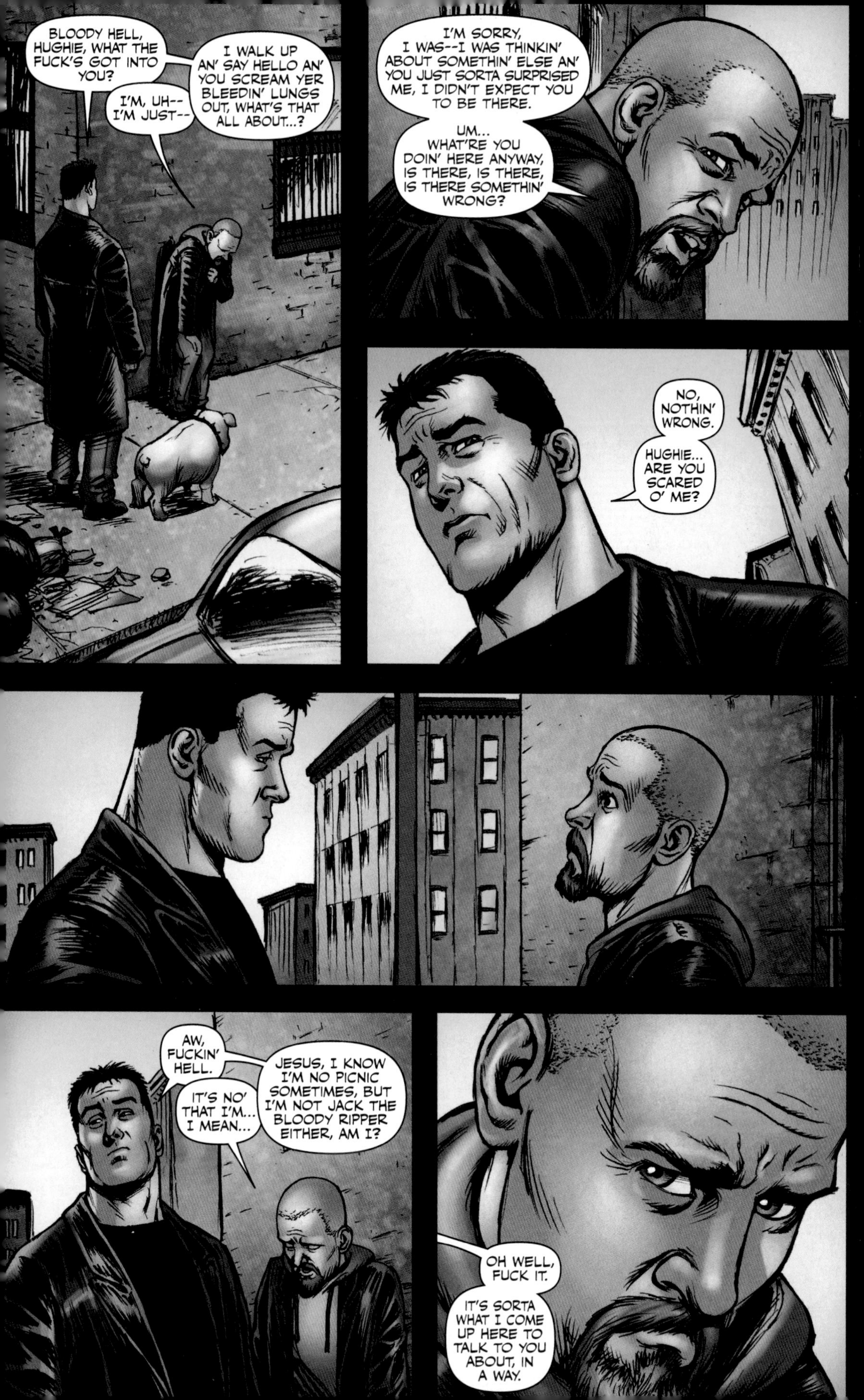
BLOODY HELL, HUGHIE, WHAT THE FUCK'S GOT INTO YOU?
I WALK UP AN' SAY HELLO AN' YOU SCREAM YER BLEEDIN' LUNGS OUT, WHAT'S THAT ALL ABOUT...?
I'M, UH-- I'M JUST--
I'M SORRY, I WAS--I WAS THINKIN' ABOUT SOMETHIN' ELSE AN' YOU JUST SORTA SURPRISED ME, I DIDN'T EXPECT YOU TO BE THERE.
UM... WHAT'RE YOU DOIN' HERE ANYWAY, IS THERE, IS THERE, IS THERE SOMETHIN' WRONG?
NO, NOTHIN' WRONG.
HUGHIE... ARE YOU SCARED O' ME?
AW, FUCKIN' HELL.
JESUS, I KNOW I'M NO PICNIC SOMETIMES, BUT I'M NOT JACK THE BLOODY RIPPER EITHER, AM I?
IT'S NO' THAT I'M... I MEAN...
OH WELL, FUCK IT.
IT'S SORTA WHAT I COME UP HERE TO TALK TO YOU ABOUT, IN A WAY.

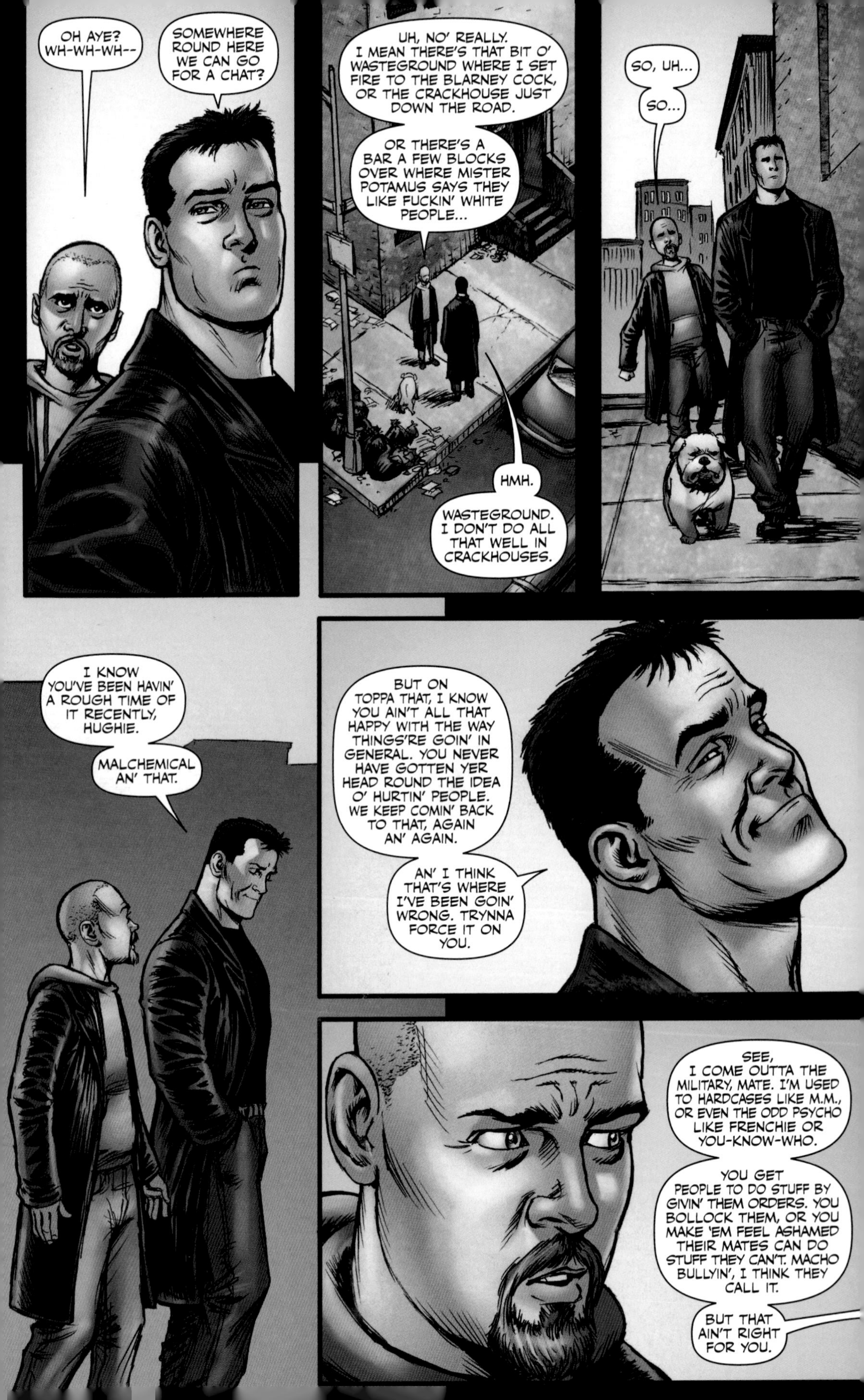
SOMEWHERE ROUND HERE WE CAN GO FOR A CHAT?
OH AYE? WH-WH-WH--
UH, NO' REALLY. I MEAN THERE'S THAT BIT O' WASTEGROUND WHERE I SET FIRE TO THE BLARNEY COCK, OR THE CRACKHOUSE JUST DOWN THE ROAD.
OR THERE'S A BAR A FEW BLOCKS OVER WHERE MISTER POTAMUS SAYS THEY LIKE FUCKIN' WHITE PEOPLE...
HMH.
WASTEGROUND. I DON'T DO ALL THAT WELL IN CRACKHOUSES.
SO, UH...
SO...
I KNOW YOU'VE BEEN HAVIN' A ROUGH TIME OF IT RECENTLY, HUGHIE.
MALCHEMICAL AN' THAT.
BUT ON TOPPA THAT, I KNOW YOU AIN'T ALL THAT HAPPY WITH THE WAY THINGS'RE GOIN' IN GENERAL. YOU NEVER HAVE GOTTEN YER HEAD ROUND THE IDEA O' HURTIN' PEOPLE. WE KEEP COMIN' BACK TO THAT, AGAIN AN' AGAIN.
AN' I THINK THAT'S WHERE I'VE BEEN GOIN' WRONG. TRYNNA FORCE IT ON YOU.
SEE, I COME OUTTA THE MILITARY, MATE. I'M USED TO HARDCASES LIKE M.M., OR EVEN THE ODD PSYCHO LIKE FRENCHIE OR YOU-KNOW-WHO.
YOU GET PEOPLE TO DO STUFF BY GIVIN' THEM ORDERS. YOU BOLLOCK THEM, OR YOU MAKE 'EM FEEL ASHAMED THEIR MATES CAN DO STUFF THEY CAN'T. MACHO BULLYIN', I THINK THEY CALL IT.
BUT THAT AIN'T RIGHT FOR YOU.

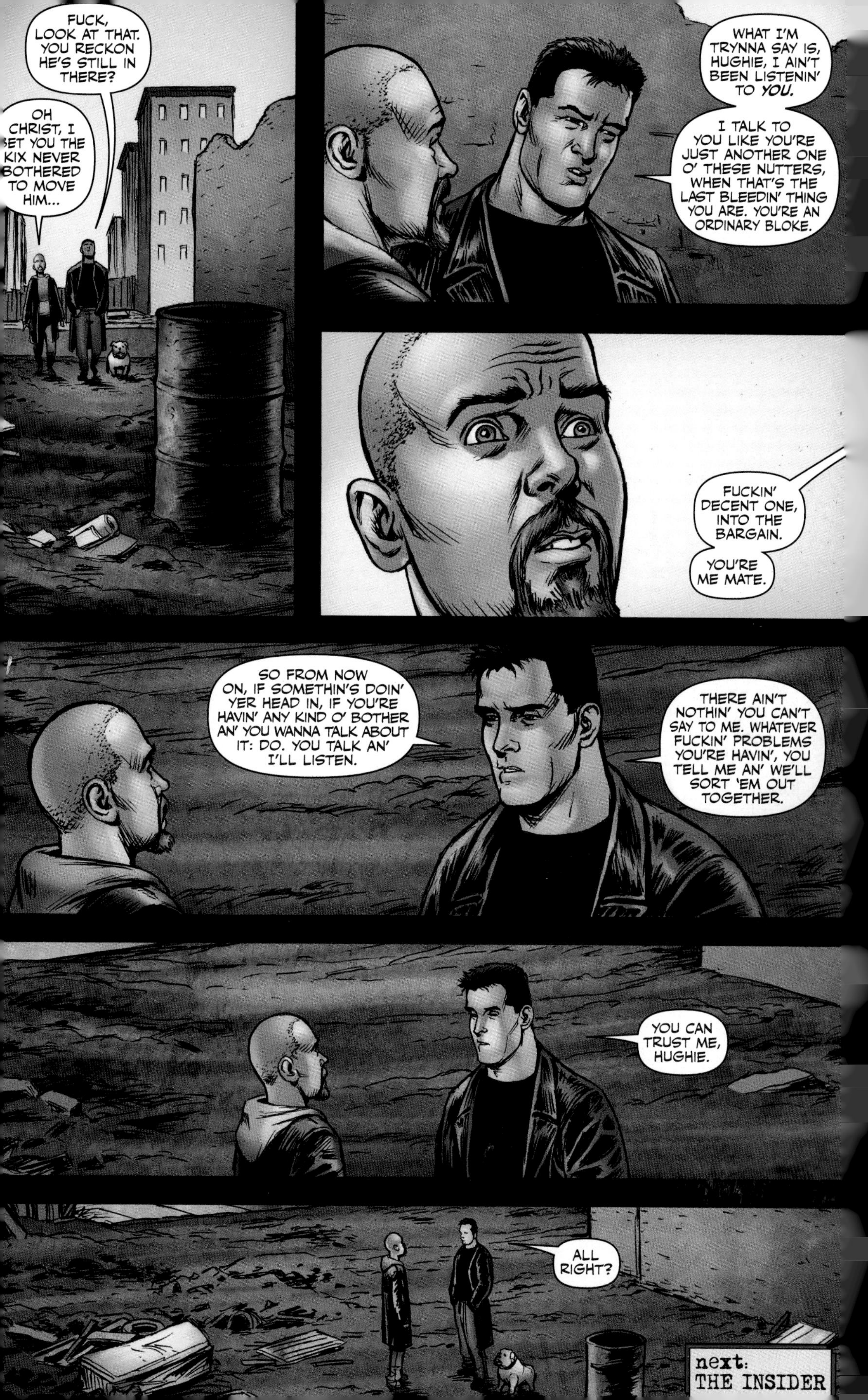
FUCK, LOOK AT THAT. YOU RECKON HE'S STILL IN THERE?
OH CHRIST, I BET YOU THE KIX NEVER BOTHERED TO MOVE HIM...
WHAT I'M TRYNNA SAY IS, HUGHIE, I AIN'T BEEN LISTENIN' TO YOU.
I TALK TO YOU LIKE YOU'RE JUST ANOTHER ONE O' THESE NUTTERS, WHEN THAT'S THE LAST BLEEDIN' THING YOU ARE. YOU'RE AN ORDINARY BLOKE.
FUCKIN' DECENT ONE, INTO THE BARGAIN.
YOU'RE ME MATE.
SO FROM NOW ON, IF SOMETHIN'S DOIN' YER HEAD IN, IF YOU'RE HAVIN' ANY KIND O' BOTHER AN' YOU WANNA TALK ABOUT IT: DO. YOU TALK AN' I'LL LISTEN.
THERE AIN'T NOTHIN' YOU CAN'T SAY TO ME. WHATEVER FUCKIN' PROBLEMS YOU'RE HAVIN', YOU TELL ME AN' WE'LL SORT 'EM OUT TOGETHER.
YOU CAN TRUST ME, HUGHIE.
ALL RIGHT?
next: THE INSIDER

#46 cover
by Darick Robertson
and Tony Aviña

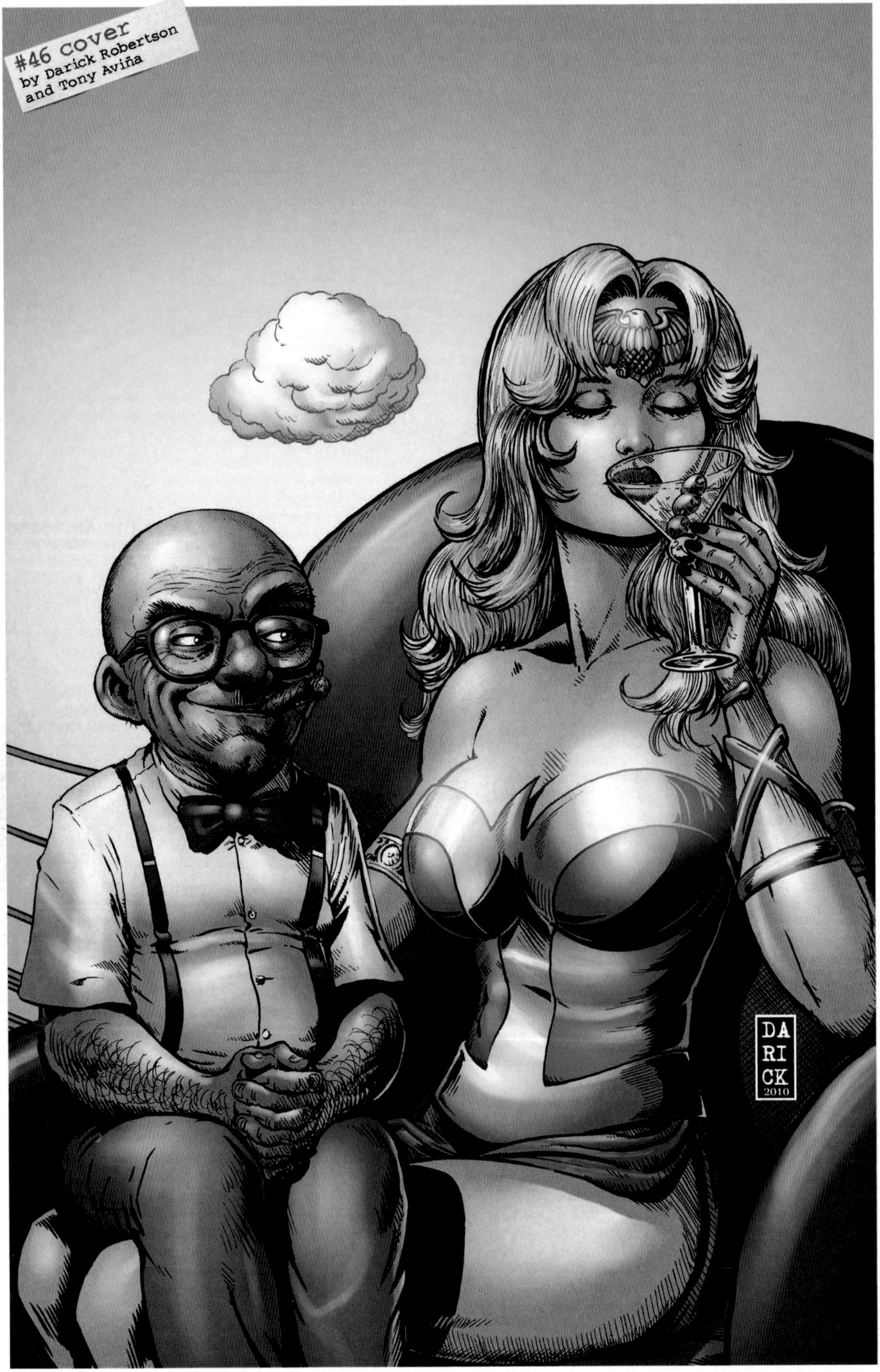
DARICK
2010

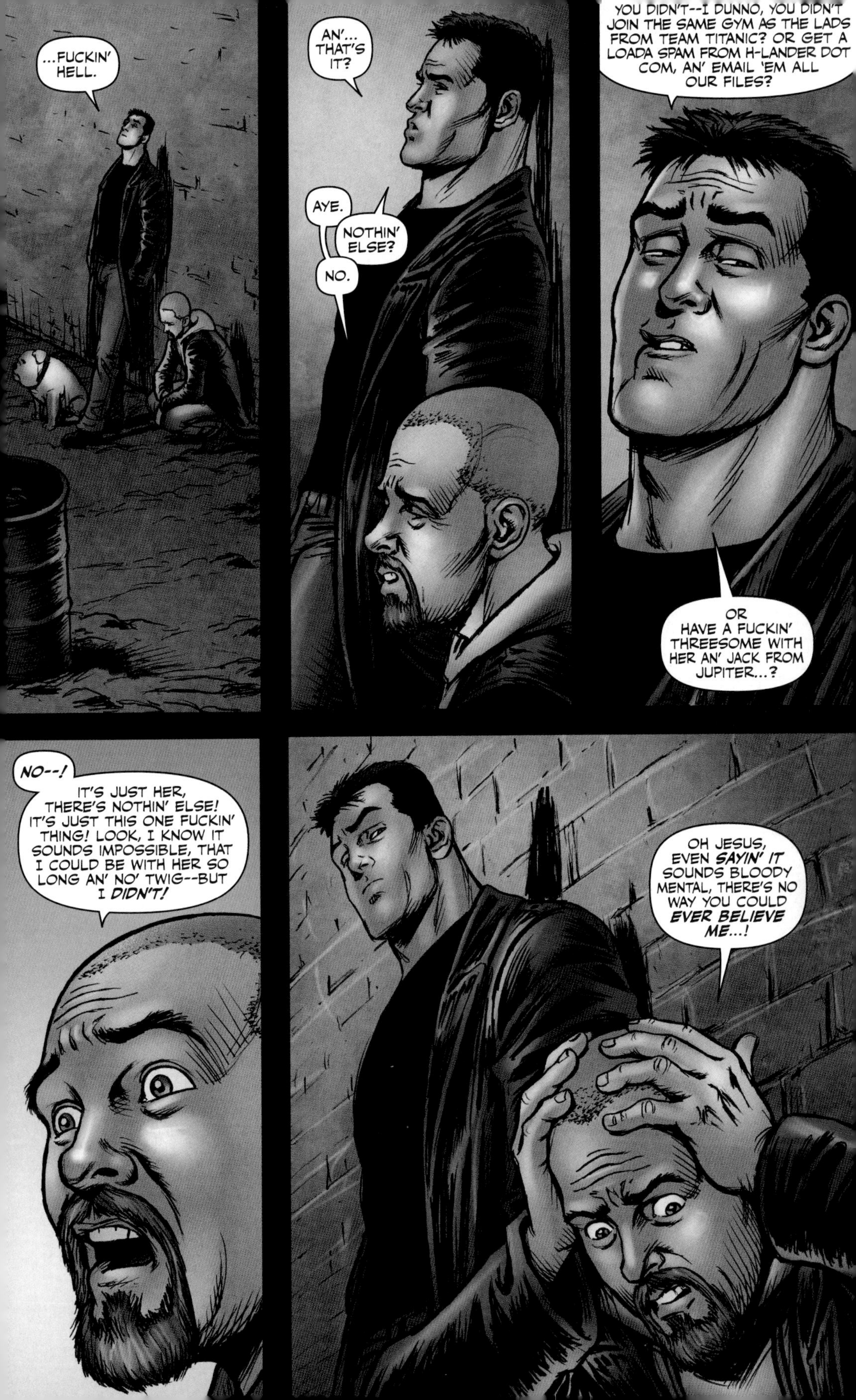
...FUCKIN' HELL.
AN'... THAT'S IT?
AYE.
NOTHIN' ELSE?
NO.
YOU DIDN'T--I DUNNO, YOU DIDN'T JOIN THE SAME GYM AS THE LADS FROM TEAM TITANIC? OR GET A LOADA SPAM FROM H-LANDER DOT COM, AN' EMAIL 'EM ALL OUR FILES?
OR HAVE A FUCKIN' THREESOME WITH HER AN' JACK FROM JUPITER...?
NO--!
IT'S JUST HER, THERE'S NOTHIN' ELSE! IT'S JUST THIS ONE FUCKIN' THING! LOOK, I KNOW IT SOUNDS IMPOSSIBLE, THAT I COULD BE WITH HER SO LONG AN' NO' TWIG--BUT I *DIDN'T!*
OH JESUS, EVEN *SAYIN' IT* SOUNDS BLOODY MENTAL, THERE'S NO WAY YOU COULD *EVER BELIEVE ME...!*

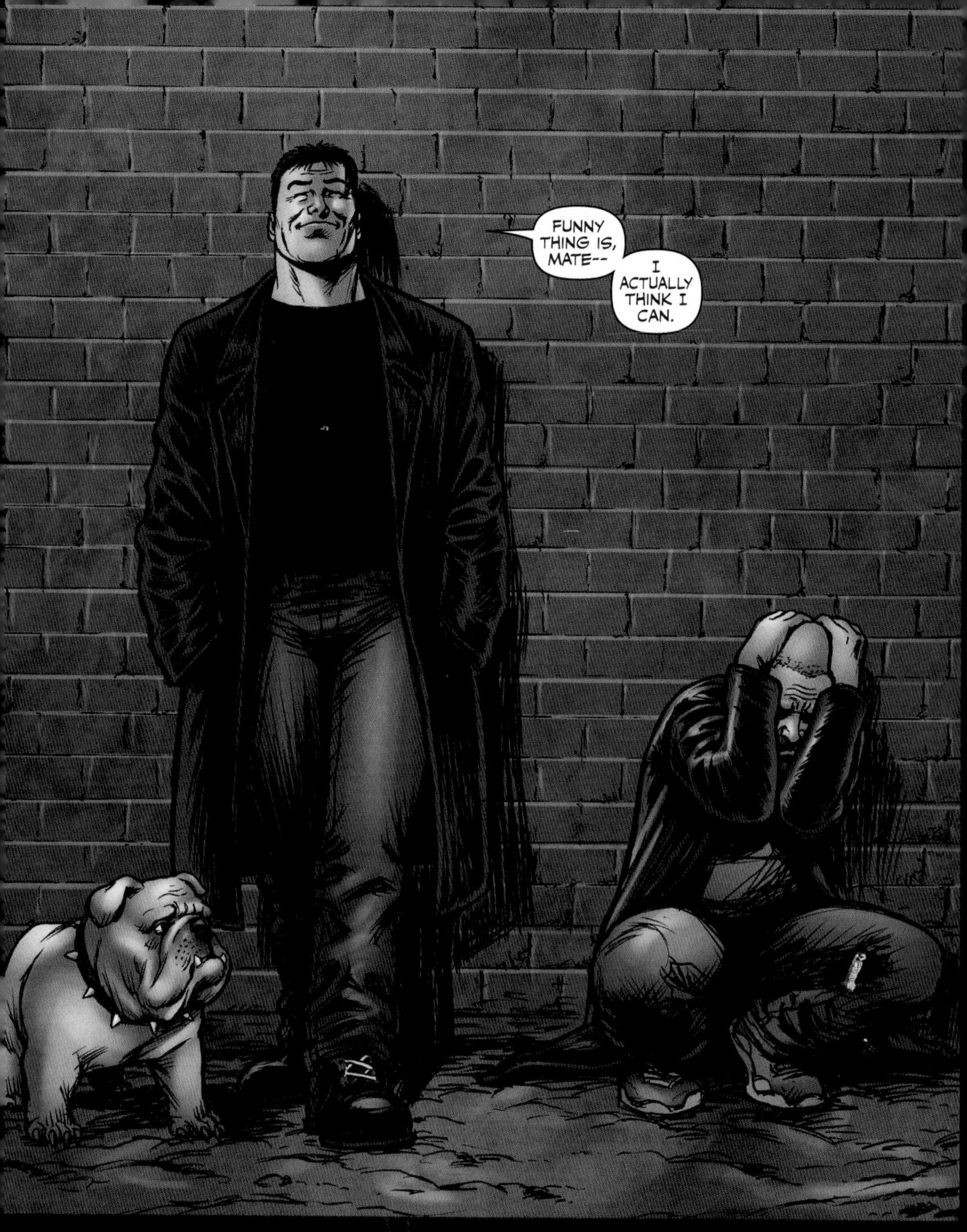
FUNNY THING IS, MATE--
I ACTUALLY THINK I CAN.

BELIEVE
part three

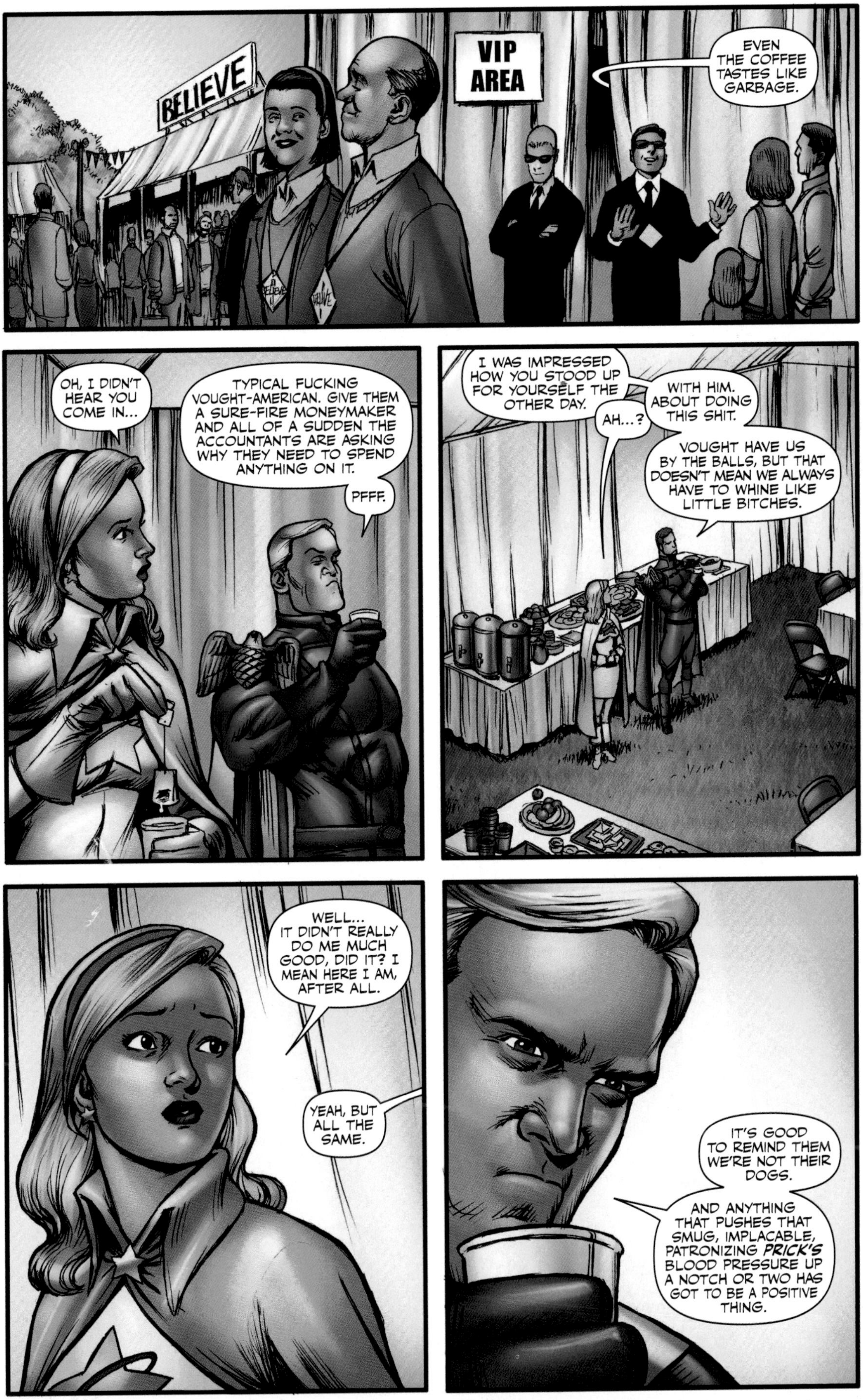
BELIEVE
VIP AREA
EVEN THE COFFEE TASTES LIKE GARBAGE.
OH, I DIDN'T HEAR YOU COME IN...
TYPICAL FUCKING VOUGHT-AMERICAN. GIVE THEM A SURE-FIRE MONEYMAKER AND ALL OF A SUDDEN THE ACCOUNTANTS ARE ASKING WHY THEY NEED TO SPEND ANYTHING ON IT.
PFFF.
I WAS IMPRESSED HOW YOU STOOD UP FOR YOURSELF THE OTHER DAY.
WITH HIM. ABOUT DOING THIS SHIT.
AH...?
VOUGHT HAVE US BY THE BALLS, BUT THAT DOESN'T MEAN WE ALWAYS HAVE TO WHINE LIKE LITTLE BITCHES.
WELL... IT DIDN'T REALLY DO ME MUCH GOOD, DID IT? I MEAN HERE I AM, AFTER ALL.
YEAH, BUT ALL THE SAME.
IT'S GOOD TO REMIND THEM WE'RE NOT THEIR DOGS.
AND ANYTHING THAT PUSHES THAT SMUG, IMPLACABLE, PATRONIZING PRICK'S BLOOD PRESSURE UP A NOTCH OR TWO HAS GOT TO BE A POSITIVE THING.

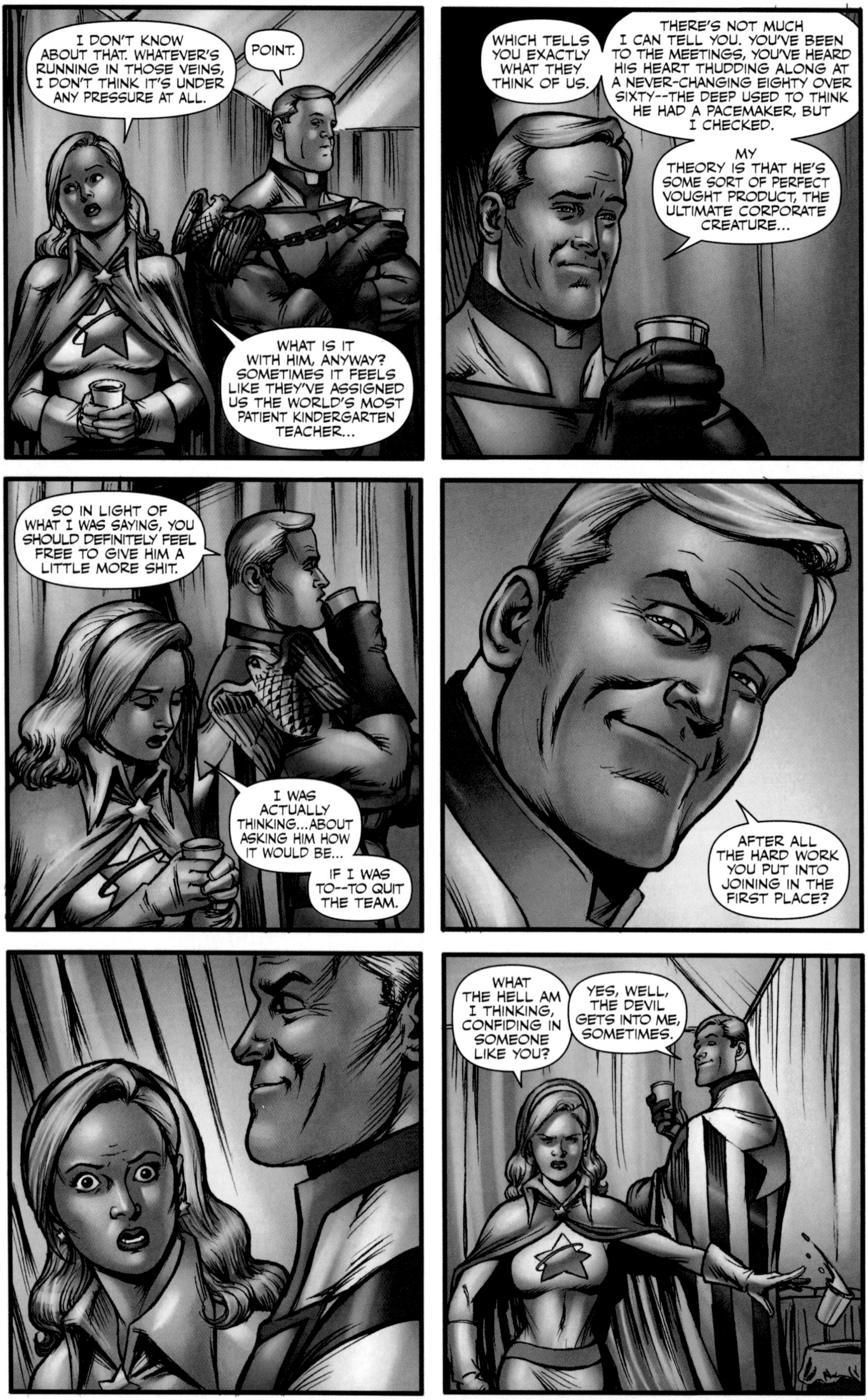
I DON'T KNOW ABOUT THAT. WHATEVER'S RUNNING IN THOSE VEINS, I DON'T THINK IT'S UNDER ANY PRESSURE AT ALL.
POINT.
WHAT IS IT WITH HIM, ANYWAY? SOMETIMES IT FEELS LIKE THEY'VE ASSIGNED US THE WORLD'S MOST PATIENT KINDERGARTEN TEACHER...
WHICH TELLS YOU EXACTLY WHAT THEY THINK OF US.
THERE'S NOT MUCH I CAN TELL YOU. YOU'VE BEEN TO THE MEETINGS, YOU'VE HEARD HIS HEART THUDDING ALONG AT A NEVER-CHANGING EIGHTY OVER SIXTY--THE DEEP USED TO THINK HE HAD A PACEMAKER, BUT I CHECKED.
MY THEORY IS THAT HE'S SOME SORT OF PERFECT VOUGHT PRODUCT, THE ULTIMATE CORPORATE CREATURE...
SO IN LIGHT OF WHAT I WAS SAYING, YOU SHOULD DEFINITELY FEEL FREE TO GIVE HIM A LITTLE MORE SHIT.
I WAS ACTUALLY THINKING...ABOUT ASKING HIM HOW IT WOULD BE...
IF I WAS TO--TO QUIT THE TEAM.
AFTER ALL THE HARD WORK YOU PUT INTO JOINING IN THE FIRST PLACE?
WHAT THE HELL AM I THINKING, CONFIDING IN SOMEONE LIKE YOU?
YES, WELL, THE DEVIL GETS INTO ME, SOMETIMES.

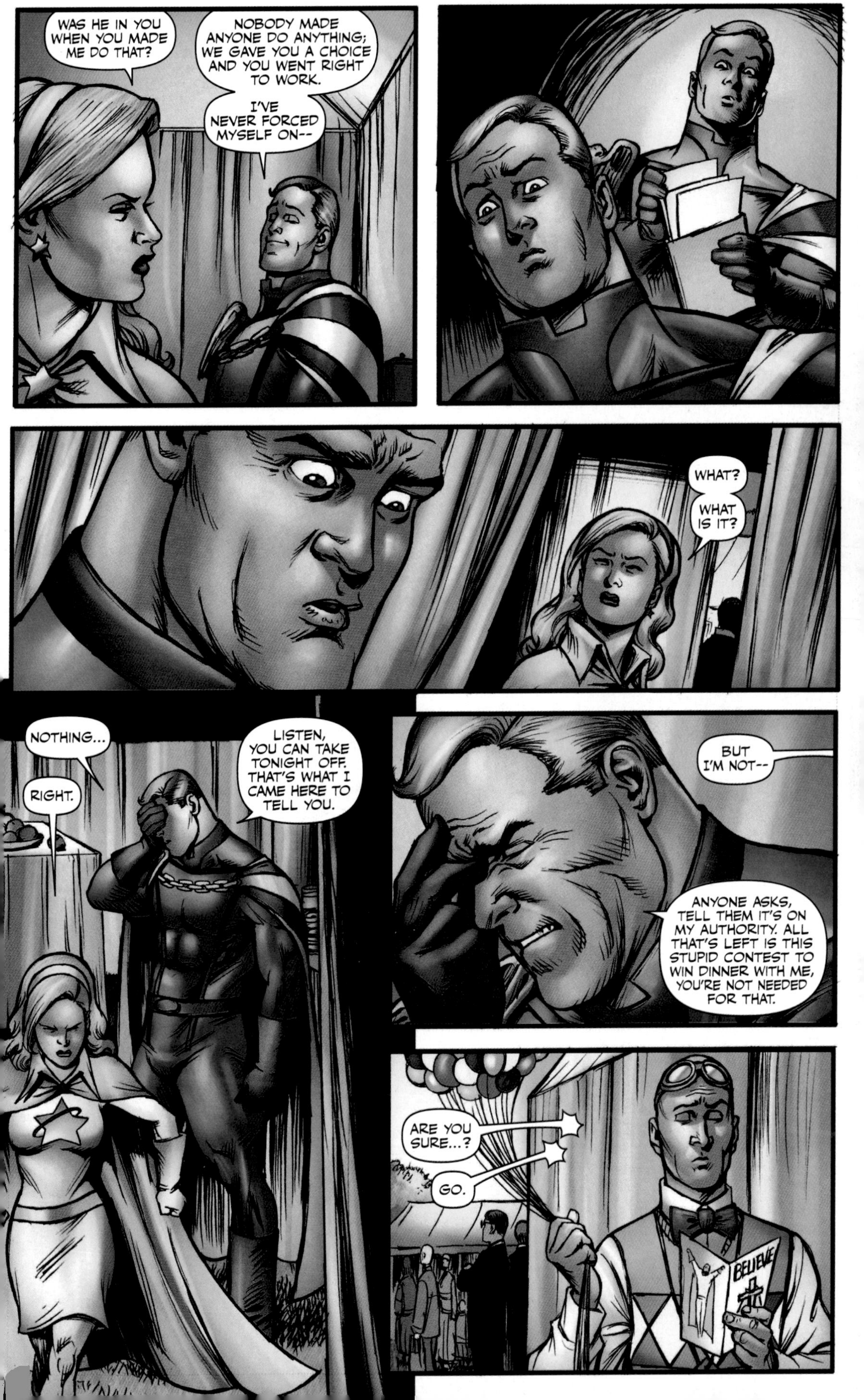
WAS HE IN YOU WHEN YOU MADE ME DO THAT?
NOBODY MADE ANYONE DO ANYTHING; WE GAVE YOU A CHOICE AND YOU WENT RIGHT TO WORK.
I'VE NEVER FORCED MYSELF ON--
WHAT?
WHAT IS IT?
NOTHING...
RIGHT.
LISTEN, YOU CAN TAKE TONIGHT OFF. THAT'S WHAT I CAME HERE TO TELL YOU.
BUT I'M NOT--
ANYONE ASKS, TELL THEM IT'S ON MY AUTHORITY. ALL THAT'S LEFT IS THIS STUPID CONTEST TO WIN DINNER WITH ME, YOU'RE NOT NEEDED FOR THAT.
ARE YOU SURE...?
GO.
BELIEVE

YOU'RE NO' GONNA KILL ME, ARE YOU?

WHAT?

YOU PROBABLY THINK SHE'S BEEN USIN' ME TO FIND STUFF OUT...

I--

FUCK, YOU THINK I'M A SPY.

HUGHIE...

NO!!

GOTTA GET WUUUH

HUGHIE, FOR FUCK'S--

FUCK'S SAKE, SON--!

AW NO-NO-NO-NO-NO--

WEREN'T YOU LISTENIN' TO A WORD I SAID JUST NOW? YOU'RE ME MATE, YOU TIT, YOU CAN TRUST ME WITH ANYTHIN'.

COME ON GET UP OFF ARSE AN' LE TRY AN' SO THIS OUT

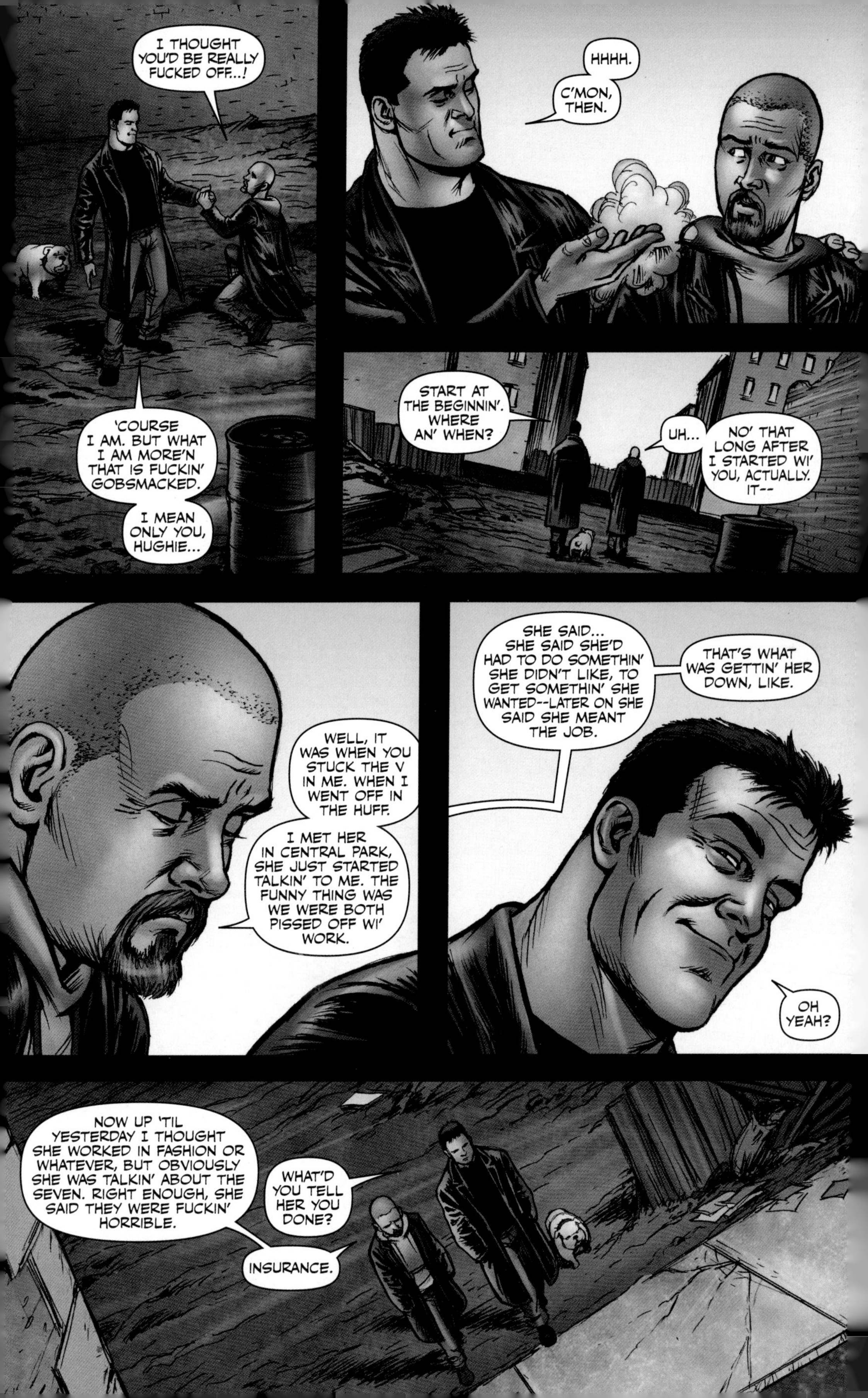
I THOUGHT YOU'D BE REALLY FUCKED OFF...!
'COURSE I AM. BUT WHAT I AM MORE'N THAT IS FUCKIN' GOBSMACKED.
I MEAN ONLY YOU, HUGHIE...
HHHH.
C'MON, THEN.
START AT THE BEGINNIN'. WHERE AN' WHEN?
UH...
NO' THAT LONG AFTER I STARTED WI' YOU, ACTUALLY. IT--
WELL, IT WAS WHEN YOU STUCK THE V IN ME. WHEN I WENT OFF IN THE HUFF.
I MET HER IN CENTRAL PARK, SHE JUST STARTED TALKIN' TO ME. THE FUNNY THING WAS WE WERE BOTH PISSED OFF WI' WORK.
SHE SAID... SHE SAID SHE'D HAD TO DO SOMETHIN' SHE DIDN'T LIKE, TO GET SOMETHIN' SHE WANTED--LATER ON SHE SAID SHE MEANT THE JOB.
THAT'S WHAT WAS GETTIN' HER DOWN, LIKE.
OH YEAH?
NOW UP 'TIL YESTERDAY I THOUGHT SHE WORKED IN FASHION OR WHATEVER, BUT OBVIOUSLY SHE WAS TALKIN' ABOUT THE SEVEN. RIGHT ENOUGH, SHE SAID THEY WERE FUCKIN' HORRIBLE.
WHAT'D YOU TELL HER YOU DONE?
INSURANCE.

WAIT A MINUTE, THIS IS THE BIRD YOU TOLD M.M. ABOUT...

AYE.

WHICH MEANS SHE'S THE ONE YOU WAS HAVIN' A NOSH ON WHEN YOU GOT THE OL' RED SAILS IN THE SUNSET, AIN'T SHE?

AYE...

HEH HEH HEH. YEAH, ALL RIGHT.

SO ANYWAY, YOU START SHAGGIN' AN' IT GETS SERIOUS-- WELL, DOES IT GET SERIOUS? HOW CLOSE ARE THE TWO O' YOU, ANYWAY?

WE-- WELL... WE...

WE'RE IN LOVE.

WORSE'N I FUCKIN' THOUGHT.

MM?

HOW D'YOU FEEL NOW YOU KNOW WHO SHE REALLY IS?

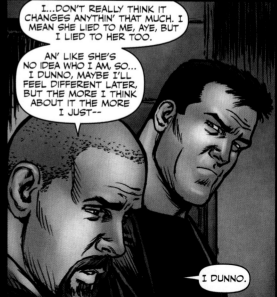

I...DON'T REALLY THINK IT CHANGES ANYTHIN' THAT MUCH. I MEAN SHE LIED TO ME, AYE, BUT I LIED TO HER TOO.

AN' LIKE SHE'S NO IDEA WHO I AM, SO... I DUNNO, MAYBE I'LL FEEL DIFFERENT LATER, BUT THE MORE I THINK ABOUT IT THE MORE I JUST--

I DUNNO.

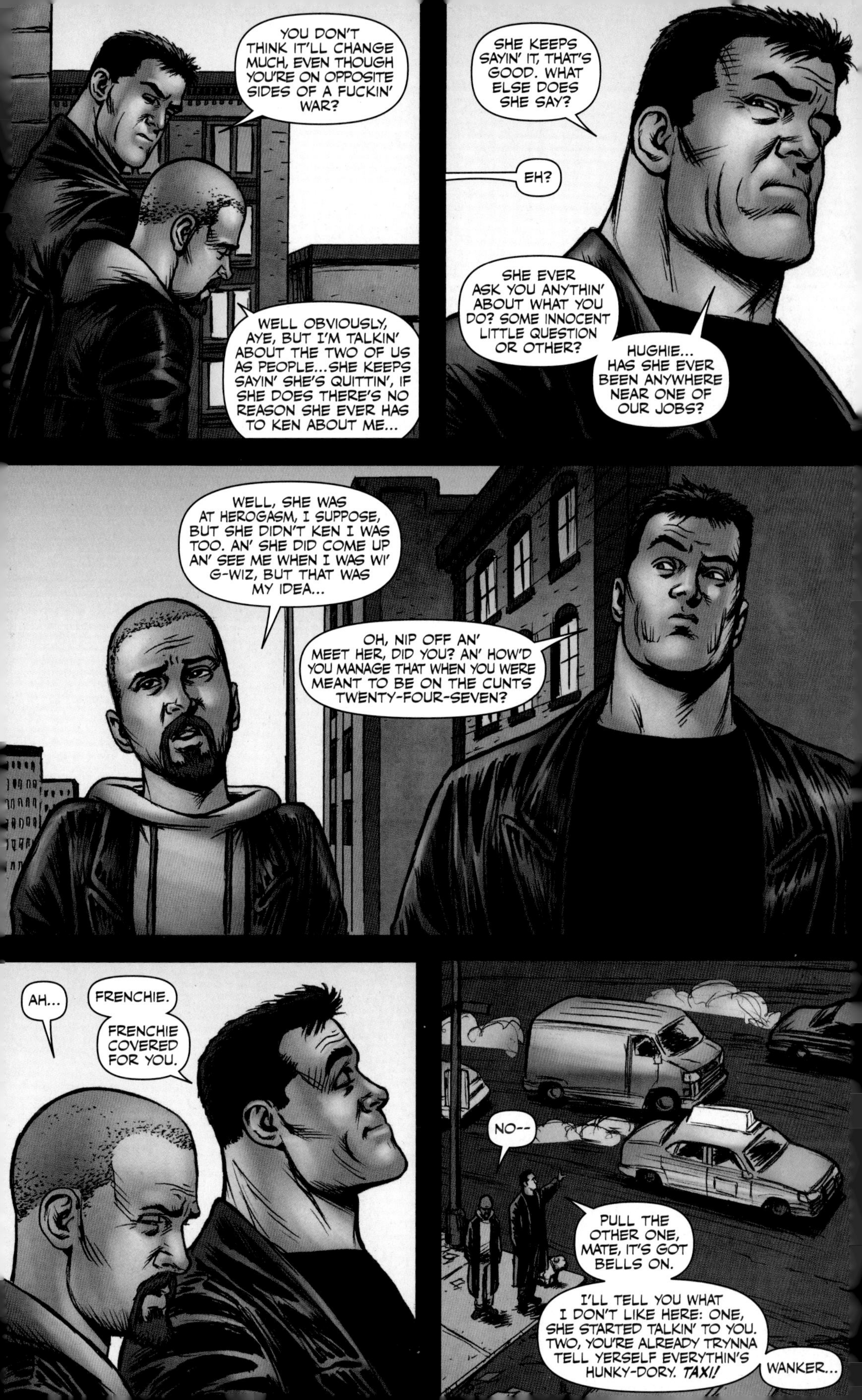
YOU DON'T THINK IT'LL CHANGE MUCH, EVEN THOUGH YOU'RE ON OPPOSITE SIDES OF A FUCKIN' WAR?
WELL OBVIOUSLY, AYE, BUT I'M TALKIN' ABOUT THE TWO OF US AS PEOPLE...SHE KEEPS SAYIN' SHE'S QUITTIN', IF SHE DOES THERE'S NO REASON SHE EVER HAS TO KEN ABOUT ME...
SHE KEEPS SAYIN' IT, THAT'S GOOD. WHAT ELSE DOES SHE SAY?
EH?
SHE EVER ASK YOU ANYTHIN' ABOUT WHAT YOU DO? SOME INNOCENT LITTLE QUESTION OR OTHER?
HUGHIE... HAS SHE EVER BEEN ANYWHERE NEAR ONE OF OUR JOBS?
WELL, SHE WAS AT HEROGASM, I SUPPOSE, BUT SHE DIDN'T KEN I WAS TOO. AN' SHE DID COME UP AN' SEE ME WHEN I WAS WI' G-WIZ, BUT THAT WAS MY IDEA...
OH, NIP OFF AN' MEET HER, DID YOU? AN' HOW'D YOU MANAGE THAT WHEN YOU WERE MEANT TO BE ON THE CUNTS TWENTY-FOUR-SEVEN?
AH...
FRENCHIE.
FRENCHIE COVERED FOR YOU.
NO--
PULL THE OTHER ONE, MATE, IT'S GOT BELLS ON.
I'LL TELL YOU WHAT I DON'T LIKE HERE: ONE, SHE STARTED TALKIN' TO YOU. TWO, YOU'RE ALREADY TRYNNA TELL YERSELF EVERYTHIN'S HUNKY-DORY. *TAXI!*
WANKER...

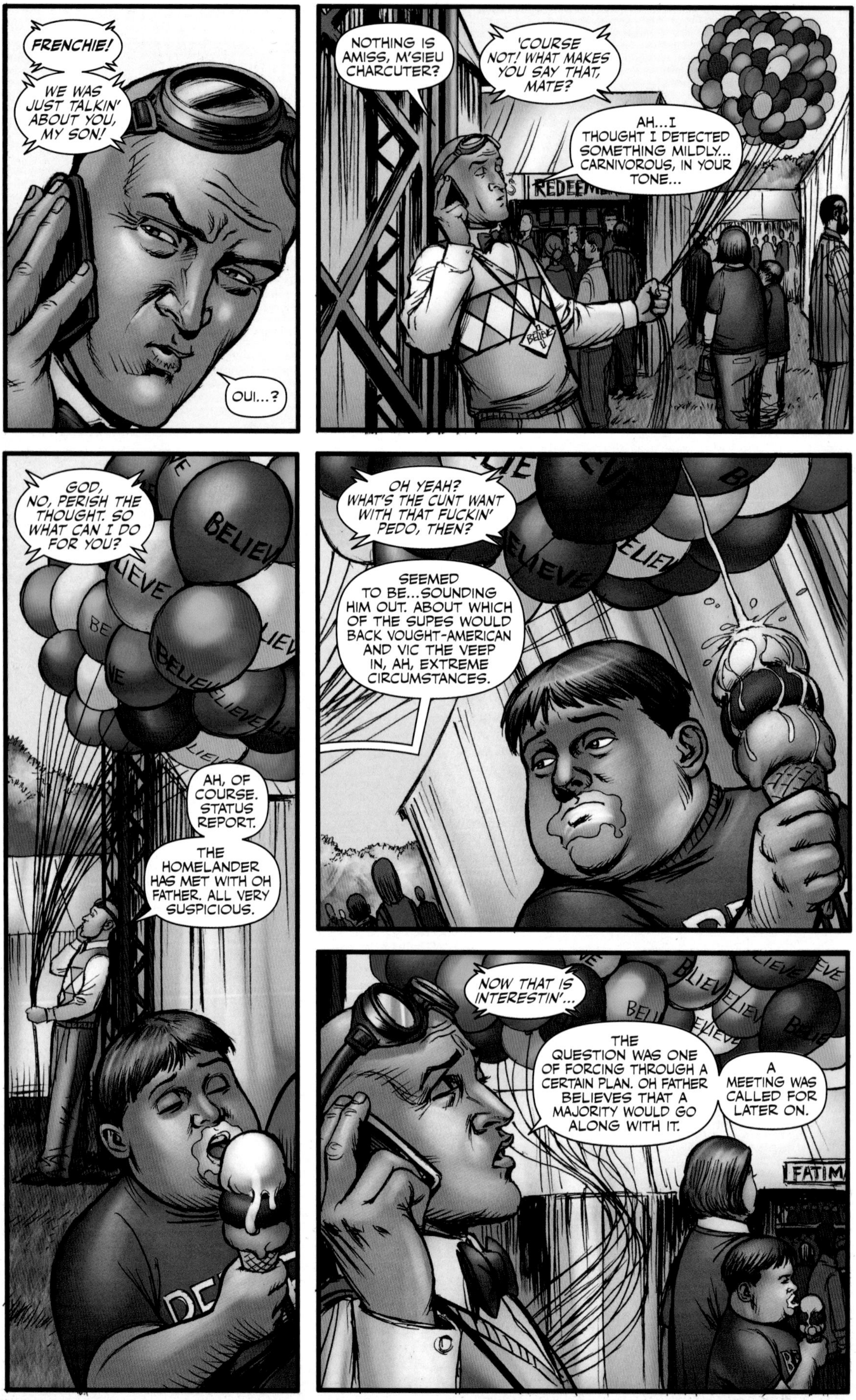
FRENCHIE!
WE WAS JUST TALKIN' ABOUT YOU, MY SON!
OUI...?
NOTHING IS AMISS, M'SIEU CHARCUTER?
'COURSE NOT! WHAT MAKES YOU SAY THAT, MATE?
AH...I THOUGHT I DETECTED SOMETHING MILDLY... CARNIVOROUS, IN YOUR TONE...
GOD, NO, PERISH THE THOUGHT. SO WHAT CAN I DO FOR YOU?
AH, OF COURSE. STATUS REPORT.
THE HOMELANDER HAS MET WITH OH FATHER. ALL VERY SUSPICIOUS.
OH YEAH? WHAT'S THE CUNT WANT WITH THAT FUCKIN' PEDO, THEN?
SEEMED TO BE...SOUNDING HIM OUT. ABOUT WHICH OF THE SUPES WOULD BACK VOUGHT-AMERICAN AND VIC THE VEEP IN, AH, EXTREME CIRCUMSTANCES.
NOW THAT IS INTERESTIN'...
THE QUESTION WAS ONE OF FORCING THROUGH A CERTAIN PLAN. OH FATHER BELIEVES THAT A MAJORITY WOULD GO ALONG WITH IT.
A MEETING WAS CALLED FOR LATER ON.

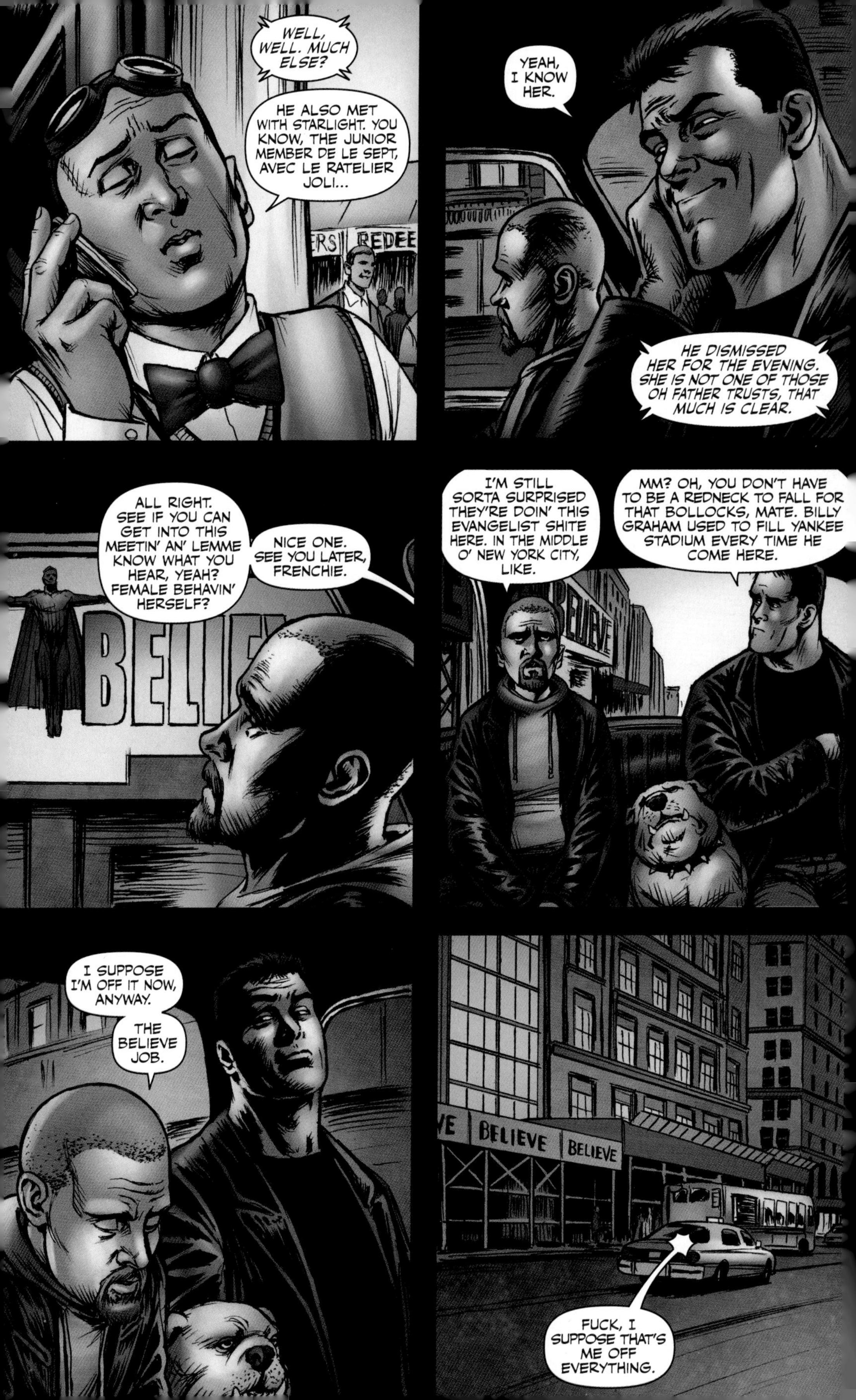
WELL, WELL. MUCH ELSE?
HE ALSO MET WITH STARLIGHT. YOU KNOW, THE JUNIOR MEMBER DE LE SEPT, AVEC LE RATELIER JOLI...
YEAH, I KNOW HER.
HE DISMISSED HER FOR THE EVENING. SHE IS NOT ONE OF THOSE OH FATHER TRUSTS, THAT MUCH IS CLEAR.
ALL RIGHT. SEE IF YOU CAN GET INTO THIS MEETIN' AN' LEMME KNOW WHAT YOU HEAR, YEAH? FEMALE BEHAVIN' HERSELF?
NICE ONE. SEE YOU LATER, FRENCHIE.
I'M STILL SORTA SURPRISED THEY'RE DOIN' THIS EVANGELIST SHITE HERE. IN THE MIDDLE O' NEW YORK CITY, LIKE.
MM? OH, YOU DON'T HAVE TO BE A REDNECK TO FALL FOR THAT BOLLOCKS, MATE. BILLY GRAHAM USED TO FILL YANKEE STADIUM EVERY TIME HE COME HERE.
I SUPPOSE I'M OFF IT NOW, ANYWAY.
THE BELIEVE JOB.
BELIEVE
BELIEVE
FUCK, I SUPPOSE THAT'S ME OFF EVERYTHING.

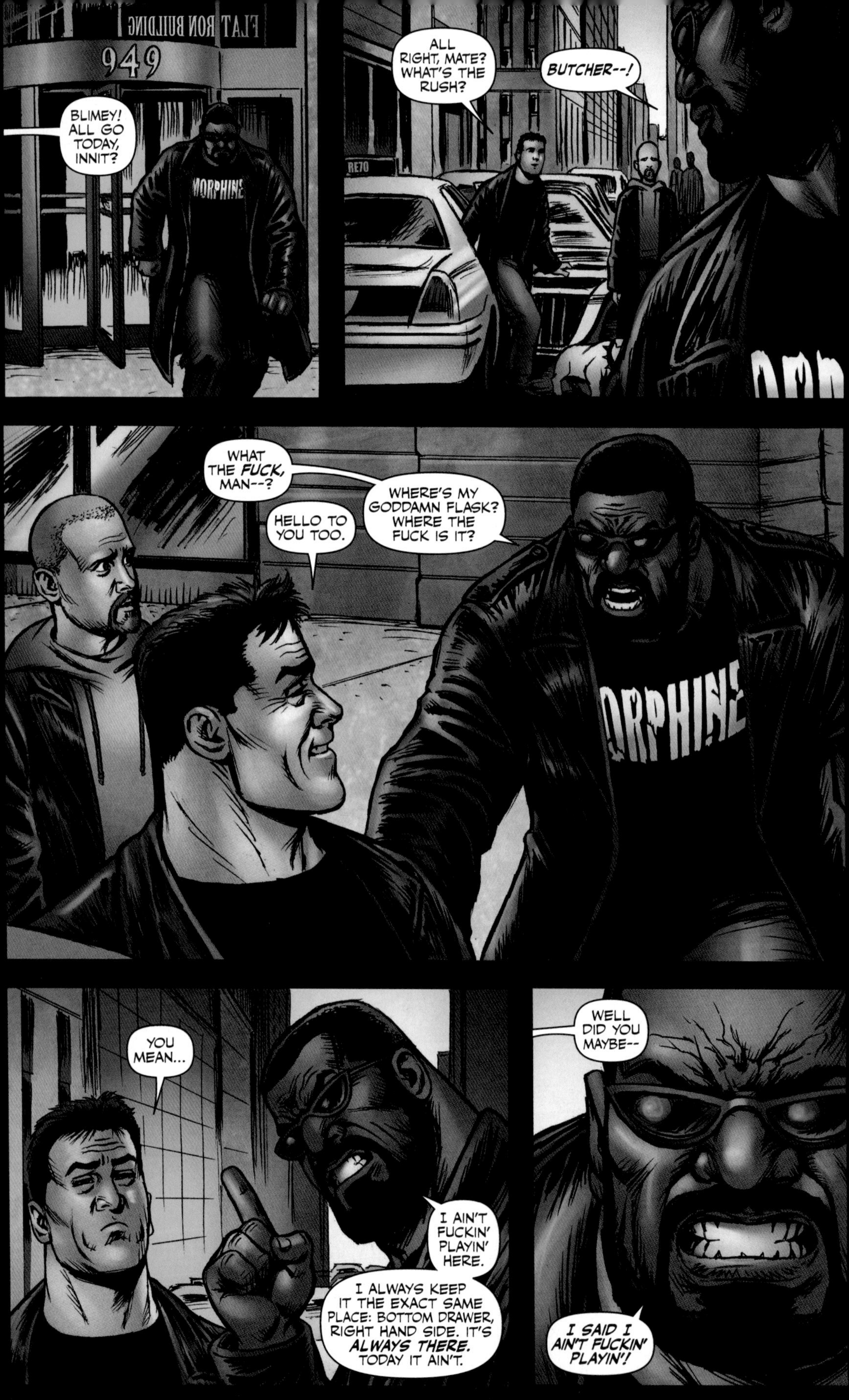
FLAT IRON BUILDING
949
BLIMEY! ALL GO TODAY, INNIT?
MORPHINE
ALL RIGHT, MATE? WHAT'S THE RUSH?
BUTCHER--!
WHAT THE *FUCK,* MAN--?
WHERE'S MY GODDAMN FLASK? WHERE THE FUCK IS IT?
HELLO TO YOU TOO.
MORPHINE
YOU MEAN...
I AIN'T FUCKIN' PLAYIN' HERE.
I ALWAYS KEEP IT THE EXACT SAME PLACE: BOTTOM DRAWER, RIGHT HAND SIDE. IT'S *ALWAYS THERE.* TODAY IT AIN'T.
WELL DID YOU MAYBE--
I SAID I AIN'T FUCKIN' PLAYIN'!

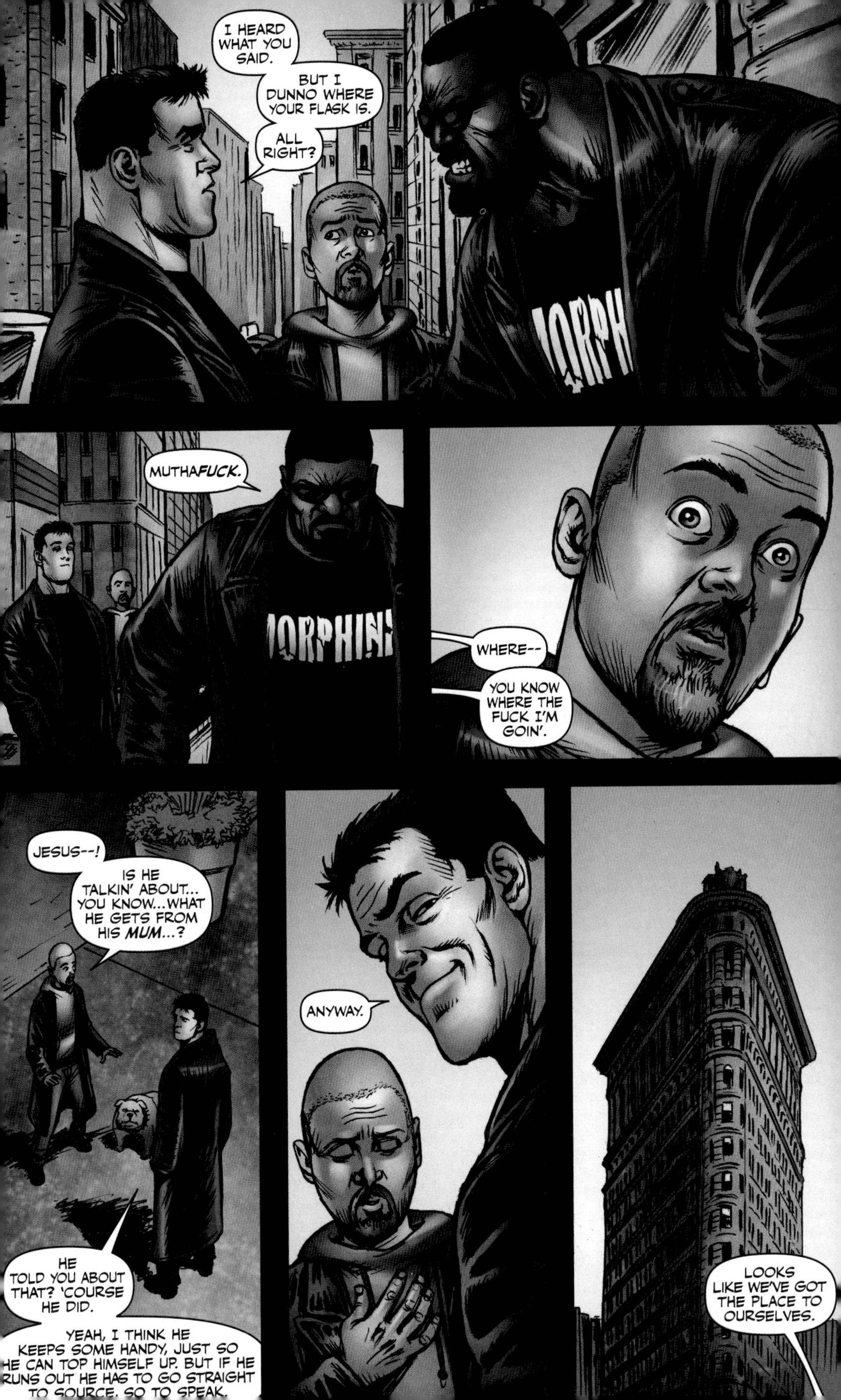
I HEARD WHAT YOU SAID.
BUT I DUNNO WHERE YOUR FLASK IS.
ALL RIGHT?
MUTHA*FUCK*.
WHERE--
YOU KNOW WHERE THE FUCK I'M GOIN'.
JESUS--!
IS HE TALKIN' ABOUT... YOU KNOW...WHAT HE GETS FROM HIS *MUM*...?
HE TOLD YOU ABOUT THAT? 'COURSE HE DID.
YEAH, I THINK HE KEEPS SOME HANDY, JUST SO HE CAN TOP HIMSELF UP. BUT IF HE RUNS OUT HE HAS TO GO STRAIGHT TO SOURCE, SO TO SPEAK.
ANYWAY.
LOOKS LIKE WE'VE GOT THE PLACE TO OURSELVES.

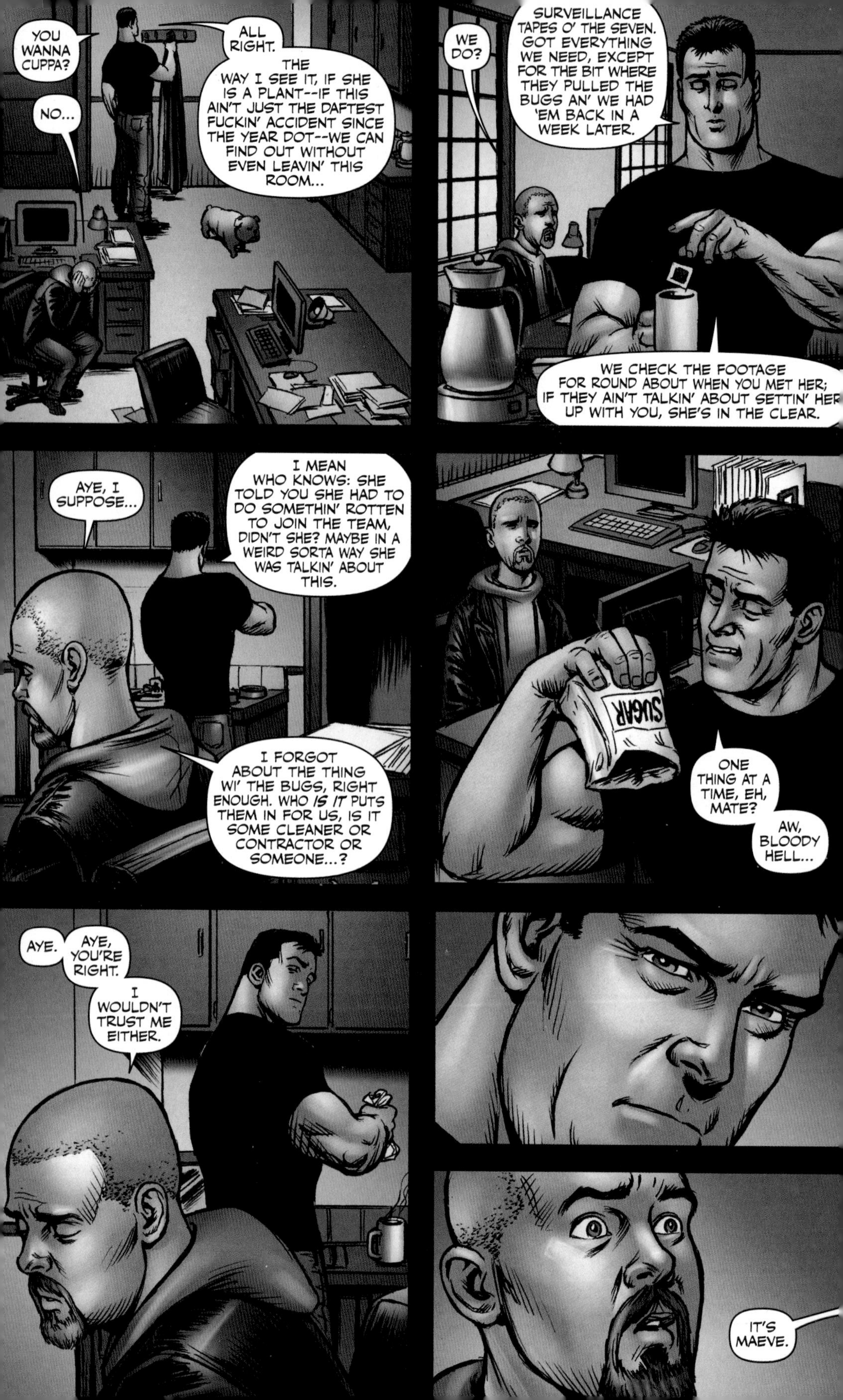
YOU WANNA CUPPA?
ALL RIGHT.
NO...
THE WAY I SEE IT, IF SHE IS A PLANT--IF THIS AIN'T JUST THE DAFTEST FUCKIN' ACCIDENT SINCE THE YEAR DOT--WE CAN FIND OUT WITHOUT EVEN LEAVIN' THIS ROOM...
WE DO?
SURVEILLANCE TAPES O' THE SEVEN. GOT EVERYTHING WE NEED, EXCEPT FOR THE BIT WHERE THEY PULLED THE BUGS AN' WE HAD 'EM BACK IN A WEEK LATER.
WE CHECK THE FOOTAGE FOR ROUND ABOUT WHEN YOU MET HER; IF THEY AIN'T TALKIN' ABOUT SETTIN' HER UP WITH YOU, SHE'S IN THE CLEAR.
AYE, I SUPPOSE...
I MEAN WHO KNOWS: SHE TOLD YOU SHE HAD TO DO SOMETHIN' ROTTEN TO JOIN THE TEAM, DIDN'T SHE? MAYBE IN A WEIRD SORTA WAY SHE WAS TALKIN' ABOUT THIS.
I FORGOT ABOUT THE THING WI' THE BUGS, RIGHT ENOUGH. WHO *IS IT* PUTS THEM IN FOR US, IS IT SOME CLEANER OR CONTRACTOR OR SOMEONE...?
SUGAR
ONE THING AT A TIME, EH, MATE?
AW, BLOODY HELL...
AYE.
AYE, YOU'RE RIGHT.
I WOULDN'T TRUST ME EITHER.
IT'S MAEVE.

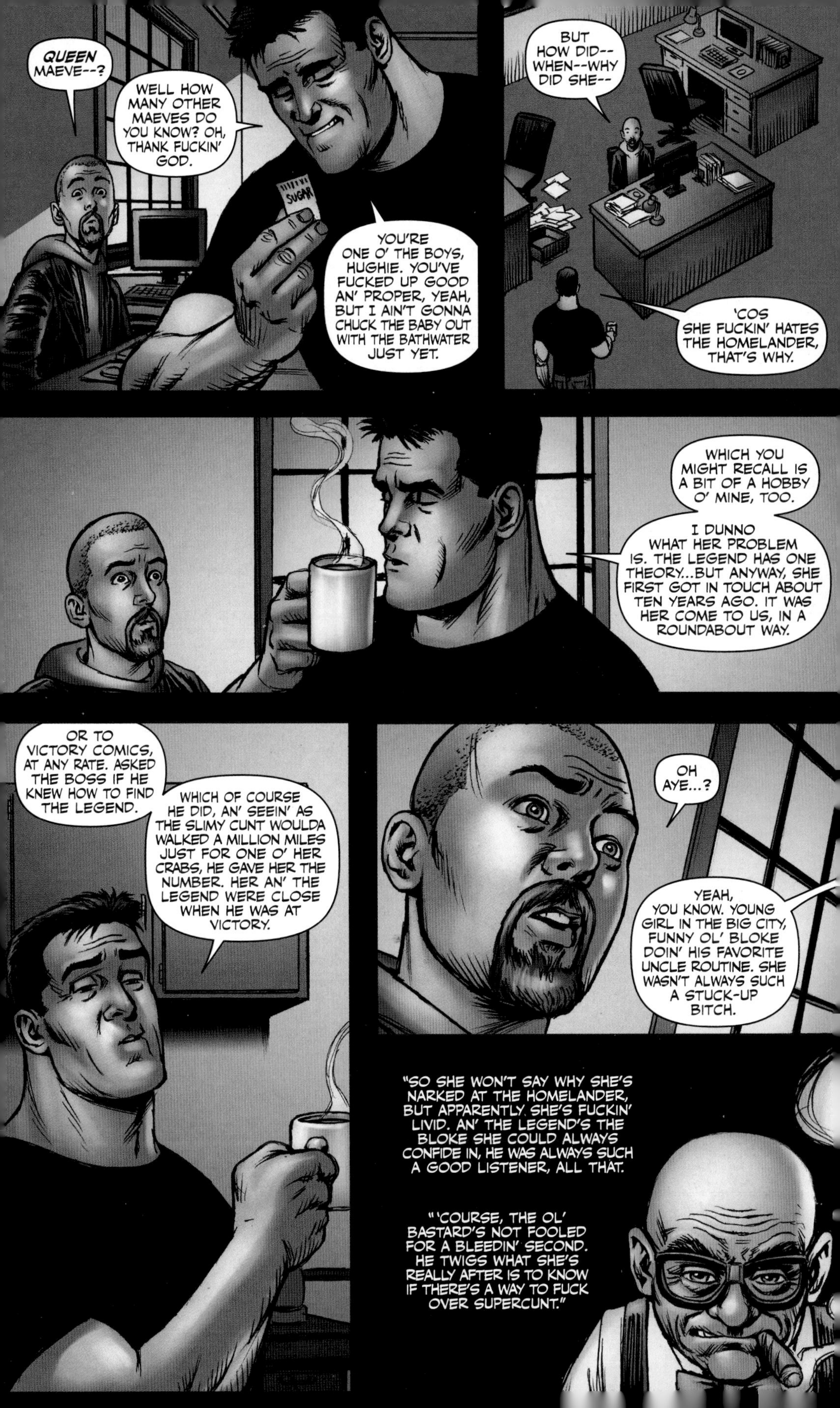
QUEEN MAEVE--?
WELL HOW MANY OTHER MAEVES DO YOU KNOW? OH, THANK FUCKIN' GOD.
SUGAR
YOU'RE ONE O' THE BOYS, HUGHIE. YOU'VE FUCKED UP GOOD AN' PROPER, YEAH, BUT I AIN'T GONNA CHUCK THE BABY OUT WITH THE BATHWATER JUST YET.
BUT HOW DID-- WHEN--WHY DID SHE--
'COS SHE FUCKIN' HATES THE HOMELANDER, THAT'S WHY.
WHICH YOU MIGHT RECALL IS A BIT OF A HOBBY O' MINE, TOO.
I DUNNO WHAT HER PROBLEM IS. THE LEGEND HAS ONE THEORY...BUT ANYWAY, SHE FIRST GOT IN TOUCH ABOUT TEN YEARS AGO. IT WAS HER COME TO US, IN A ROUNDABOUT WAY.
OR TO VICTORY COMICS, AT ANY RATE. ASKED THE BOSS IF HE KNEW HOW TO FIND THE LEGEND.
WHICH OF COURSE HE DID, AN' SEEIN' AS THE SLIMY CUNT WOULDA WALKED A MILLION MILES JUST FOR ONE O' HER CRABS, HE GAVE HER THE NUMBER. HER AN' THE LEGEND WERE CLOSE WHEN HE WAS AT VICTORY.
OH AYE...?
YEAH, YOU KNOW. YOUNG GIRL IN THE BIG CITY, FUNNY OL' BLOKE DOIN' HIS FAVORITE UNCLE ROUTINE. SHE WASN'T ALWAYS SUCH A STUCK-UP BITCH.
"SO SHE WON'T SAY WHY SHE'S NARKED AT THE HOMELANDER, BUT APPARENTLY SHE'S FUCKIN' LIVID. AN' THE LEGEND'S THE BLOKE SHE COULD ALWAYS CONFIDE IN, HE WAS ALWAYS SUCH A GOOD LISTENER, ALL THAT.
"'COURSE, THE OL' BASTARD'S NOT FOOLED FOR A BLEEDIN' SECOND. HE TWIGS WHAT SHE'S REALLY AFTER IS TO KNOW IF THERE'S A WAY TO FUCK OVER SUPERCUNT."

"SO HE BROKERS A MEETIN'. TELLS HER HE KNOWS SOME BLOKES MIGHT BE ABLE TO HELP--WHICH SHE DON'T LIKE ONE BIT, BUT SHE'S PISSED OFF ENOUGH TO GO ALONG WITH IT.

"AT THIS POINT, WE AIN'T GOT THAT MUCH ON THE SEVEN, SO WE JUMP AT THE CHANCE. NOT THAT WE DON'T PLAY IT COOL WHEN WE GO AN' SEE HER."

"NOW, SHE WON'T DO NOTHIN' THAT'LL GET HER IN SERIOUS SHIT. SHE DON'T WANNA UPSET THE APPLECART, NEITHER, IT'S PRETTY OBVIOUS SHE AIN'T ABOUT TO GIVE UP THE GOOD LIFE.

"BUT YOU CAN TELL SHE WANTS TO DO *SOMETHIN',* IT'S BURNIN' IN HER *GUT* SO SHE CAN HARDLY EVEN STAND STILL. MALLORY PLAYS IT JUST RIGHT: DROPS A HINT THAT WE'RE FEDERAL, SAYS WE DON'T WANNA FINISH THE SEVEN EITHER, FAR FROM IT--

BINGO, HER EYES LIGHT UP. YOU CAN TELL WHAT SHE'S THINKIN': PICTURES. EMBARRASSMENT. SEVERE FRUSTRATION.

FUCK WITH THE HOMELANDER, FUCK WITH THE HOMELANDER...

SO... WHAT'S SHE LIKE WHEN YOU ACTUALLY *SEE* HER...?

"BUT HOW ABOUT STICKIN' IN A COUPLA CAMERAS FOR US?"

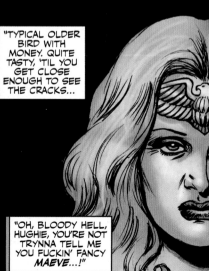

"TYPICAL OLDER BIRD WITH MONEY. QUITE TASTY, 'TIL YOU GET CLOSE ENOUGH TO SEE THE CRACKS...

"OH, BLOODY HELL, HUGHIE, YOU'RE NOT TRYNNA TELL ME YOU FUCKIN' FANCY *MAEVE...!*"

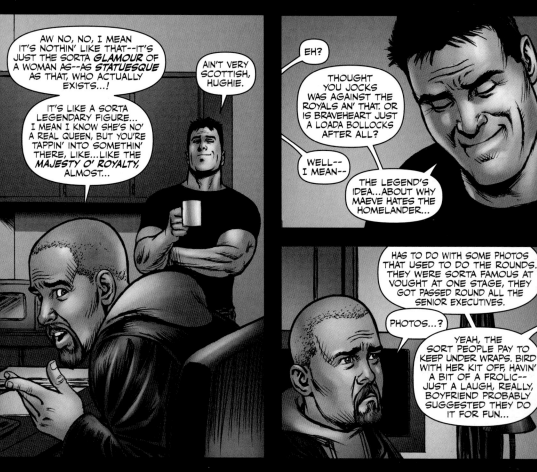

AW NO, NO, I MEAN IT'S NOTHIN' LIKE THAT--IT'S JUST THE SORTA *GLAMOUR* OF A WOMAN AS--AS *STATUESQUE* AS THAT, WHO ACTUALLY EXISTS...!

AIN'T VERY SCOTTISH, HUGHIE.

IT'S LIKE A SORTA LEGENDARY FIGURE... I MEAN I KNOW SHE'S NO' A REAL QUEEN, BUT YOU'RE TAPPIN' INTO SOMETHIN' THERE, LIKE...LIKE THE *MAJESTY O' ROYALTY*, ALMOST...

EH?

THOUGHT YOU JOCKS WAS AGAINST THE ROYALS AN' THAT. OR IS BRAVEHEART JUST A LOADA BOLLOCKS AFTER ALL?

WELL-- I MEAN--

THE LEGEND'S IDEA...ABOUT WHY MAEVE HATES THE HOMELANDER...

HAS TO DO WITH SOME PHOTOS THAT USED TO DO THE ROUNDS. THEY WERE SORTA FAMOUS AT VOUGHT AT ONE STAGE, THEY GOT PASSED ROUND ALL THE SENIOR EXECUTIVES.

PHOTOS...?

YEAH, THE SORT PEOPLE PAY TO KEEP UNDER WRAPS. BIRD WITH HER KIT OFF, HAVIN' A BIT OF A FROLIC-- JUST A LAUGH, REALLY, BOYFRIEND PROBABLY SUGGESTED THEY DO IT FOR FUN...

EXCEPT HIS MUG NEVER SHOWS UP IN ANY O' THE PICS. FUNNY, THAT.

LEGEND SAID FROM THE SIZE O' THE DONG THE BLOKE'S PROBABLY THE HOMELANDER--STANDS TO REASON HE'S THE ONE PUT 'EM OUT THERE. MAEVE'S FUCKIN' FLAMIN' OVER THIS SUDDEN AN' UNEXPECTED BETRAYAL...SO...

HAVE YOU SEEN THEM?

I MEAN DO THEY EVEN EXIST, ARE THEY JUST SOME SORTA DAFT MYTH...?

TOP DRAWER O' ME DESK, UNDER THE ENGLISH-FRENCH DICTIONARY.

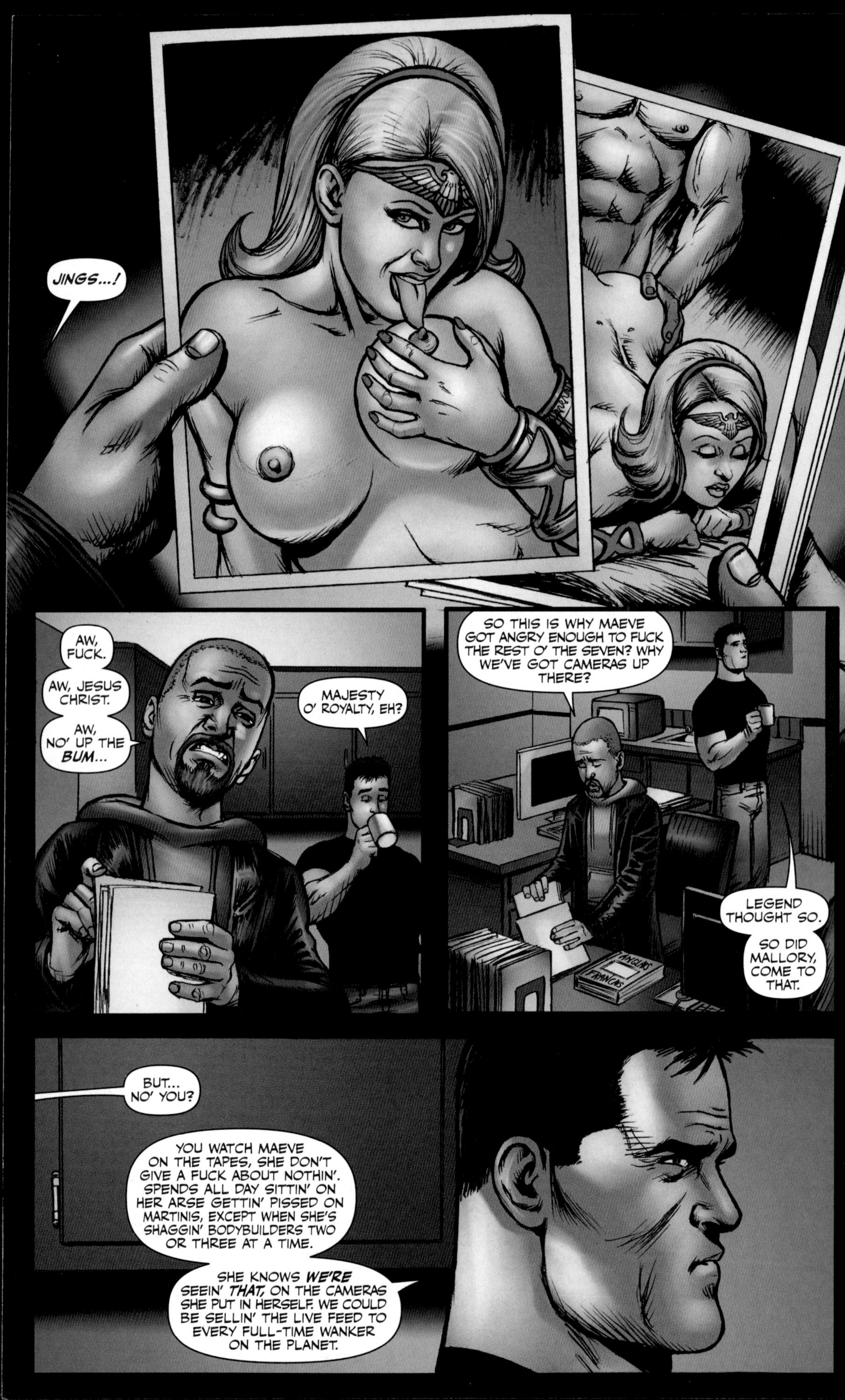
JINGS...!
AW, FUCK.
AW, JESUS CHRIST.
AW, NO' UP THE *BUM*...
MAJESTY O' ROYALTY, EH?
SO THIS IS WHY MAEVE GOT ANGRY ENOUGH TO FUCK THE REST O' THE SEVEN? WHY WE'VE GOT CAMERAS UP THERE?
LEGEND THOUGHT SO.
SO DID MALLORY, COME TO THAT.
BUT... NO' YOU?
YOU WATCH MAEVE ON THE TAPES, SHE DON'T GIVE A FUCK ABOUT NOTHIN'. SPENDS ALL DAY SITTIN' ON HER ARSE GETTIN' PISSED ON MARTINIS, EXCEPT WHEN SHE'S SHAGGIN' BODYBUILDERS TWO OR THREE AT A TIME.
SHE KNOWS *WE'RE* SEEIN' *THAT,* ON THE CAMERAS SHE PUT IN HERSELF. WE COULD BE SELLIN' THE LIVE FEED TO EVERY FULL-TIME WANKER ON THE PLANET.

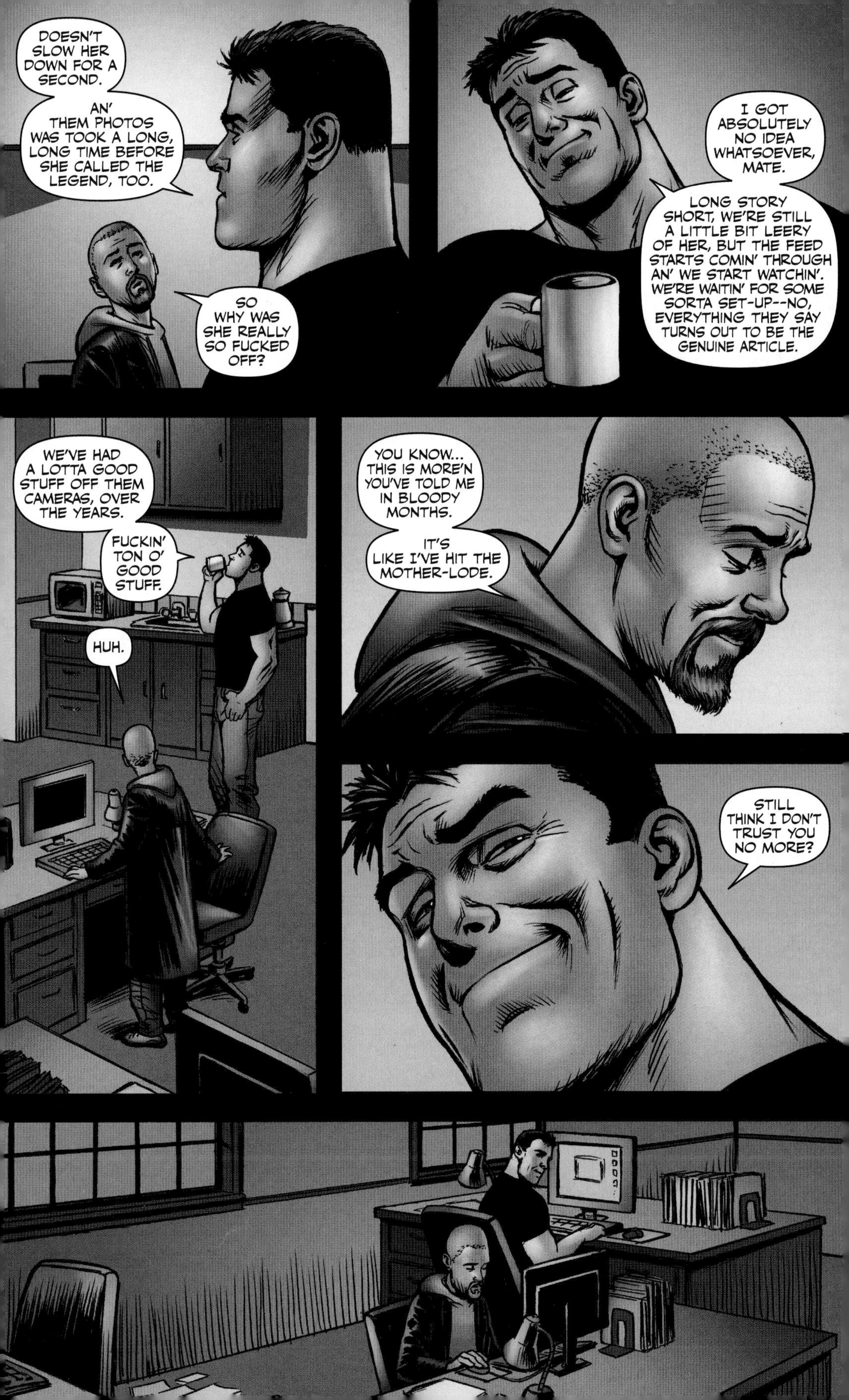
DOESN'T SLOW HER DOWN FOR A SECOND.
AN' THEM PHOTOS WAS TOOK A LONG, LONG TIME BEFORE SHE CALLED THE LEGEND, TOO.
SO WHY WAS SHE REALLY SO FUCKED OFF?
I GOT ABSOLUTELY NO IDEA WHATSOEVER, MATE.
LONG STORY SHORT, WE'RE STILL A LITTLE BIT LEERY OF HER, BUT THE FEED STARTS COMIN' THROUGH AN' WE START WATCHIN'. WE'RE WAITIN' FOR SOME SORTA SET-UP--NO, EVERYTHING THEY SAY TURNS OUT TO BE THE GENUINE ARTICLE.
WE'VE HAD A LOTTA GOOD STUFF OFF THEM CAMERAS, OVER THE YEARS.
FUCKIN' TON O' GOOD STUFF.
HUH.
YOU KNOW... THIS IS MORE'N YOU'VE TOLD ME IN BLOODY MONTHS.
IT'S LIKE I'VE HIT THE MOTHER-LODE.
STILL THINK I DON'T TRUST YOU NO MORE?

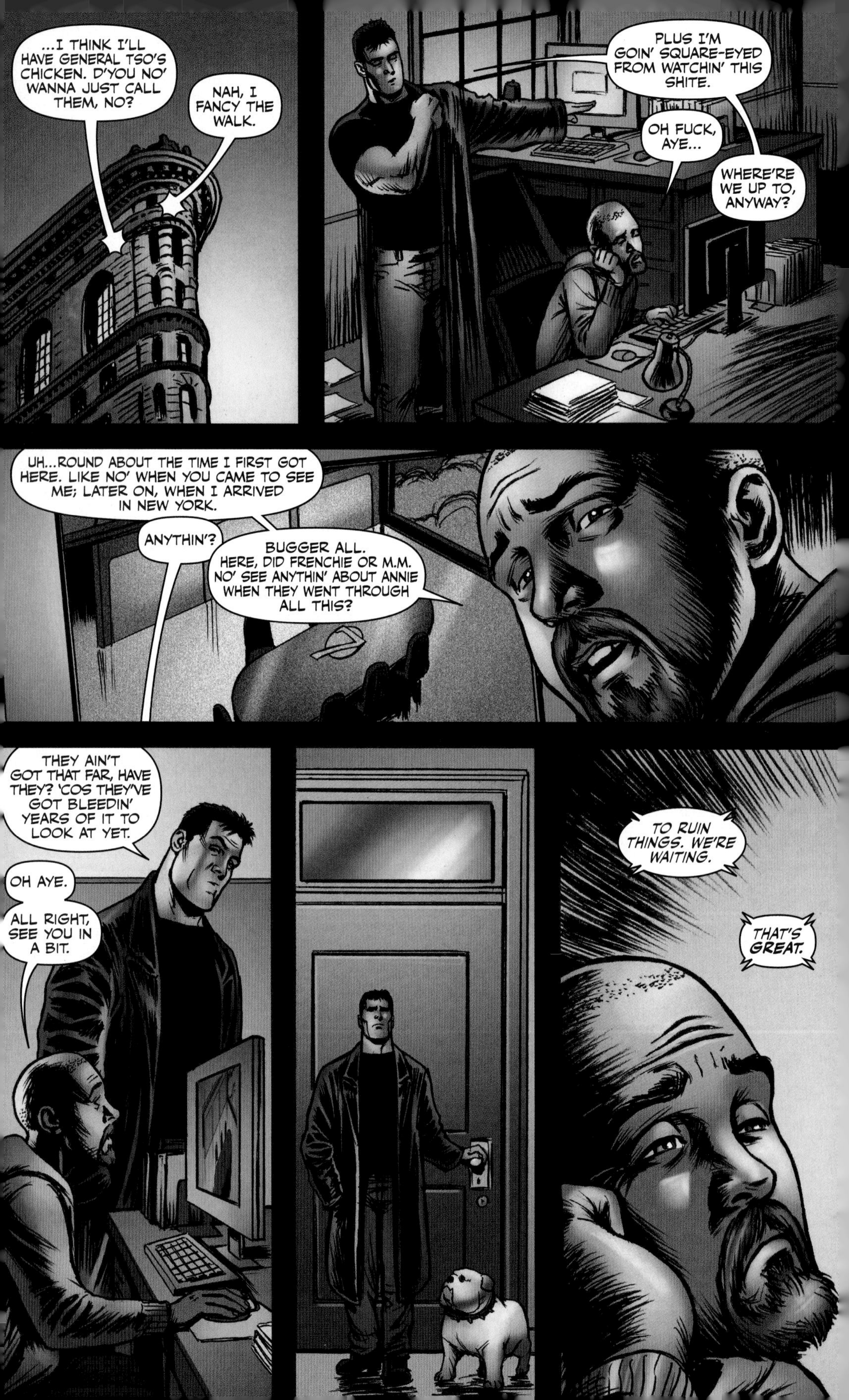

...I THINK I'LL HAVE GENERAL TSO'S CHICKEN. D'YOU NO' WANNA JUST CALL THEM, NO?
NAH, I FANCY THE WALK.
PLUS I'M GOIN' SQUARE-EYED FROM WATCHIN' THIS SHITE.
OH FUCK, AYE...
WHERE'RE WE UP TO, ANYWAY?
UH...ROUND ABOUT THE TIME I FIRST GOT HERE. LIKE NO' WHEN YOU CAME TO SEE ME; LATER ON, WHEN I ARRIVED IN NEW YORK.
ANYTHIN'?
BUGGER ALL. HERE, DID FRENCHIE OR M.M. NO' SEE ANYTHIN' ABOUT ANNIE WHEN THEY WENT THROUGH ALL THIS?
THEY AIN'T GOT THAT FAR, HAVE THEY? 'COS THEY'VE GOT BLEEDIN' YEARS OF IT TO LOOK AT YET.
OH AYE.
ALL RIGHT, SEE YOU IN A BIT.
TO RUIN THINGS. WE'RE WAITING.
THAT'S GREAT.

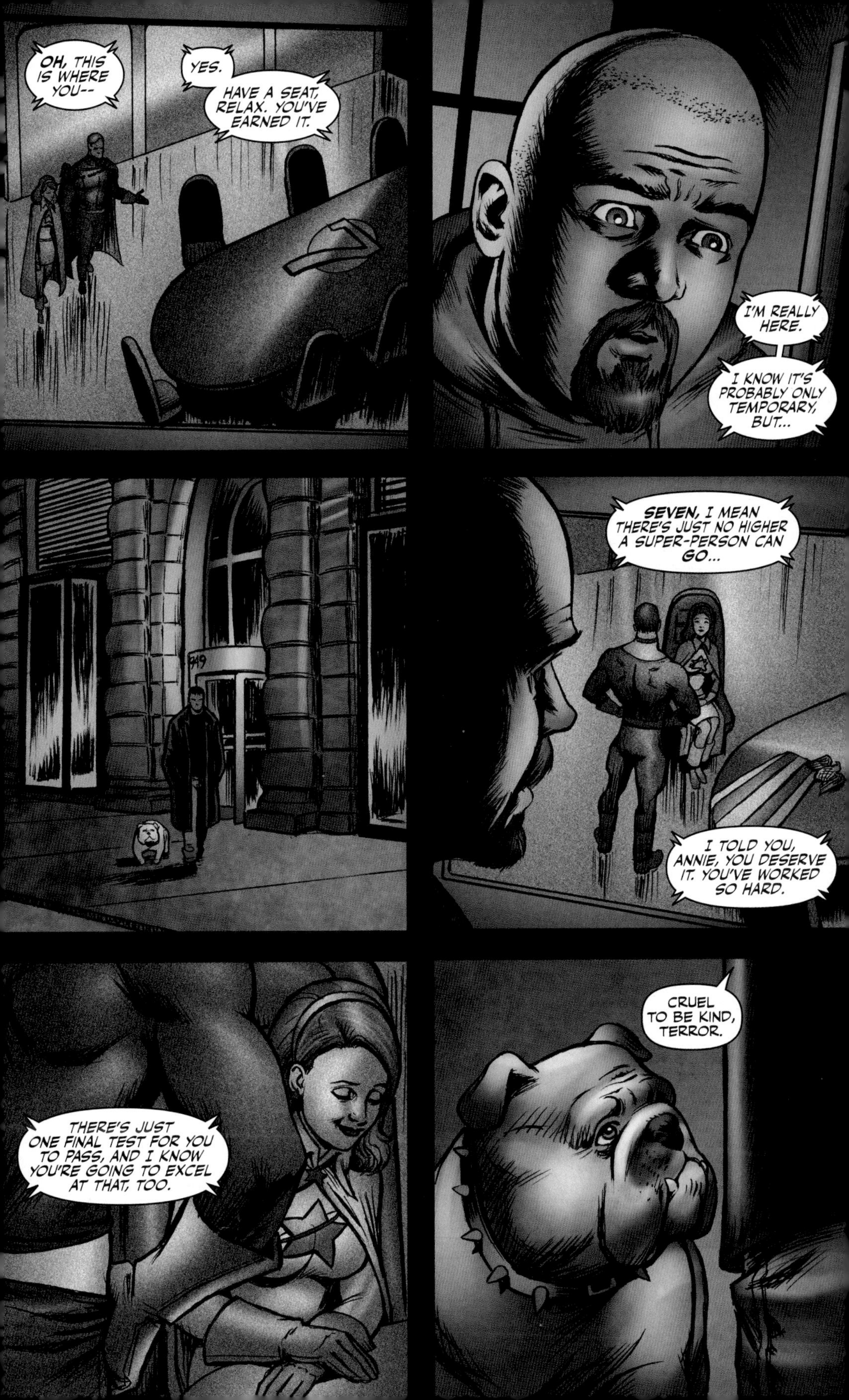
OH, THIS IS WHERE YOU--
YES.
HAVE A SEAT, RELAX. YOU'VE EARNED IT.
I'M REALLY HERE.
I KNOW IT'S PROBABLY ONLY TEMPORARY, BUT...
949
SEVEN, I MEAN THERE'S JUST NO HIGHER A SUPER-PERSON CAN GO...
I TOLD YOU, ANNIE, YOU DESERVE IT. YOU'VE WORKED SO HARD.
THERE'S JUST ONE FINAL TEST FOR YOU TO PASS, AND I KNOW YOU'RE GOING TO EXCEL AT THAT, TOO.
CRUEL TO BE KIND, TERROR.

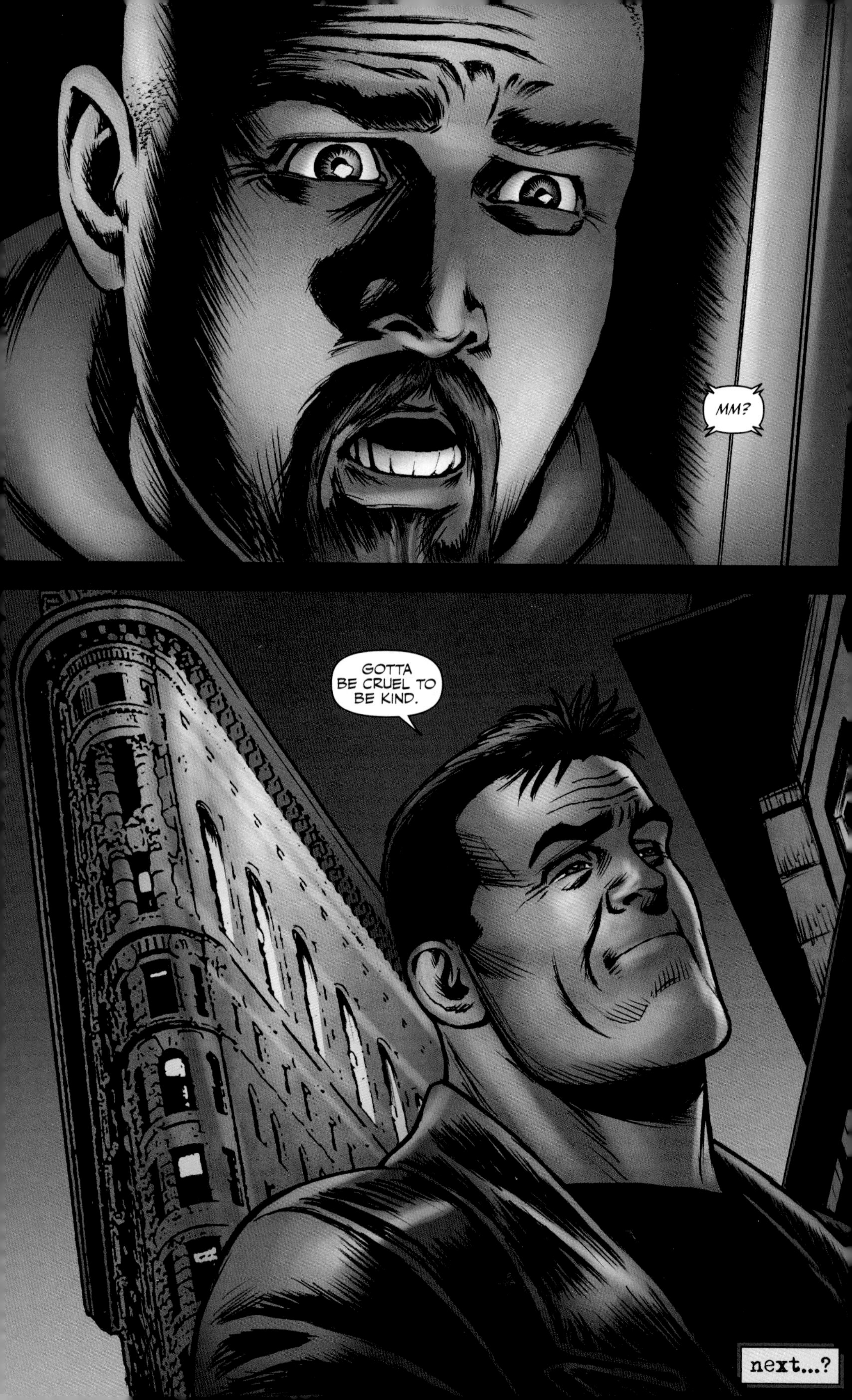
MM?
GOTTA BE CRUEL TO BE KIND.
next...?

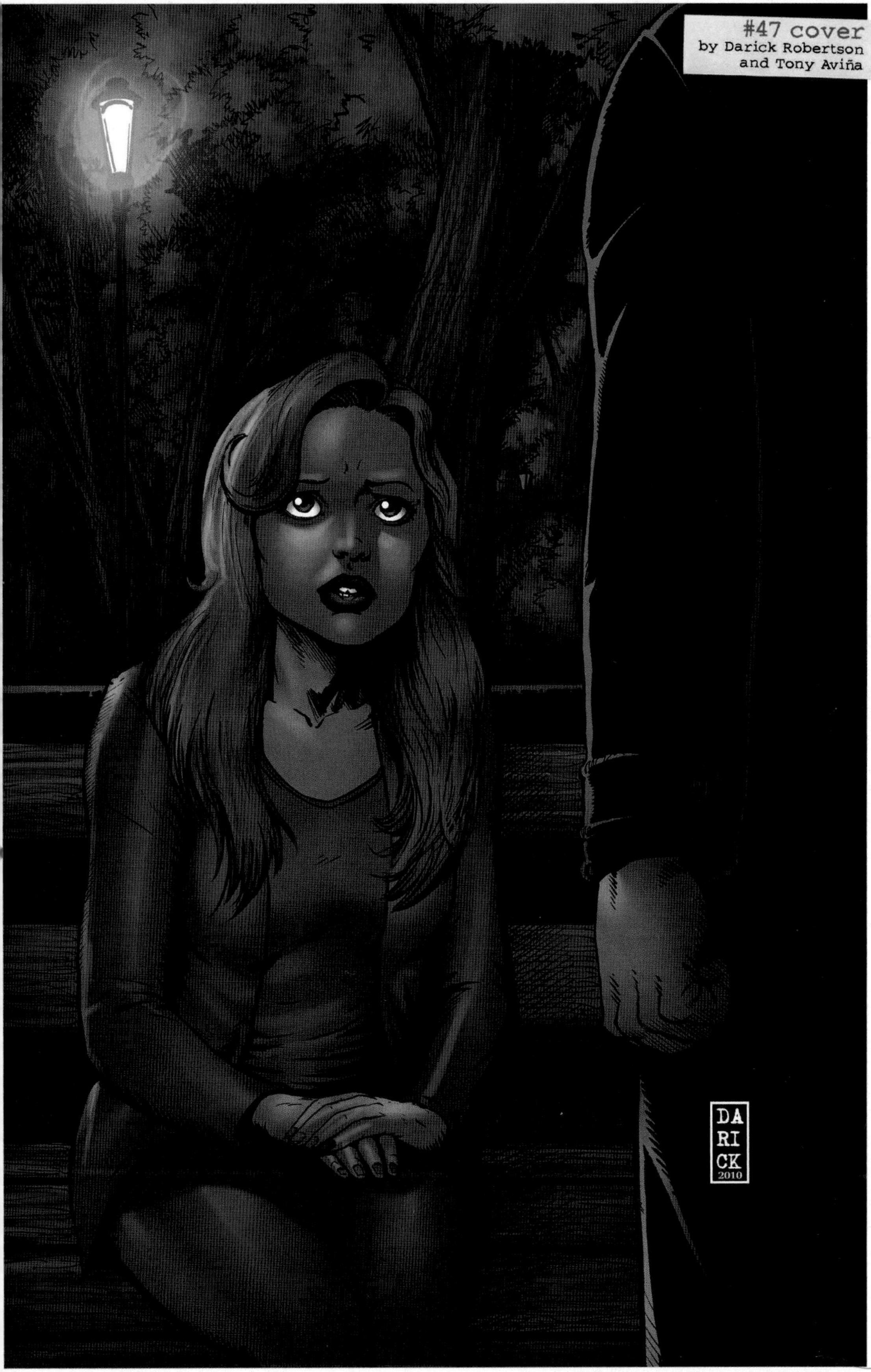
#47 cover
by Darick Robertson
and Tony Aviña
DA
RI
CK
2010

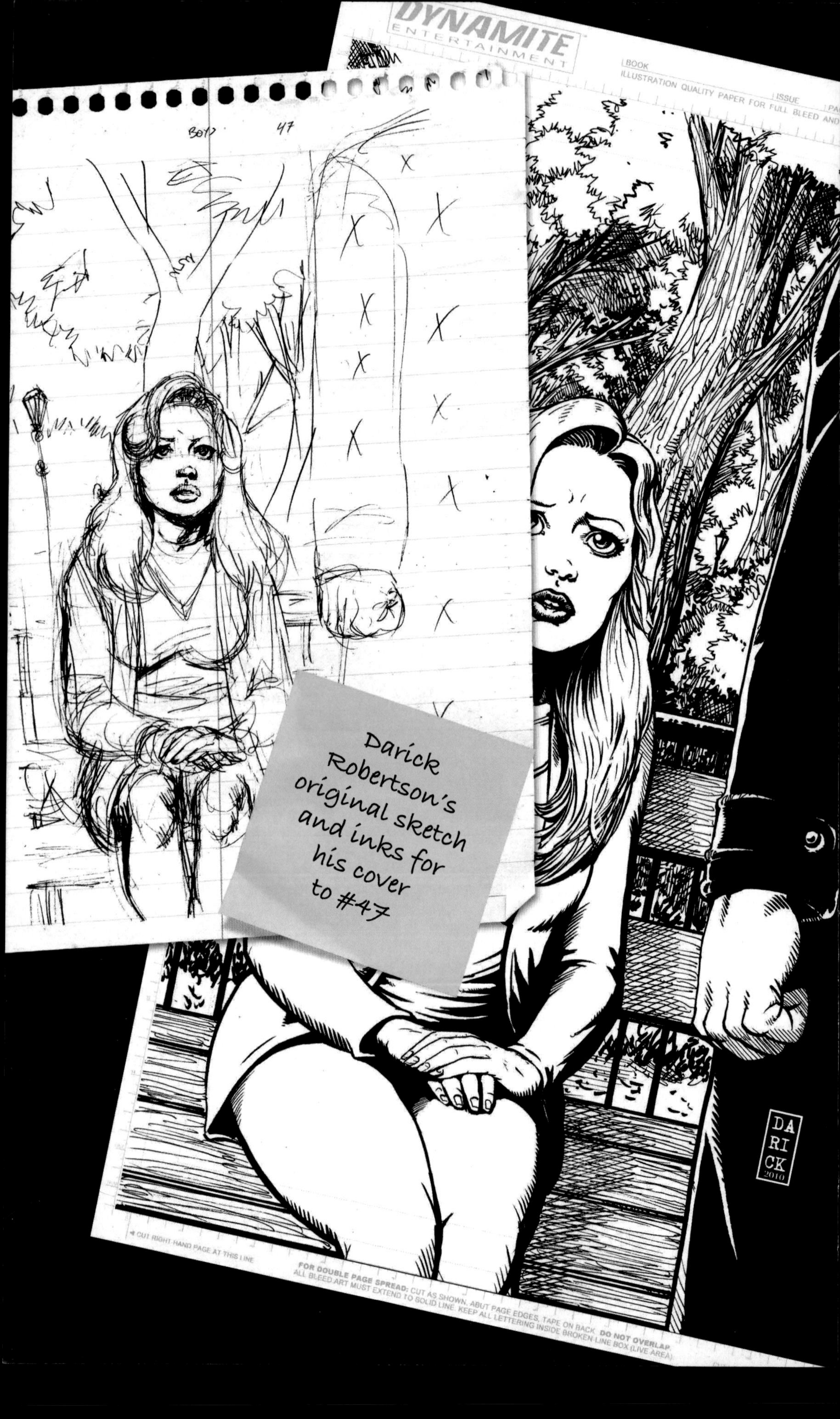

DYNAMITE ENTERTAINMENT
BOOK
ILLUSTRATION QUALITY PAPER FOR FULL BLEED AND
ISSUE
BOYS 47
Darick Robertson's original sketch and inks for his cover to #47
DA RI CK 2010
CUT RIGHT HAND PAGE AT THIS LINE
FOR DOUBLE PAGE SPREAD: CUT AS SHOWN, ABUT PAGE EDGES, TAPE ON BACK. DO NOT OVERLAP.
ALL BLEED ART MUST EXTEND TO SOLID LINE. KEEP ALL LETTERING INSIDE BROKEN LINE BOX (LIVE AREA)

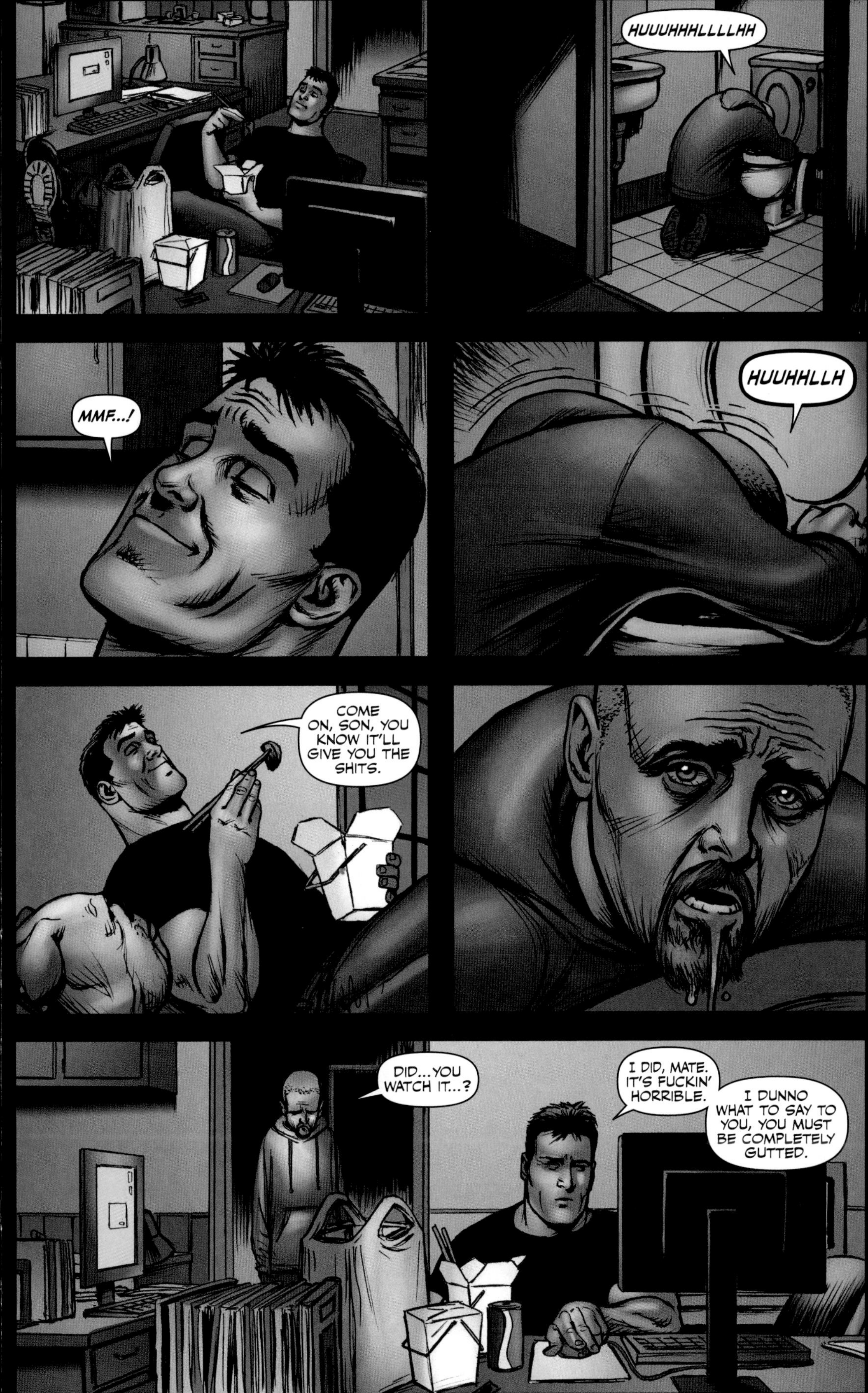
HUUUHHHLLLLLHH
MMF...!
HUUHHLLH
COME ON, SON, YOU KNOW IT'LL GIVE YOU THE SHITS.
DID...YOU WATCH IT...?
I DID, MATE. IT'S FUCKIN' HORRIBLE.
I DUNNO WHAT TO SAY TO YOU, YOU MUST BE COMPLETELY GUTTED.

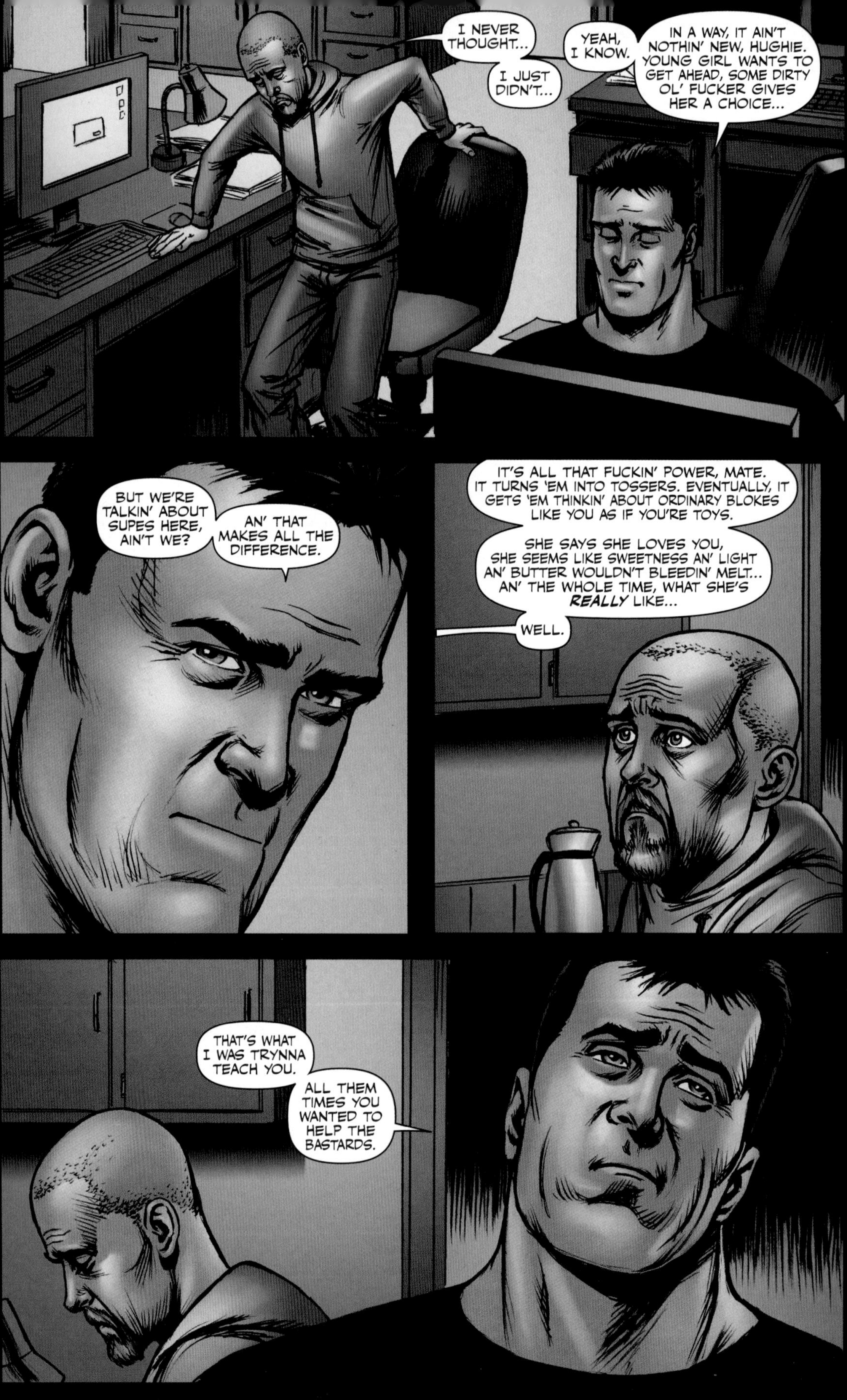
I NEVER THOUGHT...
I JUST DIDN'T...
YEAH, I KNOW.
IN A WAY, IT AIN'T NOTHIN' NEW, HUGHIE. YOUNG GIRL WANTS TO GET AHEAD, SOME DIRTY OL' FUCKER GIVES HER A CHOICE...
BUT WE'RE TALKIN' ABOUT SUPES HERE, AIN'T WE?
AN' THAT MAKES ALL THE DIFFERENCE.
IT'S ALL THAT FUCKIN' POWER, MATE. IT TURNS 'EM INTO TOSSERS. EVENTUALLY, IT GETS 'EM THINKIN' ABOUT ORDINARY BLOKES LIKE YOU AS IF YOU'RE TOYS.
SHE SAYS SHE LOVES YOU, SHE SEEMS LIKE SWEETNESS AN' LIGHT AN' BUTTER WOULDN'T BLEEDIN' MELT... AN' THE WHOLE TIME, WHAT SHE'S *REALLY* LIKE...
WELL.
THAT'S WHAT I WAS TRYNNA TEACH YOU.
ALL THEM TIMES YOU WANTED TO HELP THE BASTARDS.

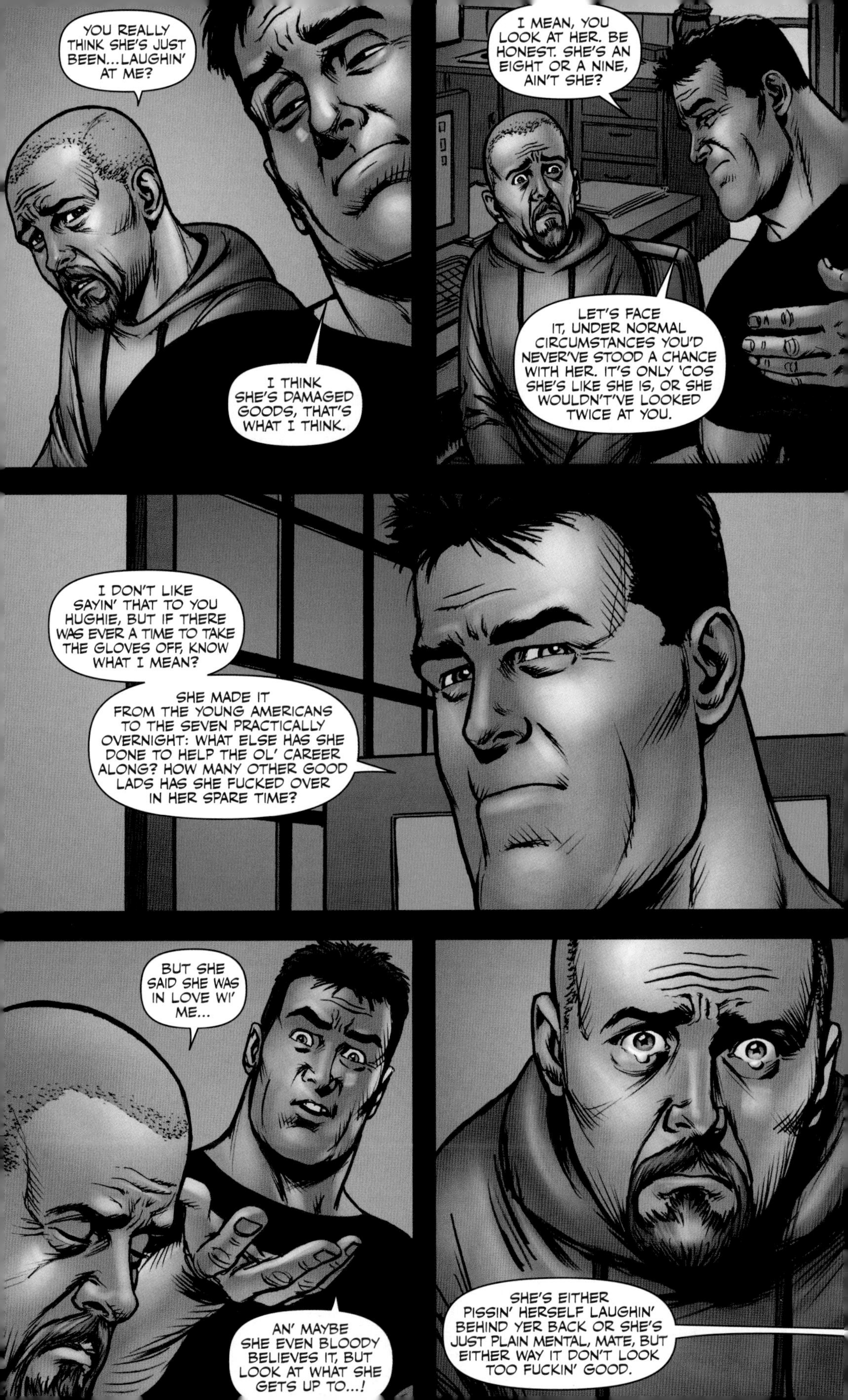
YOU REALLY THINK SHE'S JUST BEEN...LAUGHIN' AT ME?
I THINK SHE'S DAMAGED GOODS, THAT'S WHAT I THINK.
I MEAN, YOU LOOK AT HER. BE HONEST. SHE'S AN EIGHT OR A NINE, AIN'T SHE?
LET'S FACE IT, UNDER NORMAL CIRCUMSTANCES YOU'D NEVER'VE STOOD A CHANCE WITH HER. IT'S ONLY 'COS SHE'S LIKE SHE IS, OR SHE WOULDN'T'VE LOOKED TWICE AT YOU.
I DON'T LIKE SAYIN' THAT TO YOU HUGHIE, BUT IF THERE WAS EVER A TIME TO TAKE THE GLOVES OFF, KNOW WHAT I MEAN?
SHE MADE IT FROM THE YOUNG AMERICANS TO THE SEVEN PRACTICALLY OVERNIGHT: WHAT ELSE HAS SHE DONE TO HELP THE OL' CAREER ALONG? HOW MANY OTHER GOOD LADS HAS SHE FUCKED OVER IN HER SPARE TIME?
BUT SHE SAID SHE WAS IN LOVE WI' ME...
AN' MAYBE SHE EVEN BLOODY BELIEVES IT, BUT LOOK AT WHAT SHE GETS UP TO...!
SHE'S EITHER PISSIN' HERSELF LAUGHIN' BEHIND YER BACK OR SHE'S JUST PLAIN MENTAL, MATE, BUT EITHER WAY IT DON'T LOOK TOO FUCKIN' GOOD.

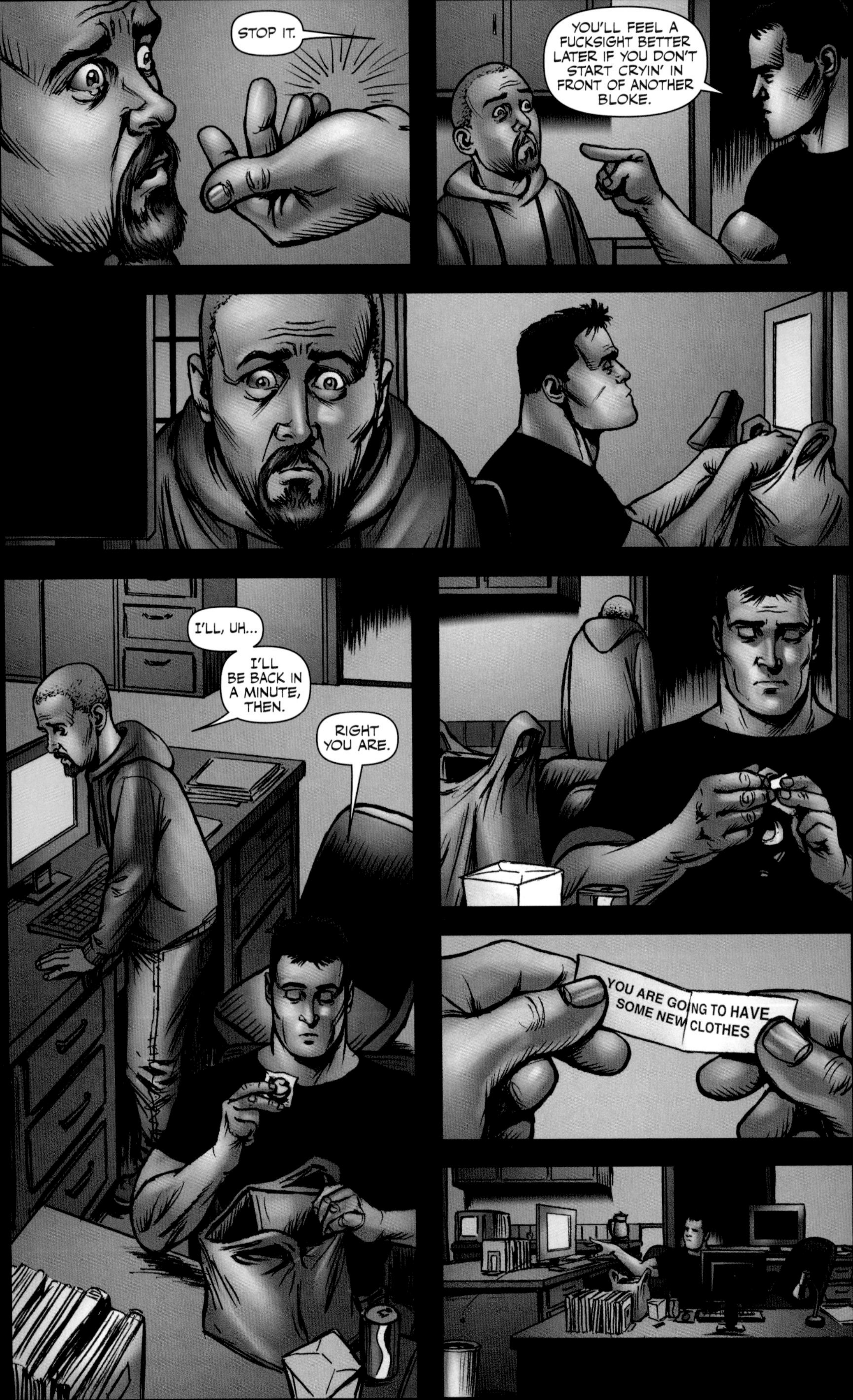
STOP IT.
YOU'LL FEEL A FUCKSIGHT BETTER LATER IF YOU DON'T START CRYIN' IN FRONT OF ANOTHER BLOKE.
I'LL, UH...
I'LL BE BACK IN A MINUTE, THEN.
RIGHT YOU ARE.
YOU ARE GOING TO HAVE SOME NEW CLOTHES

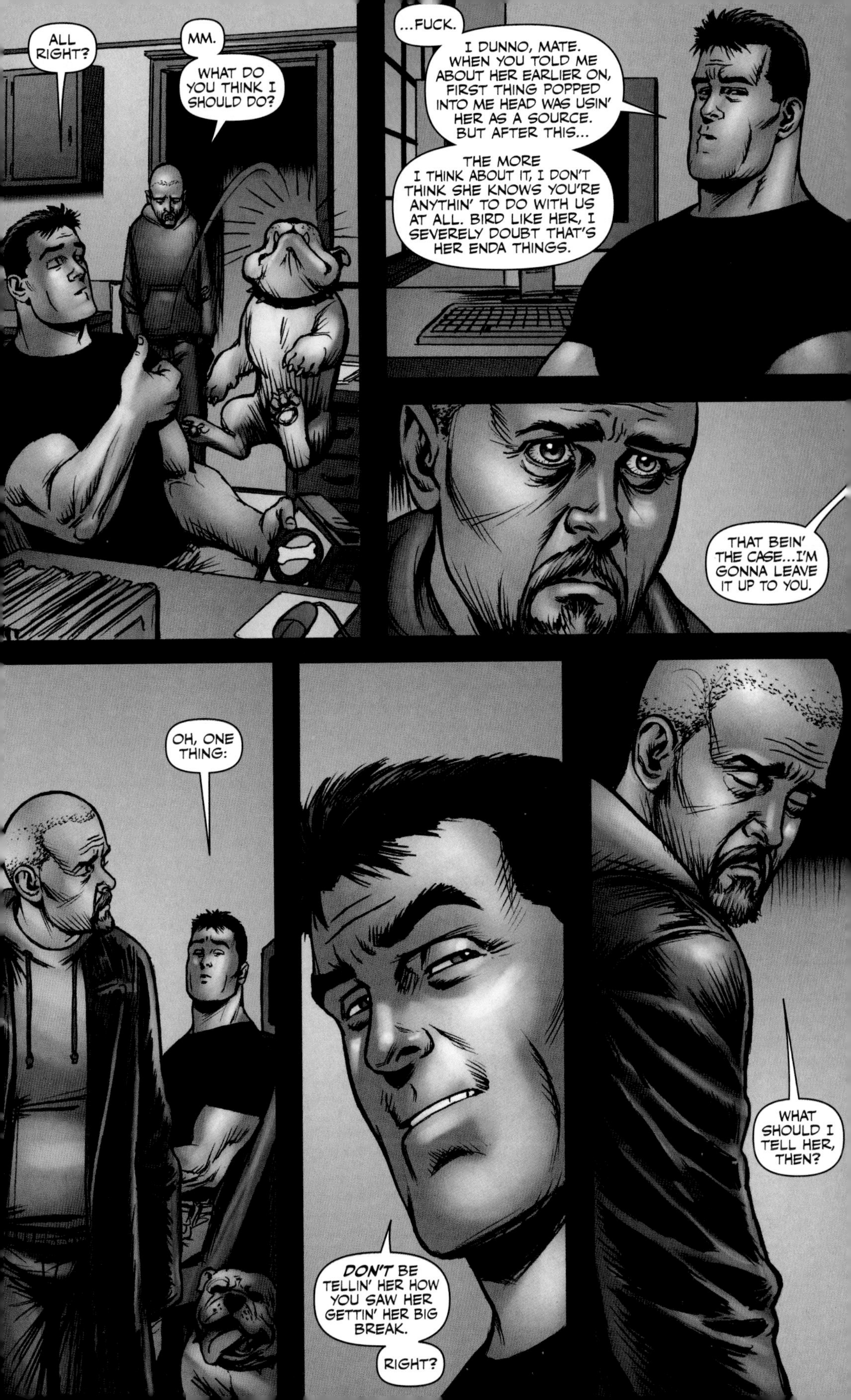
ALL RIGHT?
MM.
WHAT DO YOU THINK I SHOULD DO?
...FUCK.
I DUNNO, MATE. WHEN YOU TOLD ME ABOUT HER EARLIER ON, FIRST THING POPPED INTO ME HEAD WAS USIN' HER AS A SOURCE. BUT AFTER THIS...
THE MORE I THINK ABOUT IT, I DON'T THINK SHE KNOWS YOU'RE ANYTHIN' TO DO WITH US AT ALL. BIRD LIKE HER, I SEVERELY DOUBT THAT'S HER ENDA THINGS.
THAT BEIN' THE CASE...I'M GONNA LEAVE IT UP TO YOU.
OH, ONE THING:
WHAT SHOULD I TELL HER, THEN?
DON'T BE TELLIN' HER HOW YOU SAW HER GETTIN' HER BIG BREAK.
RIGHT?

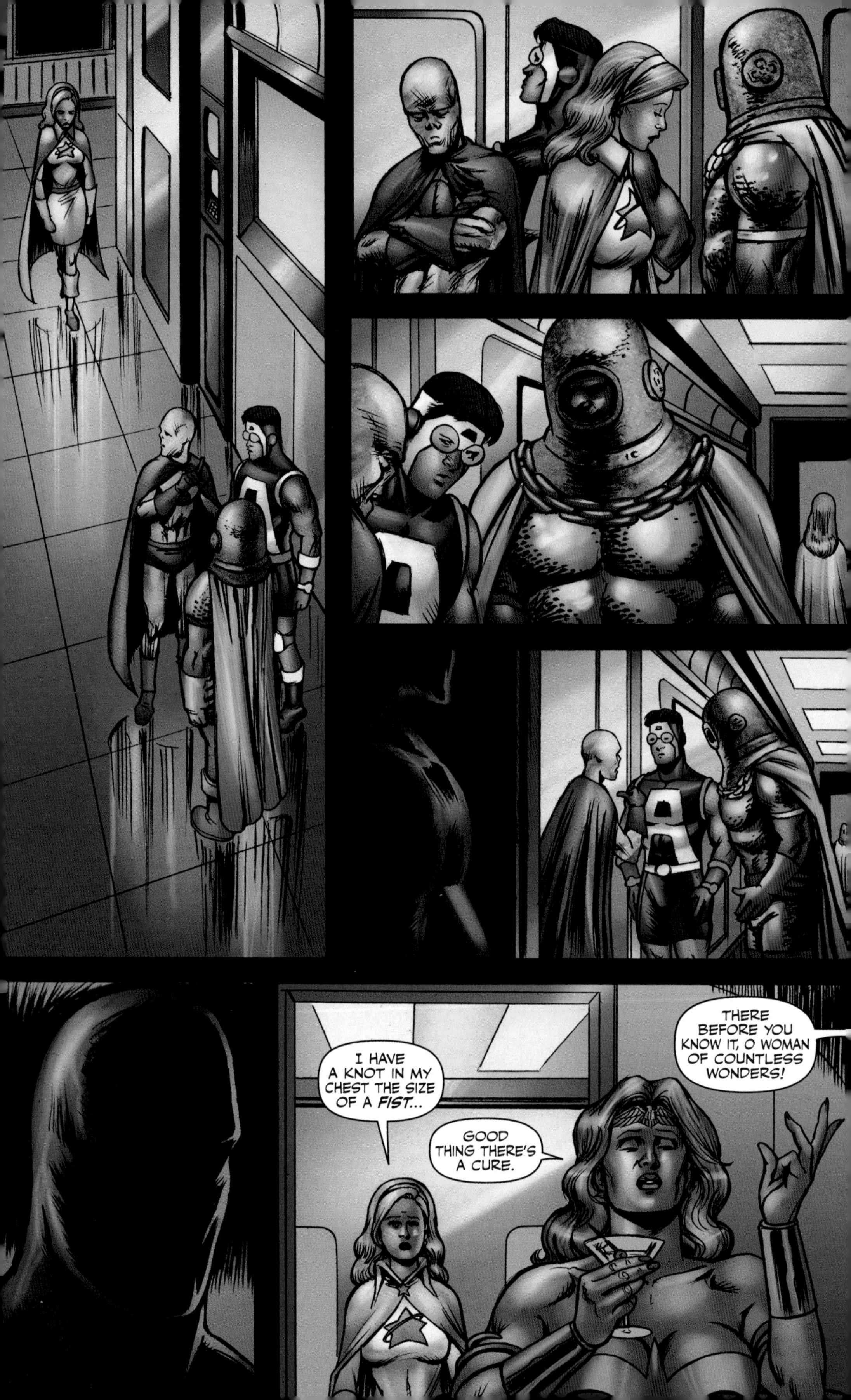
I HAVE A KNOT IN MY CHEST THE SIZE OF A FIST...
GOOD THING THERE'S A CURE.
THERE BEFORE YOU KNOW IT, O WOMAN OF COUNTLESS WONDERS!

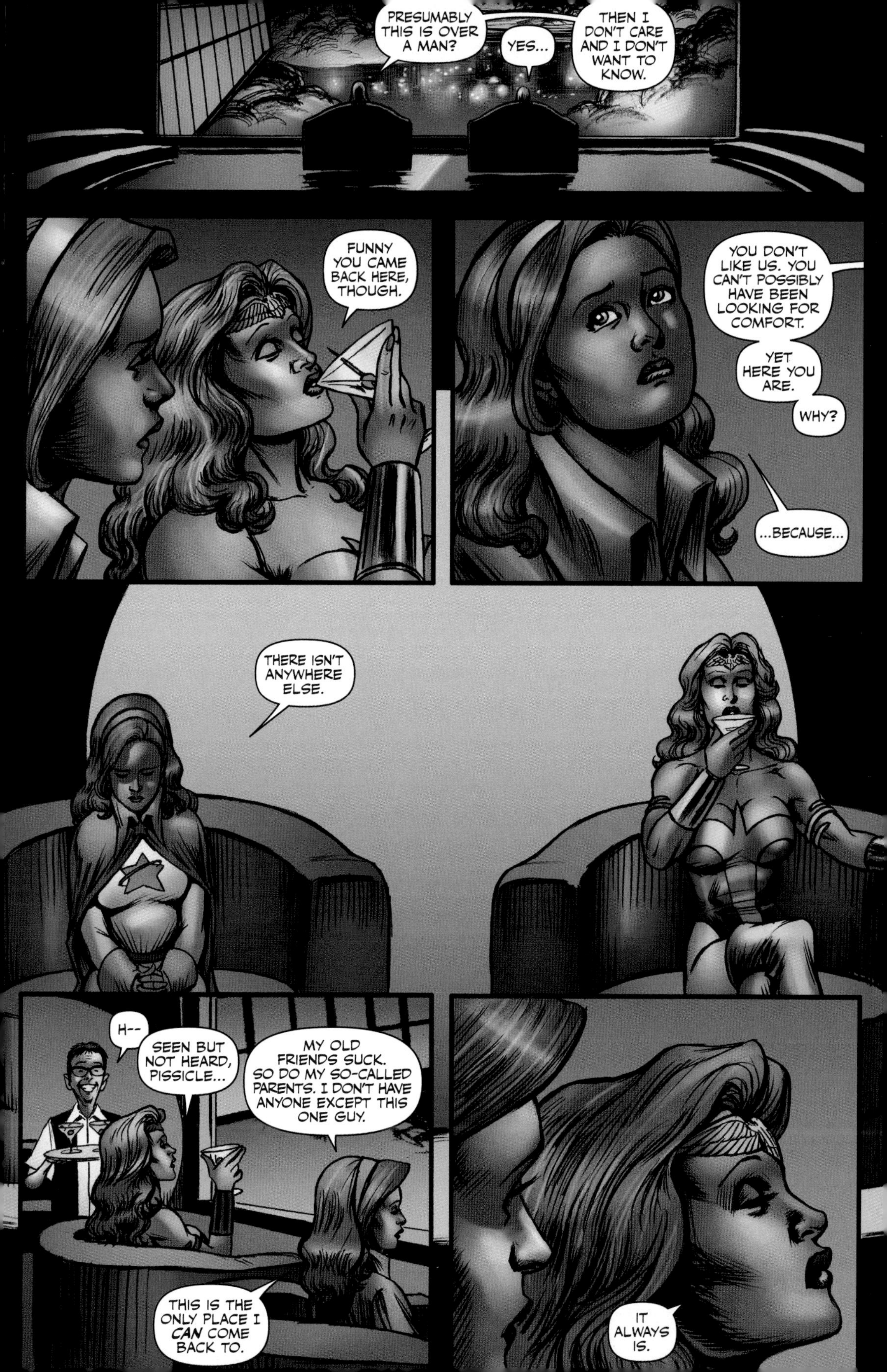
PRESUMABLY THIS IS OVER A MAN?
YES...
THEN I DON'T CARE AND I DON'T WANT TO KNOW.
FUNNY YOU CAME BACK HERE, THOUGH.
YOU DON'T LIKE US. YOU CAN'T POSSIBLY HAVE BEEN LOOKING FOR COMFORT.
YET HERE YOU ARE.
WHY?
...BECAUSE...
THERE ISN'T ANYWHERE ELSE.
H--
SEEN BUT NOT HEARD, PISSICLE...
MY OLD FRIENDS SUCK. SO DO MY SO-CALLED PARENTS. I DON'T HAVE ANYONE EXCEPT THIS ONE GUY.
THIS IS THE ONLY PLACE I *CAN* COME BACK TO.
IT ALWAYS IS.

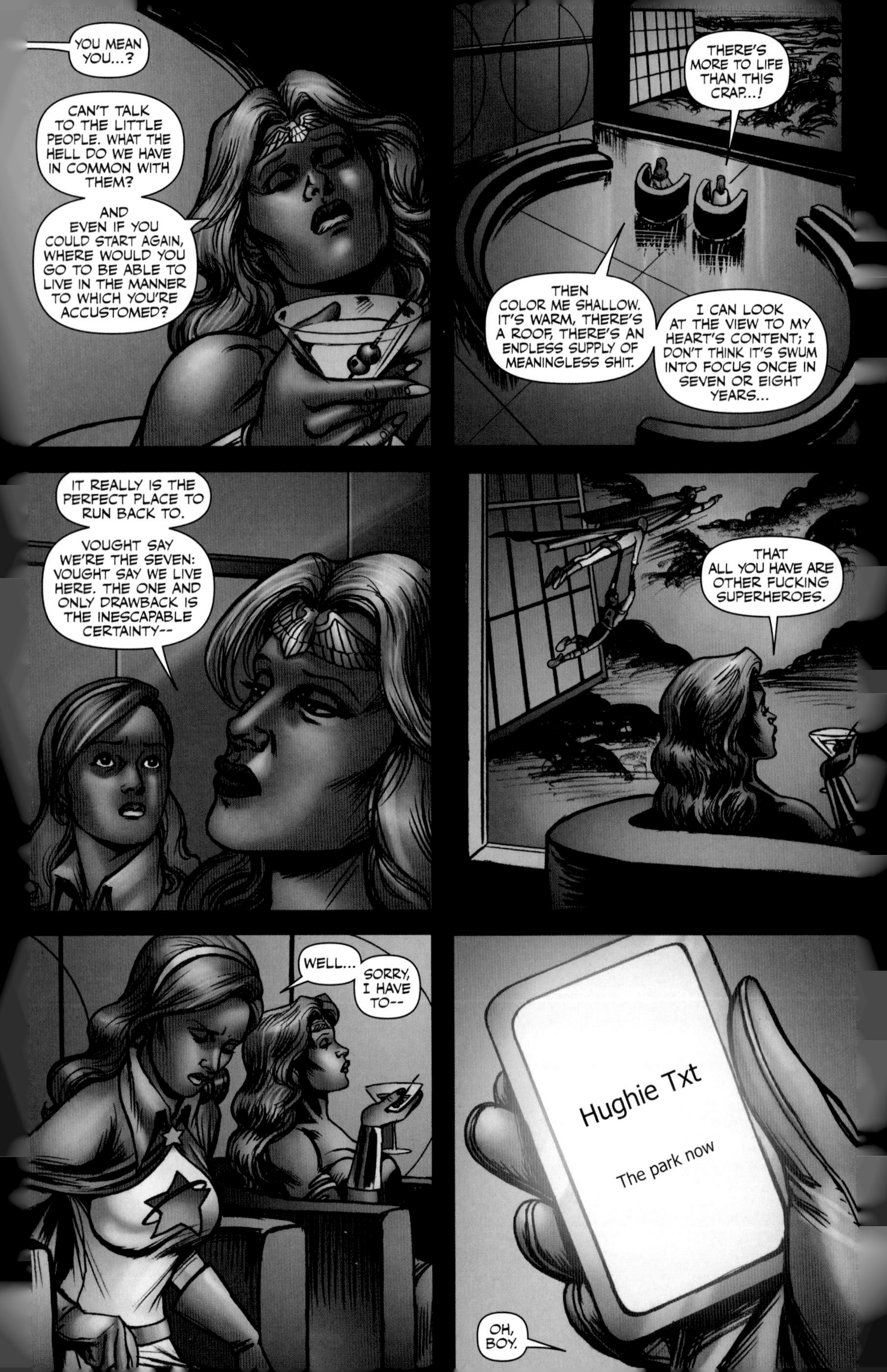
YOU MEAN YOU...?
CAN'T TALK TO THE LITTLE PEOPLE. WHAT THE HELL DO WE HAVE IN COMMON WITH THEM?
AND EVEN IF YOU COULD START AGAIN, WHERE WOULD YOU GO TO BE ABLE TO LIVE IN THE MANNER TO WHICH YOU'RE ACCUSTOMED?
THERE'S MORE TO LIFE THAN THIS CRAP...!
THEN COLOR ME SHALLOW. IT'S WARM, THERE'S A ROOF, THERE'S AN ENDLESS SUPPLY OF MEANINGLESS SHIT.
I CAN LOOK AT THE VIEW TO MY HEART'S CONTENT; I DON'T THINK IT'S SWUM INTO FOCUS ONCE IN SEVEN OR EIGHT YEARS...
IT REALLY IS THE PERFECT PLACE TO RUN BACK TO.
VOUGHT SAY WE'RE THE SEVEN: VOUGHT SAY WE LIVE HERE. THE ONE AND ONLY DRAWBACK IS THE INESCAPABLE CERTAINTY--
THAT ALL YOU HAVE ARE OTHER FUCKING SUPERHEROES.
WELL...
SORRY, I HAVE TO--
Hughie Txt
The park now
OH, BOY.

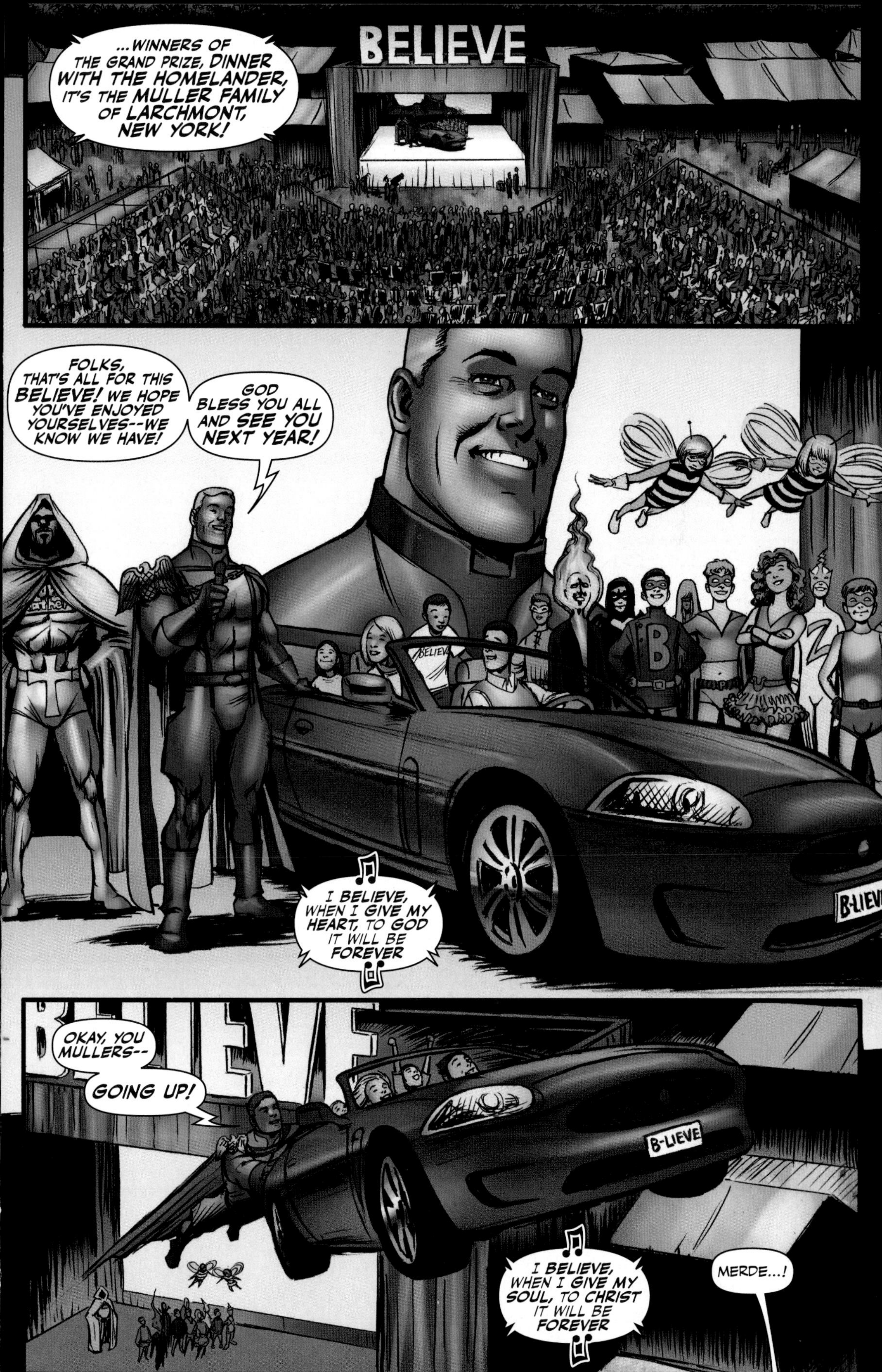

BELIEVE
...WINNERS OF THE GRAND PRIZE, DINNER WITH THE HOMELANDER, IT'S THE MULLER FAMILY OF LARCHMONT, NEW YORK!
FOLKS, THAT'S ALL FOR THIS BELIEVE! WE HOPE YOU'VE ENJOYED YOURSELVES--WE KNOW WE HAVE!
GOD BLESS YOU ALL AND SEE YOU NEXT YEAR!
I BELIEVE, WHEN I GIVE MY HEART, TO GOD IT WILL BE FOREVER
B-LIEVE
OKAY, YOU MULLERS--
GOING UP!
B-LIEVE
I BELIEVE, WHEN I GIVE MY SOUL, TO CHRIST IT WILL BE FOREVER
MERDE...!

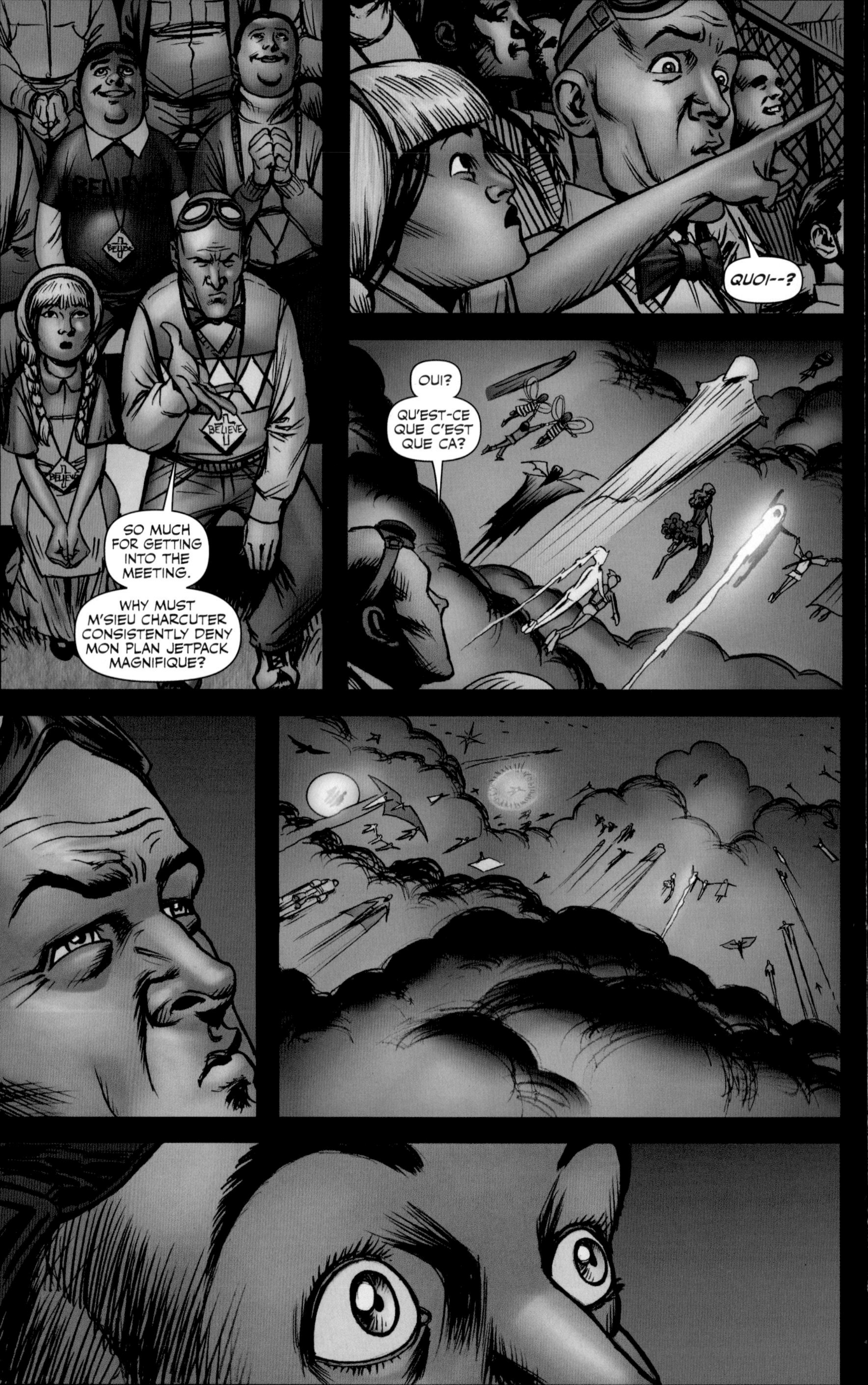

SO MUCH FOR GETTING INTO THE MEETING.
WHY MUST M'SIEU CHARCUTER CONSISTENTLY DENY MON PLAN JETPACK MAGNIFIQUE?
QUOI--?
OUI?
QU'EST-CE QUE C'EST QUE CA?

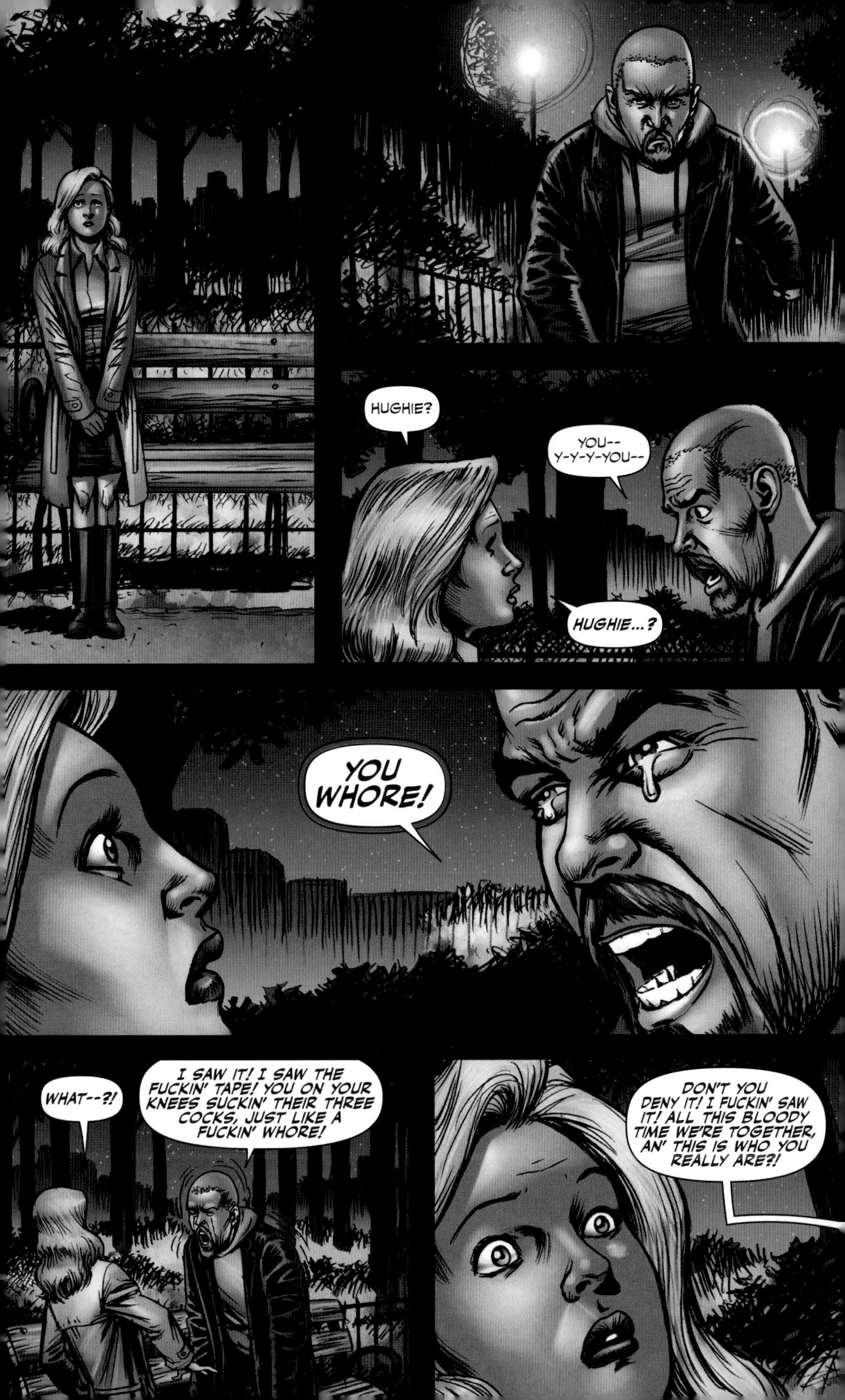
HUGHIE?
YOU--
Y-Y-Y-YOU--
HUGHIE...?
YOU WHORE!
WHAT--?!
I SAW IT! I SAW THE FUCKIN' TAPE! YOU ON YOUR KNEES SUCKIN' THEIR THREE COCKS, JUST LIKE A FUCKIN' WHORE!
DON'T YOU DENY IT! I FUCKIN' SAW IT! ALL THIS BLOODY TIME WE'RE TOGETHER, AN' THIS IS WHO YOU REALLY ARE?!

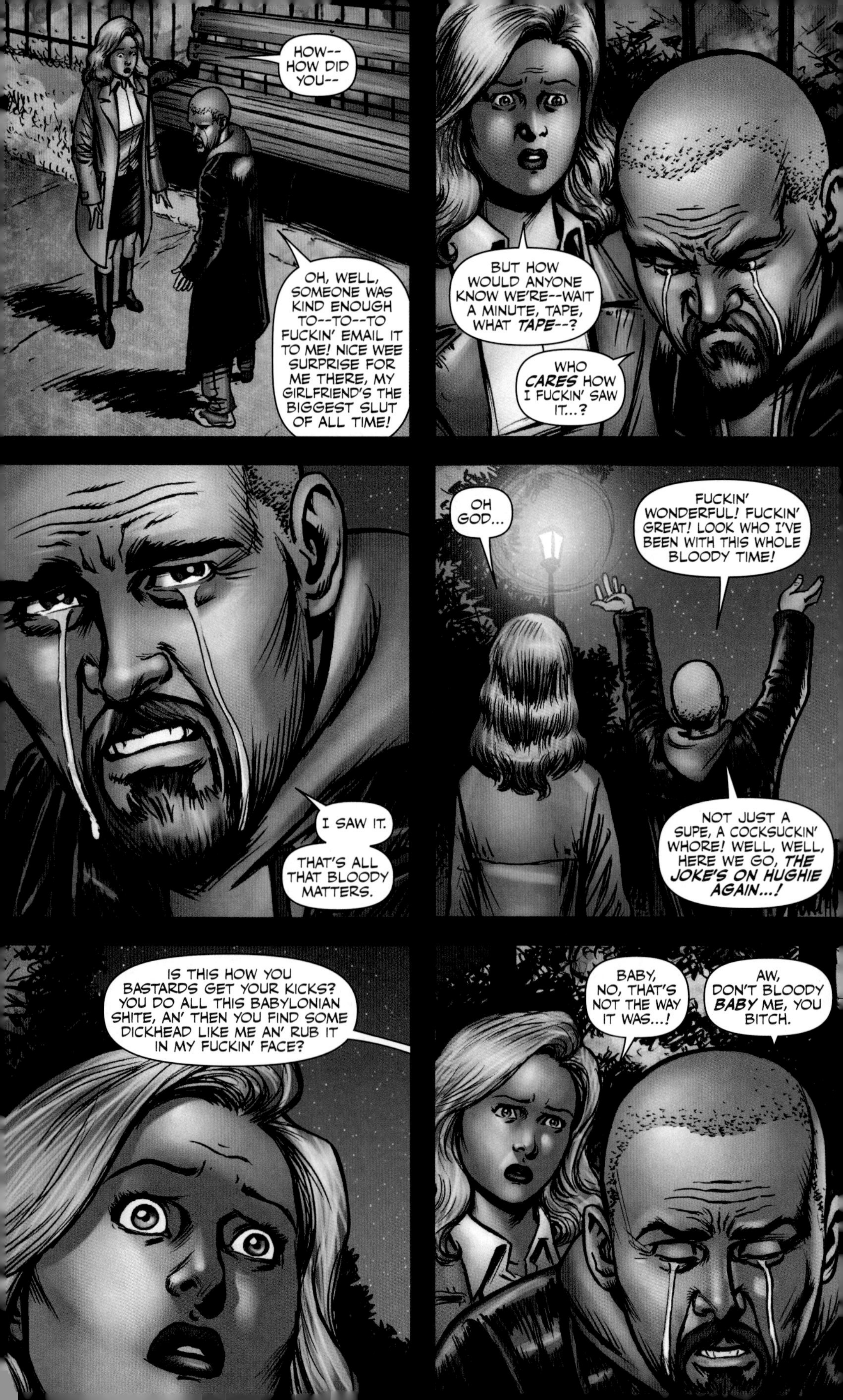
HOW-- HOW DID YOU--
OH, WELL, SOMEONE WAS KIND ENOUGH TO--TO--TO FUCKIN' EMAIL IT TO ME! NICE WEE SURPRISE FOR ME THERE, MY GIRLFRIEND'S THE BIGGEST SLUT OF ALL TIME!
BUT HOW WOULD ANYONE KNOW WE'RE--WAIT A MINUTE, TAPE, WHAT *TAPE*--?
WHO *CARES* HOW I FUCKIN' SAW IT...?
I SAW IT.
THAT'S ALL THAT BLOODY MATTERS.
OH GOD...
FUCKIN' WONDERFUL! FUCKIN' GREAT! LOOK WHO I'VE BEEN WITH THIS WHOLE BLOODY TIME!
NOT JUST A SUPE, A COCKSUCKIN' WHORE! WELL, WELL, HERE WE GO, *THE JOKE'S ON HUGHIE AGAIN...!*
IS THIS HOW YOU BASTARDS GET YOUR KICKS? YOU DO ALL THIS BABYLONIAN SHITE, AN' THEN YOU FIND SOME DICKHEAD LIKE ME AN' RUB IT IN MY FUCKIN' FACE?
BABY, NO, THAT'S NOT THE WAY IT WAS...!
AW, DON'T BLOODY *BABY* ME, YOU BITCH.

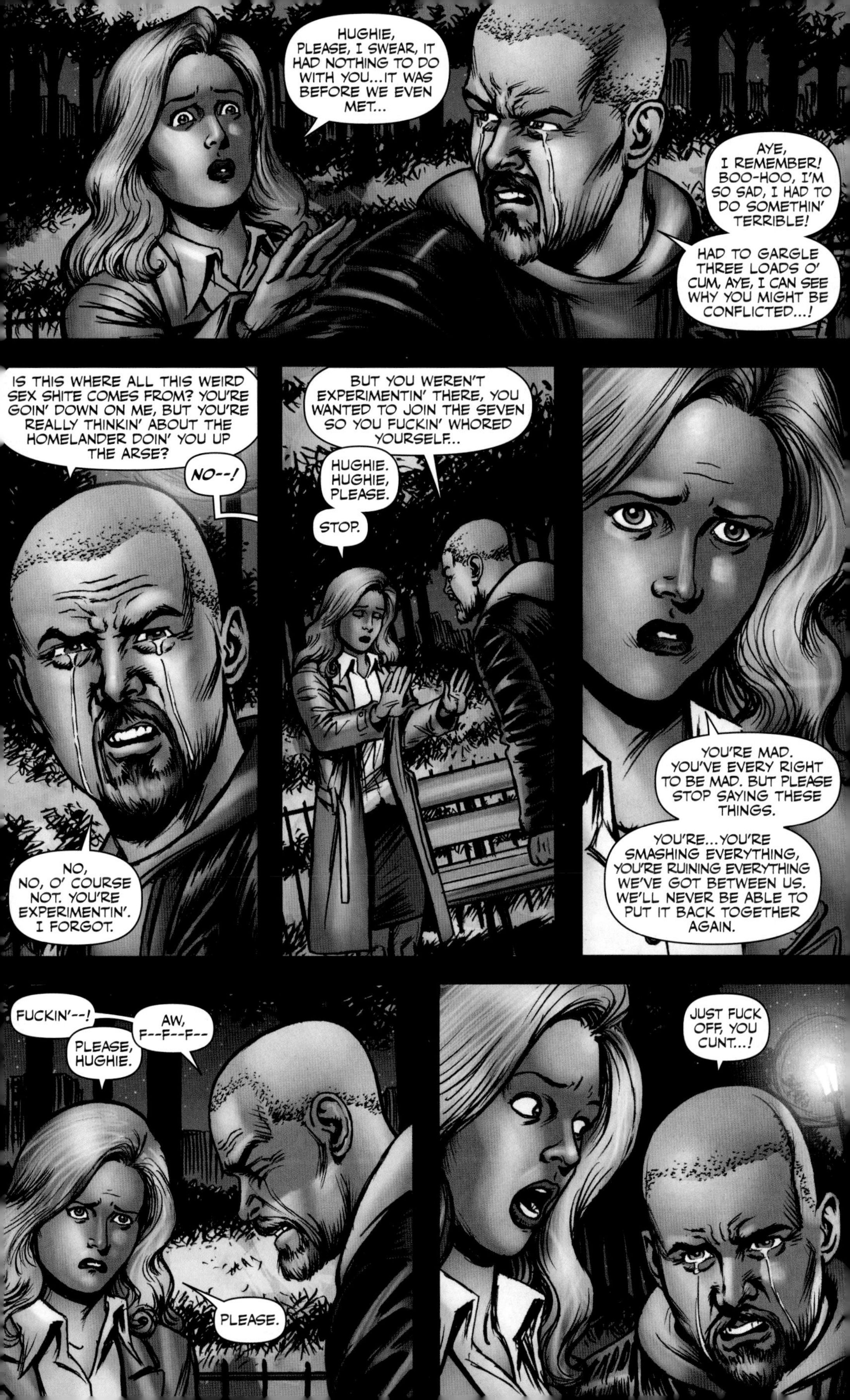

HUGHIE, PLEASE, I SWEAR, IT HAD NOTHING TO DO WITH YOU...IT WAS BEFORE WE EVEN MET...
AYE, I REMEMBER! BOO-HOO, I'M SO SAD, I HAD TO DO SOMETHIN' TERRIBLE!
HAD TO GARGLE THREE LOADS O' CUM, AYE, I CAN SEE WHY YOU MIGHT BE CONFLICTED...!
IS THIS WHERE ALL THIS WEIRD SEX SHITE COMES FROM? YOU'RE GOIN' DOWN ON ME, BUT YOU'RE REALLY THINKIN' ABOUT THE HOMELANDER DOIN' YOU UP THE ARSE?
NO--!
NO, NO, O' COURSE NOT. YOU'RE EXPERIMENTIN'. I FORGOT.
BUT YOU WEREN'T EXPERIMENTIN' THERE, YOU WANTED TO JOIN THE SEVEN SO YOU FUCKIN' WHORED YOURSELF...
HUGHIE. HUGHIE, PLEASE.
STOP.
YOU'RE MAD. YOU'VE EVERY RIGHT TO BE MAD. BUT PLEASE STOP SAYING THESE THINGS.
YOU'RE...YOU'RE SMASHING EVERYTHING, YOU'RE RUINING EVERYTHING WE'VE GOT BETWEEN US. WE'LL NEVER BE ABLE TO PUT IT BACK TOGETHER AGAIN.
FUCKIN'--!
AW, F--F--F--
PLEASE, HUGHIE.
PLEASE.
JUST FUCK OFF, YOU CUNT...!

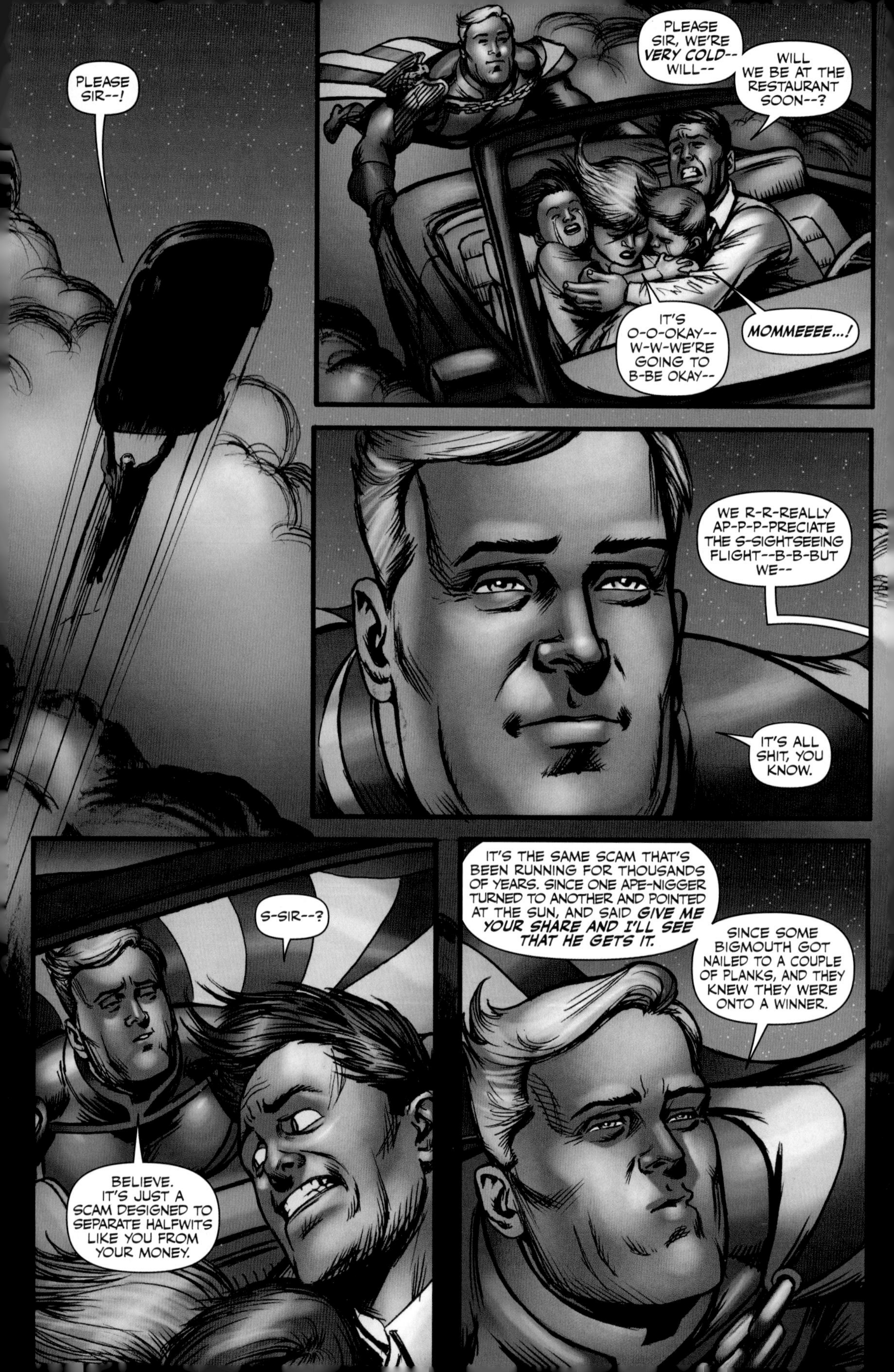
PLEASE SIR--!
PLEASE SIR, WE'RE *VERY COLD*-- WILL--
WILL WE BE AT THE RESTAURANT SOON--?
IT'S O-O-OKAY-- W-W-WE'RE GOING TO B-BE OKAY--
MOMMEEEE...!
WE R-R-REALLY AP-P-P-PRECIATE THE S-SIGHTSEEING FLIGHT--B-B-BUT WE--
IT'S ALL SHIT, YOU KNOW.
S-SIR--?
BELIEVE. IT'S JUST A SCAM DESIGNED TO SEPARATE HALFWITS LIKE YOU FROM YOUR MONEY.
IT'S THE SAME SCAM THAT'S BEEN RUNNING FOR THOUSANDS OF YEARS. SINCE ONE APE-NIGGER TURNED TO ANOTHER AND POINTED AT THE SUN, AND SAID *GIVE ME YOUR SHARE AND I'LL SEE THAT HE GETS IT.*
SINCE SOME BIGMOUTH GOT NAILED TO A COUPLE OF PLANKS, AND THEY KNEW THEY WERE ONTO A WINNER.

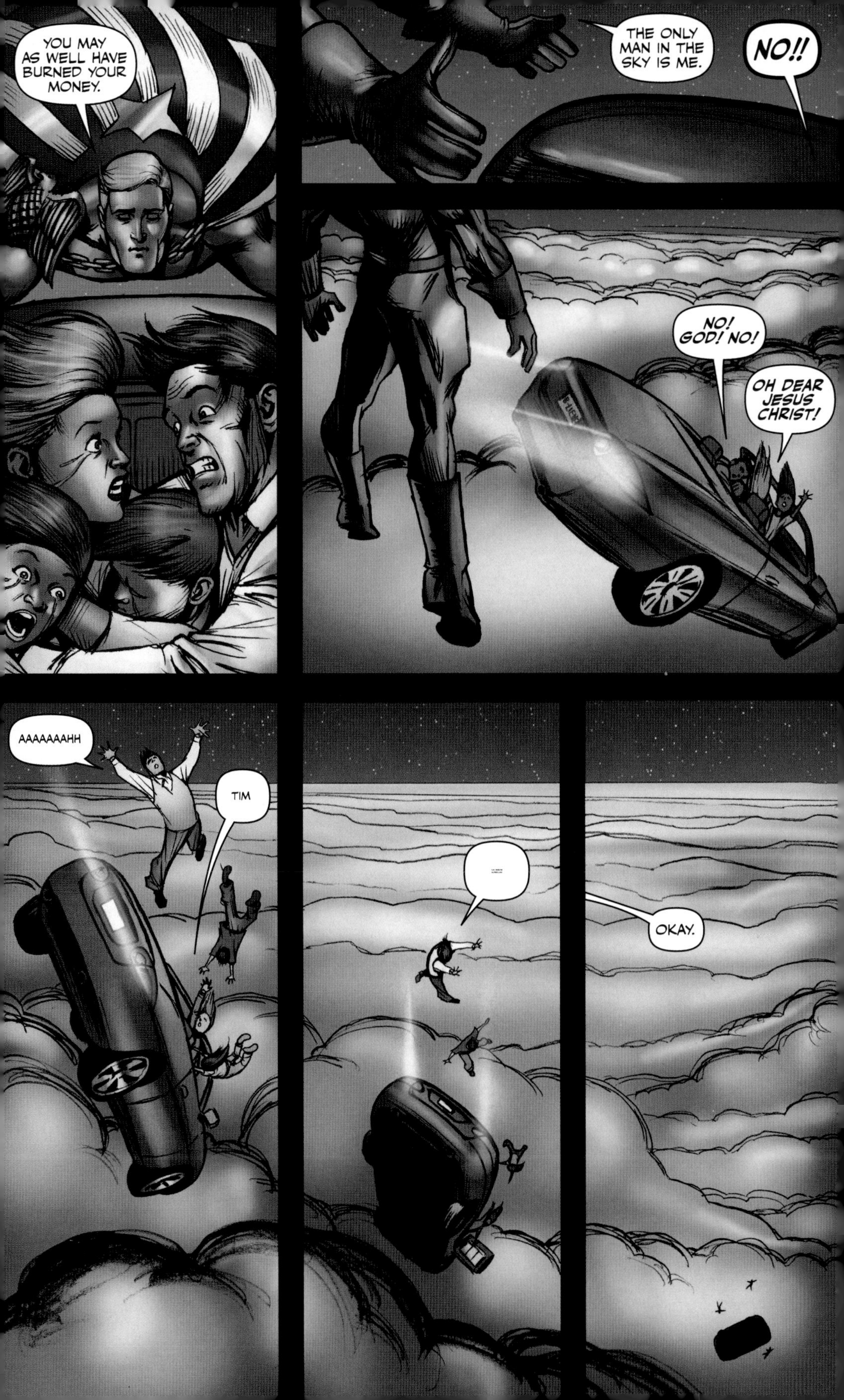
YOU MAY AS WELL HAVE BURNED YOUR MONEY.
THE ONLY MAN IN THE SKY IS ME.
NO!!
NO! GOD! NO!
OH DEAR JESUS CHRIST!
AAAAAAAHH
TIM
OKAY.

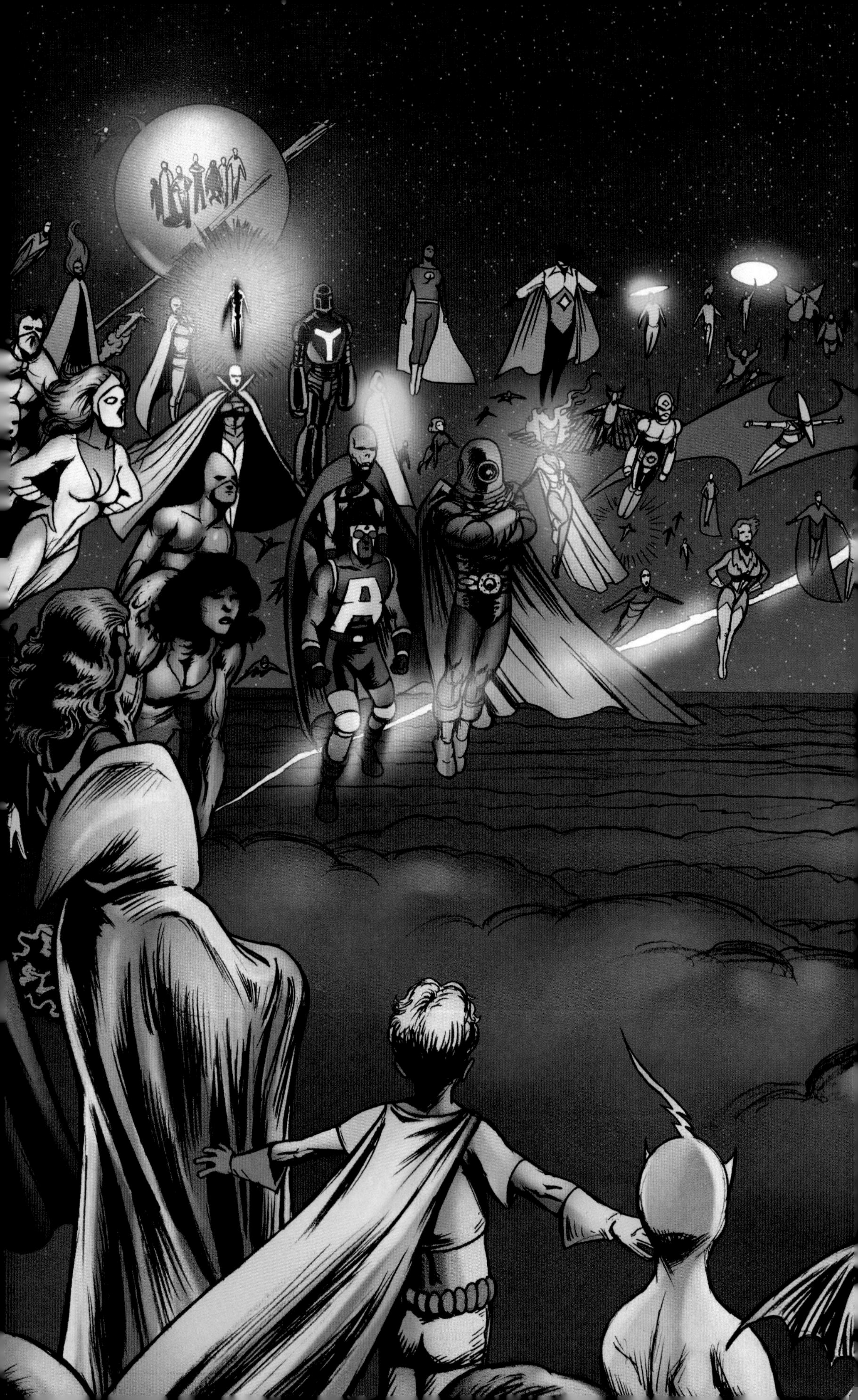

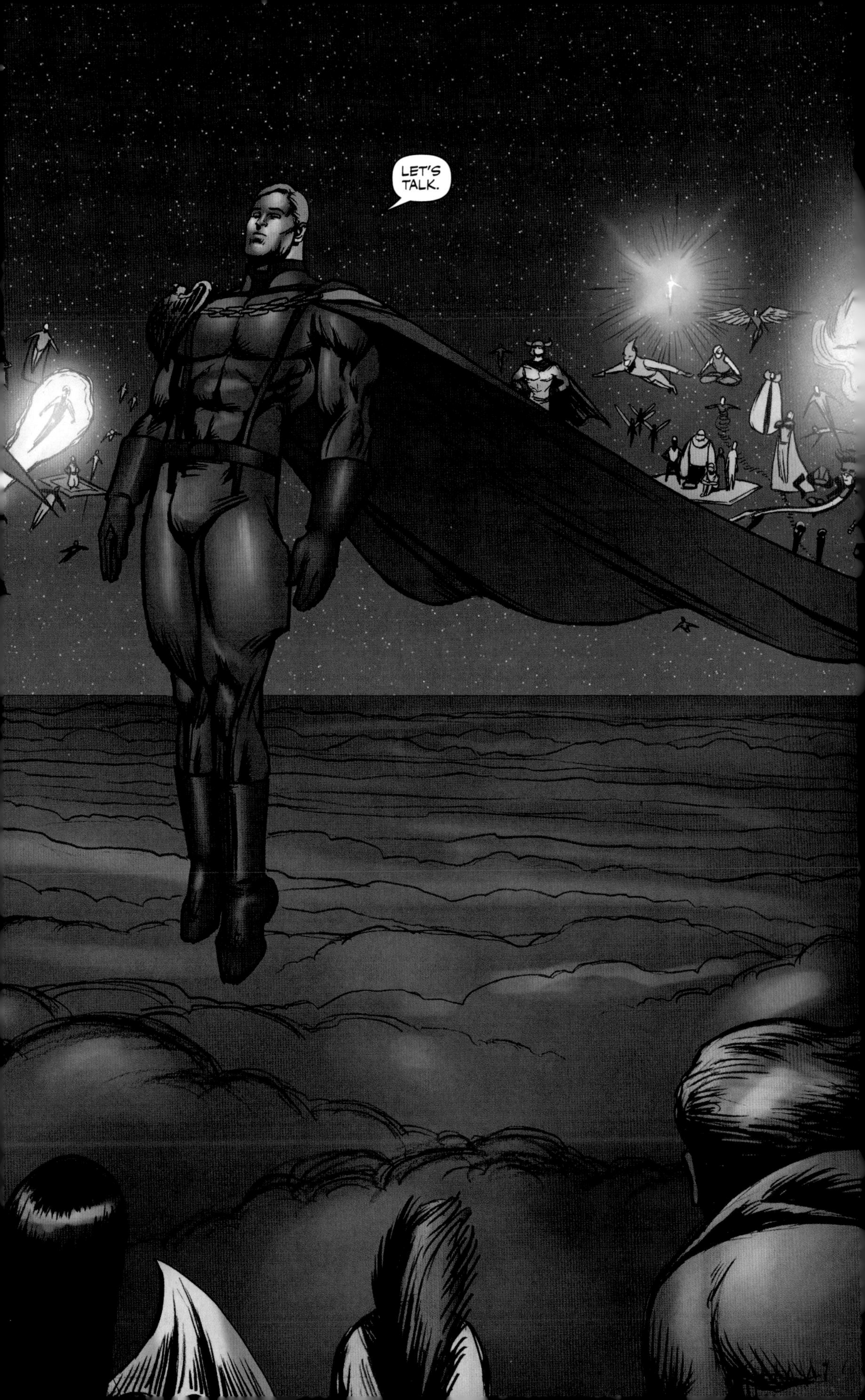
LET'S TALK.

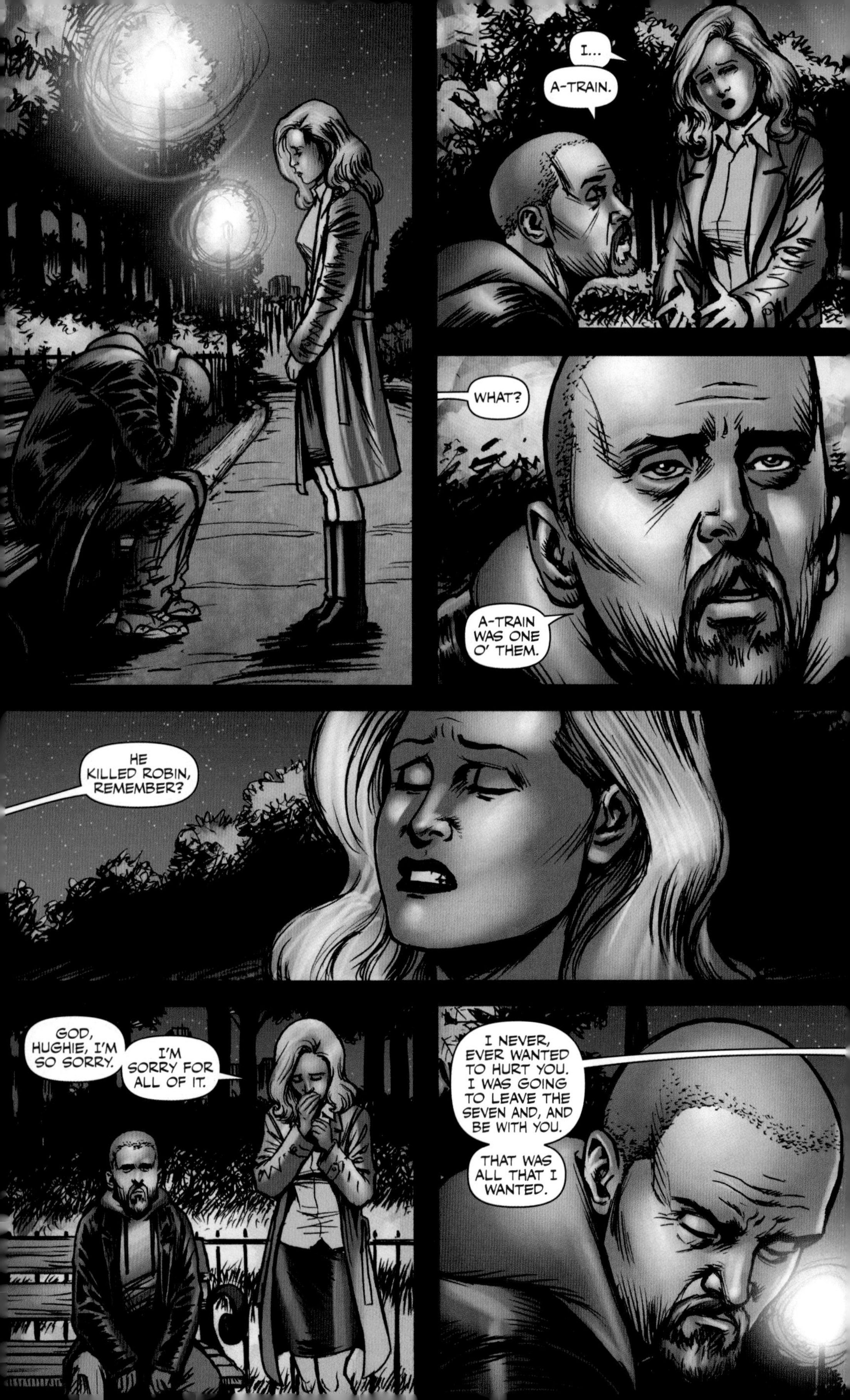
I...
A-TRAIN.
WHAT?
A-TRAIN WAS ONE O' THEM.
HE KILLED ROBIN, REMEMBER?
GOD, HUGHIE, I'M SO SORRY.
I'M SORRY FOR ALL OF IT.
I NEVER, EVER WANTED TO HURT YOU. I WAS GOING TO LEAVE THE SEVEN AND, AND BE WITH YOU.
THAT WAS ALL THAT I WANTED.

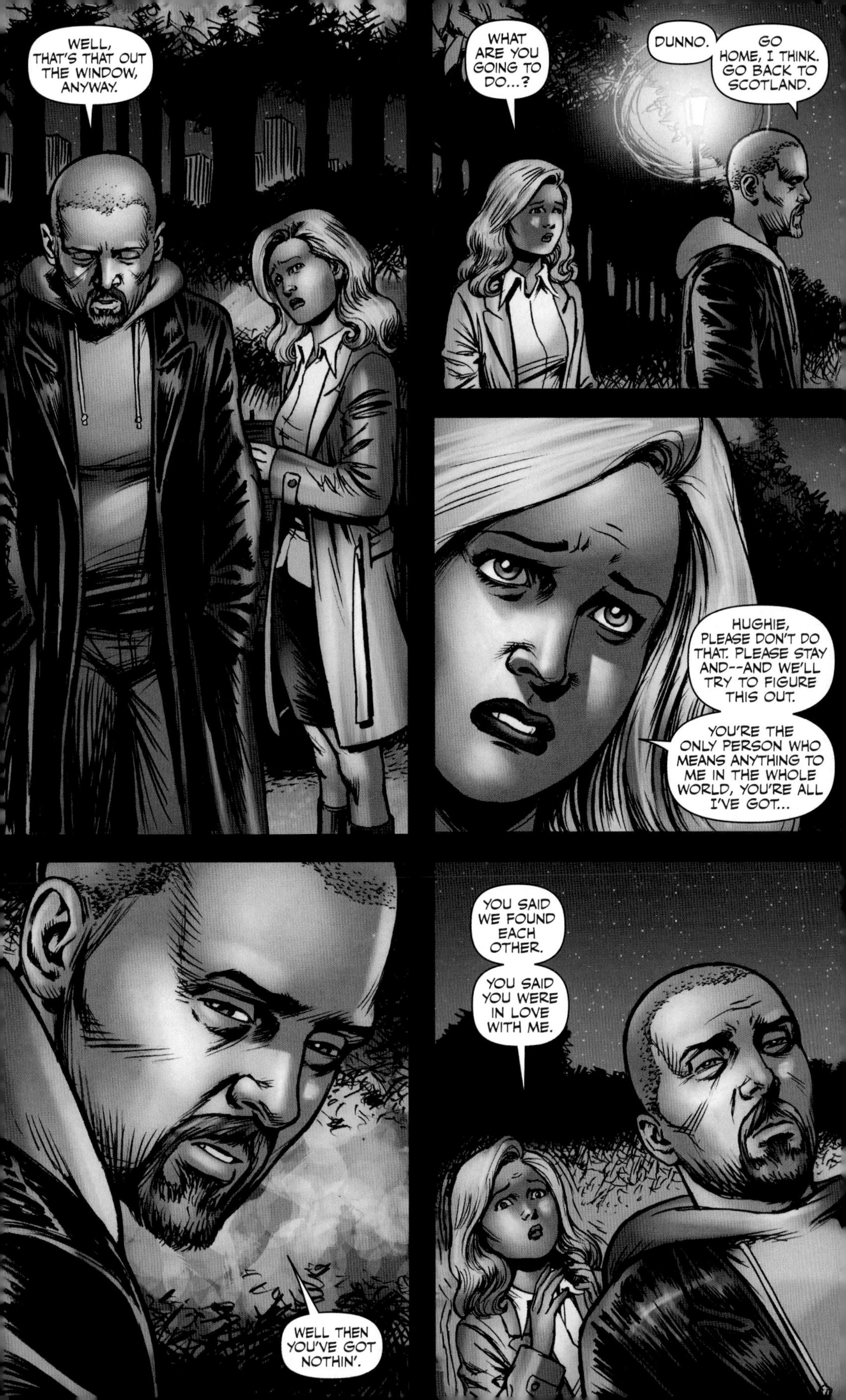
WELL, THAT'S THAT OUT THE WINDOW, ANYWAY.
WHAT ARE YOU GOING TO DO...?
DUNNO.
GO HOME, I THINK. GO BACK TO SCOTLAND.
HUGHIE, PLEASE DON'T DO THAT. PLEASE STAY AND--AND WE'LL TRY TO FIGURE THIS OUT.
YOU'RE THE ONLY PERSON WHO MEANS ANYTHING TO ME IN THE WHOLE WORLD, YOU'RE ALL I'VE GOT...
WELL THEN YOU'VE GOT NOTHIN'.
YOU SAID WE FOUND EACH OTHER.
YOU SAID YOU WERE IN LOVE WITH ME.

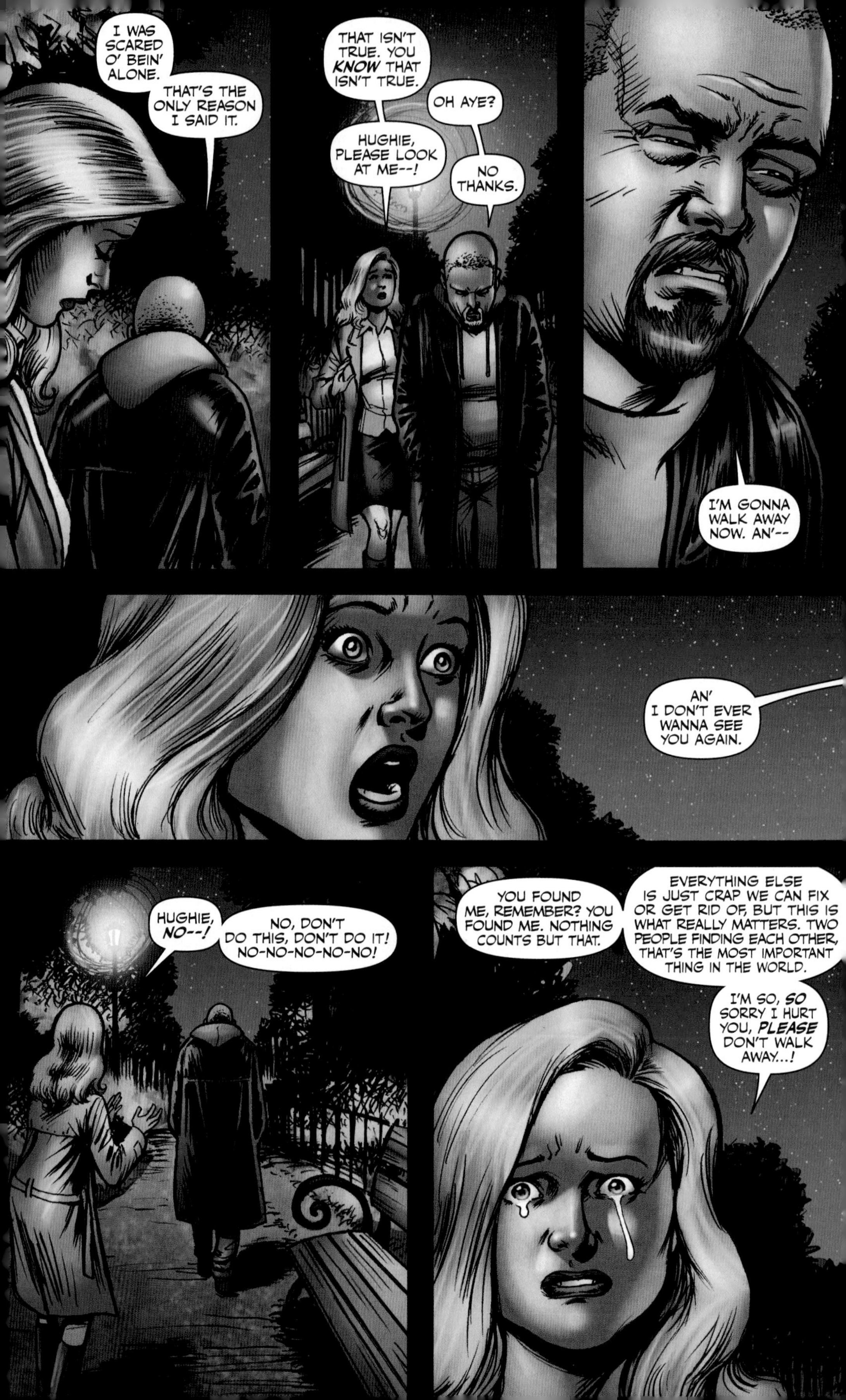
I WAS SCARED O' BEIN' ALONE.
THAT'S THE ONLY REASON I SAID IT.
THAT ISN'T TRUE. YOU *KNOW* THAT ISN'T TRUE.
OH AYE?
HUGHIE, PLEASE LOOK AT ME--!
NO THANKS.
I'M GONNA WALK AWAY NOW. AN'--
AN' I DON'T EVER WANNA SEE YOU AGAIN.
HUGHIE, *NO--!*
NO, DON'T DO THIS, DON'T DO IT! NO-NO-NO-NO-NO!
YOU FOUND ME, REMEMBER? YOU FOUND ME. NOTHING COUNTS BUT THAT.
EVERYTHING ELSE IS JUST CRAP WE CAN FIX OR GET RID OF, BUT THIS IS WHAT REALLY MATTERS. TWO PEOPLE FINDING EACH OTHER, THAT'S THE MOST IMPORTANT THING IN THE WORLD.
I'M SO, *SO* SORRY I HURT YOU, *PLEASE* DON'T WALK AWAY...!

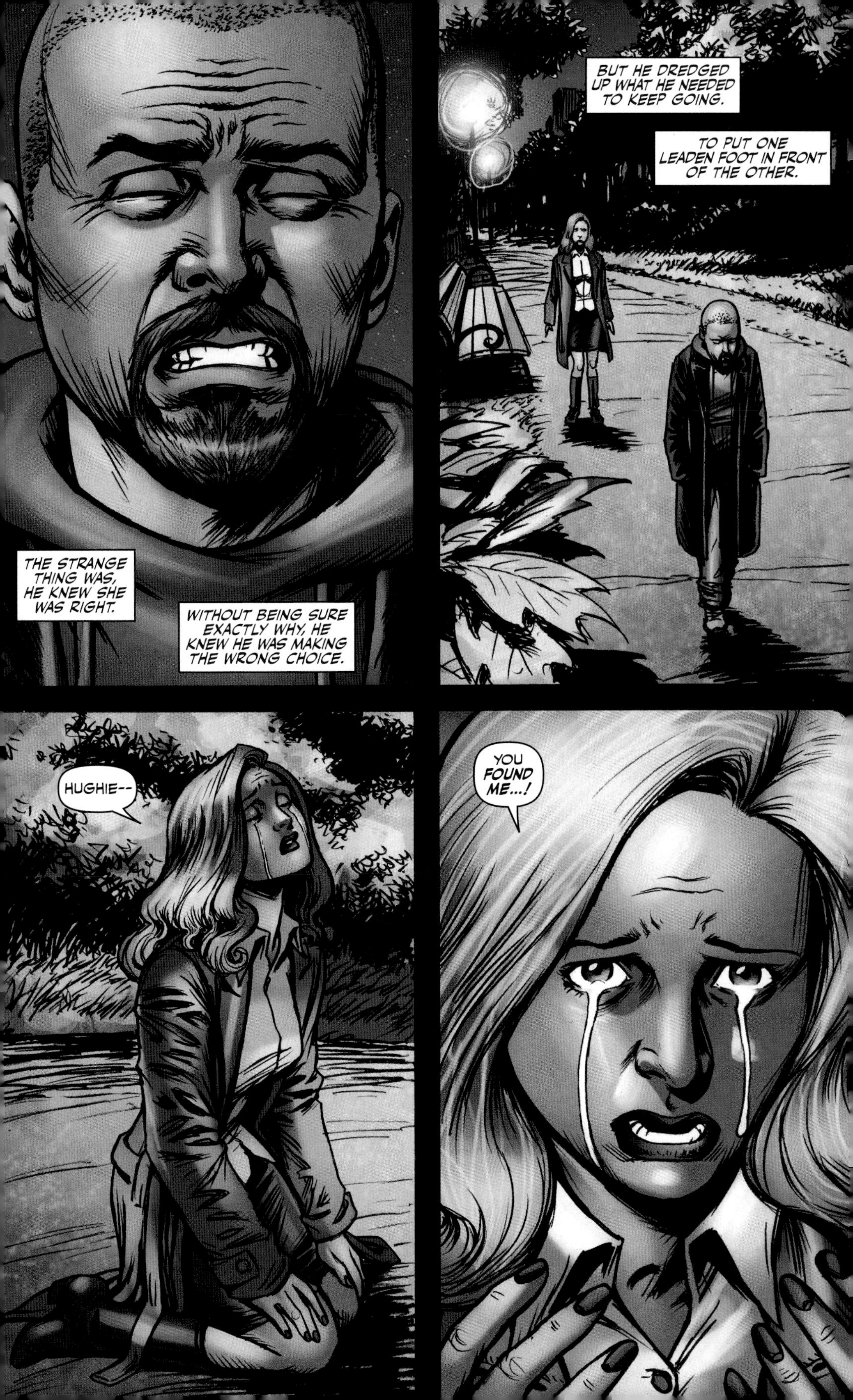
THE STRANGE THING WAS, HE KNEW SHE WAS RIGHT.
WITHOUT BEING SURE EXACTLY WHY, HE KNEW HE WAS MAKING THE WRONG CHOICE.
BUT HE DREDGED UP WHAT HE NEEDED TO KEEP GOING.
TO PUT ONE LEADEN FOOT IN FRONT OF THE OTHER.
HUGHIE--
YOU FOUND ME...!

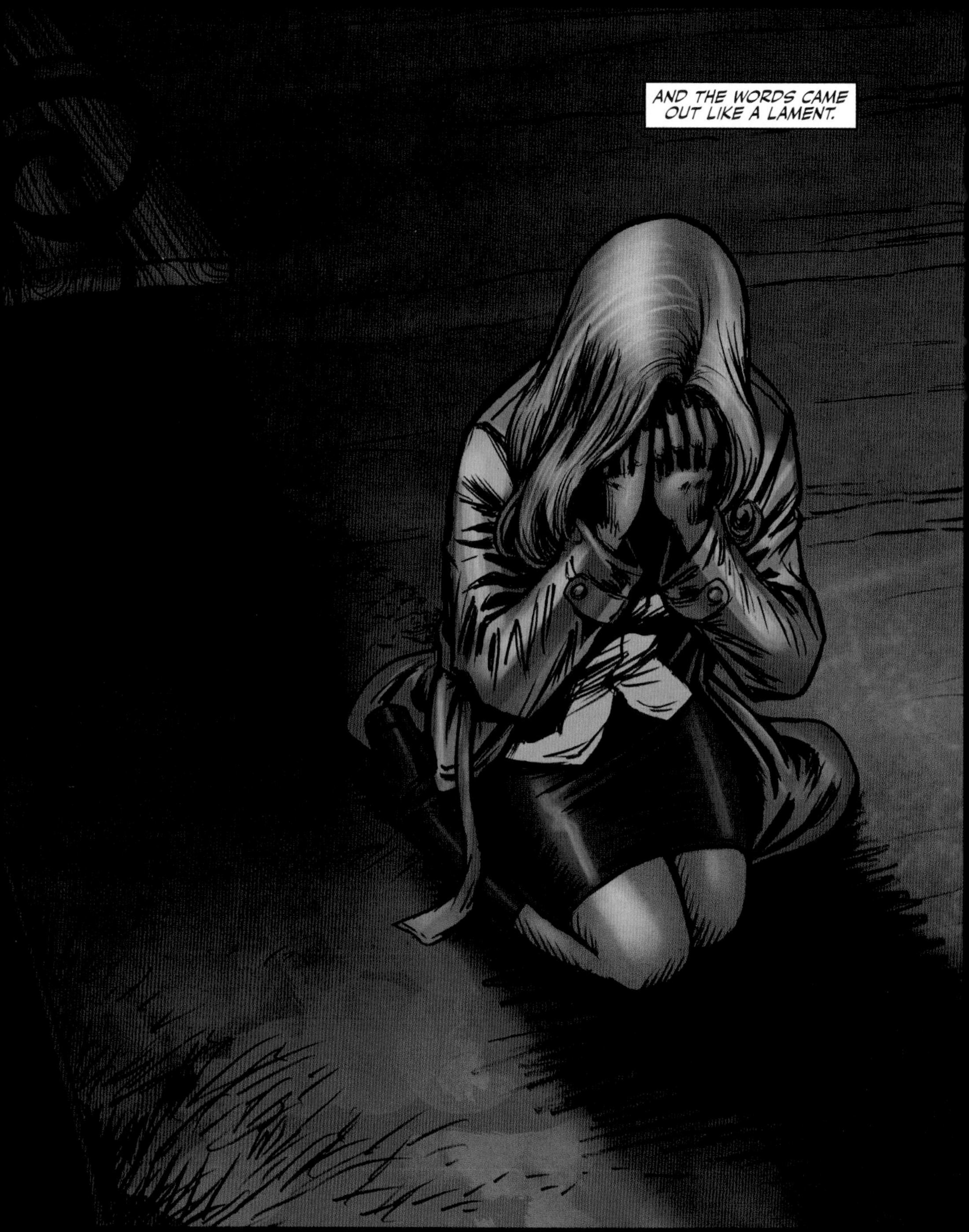
AND THE WORDS CAME OUT LIKE A LAMENT.

BELIEVE
conclusion

HIGHLAND LADDIE #1
cover

by DARICK ROBERTSON
and TONY AVIÑA

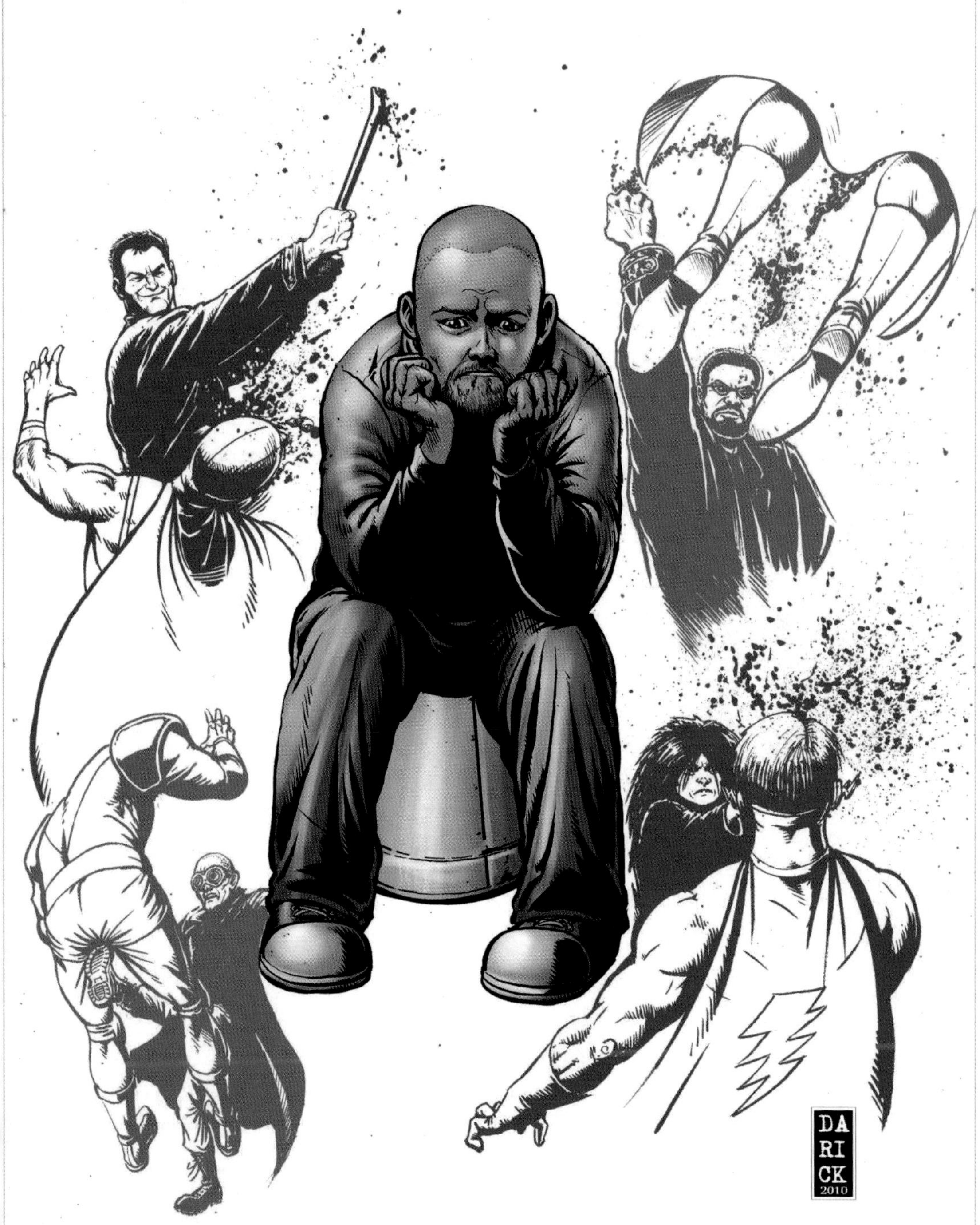
DA
RI
CK
2010

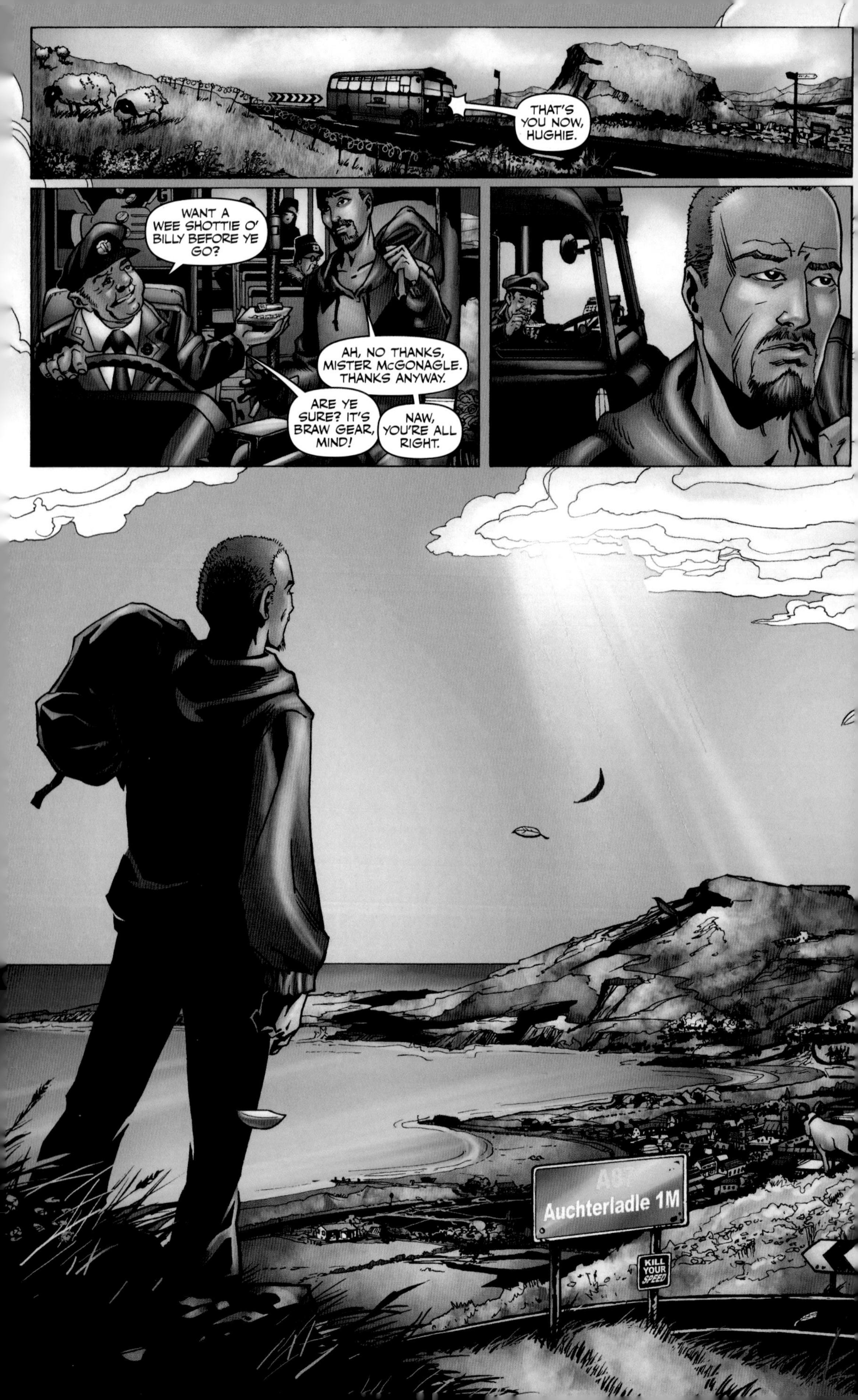
THAT'S YOU NOW, HUGHIE.
WANT A WEE SHOTTIE O' BILLY BEFORE YE GO?
AH, NO THANKS, MISTER McGONAGLE. THANKS ANYWAY.
ARE YE SURE? IT'S BRAW GEAR, MIND!
NAW, YOU'RE ALL RIGHT.
Auchterladle 1M
KILL YOUR SPEED

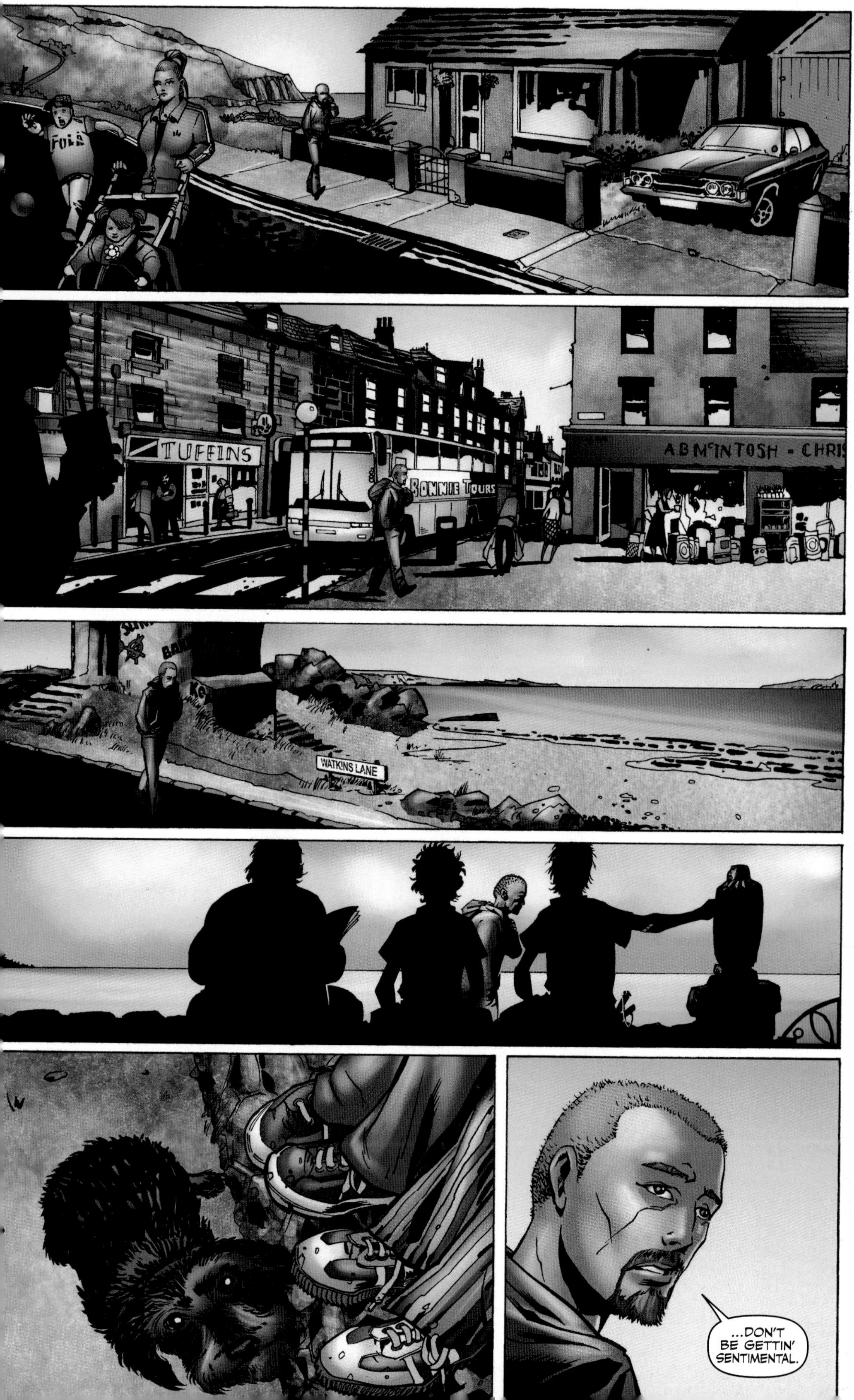
FOLA
TUFFINS
BONNIE TOURS
A.B.McINTOSH - CHRIS
WATKINS LANE
...DON'T BE GETTIN' SENTIMENTAL.

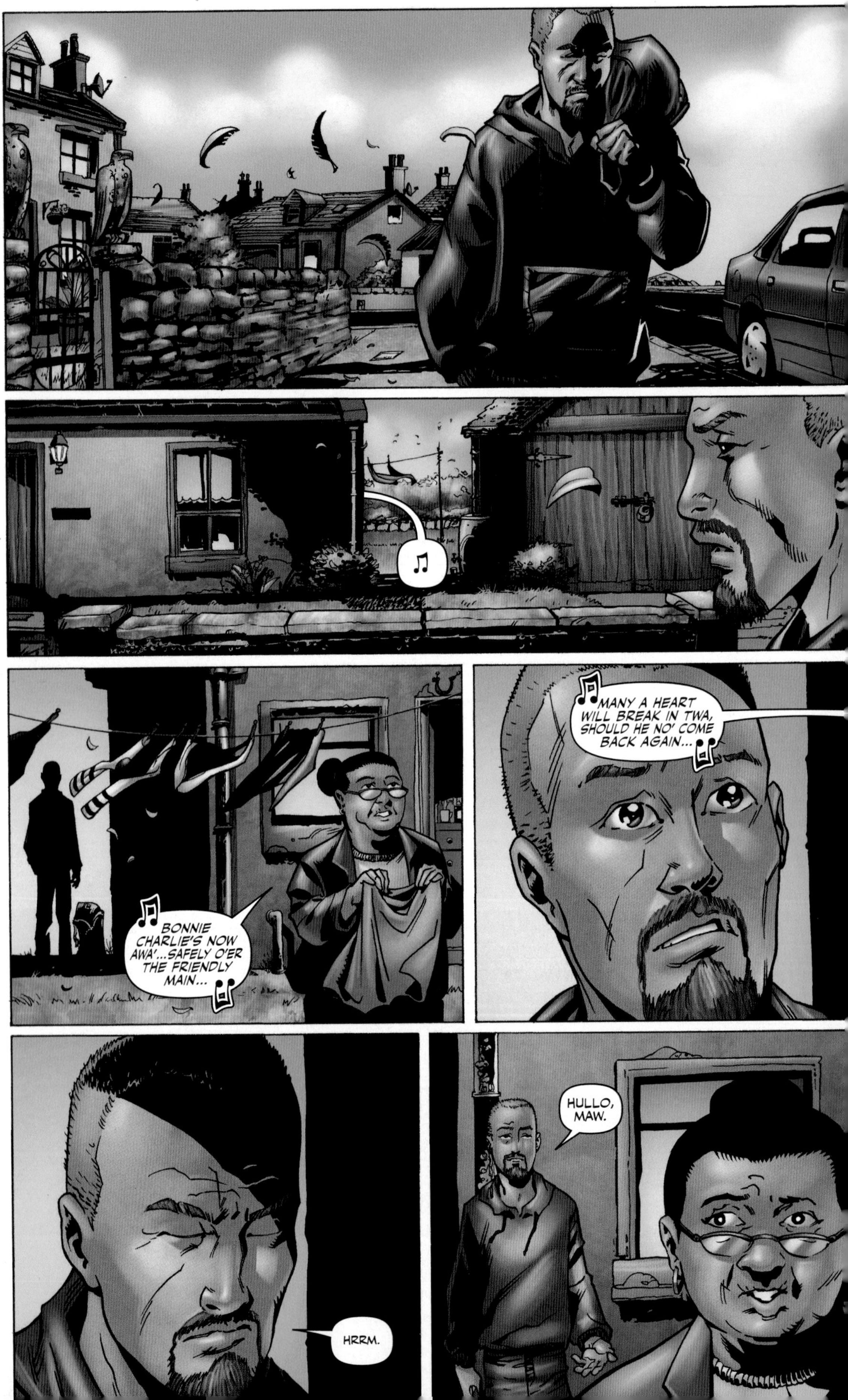
♫
♫ BONNIE CHARLIE'S NOW AWA'...SAFELY O'ER THE FRIENDLY MAIN... ♫
♫ MANY A HEART WILL BREAK IN TWA, SHOULD HE NO' COME BACK AGAIN... ♫
HRRM.
HULLO, MAW.

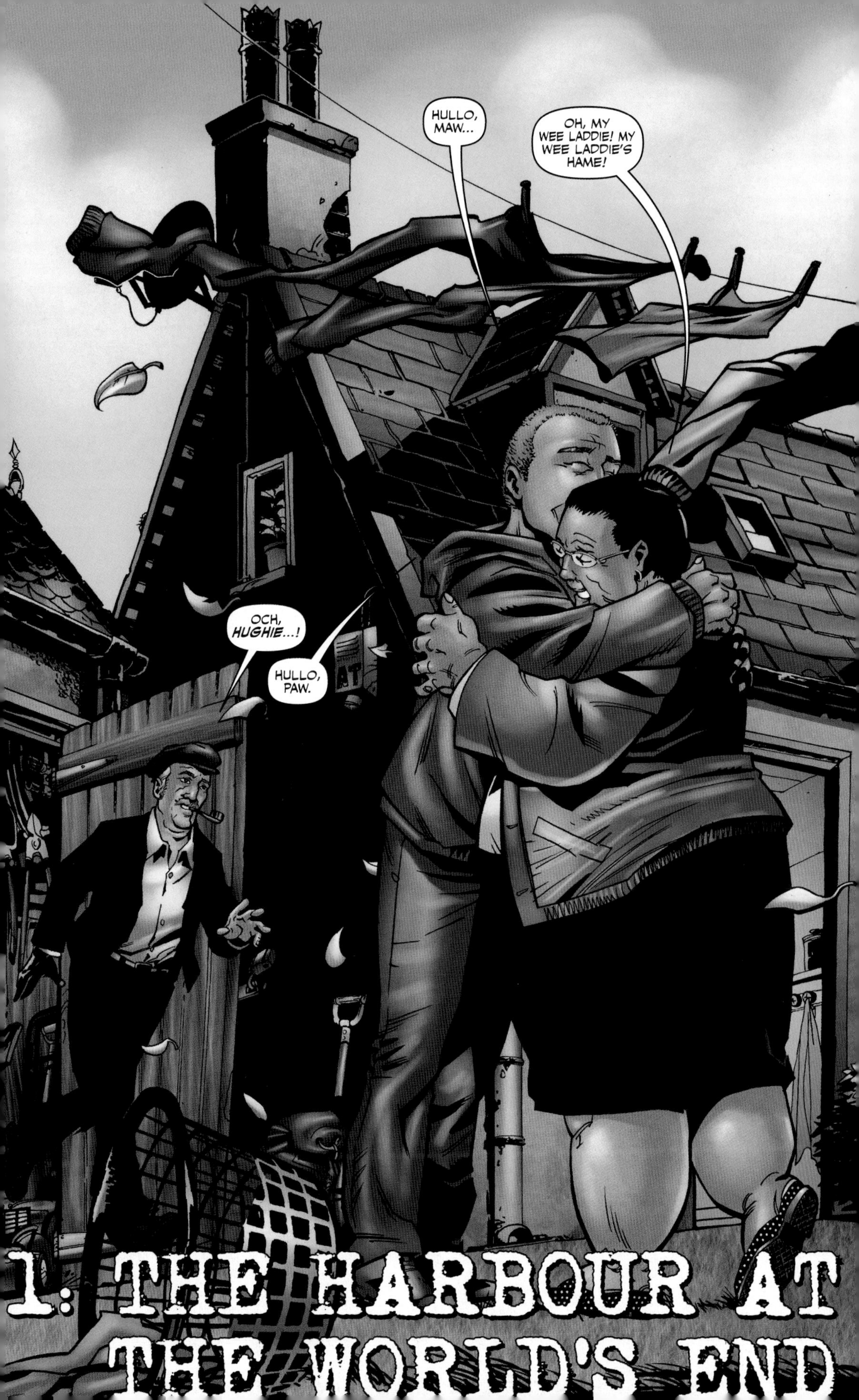
HULLO, MAW...
OH, MY WEE LADDIE! MY WEE LADDIE'S HAME!
OCH, HUGHIE...!
HULLO, PAW.
1: THE HARBOUR AT THE WORLD'S END

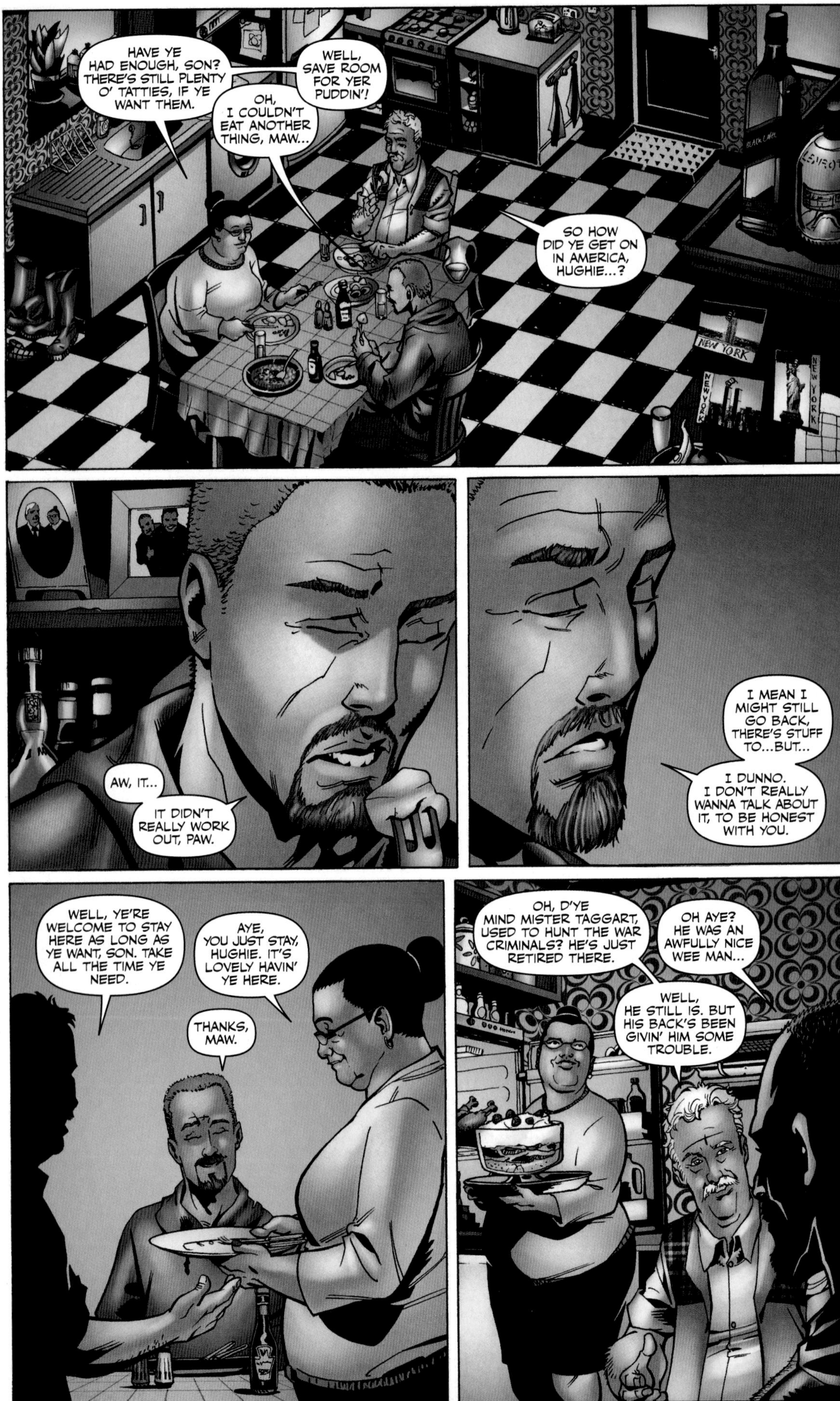
HAVE YE HAD ENOUGH, SON? THERE'S STILL PLENTY O' TATTIES, IF YE WANT THEM.
OH, I COULDN'T EAT ANOTHER THING, MAW...
WELL, SAVE ROOM FOR YER PUDDIN'!
SO HOW DID YE GET ON IN AMERICA, HUGHIE...?
NEW YORK
NEW YORK
NEW YORK
AW, IT...
IT DIDN'T REALLY WORK OUT, PAW.
I MEAN I MIGHT STILL GO BACK, THERE'S STUFF TO...BUT...
I DUNNO. I DON'T REALLY WANNA TALK ABOUT IT, TO BE HONEST WITH YOU.
WELL, YE'RE WELCOME TO STAY HERE AS LONG AS YE WANT, SON. TAKE ALL THE TIME YE NEED.
AYE, YOU JUST STAY, HUGHIE. IT'S LOVELY HAVIN' YE HERE.
THANKS, MAW.
OH, D'YE MIND MISTER TAGGART, USED TO HUNT THE WAR CRIMINALS? HE'S JUST RETIRED THERE.
OH AYE? HE WAS AN AWFULLY NICE WEE MAN...
WELL, HE STILL IS. BUT HIS BACK'S BEEN GIVIN' HIM SOME TROUBLE.

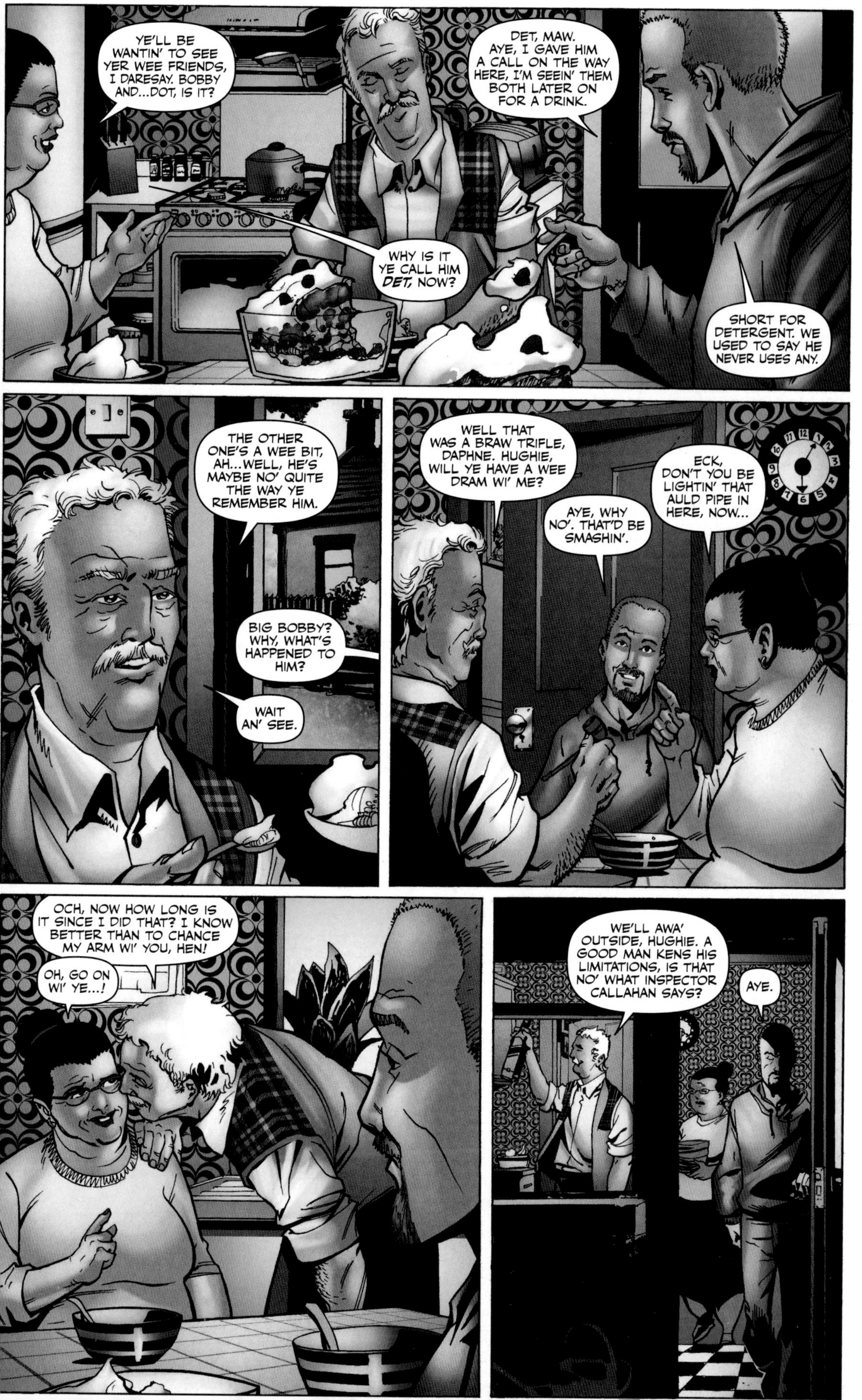
YE'LL BE WANTIN' TO SEE YER WEE FRIENDS, I DARESAY. BOBBY AND...DOT, IS IT?
DET, MAW. AYE, I GAVE HIM A CALL ON THE WAY HERE, I'M SEEIN' THEM BOTH LATER ON FOR A DRINK.
WHY IS IT YE CALL HIM *DET*, NOW?
SHORT FOR DETERGENT. WE USED TO SAY HE NEVER USES ANY.
THE OTHER ONE'S A WEE BIT, AH...WELL, HE'S MAYBE NO' QUITE THE WAY YE REMEMBER HIM.
BIG BOBBY? WHY, WHAT'S HAPPENED TO HIM?
WAIT AN' SEE.
WELL THAT WAS A BRAW TRIFLE, DAPHNE. HUGHIE, WILL YE HAVE A WEE DRAM WI' ME?
AYE, WHY NO'. THAT'D BE SMASHIN'.
ECK, DON'T YOU BE LIGHTIN' THAT AULD PIPE IN HERE, NOW...
OCH, NOW HOW LONG IS IT SINCE I DID THAT? I KNOW BETTER THAN TO CHANCE MY ARM WI' YOU, HEN!
OH, GO ON WI' YE...!
WE'LL AWA' OUTSIDE, HUGHIE. A GOOD MAN KENS HIS LIMITATIONS, IS THAT NO' WHAT INSPECTOR CALLAHAN SAYS?
AYE.

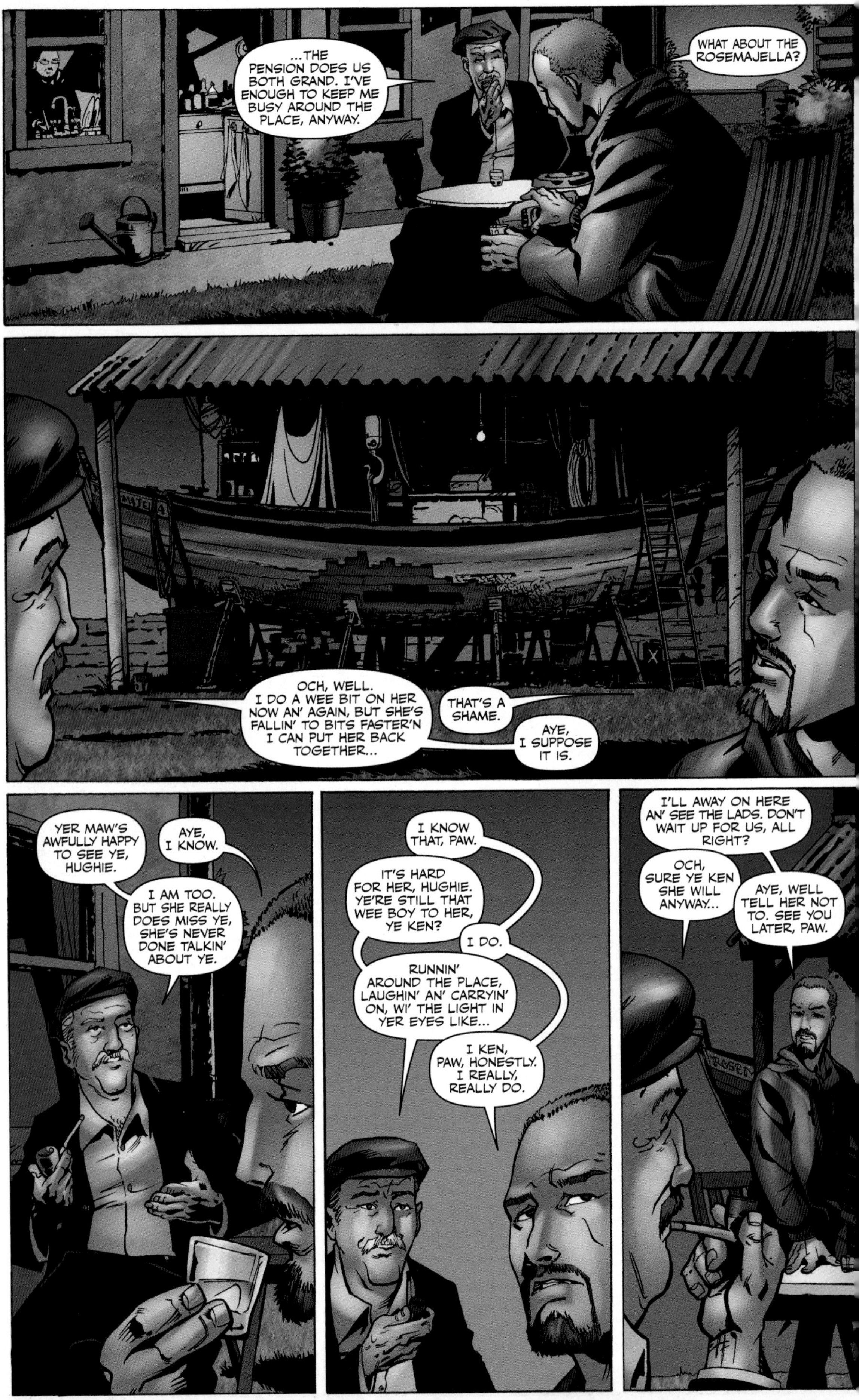
...THE PENSION DOES US BOTH GRAND. I'VE ENOUGH TO KEEP ME BUSY AROUND THE PLACE, ANYWAY.
WHAT ABOUT THE ROSEMAJELLA?
OCH, WELL. I DO A WEE BIT ON HER NOW AN' AGAIN, BUT SHE'S FALLIN' TO BITS FASTER'N I CAN PUT HER BACK TOGETHER...
THAT'S A SHAME.
AYE, I SUPPOSE IT IS.
YER MAW'S AWFULLY HAPPY TO SEE YE, HUGHIE.
AYE, I KNOW.
I AM TOO. BUT SHE REALLY DOES MISS YE, SHE'S NEVER DONE TALKIN' ABOUT YE.
I KNOW THAT, PAW.
IT'S HARD FOR HER, HUGHIE. YE'RE STILL THAT WEE BOY TO HER, YE KEN?
I DO.
RUNNIN' AROUND THE PLACE, LAUGHIN' AN' CARRYIN' ON, WI' THE LIGHT IN YER EYES LIKE...
I KEN, PAW, HONESTLY. I REALLY, REALLY DO.
I'LL AWAY ON HERE AN' SEE THE LADS. DON'T WAIT UP FOR US, ALL RIGHT?
OCH, SURE YE KEN SHE WILL ANYWAY...
AYE, WELL TELL HER NOT TO. SEE YOU LATER, PAW.

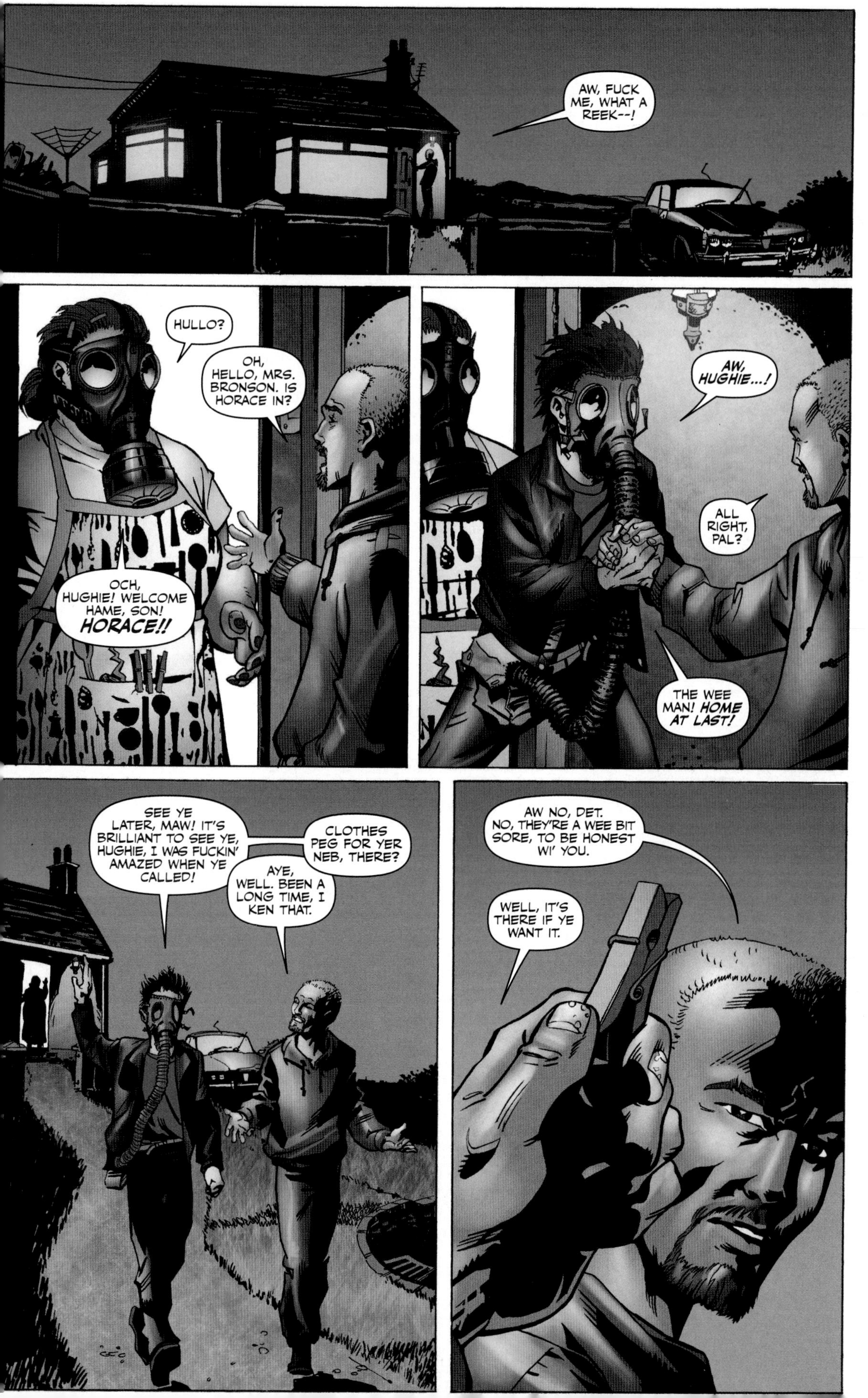
AW, FUCK ME, WHAT A REEK--!
HULLO?
OH, HELLO, MRS. BRONSON. IS HORACE IN?
OCH, HUGHIE! WELCOME HAME, SON! HORACE!!
AW, HUGHIE...!
ALL RIGHT, PAL?
THE WEE MAN! HOME AT LAST!
SEE YE LATER, MAW! IT'S BRILLIANT TO SEE YE, HUGHIE, I WAS FUCKIN' AMAZED WHEN YE CALLED!
AYE, WELL. BEEN A LONG TIME, I KEN THAT.
CLOTHES PEG FOR YER NEB, THERE?
AW NO, DET. NO, THEY'RE A WEE BIT SORE, TO BE HONEST WI' YOU.
WELL, IT'S THERE IF YE WANT IT.

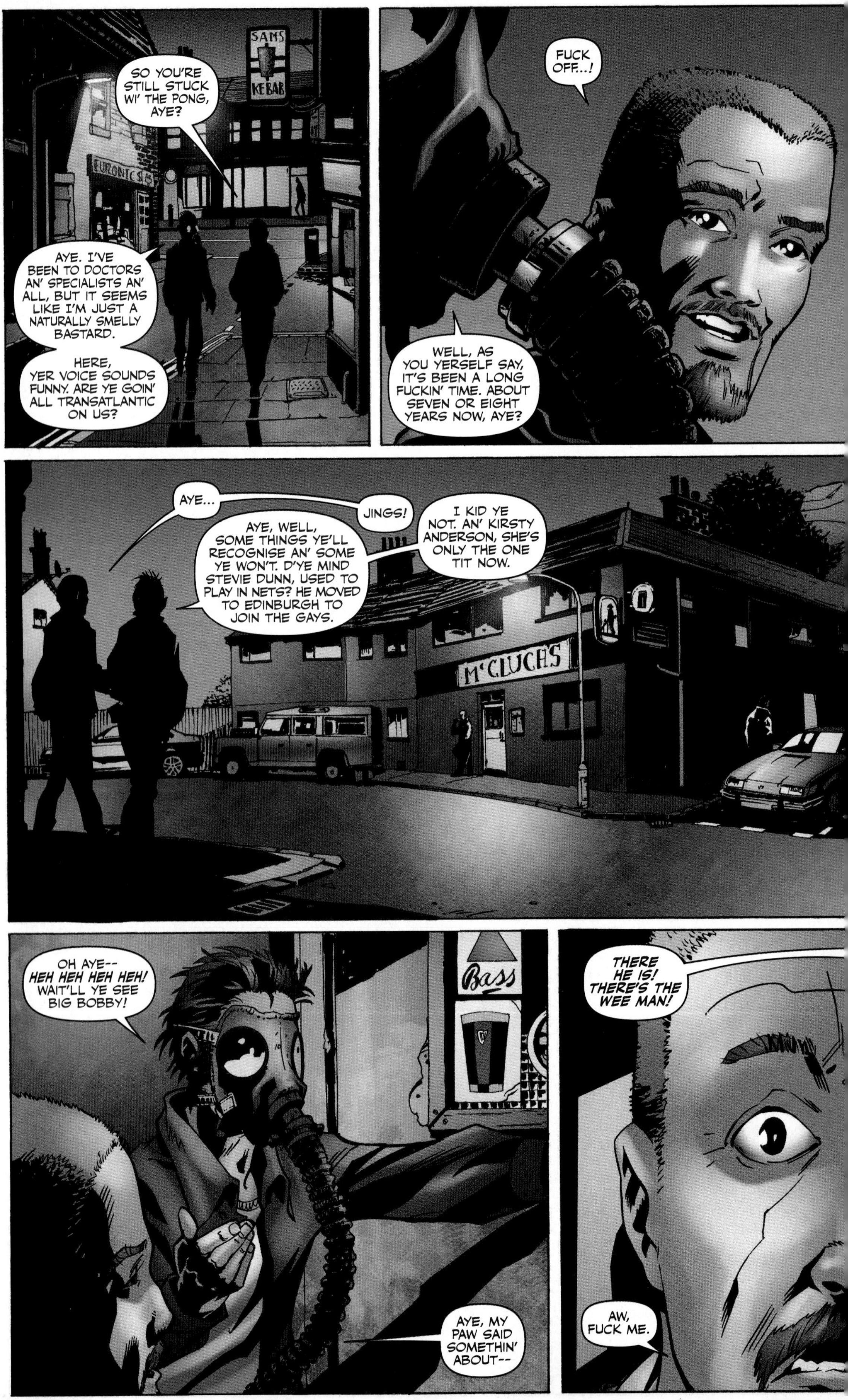
SAMS KEBAB
EURONICS
SO YOU'RE STILL STUCK WI' THE PONG, AYE?
AYE. I'VE BEEN TO DOCTORS AN' SPECIALISTS AN' ALL, BUT IT SEEMS LIKE I'M JUST A NATURALLY SMELLY BASTARD.
HERE, YER VOICE SOUNDS FUNNY. ARE YE GOIN' ALL TRANSATLANTIC ON US?
FUCK OFF...!
WELL, AS YOU YERSELF SAY, IT'S BEEN A LONG FUCKIN' TIME. ABOUT SEVEN OR EIGHT YEARS NOW, AYE?
AYE...
AYE, WELL, SOME THINGS YE'LL RECOGNISE AN' SOME YE WON'T. D'YE MIND STEVIE DUNN, USED TO PLAY IN NETS? HE MOVED TO EDINBURGH TO JOIN THE GAYS.
JINGS!
I KID YE NOT. AN' KIRSTY ANDERSON, SHE'S ONLY THE ONE TIT NOW.
McCLUCH'S
OH AYE-- HEH HEH HEH HEH! WAIT'LL YE SEE BIG BOBBY!
Bass
AYE, MY PAW SAID SOMETHIN' ABOUT--
THERE HE IS! THERE'S THE WEE MAN!
AW, FUCK ME.

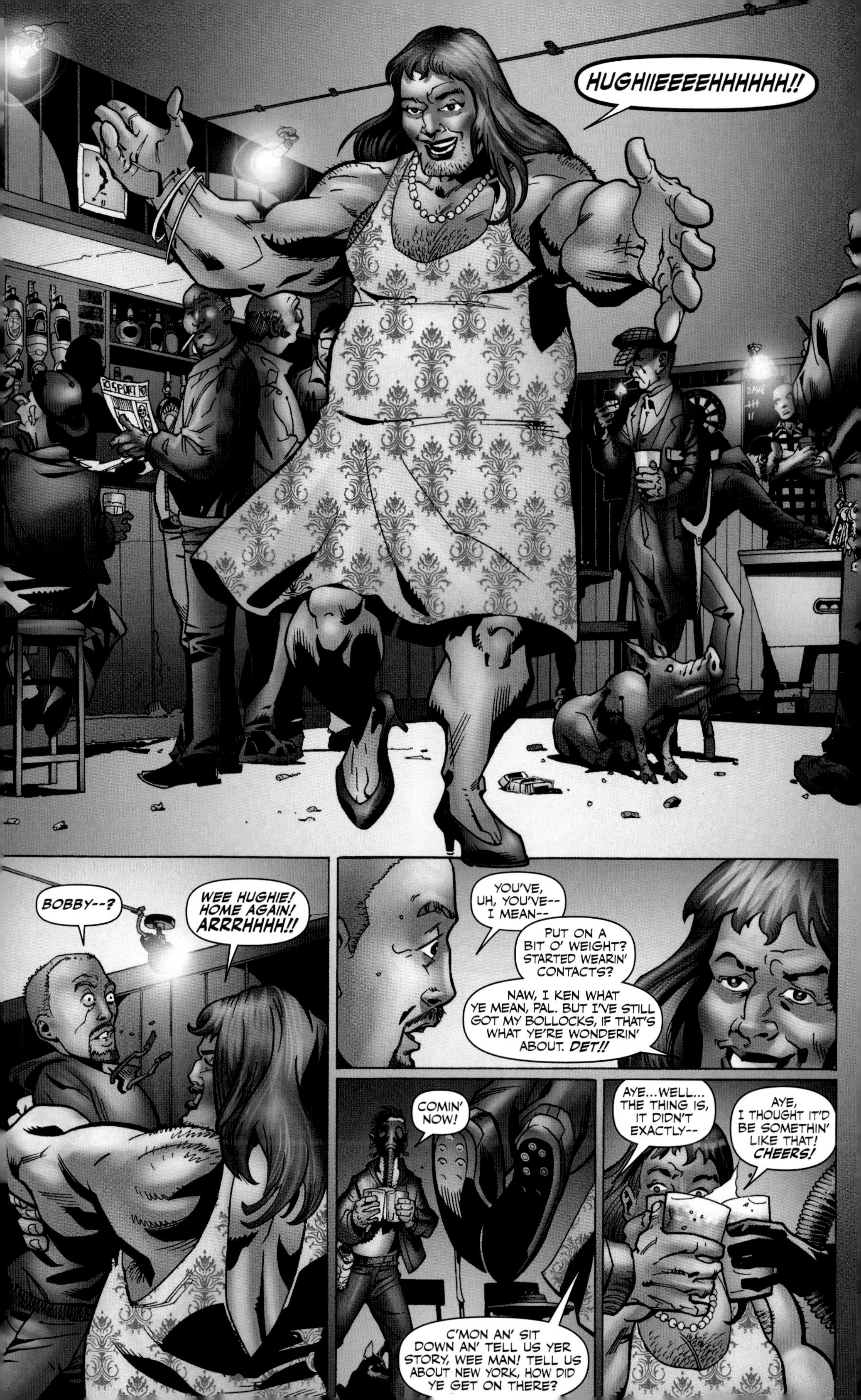
HUGHIIEEEEHHHHHH!!
BOBBY--?
WEE HUGHIE! HOME AGAIN! ARRRHHHH!!
YOU'VE, UH, YOU'VE-- I MEAN--
PUT ON A BIT O' WEIGHT? STARTED WEARIN' CONTACTS?
NAW, I KEN WHAT YE MEAN, PAL. BUT I'VE STILL GOT MY BOLLOCKS, IF THAT'S WHAT YE'RE WONDERIN' ABOUT. DET!!
COMIN' NOW!
C'MON AN' SIT DOWN AN' TELL US YER STORY, WEE MAN! TELL US ABOUT NEW YORK, HOW DID YE GET ON THERE?
AYE...WELL... THE THING IS, IT DIDN'T EXACTLY--
AYE, I THOUGHT IT'D BE SOMETHIN' LIKE THAT! CHEERS!

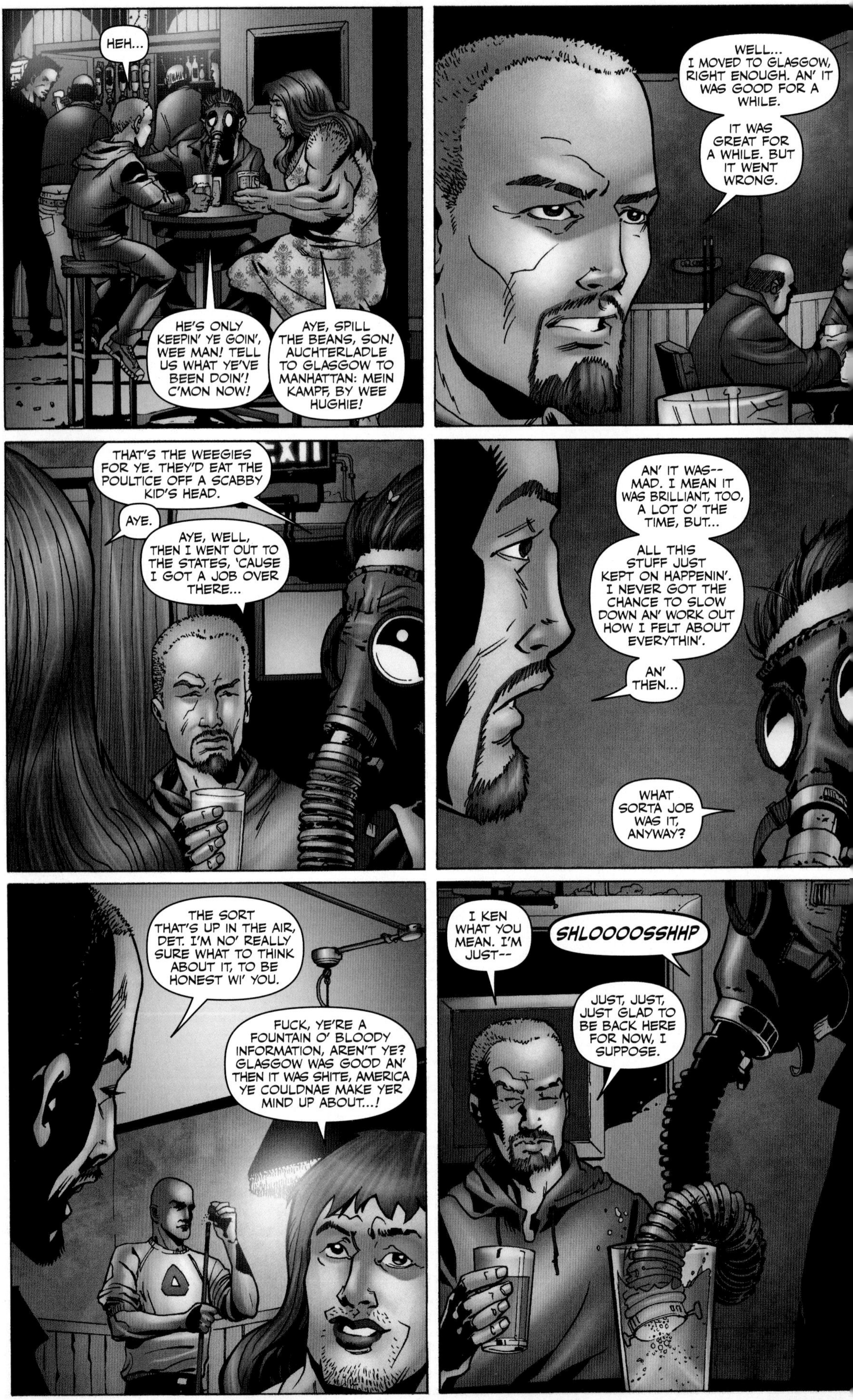
HEH...
HE'S ONLY KEEPIN' YE GOIN', WEE MAN! TELL US WHAT YE'VE BEEN DOIN'! C'MON NOW!
AYE, SPILL THE BEANS, SON! AUCHTERLADLE TO GLASGOW TO MANHATTAN: MEIN KAMPF, BY WEE HUGHIE!
WELL... I MOVED TO GLASGOW, RIGHT ENOUGH. AN' IT WAS GOOD FOR A WHILE.
IT WAS GREAT FOR A WHILE. BUT IT WENT WRONG.
THAT'S THE WEEGIES FOR YE. THEY'D EAT THE POULTICE OFF A SCABBY KID'S HEAD.
AYE.
AYE, WELL, THEN I WENT OUT TO THE STATES, 'CAUSE I GOT A JOB OVER THERE...
EXIT
AN' IT WAS-- MAD. I MEAN IT WAS BRILLIANT, TOO, A LOT O' THE TIME, BUT...
ALL THIS STUFF JUST KEPT ON HAPPENIN'. I NEVER GOT THE CHANCE TO SLOW DOWN AN' WORK OUT HOW I FELT ABOUT EVERYTHIN'.
AN' THEN...
WHAT SORTA JOB WAS IT, ANYWAY?
THE SORT THAT'S UP IN THE AIR, DET. I'M NO' REALLY SURE WHAT TO THINK ABOUT IT, TO BE HONEST WI' YOU.
FUCK, YE'RE A FOUNTAIN O' BLOODY INFORMATION, AREN'T YE? GLASGOW WAS GOOD AN' THEN IT WAS SHITE, AMERICA YE COULDNAE MAKE YER MIND UP ABOUT...!
I KEN WHAT YOU MEAN. I'M JUST--
SHLOOOOSSHHP
JUST, JUST, JUST GLAD TO BE BACK HERE FOR NOW, I SUPPOSE.

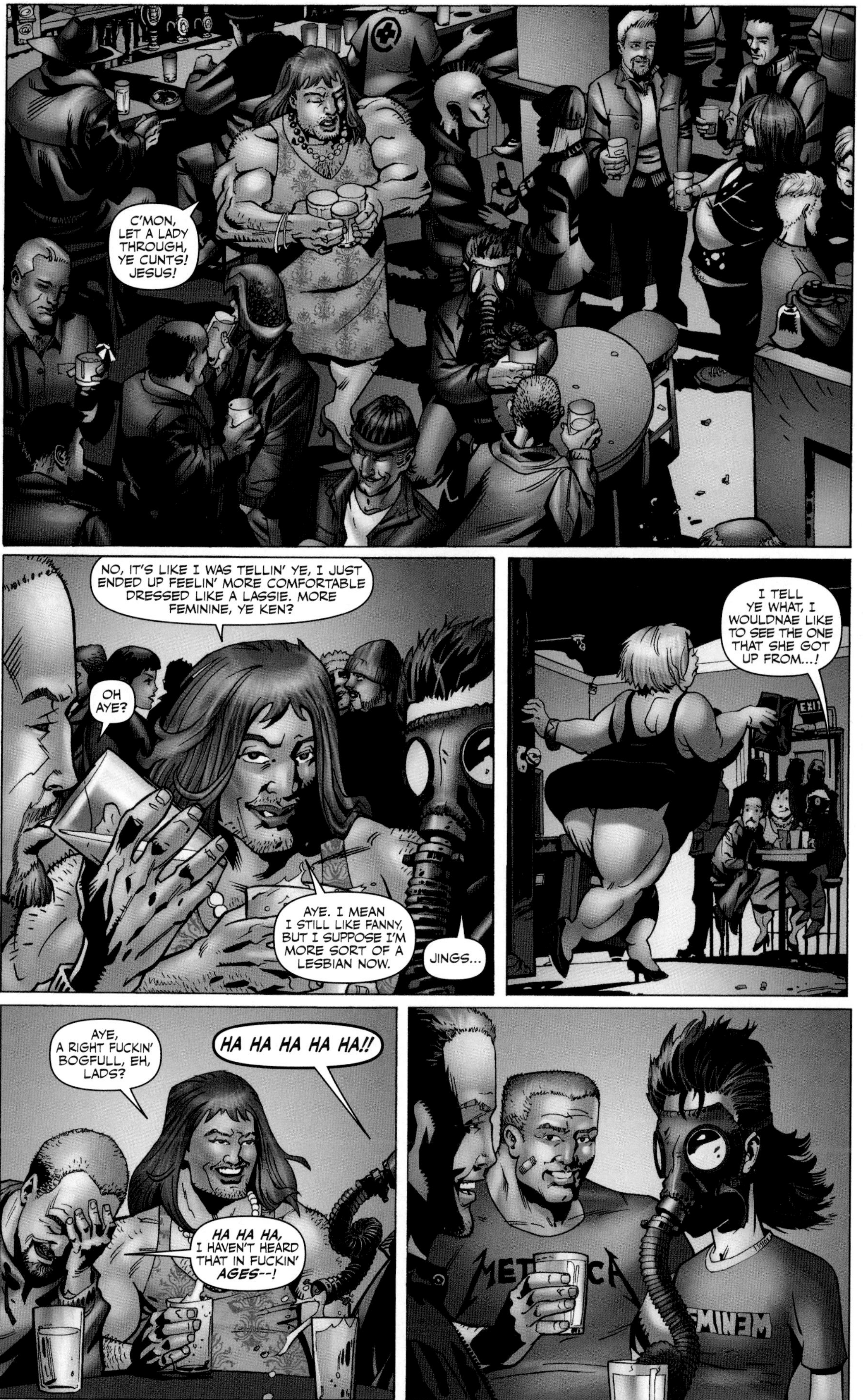
C'MON, LET A LADY THROUGH, YE CUNTS! JESUS!
NO, IT'S LIKE I WAS TELLIN' YE, I JUST ENDED UP FEELIN' MORE COMFORTABLE DRESSED LIKE A LASSIE. MORE FEMININE, YE KEN?
OH AYE?
AYE. I MEAN I STILL LIKE FANNY, BUT I SUPPOSE I'M MORE SORT OF A LESBIAN NOW.
JINGS...
I TELL YE WHAT, I WOULDNAE LIKE TO SEE THE ONE THAT SHE GOT UP FROM...!
AYE, A RIGHT FUCKIN' BOGFULL, EH, LADS?
HA HA HA HA HA!!
HA HA HA, I HAVEN'T HEARD THAT IN FUCKIN' AGES--!

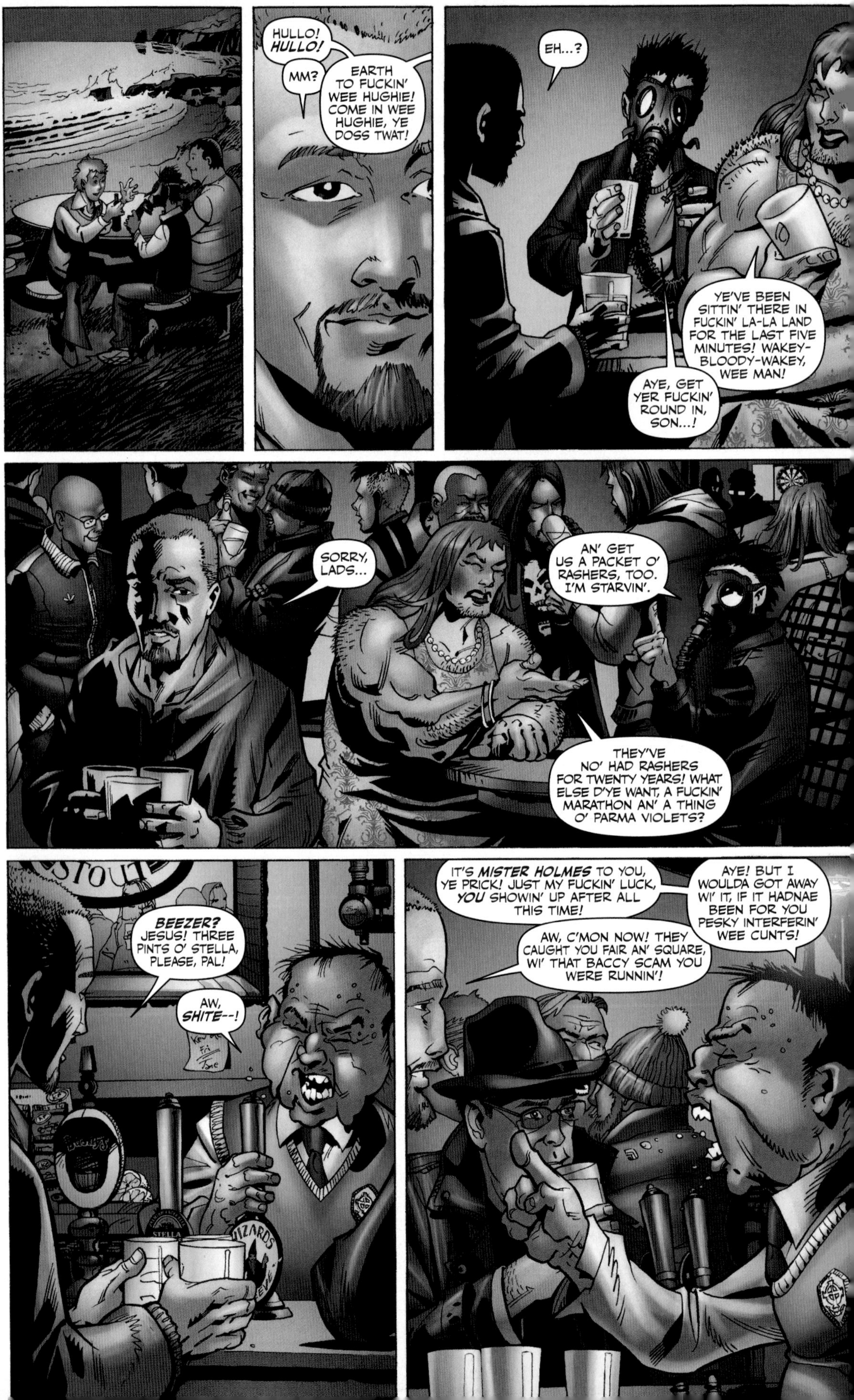
HULLO! *HULLO!*
MM?
EARTH TO FUCKIN' WEE HUGHIE! COME IN WEE HUGHIE, YE DOSS TWAT!
EH...?
YE'VE BEEN SITTIN' THERE IN FUCKIN' LA-LA LAND FOR THE LAST FIVE MINUTES! WAKEY-BLOODY-WAKEY, WEE MAN!
AYE, GET YER FUCKIN' ROUND IN, SON...!
SORRY, LADS...
AN' GET US A PACKET O' RASHERS, TOO. I'M STARVIN'.
THEY'VE NO' HAD RASHERS FOR TWENTY YEARS! WHAT ELSE D'YE WANT, A FUCKIN' MARATHON AN' A THING O' PARMA VIOLETS?
BEEZER? JESUS! THREE PINTS O' STELLA, PLEASE, PAL!
AW, *SHITE--!*
IT'S *MISTER HOLMES* TO YOU, YE PRICK! JUST MY FUCKIN' LUCK, *YOU* SHOWIN' UP AFTER ALL THIS TIME!
AYE! BUT I WOULDA GOT AWAY WI' IT, IF IT HADNAE BEEN FOR YOU PESKY INTERFERIN' WEE CUNTS!
AW, C'MON NOW! THEY CAUGHT YOU FAIR AN' SQUARE, WI' THAT BACCY SCAM YOU WERE RUNNIN'!

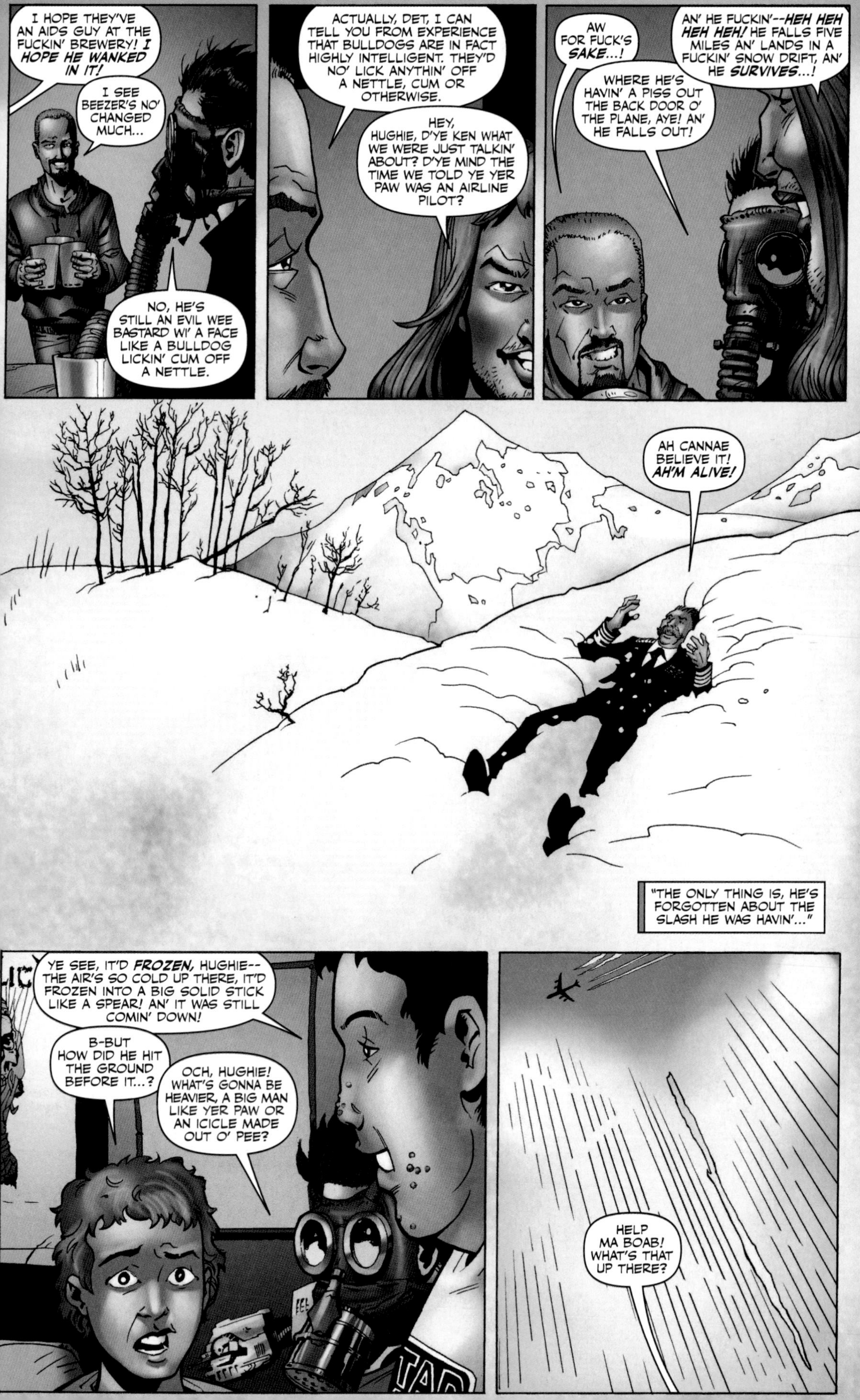
I HOPE THEY'VE AN AIDS GUY AT THE FUCKIN' BREWERY! I HOPE HE WANKED IN IT!
I SEE BEEZER'S NO' CHANGED MUCH...
NO, HE'S STILL AN EVIL WEE BASTARD WI' A FACE LIKE A BULLDOG LICKIN' CUM OFF A NETTLE.
ACTUALLY, DET, I CAN TELL YOU FROM EXPERIENCE THAT BULLDOGS ARE IN FACT HIGHLY INTELLIGENT. THEY'D NO' LICK ANYTHIN' OFF A NETTLE, CUM OR OTHERWISE.
HEY, HUGHIE, D'YE KEN WHAT WE WERE JUST TALKIN' ABOUT? D'YE MIND THE TIME WE TOLD YE YER PAW WAS AN AIRLINE PILOT?
AW FOR FUCK'S SAKE...!
WHERE HE'S HAVIN' A PISS OUT THE BACK DOOR O' THE PLANE, AYE! AN' HE FALLS OUT!
AN' HE FUCKIN'--HEH HEH HEH HEH! HE FALLS FIVE MILES AN' LANDS IN A FUCKIN' SNOW DRIFT, AN' HE SURVIVES...!
AH CANNAE BELIEVE IT! AH'M ALIVE!
"THE ONLY THING IS, HE'S FORGOTTEN ABOUT THE SLASH HE WAS HAVIN'..."
YE SEE, IT'D FROZEN, HUGHIE--THE AIR'S SO COLD UP THERE, IT'D FROZEN INTO A BIG SOLID STICK LIKE A SPEAR! AN' IT WAS STILL COMIN' DOWN!
B-BUT HOW DID HE HIT THE GROUND BEFORE IT...?
OCH, HUGHIE! WHAT'S GONNA BE HEAVIER, A BIG MAN LIKE YER PAW OR AN ICICLE MADE OUT O' PEE?
HELP MA BOAB! WHAT'S THAT UP THERE?

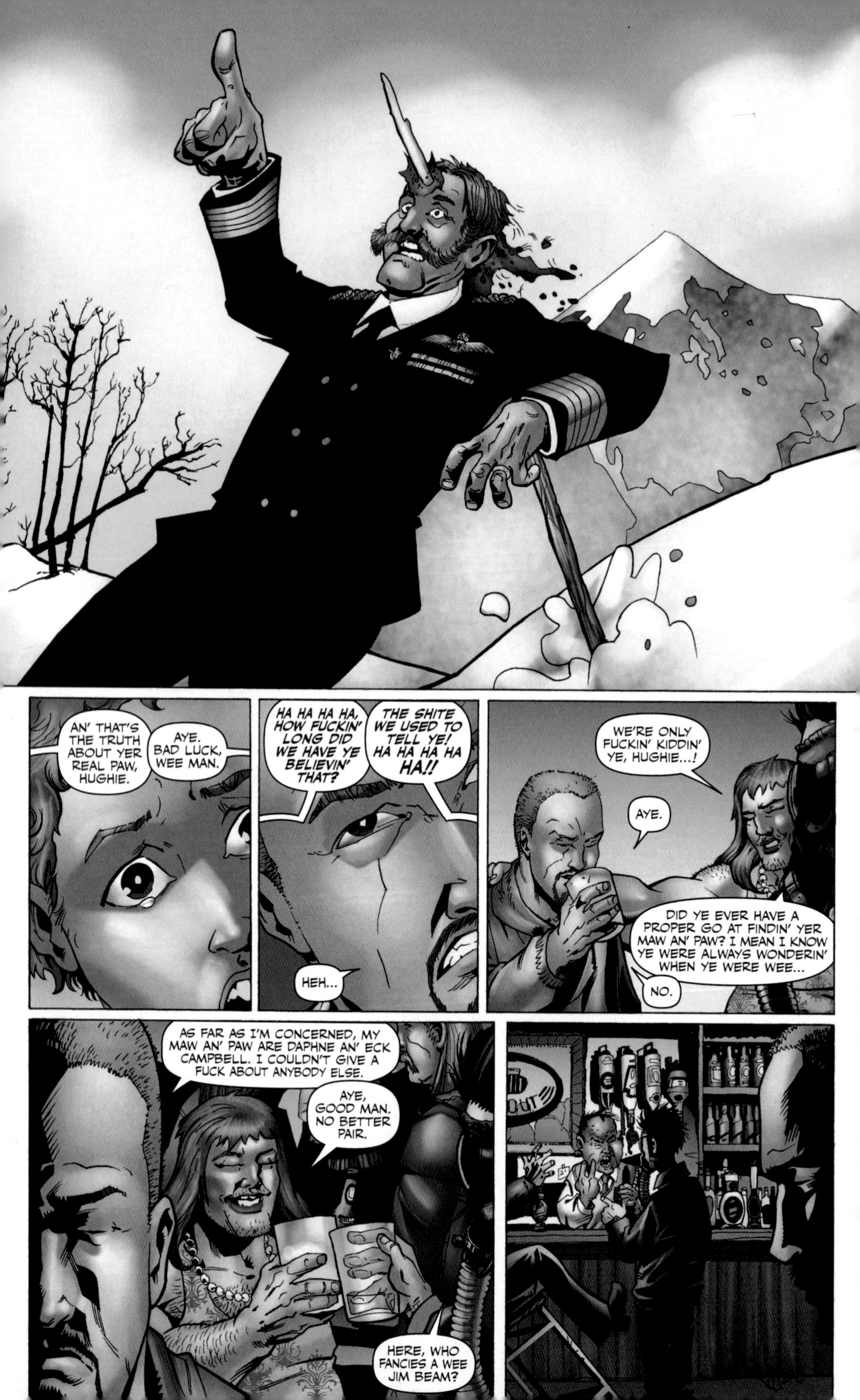
AN' THAT'S THE TRUTH ABOUT YER REAL PAW, HUGHIE.
AYE. BAD LUCK, WEE MAN.
HA HA HA HA, HOW FUCKIN' LONG DID WE HAVE YE BELIEVIN' THAT?
THE SHITE WE USED TO TELL YE! HA HA HA HA HA!!
HEH...
WE'RE ONLY FUCKIN' KIDDIN' YE, HUGHIE...!
AYE.
DID YE EVER HAVE A PROPER GO AT FINDIN' YER MAW AN' PAW? I MEAN I KNOW YE WERE ALWAYS WONDERIN' WHEN YE WERE WEE...
NO.
AS FAR AS I'M CONCERNED, MY MAW AN' PAW ARE DAPHNE AN' ECK CAMPBELL. I COULDN'T GIVE A FUCK ABOUT ANYBODY ELSE.
AYE, GOOD MAN. NO BETTER PAIR.
HERE, WHO FANCIES A WEE JIM BEAM?

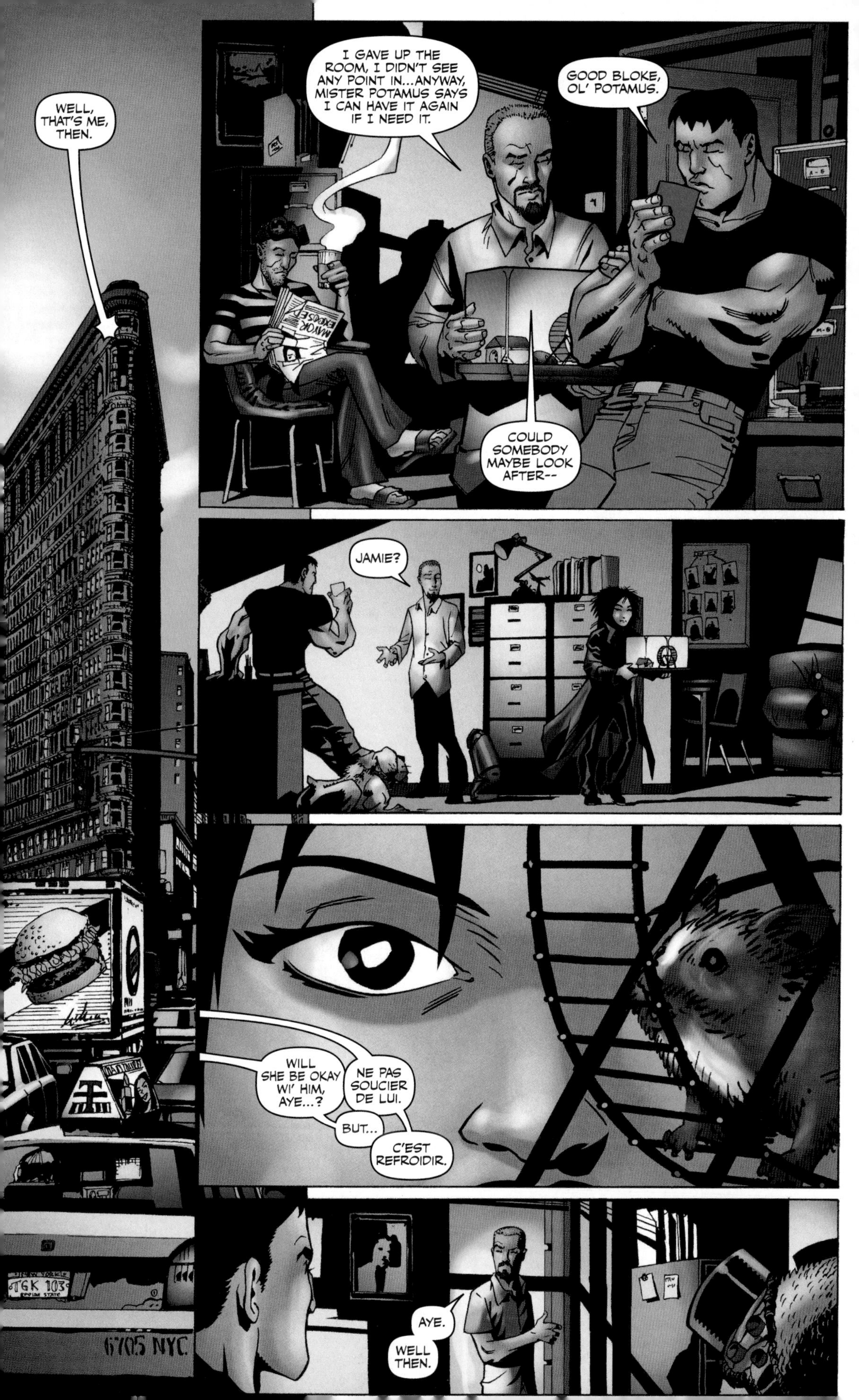
WELL, THAT'S ME, THEN.
I GAVE UP THE ROOM, I DIDN'T SEE ANY POINT IN...ANYWAY, MISTER POTAMUS SAYS I CAN HAVE IT AGAIN IF I NEED IT.
GOOD BLOKE, OL' POTAMUS.
MAYOR EXPOSED
COULD SOMEBODY MAYBE LOOK AFTER--
JAMIE?
WILL SHE BE OKAY WI' HIM, AYE...?
NE PAS SOUCIER DE LUI.
BUT...
C'EST REFROIDIR.
AYE.
WELL THEN.
NEW YORK
JGK 103
EMPIRE STATE
6705 NYC

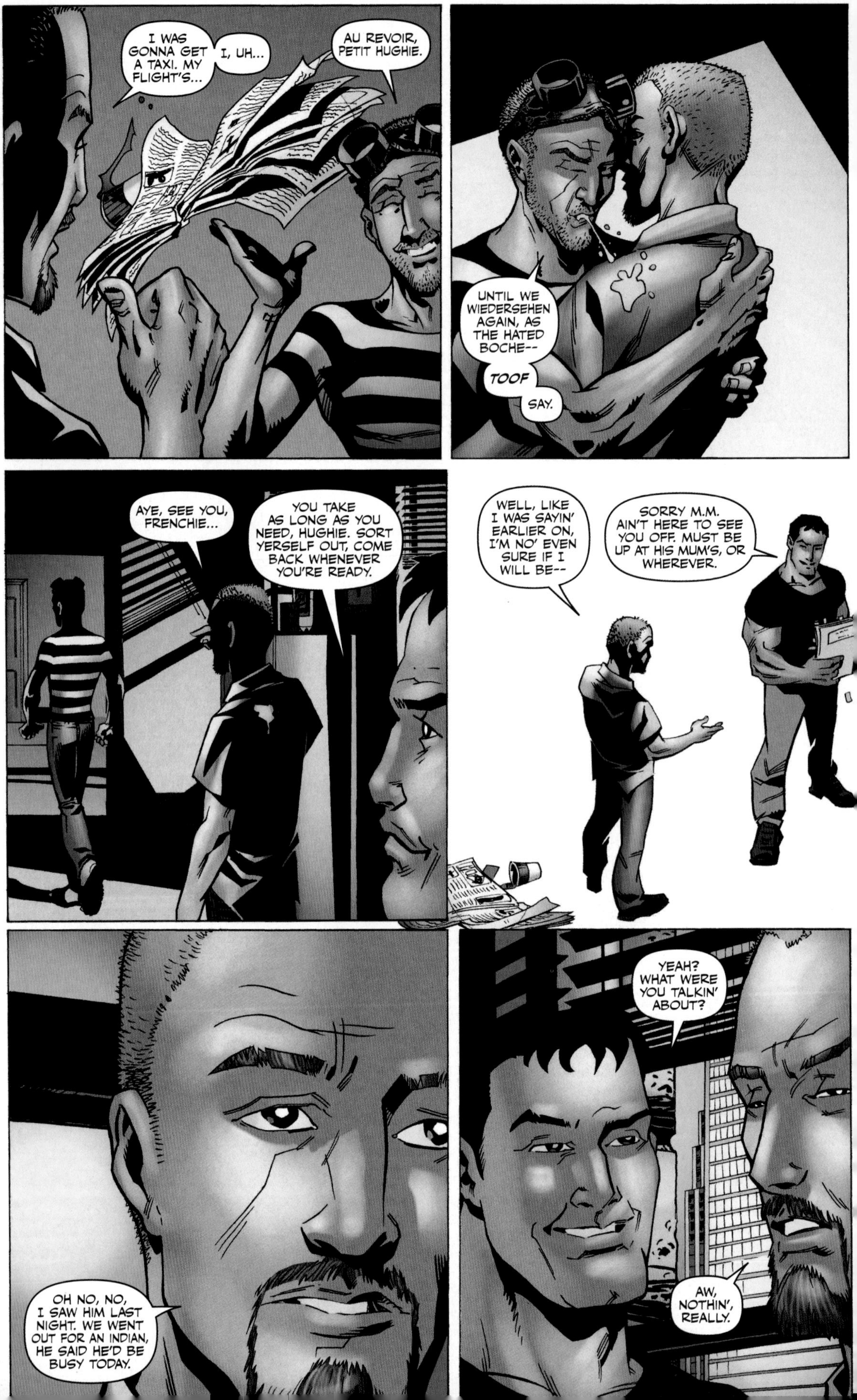
I WAS GONNA GET A TAXI. MY FLIGHT'S...
I, UH...
AU REVOIR, PETIT HUGHIE.
UNTIL WE WIEDERSEHEN AGAIN, AS THE HATED BOCHE--
TOOF
SAY.
AYE, SEE YOU, FRENCHIE...
YOU TAKE AS LONG AS YOU NEED, HUGHIE. SORT YERSELF OUT, COME BACK WHENEVER YOU'RE READY.
WELL, LIKE I WAS SAYIN' EARLIER ON, I'M NO' EVEN SURE IF I WILL BE--
SORRY M.M. AIN'T HERE TO SEE YOU OFF. MUST BE UP AT HIS MUM'S, OR WHEREVER.
OH NO, NO, I SAW HIM LAST NIGHT. WE WENT OUT FOR AN INDIAN, HE SAID HE'D BE BUSY TODAY.
YEAH? WHAT WERE YOU TALKIN' ABOUT?
AW, NOTHIN', REALLY.

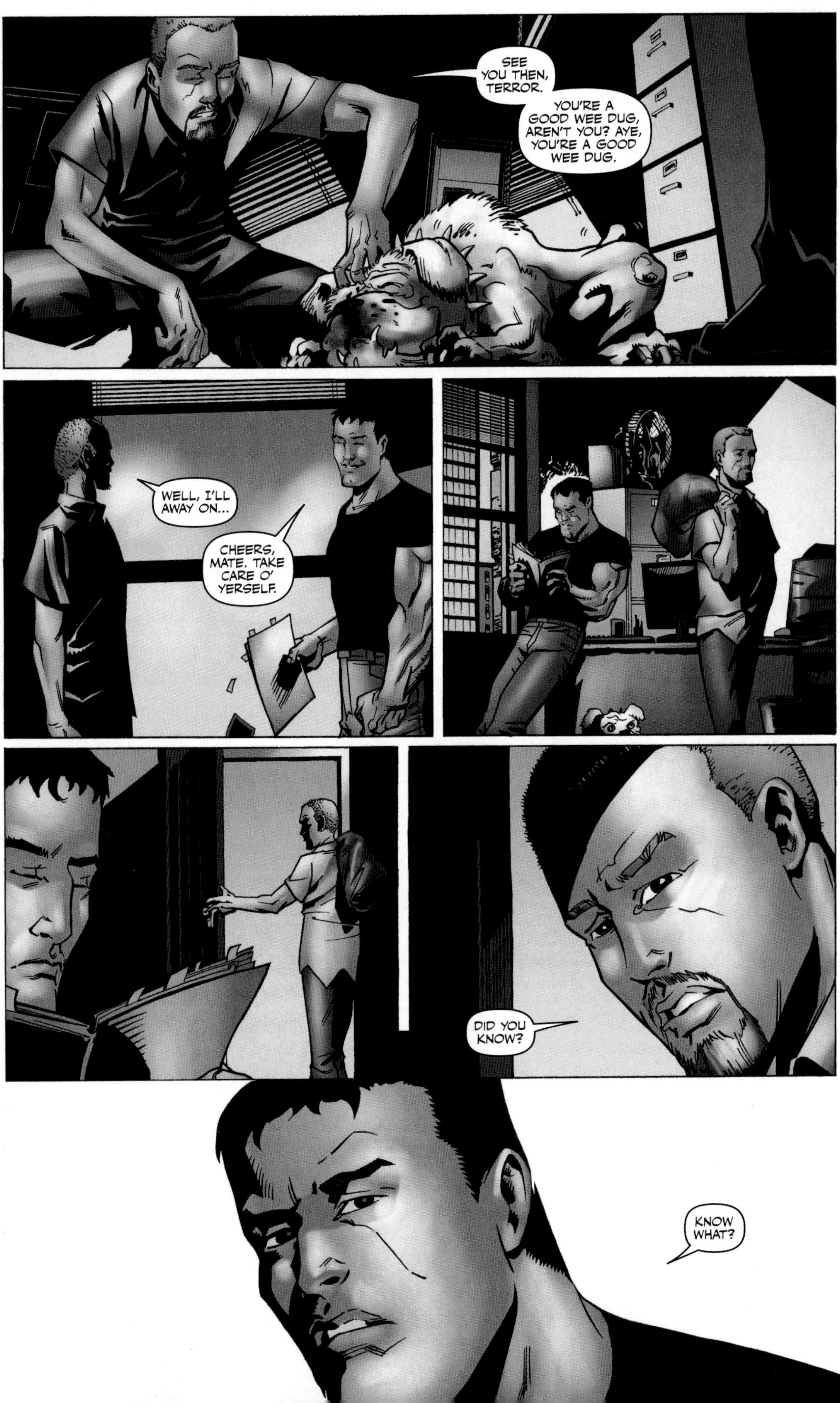
SEE YOU THEN, TERROR.
YOU'RE A GOOD WEE DUG, AREN'T YOU? AYE, YOU'RE A GOOD WEE DUG.
WELL, I'LL AWAY ON...
CHEERS, MATE. TAKE CARE O' YERSELF.
DID YOU KNOW?
KNOW WHAT?

PWORRNK

AYE, GET IT ALL OUT, SON. IT'S DOIN' YE NO GOOD.

ARE YE HEADIN' ON, ARE YE?

AYE, I THOUGHT I'D TAKE A WEE WALK DOWN THE SHORE. I'M NO' THAT TIRED YET.

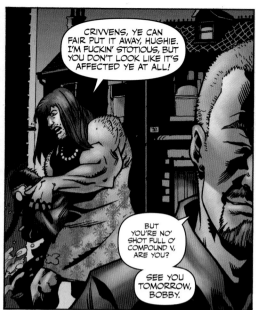

CRIVVENS, YE CAN FAIR PUT IT AWAY, HUGHIE. I'M FUCKIN' STOTIOUS, BUT YOU DON'T LOOK LIKE IT'S AFFECTED YE AT ALL!

BUT YOU'RE NO' SHOT FULL O' COMPOUND V, ARE YOU?

SEE YOU TOMORROW, BOBBY.

'EVENING.

HULLO THERE. ARE YOU PAINTIN' A PICTURE, AYE?

THAT I AM.

AW, THAT'S VERY GOOD...!

TRYING TO CAPTURE THE SIMMER DIM.

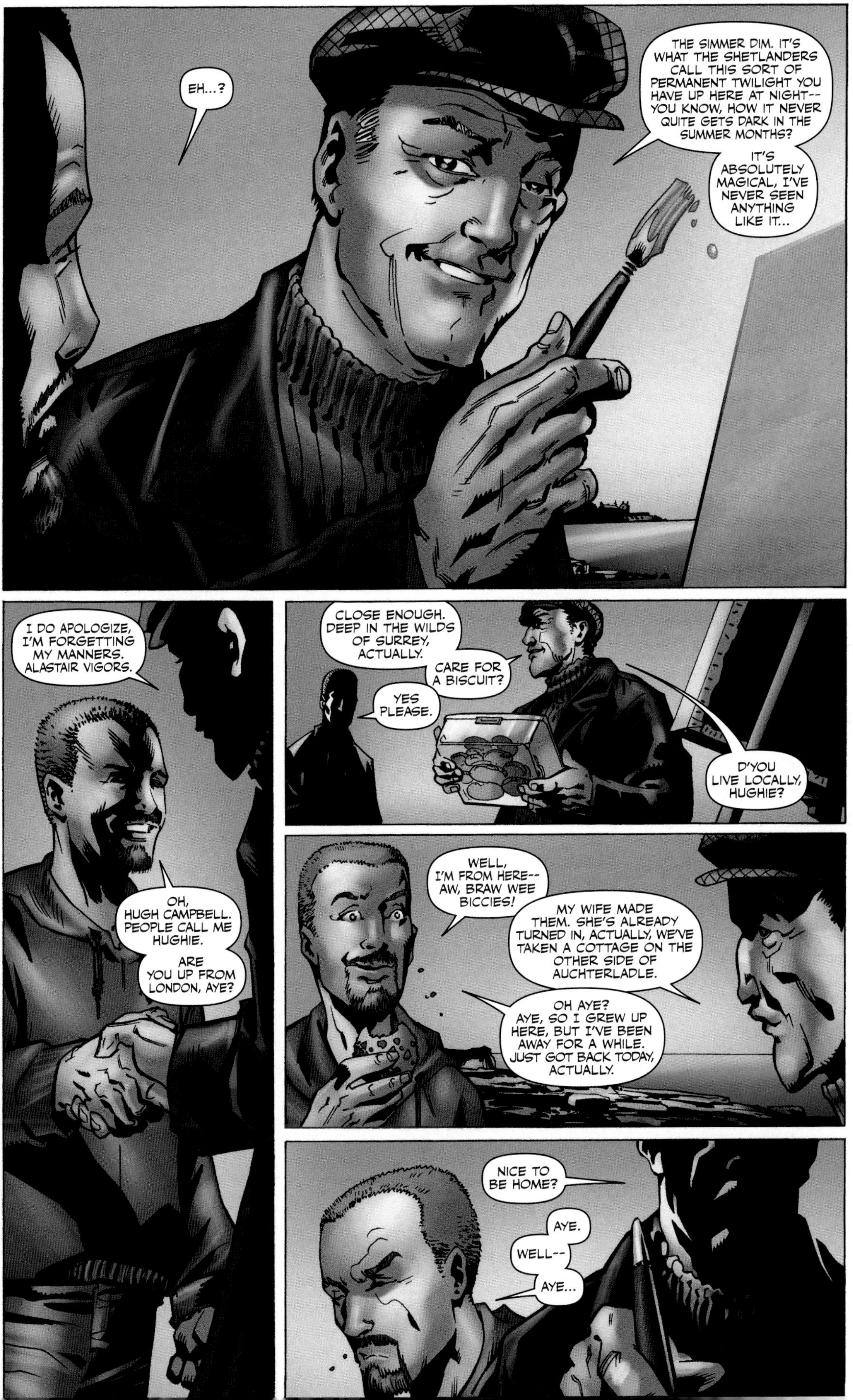
EH...?
THE SIMMER DIM. IT'S WHAT THE SHETLANDERS CALL THIS SORT OF PERMANENT TWILIGHT YOU HAVE UP HERE AT NIGHT-- YOU KNOW, HOW IT NEVER QUITE GETS DARK IN THE SUMMER MONTHS?
IT'S ABSOLUTELY MAGICAL, I'VE NEVER SEEN ANYTHING LIKE IT...
I DO APOLOGIZE, I'M FORGETTING MY MANNERS. ALASTAIR VIGORS.
OH, HUGH CAMPBELL. PEOPLE CALL ME HUGHIE.
ARE YOU UP FROM LONDON, AYE?
CLOSE ENOUGH. DEEP IN THE WILDS OF SURREY, ACTUALLY.
CARE FOR A BISCUIT?
YES PLEASE.
D'YOU LIVE LOCALLY, HUGHIE?
WELL, I'M FROM HERE-- AW, BRAW WEE BICCIES!
MY WIFE MADE THEM. SHE'S ALREADY TURNED IN, ACTUALLY, WE'VE TAKEN A COTTAGE ON THE OTHER SIDE OF AUCHTERLADLE.
OH AYE? AYE, SO I GREW UP HERE, BUT I'VE BEEN AWAY FOR A WHILE. JUST GOT BACK TODAY, ACTUALLY.
NICE TO BE HOME?
AYE.
WELL--
AYE...

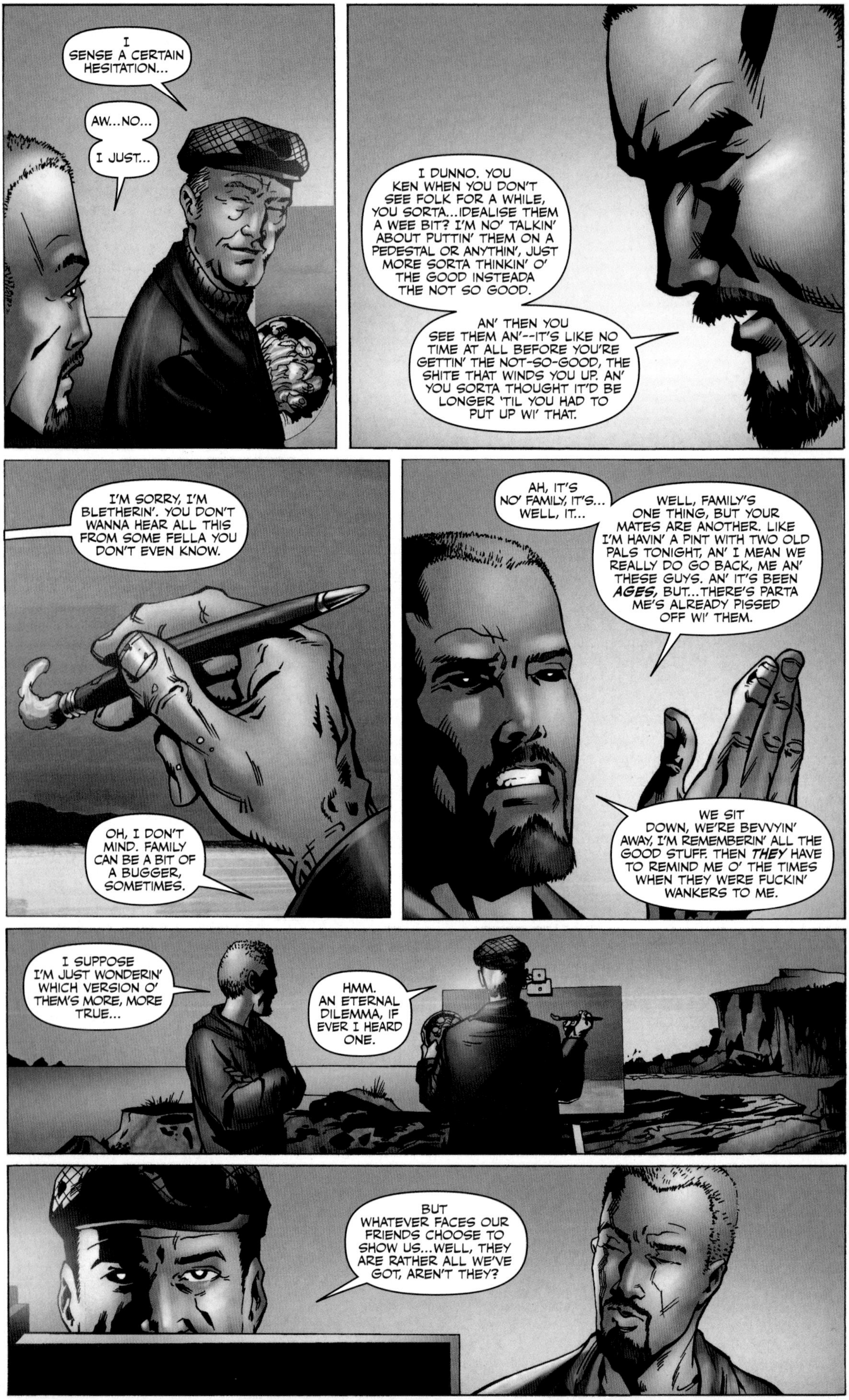
I SENSE A CERTAIN HESITATION...
AW...NO...
I JUST...
I DUNNO. YOU KEN WHEN YOU DON'T SEE FOLK FOR A WHILE, YOU SORTA...IDEALISE THEM A WEE BIT? I'M NO' TALKIN' ABOUT PUTTIN' THEM ON A PEDESTAL OR ANYTHIN', JUST MORE SORTA THINKIN' O' THE GOOD INSTEADA THE NOT SO GOOD.
AN' THEN YOU SEE THEM AN'--IT'S LIKE NO TIME AT ALL BEFORE YOU'RE GETTIN' THE NOT-SO-GOOD, THE SHITE THAT WINDS YOU UP. AN' YOU SORTA THOUGHT IT'D BE LONGER 'TIL YOU HAD TO PUT UP WI' THAT.
I'M SORRY, I'M BLETHERIN'. YOU DON'T WANNA HEAR ALL THIS FROM SOME FELLA YOU DON'T EVEN KNOW.
OH, I DON'T MIND. FAMILY CAN BE A BIT OF A BUGGER, SOMETIMES.
AH, IT'S NO' FAMILY, IT'S... WELL, IT...
WELL, FAMILY'S ONE THING, BUT YOUR MATES ARE ANOTHER. LIKE I'M HAVIN' A PINT WITH TWO OLD PALS TONIGHT, AN' I MEAN WE REALLY DO GO BACK, ME AN' THESE GUYS. AN' IT'S BEEN *AGES*, BUT...THERE'S PARTA ME'S ALREADY PISSED OFF WI' THEM.
WE SIT DOWN, WE'RE BEVVYIN' AWAY, I'M REMEMBERIN' ALL THE GOOD STUFF. THEN *THEY* HAVE TO REMIND ME O' THE TIMES WHEN THEY WERE FUCKIN' WANKERS TO ME.
I SUPPOSE I'M JUST WONDERIN' WHICH VERSION O' THEM'S MORE, MORE TRUE...
HMM. AN ETERNAL DILEMMA, IF EVER I HEARD ONE.
BUT WHATEVER FACES OUR FRIENDS CHOOSE TO SHOW US...WELL, THEY ARE RATHER ALL WE'VE GOT, AREN'T THEY?

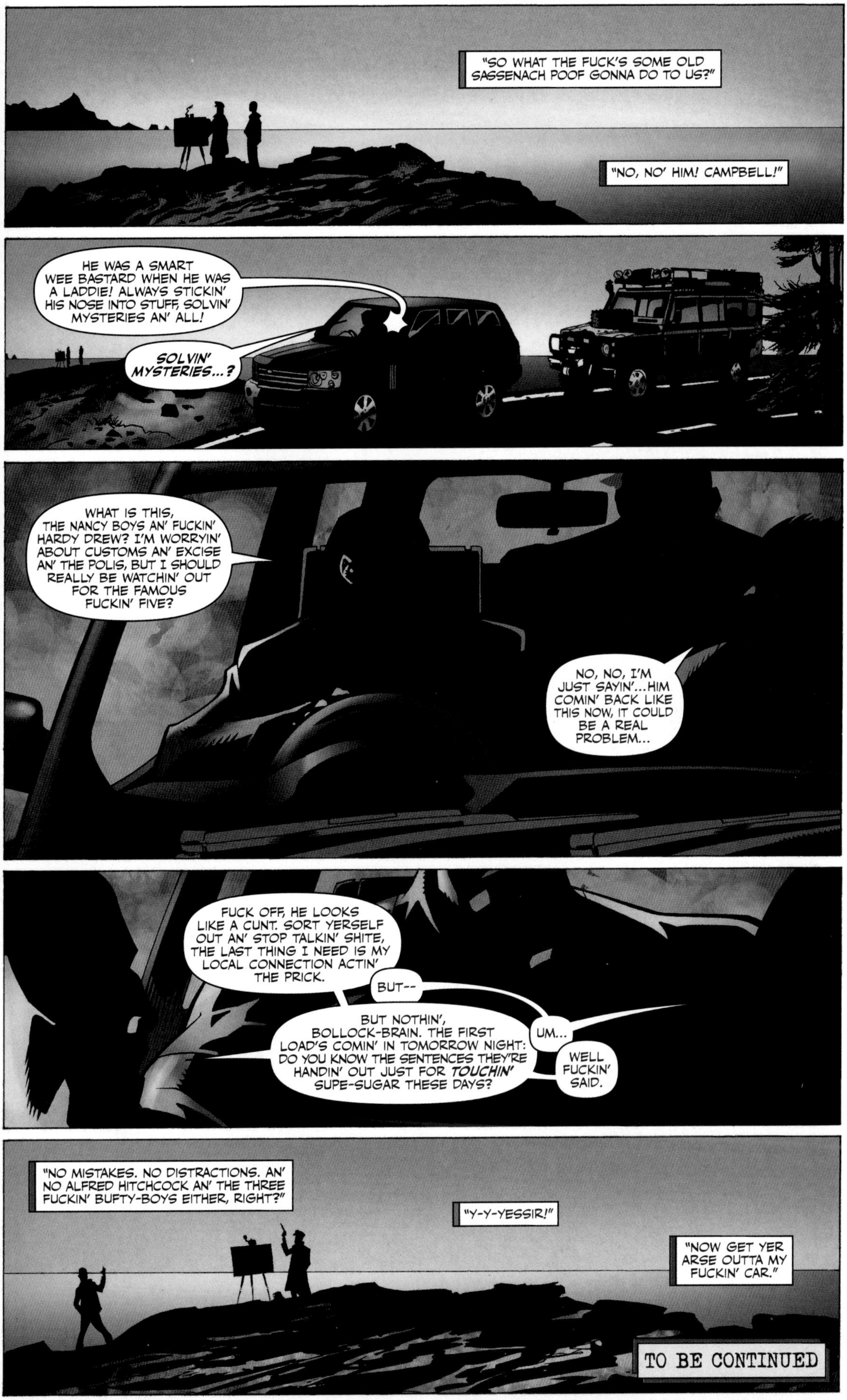
"SO WHAT THE FUCK'S SOME OLD SASSENACH POOF GONNA DO TO US?"
"NO, NO' HIM! CAMPBELL!"
HE WAS A SMART WEE BASTARD WHEN HE WAS A LADDIE! ALWAYS STICKIN' HIS NOSE INTO STUFF, SOLVIN' MYSTERIES AN' ALL!
SOLVIN' MYSTERIES...?
WHAT IS THIS, THE NANCY BOYS AN' FUCKIN' HARDY DREW? I'M WORRYIN' ABOUT CUSTOMS AN' EXCISE AN' THE POLIS, BUT I SHOULD REALLY BE WATCHIN' OUT FOR THE FAMOUS FUCKIN' FIVE?
NO, NO, I'M JUST SAYIN'...HIM COMIN' BACK LIKE THIS NOW, IT COULD BE A REAL PROBLEM...
FUCK OFF, HE LOOKS LIKE A CUNT. SORT YERSELF OUT AN' STOP TALKIN' SHITE, THE LAST THING I NEED IS MY LOCAL CONNECTION ACTIN' THE PRICK.
BUT--
BUT NOTHIN', BOLLOCK-BRAIN. THE FIRST LOAD'S COMIN' IN TOMORROW NIGHT: DO YOU KNOW THE SENTENCES THEY'RE HANDIN' OUT JUST FOR *TOUCHIN'* SUPE-SUGAR THESE DAYS?
UM...
WELL FUCKIN' SAID.
"NO MISTAKES. NO DISTRACTIONS. AN' NO ALFRED HITCHCOCK AN' THE THREE FUCKIN' BUFTY-BOYS EITHER, RIGHT?"
"Y-Y-YESSIR!"
"NOW GET YER ARSE OUTTA MY FUCKIN' CAR."
TO BE CONTINUED

HIGHLAND LADDIE #2
cover

by DARICK ROBERTSON
and TONY AVIÑA

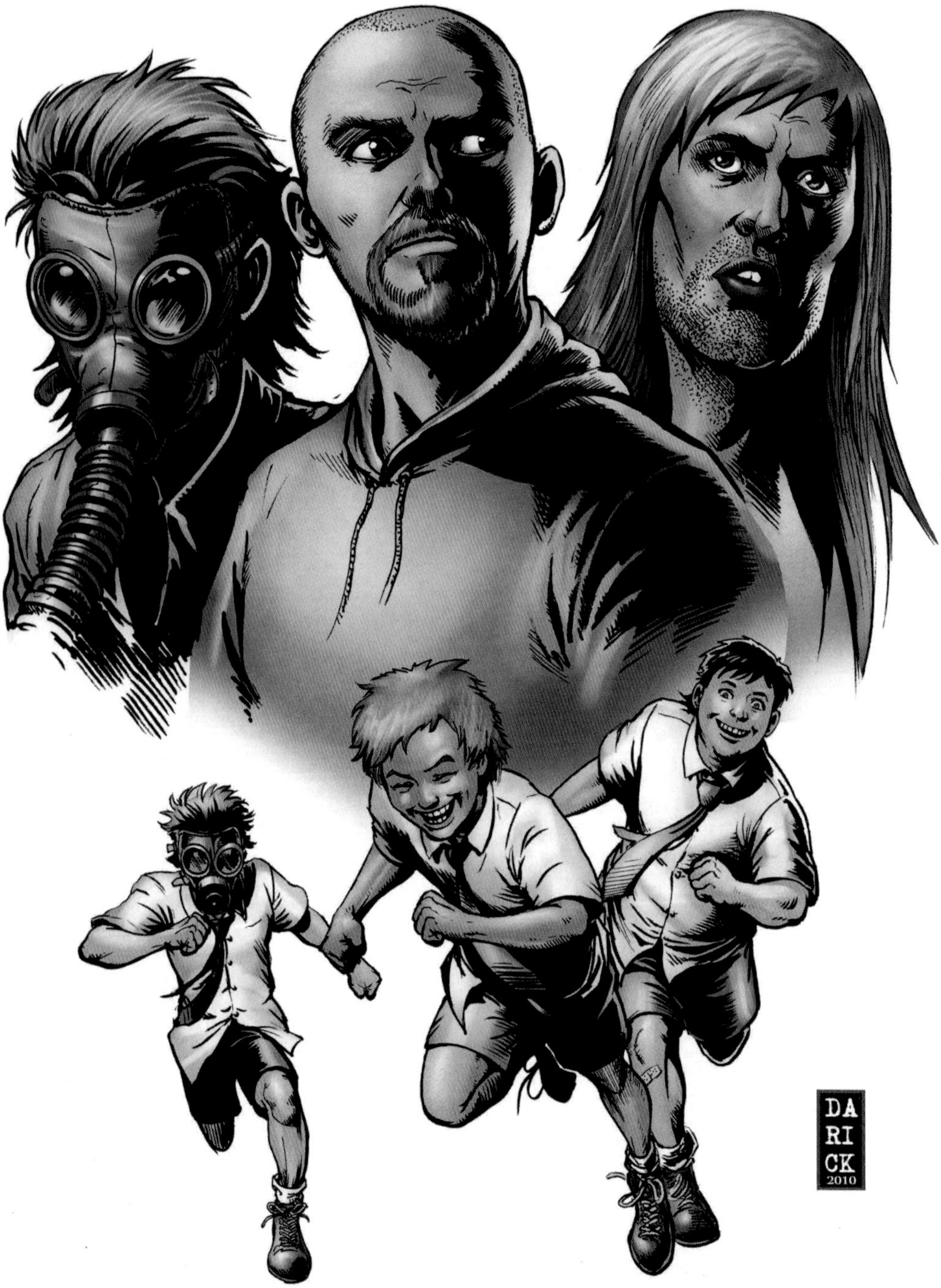
DA
RI
CK
2010

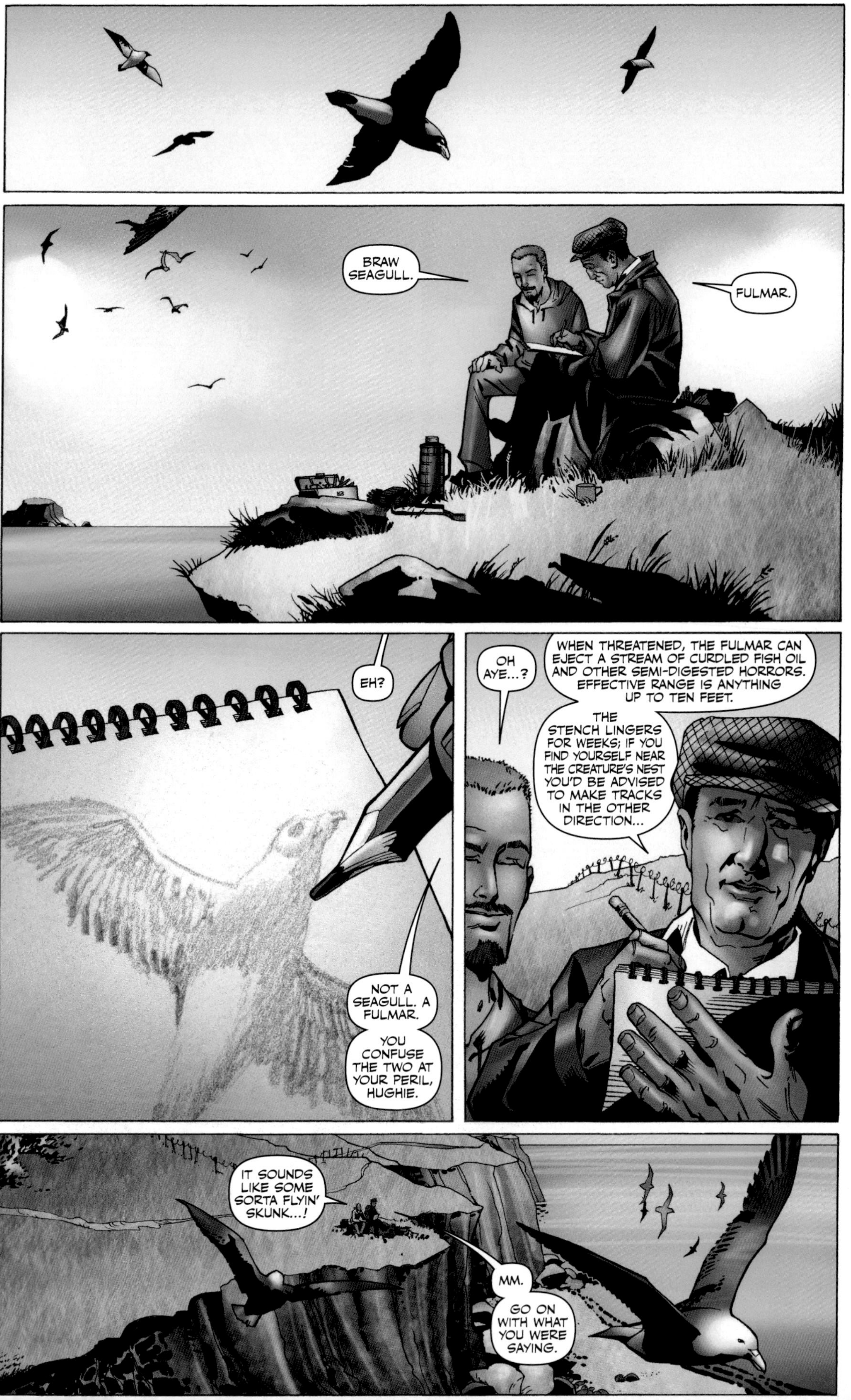
BRAW SEAGULL.
FULMAR.
EH?
NOT A SEAGULL. A FULMAR.
YOU CONFUSE THE TWO AT YOUR PERIL, HUGHIE.
OH AYE...?
WHEN THREATENED, THE FULMAR CAN EJECT A STREAM OF CURDLED FISH OIL AND OTHER SEMI-DIGESTED HORRORS. EFFECTIVE RANGE IS ANYTHING UP TO TEN FEET.
THE STENCH LINGERS FOR WEEKS; IF YOU FIND YOURSELF NEAR THE CREATURE'S NEST YOU'D BE ADVISED TO MAKE TRACKS IN THE OTHER DIRECTION...
IT SOUNDS LIKE SOME SORTA FLYIN' SKUNK...!
MM.
GO ON WITH WHAT YOU WERE SAYING.

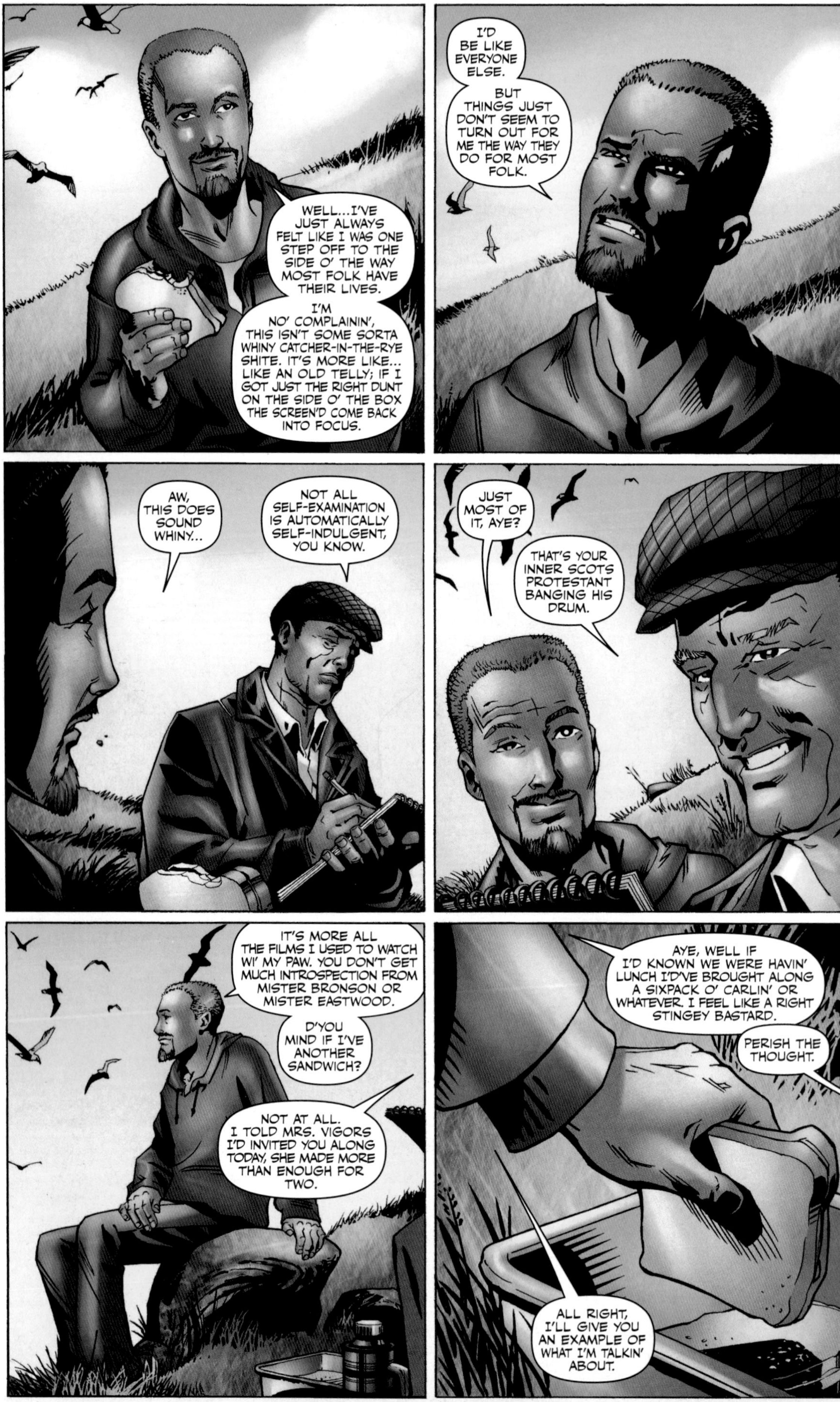
WELL...I'VE JUST ALWAYS FELT LIKE I WAS ONE STEP OFF TO THE SIDE O' THE WAY MOST FOLK HAVE THEIR LIVES.
I'M NO' COMPLAININ', THIS ISN'T SOME SORTA WHINY CATCHER-IN-THE-RYE SHITE. IT'S MORE LIKE... LIKE AN OLD TELLY; IF I GOT JUST THE RIGHT DUNT ON THE SIDE O' THE BOX THE SCREEN'D COME BACK INTO FOCUS.
I'D BE LIKE EVERYONE ELSE.
BUT THINGS JUST DON'T SEEM TO TURN OUT FOR ME THE WAY THEY DO FOR MOST FOLK.
AW, THIS DOES SOUND WHINY...
NOT ALL SELF-EXAMINATION IS AUTOMATICALLY SELF-INDULGENT, YOU KNOW.
JUST MOST OF IT, AYE?
THAT'S YOUR INNER SCOTS PROTESTANT BANGING HIS DRUM.
IT'S MORE ALL THE FILMS I USED TO WATCH WI' MY PAW. YOU DON'T GET MUCH INTROSPECTION FROM MISTER BRONSON OR MISTER EASTWOOD.
D'YOU MIND IF I'VE ANOTHER SANDWICH?
NOT AT ALL. I TOLD MRS. VIGORS I'D INVITED YOU ALONG TODAY, SHE MADE MORE THAN ENOUGH FOR TWO.
AYE, WELL IF I'D KNOWN WE WERE HAVIN' LUNCH I'D'VE BROUGHT ALONG A SIXPACK O' CARLIN' OR WHATEVER. I FEEL LIKE A RIGHT STINGEY BASTARD.
PERISH THE THOUGHT.
ALL RIGHT, I'LL GIVE YOU AN EXAMPLE OF WHAT I'M TALKIN' ABOUT.

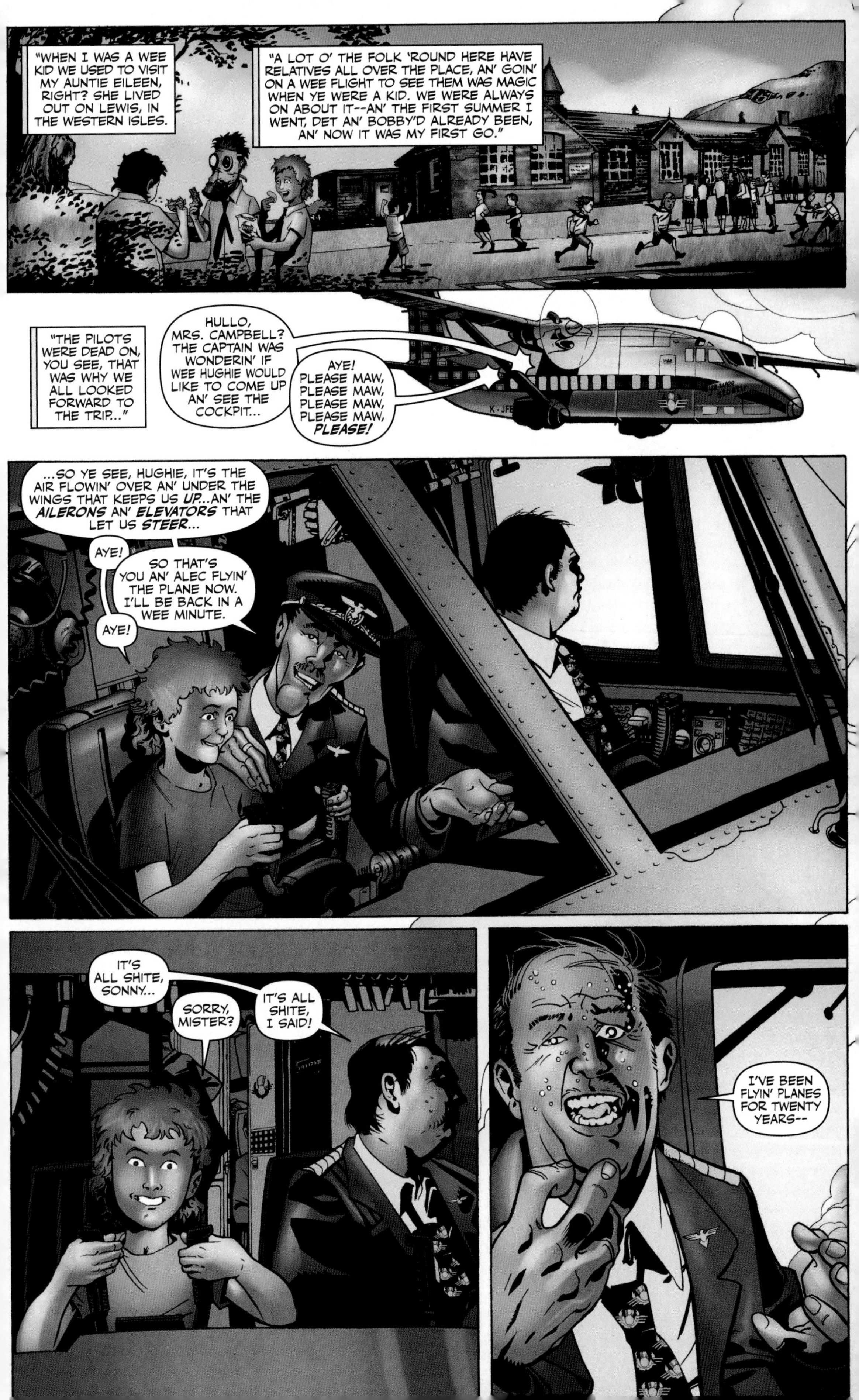
"WHEN I WAS A WEE KID WE USED TO VISIT MY AUNTIE EILEEN, RIGHT? SHE LIVED OUT ON LEWIS, IN THE WESTERN ISLES.
"A LOT O' THE FOLK 'ROUND HERE HAVE RELATIVES ALL OVER THE PLACE, AN' GOIN' ON A WEE FLIGHT TO SEE THEM WAS MAGIC WHEN YE WERE A KID. WE WERE ALWAYS ON ABOUT IT--AN' THE FIRST SUMMER I WENT, DET AN' BOBBY'D ALREADY BEEN, AN' NOW IT WAS MY FIRST GO."
"THE PILOTS WERE DEAD ON, YOU SEE, THAT WAS WHY WE ALL LOOKED FORWARD TO THE TRIP..."
HULLO, MRS. CAMPBELL? THE CAPTAIN WAS WONDERIN' IF WEE HUGHIE WOULD LIKE TO COME UP AN' SEE THE COCKPIT...
AYE! PLEASE MAW, PLEASE MAW, PLEASE MAW, PLEASE MAW, PLEASE!
...SO YE SEE, HUGHIE, IT'S THE AIR FLOWIN' OVER AN' UNDER THE WINGS THAT KEEPS US UP...AN' THE AILERONS AN' ELEVATORS THAT LET US STEER...
AYE!
SO THAT'S YOU AN' ALEC FLYIN' THE PLANE NOW. I'LL BE BACK IN A WEE MINUTE.
AYE!
IT'S ALL SHITE, SONNY...
SORRY, MISTER?
IT'S ALL SHITE, I SAID!
I'VE BEEN FLYIN' PLANES FOR TWENTY YEARS--

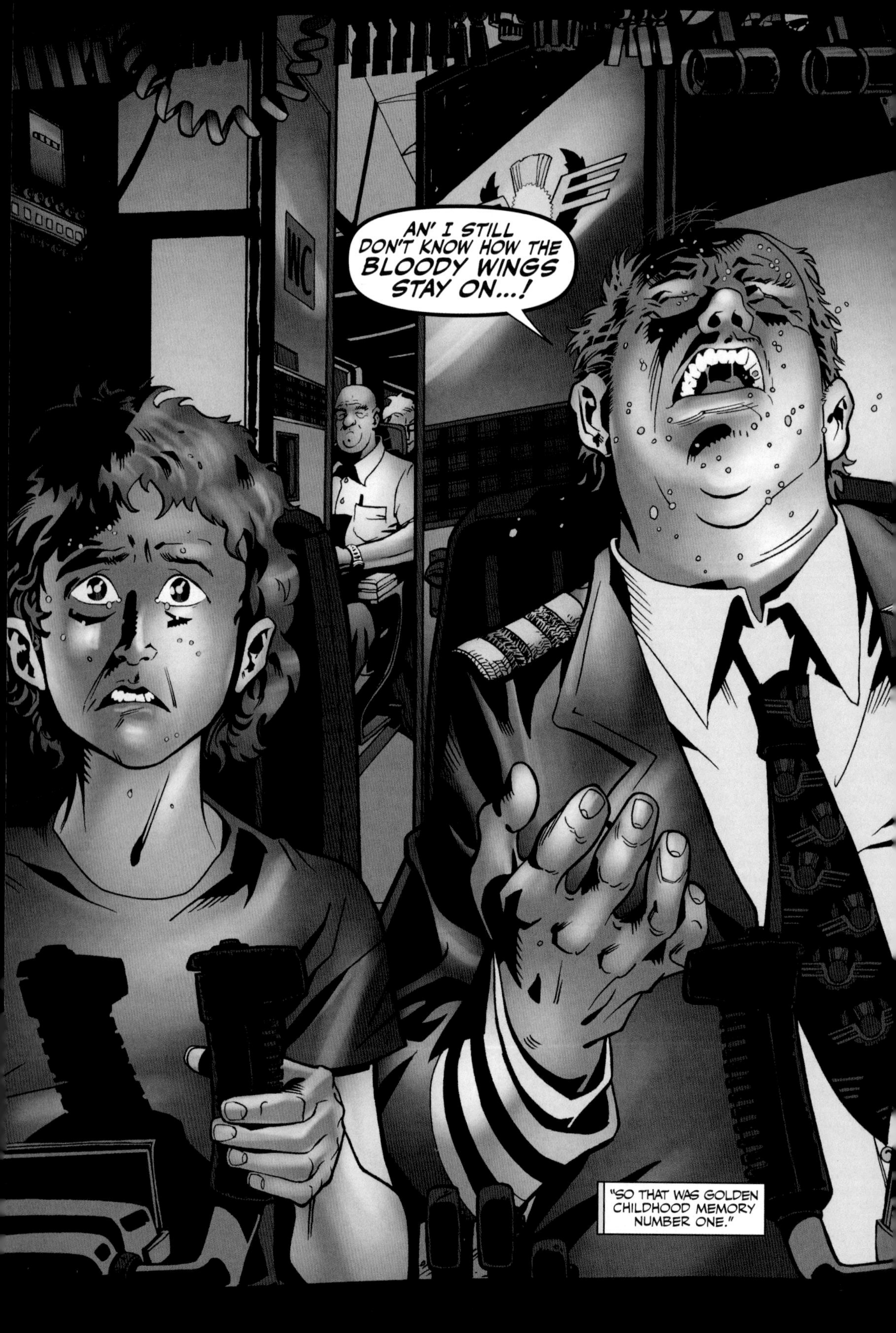
WC
AN' I STILL DON'T KNOW HOW THE BLOODY WINGS STAY ON...!
"SO THAT WAS GOLDEN CHILDHOOD MEMORY NUMBER ONE."

2: GREAT GLASS ELEVATOR

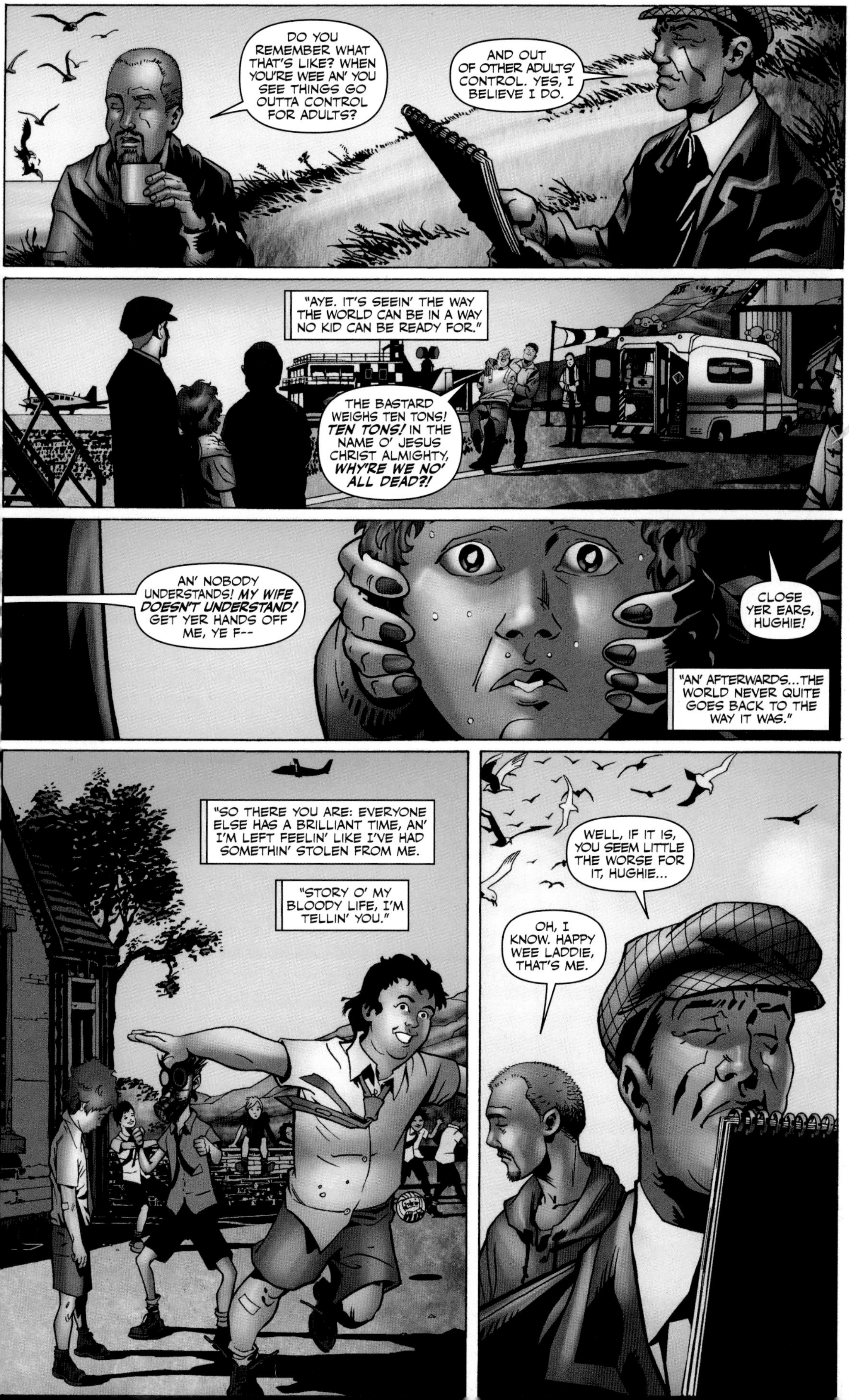
DO YOU REMEMBER WHAT THAT'S LIKE? WHEN YOU'RE WEE AN' YOU SEE THINGS GO OUTTA CONTROL FOR ADULTS?
AND OUT OF OTHER ADULTS' CONTROL. YES, I BELIEVE I DO.
"AYE. IT'S SEEIN' THE WAY THE WORLD CAN BE IN A WAY NO KID CAN BE READY FOR."
THE BASTARD WEIGHS TEN TONS! TEN TONS! IN THE NAME O' JESUS CHRIST ALMIGHTY, WHY'RE WE NO' ALL DEAD?!
AN' NOBODY UNDERSTANDS! MY WIFE DOESN'T UNDERSTAND! GET YER HANDS OFF ME, YE F--
CLOSE YER EARS, HUGHIE!
"AN' AFTERWARDS...THE WORLD NEVER QUITE GOES BACK TO THE WAY IT WAS."
"SO THERE YOU ARE: EVERYONE ELSE HAS A BRILLIANT TIME, AN' I'M LEFT FEELIN' LIKE I'VE HAD SOMETHIN' STOLEN FROM ME.
"STORY O' MY BLOODY LIFE, I'M TELLIN' YOU."
WELL, IF IT IS, YOU SEEM LITTLE THE WORSE FOR IT, HUGHIE...
OH, I KNOW. HAPPY WEE LADDIE, THAT'S ME.

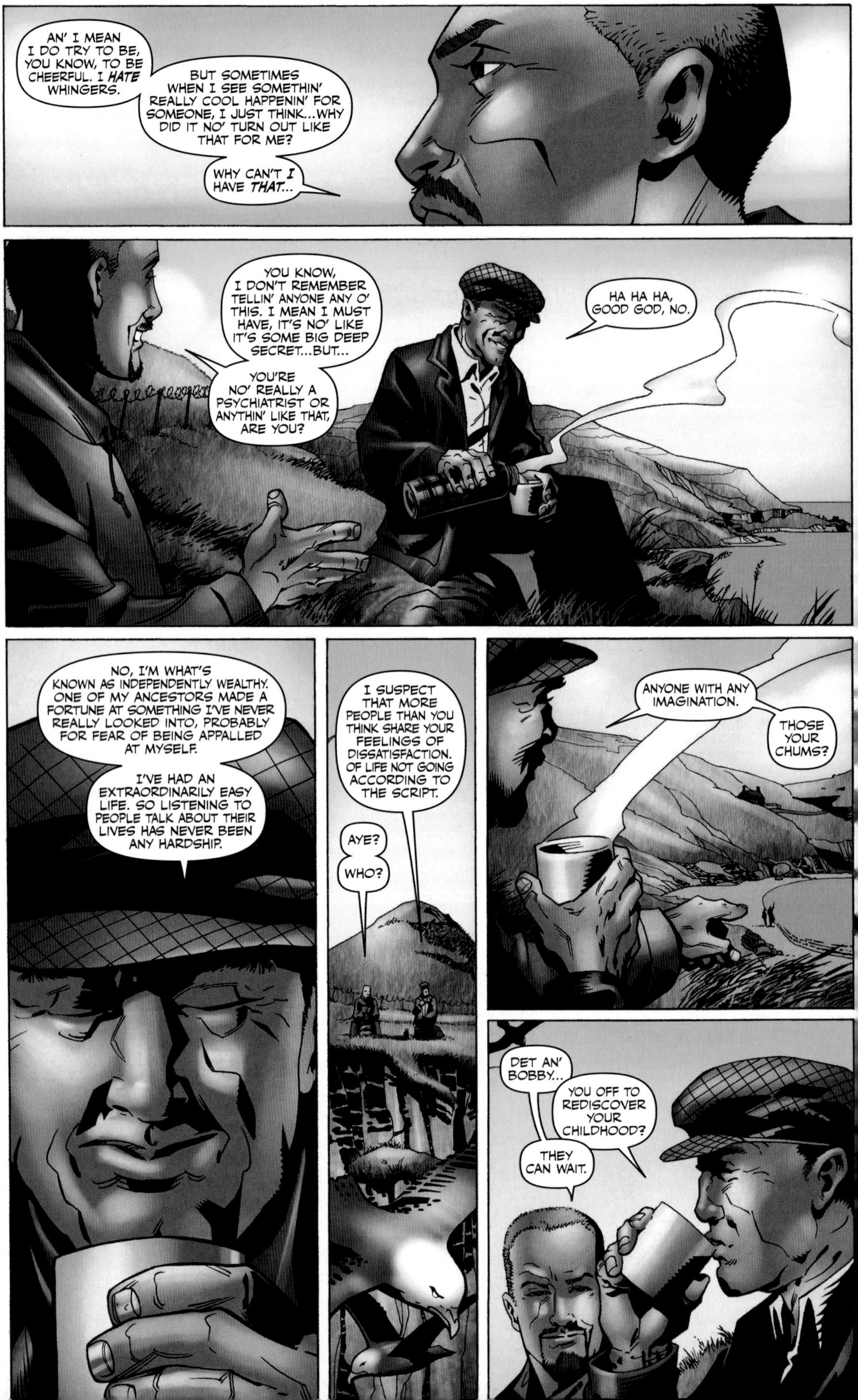
AN' I MEAN I DO TRY TO BE, YOU KNOW, TO BE CHEERFUL. I *HATE* WHINGERS.
BUT SOMETIMES WHEN I SEE SOMETHIN' REALLY COOL HAPPENIN' FOR SOMEONE, I JUST THINK...WHY DID IT NO' TURN OUT LIKE THAT FOR ME?
WHY CAN'T *I* HAVE *THAT*...
YOU KNOW, I DON'T REMEMBER TELLIN' ANYONE ANY O' THIS. I MEAN I MUST HAVE, IT'S NO' LIKE IT'S SOME BIG DEEP SECRET...BUT...
YOU'RE NO' REALLY A PSYCHIATRIST OR ANYTHIN' LIKE THAT, ARE YOU?
HA HA HA, GOOD GOD, NO.
NO, I'M WHAT'S KNOWN AS INDEPENDENTLY WEALTHY. ONE OF MY ANCESTORS MADE A FORTUNE AT SOMETHING I'VE NEVER REALLY LOOKED INTO, PROBABLY FOR FEAR OF BEING APPALLED AT MYSELF.
I'VE HAD AN EXTRAORDINARILY EASY LIFE. SO LISTENING TO PEOPLE TALK ABOUT THEIR LIVES HAS NEVER BEEN ANY HARDSHIP.
I SUSPECT THAT MORE PEOPLE THAN YOU THINK SHARE YOUR FEELINGS OF DISSATISFACTION. OF LIFE NOT GOING ACCORDING TO THE SCRIPT.
AYE?
WHO?
ANYONE WITH ANY IMAGINATION.
THOSE YOUR CHUMS?
DET AN' BOBBY...
YOU OFF TO REDISCOVER YOUR CHILDHOOD?
THEY CAN WAIT.

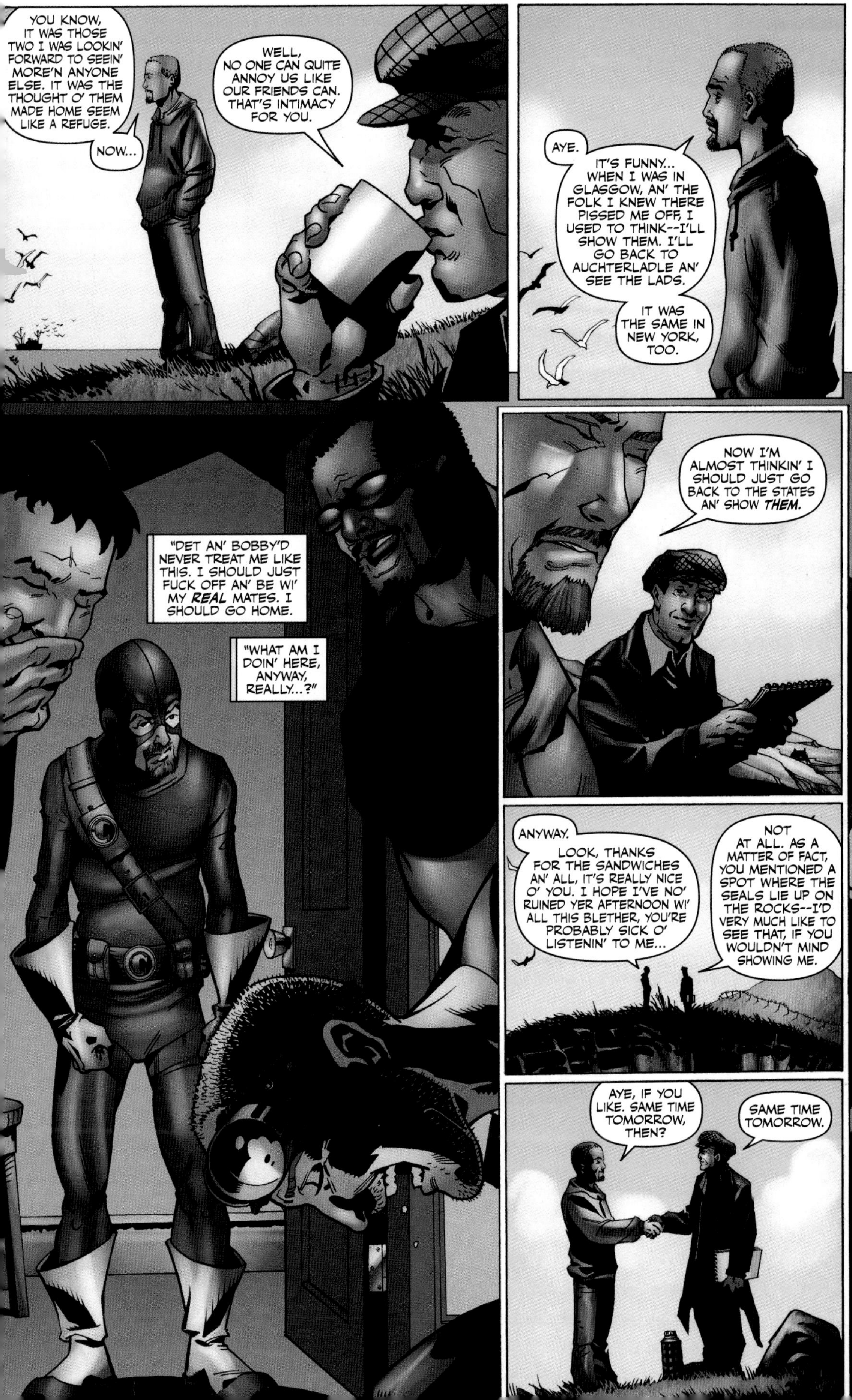
YOU KNOW, IT WAS THOSE TWO I WAS LOOKIN' FORWARD TO SEEIN' MORE'N ANYONE ELSE. IT WAS THE THOUGHT O' THEM MADE HOME SEEM LIKE A REFUGE.
NOW...
WELL, NO ONE CAN QUITE ANNOY US LIKE OUR FRIENDS CAN. THAT'S INTIMACY FOR YOU.
AYE.
IT'S FUNNY... WHEN I WAS IN GLASGOW, AN' THE FOLK I KNEW THERE PISSED ME OFF, I USED TO THINK--I'LL SHOW THEM. I'LL GO BACK TO AUCHTERLADLE AN' SEE THE LADS.
IT WAS THE SAME IN NEW YORK, TOO.
"DET AN' BOBBY'D NEVER TREAT ME LIKE THIS. I SHOULD JUST FUCK OFF AN' BE WI' MY ***REAL*** MATES. I SHOULD GO HOME.
"WHAT AM I DOIN' HERE, ANYWAY, REALLY...?"
NOW I'M ALMOST THINKIN' I SHOULD JUST GO BACK TO THE STATES AN' SHOW ***THEM.***
ANYWAY.
LOOK, THANKS FOR THE SANDWICHES AN' ALL, IT'S REALLY NICE O' YOU. I HOPE I'VE NO' RUINED YER AFTERNOON WI' ALL THIS BLETHER, YOU'RE PROBABLY SICK O' LISTENIN' TO ME...
NOT AT ALL. AS A MATTER OF FACT, YOU MENTIONED A SPOT WHERE THE SEALS LIE UP ON THE ROCKS--I'D VERY MUCH LIKE TO SEE THAT, IF YOU WOULDN'T MIND SHOWING ME.
AYE, IF YOU LIKE. SAME TIME TOMORROW, THEN?
SAME TIME TOMORROW.

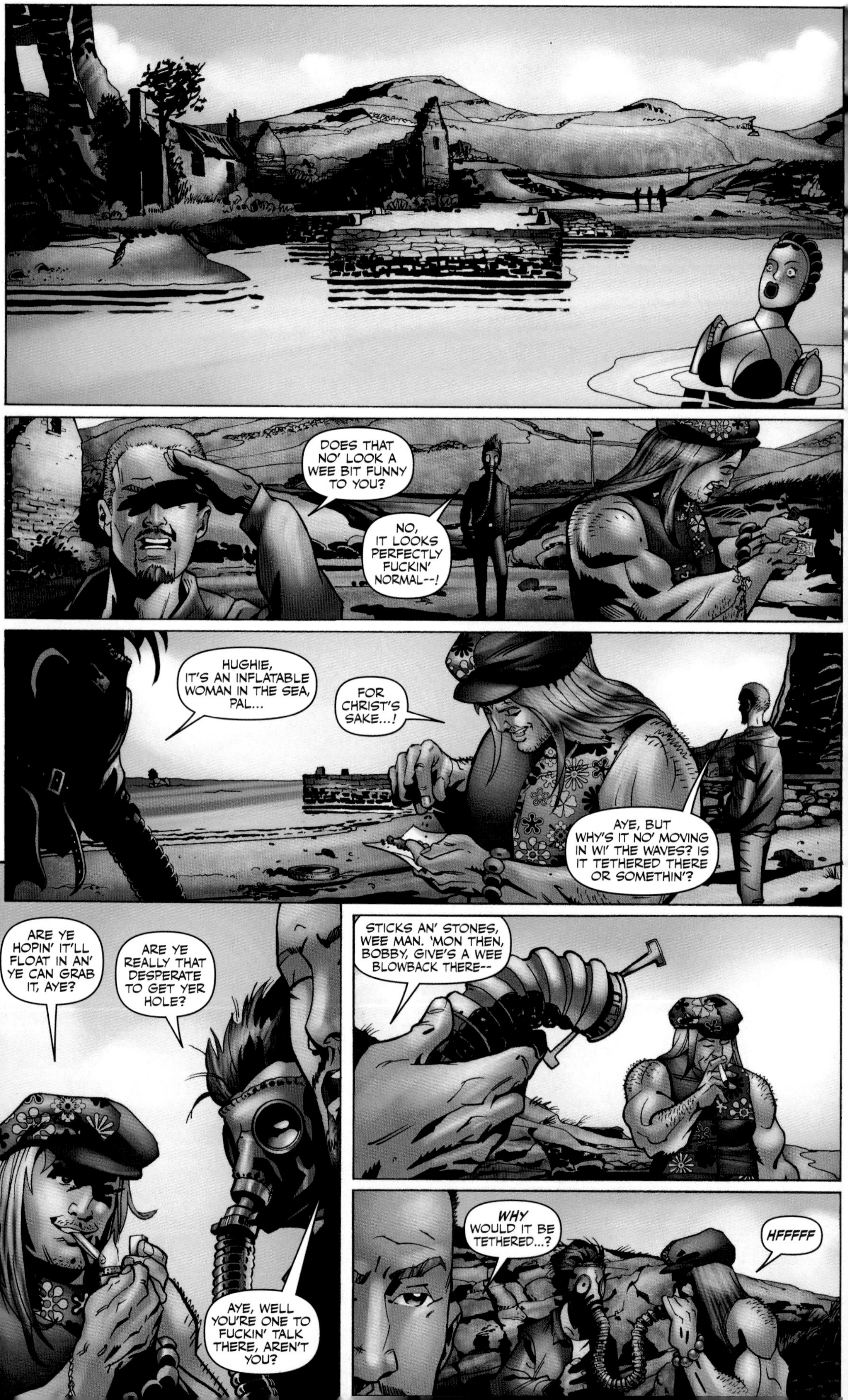
DOES THAT NO' LOOK A WEE BIT FUNNY TO YOU?
NO, IT LOOKS PERFECTLY FUCKIN' NORMAL--!
HUGHIE, IT'S AN INFLATABLE WOMAN IN THE SEA, PAL...
FOR CHRIST'S SAKE...!
AYE, BUT WHY'S IT NO' MOVING IN WI' THE WAVES? IS IT TETHERED THERE OR SOMETHIN'?
ARE YE HOPIN' IT'LL FLOAT IN AN' YE CAN GRAB IT, AYE?
ARE YE REALLY THAT DESPERATE TO GET YER HOLE?
AYE, WELL YOU'RE ONE TO FUCKIN' TALK THERE, AREN'T YOU?
STICKS AN' STONES, WEE MAN. 'MON THEN, BOBBY, GIVE'S A WEE BLOWBACK THERE--
WHY WOULD IT BE TETHERED...?
HFFFFF

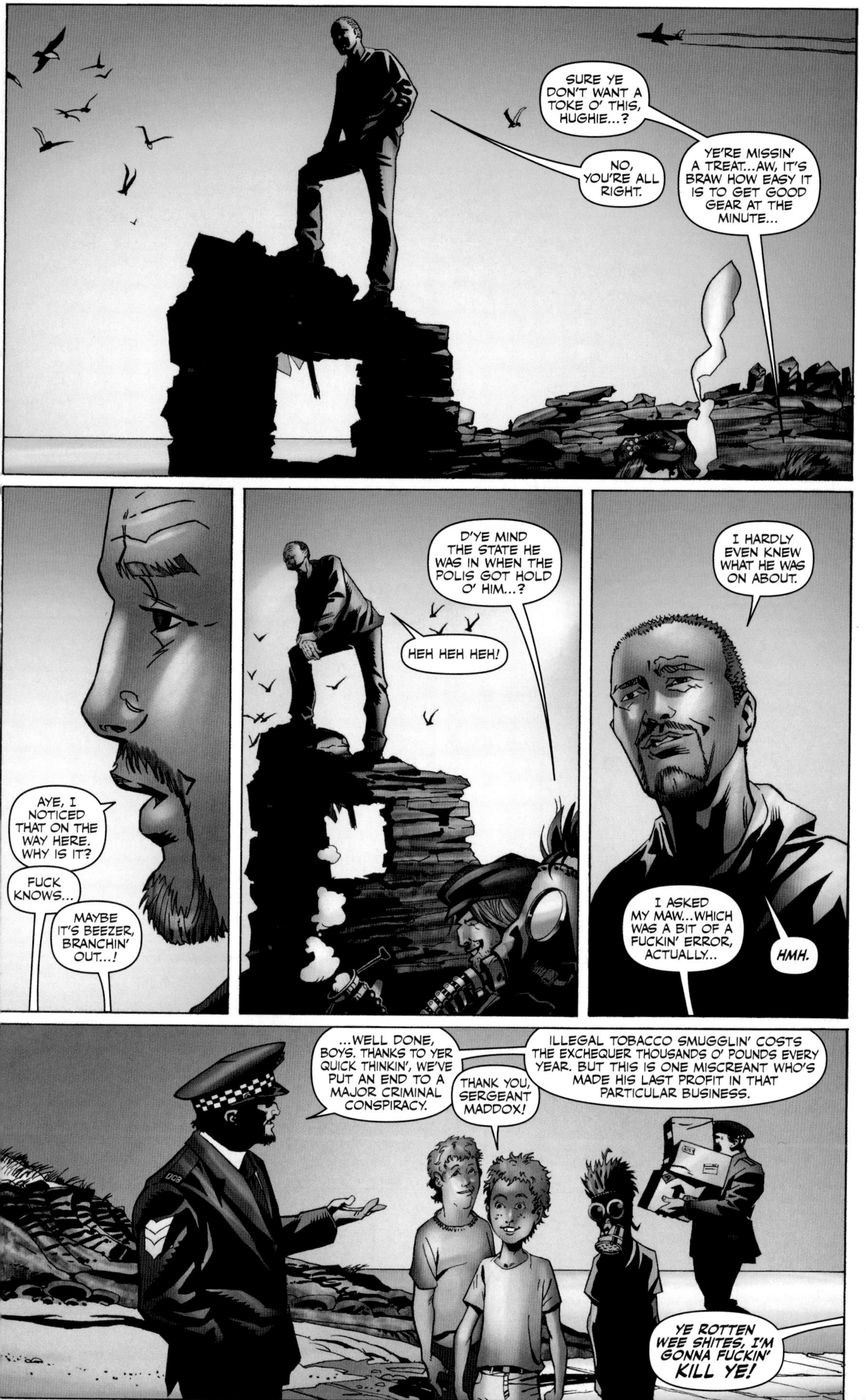
SURE YE DON'T WANT A TOKE O' THIS, HUGHIE...?
NO, YOU'RE ALL RIGHT.
YE'RE MISSIN' A TREAT...AW, IT'S BRAW HOW EASY IT IS TO GET GOOD GEAR AT THE MINUTE...
AYE, I NOTICED THAT ON THE WAY HERE. WHY IS IT?
FUCK KNOWS...
MAYBE IT'S BEEZER, BRANCHIN' OUT...!
D'YE MIND THE STATE HE WAS IN WHEN THE POLIS GOT HOLD O' HIM...?
HEH HEH HEH!
I HARDLY EVEN KNEW WHAT HE WAS ON ABOUT.
I ASKED MY MAW...WHICH WAS A BIT OF A FUCKIN' ERROR, ACTUALLY...
HMH.
...WELL DONE, BOYS. THANKS TO YER QUICK THINKIN', WE'VE PUT AN END TO A MAJOR CRIMINAL CONSPIRACY.
THANK YOU, SERGEANT MADDOX!
ILLEGAL TOBACCO SMUGGLIN' COSTS THE EXCHEQUER THOUSANDS O' POUNDS EVERY YEAR. BUT THIS IS ONE MISCREANT WHO'S MADE HIS LAST PROFIT IN THAT PARTICULAR BUSINESS.
YE ROTTEN WEE SHITES, I'M GONNA FUCKIN' KILL YE!

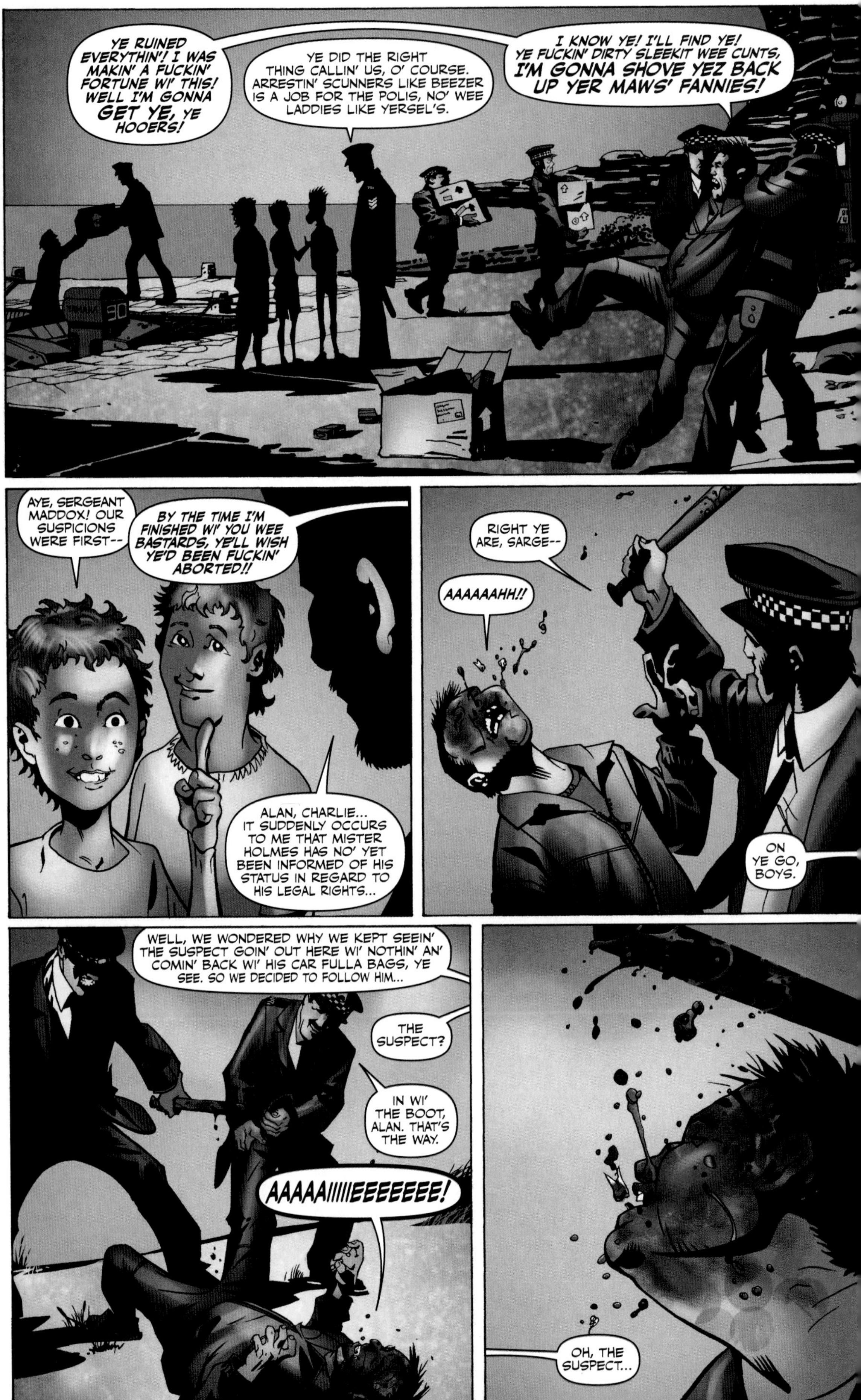
YE RUINED EVERYTHIN'! I WAS MAKIN' A FUCKIN' FORTUNE WI' THIS! WELL I'M GONNA GET YE, YE HOOERS!
YE DID THE RIGHT THING CALLIN' US, O' COURSE. ARRESTIN' SCUNNERS LIKE BEEZER IS A JOB FOR THE POLIS, NO' WEE LADDIES LIKE YERSEL'S.
I KNOW YE! I'LL FIND YE! YE FUCKIN' DIRTY SLEEKIT WEE CUNTS, I'M GONNA SHOVE YEZ BACK UP YER MAWS' FANNIES!
AYE, SERGEANT MADDOX! OUR SUSPICIONS WERE FIRST--
BY THE TIME I'M FINISHED WI' YOU WEE BASTARDS, YE'LL WISH YE'D BEEN FUCKIN' ABORTED!!
ALAN, CHARLIE... IT SUDDENLY OCCURS TO ME THAT MISTER HOLMES HAS NO' YET BEEN INFORMED OF HIS STATUS IN REGARD TO HIS LEGAL RIGHTS...
RIGHT YE ARE, SARGE--
AAAAAAHH!!
ON YE GO, BOYS.
WELL, WE WONDERED WHY WE KEPT SEEIN' THE SUSPECT GOIN' OUT HERE WI' NOTHIN' AN' COMIN' BACK WI' HIS CAR FULLA BAGS, YE SEE. SO WE DECIDED TO FOLLOW HIM...
THE SUSPECT?
IN WI' THE BOOT, ALAN. THAT'S THE WAY.
AAAAAIIIIIEEEEEEE!
OH, THE SUSPECT...

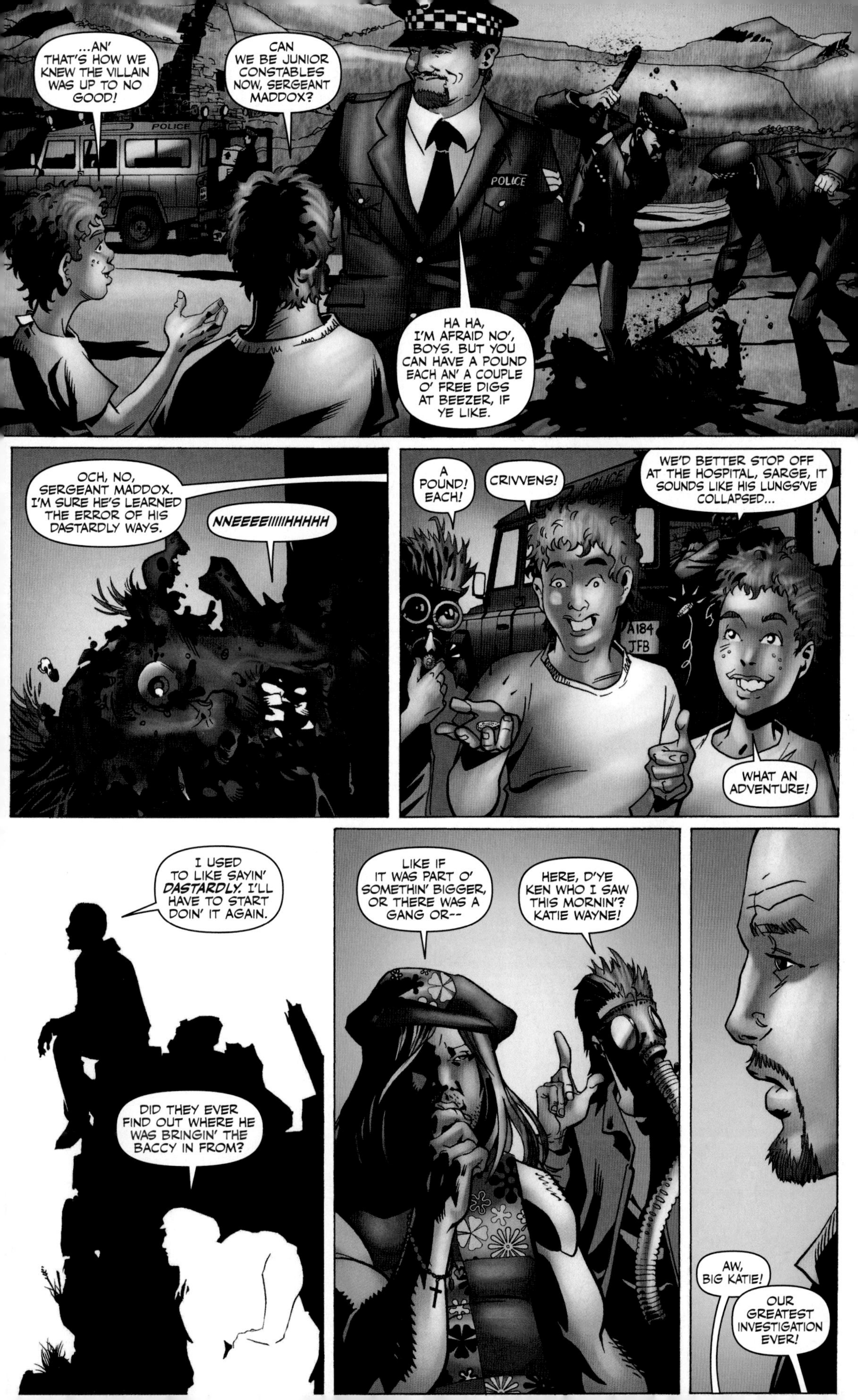
...AN' THAT'S HOW WE KNEW THE VILLAIN WAS UP TO NO GOOD!
CAN WE BE JUNIOR CONSTABLES NOW, SERGEANT MADDOX?
POLICE
POLICE
HA HA, I'M AFRAID NO', BOYS. BUT YOU CAN HAVE A POUND EACH AN' A COUPLE O' FREE DIGS AT BEEZER, IF YE LIKE.
OCH, NO, SERGEANT MADDOX. I'M SURE HE'S LEARNED THE ERROR OF HIS DASTARDLY WAYS.
NNEEEEIIIIIHHHHH
A POUND! EACH!
CRIVVENS!
WE'D BETTER STOP OFF AT THE HOSPITAL, SARGE, IT SOUNDS LIKE HIS LUNGS'VE COLLAPSED...
A184 JFB
WHAT AN ADVENTURE!
I USED TO LIKE SAYIN' DASTARDLY. I'LL HAVE TO START DOIN' IT AGAIN.
DID THEY EVER FIND OUT WHERE HE WAS BRINGIN' THE BACCY IN FROM?
LIKE IF IT WAS PART O' SOMETHIN' BIGGER, OR THERE WAS A GANG OR--
HERE, D'YE KEN WHO I SAW THIS MORNIN'? KATIE WAYNE!
AW, BIG KATIE!
OUR GREATEST INVESTIGATION EVER!

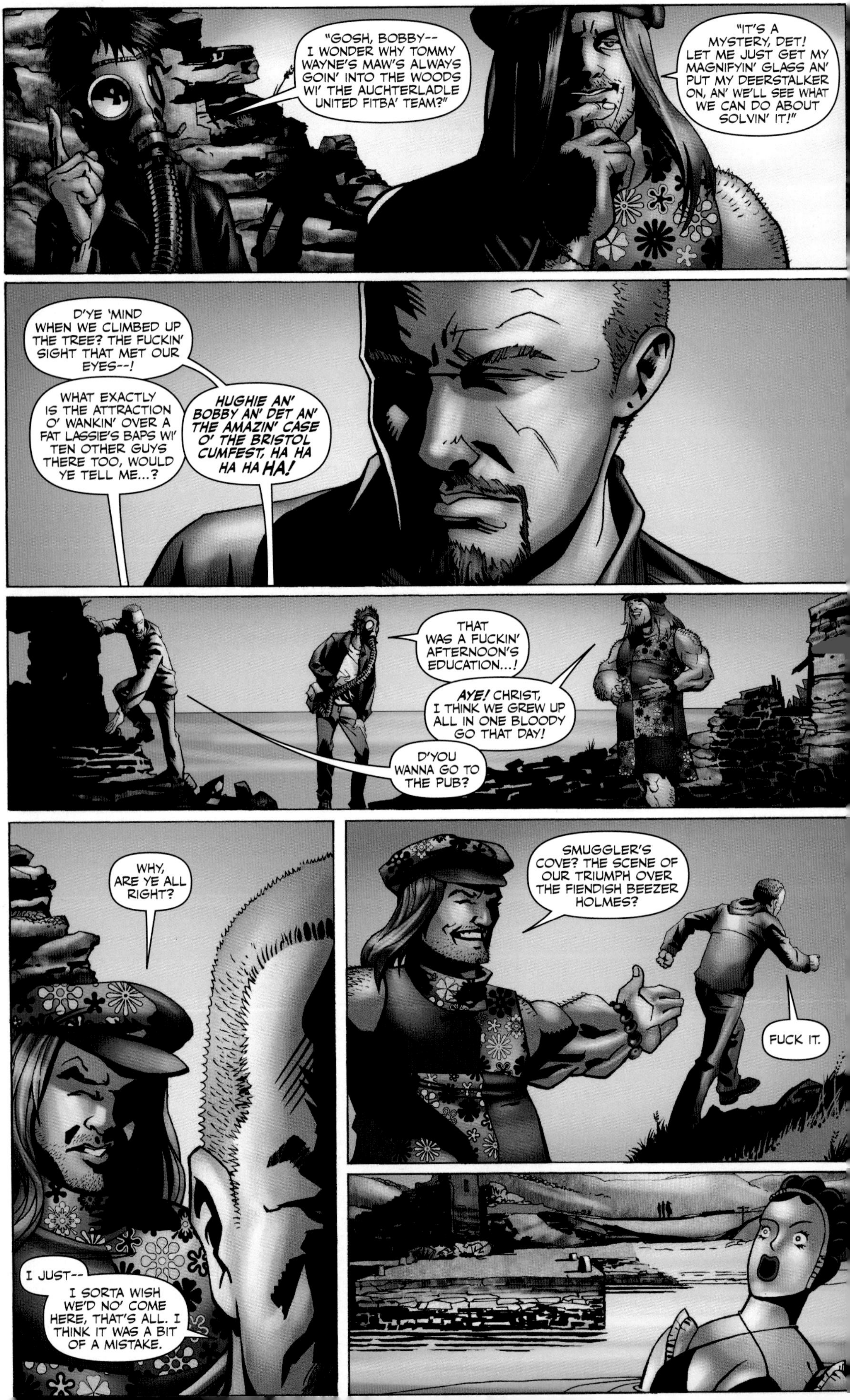
"GOSH, BOBBY-- I WONDER WHY TOMMY WAYNE'S MAW'S ALWAYS GOIN' INTO THE WOODS WI' THE AUCHTERLADLE UNITED FITBA' TEAM?"
"IT'S A MYSTERY, DET! LET ME JUST GET MY MAGNIFYIN' GLASS AN' PUT MY DEERSTALKER ON, AN' WE'LL SEE WHAT WE CAN DO ABOUT SOLVIN' IT!"
D'YE 'MIND WHEN WE CLIMBED UP THE TREE? THE FUCKIN' SIGHT THAT MET OUR EYES--!
HUGHIE AN' BOBBY AN' DET AN' THE AMAZIN' CASE O' THE BRISTOL CUMFEST, HA HA HA HA HA!
WHAT EXACTLY IS THE ATTRACTION O' WANKIN' OVER A FAT LASSIE'S BAPS WI' TEN OTHER GUYS THERE TOO, WOULD YE TELL ME...?
THAT WAS A FUCKIN' AFTERNOON'S EDUCATION...!
AYE! CHRIST, I THINK WE GREW UP ALL IN ONE BLOODY GO THAT DAY!
D'YOU WANNA GO TO THE PUB?
WHY, ARE YE ALL RIGHT?
I JUST-- I SORTA WISH WE'D NO' COME HERE, THAT'S ALL. I THINK IT WAS A BIT OF A MISTAKE.
SMUGGLER'S COVE? THE SCENE OF OUR TRIUMPH OVER THE FIENDISH BEEZER HOLMES?
FUCK IT.

YOU AIN'T HUNGRY?

AH...

OR YOU HAVIN' SECOND THOUGHTS?

NO, I'M GOIN'. I'M DEFINITELY GOIN'.

BUT YOU AIN'T GONNA TALK ABOUT THIS MYSTERY CHICK...

UH-UH.

I WANNA TALK ABOUT OUR BOSS.

YEAH?

WE'RE MEANT TO BE A C.I.A. TEAM...A TEAM WI' C.I.A. BACKIN', ANYWAY...AN' IT'S OUR JOB TO KEEP AN EYE ON SUPERHEROES. THE WORD I ALWAYS USED TO HEAR WAS MANAGEMENT.

BUT I ASKED THE LEGEND ABOUT THAT, AN' HE TOLD ME THE SEVEN--THEM IN PARTICULAR--WERE REALLY A TARGET. HE SAID THEY WERE BUTCHER'S TARGET, HE ASKED ME IF I THOUGHT SOMEONE LIKE BUTCHER'D EVER BE INTERESTED IN MANAGIN' ANYTHIN'.

YOU ASK THE MAN HIMSELF ABOUT THIS?

OH, SHIT.

AYE, BUT I FUCKED UP THERE. I MENTIONED HIS WIFE.

I SORTA DID IT AGAIN RECENTLY THERE. I DUNNO WHAT'S THE MATTER WI' ME.

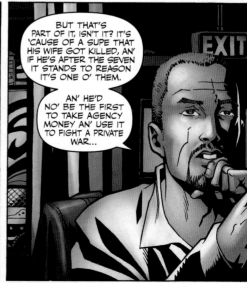

BUT THAT'S PART OF IT, ISN'T IT? IT'S 'CAUSE OF A SUPE THAT HIS WIFE GOT KILLED, AN' IF HE'S AFTER THE SEVEN IT STANDS TO REASON IT'S ONE O' THEM.

AN' HE'D NO' BE THE FIRST TO TAKE AGENCY MONEY AN' USE IT TO FIGHT A PRIVATE WAR...

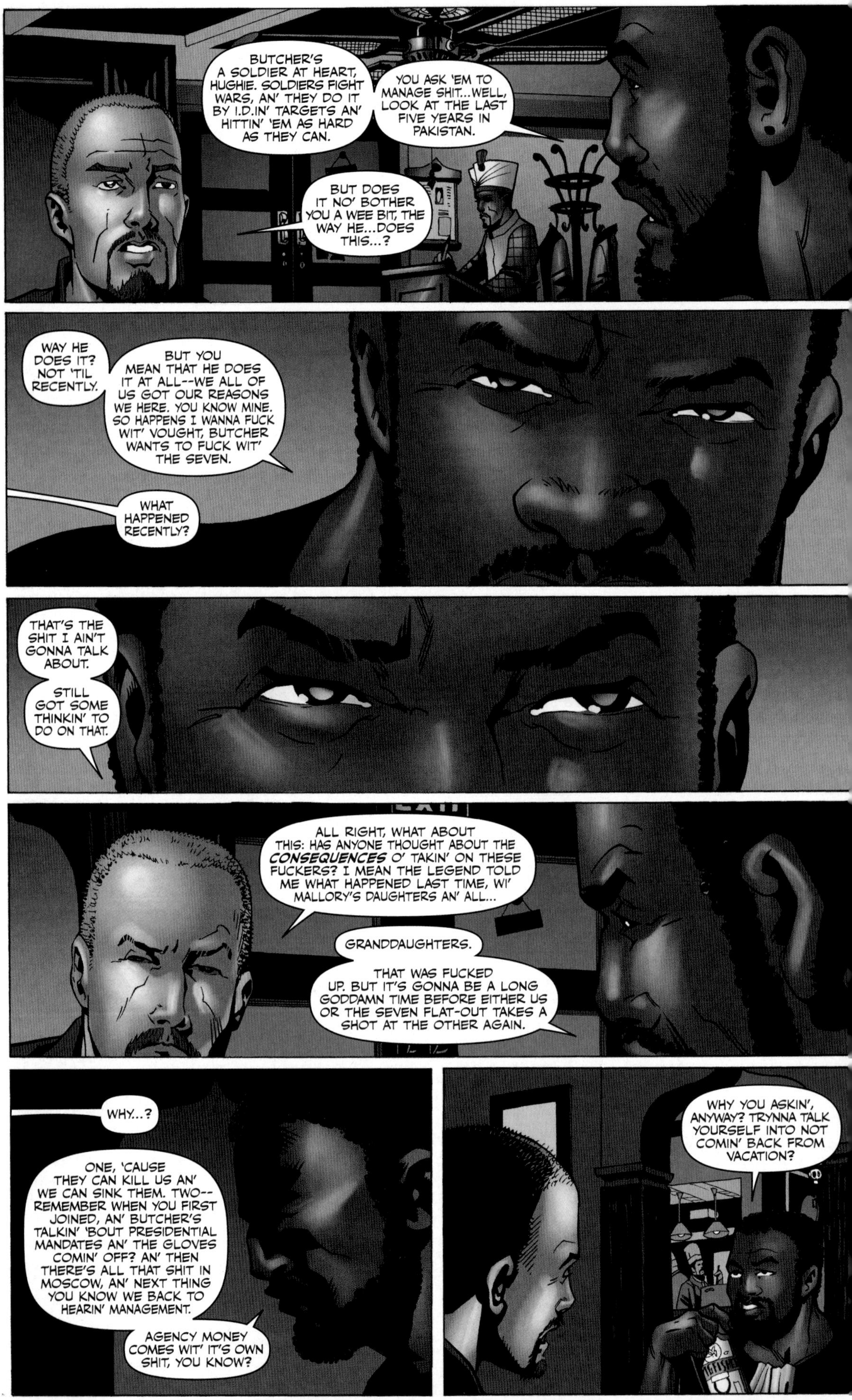
BUTCHER'S A SOLDIER AT HEART, HUGHIE. SOLDIERS FIGHT WARS, AN' THEY DO IT BY I.D.IN' TARGETS AN' HITTIN' 'EM AS HARD AS THEY CAN.
YOU ASK 'EM TO MANAGE SHIT...WELL, LOOK AT THE LAST FIVE YEARS IN PAKISTAN.
BUT DOES IT NO' BOTHER YOU A WEE BIT, THE WAY HE...DOES THIS...?
WAY HE DOES IT? NOT 'TIL RECENTLY.
BUT YOU MEAN THAT HE DOES IT AT ALL--WE ALL OF US GOT OUR REASONS WE HERE. YOU KNOW MINE. SO HAPPENS I WANNA FUCK WIT' VOUGHT, BUTCHER WANTS TO FUCK WIT' THE SEVEN.
WHAT HAPPENED RECENTLY?
THAT'S THE SHIT I AIN'T GONNA TALK ABOUT.
STILL GOT SOME THINKIN' TO DO ON THAT.
ALL RIGHT, WHAT ABOUT THIS: HAS ANYONE THOUGHT ABOUT THE *CONSEQUENCES* O' TAKIN' ON THESE FUCKERS? I MEAN THE LEGEND TOLD ME WHAT HAPPENED LAST TIME, WI' MALLORY'S DAUGHTERS AN' ALL...
GRANDDAUGHTERS.
THAT WAS FUCKED UP. BUT IT'S GONNA BE A LONG GODDAMN TIME BEFORE EITHER US OR THE SEVEN FLAT-OUT TAKES A SHOT AT THE OTHER AGAIN.
WHY...?
ONE, 'CAUSE THEY CAN KILL US AN' WE CAN SINK THEM. TWO-- REMEMBER WHEN YOU FIRST JOINED, AN' BUTCHER'S TALKIN' 'BOUT PRESIDENTIAL MANDATES AN' THE GLOVES COMIN' OFF? AN' THEN THERE'S ALL THAT SHIT IN MOSCOW, AN' NEXT THING YOU KNOW WE BACK TO HEARIN' MANAGEMENT.
AGENCY MONEY COMES WIT' IT'S OWN SHIT, YOU KNOW?
WHY YOU ASKIN', ANYWAY? TRYNNA TALK YOURSELF INTO NOT COMIN' BACK FROM VACATION?

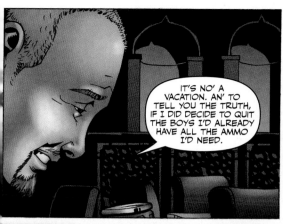

IT'S NO' A VACATION. AN' TO TELL YOU THE TRUTH, IF I DID DECIDE TO QUIT THE BOYS I'D ALREADY HAVE ALL THE AMMO I'D NEED.

HOW SO?

THE FUCKIN' *CARNAGE*...!

THE MURDER, THE DISMEMBERMENT, THE SHEER FUCKIN' AMOUNT O' *VIOLENCE* I'VE SEEN...THE THINGS I'VE DONE AN' HAD DONE TO ME, WI' PAYBACK AN' HEROGASM AN' EVERYTHIN'...

NOTHIN' HAPPENED TO YOU AT HEROGASM. YOU TALKIN' 'BOUT WHEN YOU FELL AN' HIT YOUR HEAD?

OH--NO, NO, THAT WAS MORE WHERE IT WAS WHAT I SAW. YOU KNOW WHAT I MEAN.

I DUNNO IF THIS REALLY MEANS MUCH TO YOU, I KNOW YOU WERE IN THE ARMY TOO...

YEAH, BUT I'M SWEETNESS AN' MUTHAFUCKIN' LIGHT. FILLED FROM GODDAMN HEAD TO TOE WIT' LOVE.

WELL, I WOULDN'T GO THAT FAR. BUT I WILL MISS YOU, LIKE...

GET THE FUCK OUTTA HERE.

AYE, WELL RIGHT ENOUGH, I SUPPOSE I'D BETTER GET THE BILL. THE CHECK.

WILL YOU BE IN THE OFFICE TOMORROW, WI' THE OTHERS?

NO.

NO?

NO.

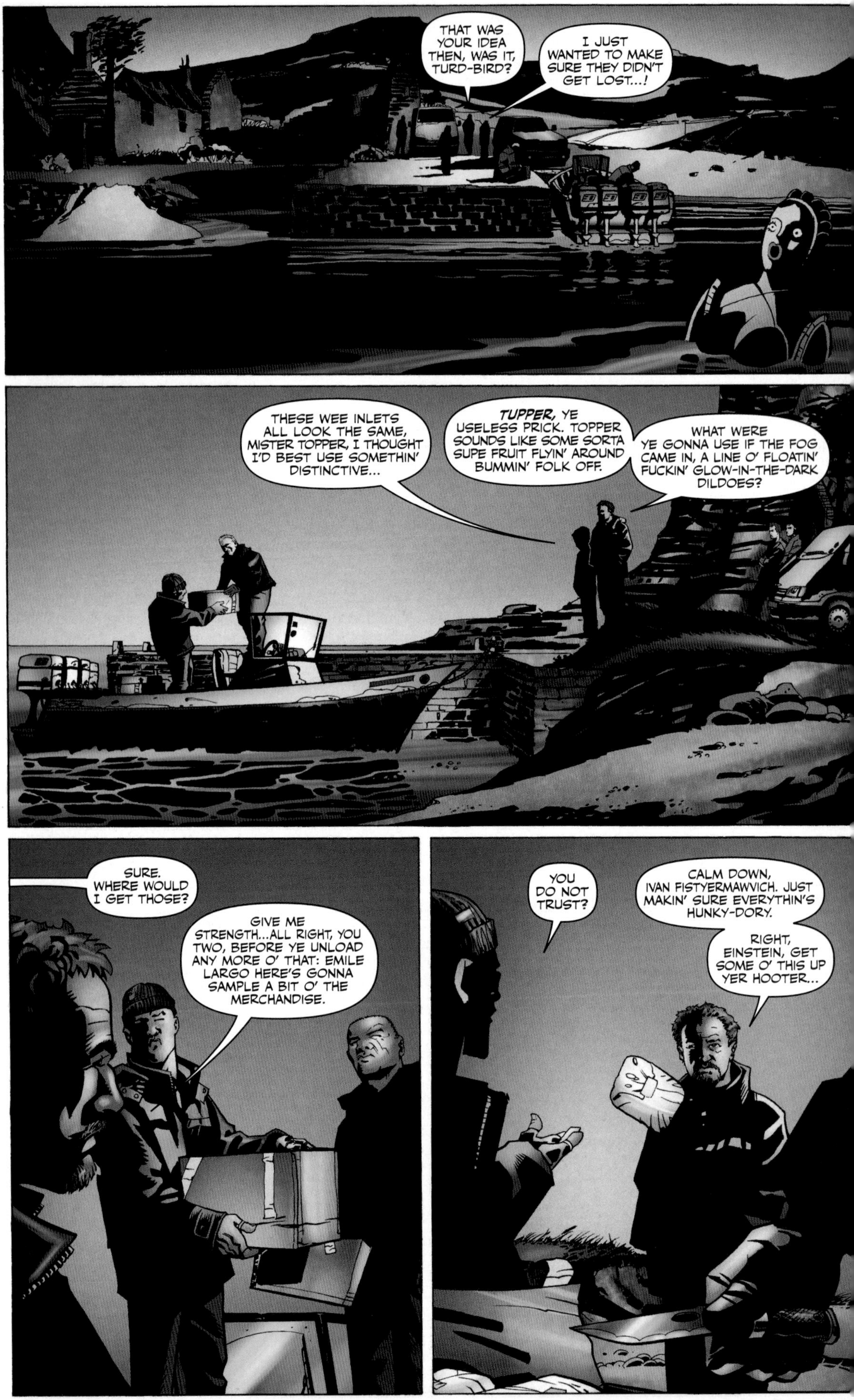
THAT WAS YOUR IDEA THEN, WAS IT, TURD-BIRD?
I JUST WANTED TO MAKE SURE THEY DIDN'T GET LOST...!
THESE WEE INLETS ALL LOOK THE SAME, MISTER TOPPER, I THOUGHT I'D BEST USE SOMETHIN' DISTINCTIVE...
TUPPER, YE USELESS PRICK. TOPPER SOUNDS LIKE SOME SORTA SUPE FRUIT FLYIN' AROUND BUMMIN' FOLK OFF.
WHAT WERE YE GONNA USE IF THE FOG CAME IN, A LINE O' FLOATIN' FUCKIN' GLOW-IN-THE-DARK DILDOES?
SURE. WHERE WOULD I GET THOSE?
GIVE ME STRENGTH...ALL RIGHT, YOU TWO, BEFORE YE UNLOAD ANY MORE O' THAT: EMILE LARGO HERE'S GONNA SAMPLE A BIT O' THE MERCHANDISE.
YOU DO NOT TRUST?
CALM DOWN, IVAN FISTYERMAWVICH. JUST MAKIN' SURE EVERYTHIN'S HUNKY-DORY.
RIGHT, EINSTEIN, GET SOME O' THIS UP YER HOOTER...

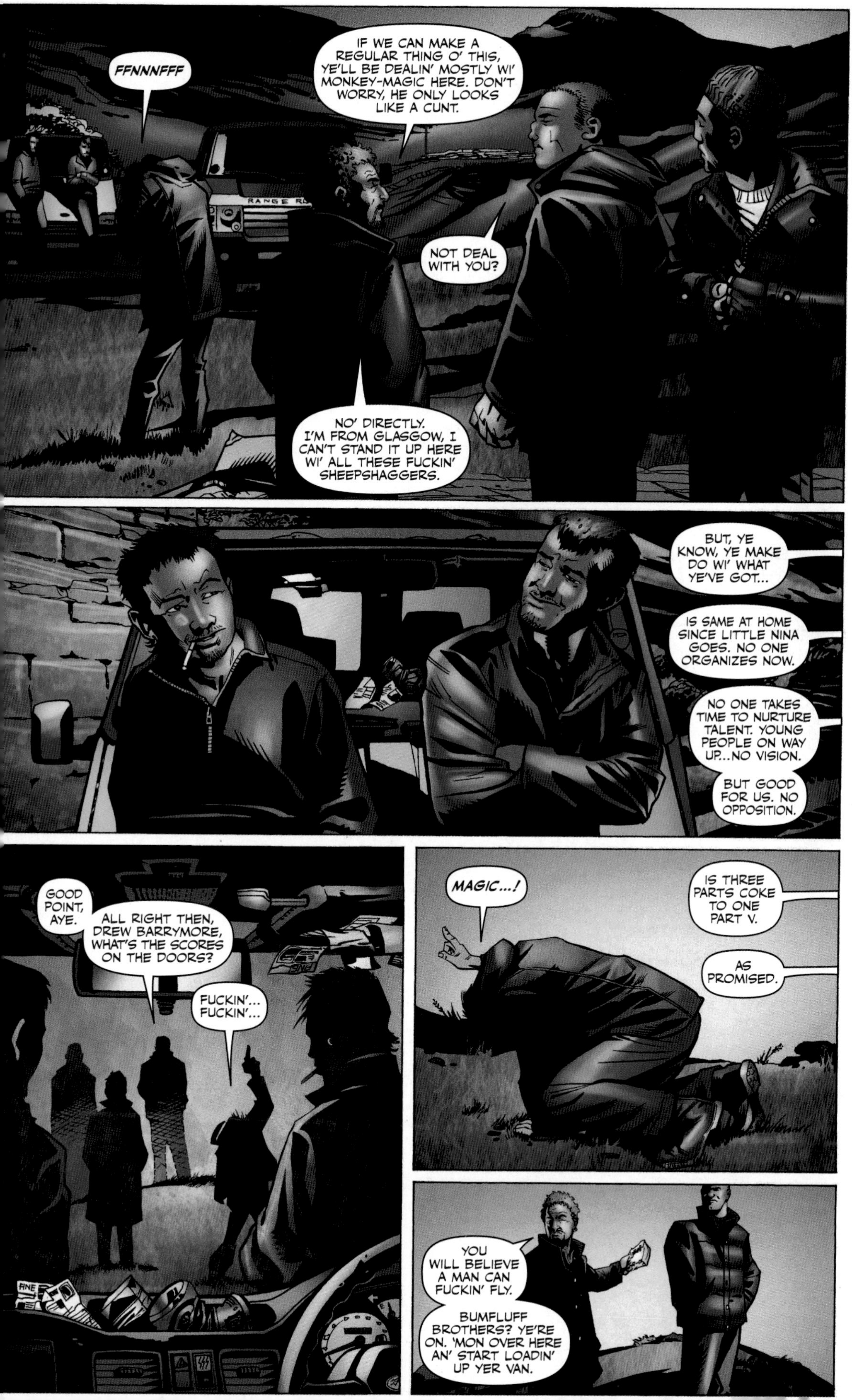
FFNNNFFF
IF WE CAN MAKE A REGULAR THING O' THIS, YE'LL BE DEALIN' MOSTLY WI' MONKEY-MAGIC HERE. DON'T WORRY, HE ONLY LOOKS LIKE A CUNT.
NOT DEAL WITH YOU?
NO' DIRECTLY. I'M FROM GLASGOW, I CAN'T STAND IT UP HERE WI' ALL THESE FUCKIN' SHEEPSHAGGERS.
BUT, YE KNOW, YE MAKE DO WI' WHAT YE'VE GOT...
IS SAME AT HOME SINCE LITTLE NINA GOES. NO ONE ORGANIZES NOW.
NO ONE TAKES TIME TO NURTURE TALENT. YOUNG PEOPLE ON WAY UP...NO VISION.
BUT GOOD FOR US. NO OPPOSITION.
GOOD POINT, AYE.
ALL RIGHT THEN, DREW BARRYMORE, WHAT'S THE SCORES ON THE DOORS?
FUCKIN'... FUCKIN'...
MAGIC...!
IS THREE PARTS COKE TO ONE PART V.
AS PROMISED.
YOU WILL BELIEVE A MAN CAN FUCKIN' FLY.
BUMFLUFF BROTHERS? YE'RE ON. 'MON OVER HERE AN' START LOADIN' UP YER VAN.

AYE, WELL, JUST A MINUTE THERE. WE WANTED A WEE WORD BEFORE WE WENT ANY FURTHER.

OH AYE?

AYE. WE WERE JUST LISTENIN' TO WHAT YE WERE SAYIN' TO THESE TWO BOYS HERE, YE KEN?

IT SOUNDS TO US LIKE YE'VE GOT QUITE A MAJOR OPERATION HERE. LIKE AN INTERNATIONAL SORTA THING.

AN' WE WERE THINKIN'...WELL, WE'RE THE ONES'VE GOTTA DRIVE THIS GEAR ALL OVER THE HIGHLANDS-- NO' TO MENTION THE BIG DELIVERIES IN DUNDEE AN' GLASGOW...

SO WE THOUGHT, LIKE, WI' ALL THIS CASH YE'RE GONNA BE MAKIN', YE COULD AFFORD TO PAY US SOME PROPER--

AW, FOR FUCK'S SAKE...HERE, CUNTOSAURUS? I THOUGHT I TOLD YE TO HIRE SOMEONE RELIABLE?

MMMMMMM

BRILLIANT. OKAY THEN, WHAT IF I WAS TO OPEN THE NEGOTIATIONS BY TELLIN' YOU TWO FUDGE-MERCHANTS TO FUCK OFF?

WE COULD DO THAT. WE COULD FUCK OFF.

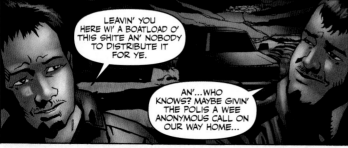

LEAVIN' YOU HERE WI' A BOATLOAD O' THIS SHITE AN' NOBODY TO DISTRIBUTE IT FOR YE.

AN'...WHO KNOWS? MAYBE GIVIN' THE POLIS A WEE ANONYMOUS CALL ON OUR WAY HOME...

SOME INTERESTIN' THOUGHTS THERE.

SARAH!

RANGE R

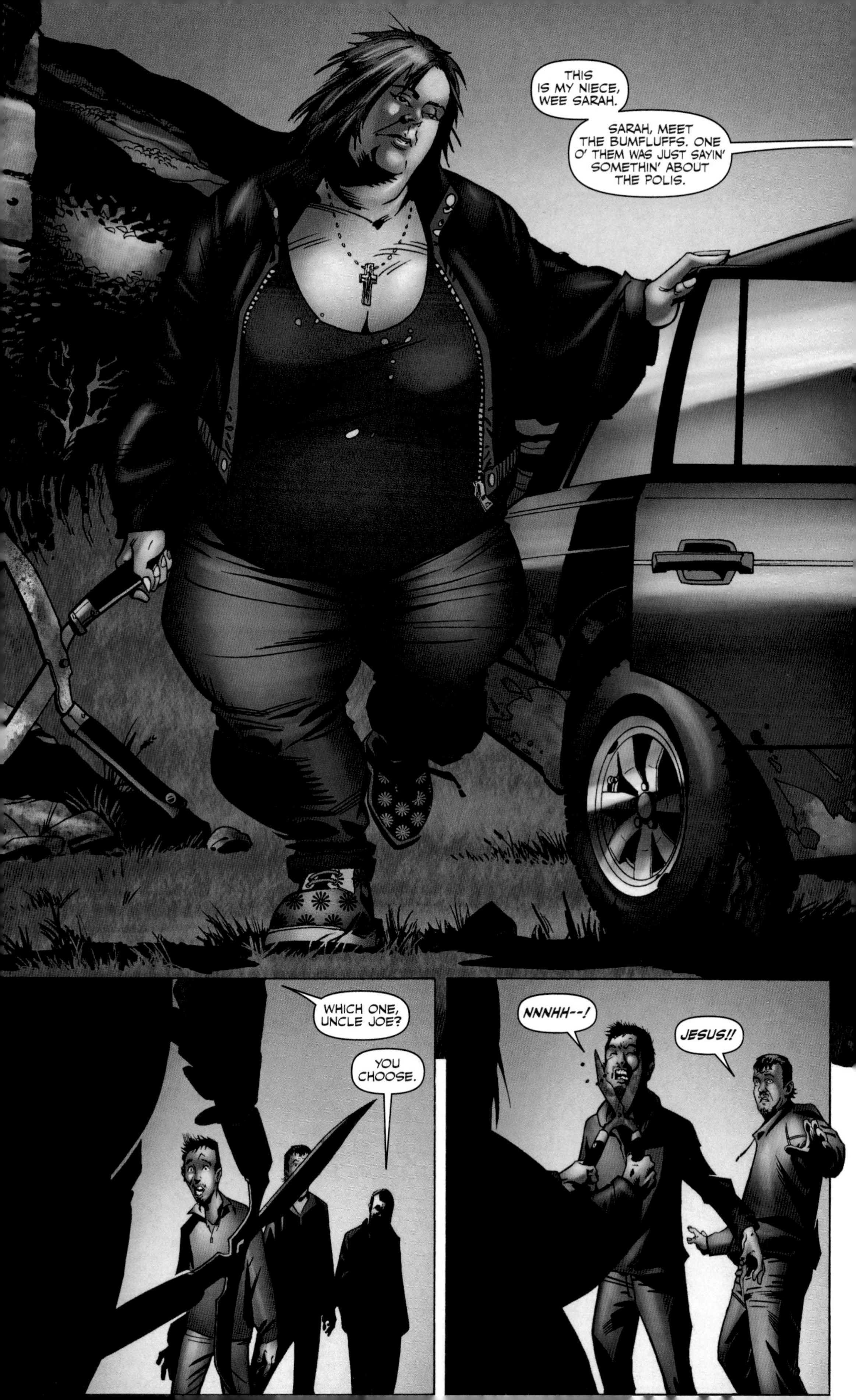
THIS IS MY NIECE, WEE SARAH.
SARAH, MEET THE BUMFLUFFS. ONE O' THEM WAS JUST SAYIN' SOMETHIN' ABOUT THE POLIS.
WHICH ONE, UNCLE JOE?
YOU CHOOSE.
NNNHH--!
JESUS!!

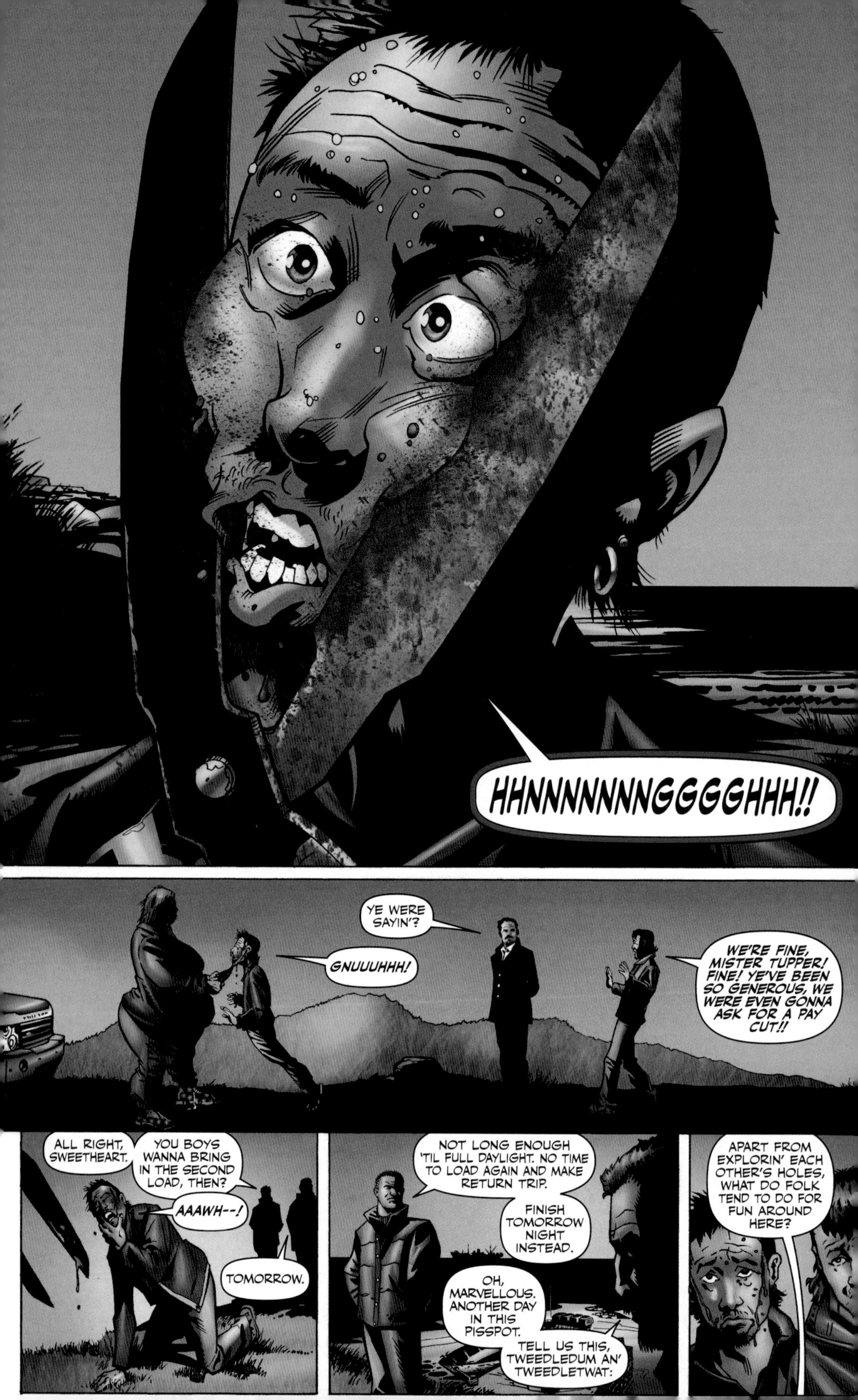
HHNNNNNNNGGGGHHH!!
YE WERE SAYIN'?
GNUUUHHH!
WE'RE FINE, MISTER TUPPER! FINE! YE'VE BEEN SO GENEROUS, WE WERE EVEN GONNA ASK FOR A PAY CUT!!
ALL RIGHT, SWEETHEART.
YOU BOYS WANNA BRING IN THE SECOND LOAD, THEN?
AAAWH--!
TOMORROW.
NOT LONG ENOUGH 'TIL FULL DAYLIGHT. NO TIME TO LOAD AGAIN AND MAKE RETURN TRIP.
FINISH TOMORROW NIGHT INSTEAD.
OH, MARVELLOUS. ANOTHER DAY IN THIS PISSPOT.
TELL US THIS, TWEEDLEDUM AN' TWEEDLETWAT:
APART FROM EXPLORIN' EACH OTHER'S HOLES, WHAT DO FOLK TEND TO DO FOR FUN AROUND HERE?

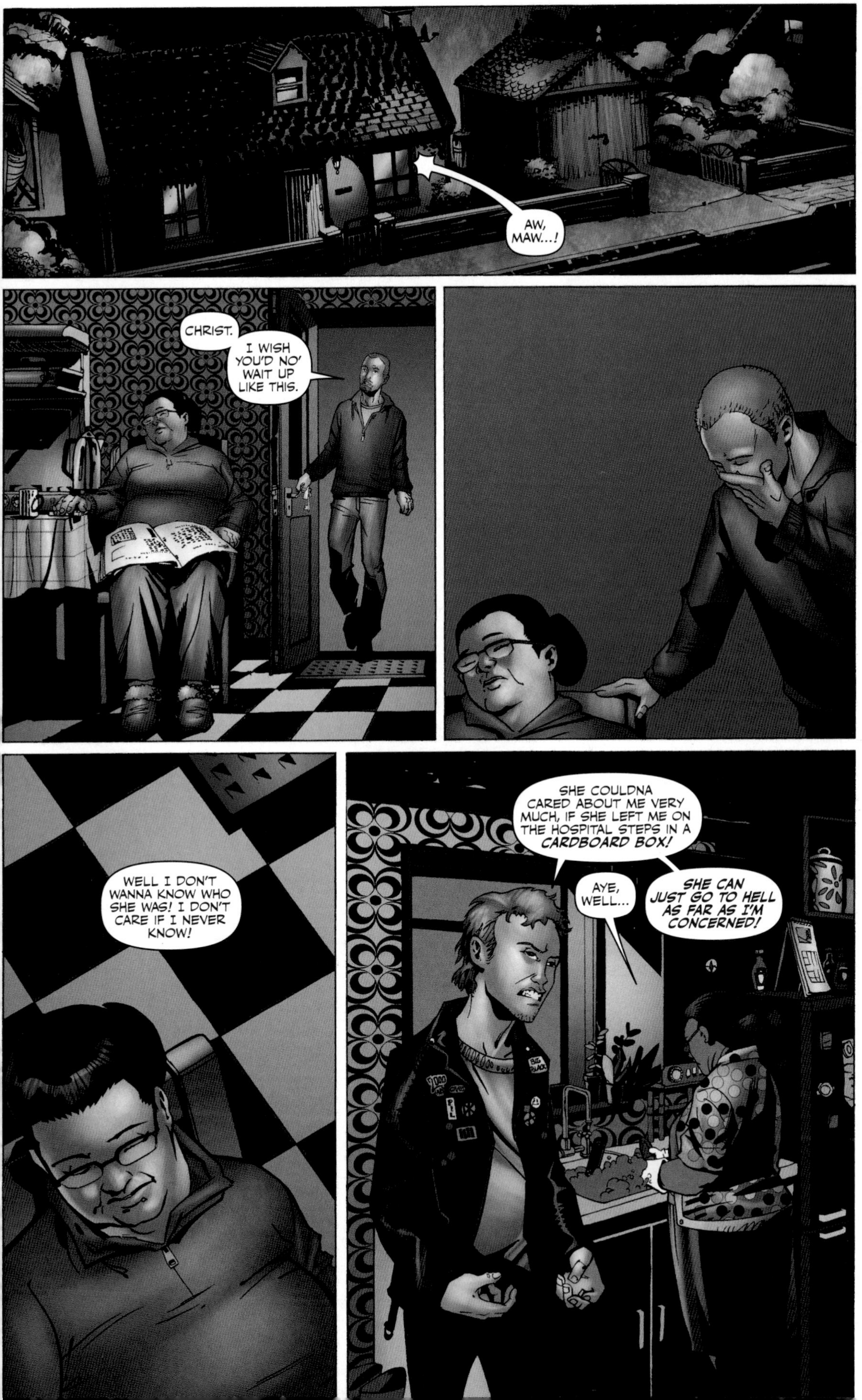
AW, MAW...!
CHRIST.
I WISH YOU'D NO' WAIT UP LIKE THIS.
WELL I DON'T WANNA KNOW WHO SHE WAS! I DON'T CARE IF I NEVER KNOW!
SHE COULDNA CARED ABOUT ME VERY MUCH, IF SHE LEFT ME ON THE HOSPITAL STEPS IN A *CARDBOARD BOX!*
AYE, WELL...
SHE CAN JUST GO TO HELL AS FAR AS I'M CONCERNED!

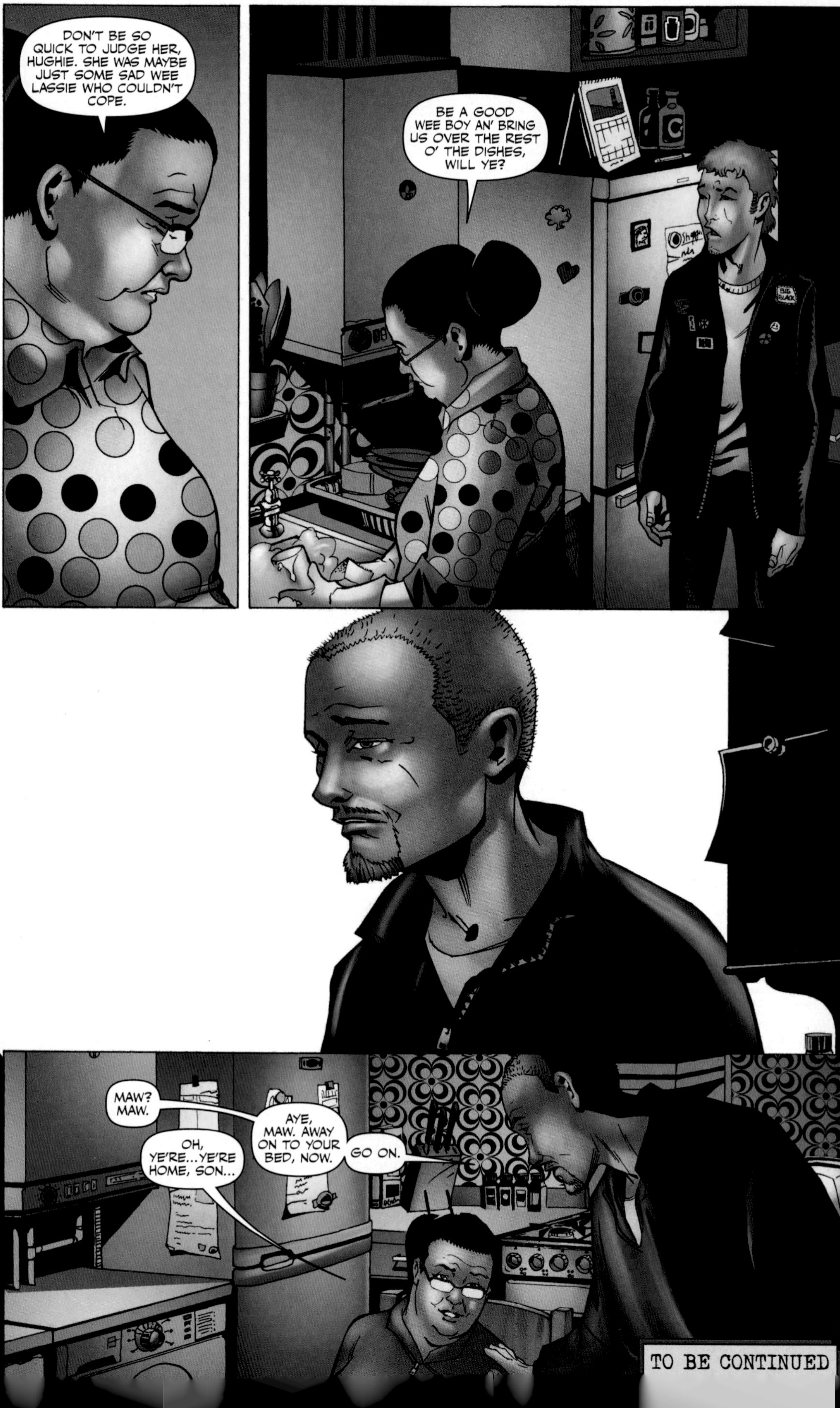
DON'T BE SO QUICK TO JUDGE HER, HUGHIE. SHE WAS MAYBE JUST SOME SAD WEE LASSIE WHO COULDN'T COPE.
BE A GOOD WEE BOY AN' BRING US OVER THE REST O' THE DISHES, WILL YE?
MAW? MAW.
OH, YE'RE...YE'RE HOME, SON...
AYE, MAW. AWAY ON TO YOUR BED, NOW.
GO ON.
TO BE CONTINUED

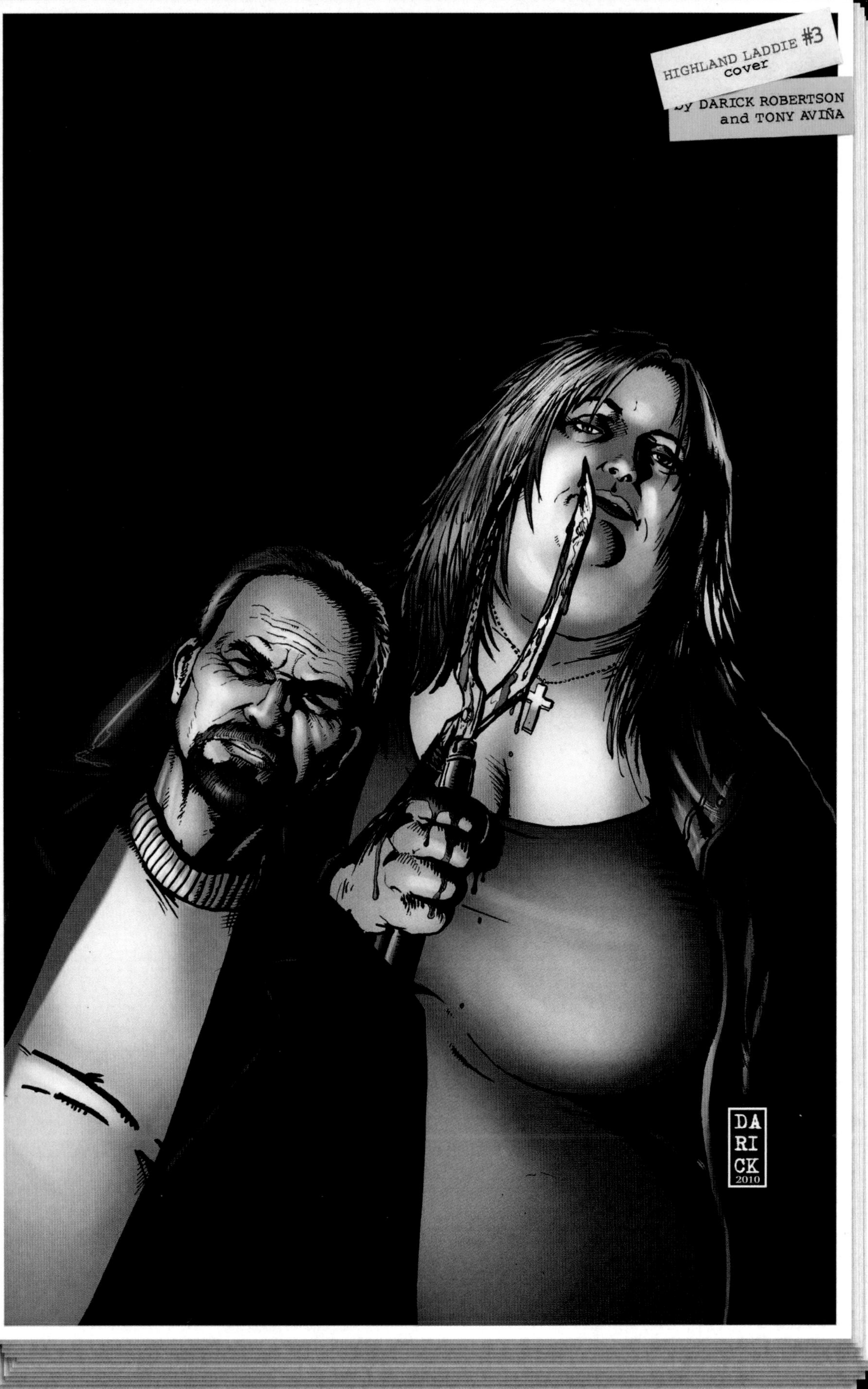
HIGHLAND LADDIE #3
cover
by DARICK ROBERTSON
and TONY AVIÑA
DA
RI
CK
2010

"AUNTIE MARY WAS...

"SHE WAS A FRAIL WEE WOMAN. SHE WAS NICE, BUT SHE WAS VAGUE. IT WASN'T SO MUCH THAT SHE'D LOSE TRACK O' WHERE SHE WAS, AS SHE'D FORGET THAT SHE WAS THERE AT ALL.

"ONE TIME SHE CAME TO STAY WI' US, AN' SHE GOT OUT O' THE BATH AN' WENT OUT THE BACK DOOR AN' KEPT GOIN'. SHE WENT LEFT INSTEAD O' RIGHT, OR SHE'D'VE JUST GONE BACK TO THE SPARE ROOM."

"IT WAS ONE IN THE MORNIN' BEFORE MAW AN' PAW TWIGGED SHE WAS GONE.

"SHE WOULDN'T SAY BOO TO A GOOSE, EITHER. NEVER ASKED FOR ANYTHIN'. THAT'S WHY SHE WAS SO THIN, MAW SAID, 'CAUSE SHE WOULDN'T ASK ANYONE FOR SOMETHIN' TO EAT AN' SHE KEPT FORGETTIN' TO FEED HERSELF.

"THAT'S WHAT WE THOUGHT IT WAS, AT LEAST."

"I LIKED AUNTIE MARY, I THOUGHT SHE WAS LOVELY. SHE WAS REALLY KIND, AN' IT WAS DEAD EASY BEATIN' HER AT MONOPOLY OR WHATEVER.

"YOU KEN WHAT IT'S LIKE AT THAT AGE, BUT YOU HAVEN'T A BLOODY CLUE."

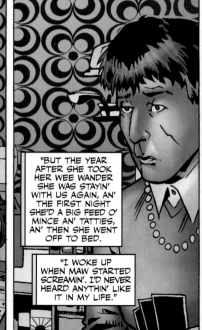

"BUT THE YEAR AFTER SHE TOOK HER WEE WANDER SHE WAS STAYIN' WITH US AGAIN, AN' THE FIRST NIGHT SHE'D A BIG FEED O' MINCE AN' TATTIES, AN' THEN SHE WENT OFF TO BED.

"I WOKE UP WHEN MAW STARTED SCREAMIN'. I'D NEVER HEARD ANYTHIN' LIKE IT IN MY LIFE."

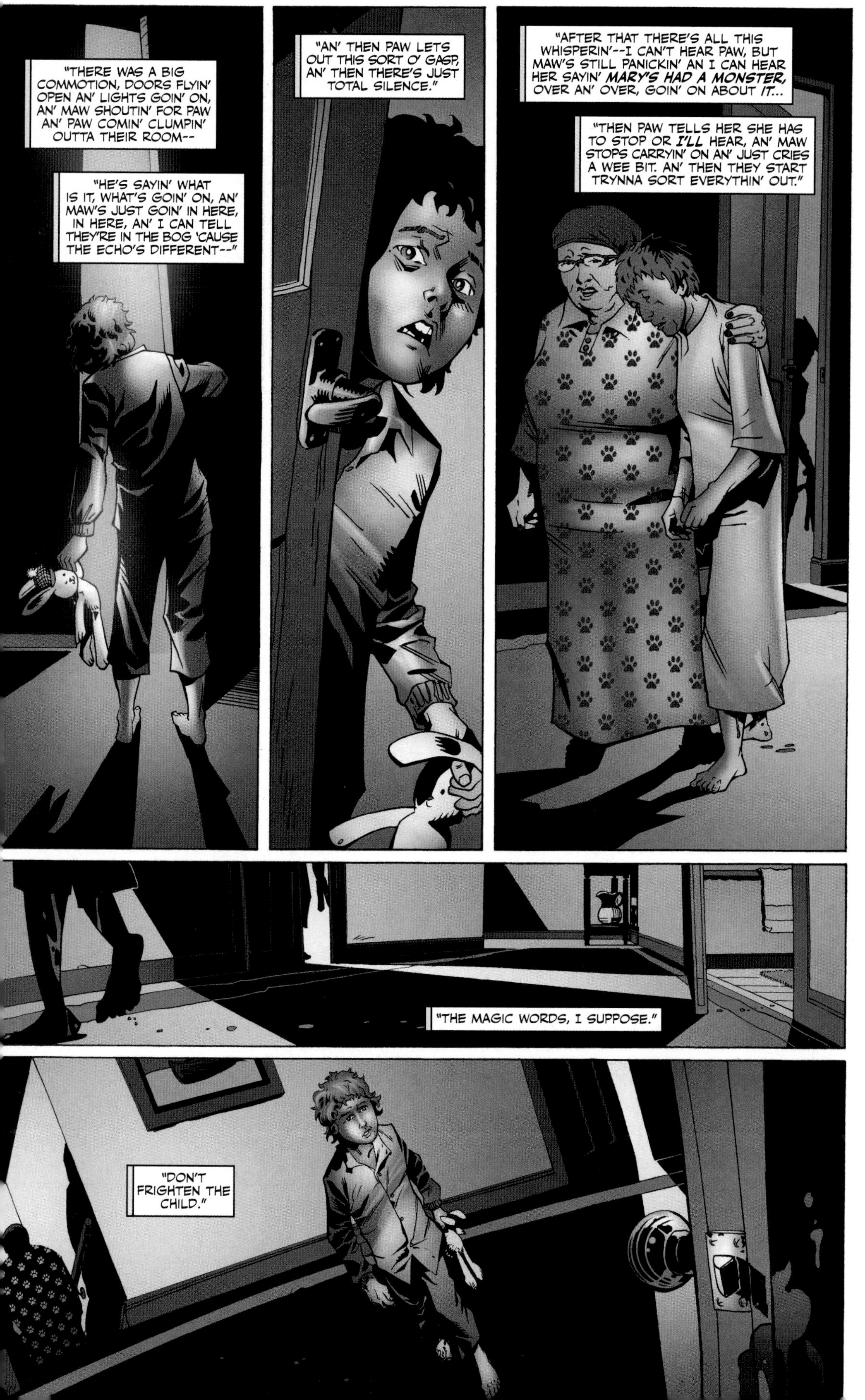
"THERE WAS A BIG COMMOTION, DOORS FLYIN' OPEN AN' LIGHTS GOIN' ON, AN' MAW SHOUTIN' FOR PAW AN' PAW COMIN' CLUMPIN' OUTTA THEIR ROOM--
"HE'S SAYIN' WHAT IS IT, WHAT'S GOIN' ON, AN' MAW'S JUST GOIN' IN HERE, IN HERE, AN' I CAN TELL THEY'RE IN THE BOG 'CAUSE THE ECHO'S DIFFERENT--"
"AN' THEN PAW LETS OUT THIS SORT O' GASP, AN' THEN THERE'S JUST TOTAL SILENCE."
"AFTER THAT THERE'S ALL THIS WHISPERIN'--I CAN'T HEAR PAW, BUT MAW'S STILL PANICKIN' AN I CAN HEAR HER SAYIN' ***MARY'S HAD A MONSTER,*** OVER AN' OVER, GOIN' ON ABOUT *IT*...
"THEN PAW TELLS HER SHE HAS TO STOP OR ***I'LL*** HEAR, AN' MAW STOPS CARRYIN' ON AN' JUST CRIES A WEE BIT. AN' THEN THEY START TRYNNA SORT EVERYTHIN' OUT."
"THE MAGIC WORDS, I SUPPOSE."
"DON'T FRIGHTEN THE CHILD."

"I'D NEVER SEEN A LOOK LIKE THAT FROM PAW BEFORE.

"TO ME HE WAS ALWAYS HAPPY, AN' KIND, AN' WARM, AN' STRONG. HE WAS NEVER NERVOUS. NEVER *LOST.*"

"I DIDN'T KNOW WHAT TO MAKE OF ANY OF IT."

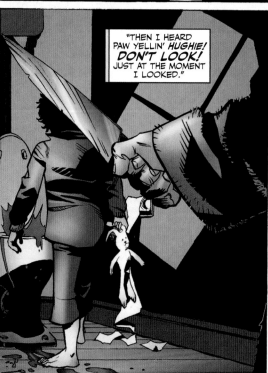

"THEN I HEARD PAW YELLIN' *HUGHIE! DON'T LOOK!* JUST AT THE MOMENT I LOOKED."

HAD SHE... MISCARRIED INTO THE...?

NO, IT WAS A TAPEWORM.

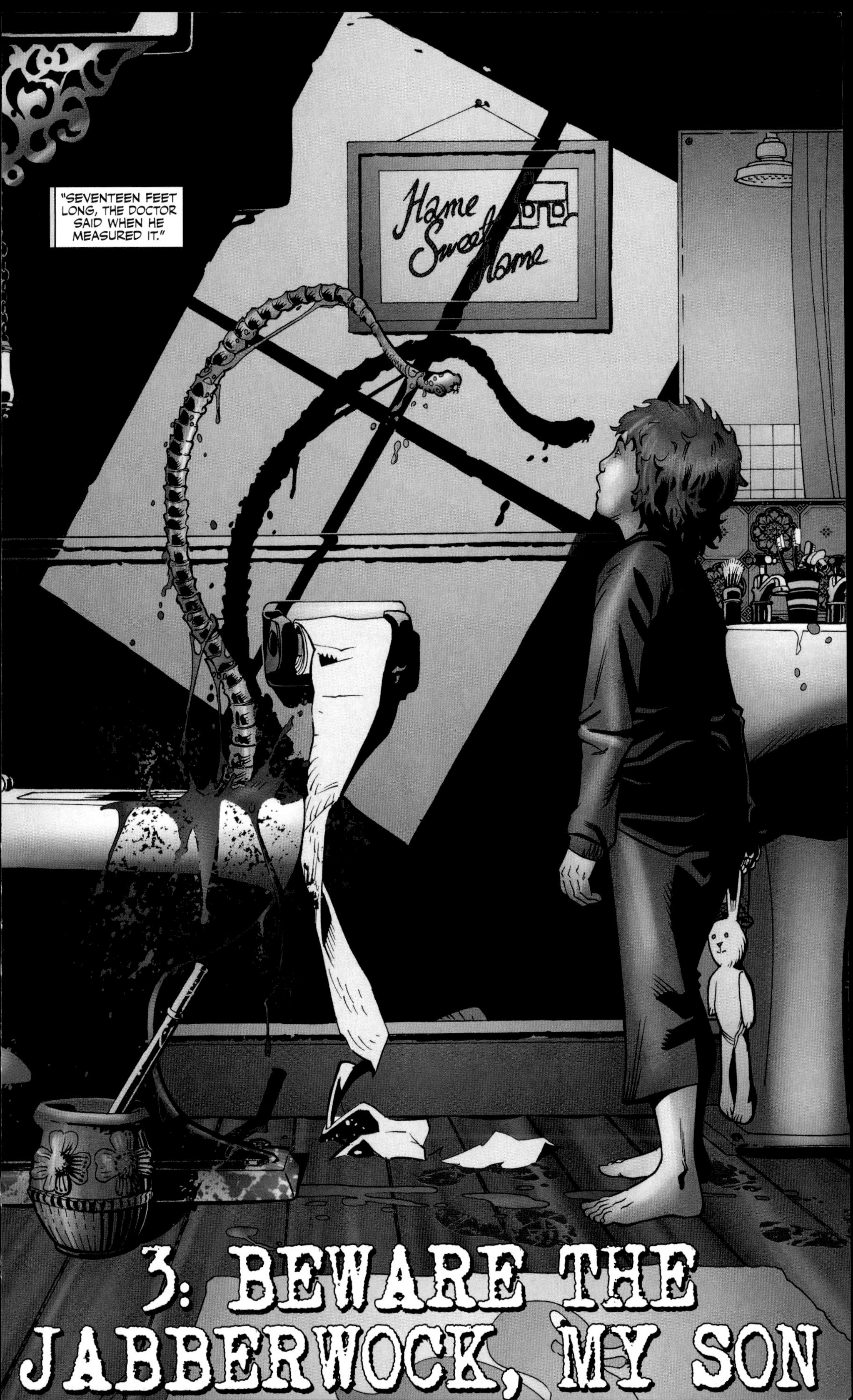
"SEVENTEEN FEET LONG, THE DOCTOR SAID WHEN HE MEASURED IT."
Home Sweet Home

3: BEWARE THE JABBERWOCK, MY SON

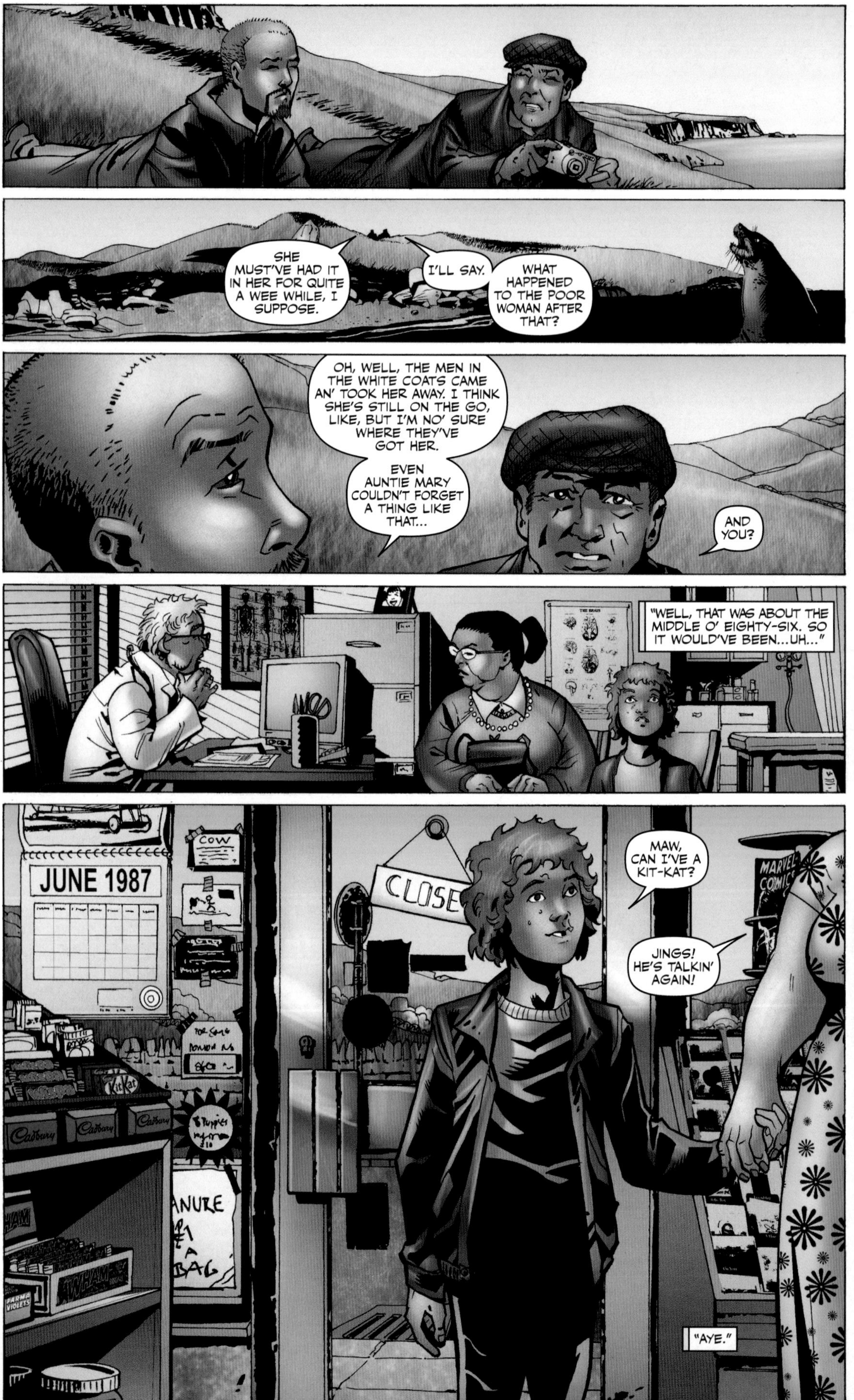
SHE MUST'VE HAD IT IN HER FOR QUITE A WEE WHILE, I SUPPOSE.
I'LL SAY.
WHAT HAPPENED TO THE POOR WOMAN AFTER THAT?
OH, WELL, THE MEN IN THE WHITE COATS CAME AN' TOOK HER AWAY. I THINK SHE'S STILL ON THE GO, LIKE, BUT I'M NO' SURE WHERE THEY'VE GOT HER.
EVEN AUNTIE MARY COULDN'T FORGET A THING LIKE THAT...
AND YOU?
"WELL, THAT WAS ABOUT THE MIDDLE O' EIGHTY-SIX. SO IT WOULD'VE BEEN...UH..."
THE BRAIN
JUNE 1987
COW
CLOSE
MARVEL COMICS
KitKat
Cadbury
Cadbury
Cadbury
MANURE
BAG
WHAM
PARMA VIOLETS
MAW, CAN I'VE A KIT-KAT?
JINGS! HE'S TALKIN' AGAIN!
"AYE."

YOU SEE, I THINK THAT'S WHY I'M NEVER GONNA BE...

WHY I CAN'T...

AW, JUST WHY I'M NO' ANY SORT O' TOUGH GUY, I SUPPOSE.

TOO SQUEAMISH.

ANYTHIN' MENTAL HAPPENS TO ME, I ALWAYS GO BACK TO THAT MOMENT. I REMEMBER GOIN' COLD AN' TINGLY, AN' THEN JUST SHUTTIN' DOWN.

DOES THAT TROUBLE YOU?

SO LONG AS I'VE GOT YOU ON THE PSYCHIATRIST'S ROCKY SHORE, I MEAN.

HMH.

THERE'S A BIG BOY NOW, YOU COULD GET A NICE ONE O' HIM.

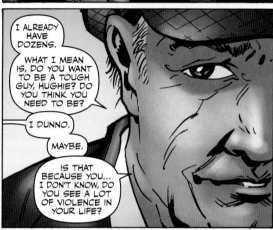

I ALREADY HAVE DOZENS.

WHAT I MEAN IS, DO YOU WANT TO BE A TOUGH GUY, HUGHIE? DO YOU THINK YOU NEED TO BE?

I DUNNO.

MAYBE.

IS THAT BECAUSE YOU... I DON'T KNOW, DO YOU SEE A LOT OF VIOLENCE IN YOUR LIFE?

"ARE YOU FUCKIN' KIDDIN' M--

"UM.

"IT DEPENDS WHAT YOU MEAN BY A LOT."

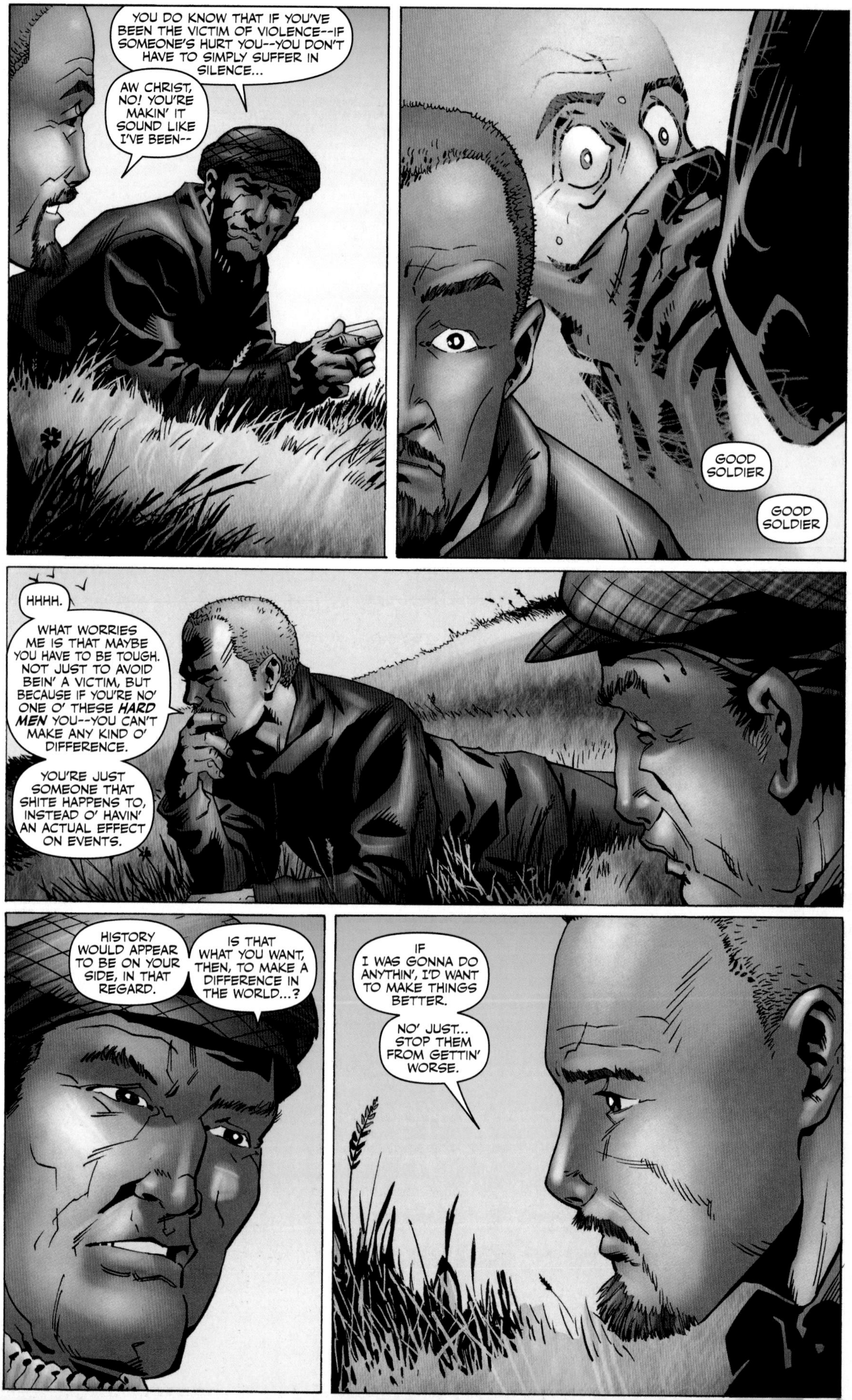

YOU DO KNOW THAT IF YOU'VE BEEN THE VICTIM OF VIOLENCE--IF SOMEONE'S HURT YOU--YOU DON'T HAVE TO SIMPLY SUFFER IN SILENCE...
AW CHRIST, NO! YOU'RE MAKIN' IT SOUND LIKE I'VE BEEN--
GOOD SOLDIER
GOOD SOLDIER
HHHH.
WHAT WORRIES ME IS THAT MAYBE YOU HAVE TO BE TOUGH. NOT JUST TO AVOID BEIN' A VICTIM, BUT BECAUSE IF YOU'RE NO' ONE O' THESE HARD MEN YOU--YOU CAN'T MAKE ANY KIND O' DIFFERENCE.
YOU'RE JUST SOMEONE THAT SHITE HAPPENS TO, INSTEAD O' HAVIN' AN ACTUAL EFFECT ON EVENTS.
HISTORY WOULD APPEAR TO BE ON YOUR SIDE, IN THAT REGARD.
IS THAT WHAT YOU WANT, THEN, TO MAKE A DIFFERENCE IN THE WORLD...?
IF I WAS GONNA DO ANYTHIN', I'D WANT TO MAKE THINGS BETTER.
NO' JUST... STOP THEM FROM GETTIN' WORSE.

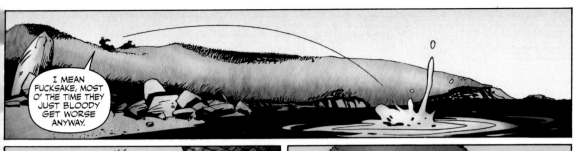

I MEAN FUCKSAKE, MOST O' THE TIME THEY JUST BLOODY GET WORSE ANYWAY.

I DON'T KNOW ENOUGH ABOUT WHAT YOU DO TO SAY ONE WAY OR THE OTHER, HUGHIE.

I HAVE NO PAT ANSWERS FOR YOU TODAY.

AW, IT DOES ME GOOD TO TALK.

THAT'S WHY I CAME HOME IN THE FIRST PLACE, REALLY. SORT MY HEAD OUT. DECIDE HOW I FEEL ABOUT THINGS.

INSTEAD MY PALS JUST WIND ME UP TO FUCK, AN' MY MAW AN' PAW...

YOU DON'T GET ON WITH THEM?

IT'S NO' THAT. THEY'RE THE NICEST, MOST DECENT FOLK YOU COULD EVER HOPE TO MEET, I FEEL LIKE A *BASTARD* COMPLAININ' ABOUT THEM.

THEY'RE JUST A WEE BIT MUCH IN A DIFFERENT WAY.

D'YOU GET ANY GOOD PHOTIES THERE, THEN?

HAVE A LOOK.

AW, YEAH.

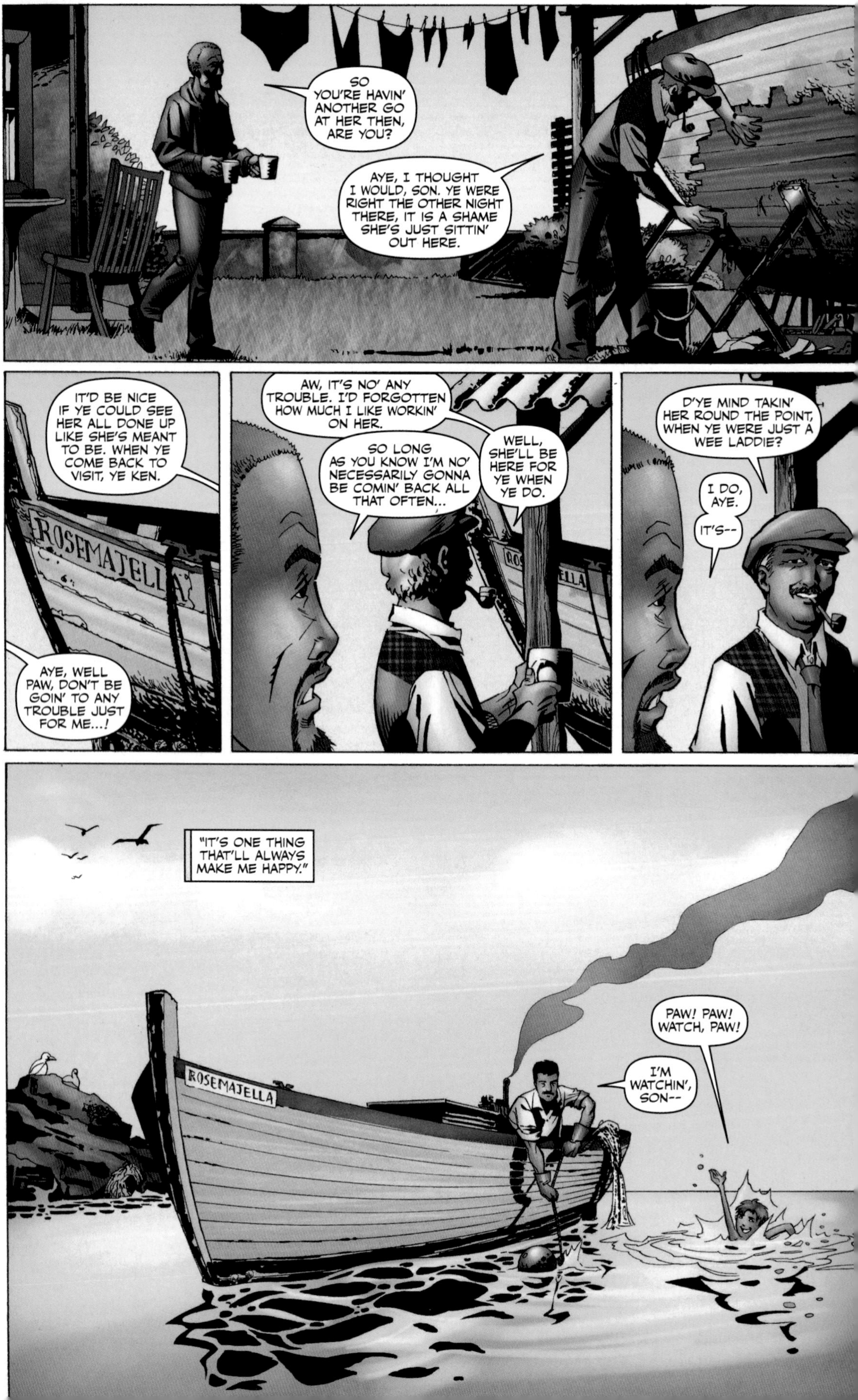
SO YOU'RE HAVIN' ANOTHER GO AT HER THEN, ARE YOU?
AYE, I THOUGHT I WOULD, SON. YE WERE RIGHT THE OTHER NIGHT THERE, IT IS A SHAME SHE'S JUST SITTIN' OUT HERE.
IT'D BE NICE IF YE COULD SEE HER ALL DONE UP LIKE SHE'S MEANT TO BE. WHEN YE COME BACK TO VISIT, YE KEN.
ROSEMAJELLA
AYE, WELL PAW, DON'T BE GOIN' TO ANY TROUBLE JUST FOR ME...!
AW, IT'S NO' ANY TROUBLE. I'D FORGOTTEN HOW MUCH I LIKE WORKIN' ON HER.
SO LONG AS YOU KNOW I'M NO' NECESSARILY GONNA BE COMIN' BACK ALL THAT OFTEN...
WELL, SHE'LL BE HERE FOR YE WHEN YE DO.
D'YE MIND TAKIN' HER ROUND THE POINT, WHEN YE WERE JUST A WEE LADDIE?
I DO, AYE.
IT'S--
"IT'S ONE THING THAT'LL ALWAYS MAKE ME HAPPY."
ROSEMAJELLA
PAW! PAW! WATCH, PAW!
I'M WATCHIN', SON--

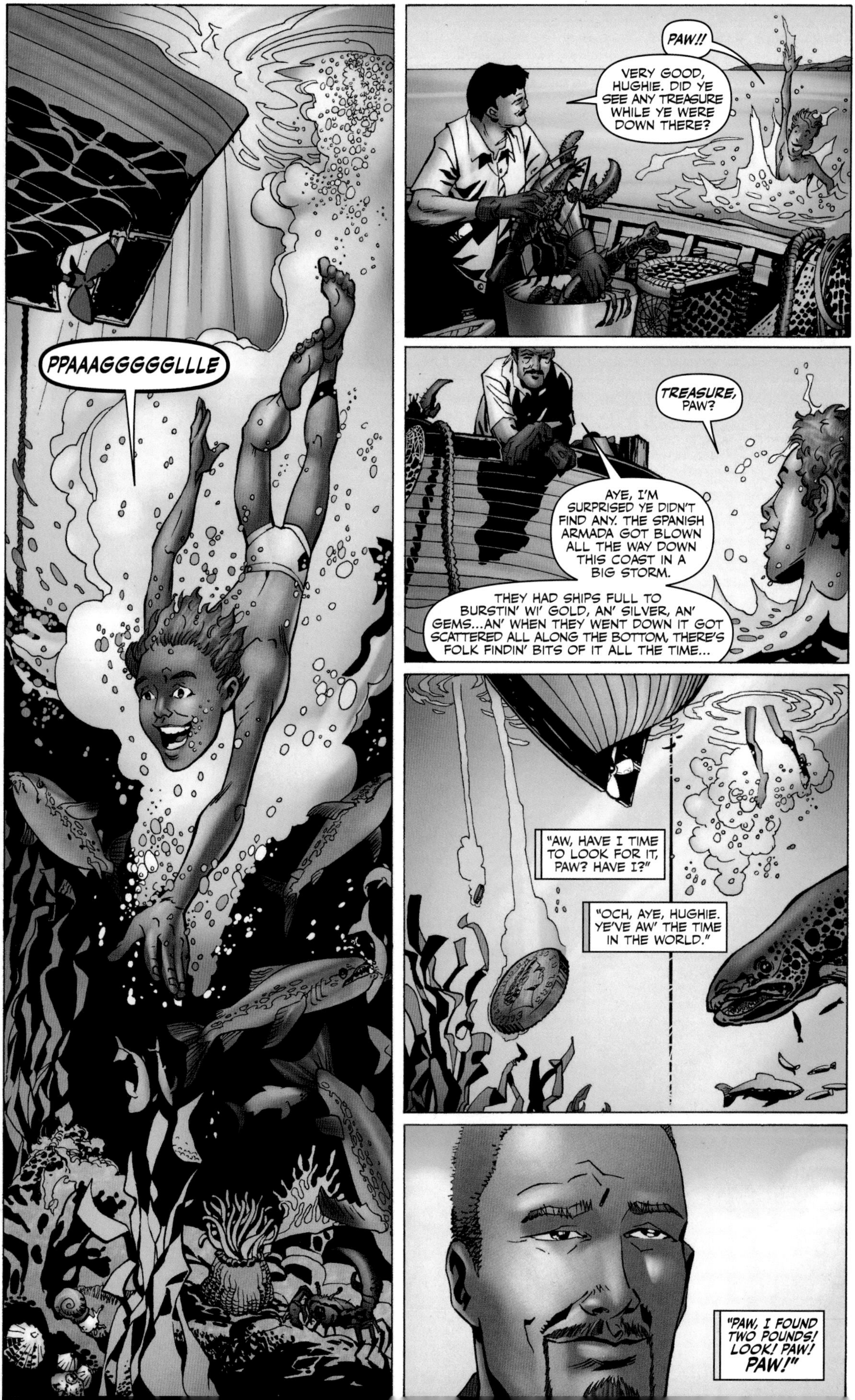
PPAAAGGGGGLLLE
PAW!!
VERY GOOD, HUGHIE. DID YE SEE ANY TREASURE WHILE YE WERE DOWN THERE?
TREASURE, PAW?
AYE, I'M SURPRISED YE DIDN'T FIND ANY. THE SPANISH ARMADA GOT BLOWN ALL THE WAY DOWN THIS COAST IN A BIG STORM.
THEY HAD SHIPS FULL TO BURSTIN' WI' GOLD, AN' SILVER, AN' GEMS...AN' WHEN THEY WENT DOWN IT GOT SCATTERED ALL ALONG THE BOTTOM, THERE'S FOLK FINDIN' BITS OF IT ALL THE TIME...
"AW, HAVE I TIME TO LOOK FOR IT, PAW? HAVE I?"
"OCH, AYE, HUGHIE. YE'VE AW' THE TIME IN THE WORLD."
"PAW, I FOUND TWO POUNDS! LOOK! PAW! PAW!"

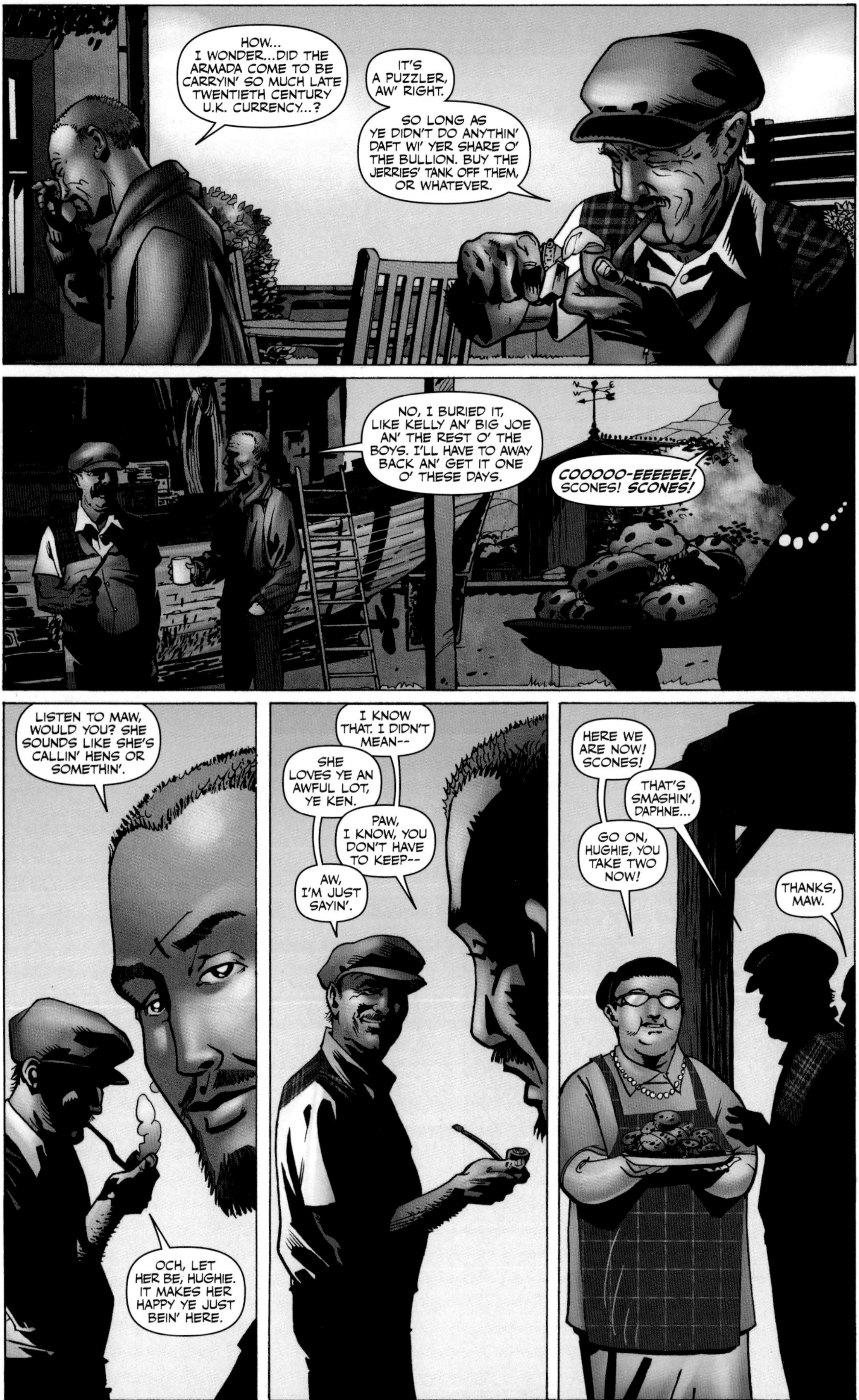
HOW... I WONDER...DID THE ARMADA COME TO BE CARRYIN' SO MUCH LATE TWENTIETH CENTURY U.K. CURRENCY...?
IT'S A PUZZLER, AW' RIGHT.
SO LONG AS YE DIDN'T DO ANYTHIN' DAFT WI' YER SHARE O' THE BULLION. BUY THE JERRIES' TANK OFF THEM, OR WHATEVER.
NO, I BURIED IT, LIKE KELLY AN' BIG JOE AN' THE REST O' THE BOYS. I'LL HAVE TO AWAY BACK AN' GET IT ONE O' THESE DAYS.
COOOOO-EEEEEE! SCONES! SCONES!
LISTEN TO MAW, WOULD YOU? SHE SOUNDS LIKE SHE'S CALLIN' HENS OR SOMETHIN'.
OCH, LET HER BE, HUGHIE. IT MAKES HER HAPPY YE JUST BEIN' HERE.
I KNOW THAT. I DIDN'T MEAN--
SHE LOVES YE AN AWFUL LOT, YE KEN.
PAW, I KNOW, YOU DON'T HAVE TO KEEP--
AW, I'M JUST SAYIN'.
HERE WE ARE NOW! SCONES!
THAT'S SMASHIN', DAPHNE...
GO ON, HUGHIE, YOU TAKE TWO NOW!
THANKS, MAW.

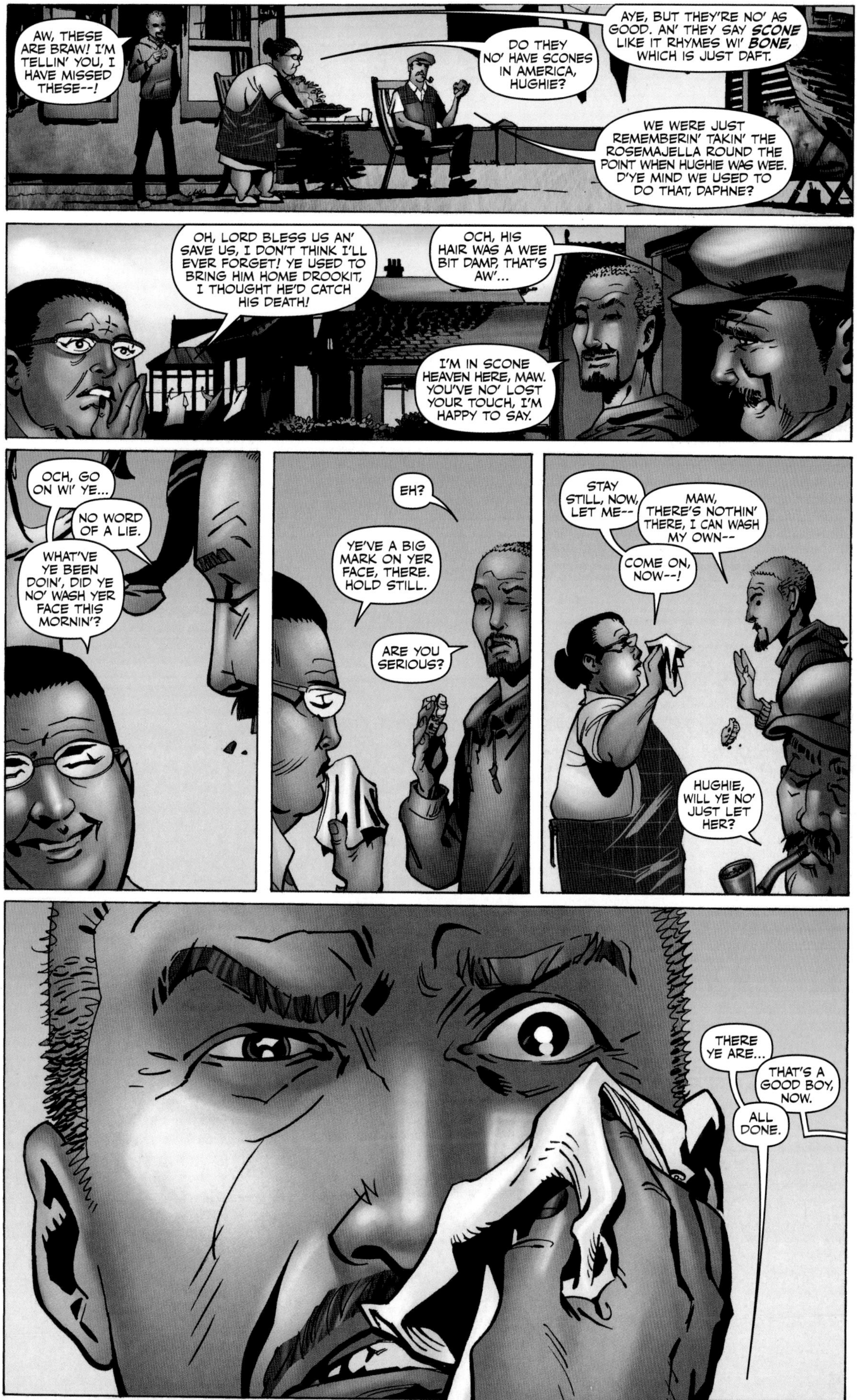
AW, THESE ARE BRAW! I'M TELLIN' YOU, I HAVE MISSED THESE--!
DO THEY NO' HAVE SCONES IN AMERICA, HUGHIE?
AYE, BUT THEY'RE NO' AS GOOD. AN' THEY SAY *SCONE* LIKE IT RHYMES WI' *BONE*, WHICH IS JUST DAFT.
WE WERE JUST REMEMBERIN' TAKIN' THE ROSEMAJELLA ROUND THE POINT WHEN HUGHIE WAS WEE. D'YE MIND WE USED TO DO THAT, DAPHNE?
OH, LORD BLESS US AN' SAVE US, I DON'T THINK I'LL EVER FORGET! YE USED TO BRING HIM HOME DROOKIT, I THOUGHT HE'D CATCH HIS DEATH!
OCH, HIS HAIR WAS A WEE BIT DAMP, THAT'S AW'...
I'M IN SCONE HEAVEN HERE, MAW. YOU'VE NO' LOST YOUR TOUCH, I'M HAPPY TO SAY.
OCH, GO ON WI' YE...
NO WORD OF A LIE.
WHAT'VE YE BEEN DOIN', DID YE NO' WASH YER FACE THIS MORNIN'?
EH?
YE'VE A BIG MARK ON YER FACE, THERE. HOLD STILL.
ARE YOU SERIOUS?
STAY STILL, NOW, LET ME--
MAW, THERE'S NOTHIN' THERE, I CAN WASH MY OWN--
COME ON, NOW--!
HUGHIE, WILL YE NO' JUST LET HER?
THERE YE ARE...
THAT'S A GOOD BOY, NOW.
ALL DONE.

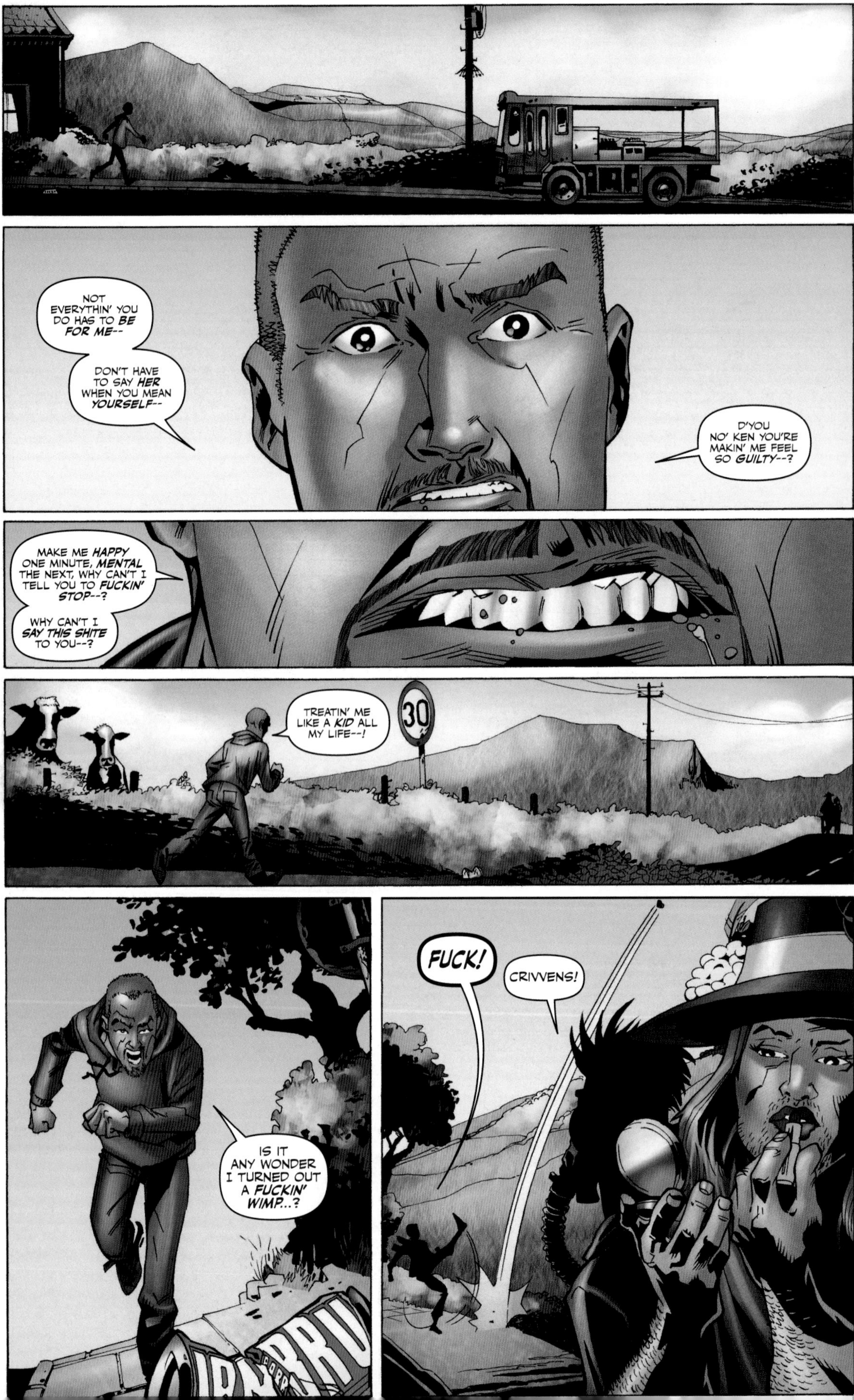
NOT EVERYTHIN' YOU DO HAS TO *BE FOR ME*--
DON'T HAVE TO SAY *HER* WHEN YOU MEAN *YOURSELF*--
D'YOU NO' KEN YOU'RE MAKIN' ME FEEL SO *GUILTY*--?
MAKE ME *HAPPY* ONE MINUTE, *MENTAL* THE NEXT, WHY CAN'T I TELL YOU TO *FUCKIN' STOP*--?
WHY CAN'T I *SAY THIS SHITE* TO YOU--?
TREATIN' ME LIKE A *KID* ALL MY LIFE--!
30
IS IT ANY WONDER I TURNED OUT A *FUCKIN' WIMP*...?
FUCK!
CRIVVENS!

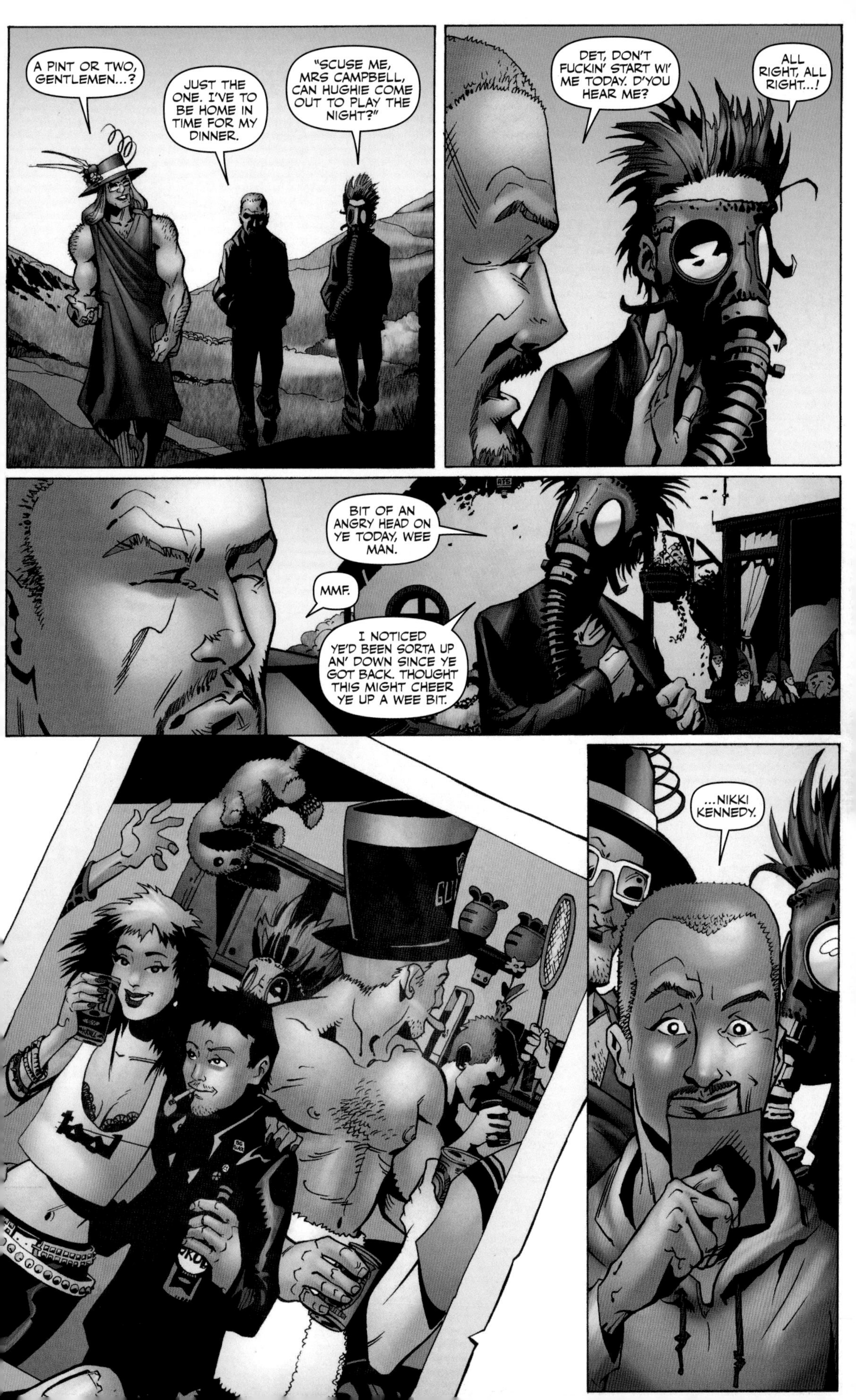
A PINT OR TWO, GENTLEMEN...?
JUST THE ONE. I'VE TO BE HOME IN TIME FOR MY DINNER.
"SCUSE ME, MRS CAMPBELL, CAN HUGHIE COME OUT TO PLAY THE NIGHT?"
DET, DON'T FUCKIN' START WI' ME TODAY. D'YOU HEAR ME?
ALL RIGHT, ALL RIGHT...!
BIT OF AN ANGRY HEAD ON YE TODAY, WEE MAN.
MMF.
I NOTICED YE'D BEEN SORTA UP AN' DOWN SINCE YE GOT BACK. THOUGHT THIS MIGHT CHEER YE UP A WEE BIT.
...NIKKI KENNEDY.

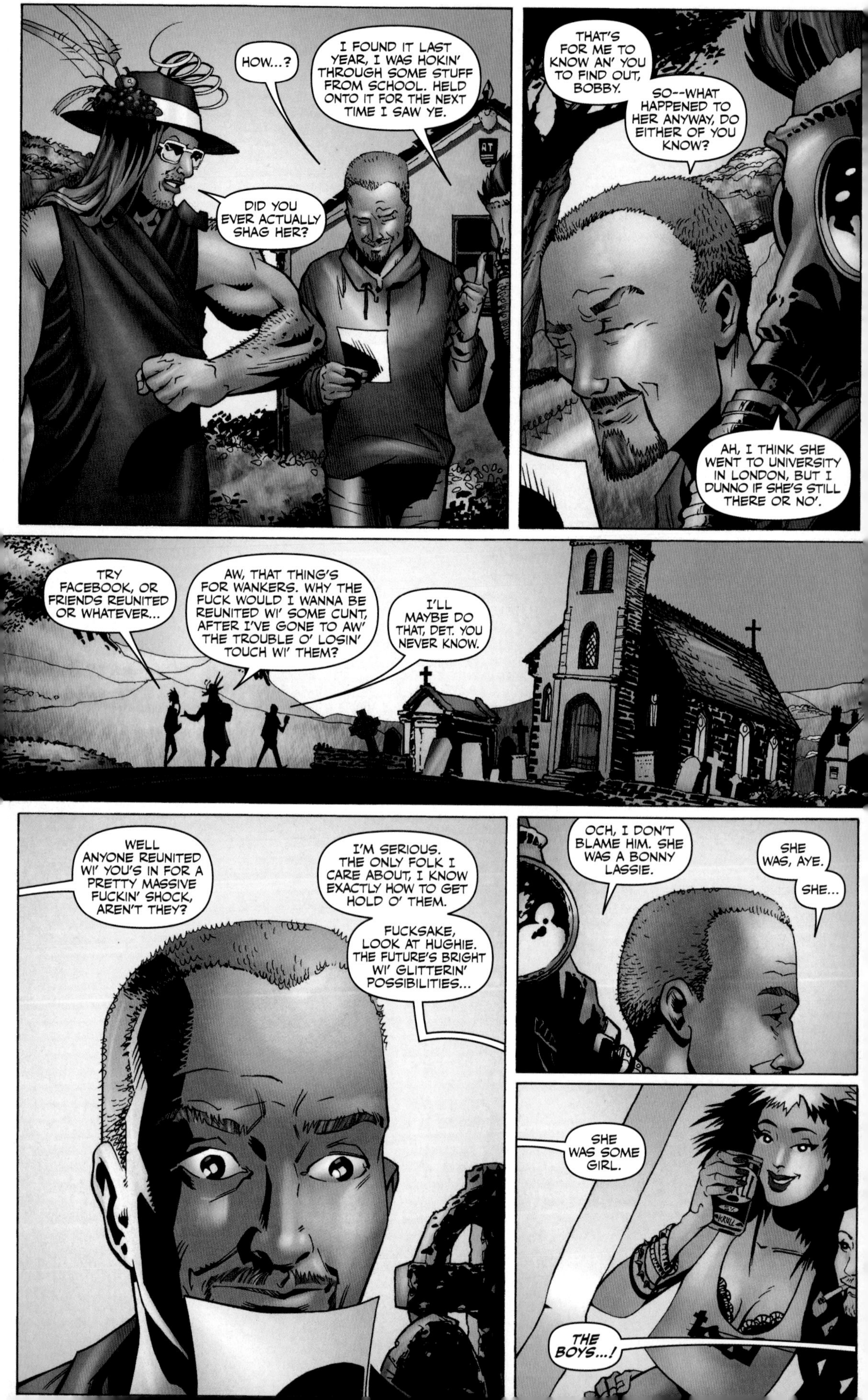
HOW...?
I FOUND IT LAST YEAR, I WAS HOKIN' THROUGH SOME STUFF FROM SCHOOL. HELD ONTO IT FOR THE NEXT TIME I SAW YE.
DID YOU EVER ACTUALLY SHAG HER?
THAT'S FOR ME TO KNOW AN' YOU TO FIND OUT, BOBBY.
SO--WHAT HAPPENED TO HER ANYWAY, DO EITHER OF YOU KNOW?
AH, I THINK SHE WENT TO UNIVERSITY IN LONDON, BUT I DUNNO IF SHE'S STILL THERE OR NO'.
TRY FACEBOOK, OR FRIENDS REUNITED OR WHATEVER...
AW, THAT THING'S FOR WANKERS. WHY THE FUCK WOULD I WANNA BE REUNITED WI' SOME CUNT, AFTER I'VE GONE TO AW' THE TROUBLE O' LOSIN' TOUCH WI' THEM?
I'LL MAYBE DO THAT, DET. YOU NEVER KNOW.
WELL ANYONE REUNITED WI' YOU'S IN FOR A PRETTY MASSIVE FUCKIN' SHOCK, AREN'T THEY?
I'M SERIOUS. THE ONLY FOLK I CARE ABOUT, I KNOW EXACTLY HOW TO GET HOLD O' THEM.
FUCKSAKE, LOOK AT HUGHIE. THE FUTURE'S BRIGHT WI' GLITTERIN' POSSIBILITIES...
OCH, I DON'T BLAME HIM. SHE WAS A BONNY LASSIE.
SHE WAS, AYE.
SHE...
SHE WAS SOME GIRL.
THE BOYS...!

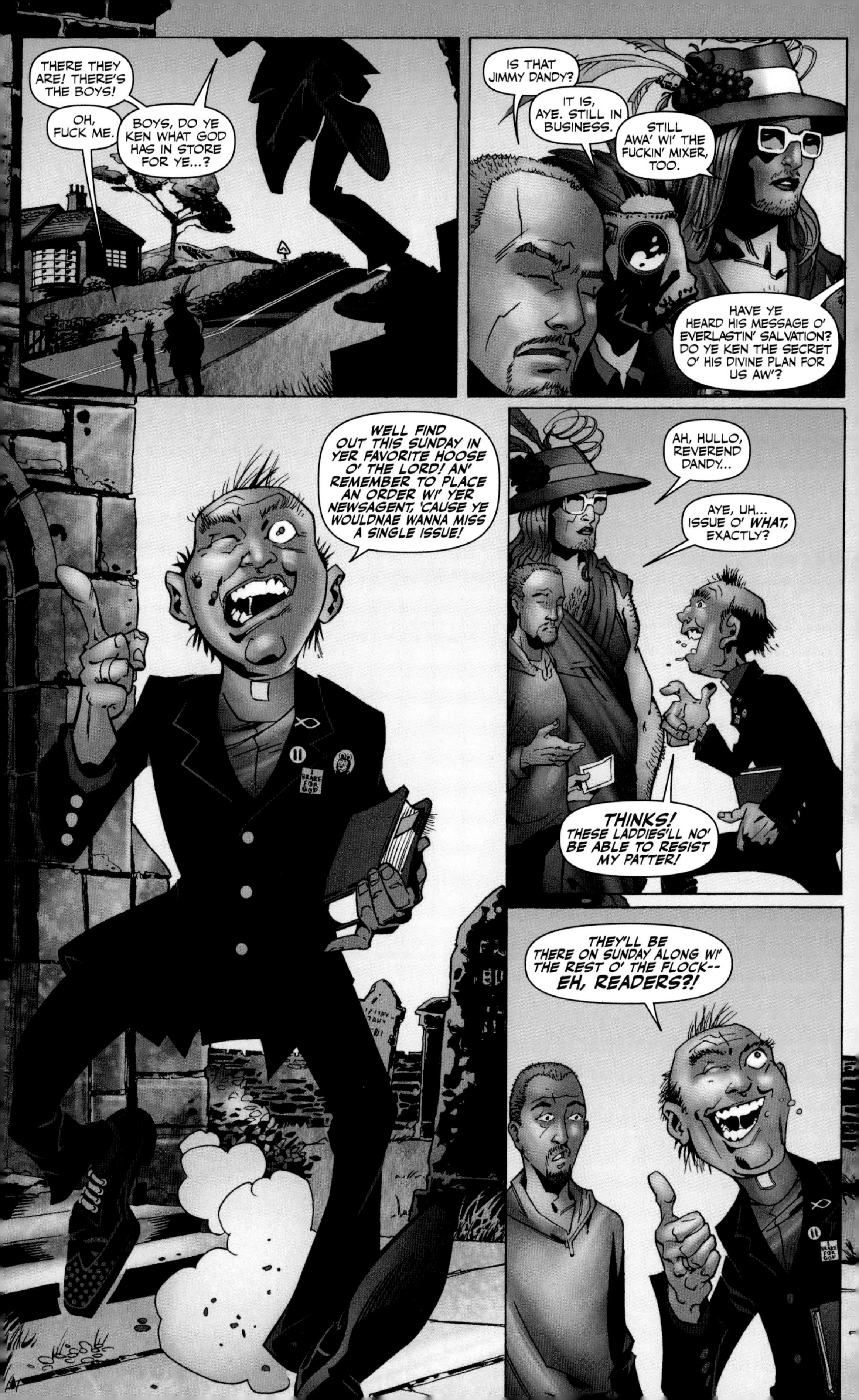

THERE THEY ARE! THERE'S THE BOYS!
OH, FUCK ME.
BOYS, DO YE KEN WHAT GOD HAS IN STORE FOR YE...?
IS THAT JIMMY DANDY?
IT IS, AYE. STILL IN BUSINESS.
STILL AWA' WI' THE FUCKIN' MIXER, TOO.
HAVE YE HEARD HIS MESSAGE O' EVERLASTIN' SALVATION? DO YE KEN THE SECRET O' HIS DIVINE PLAN FOR US AW'?
WELL FIND OUT THIS SUNDAY IN YER FAVORITE HOOSE O' THE LORD! AN' REMEMBER TO PLACE AN ORDER WI' YER NEWSAGENT, 'CAUSE YE WOULDNAE WANNA MISS A SINGLE ISSUE!
I BRAKE FOR GOD
AH, HULLO, REVEREND DANDY...
AYE, UH... ISSUE O' WHAT, EXACTLY?
THINKS! THESE LADDIES'LL NO' BE ABLE TO RESIST MY PATTER!
THEY'LL BE THERE ON SUNDAY ALONG WI' THE REST O' THE FLOCK-- EH, READERS?!

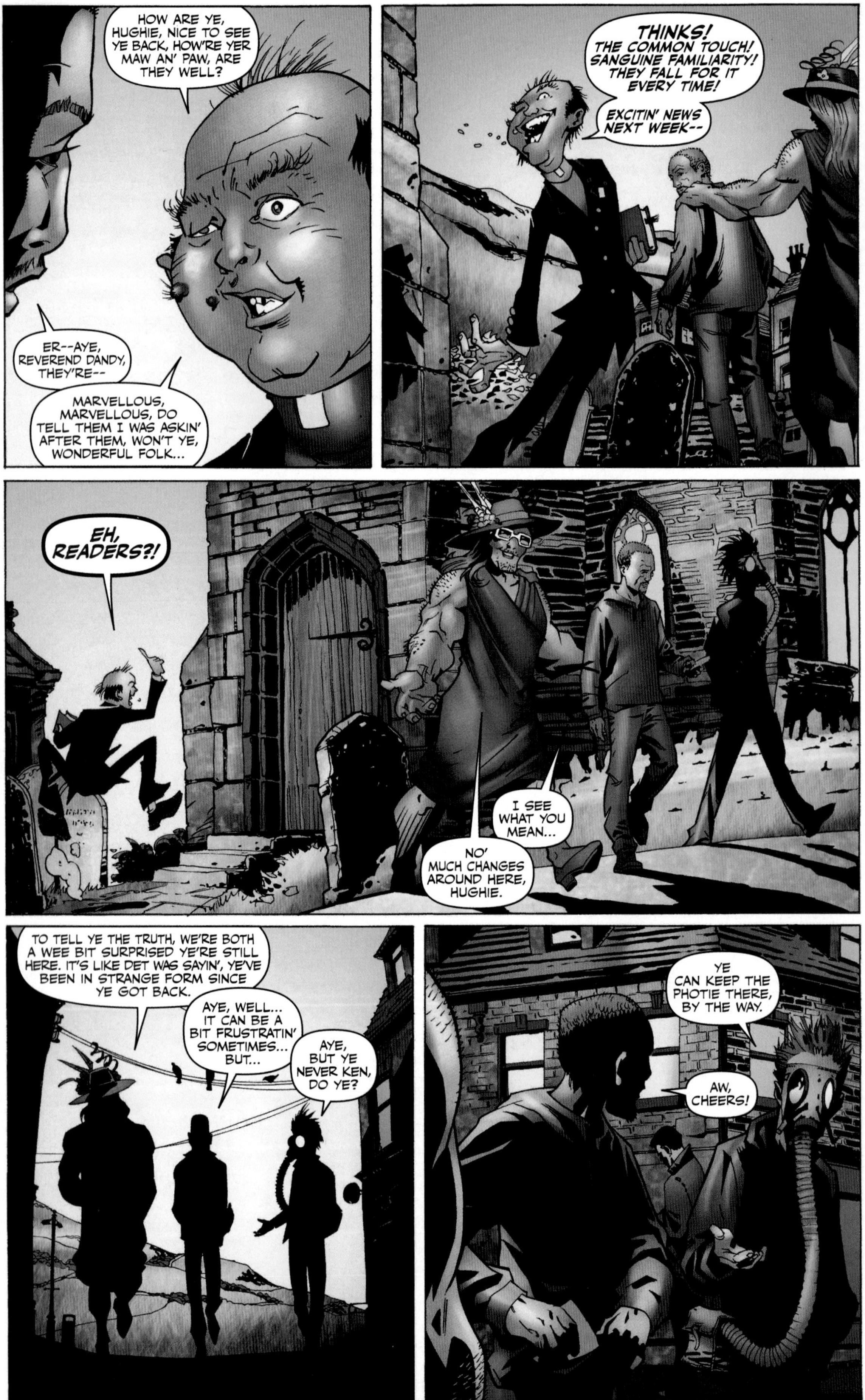

HOW ARE YE, HUGHIE, NICE TO SEE YE BACK, HOW'RE YER MAW AN' PAW, ARE THEY WELL?
ER--AYE, REVEREND DANDY, THEY'RE--
MARVELLOUS, MARVELLOUS, DO TELL THEM I WAS ASKIN' AFTER THEM, WON'T YE, WONDERFUL FOLK...
THINKS! THE COMMON TOUCH! SANGUINE FAMILIARITY! THEY FALL FOR IT EVERY TIME!
EXCITIN' NEWS NEXT WEEK--
EH, READERS?!
I SEE WHAT YOU MEAN...
NO' MUCH CHANGES AROUND HERE, HUGHIE.
TO TELL YE THE TRUTH, WE'RE BOTH A WEE BIT SURPRISED YE'RE STILL HERE. IT'S LIKE DET WAS SAYIN', YE'VE BEEN IN STRANGE FORM SINCE YE GOT BACK.
AYE, WELL... IT CAN BE A BIT FRUSTRATIN' SOMETIMES... BUT...
AYE, BUT YE NEVER KEN, DO YE?
YE CAN KEEP THE PHOTIE THERE, BY THE WAY.
AW, CHEERS!

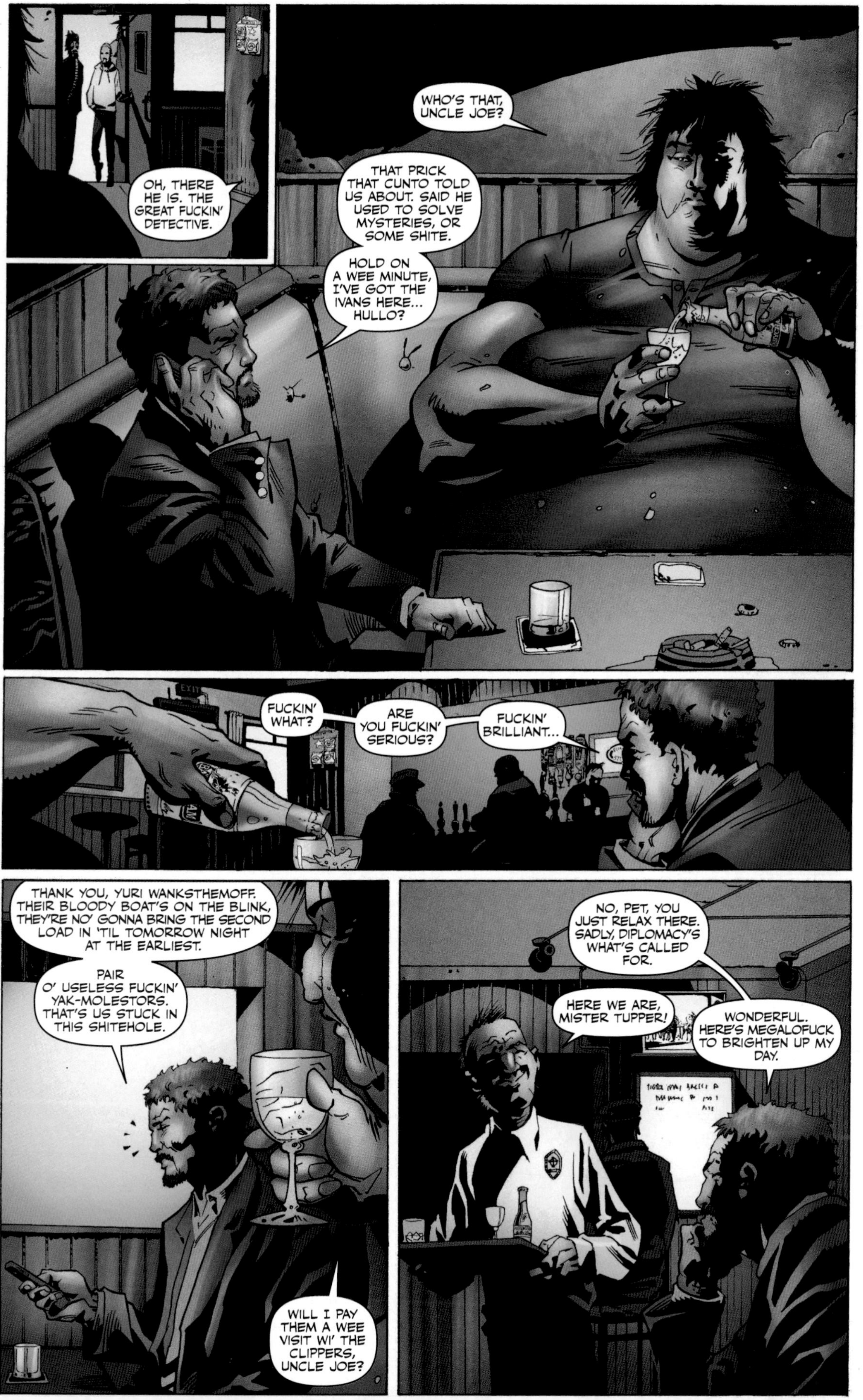
OH, THERE HE IS. THE GREAT FUCKIN' DETECTIVE.
WHO'S THAT, UNCLE JOE?
THAT PRICK THAT CUNTO TOLD US ABOUT. SAID HE USED TO SOLVE MYSTERIES, OR SOME SHITE.
HOLD ON A WEE MINUTE, I'VE GOT THE IVANS HERE... HULLO?
FUCKIN' WHAT?
ARE YOU FUCKIN' SERIOUS?
FUCKIN' BRILLIANT...
THANK YOU, YURI WANKSTHEMOFF. THEIR BLOODY BOAT'S ON THE BLINK, THEY'RE NO' GONNA BRING THE SECOND LOAD IN 'TIL TOMORROW NIGHT AT THE EARLIEST.
PAIR O' USELESS FUCKIN' YAK-MOLESTORS. THAT'S US STUCK IN THIS SHITEHOLE.
WILL I PAY THEM A WEE VISIT WI' THE CLIPPERS, UNCLE JOE?
NO, PET, YOU JUST RELAX THERE. SADLY, DIPLOMACY'S WHAT'S CALLED FOR.
HERE WE ARE, MISTER TUPPER!
WONDERFUL. HERE'S MEGALOFUCK TO BRIGHTEN UP MY DAY.

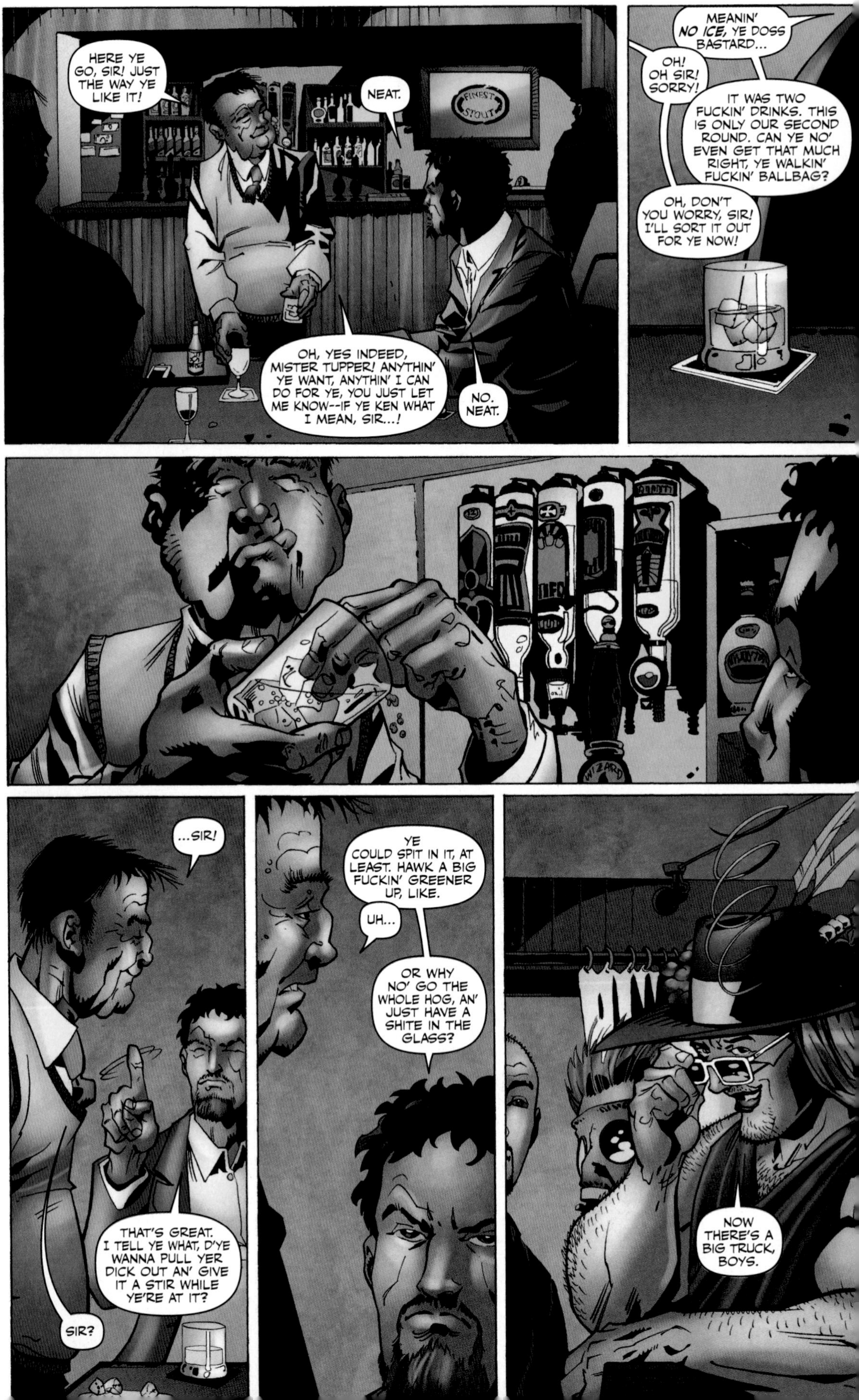
HERE YE GO, SIR! JUST THE WAY YE LIKE IT!
NEAT.
OH, YES INDEED, MISTER TUPPER! ANYTHIN' YE WANT, ANYTHIN' I CAN DO FOR YE, YOU JUST LET ME KNOW--IF YE KEN WHAT I MEAN, SIR...!
NO. NEAT.
FINEST STOUT
MEANIN' NO ICE, YE DOSS BASTARD...
OH! OH SIR! SORRY!
IT WAS TWO FUCKIN' DRINKS. THIS IS ONLY OUR SECOND ROUND. CAN YE NO' EVEN GET THAT MUCH RIGHT, YE WALKIN' FUCKIN' BALLBAG?
OH, DON'T YOU WORRY, SIR! I'LL SORT IT OUT FOR YE NOW!
...SIR!
THAT'S GREAT. I TELL YE WHAT, D'YE WANNA PULL YER DICK OUT AN' GIVE IT A STIR WHILE YE'RE AT IT?
SIR?
YE COULD SPIT IN IT, AT LEAST. HAWK A BIG FUCKIN' GREENER UP, LIKE.
UH...
OR WHY NO' GO THE WHOLE HOG, AN' JUST HAVE A SHITE IN THE GLASS?
NOW THERE'S A BIG TRUCK, BOYS.

WHO? *HER?*

THE FUCKIN' BRONTO WI' BEEZER'S PAL?

THE DEEPER THE CUSHION, DET, MY LAD. I SEE SOME RED-HOT GIRL-ON-GIRL ACTION IN MY IMMEDIATE FUTURE.

AYE, WELL YE'RE RIGHT THERE, BECAUSE I THINK WE'RE LOOKIN' AT MISS STRAP-ON OWNER TWO THOUSAND AN' SEVEN!

AS A MATTER O' FACT, I'D BE FUCKIN' AMAZED IF SHE NEEDED THE STRAP-ON...

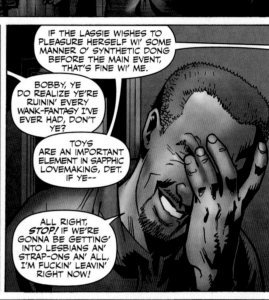

IF THE LASSIE WISHES TO PLEASURE HERSELF WI' SOME MANNER O' SYNTHETIC DONG BEFORE THE MAIN EVENT, THAT'S FINE WI' ME.

BOBBY, YE DO REALIZE YE'RE RUININ' EVERY WANK-FANTASY I'VE EVER HAD, DON'T YE?

TOYS ARE AN IMPORTANT ELEMENT IN SAPPHIC LOVEMAKING, DET. IF YE--

ALL RIGHT, *STOP!* IF WE'RE GONNA BE GETTING' INTO LESBIANS AN' STRAP-ONS AN' ALL, I'M FUCKIN' LEAVIN' RIGHT NOW!

"LINES YE DON'T HEAR VERY FUCKIN' OFTEN..."

HA!!

HA HA HA HA, YE PAIR O' WANKERS--!

ALL RIGHT, FUCK IT, I'M GETTING' ANOTHER ROUND IN! DINNER CAN BLOODY WELL WAIT!

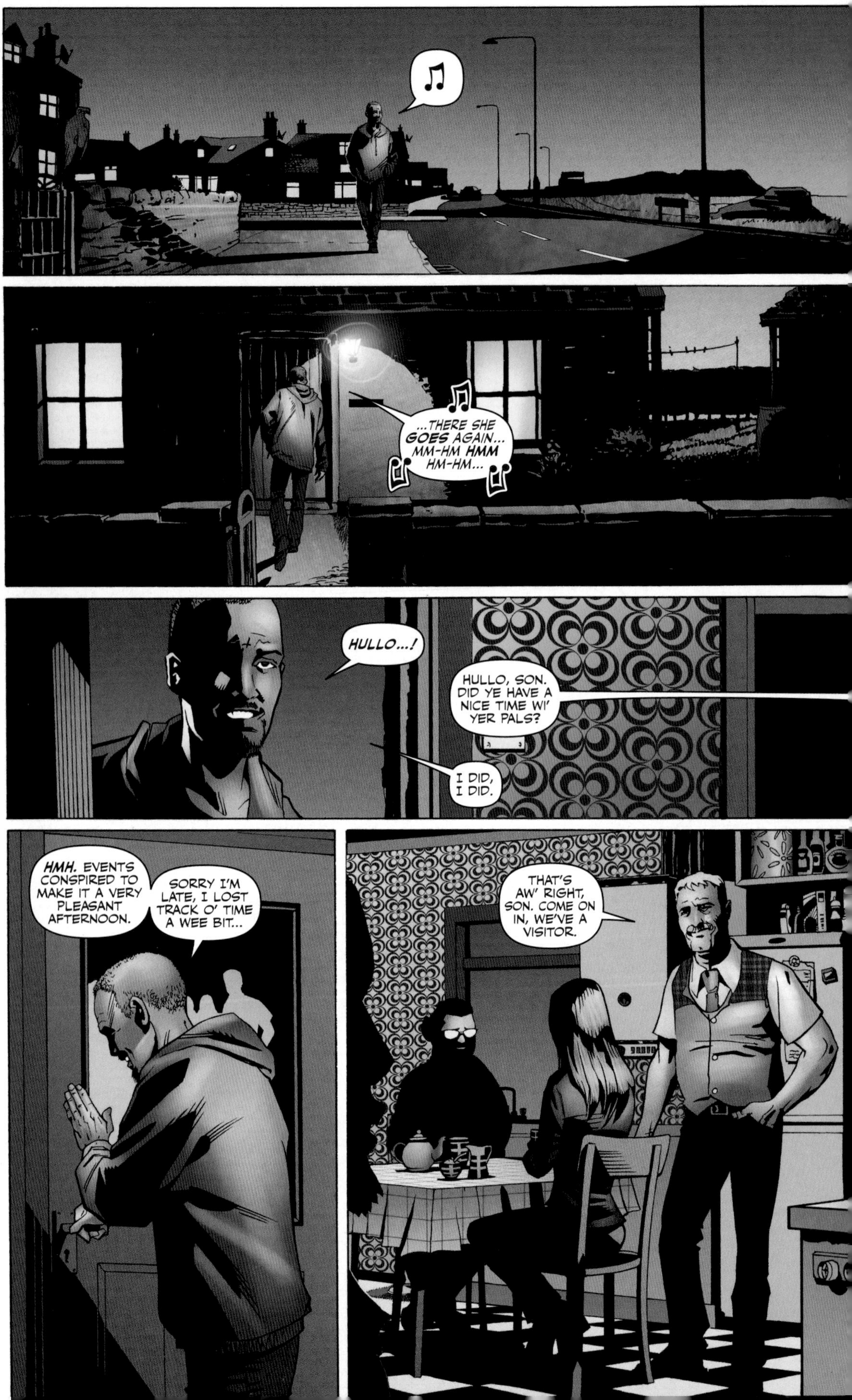
♫
...THERE SHE GOES AGAIN... MM-HM HMM HM-HM...
HULLO...!
HULLO, SON. DID YE HAVE A NICE TIME WI' YER PALS?
I DID, I DID.
HMH. EVENTS CONSPIRED TO MAKE IT A VERY PLEASANT AFTERNOON.
SORRY I'M LATE, I LOST TRACK O' TIME A WEE BIT...
THAT'S AW' RIGHT, SON. COME ON IN, WE'VE A VISITOR.

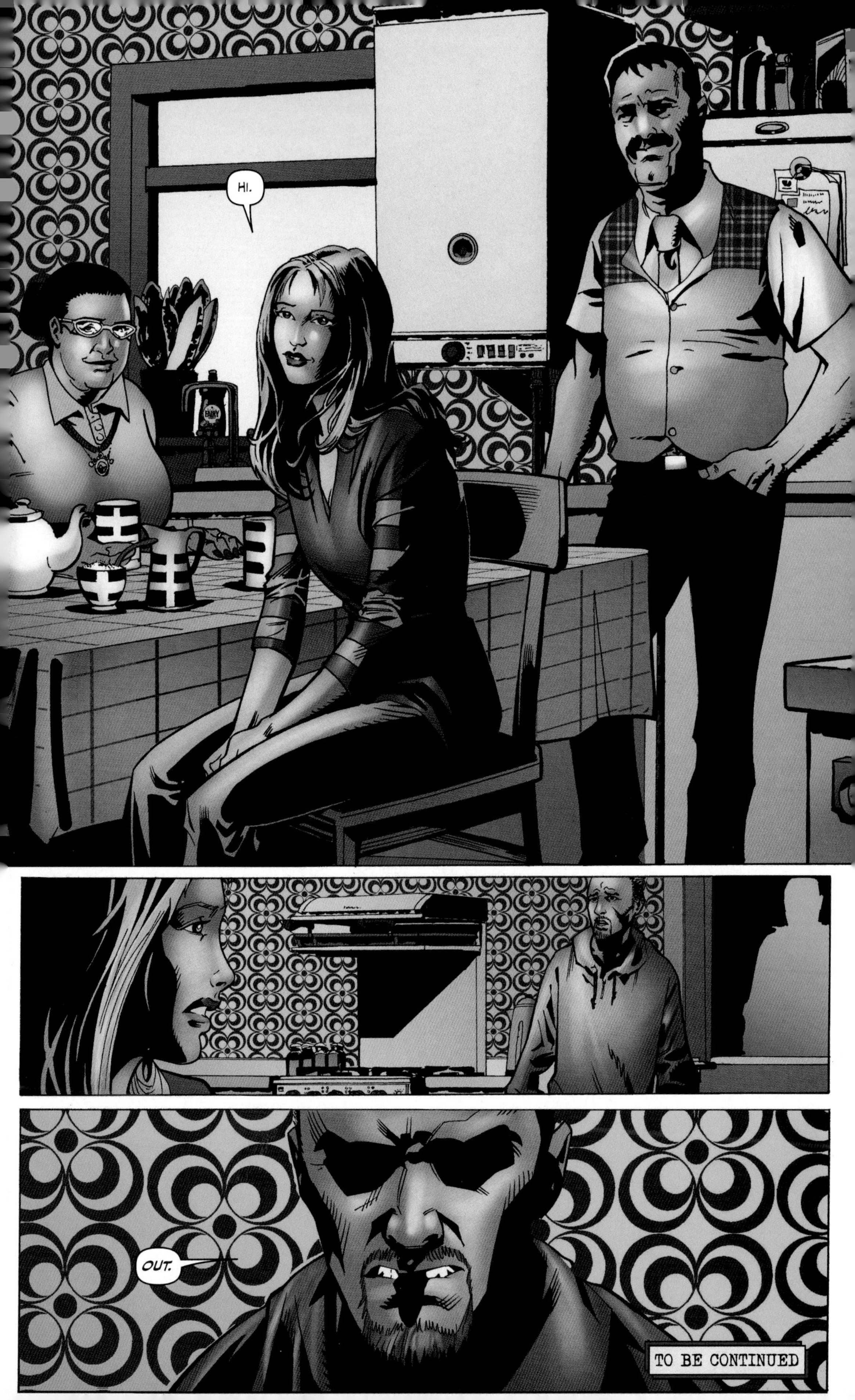
HI.
OUT.
TO BE CONTINUED

HIGHLAND LADDIE #4
cover

by DARICK ROBERTSON
and TONY AVIÑA

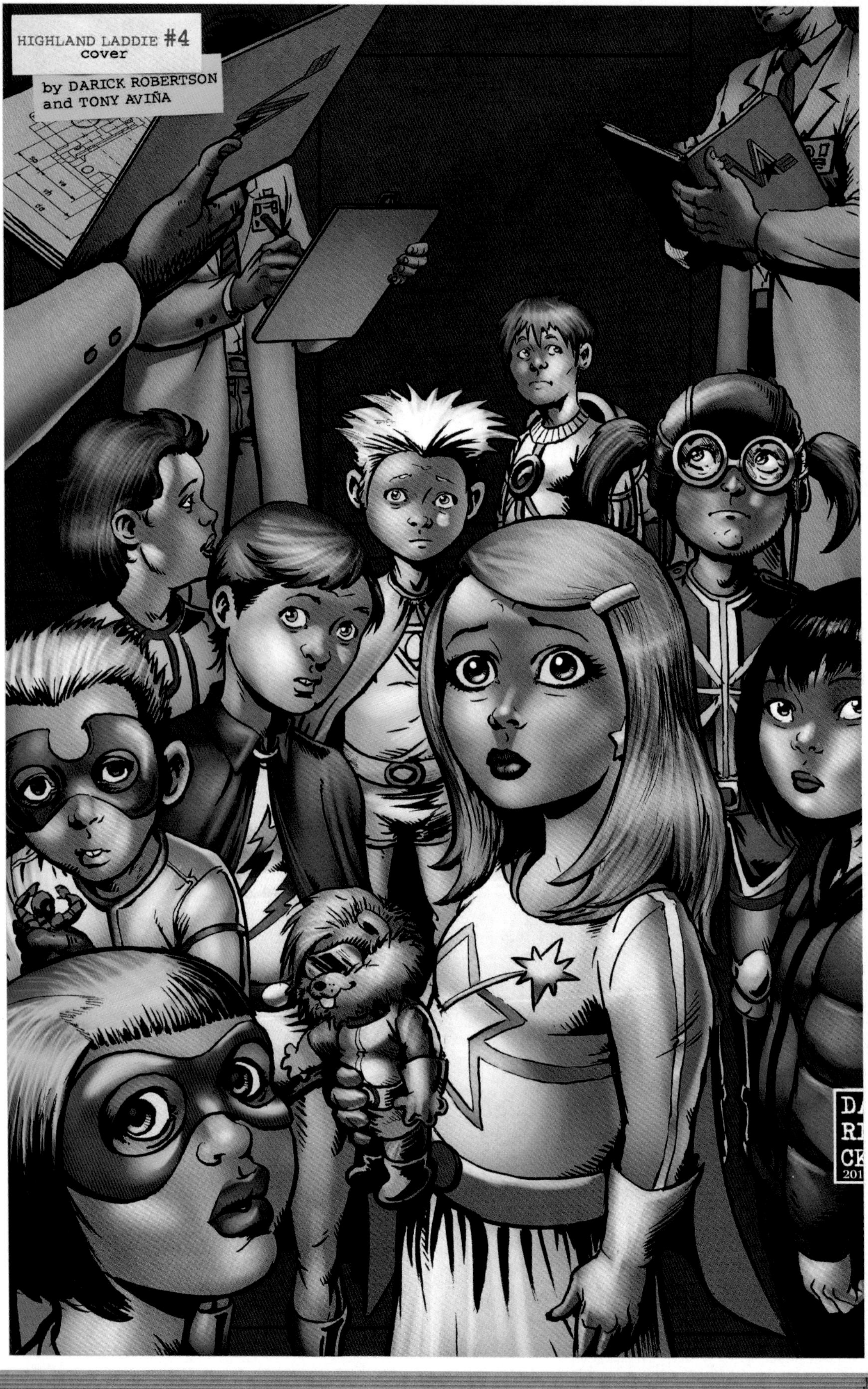

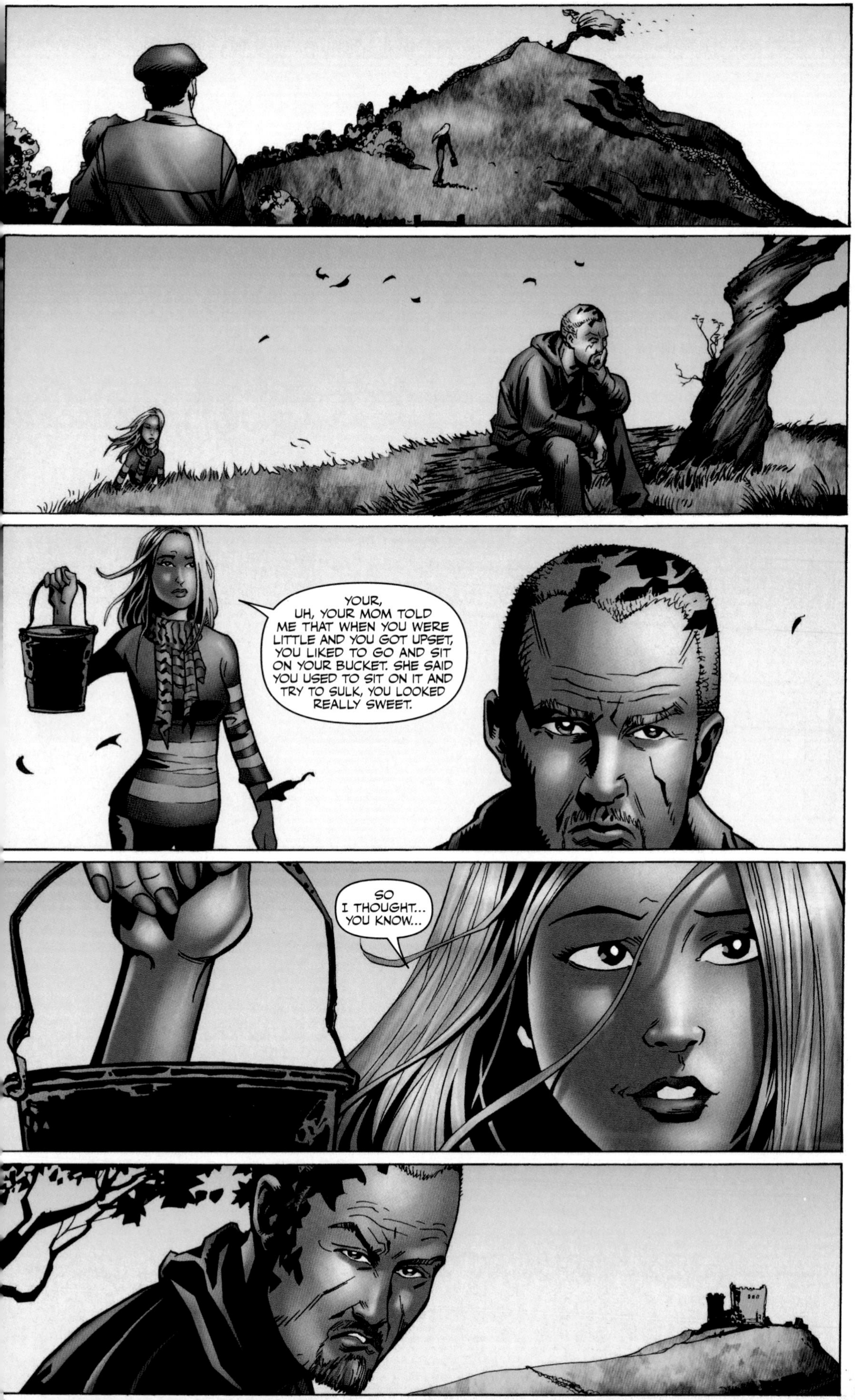
YOUR, UH, YOUR MOM TOLD ME THAT WHEN YOU WERE LITTLE AND YOU GOT UPSET, YOU LIKED TO GO AND SIT ON YOUR BUCKET. SHE SAID YOU USED TO SIT ON IT AND TRY TO SULK, YOU LOOKED REALLY SWEET.
SO I THOUGHT... YOU KNOW...

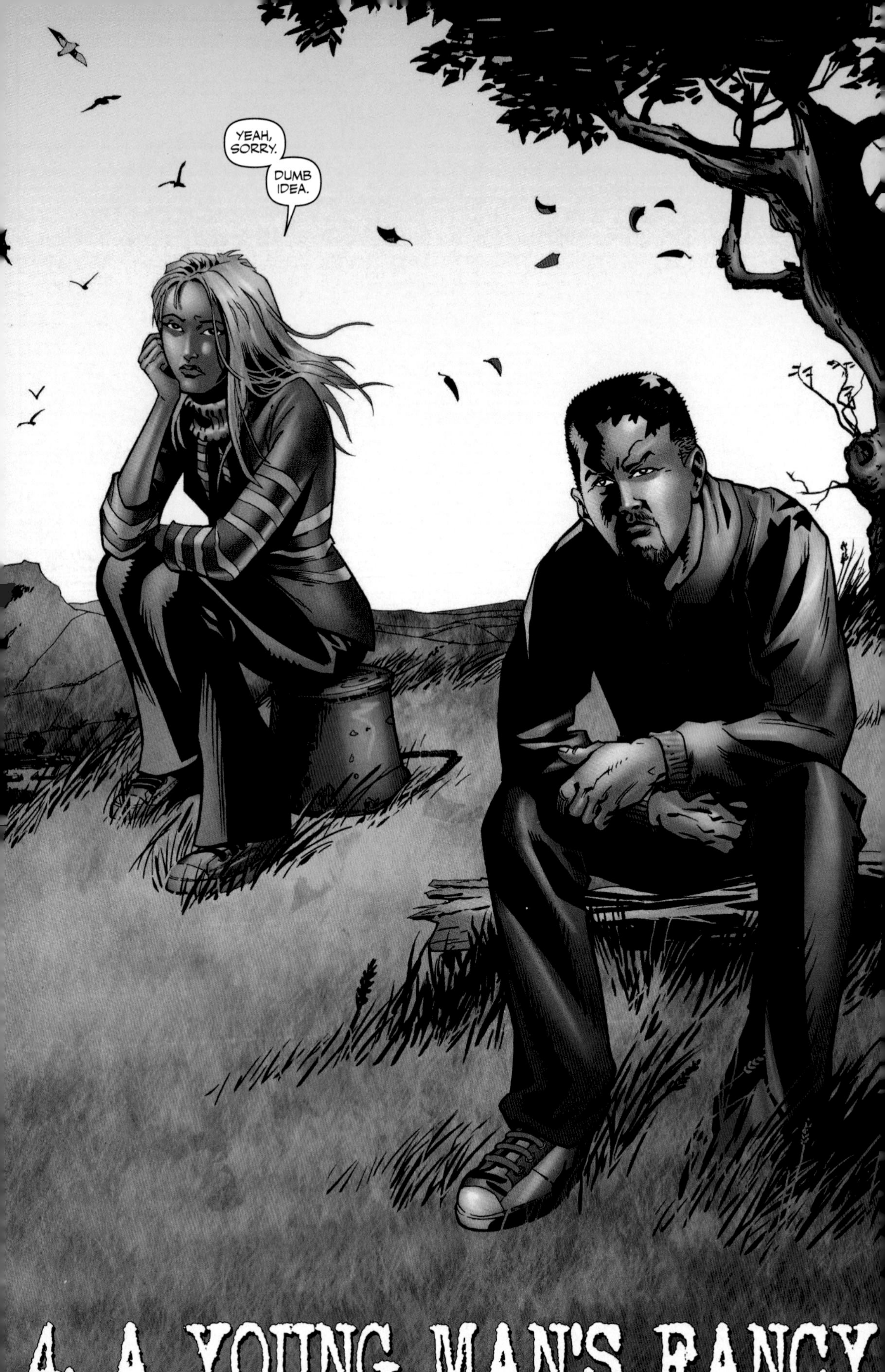
YEAH, SORRY.
DUMB IDEA.

4: A YOUNG MAN'S FANCY

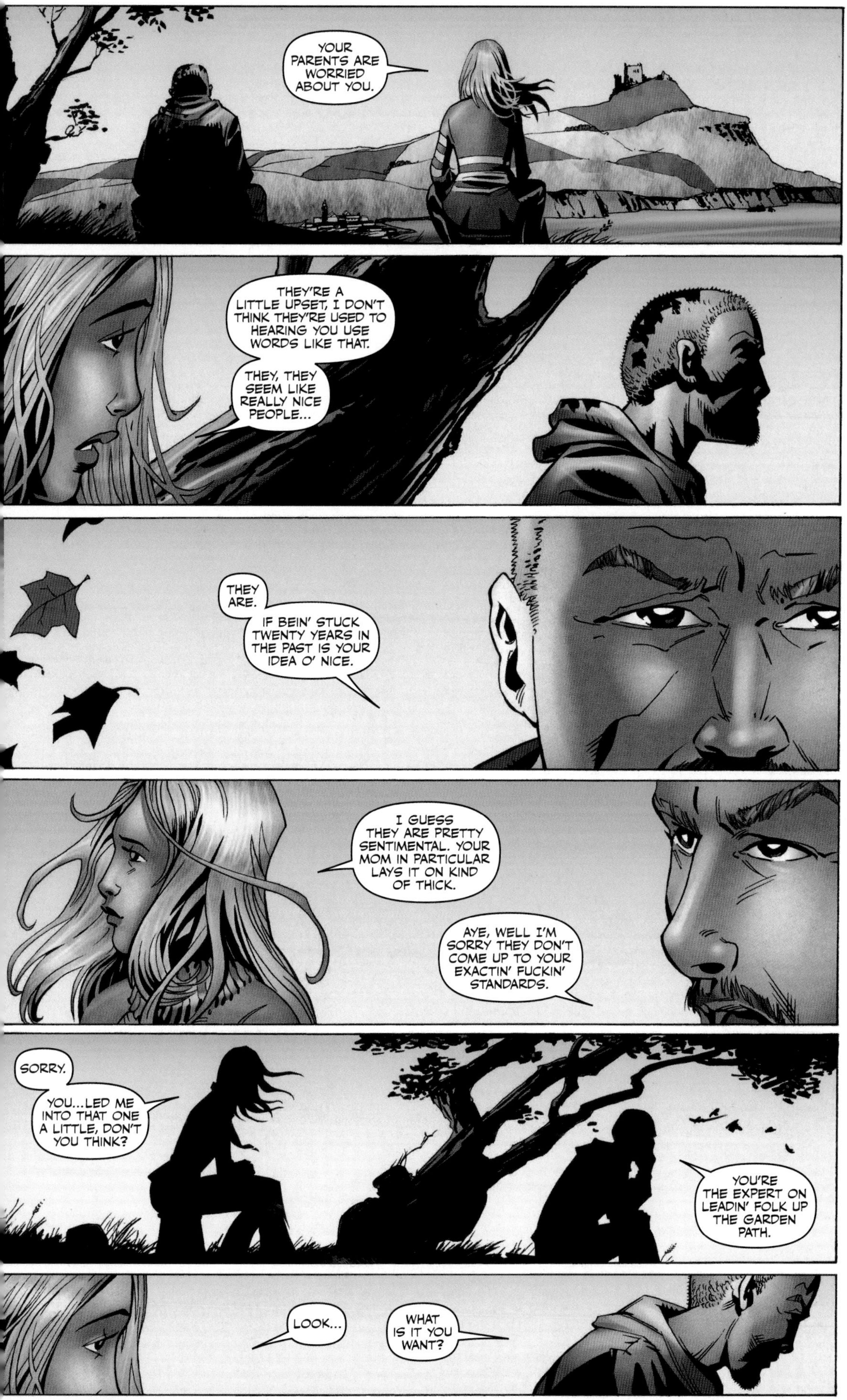
YOUR PARENTS ARE WORRIED ABOUT YOU.
THEY'RE A LITTLE UPSET, I DON'T THINK THEY'RE USED TO HEARING YOU USE WORDS LIKE THAT.
THEY, THEY SEEM LIKE REALLY NICE PEOPLE...
THEY ARE.
IF BEIN' STUCK TWENTY YEARS IN THE PAST IS YOUR IDEA O' NICE.
I GUESS THEY ARE PRETTY SENTIMENTAL. YOUR MOM IN PARTICULAR LAYS IT ON KIND OF THICK.
AYE, WELL I'M SORRY THEY DON'T COME UP TO YOUR EXACTIN' FUCKIN' STANDARDS.
SORRY.
YOU...LED ME INTO THAT ONE A LITTLE, DON'T YOU THINK?
YOU'RE THE EXPERT ON LEADIN' FOLK UP THE GARDEN PATH.
LOOK...
WHAT IS IT YOU WANT?

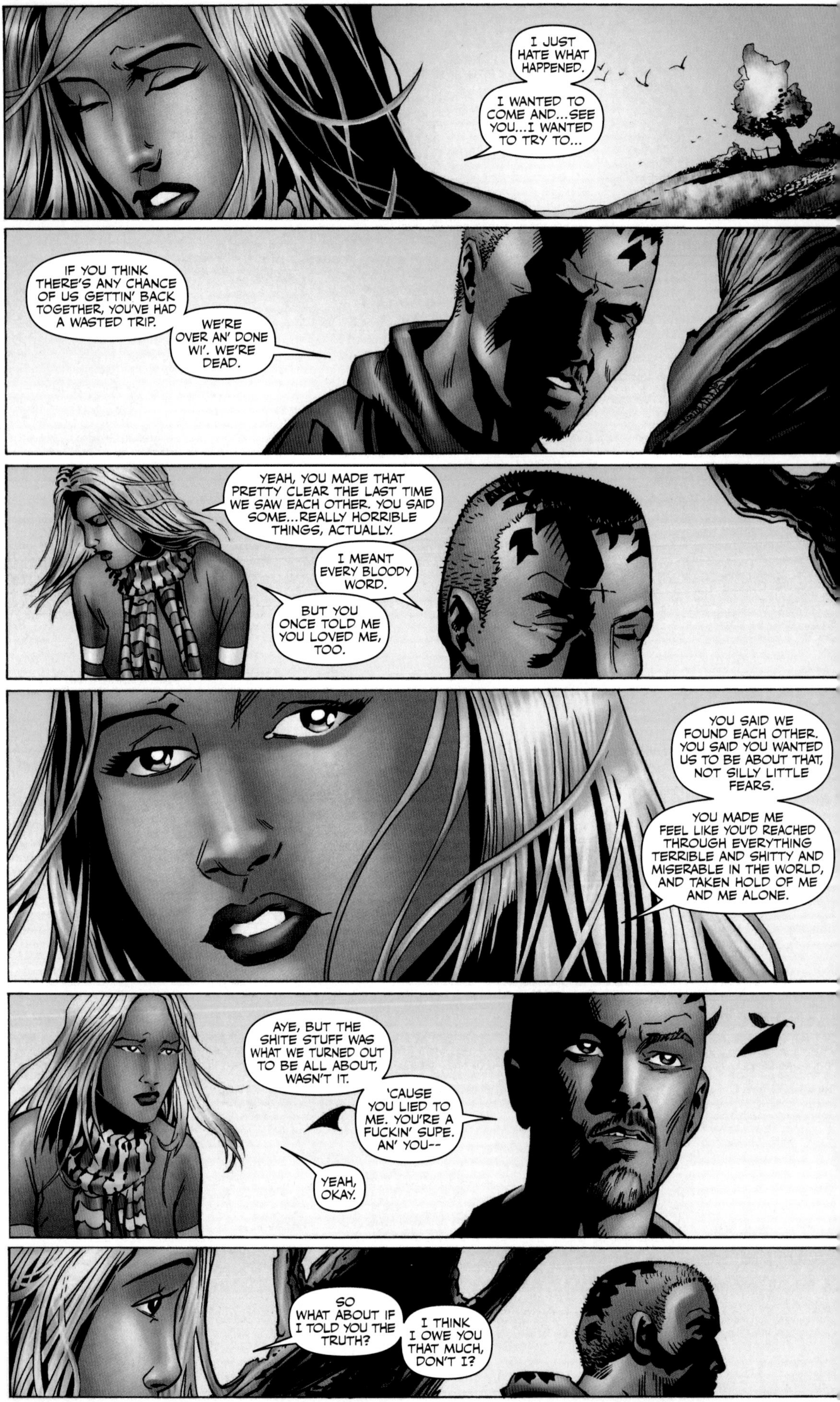
I JUST HATE WHAT HAPPENED.
I WANTED TO COME AND...SEE YOU...I WANTED TO TRY TO...
IF YOU THINK THERE'S ANY CHANCE OF US GETTIN' BACK TOGETHER, YOU'VE HAD A WASTED TRIP.
WE'RE OVER AN' DONE WI'. WE'RE DEAD.
YEAH, YOU MADE THAT PRETTY CLEAR THE LAST TIME WE SAW EACH OTHER. YOU SAID SOME...REALLY HORRIBLE THINGS, ACTUALLY.
I MEANT EVERY BLOODY WORD.
BUT YOU ONCE TOLD ME YOU LOVED ME, TOO.
YOU SAID WE FOUND EACH OTHER. YOU SAID YOU WANTED US TO BE ABOUT THAT, NOT SILLY LITTLE FEARS.
YOU MADE ME FEEL LIKE YOU'D REACHED THROUGH EVERYTHING TERRIBLE AND SHITTY AND MISERABLE IN THE WORLD, AND TAKEN HOLD OF ME AND ME ALONE.
AYE, BUT THE SHITE STUFF WAS WHAT WE TURNED OUT TO BE ALL ABOUT, WASN'T IT.
'CAUSE YOU LIED TO ME. YOU'RE A FUCKIN' SUPE. AN' YOU--
YEAH, OKAY.
SO WHAT ABOUT IF I TOLD YOU THE TRUTH?
I THINK I OWE YOU THAT MUCH, DON'T I?

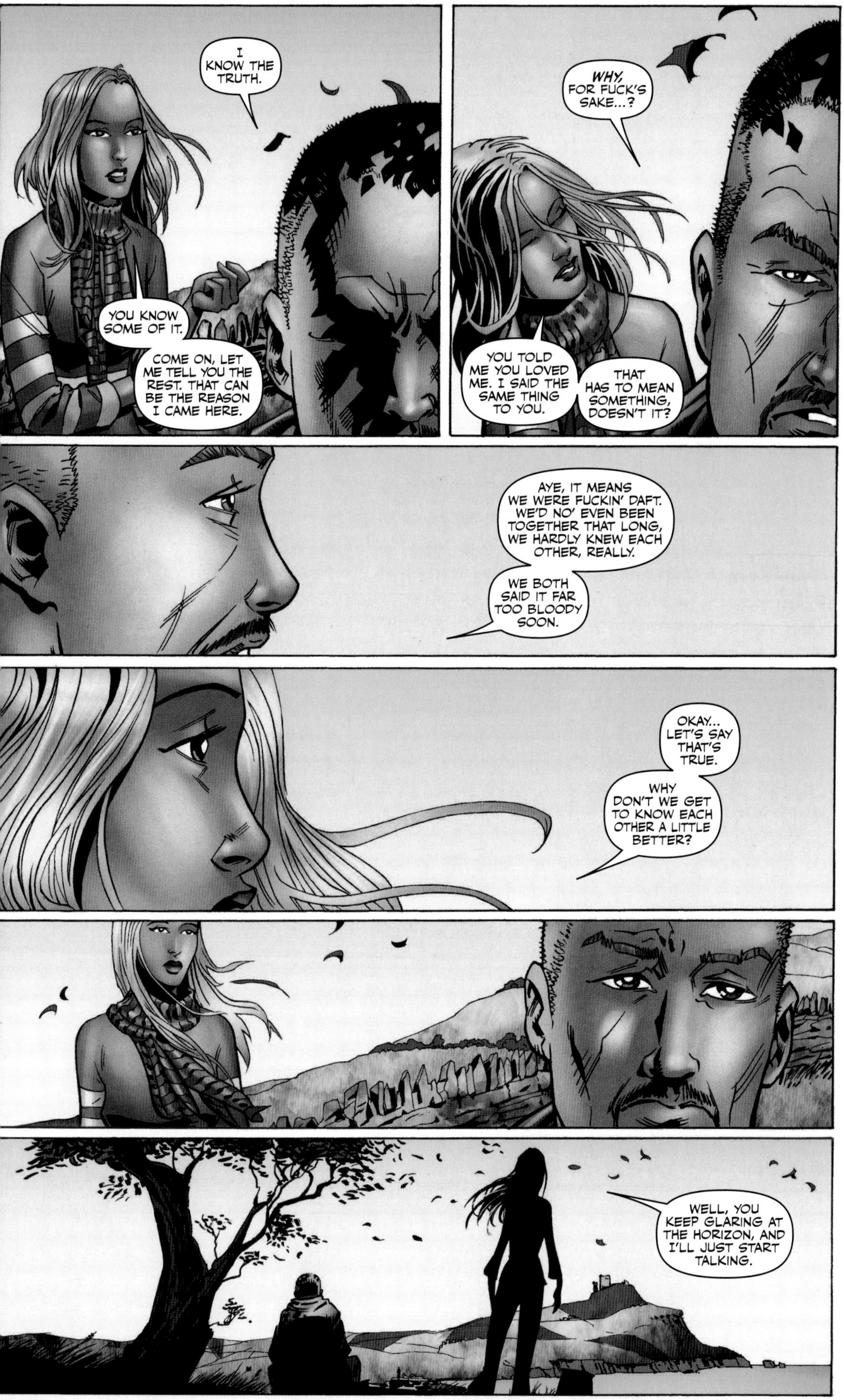
I KNOW THE TRUTH.
YOU KNOW SOME OF IT.
COME ON, LET ME TELL YOU THE REST. THAT CAN BE THE REASON I CAME HERE.
WHY, FOR FUCK'S SAKE...?
YOU TOLD ME YOU LOVED ME. I SAID THE SAME THING TO YOU.
THAT HAS TO MEAN SOMETHING, DOESN'T IT?
AYE, IT MEANS WE WERE FUCKIN' DAFT. WE'D NO' EVEN BEEN TOGETHER THAT LONG, WE HARDLY KNEW EACH OTHER, REALLY.
WE BOTH SAID IT FAR TOO BLOODY SOON.
OKAY... LET'S SAY THAT'S TRUE.
WHY DON'T WE GET TO KNOW EACH OTHER A LITTLE BETTER?
WELL, YOU KEEP GLARING AT THE HORIZON, AND I'LL JUST START TALKING.

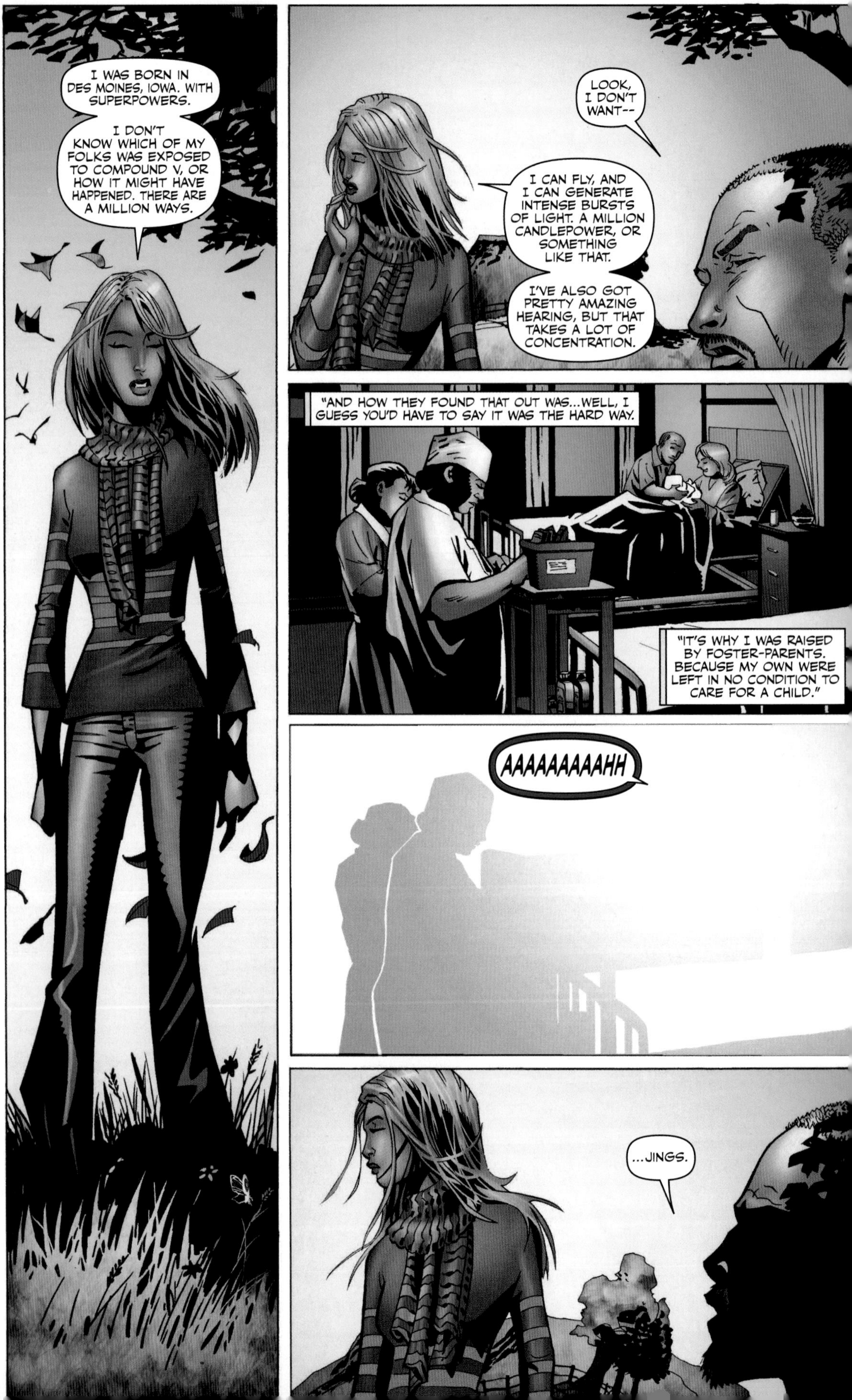
I WAS BORN IN DES MOINES, IOWA. WITH SUPERPOWERS.
I DON'T KNOW WHICH OF MY FOLKS WAS EXPOSED TO COMPOUND V, OR HOW IT MIGHT HAVE HAPPENED. THERE ARE A MILLION WAYS.
LOOK, I DON'T WANT--
I CAN FLY, AND I CAN GENERATE INTENSE BURSTS OF LIGHT. A MILLION CANDLEPOWER, OR SOMETHING LIKE THAT.
I'VE ALSO GOT PRETTY AMAZING HEARING, BUT THAT TAKES A LOT OF CONCENTRATION.
"AND HOW THEY FOUND THAT OUT WAS...WELL, I GUESS YOU'D HAVE TO SAY IT WAS THE HARD WAY.
"IT'S WHY I WAS RAISED BY FOSTER-PARENTS. BECAUSE MY OWN WERE LEFT IN NO CONDITION TO CARE FOR A CHILD."
AAAAAAAAAHH
...JINGS.

"VOUGHT-AMERICAN WERE ON THE CASE RIGHT AWAY. THEY HAVE PEOPLE READY--SOMETIMES HUNTERS, SOMETIMES JUST LAWYERS. BUT THEY GET WORD FROM A HOSPITAL, OR LOCAL LAW ENFORCEMENT, OR WHOEVER IT IS CALLS THE ONE-EIGHT-HUNDRED NUMBER...

"AND THEY OPEN A FILE."

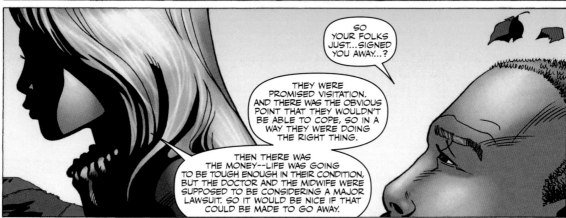

SO YOUR FOLKS JUST...SIGNED YOU AWAY...?

THEY WERE PROMISED VISITATION. AND THERE WAS THE OBVIOUS POINT THAT THEY WOULDN'T BE ABLE TO COPE, SO IN A WAY THEY WERE DOING THE RIGHT THING.

THEN THERE WAS THE MONEY--LIFE WAS GOING TO BE TOUGH ENOUGH IN THEIR CONDITION, BUT THE DOCTOR AND THE MIDWIFE WERE SUPPOSED TO BE CONSIDERING A MAJOR LAWSUIT. SO IT WOULD BE NICE IF THAT COULD BE MADE TO GO AWAY.

ONE WAY OR ANOTHER, THEY WERE HELPED TO UNDERSTAND HOW THINGS WOULD BE.

I THINK VOUGHT EVEN THREW IN A COUPLE OF SEEING-EYE DOGS.

I FOUND OUT ABOUT ALL OF THIS LATER. I SAW MY REAL FOLKS ABOUT ONCE A YEAR, AND WHEN I WAS SIXTEEN THEY TOLD ME AS MUCH AS THEY THOUGHT THE NON-DISCLOSURE CLAUSE WOULD LET THEM.

ACTUALLY, THEY WEREN'T ALL THAT DISCRETE ABOUT IT, REALLY.

I THINK I WAS JUST CAREFUL NOT TO READ TOO DEEP BETWEEN THE LINES, BECAUSE BY THEN THE COURSE OF MY LIFE WAS SET IN STONE.

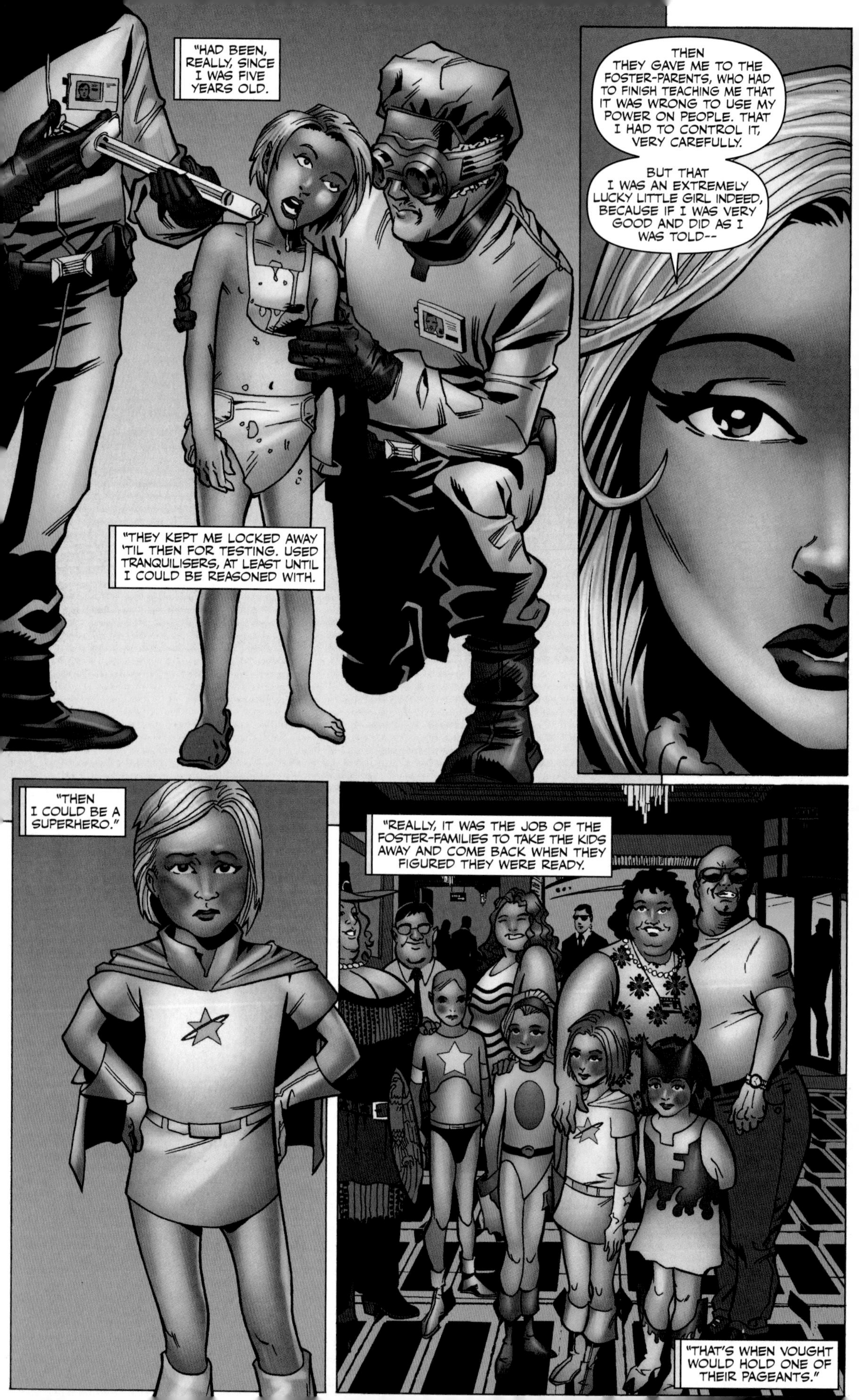
"HAD BEEN, REALLY, SINCE I WAS FIVE YEARS OLD.
"THEY KEPT ME LOCKED AWAY 'TIL THEN FOR TESTING. USED TRANQUILISERS, AT LEAST UNTIL I COULD BE REASONED WITH.
THEN THEY GAVE ME TO THE FOSTER-PARENTS, WHO HAD TO FINISH TEACHING ME THAT IT WAS WRONG TO USE MY POWER ON PEOPLE. THAT I HAD TO CONTROL IT, VERY CAREFULLY.
BUT THAT I WAS AN EXTREMELY LUCKY LITTLE GIRL INDEED, BECAUSE IF I WAS VERY GOOD AND DID AS I WAS TOLD--
"THEN I COULD BE A SUPERHERO."
"REALLY, IT WAS THE JOB OF THE FOSTER-FAMILIES TO TAKE THE KIDS AWAY AND COME BACK WHEN THEY FIGURED THEY WERE READY.
"THAT'S WHEN VOUGHT WOULD HOLD ONE OF THEIR PAGEANTS."

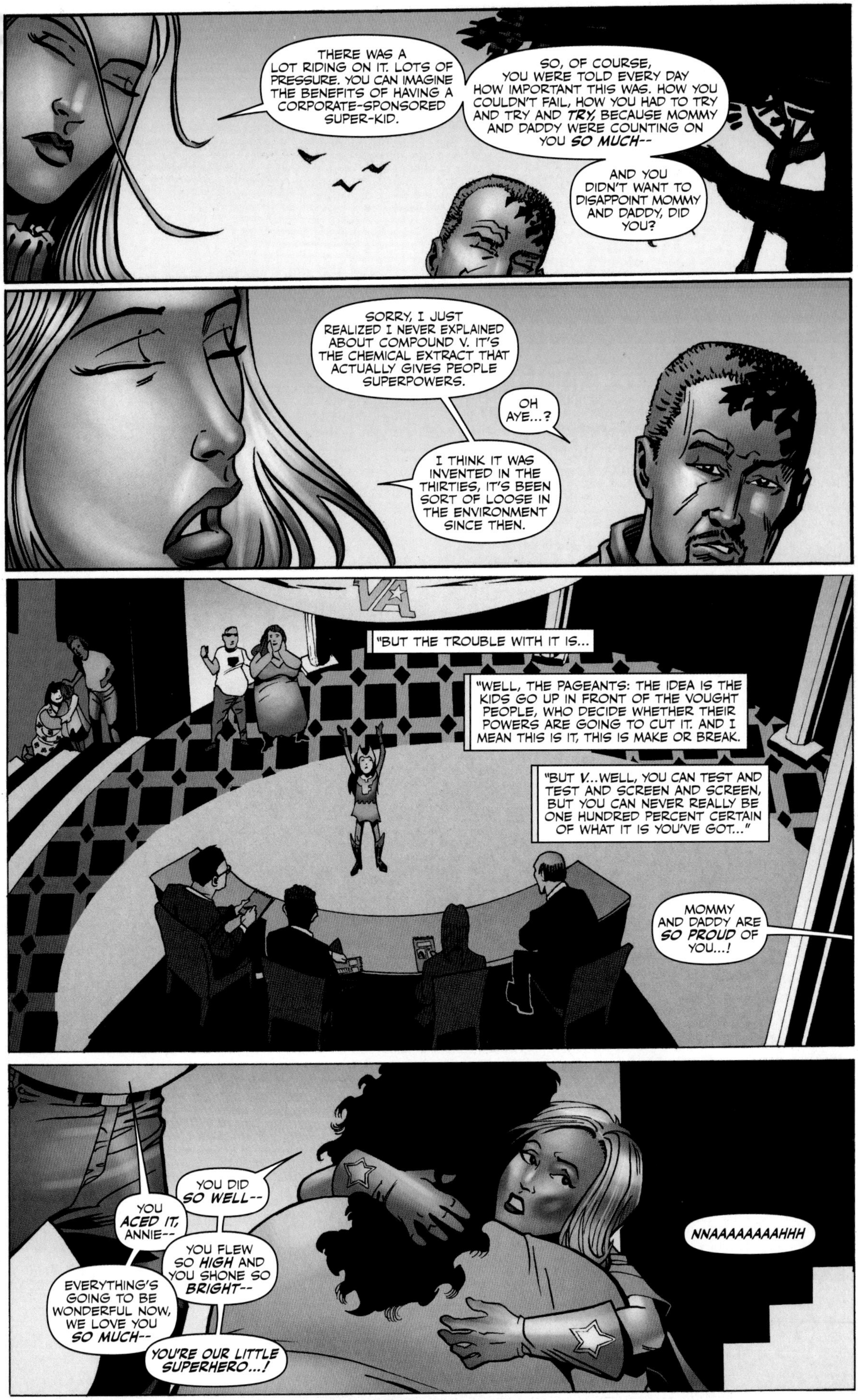
THERE WAS A LOT RIDING ON IT. LOTS OF PRESSURE. YOU CAN IMAGINE THE BENEFITS OF HAVING A CORPORATE-SPONSORED SUPER-KID.
SO, OF COURSE, YOU WERE TOLD EVERY DAY HOW IMPORTANT THIS WAS. HOW YOU COULDN'T FAIL, HOW YOU HAD TO TRY AND TRY AND *TRY,* BECAUSE MOMMY AND DADDY WERE COUNTING ON YOU *SO MUCH*--
AND YOU DIDN'T WANT TO DISAPPOINT MOMMY AND DADDY, DID YOU?
SORRY, I JUST REALIZED I NEVER EXPLAINED ABOUT COMPOUND V. IT'S THE CHEMICAL EXTRACT THAT ACTUALLY GIVES PEOPLE SUPERPOWERS.
OH AYE...?
I THINK IT WAS INVENTED IN THE THIRTIES, IT'S BEEN SORT OF LOOSE IN THE ENVIRONMENT SINCE THEN.
VA
"BUT THE TROUBLE WITH IT IS...
"WELL, THE PAGEANTS: THE IDEA IS THE KIDS GO UP IN FRONT OF THE VOUGHT PEOPLE, WHO DECIDE WHETHER THEIR POWERS ARE GOING TO CUT IT. AND I MEAN THIS IS IT, THIS IS MAKE OR BREAK.
"BUT *V*...WELL, YOU CAN TEST AND TEST AND SCREEN AND SCREEN, BUT YOU CAN NEVER REALLY BE ONE HUNDRED PERCENT CERTAIN OF WHAT IT IS YOU'VE GOT..."
MOMMY AND DADDY ARE *SO PROUD* OF YOU...!
YOU DID *SO WELL*--
YOU *ACED IT,* ANNIE--
YOU FLEW SO *HIGH* AND YOU SHONE SO *BRIGHT*--
EVERYTHING'S GOING TO BE WONDERFUL NOW, WE LOVE YOU *SO MUCH*--
YOU'RE OUR LITTLE SUPERHERO...!
NNAAAAAAAAHHH

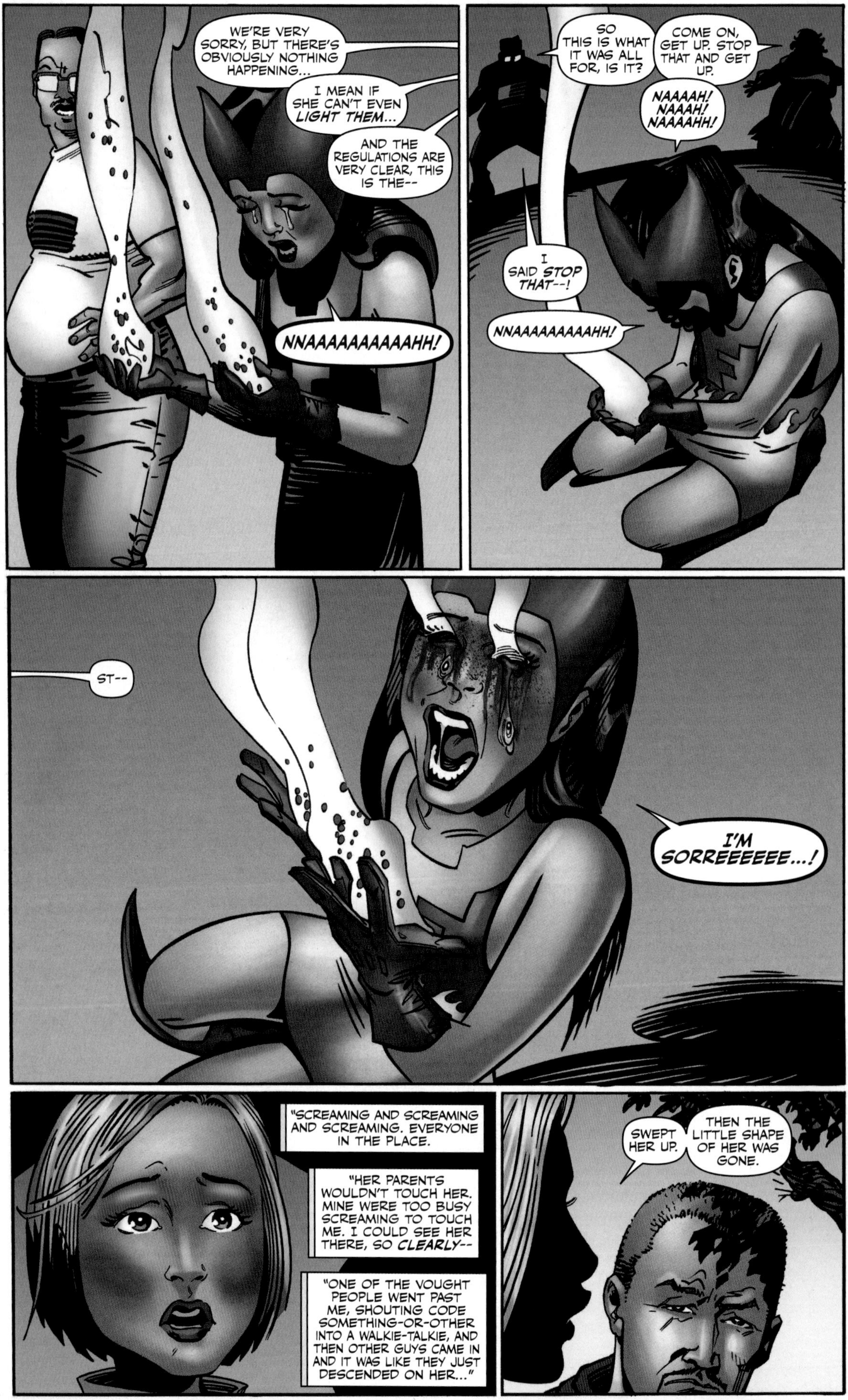
WE'RE VERY SORRY, BUT THERE'S OBVIOUSLY NOTHING HAPPENING...
I MEAN IF SHE CAN'T EVEN *LIGHT THEM*...
AND THE REGULATIONS ARE VERY CLEAR, THIS IS THE--
NNAAAAAAAAAAHH!
SO THIS IS WHAT IT WAS ALL FOR, IS IT?
COME ON, GET UP. STOP THAT AND GET UP.
NAAAAH! NAAAH! NAAAAHH!
I SAID *STOP THAT*--!
NNAAAAAAAAAAHH!
ST--
I'M SORREEEEEE...!
"SCREAMING AND SCREAMING AND SCREAMING. EVERYONE IN THE PLACE.
"HER PARENTS WOULDN'T TOUCH HER. MINE WERE TOO BUSY SCREAMING TO TOUCH ME. I COULD SEE HER THERE, SO *CLEARLY*--
"ONE OF THE VOUGHT PEOPLE WENT PAST ME, SHOUTING CODE SOMETHING-OR-OTHER INTO A WALKIE-TALKIE, AND THEN OTHER GUYS CAME IN AND IT WAS LIKE THEY JUST DESCENDED ON HER..."
SWEPT HER UP.
THEN THE LITTLE SHAPE OF HER WAS GONE.

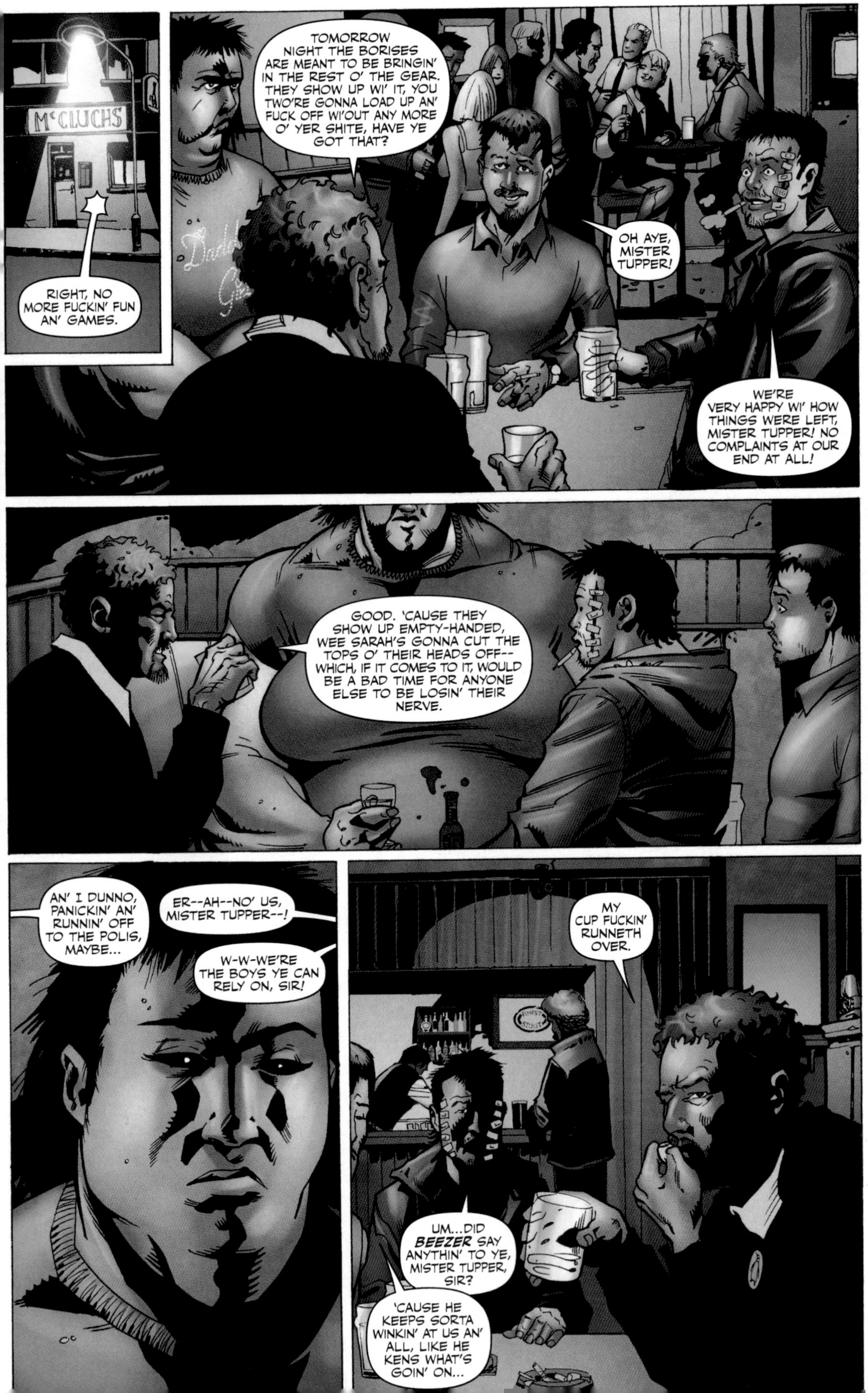
RIGHT, NO MORE FUCKIN' FUN AN' GAMES.
M^cCLUCHS
TOMORROW NIGHT THE BORISES ARE MEANT TO BE BRINGIN' IN THE REST O' THE GEAR. THEY SHOW UP WI' IT, YOU TWO'RE GONNA LOAD UP AN' FUCK OFF WI'OUT ANY MORE O' YER SHITE, HAVE YE GOT THAT?
OH AYE, MISTER TUPPER!
WE'RE VERY HAPPY WI' HOW THINGS WERE LEFT, MISTER TUPPER! NO COMPLAINTS AT OUR END AT ALL!
GOOD. 'CAUSE THEY SHOW UP EMPTY-HANDED, WEE SARAH'S GONNA CUT THE TOPS O' THEIR HEADS OFF-- WHICH, IF IT COMES TO IT, WOULD BE A BAD TIME FOR ANYONE ELSE TO BE LOSIN' THEIR NERVE.
AN' I DUNNO, PANICKIN' AN' RUNNIN' OFF TO THE POLIS, MAYBE...
ER--AH--NO' US, MISTER TUPPER--!
W-W-WE'RE THE BOYS YE CAN RELY ON, SIR!
MY CUP FUCKIN' RUNNETH OVER.
UM...DID BEEZER SAY ANYTHIN' TO YE, MISTER TUPPER, SIR?
'CAUSE HE KEEPS SORTA WINKIN' AT US AN' ALL, LIKE HE KENS WHAT'S GOIN' ON...

AYE, HE'S HAD HIS TONGUE UP MY CRACK EVER SINCE I CAME IN HERE. BUT ALL HE KENS IS THAT IF I'M HANGIN' AROUND THIS DUMP I MUST BE UP TO SOMETHIN', SO HE'S HOPIN' I'LL BRING HIM IN FOR A SLICE O' THE PIE.

HE'S FUCKIN' WELL DREAMIN'. THE LAST TIME I TRUSTED THE DOSS CUNT I LOST FIVE GRAND'S WORTH O' BACCY.

AYE, YOU KEEP ON WAVIN', FUCK-FLAPS.

THAT'S WHY I'VE GOT YER BOSS ON THIS ONE. HE'S A PRICK, BUT HE SEEMS TO MORE OR LESS KEN WHAT HE'S DOIN'.

BOSS? YE MEAN--?

THAT BIG FRUIT'S NO' OUR BOSS, HE'S JUST THIS WANKER WAS AHEAD O' US IN SCHOOL!

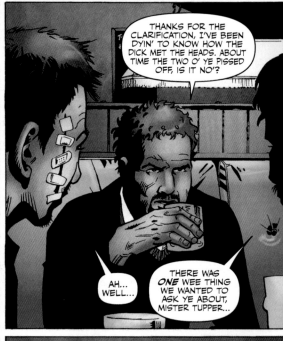

THANKS FOR THE CLARIFICATION, I'VE BEEN DYIN' TO KNOW HOW THE DICK MET THE HEADS. ABOUT TIME THE TWO O' YE PISSED OFF, IS IT NO'?

AH... WELL...

THERE WAS ONE WEE THING WE WANTED TO ASK YE ABOUT, MISTER TUPPER...

OH AYE?

WE, WE GOT A BIT WORRIED ABOUT WHAT WE'RE DOIN', YE KEN? WI' THE--THE GEAR, LIKE...

AYE, I MEAN YE HEAR ALL SORTS O' THINGS, DON'T YE?

SO WE HAD A WEE GOOGLE. HERE.

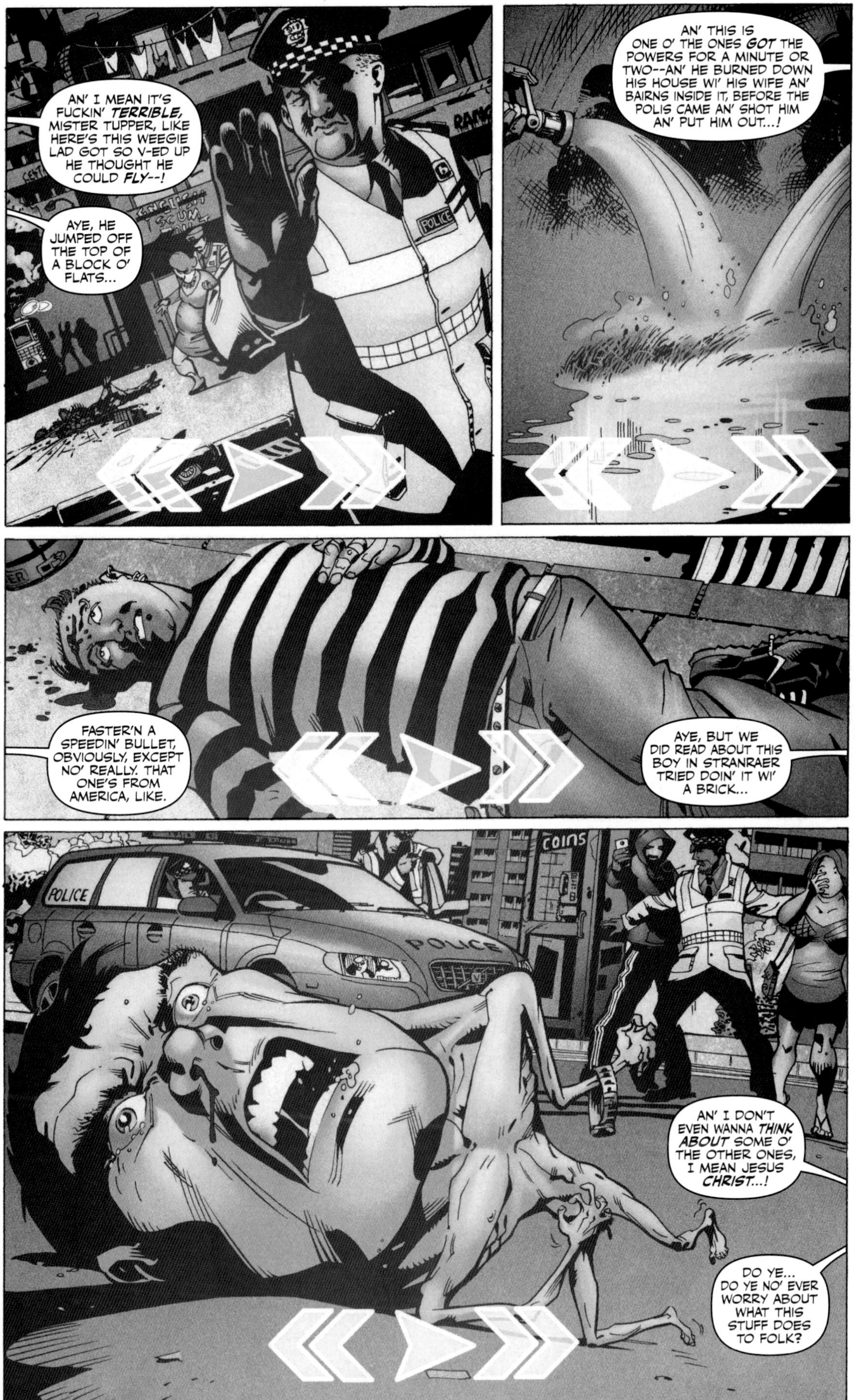

AN' I MEAN IT'S FUCKIN' ***TERRIBLE,*** MISTER TUPPER, LIKE HERE'S THIS WEEGIE LAD GOT SO V-ED UP HE THOUGHT HE COULD ***FLY--!***
AYE, HE JUMPED OFF THE TOP OF A BLOCK O' FLATS...
POLICE
AN' THIS IS ONE O' THE ONES ***GOT*** THE POWERS FOR A MINUTE OR TWO--AN' HE BURNED DOWN HIS HOUSE WI' HIS WIFE AN' BAIRNS INSIDE IT, BEFORE THE POLIS CAME AN' SHOT HIM AN' PUT HIM OUT...!
FASTER'N A SPEEDIN' BULLET, OBVIOUSLY, EXCEPT NO' REALLY. THAT ONE'S FROM AMERICA, LIKE.
AYE, BUT WE DID READ ABOUT THIS BOY IN STRANRAER TRIED DOIN' IT WI' A BRICK...
POLICE
COINS
POLICE
AN' I DON'T EVEN WANNA ***THINK ABOUT*** SOME O' THE OTHER ONES, I MEAN JESUS ***CHRIST...!***
DO YE... DO YE NO' EVER WORRY ABOUT WHAT THIS STUFF DOES TO FOLK?

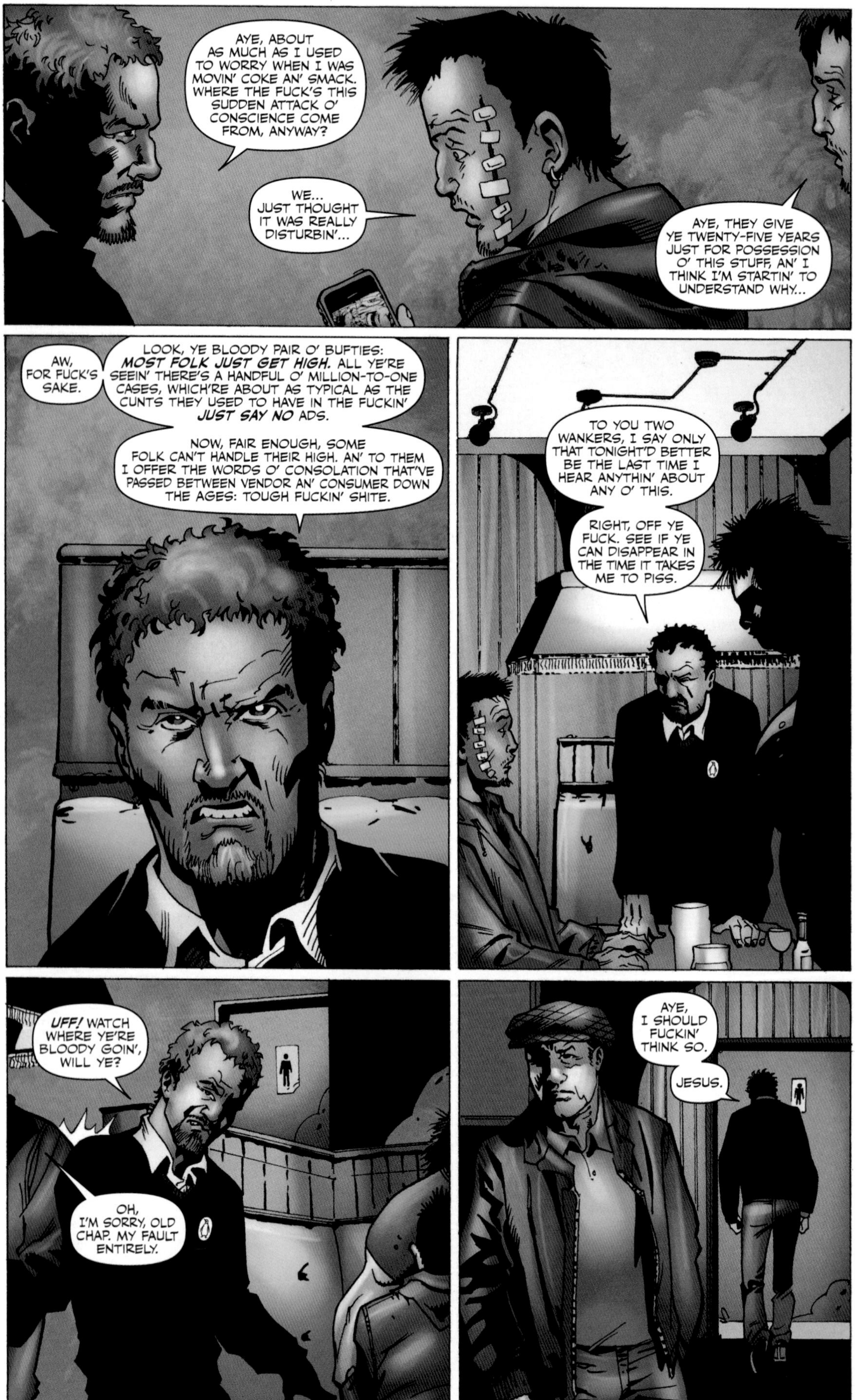
AYE, ABOUT AS MUCH AS I USED TO WORRY WHEN I WAS MOVIN' COKE AN' SMACK. WHERE THE FUCK'S THIS SUDDEN ATTACK O' CONSCIENCE COME FROM, ANYWAY?
WE... JUST THOUGHT IT WAS REALLY DISTURBIN'...
AYE, THEY GIVE YE TWENTY-FIVE YEARS JUST FOR POSSESSION O' THIS STUFF, AN' I THINK I'M STARTIN' TO UNDERSTAND WHY...
AW, FOR FUCK'S SAKE.
LOOK, YE BLOODY PAIR O' BUFTIES: *MOST FOLK JUST GET HIGH.* ALL YE'RE SEEIN' THERE'S A HANDFUL O' MILLION-TO-ONE CASES, WHICH'RE ABOUT AS TYPICAL AS THE CUNTS THEY USED TO HAVE IN THE FUCKIN' *JUST SAY NO* ADS.
NOW, FAIR ENOUGH, SOME FOLK CAN'T HANDLE THEIR HIGH. AN' TO THEM I OFFER THE WORDS O' CONSOLATION THAT'VE PASSED BETWEEN VENDOR AN' CONSUMER DOWN THE AGES: TOUGH FUCKIN' SHITE.
TO YOU TWO WANKERS, I SAY ONLY THAT TONIGHT'D BETTER BE THE LAST TIME I HEAR ANYTHIN' ABOUT ANY O' THIS.
RIGHT, OFF YE FUCK. SEE IF YE CAN DISAPPEAR IN THE TIME IT TAKES ME TO PISS.
UFF! WATCH WHERE YE'RE BLOODY GOIN', WILL YE?
OH, I'M SORRY, OLD CHAP. MY FAULT ENTIRELY.
AYE, I SHOULD FUCKIN' THINK SO.
JESUS.

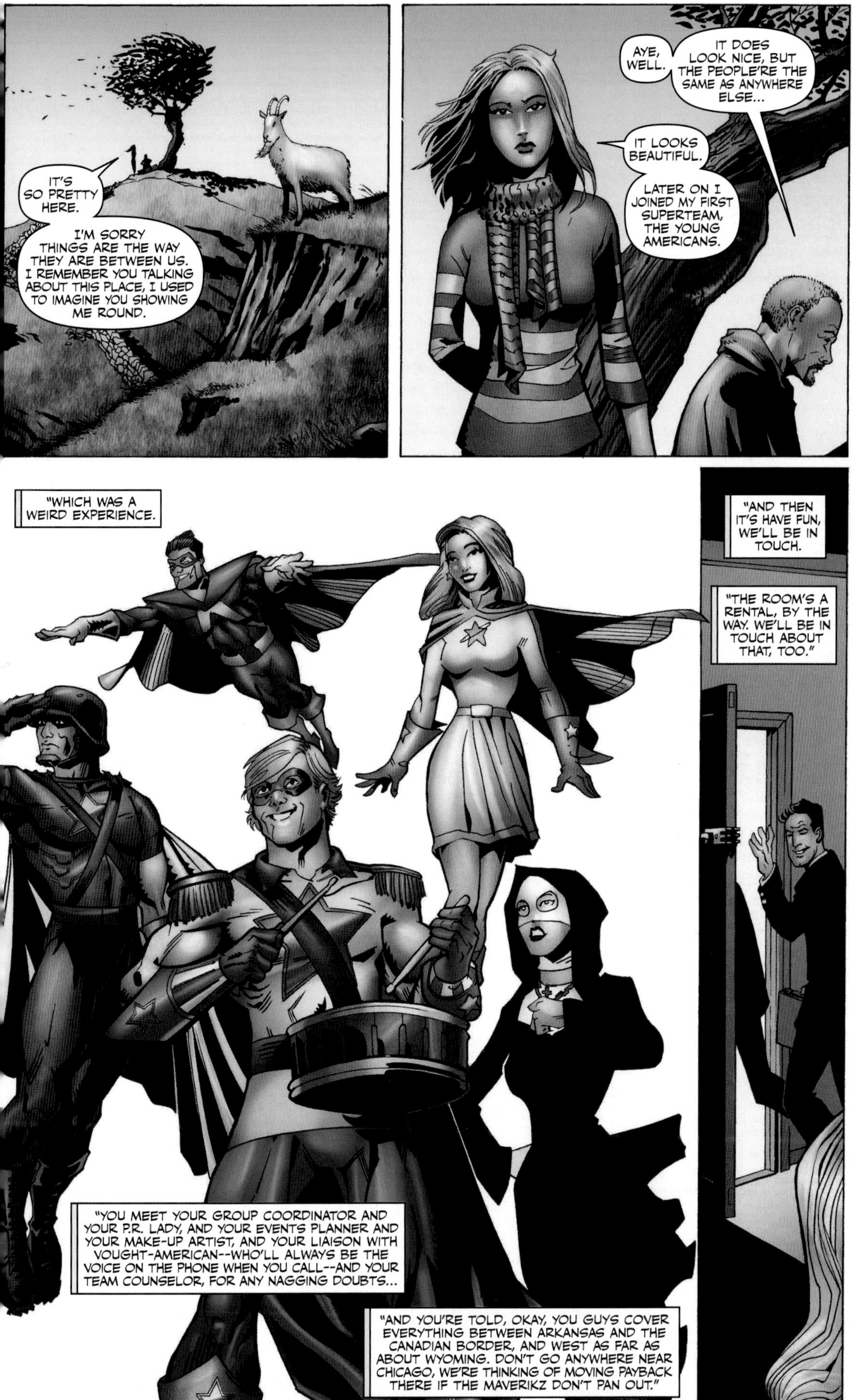
IT'S SO PRETTY HERE.
I'M SORRY THINGS ARE THE WAY THEY ARE BETWEEN US. I REMEMBER YOU TALKING ABOUT THIS PLACE, I USED TO IMAGINE YOU SHOWING ME ROUND.
AYE, WELL.
IT DOES LOOK NICE, BUT THE PEOPLE'RE THE SAME AS ANYWHERE ELSE...
IT LOOKS BEAUTIFUL.
LATER ON I JOINED MY FIRST SUPERTEAM, THE YOUNG AMERICANS.
"WHICH WAS A WEIRD EXPERIENCE.
"AND THEN IT'S HAVE FUN, WE'LL BE IN TOUCH.
"THE ROOM'S A RENTAL, BY THE WAY. WE'LL BE IN TOUCH ABOUT THAT, TOO."
"YOU MEET YOUR GROUP COORDINATOR AND YOUR P.R. LADY, AND YOUR EVENTS PLANNER AND YOUR MAKE-UP ARTIST, AND YOUR LIAISON WITH VOUGHT-AMERICAN--WHO'LL ALWAYS BE THE VOICE ON THE PHONE WHEN YOU CALL--AND YOUR TEAM COUNSELOR, FOR ANY NAGGING DOUBTS...
"AND YOU'RE TOLD, OKAY, YOU GUYS COVER EVERYTHING BETWEEN ARKANSAS AND THE CANADIAN BORDER, AND WEST AS FAR AS ABOUT WYOMING. DON'T GO ANYWHERE NEAR CHICAGO, WE'RE THINKING OF MOVING PAYBACK THERE IF THE MAVERIKZ DON'T PAN OUT."

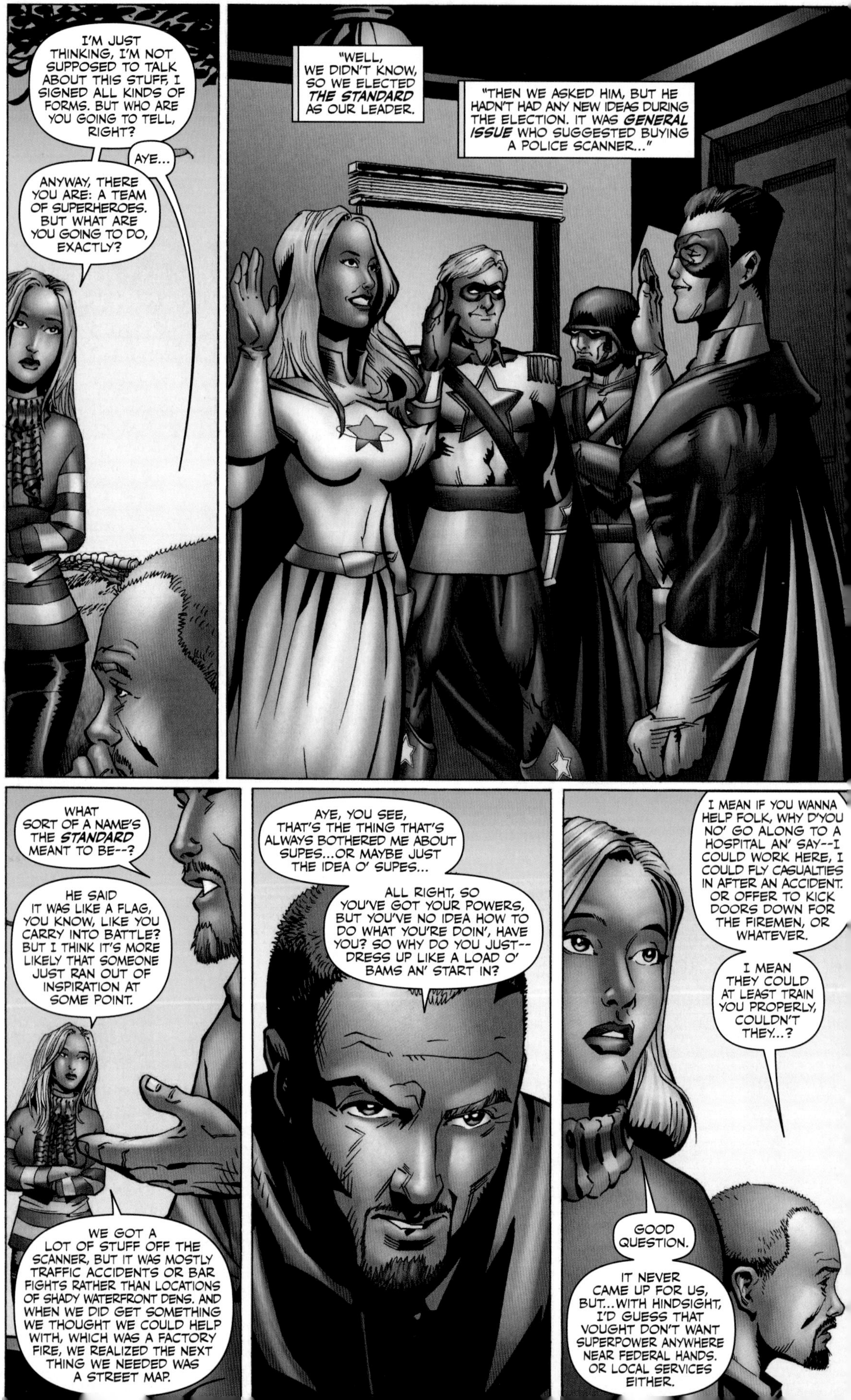
I'M JUST THINKING, I'M NOT SUPPOSED TO TALK ABOUT THIS STUFF, I SIGNED ALL KINDS OF FORMS. BUT WHO ARE YOU GOING TO TELL, RIGHT?
AYE...
ANYWAY, THERE YOU ARE: A TEAM OF SUPERHEROES. BUT WHAT ARE YOU GOING TO DO, EXACTLY?
"WELL, WE DIDN'T KNOW, SO WE ELECTED THE STANDARD AS OUR LEADER.
"THEN WE ASKED HIM, BUT HE HADN'T HAD ANY NEW IDEAS DURING THE ELECTION. IT WAS GENERAL ISSUE WHO SUGGESTED BUYING A POLICE SCANNER..."
WHAT SORT OF A NAME'S THE STANDARD MEANT TO BE--?
HE SAID IT WAS LIKE A FLAG, YOU KNOW, LIKE YOU CARRY INTO BATTLE? BUT I THINK IT'S MORE LIKELY THAT SOMEONE JUST RAN OUT OF INSPIRATION AT SOME POINT.
WE GOT A LOT OF STUFF OFF THE SCANNER, BUT IT WAS MOSTLY TRAFFIC ACCIDENTS OR BAR FIGHTS RATHER THAN LOCATIONS OF SHADY WATERFRONT DENS. AND WHEN WE DID GET SOMETHING WE THOUGHT WE COULD HELP WITH, WHICH WAS A FACTORY FIRE, WE REALIZED THE NEXT THING WE NEEDED WAS A STREET MAP.
AYE, YOU SEE, THAT'S THE THING THAT'S ALWAYS BOTHERED ME ABOUT SUPES...OR MAYBE JUST THE IDEA O' SUPES...
ALL RIGHT, SO YOU'VE GOT YOUR POWERS, BUT YOU'VE NO IDEA HOW TO DO WHAT YOU'RE DOIN', HAVE YOU? SO WHY DO YOU JUST--DRESS UP LIKE A LOAD O' BAMS AN' START IN?
I MEAN IF YOU WANNA HELP FOLK, WHY D'YOU NO' GO ALONG TO A HOSPITAL AN' SAY--I COULD WORK HERE, I COULD FLY CASUALTIES IN AFTER AN ACCIDENT. OR OFFER TO KICK DOORS DOWN FOR THE FIREMEN, OR WHATEVER.
I MEAN THEY COULD AT LEAST TRAIN YOU PROPERLY, COULDN'T THEY...?
GOOD QUESTION.
IT NEVER CAME UP FOR US, BUT...WITH HINDSIGHT, I'D GUESS THAT VOUGHT DON'T WANT SUPERPOWER ANYWHERE NEAR FEDERAL HANDS. OR LOCAL SERVICES EITHER.

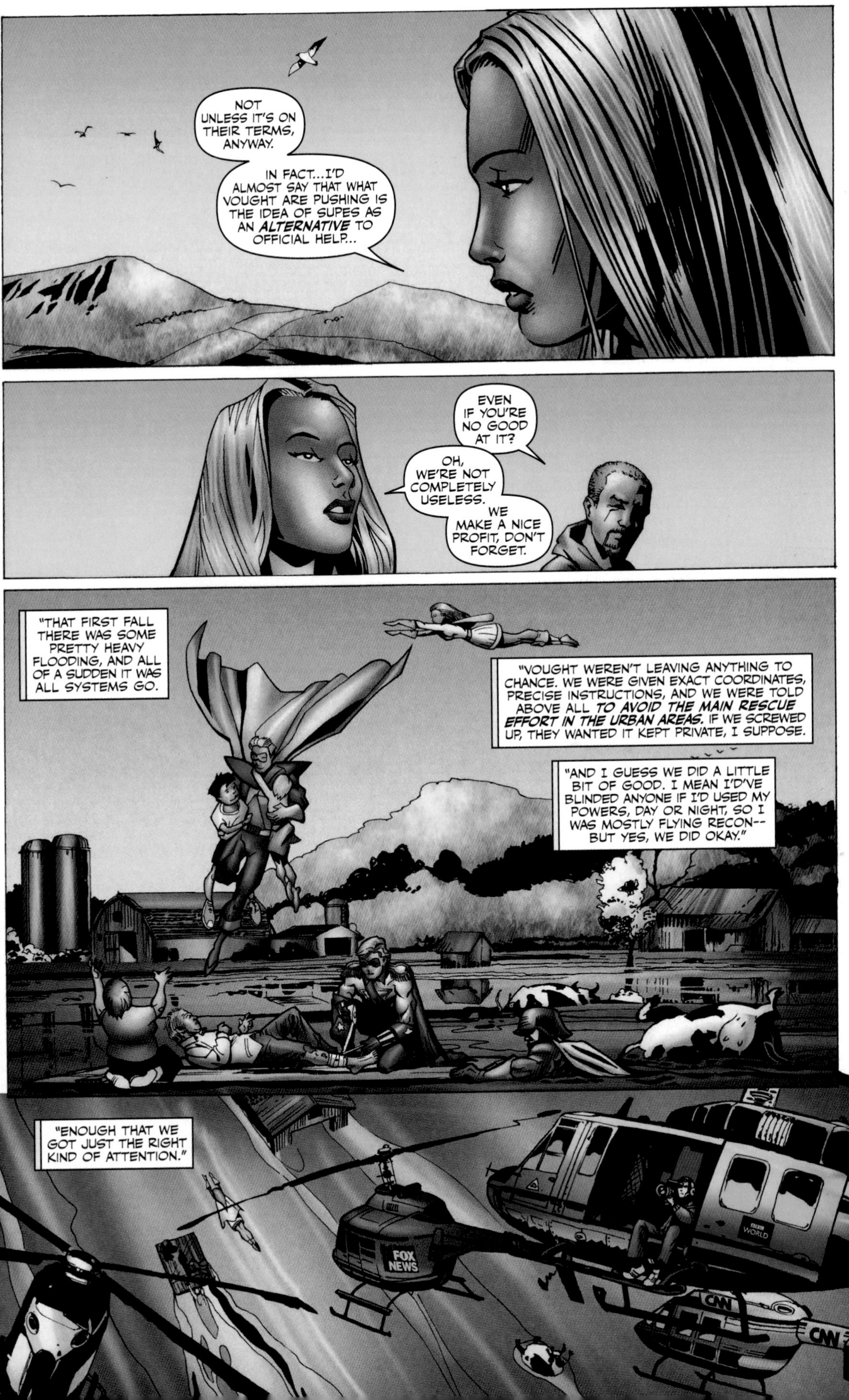

NOT UNLESS IT'S ON THEIR TERMS, ANYWAY.
IN FACT...I'D ALMOST SAY THAT WHAT VOUGHT ARE PUSHING IS THE IDEA OF SUPES AS AN *ALTERNATIVE* TO OFFICIAL HELP...
EVEN IF YOU'RE NO GOOD AT IT?
OH, WE'RE NOT COMPLETELY USELESS.
WE MAKE A NICE PROFIT, DON'T FORGET.
"THAT FIRST FALL THERE WAS SOME PRETTY HEAVY FLOODING, AND ALL OF A SUDDEN IT WAS ALL SYSTEMS GO.
"VOUGHT WEREN'T LEAVING ANYTHING TO CHANCE. WE WERE GIVEN EXACT COORDINATES, PRECISE INSTRUCTIONS, AND WE WERE TOLD ABOVE ALL ***TO AVOID THE MAIN RESCUE EFFORT IN THE URBAN AREAS.*** IF WE SCREWED UP, THEY WANTED IT KEPT PRIVATE, I SUPPOSE.
"AND I GUESS WE DID A LITTLE BIT OF GOOD. I MEAN I'D'VE BLINDED ANYONE IF I'D USED MY POWERS, DAY OR NIGHT, SO I WAS MOSTLY FLYING RECON--BUT YES, WE DID OKAY."
"ENOUGH THAT WE GOT JUST THE RIGHT KIND OF ATTENTION."
FOX NEWS
BBC WORLD
CNN
CNN

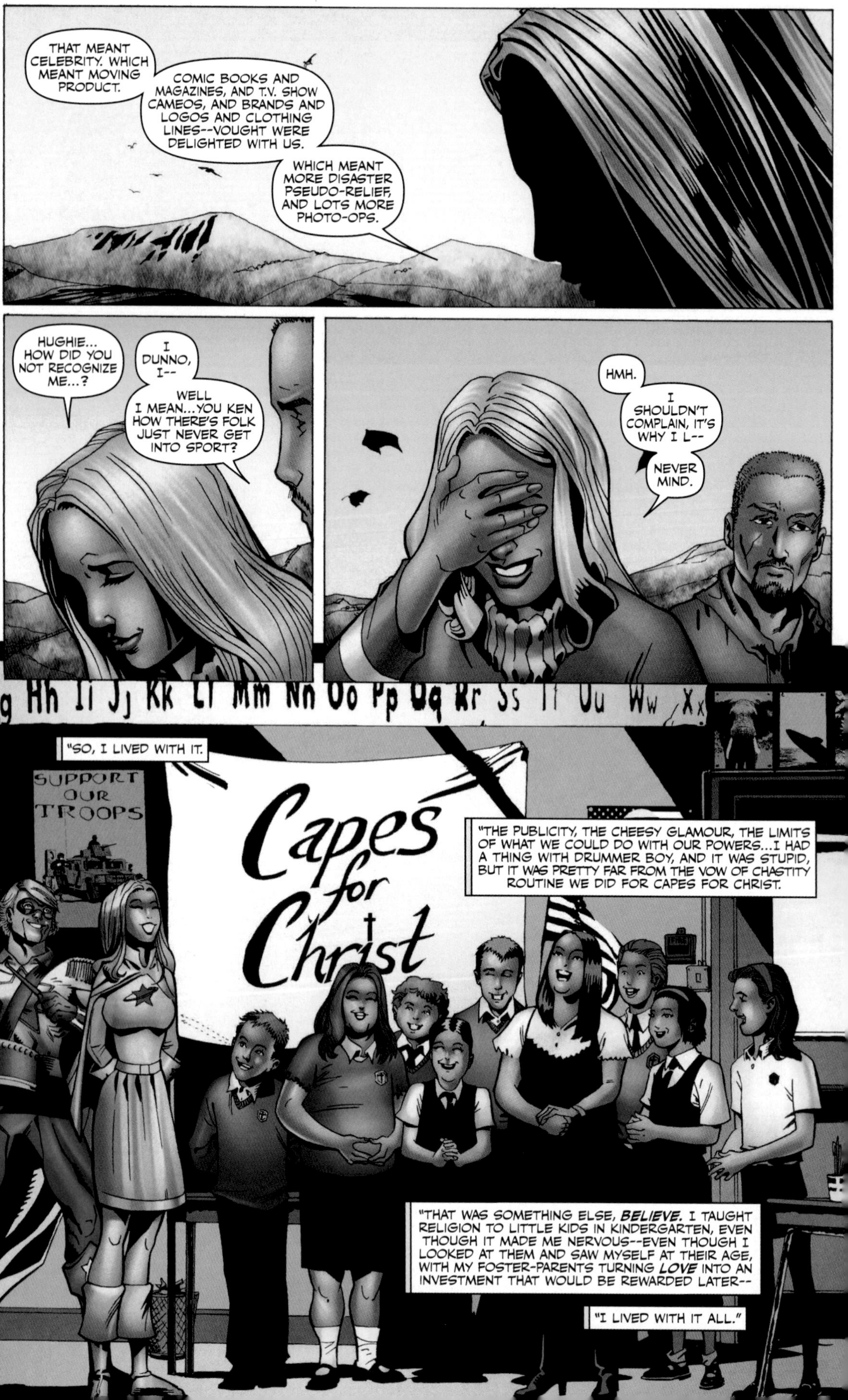
THAT MEANT CELEBRITY. WHICH MEANT MOVING PRODUCT.
COMIC BOOKS AND MAGAZINES, AND T.V. SHOW CAMEOS, AND BRANDS AND LOGOS AND CLOTHING LINES--VOUGHT WERE DELIGHTED WITH US.
WHICH MEANT MORE DISASTER PSEUDO-RELIEF, AND LOTS MORE PHOTO-OPS.
HUGHIE... HOW DID YOU NOT RECOGNIZE ME...?
I DUNNO, I--
WELL I MEAN...YOU KEN HOW THERE'S FOLK JUST NEVER GET INTO SPORT?
HMH.
I SHOULDN'T COMPLAIN, IT'S WHY I L--
NEVER MIND.
"SO, I LIVED WITH IT.
SUPPORT OUR TROOPS
Capes for Christ
"THE PUBLICITY, THE CHEESY GLAMOUR, THE LIMITS OF WHAT WE COULD DO WITH OUR POWERS...I HAD A THING WITH DRUMMER BOY, AND IT WAS STUPID, BUT IT WAS PRETTY FAR FROM THE VOW OF CHASTITY ROUTINE WE DID FOR CAPES FOR CHRIST.
"THAT WAS SOMETHING ELSE, *BELIEVE.* I TAUGHT RELIGION TO LITTLE KIDS IN KINDERGARTEN, EVEN THOUGH IT MADE ME NERVOUS--EVEN THOUGH I LOOKED AT THEM AND SAW MYSELF AT THEIR AGE, WITH MY FOSTER-PARENTS TURNING *LOVE* INTO AN INVESTMENT THAT WOULD BE REWARDED LATER--
"I LIVED WITH IT ALL."

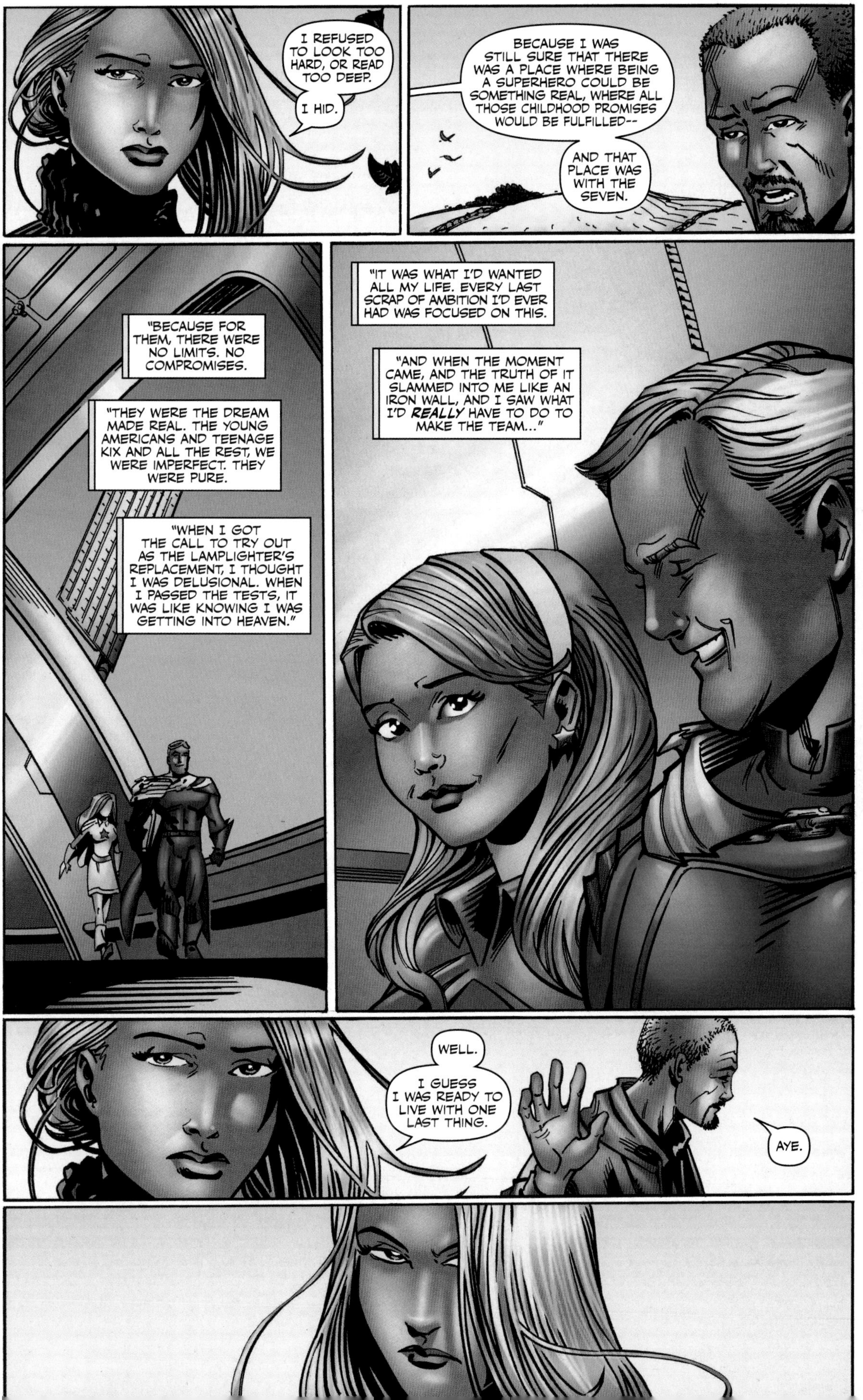
I REFUSED TO LOOK TOO HARD, OR READ TOO DEEP.
I HID.
BECAUSE I WAS STILL SURE THAT THERE WAS A PLACE WHERE BEING A SUPERHERO COULD BE SOMETHING REAL, WHERE ALL THOSE CHILDHOOD PROMISES WOULD BE FULFILLED--
AND THAT PLACE WAS WITH THE SEVEN.
"BECAUSE FOR THEM, THERE WERE NO LIMITS. NO COMPROMISES.
"THEY WERE THE DREAM MADE REAL. THE YOUNG AMERICANS AND TEENAGE KIX AND ALL THE REST, WE WERE IMPERFECT. THEY WERE PURE.
"WHEN I GOT THE CALL TO TRY OUT AS THE LAMPLIGHTER'S REPLACEMENT, I THOUGHT I WAS DELUSIONAL. WHEN I PASSED THE TESTS, IT WAS LIKE KNOWING I WAS GETTING INTO HEAVEN."
"IT WAS WHAT I'D WANTED ALL MY LIFE. EVERY LAST SCRAP OF AMBITION I'D EVER HAD WAS FOCUSED ON THIS.
"AND WHEN THE MOMENT CAME, AND THE TRUTH OF IT SLAMMED INTO ME LIKE AN IRON WALL, AND I SAW WHAT I'D *REALLY* HAVE TO DO TO MAKE THE TEAM..."
WELL.
I GUESS I WAS READY TO LIVE WITH ONE LAST THING.
AYE.

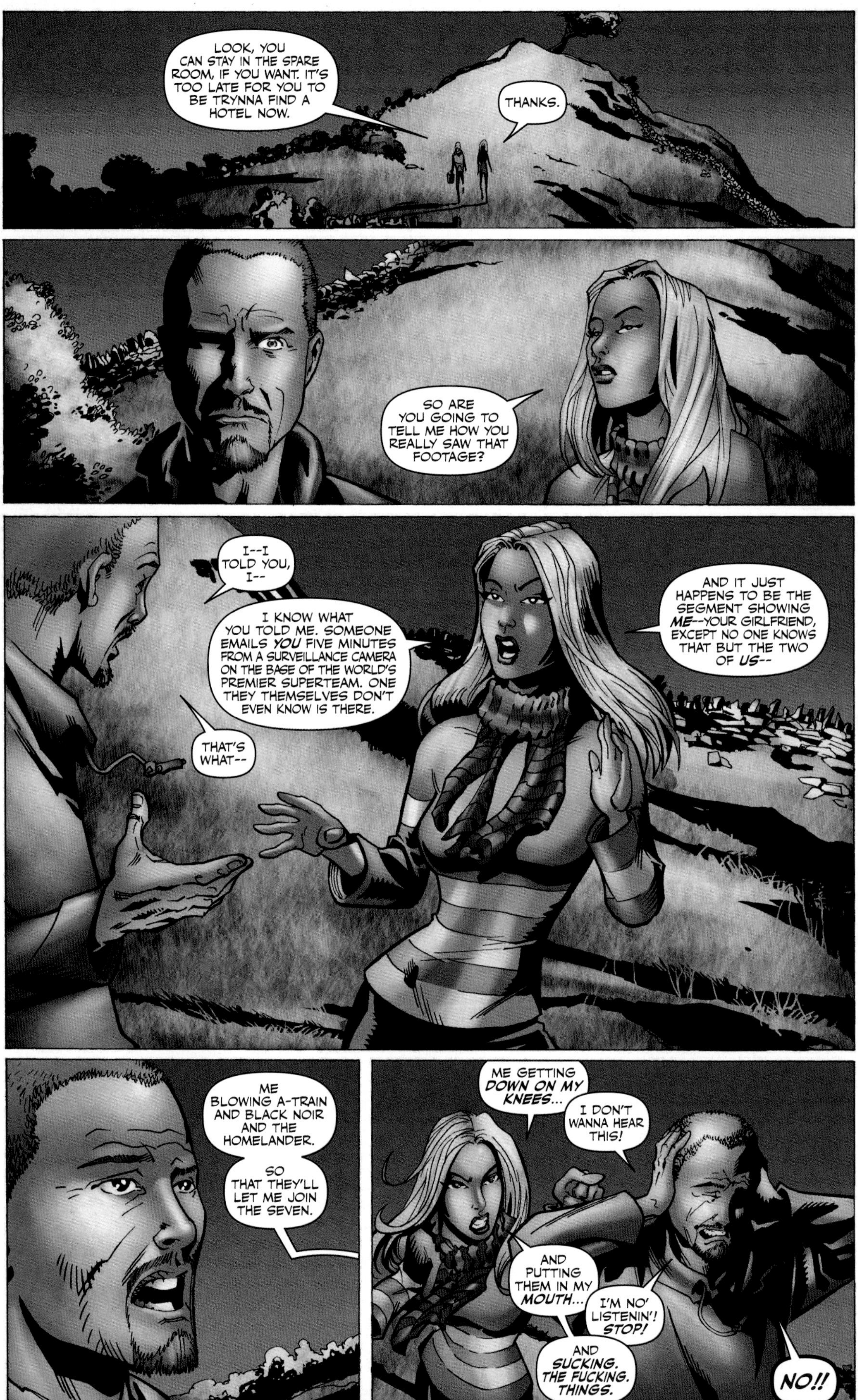
LOOK, YOU CAN STAY IN THE SPARE ROOM, IF YOU WANT. IT'S TOO LATE FOR YOU TO BE TRYNNA FIND A HOTEL NOW.
THANKS.
SO ARE YOU GOING TO TELL ME HOW YOU REALLY SAW THAT FOOTAGE?
I--I TOLD YOU, I--
I KNOW WHAT YOU TOLD ME. SOMEONE EMAILS *YOU* FIVE MINUTES FROM A SURVEILLANCE CAMERA ON THE BASE OF THE WORLD'S PREMIER SUPERTEAM. ONE THEY THEMSELVES DON'T EVEN KNOW IS THERE.
THAT'S WHAT--
AND IT JUST HAPPENS TO BE THE SEGMENT SHOWING *ME*--YOUR GIRLFRIEND, EXCEPT NO ONE KNOWS THAT BUT THE TWO OF *US*--
ME BLOWING A-TRAIN AND BLACK NOIR AND THE HOMELANDER.
SO THAT THEY'LL LET ME JOIN THE SEVEN.
ME GETTING *DOWN ON MY KNEES*...
I DON'T WANNA HEAR THIS!
AND PUTTING THEM IN MY *MOUTH*...
I'M NO' LISTENIN'! *STOP!*
AND *SUCKING. THE FUCKING. THINGS.*
NO!!

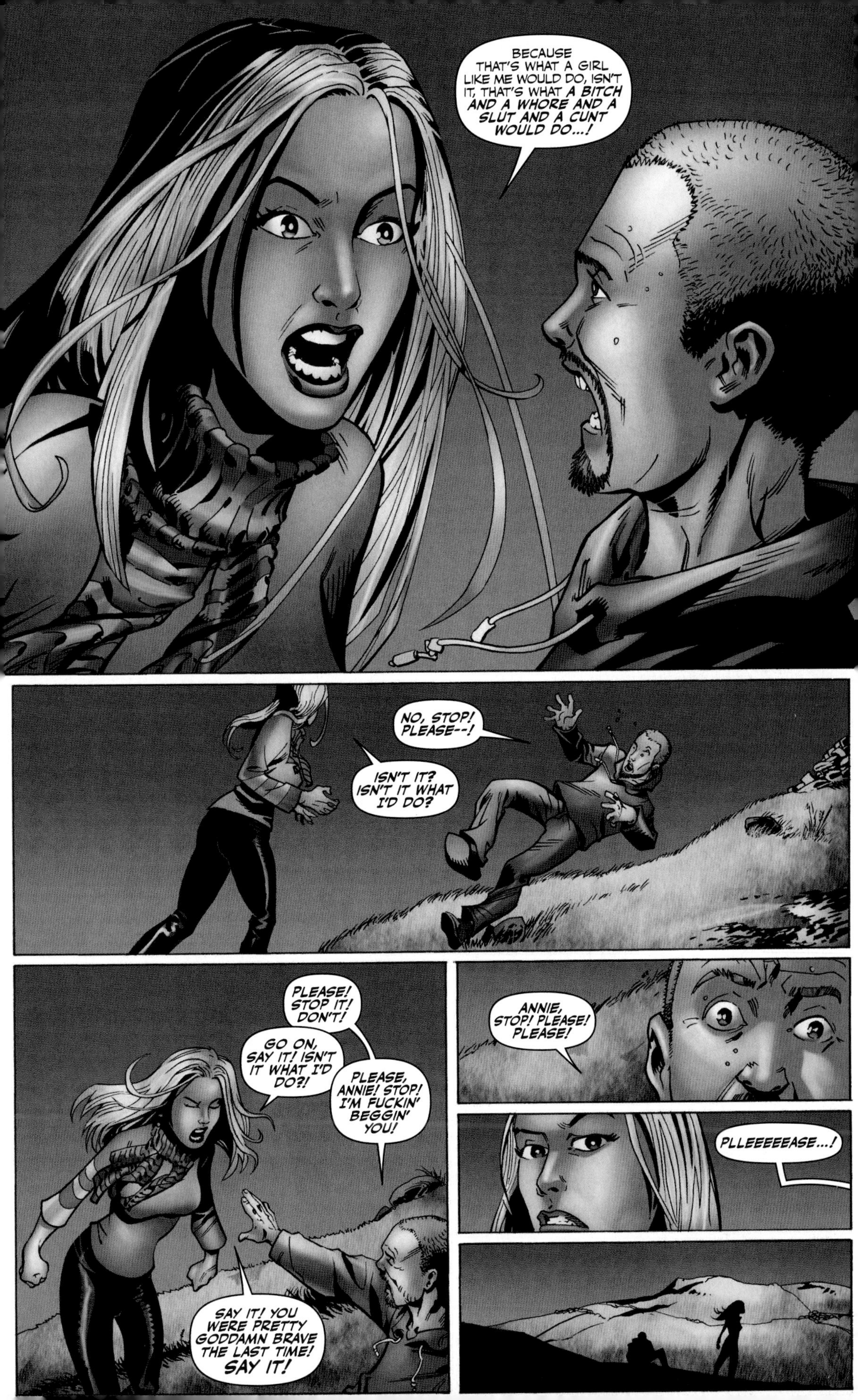
BECAUSE THAT'S WHAT A GIRL LIKE ME WOULD DO, ISN'T IT, THAT'S WHAT A BITCH AND A WHORE AND A SLUT AND A CUNT WOULD DO...!
NO, STOP! PLEASE--!
ISN'T IT? ISN'T IT WHAT I'D DO?
PLEASE! STOP IT! DON'T!
GO ON, SAY IT! ISN'T IT WHAT I'D DO?!
PLEASE, ANNIE! STOP! I'M FUCKIN' BEGGIN' YOU!
SAY IT! YOU WERE PRETTY GODDAMN BRAVE THE LAST TIME! SAY IT!
ANNIE, STOP! PLEASE! PLEASE!
PLLEEEEEASE...!

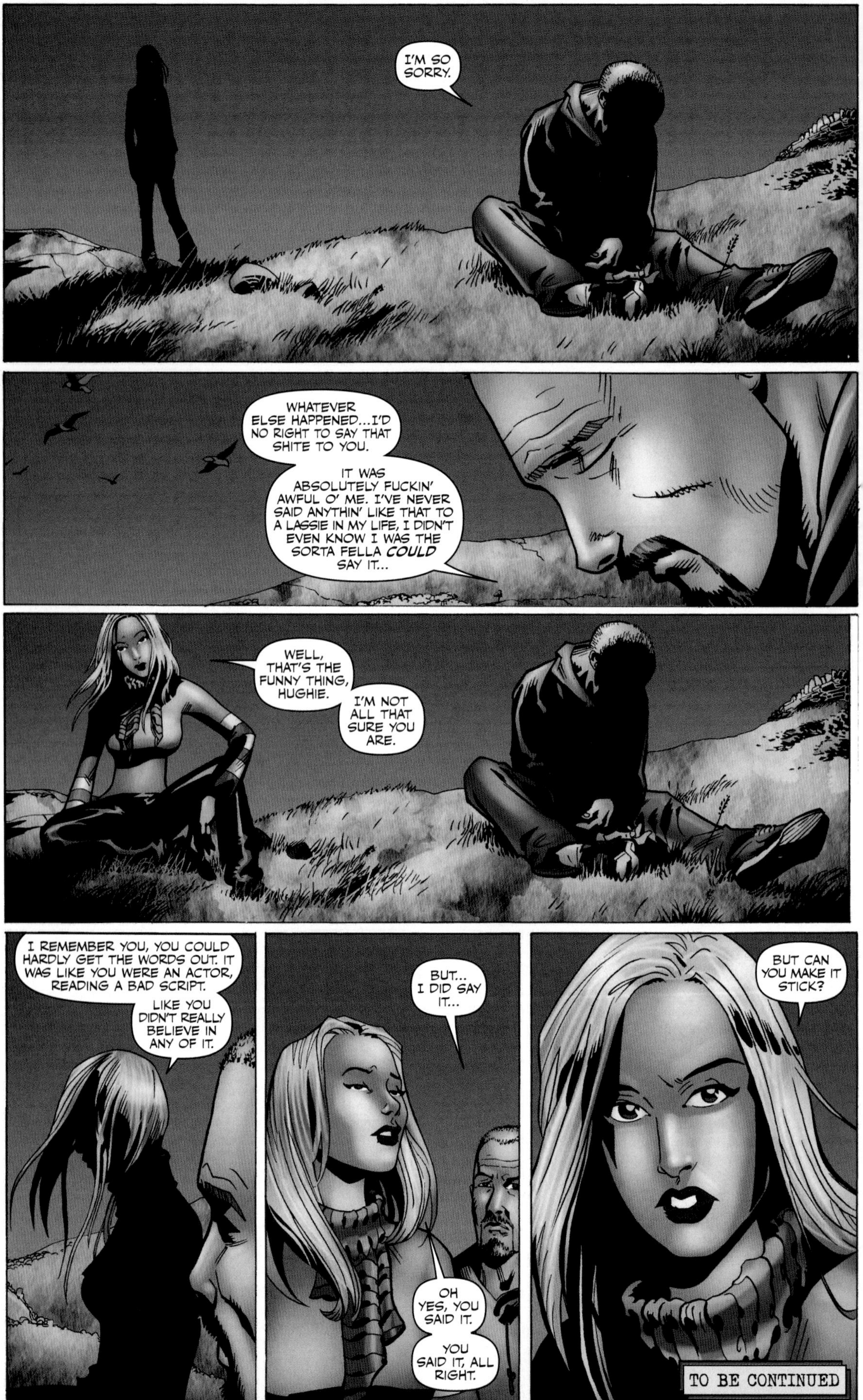
I'M SO SORRY.
WHATEVER ELSE HAPPENED...I'D NO RIGHT TO SAY THAT SHITE TO YOU.
IT WAS ABSOLUTELY FUCKIN' AWFUL O' ME. I'VE NEVER SAID ANYTHIN' LIKE THAT TO A LASSIE IN MY LIFE, I DIDN'T EVEN KNOW I WAS THE SORTA FELLA *COULD* SAY IT...
WELL, THAT'S THE FUNNY THING, HUGHIE.
I'M NOT ALL THAT SURE YOU ARE.
I REMEMBER YOU, YOU COULD HARDLY GET THE WORDS OUT. IT WAS LIKE YOU WERE AN ACTOR, READING A BAD SCRIPT.
LIKE YOU DIDN'T REALLY BELIEVE IN ANY OF IT.
BUT... I DID SAY IT...
OH YES, YOU SAID IT.
YOU SAID IT, ALL RIGHT.
BUT CAN YOU MAKE IT STICK?
TO BE CONTINUED

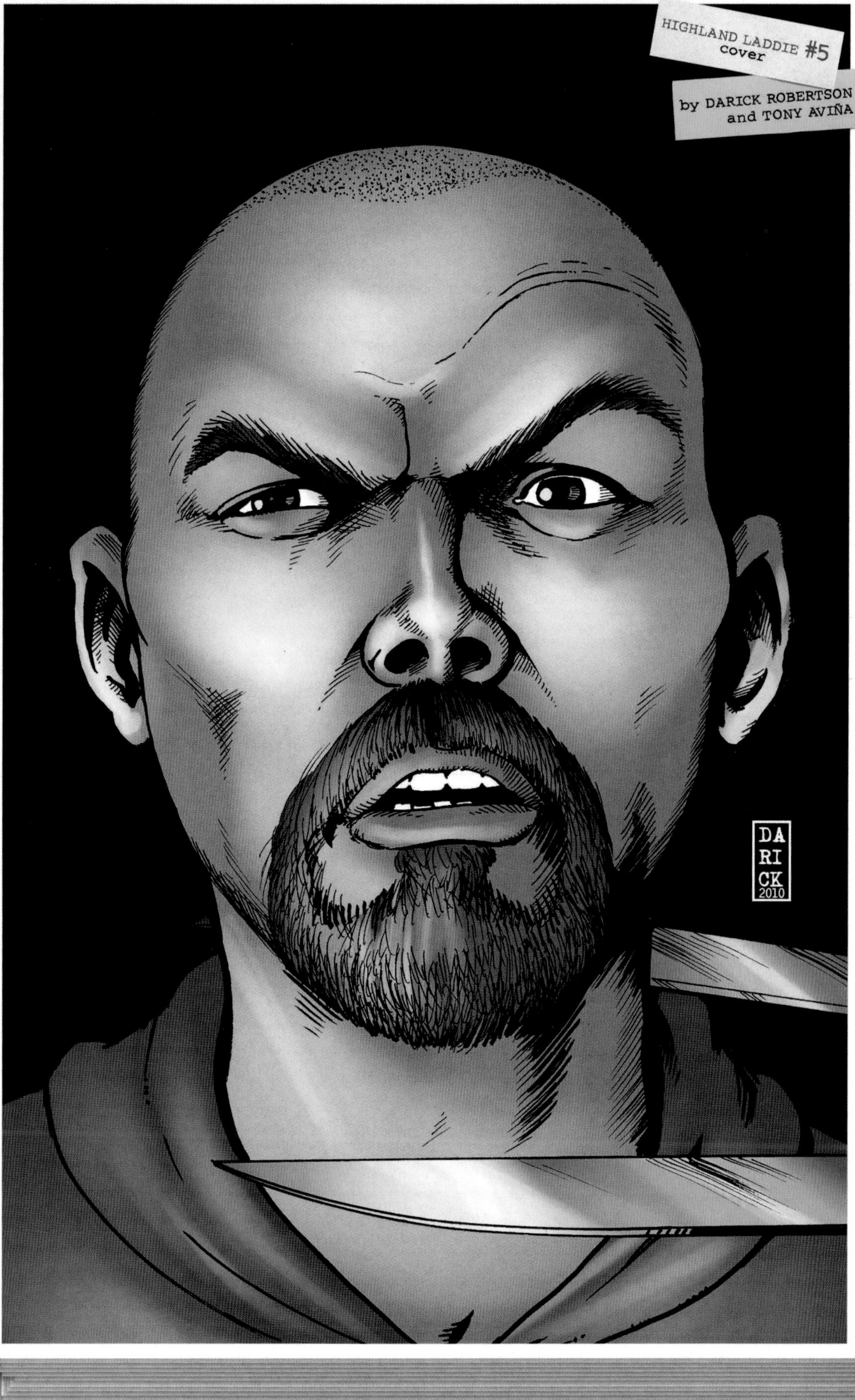
HIGHLAND LADDIE #5
cover
by DARICK ROBERTSON
and TONY AVIÑA
DA
RI
CK
2010

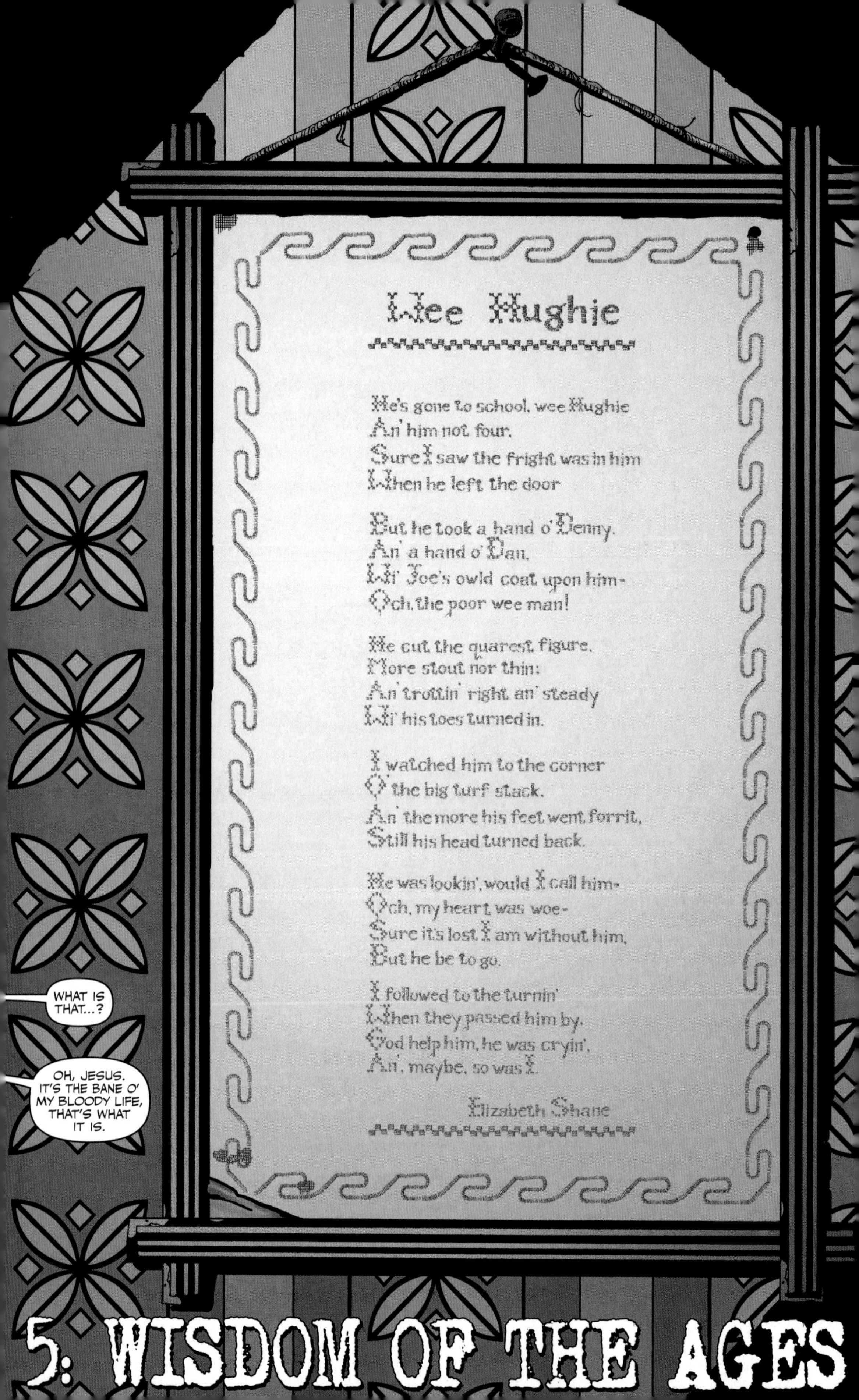

Wee Hughie
He's gone to school, wee Hughie
An' him not four.
Sure I saw the fright was in him
When he left the door
But he took a hand o' Denny.
An' a hand o' Dan,
Wi' Joe's owld coat upon him-
Och, the poor wee man!
He cut the quarest figure,
More stout nor thin:
An' trottin' right an' steady
Wi' his toes turned in.
I watched him to the corner
O' the big turf stack,
An' the more his feet went forrit,
Still his head turned back.
He was lookin', would I call him-
Och, my heart was woe-
Sure it's lost I am without him,
But he be to go.
I followed to the turnin'
When they passed him by,
God help him, he was cryin',
An', maybe, so was I.
Elizabeth Shane
WHAT IS THAT...?
OH, JESUS. IT'S THE BANE O' MY BLOODY LIFE, THAT'S WHAT IT IS.
5: WISDOM OF THE AGES

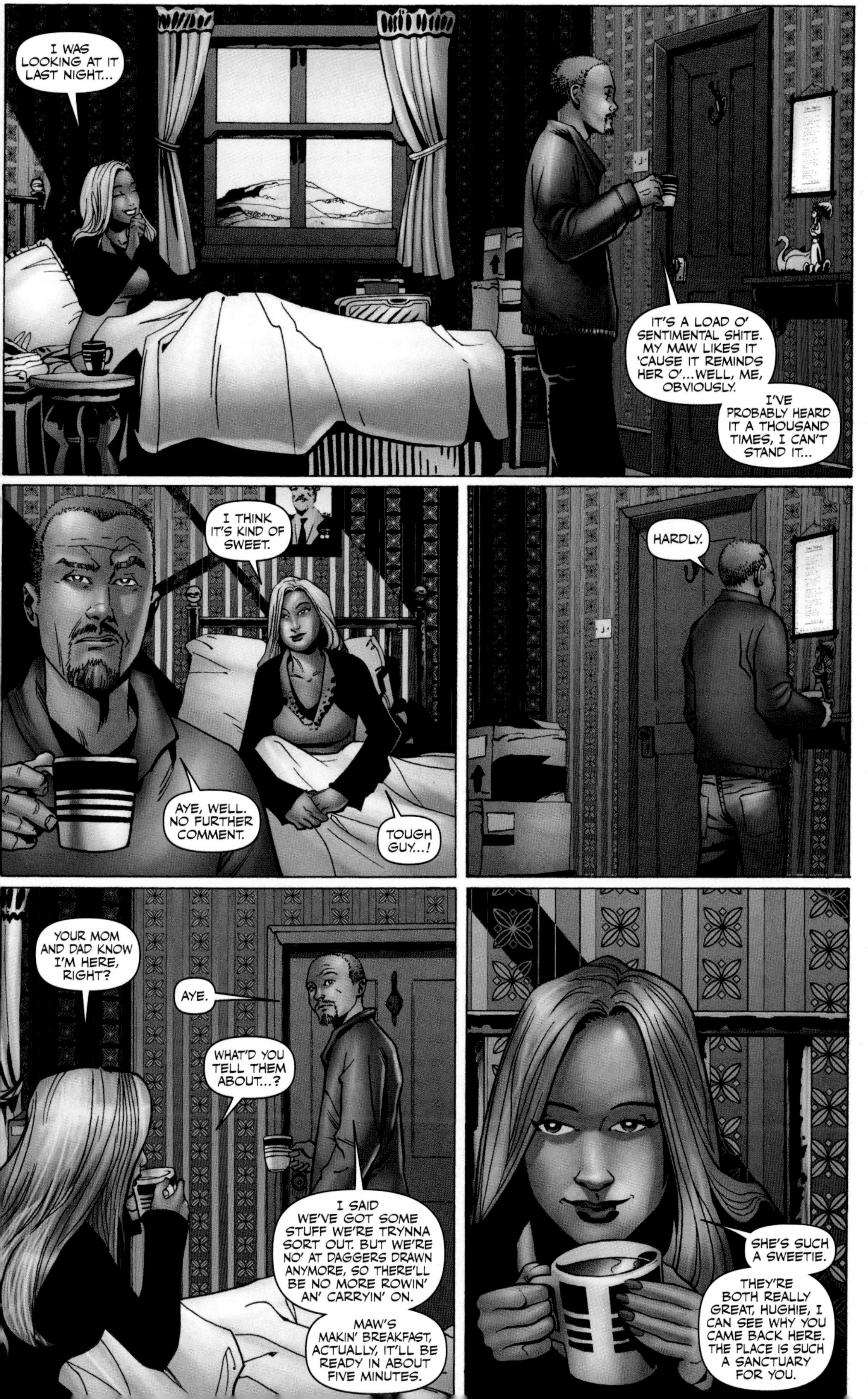
I WAS LOOKING AT IT LAST NIGHT...
IT'S A LOAD O' SENTIMENTAL SHITE. MY MAW LIKES IT 'CAUSE IT REMINDS HER O'...WELL, ME, OBVIOUSLY.
I'VE PROBABLY HEARD IT A THOUSAND TIMES, I CAN'T STAND IT...
I THINK IT'S KIND OF SWEET.
AYE, WELL. NO FURTHER COMMENT.
TOUGH GUY...!
HARDLY.
YOUR MOM AND DAD KNOW I'M HERE, RIGHT?
AYE.
WHAT'D YOU TELL THEM ABOUT...?
I SAID WE'VE GOT SOME STUFF WE'RE TRYNNA SORT OUT. BUT WE'RE NO' AT DAGGERS DRAWN ANYMORE, SO THERE'LL BE NO MORE ROWIN' AN' CARRYIN' ON.
MAW'S MAKIN' BREAKFAST, ACTUALLY, IT'LL BE READY IN ABOUT FIVE MINUTES.
SHE'S SUCH A SWEETIE.
THEY'RE BOTH REALLY GREAT, HUGHIE, I CAN SEE WHY YOU CAME BACK HERE. THE PLACE IS SUCH A SANCTUARY FOR YOU.

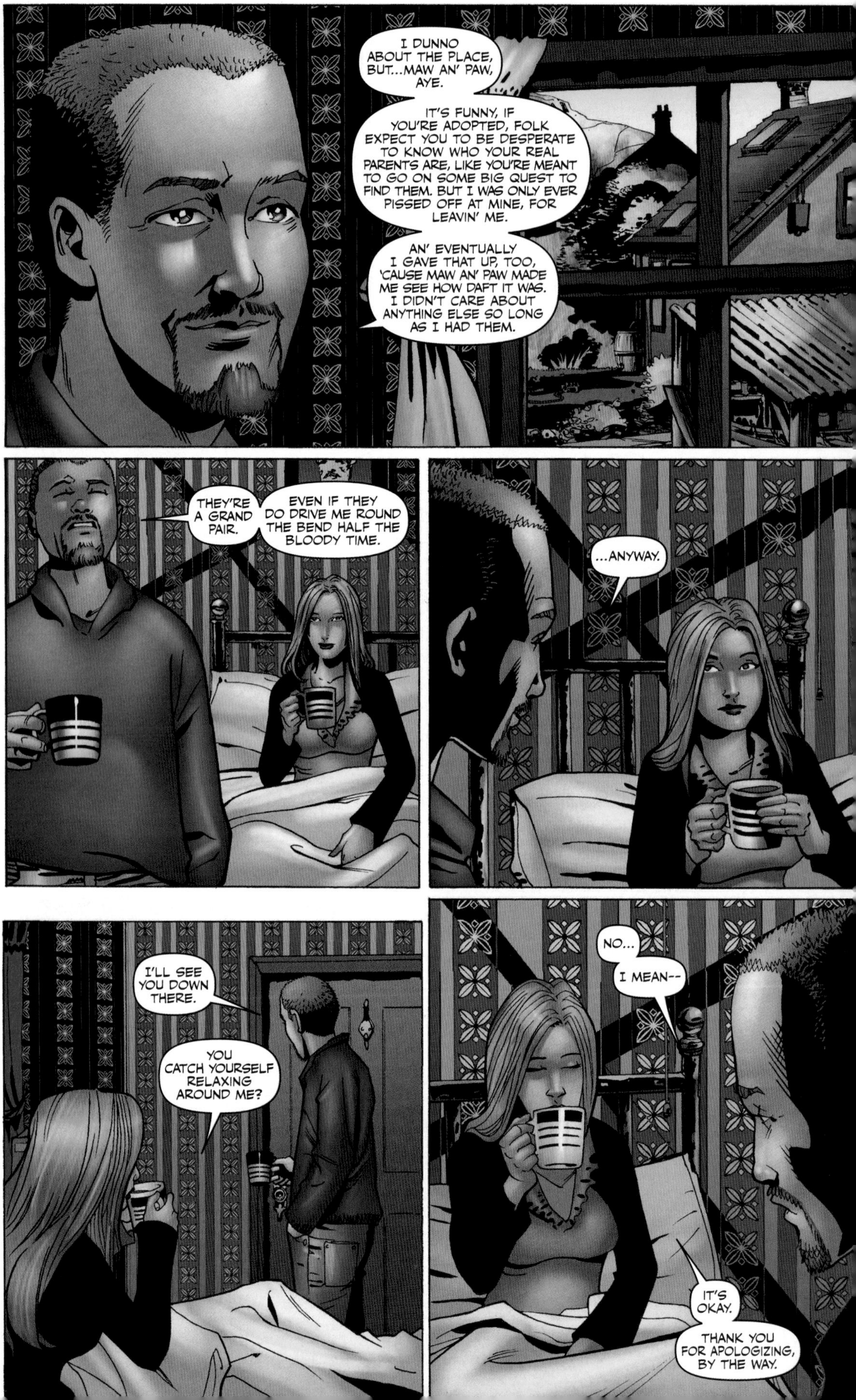
I DUNNO ABOUT THE PLACE, BUT...MAW AN' PAW, AYE.
IT'S FUNNY, IF YOU'RE ADOPTED, FOLK EXPECT YOU TO BE DESPERATE TO KNOW WHO YOUR REAL PARENTS ARE, LIKE YOU'RE MEANT TO GO ON SOME BIG QUEST TO FIND THEM. BUT I WAS ONLY EVER PISSED OFF AT MINE, FOR LEAVIN' ME.
AN' EVENTUALLY I GAVE THAT UP, TOO, 'CAUSE MAW AN' PAW MADE ME SEE HOW DAFT IT WAS. I DIDN'T CARE ABOUT ANYTHING ELSE SO LONG AS I HAD THEM.
THEY'RE A GRAND PAIR.
EVEN IF THEY DO DRIVE ME ROUND THE BEND HALF THE BLOODY TIME.
...ANYWAY.
I'LL SEE YOU DOWN THERE.
YOU CATCH YOURSELF RELAXING AROUND ME?
NO...
I MEAN--
IT'S OKAY.
THANK YOU FOR APOLOGIZING, BY THE WAY.

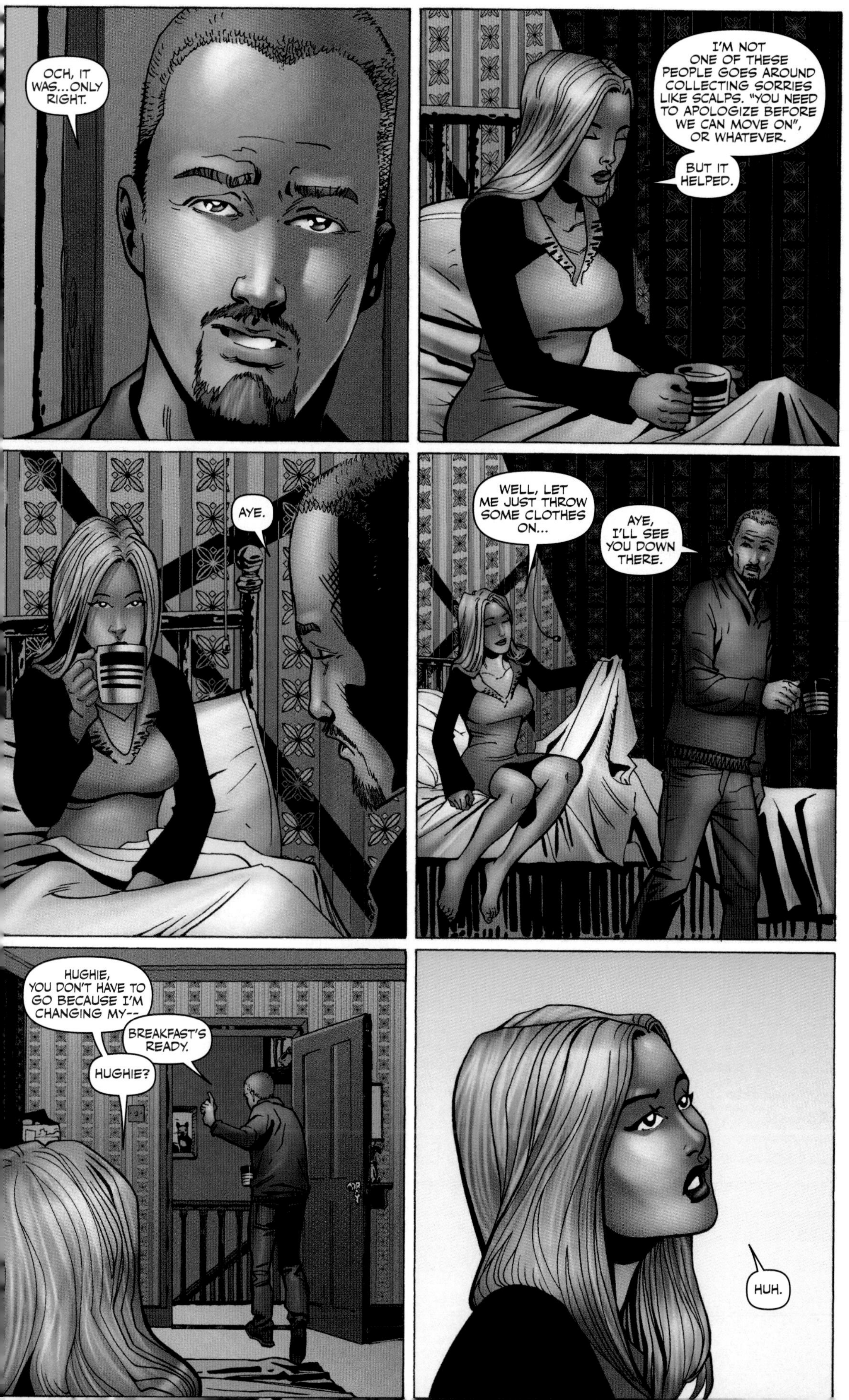
OCH, IT WAS...ONLY RIGHT.
I'M NOT ONE OF THESE PEOPLE GOES AROUND COLLECTING SORRIES LIKE SCALPS. "YOU NEED TO APOLOGIZE BEFORE WE CAN MOVE ON", OR WHATEVER.
BUT IT HELPED.
AYE.
WELL, LET ME JUST THROW SOME CLOTHES ON...
AYE, I'LL SEE YOU DOWN THERE.
HUGHIE, YOU DON'T HAVE TO GO BECAUSE I'M CHANGING MY--
BREAKFAST'S READY.
HUGHIE?
HUH.

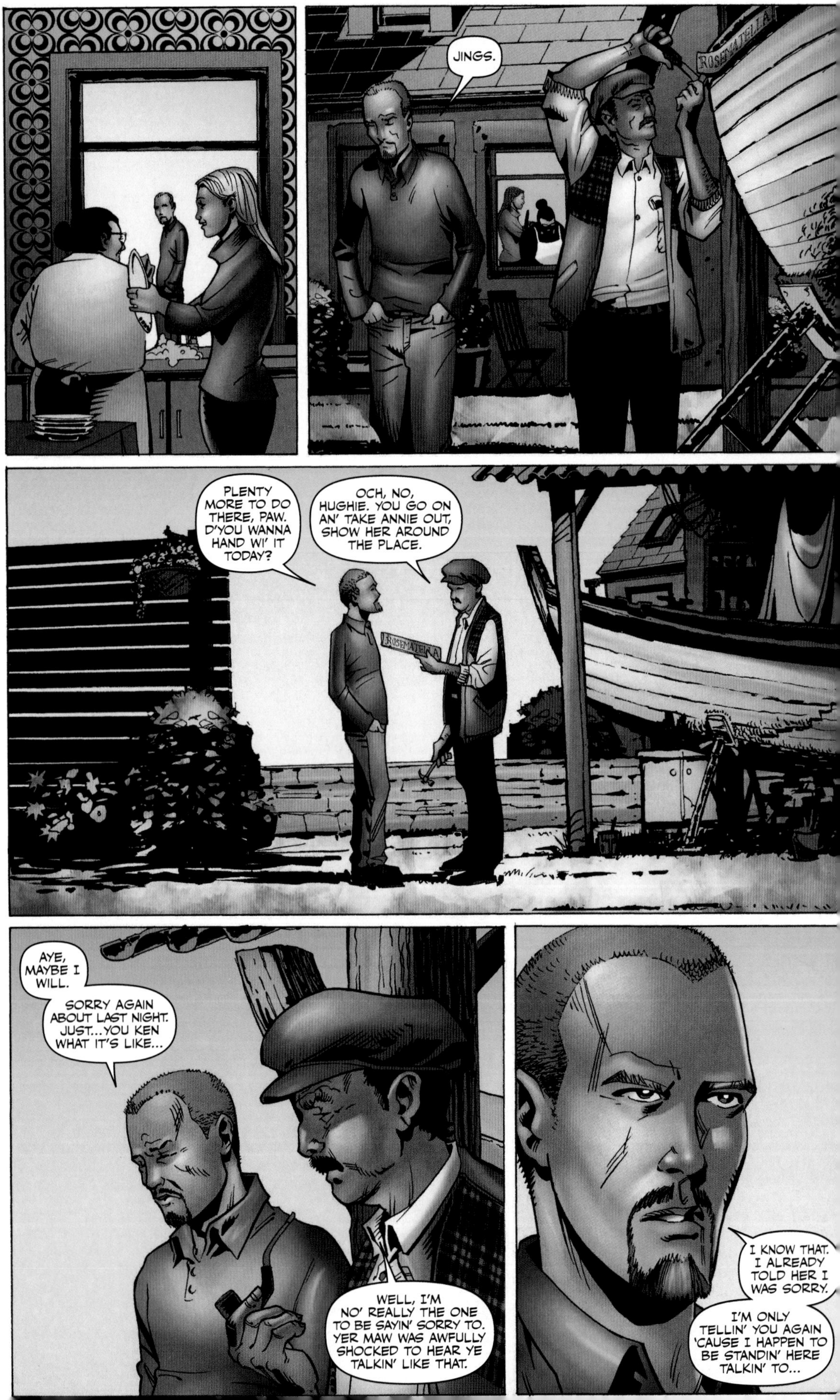
ROSEMATELLA
JINGS.
PLENTY MORE TO DO THERE, PAW. D'YOU WANNA HAND WI' IT TODAY?
OCH, NO, HUGHIE. YOU GO ON AN' TAKE ANNIE OUT, SHOW HER AROUND THE PLACE.
ROSEMATELLA
AYE, MAYBE I WILL.
SORRY AGAIN ABOUT LAST NIGHT. JUST...YOU KEN WHAT IT'S LIKE...
WELL, I'M NO' REALLY THE ONE TO BE SAYIN' SORRY TO. YER MAW WAS AWFULLY SHOCKED TO HEAR YE TALKIN' LIKE THAT.
I KNOW THAT. I ALREADY TOLD HER I WAS SORRY.
I'M ONLY TELLIN' YOU AGAIN 'CAUSE I HAPPEN TO BE STANDIN' HERE TALKIN' TO...

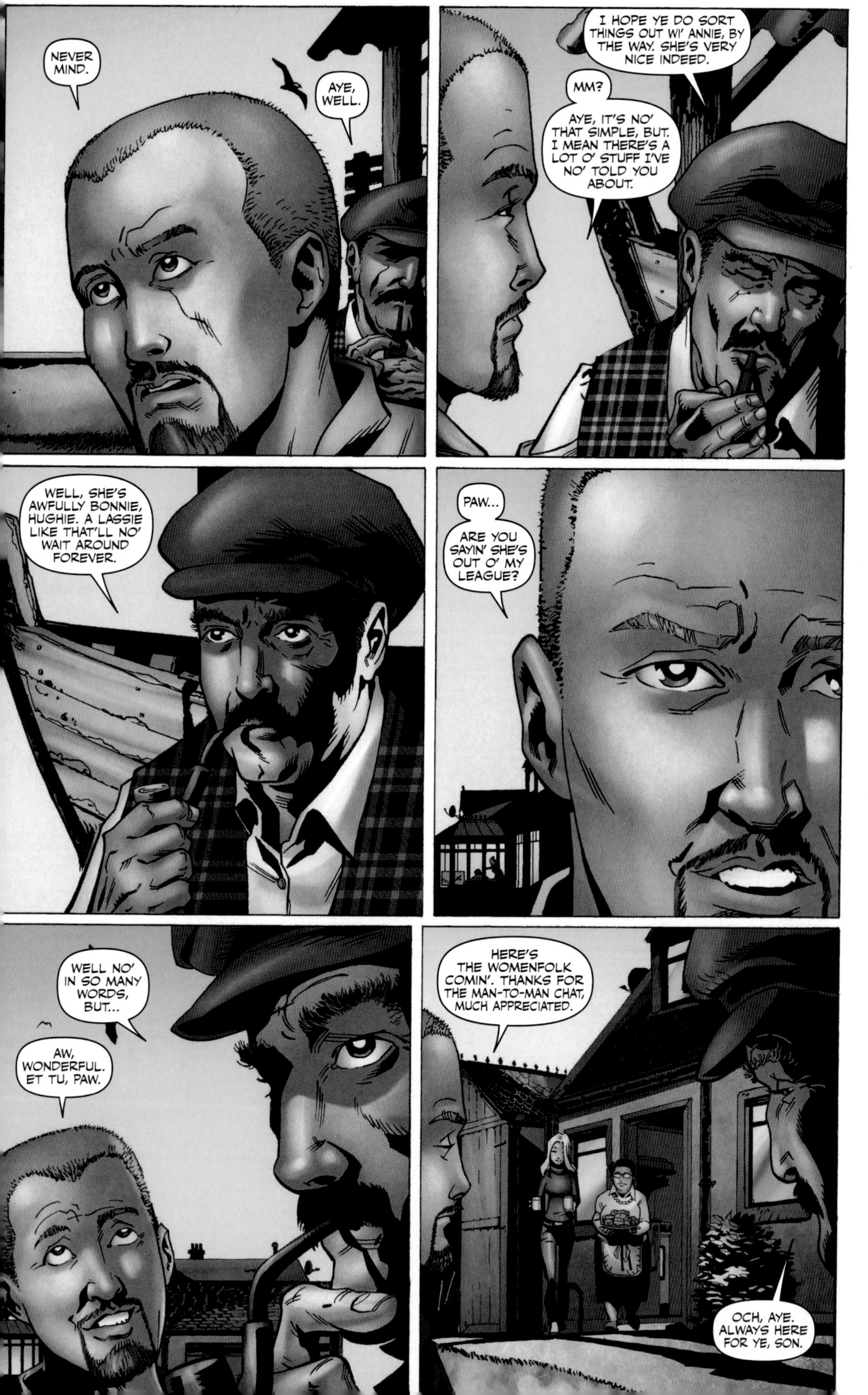
NEVER MIND.
AYE, WELL.
I HOPE YE DO SORT THINGS OUT WI' ANNIE, BY THE WAY. SHE'S VERY NICE INDEED.
MM?
AYE, IT'S NO' THAT SIMPLE, BUT. I MEAN THERE'S A LOT O' STUFF I'VE NO' TOLD YOU ABOUT.
WELL, SHE'S AWFULLY BONNIE, HUGHIE. A LASSIE LIKE THAT'LL NO' WAIT AROUND FOREVER.
PAW...
ARE YOU SAYIN' SHE'S OUT O' MY LEAGUE?
WELL NO' IN SO MANY WORDS, BUT...
AW, WONDERFUL. ET TU, PAW.
HERE'S THE WOMENFOLK COMIN'. THANKS FOR THE MAN-TO-MAN CHAT, MUCH APPRECIATED.
OCH, AYE. ALWAYS HERE FOR YE, SON.

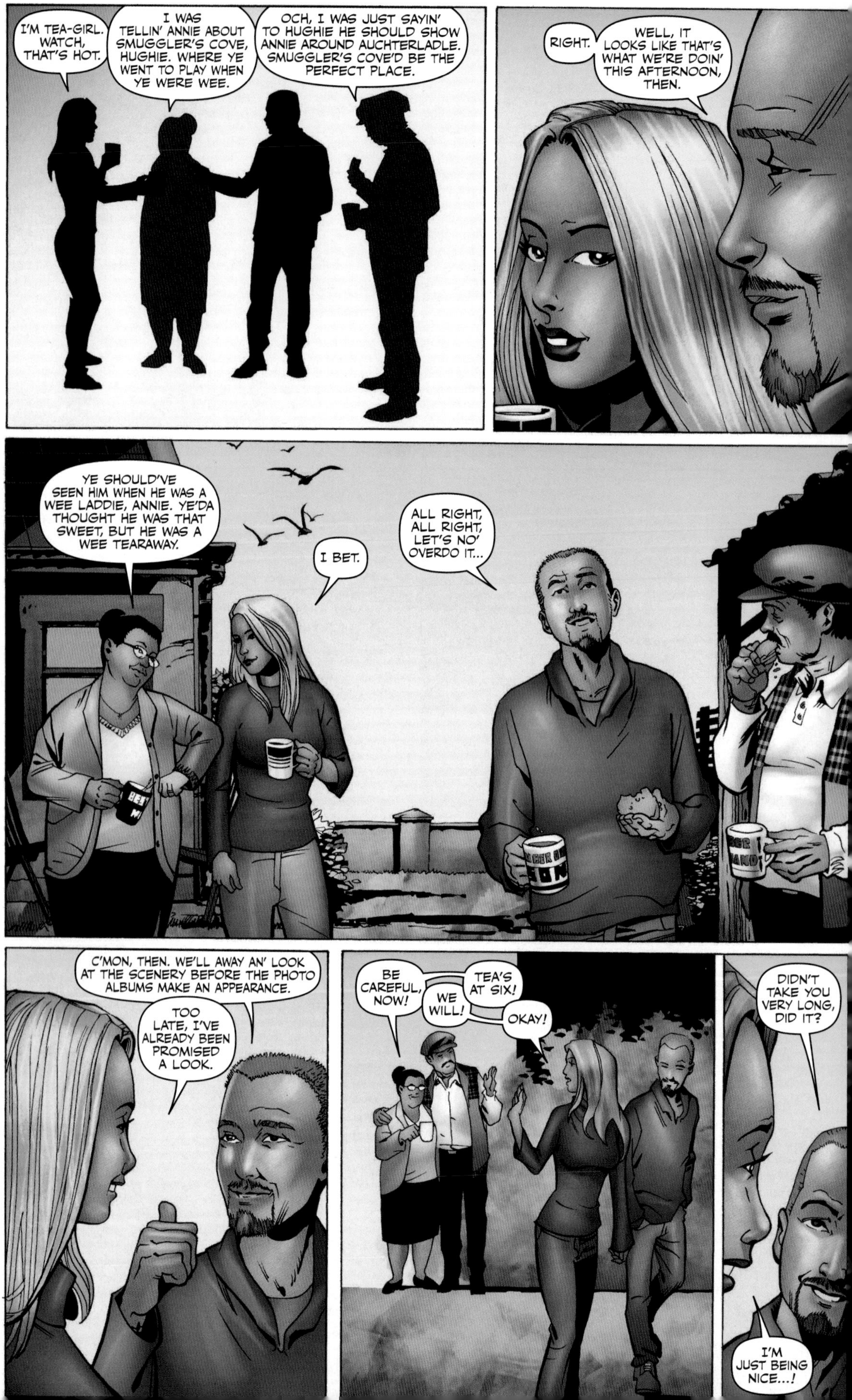
I'M TEA-GIRL. WATCH, THAT'S HOT.
I WAS TELLIN' ANNIE ABOUT SMUGGLER'S COVE, HUGHIE. WHERE YE WENT TO PLAY WHEN YE WERE WEE.
OCH, I WAS JUST SAYIN' TO HUGHIE HE SHOULD SHOW ANNIE AROUND AUCHTERLADLE. SMUGGLER'S COVE'D BE THE PERFECT PLACE.
RIGHT.
WELL, IT LOOKS LIKE THAT'S WHAT WE'RE DOIN' THIS AFTERNOON, THEN.
YE SHOULD'VE SEEN HIM WHEN HE WAS A WEE LADDIE, ANNIE. YE'DA THOUGHT HE WAS THAT SWEET, BUT HE WAS A WEE TEARAWAY.
I BET.
ALL RIGHT, ALL RIGHT, LET'S NO' OVERDO IT...
C'MON, THEN. WE'LL AWAY AN' LOOK AT THE SCENERY BEFORE THE PHOTO ALBUMS MAKE AN APPEARANCE.
TOO LATE, I'VE ALREADY BEEN PROMISED A LOOK.
BE CAREFUL, NOW!
WE WILL!
TEA'S AT SIX!
OKAY!
DIDN'T TAKE YOU VERY LONG, DID IT?
I'M JUST BEING NICE...!

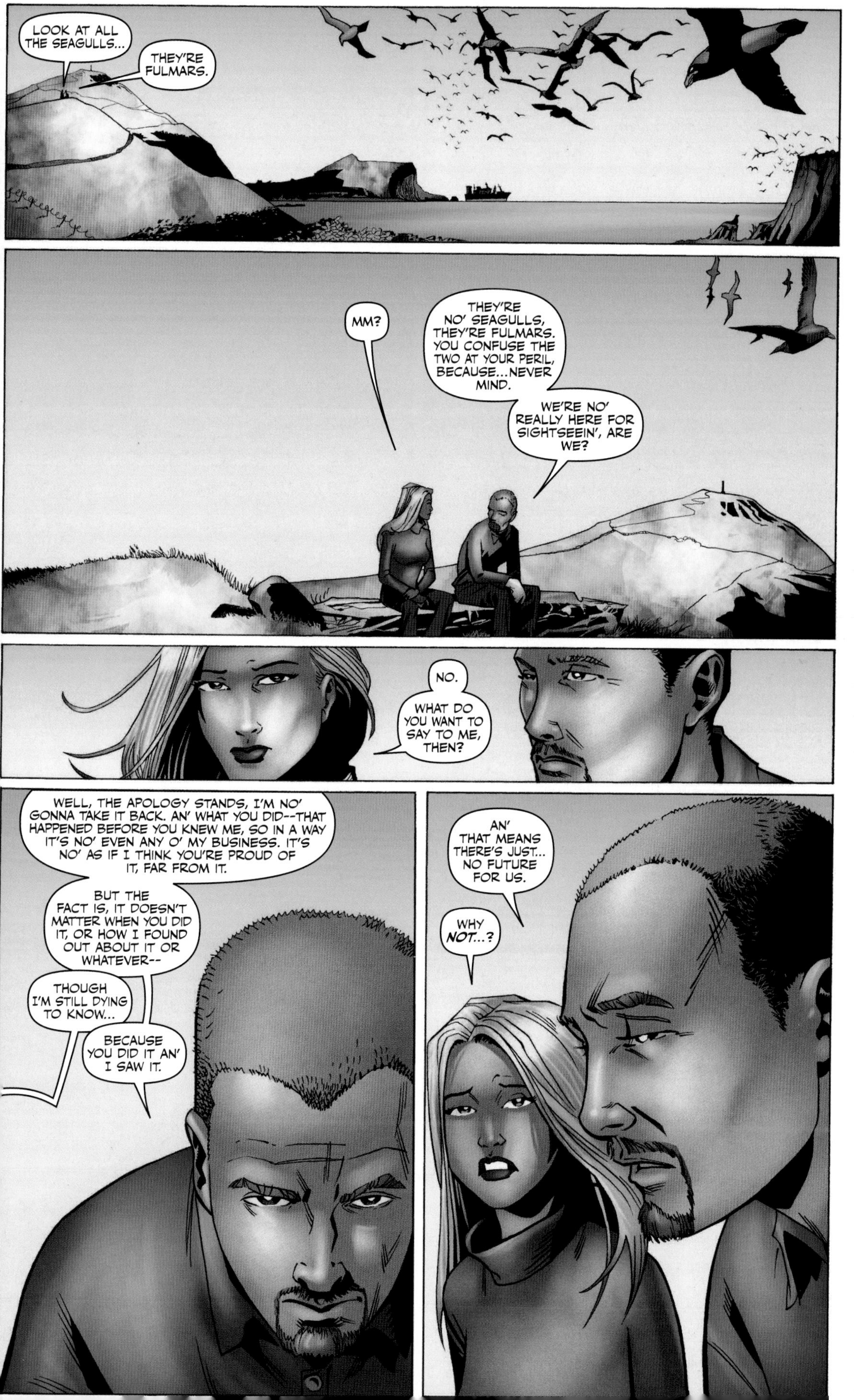
LOOK AT ALL THE SEAGULLS...
THEY'RE FULMARS.
MM?
THEY'RE NO' SEAGULLS, THEY'RE FULMARS. YOU CONFUSE THE TWO AT YOUR PERIL, BECAUSE...NEVER MIND.
WE'RE NO' REALLY HERE FOR SIGHTSEEIN', ARE WE?
NO.
WHAT DO YOU WANT TO SAY TO ME, THEN?
WELL, THE APOLOGY STANDS, I'M NO' GONNA TAKE IT BACK. AN' WHAT YOU DID--THAT HAPPENED BEFORE YOU KNEW ME, SO IN A WAY IT'S NO' EVEN ANY O' MY BUSINESS. IT'S NO' AS IF I THINK YOU'RE PROUD OF IT, FAR FROM IT.
BUT THE FACT IS, IT DOESN'T MATTER WHEN YOU DID IT, OR HOW I FOUND OUT ABOUT IT OR WHATEVER--
THOUGH I'M STILL DYING TO KNOW...
BECAUSE YOU DID IT AN' I SAW IT.
AN' THAT MEANS THERE'S JUST... NO FUTURE FOR US.
WHY *NOT*...?

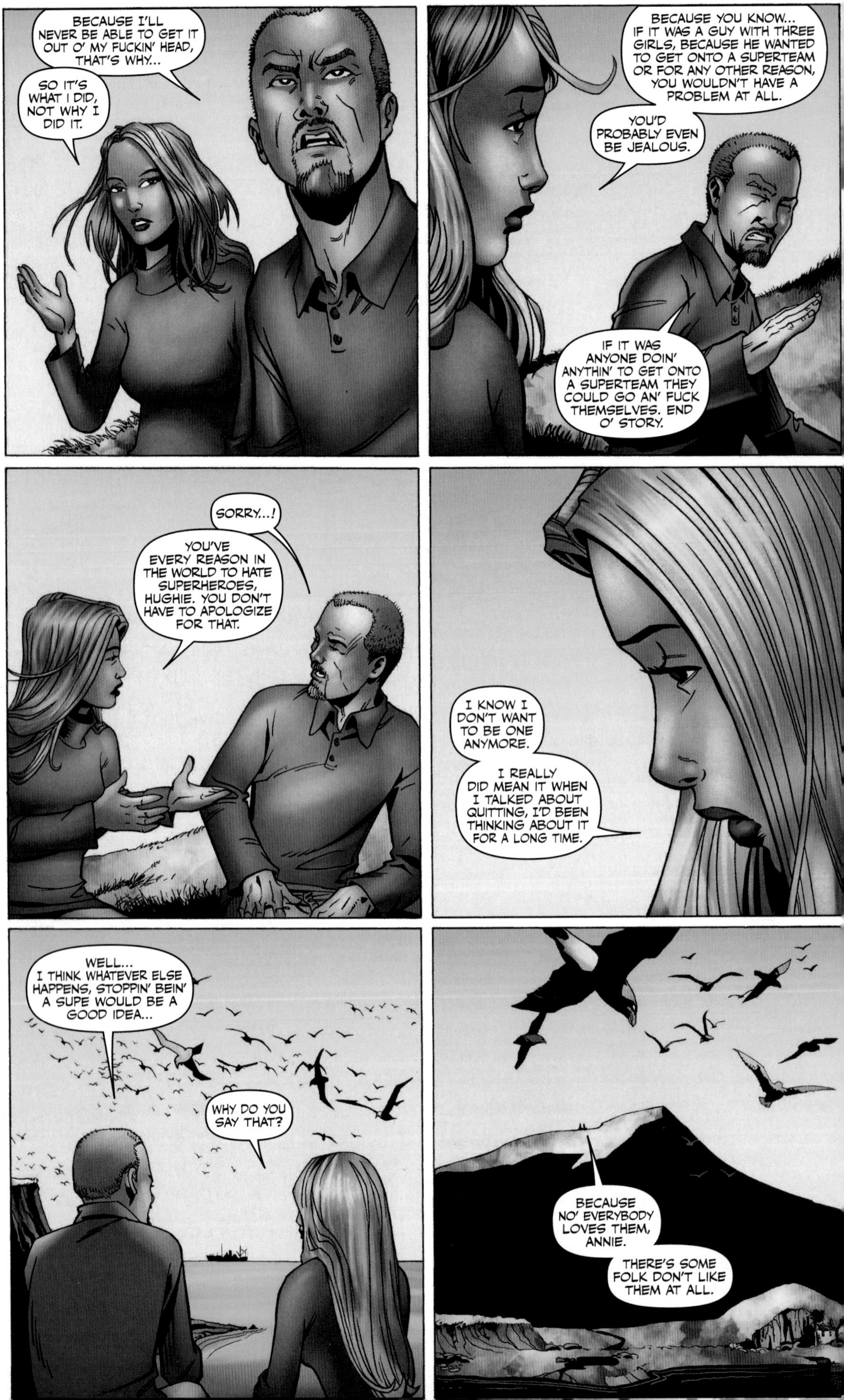
BECAUSE I'LL NEVER BE ABLE TO GET IT OUT O' MY FUCKIN' HEAD, THAT'S WHY...
SO IT'S WHAT I DID, NOT WHY I DID IT.
BECAUSE YOU KNOW... IF IT WAS A GUY WITH THREE GIRLS, BECAUSE HE WANTED TO GET ONTO A SUPERTEAM OR FOR ANY OTHER REASON, YOU WOULDN'T HAVE A PROBLEM AT ALL.
YOU'D PROBABLY EVEN BE JEALOUS.
IF IT WAS ANYONE DOIN' ANYTHIN' TO GET ONTO A SUPERTEAM THEY COULD GO AN' FUCK THEMSELVES. END O' STORY.
SORRY...!
YOU'VE EVERY REASON IN THE WORLD TO HATE SUPERHEROES, HUGHIE. YOU DON'T HAVE TO APOLOGIZE FOR THAT.
I KNOW I DON'T WANT TO BE ONE ANYMORE.
I REALLY DID MEAN IT WHEN I TALKED ABOUT QUITTING, I'D BEEN THINKING ABOUT IT FOR A LONG TIME.
WELL... I THINK WHATEVER ELSE HAPPENS, STOPPIN' BEIN' A SUPE WOULD BE A GOOD IDEA...
WHY DO YOU SAY THAT?
BECAUSE NO' EVERYBODY LOVES THEM, ANNIE.
THERE'S SOME FOLK DON'T LIKE THEM AT ALL.

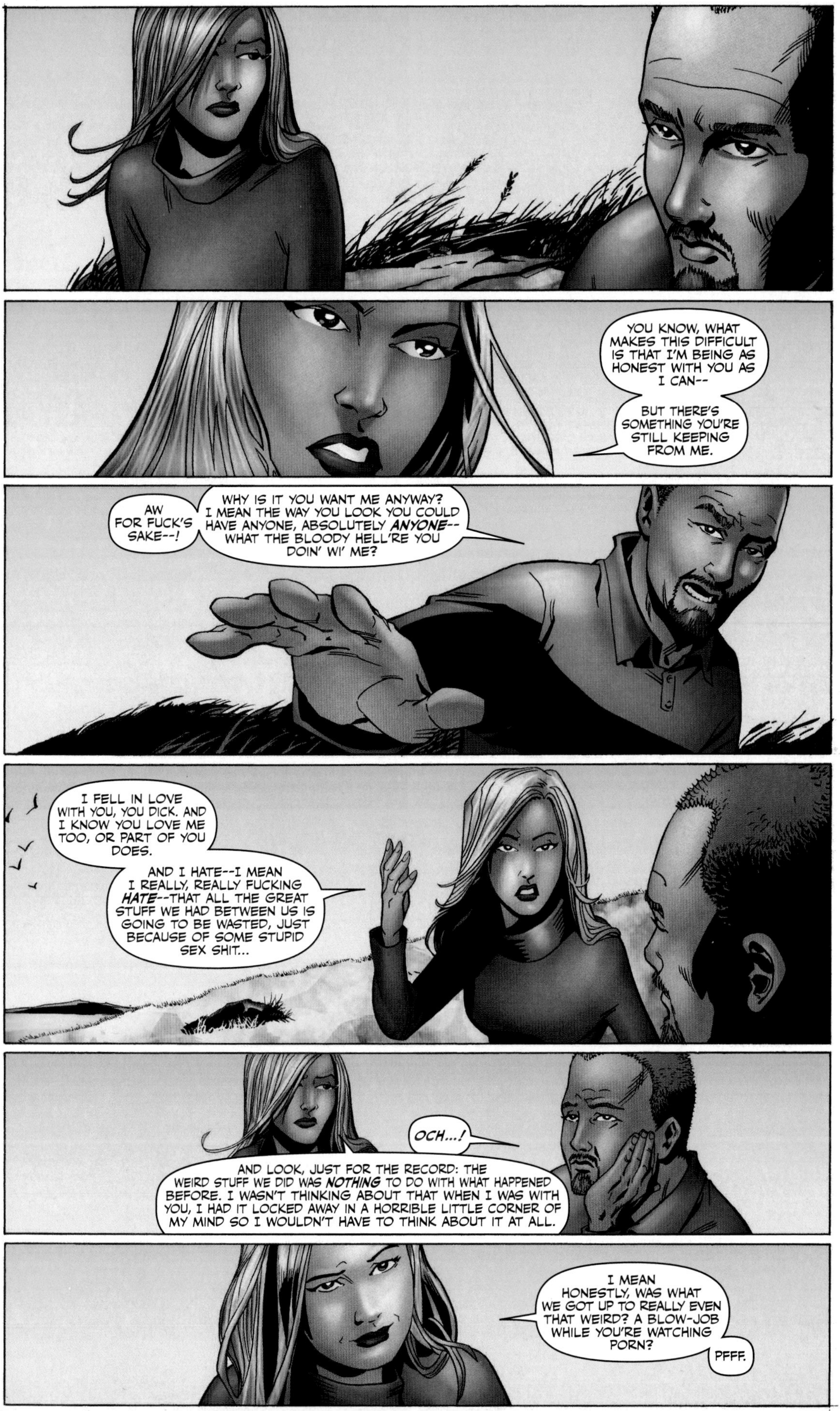
YOU KNOW, WHAT MAKES THIS DIFFICULT IS THAT I'M BEING AS HONEST WITH YOU AS I CAN--
BUT THERE'S SOMETHING YOU'RE STILL KEEPING FROM ME.
AW FOR FUCK'S SAKE--!
WHY IS IT YOU WANT ME ANYWAY? I MEAN THE WAY YOU LOOK YOU COULD HAVE ANYONE, ABSOLUTELY ANYONE-- WHAT THE BLOODY HELL'RE YOU DOIN' WI' ME?
I FELL IN LOVE WITH YOU, YOU DICK. AND I KNOW YOU LOVE ME TOO, OR PART OF YOU DOES.
AND I HATE--I MEAN I REALLY, REALLY FUCKING HATE--THAT ALL THE GREAT STUFF WE HAD BETWEEN US IS GOING TO BE WASTED, JUST BECAUSE OF SOME STUPID SEX SHIT...
OCH...!
AND LOOK, JUST FOR THE RECORD: THE WEIRD STUFF WE DID WAS NOTHING TO DO WITH WHAT HAPPENED BEFORE. I WASN'T THINKING ABOUT THAT WHEN I WAS WITH YOU, I HAD IT LOCKED AWAY IN A HORRIBLE LITTLE CORNER OF MY MIND SO I WOULDN'T HAVE TO THINK ABOUT IT AT ALL.
I MEAN HONESTLY, WAS WHAT WE GOT UP TO REALLY EVEN THAT WEIRD? A BLOW-JOB WHILE YOU'RE WATCHING PORN?
PFFF.

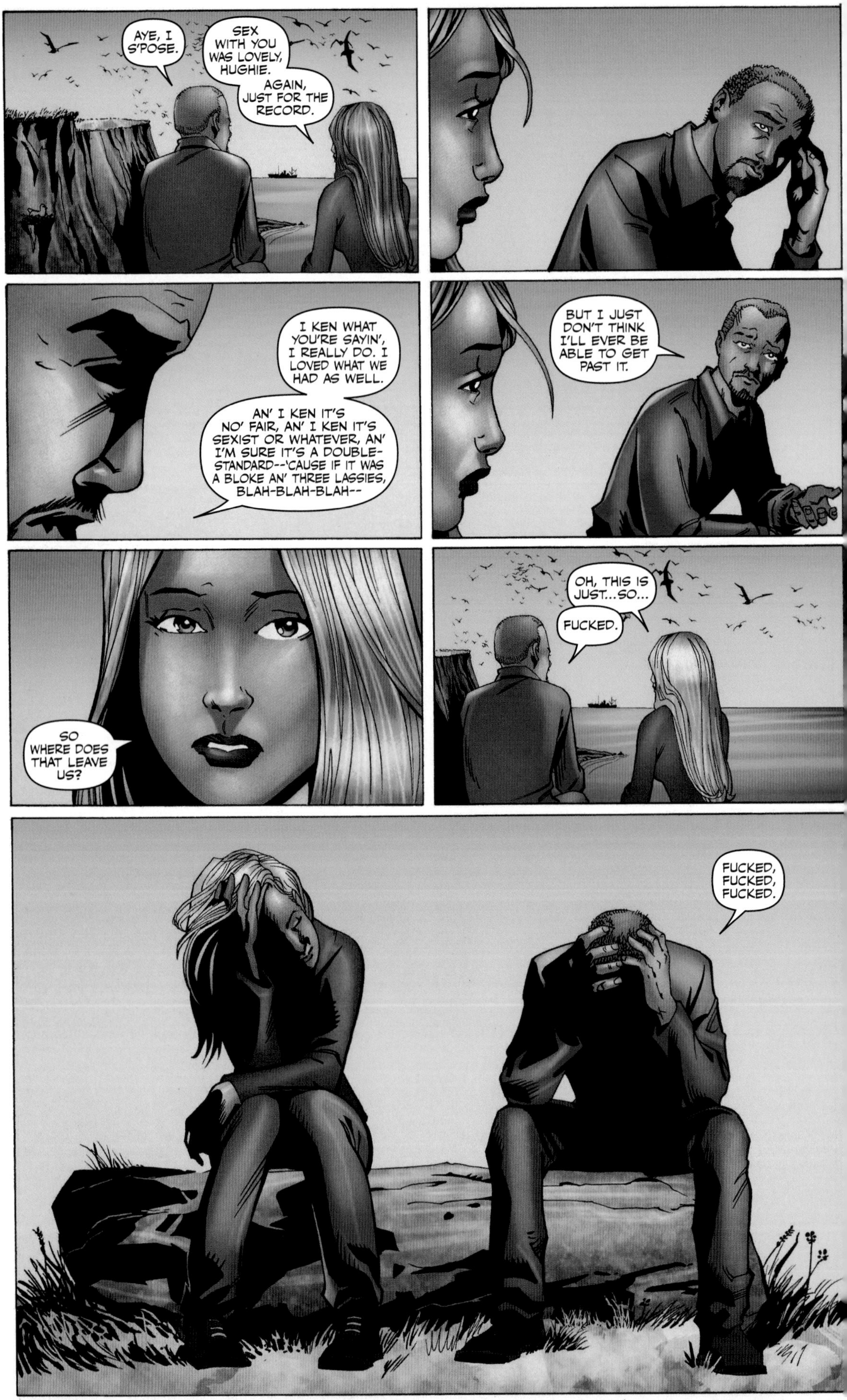
AYE, I S'POSE.
SEX WITH YOU WAS LOVELY, HUGHIE.
AGAIN, JUST FOR THE RECORD.
I KEN WHAT YOU'RE SAYIN', I REALLY DO. I LOVED WHAT WE HAD AS WELL.
AN' I KEN IT'S NO' FAIR, AN' I KEN IT'S SEXIST OR WHATEVER, AN' I'M SURE IT'S A DOUBLE-STANDARD--'CAUSE IF IT WAS A BLOKE AN' THREE LASSIES, BLAH-BLAH-BLAH--
BUT I JUST DON'T THINK I'LL EVER BE ABLE TO GET PAST IT.
SO WHERE DOES THAT LEAVE US?
OH, THIS IS JUST...SO...
FUCKED.
FUCKED, FUCKED, FUCKED.

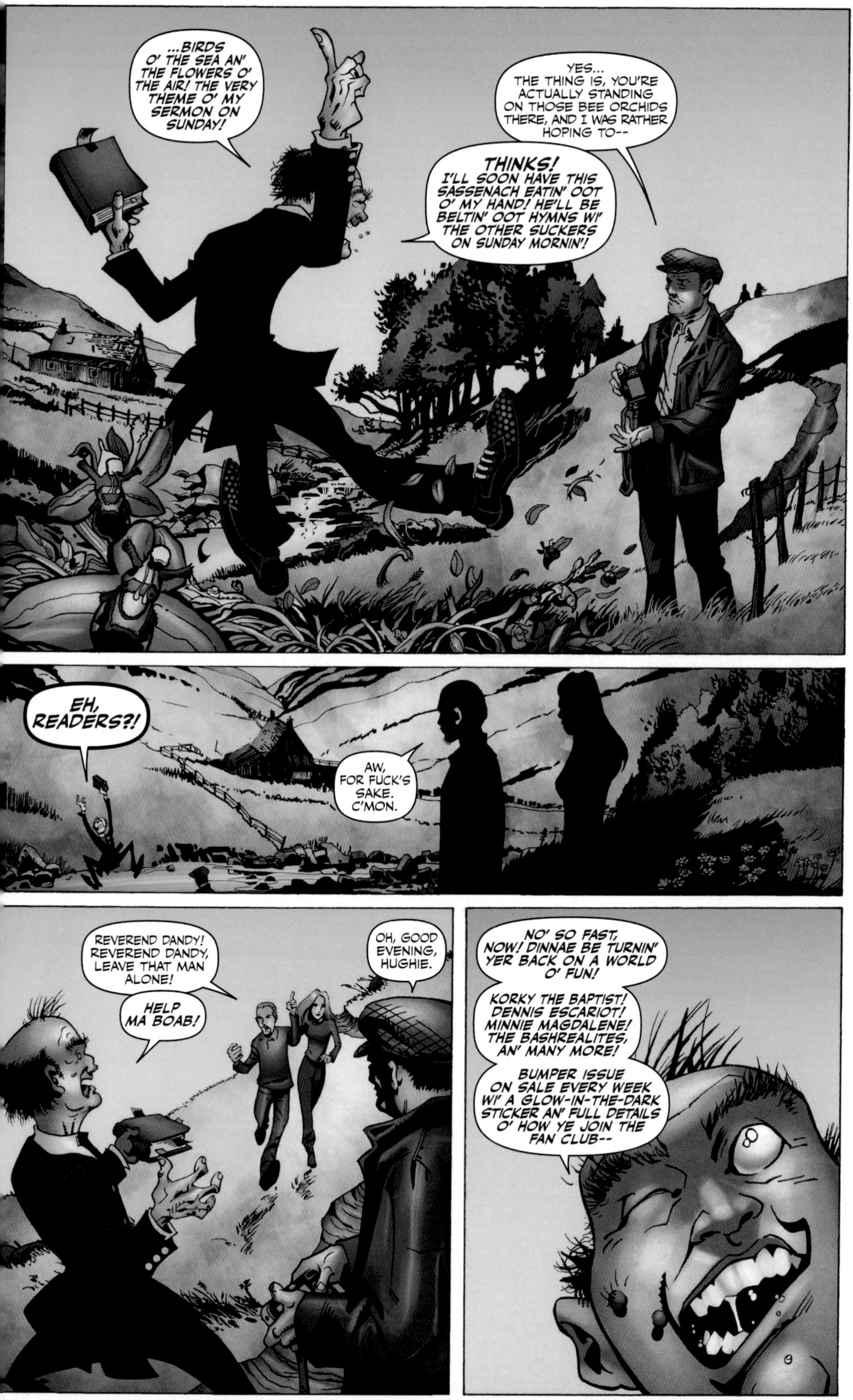

...BIRDS O' THE SEA AN' THE FLOWERS O' THE AIR! THE VERY THEME O' MY SERMON ON SUNDAY!
YES... THE THING IS, YOU'RE ACTUALLY STANDING ON THOSE BEE ORCHIDS THERE, AND I WAS RATHER HOPING TO--
THINKS! I'LL SOON HAVE THIS SASSENACH EATIN' OOT O' MY HAND! HE'LL BE BELTIN' OOT HYMNS WI' THE OTHER SUCKERS ON SUNDAY MORNIN'!
EH, READERS?!
AW, FOR FUCK'S SAKE. C'MON.
REVEREND DANDY! REVEREND DANDY, LEAVE THAT MAN ALONE!
HELP MA BOAB!
OH, GOOD EVENING, HUGHIE.
NO' SO FAST, NOW! DINNAE BE TURNIN' YER BACK ON A WORLD O' FUN!
KORKY THE BAPTIST! DENNIS ESCARIOT! MINNIE MAGDALENE! THE BASHREALITES, AN' MANY MORE!
BUMPER ISSUE ON SALE EVERY WEEK WI' A GLOW-IN-THE-DARK STICKER AN' FULL DETAILS O' HOW YE JOIN THE FAN CLUB--

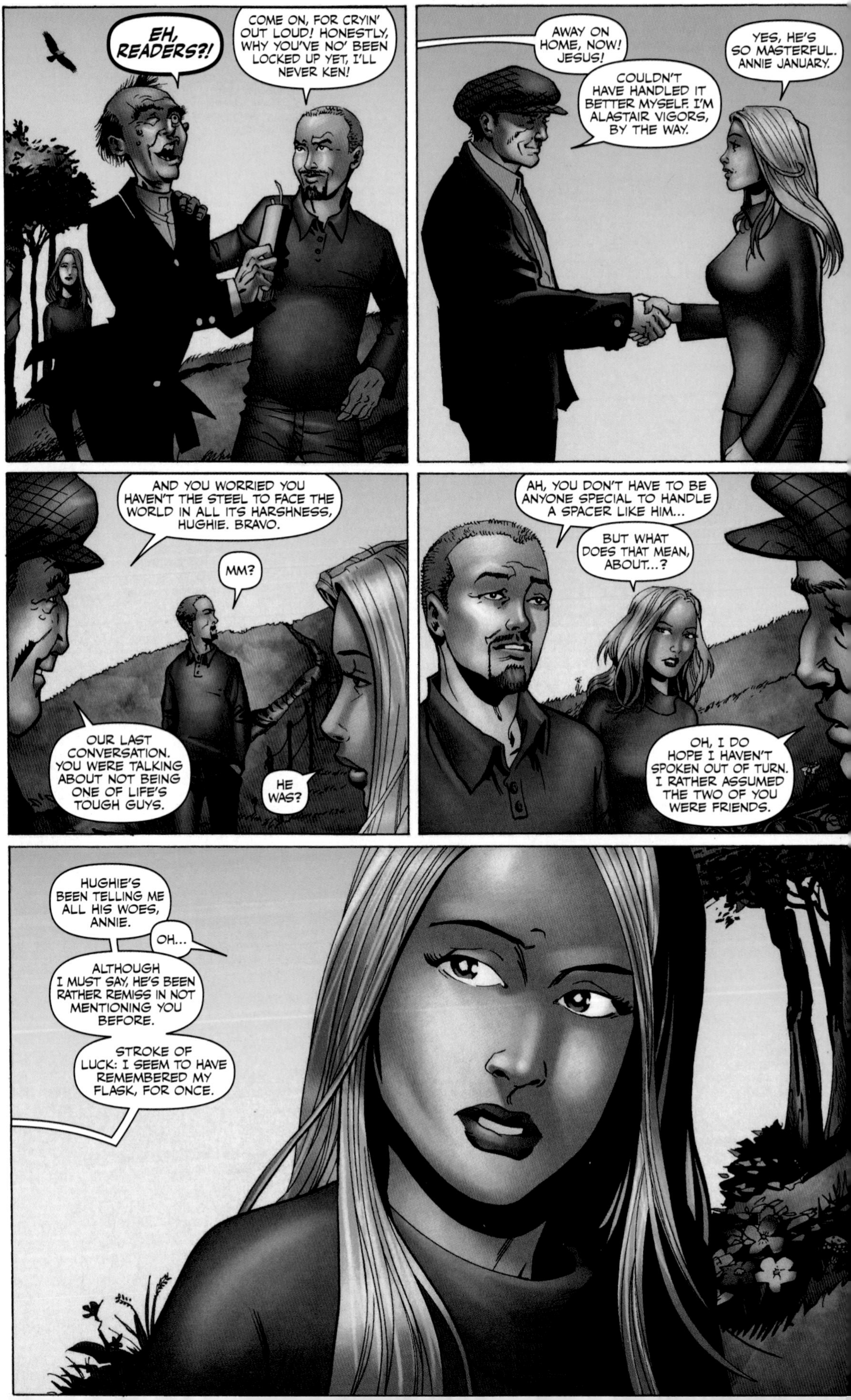
EH, READERS?!
COME ON, FOR CRYIN' OUT LOUD! HONESTLY, WHY YOU'VE NO' BEEN LOCKED UP YET, I'LL NEVER KEN!
AWAY ON HOME, NOW! JESUS!
COULDN'T HAVE HANDLED IT BETTER MYSELF. I'M ALASTAIR VIGORS, BY THE WAY.
YES, HE'S SO MASTERFUL. ANNIE JANUARY.
AND YOU WORRIED YOU HAVEN'T THE STEEL TO FACE THE WORLD IN ALL ITS HARSHNESS, HUGHIE. BRAVO.
MM?
OUR LAST CONVERSATION. YOU WERE TALKING ABOUT NOT BEING ONE OF LIFE'S TOUGH GUYS.
HE WAS?
AH, YOU DON'T HAVE TO BE ANYONE SPECIAL TO HANDLE A SPACER LIKE HIM...
BUT WHAT DOES THAT MEAN, ABOUT...?
OH, I DO HOPE I HAVEN'T SPOKEN OUT OF TURN. I RATHER ASSUMED THE TWO OF YOU WERE FRIENDS.
HUGHIE'S BEEN TELLING ME ALL HIS WOES, ANNIE.
OH...
ALTHOUGH I MUST SAY, HE'S BEEN RATHER REMISS IN NOT MENTIONING YOU BEFORE.
STROKE OF LUCK: I SEEM TO HAVE REMEMBERED MY FLASK, FOR ONCE.

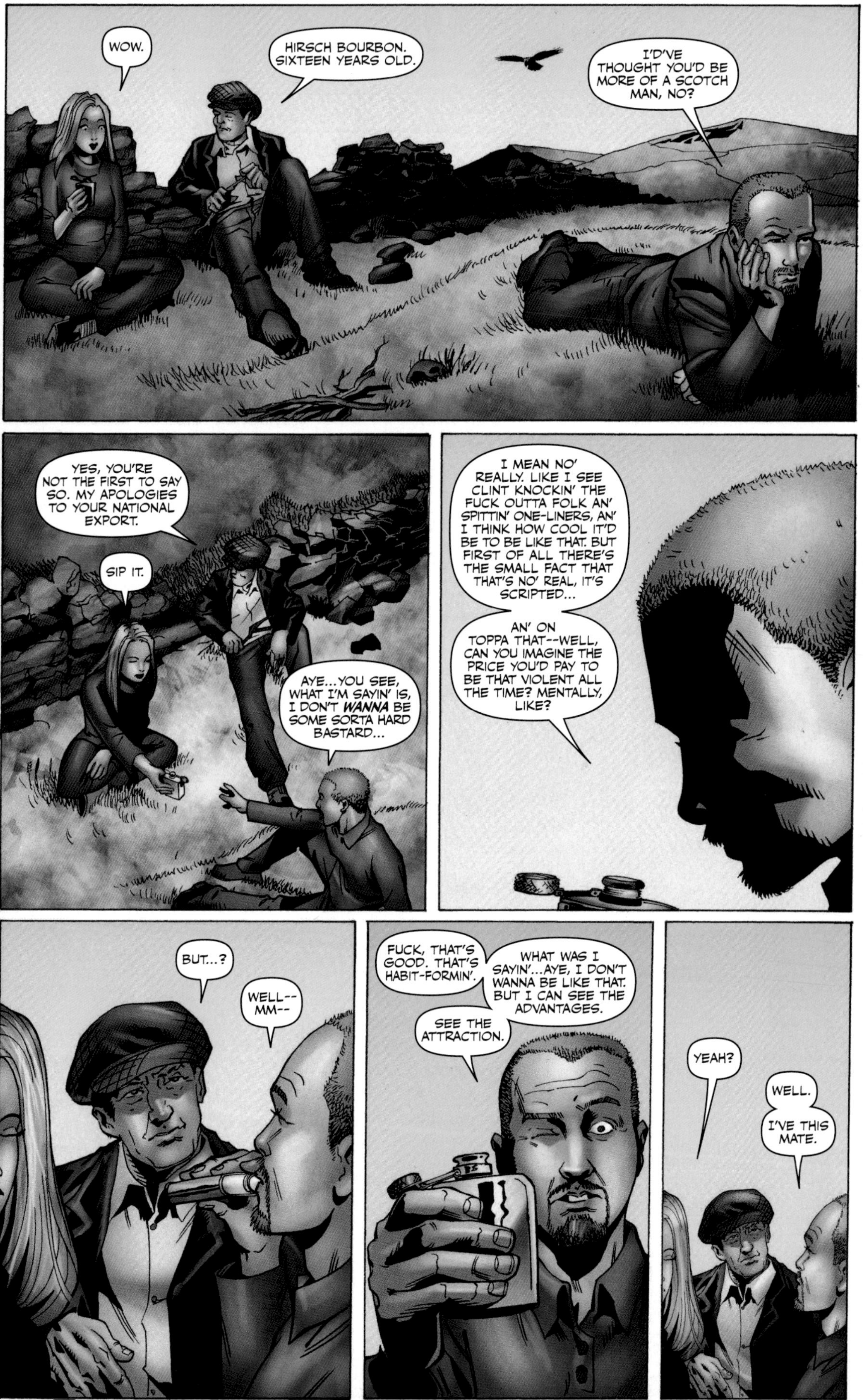

WOW.
HIRSCH BOURBON. SIXTEEN YEARS OLD.
I'D'VE THOUGHT YOU'D BE MORE OF A SCOTCH MAN, NO?
YES, YOU'RE NOT THE FIRST TO SAY SO. MY APOLOGIES TO YOUR NATIONAL EXPORT.
SIP IT.
AYE...YOU SEE, WHAT I'M SAYIN' IS, I DON'T ***WANNA*** BE SOME SORTA HARD BASTARD...
I MEAN NO' REALLY. LIKE I SEE CLINT KNOCKIN' THE FUCK OUTTA FOLK AN' SPITTIN' ONE-LINERS, AN' I THINK HOW COOL IT'D BE TO BE LIKE THAT. BUT FIRST OF ALL THERE'S THE SMALL FACT THAT THAT'S NO' REAL, IT'S SCRIPTED...
AN' ON TOPPA THAT--WELL, CAN YOU IMAGINE THE PRICE YOU'D PAY TO BE THAT VIOLENT ALL THE TIME? MENTALLY, LIKE?
BUT...?
WELL-- MM--
FUCK, THAT'S GOOD. THAT'S HABIT-FORMIN'.
WHAT WAS I SAYIN'...AYE, I DON'T WANNA BE LIKE THAT. BUT I CAN SEE THE ADVANTAGES.
SEE THE ATTRACTION.
YEAH?
WELL.
I'VE THIS MATE.

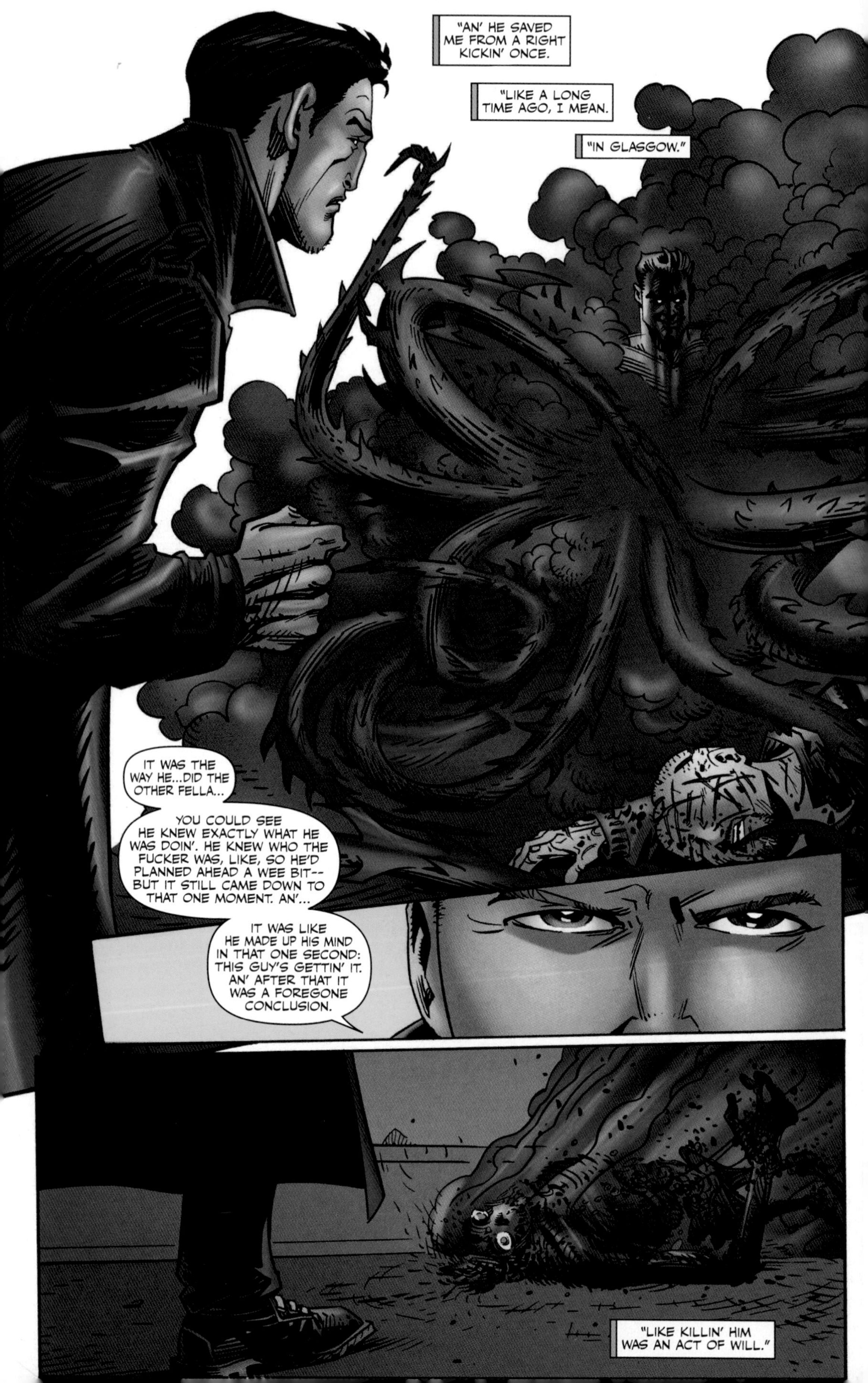
"AN' HE SAVED ME FROM A RIGHT KICKIN' ONCE.
"LIKE A LONG TIME AGO, I MEAN.
"IN GLASGOW."
IT WAS THE WAY HE...DID THE OTHER FELLA...
YOU COULD SEE HE KNEW EXACTLY WHAT HE WAS DOIN'. HE KNEW WHO THE FUCKER WAS, LIKE, SO HE'D PLANNED AHEAD A WEE BIT-- BUT IT STILL CAME DOWN TO THAT ONE MOMENT. AN'...
IT WAS LIKE HE MADE UP HIS MIND IN THAT ONE SECOND: THIS GUY'S GETTIN' IT. AN' AFTER THAT IT WAS A FOREGONE CONCLUSION.
"LIKE KILLIN' HIM WAS AN ACT OF WILL."

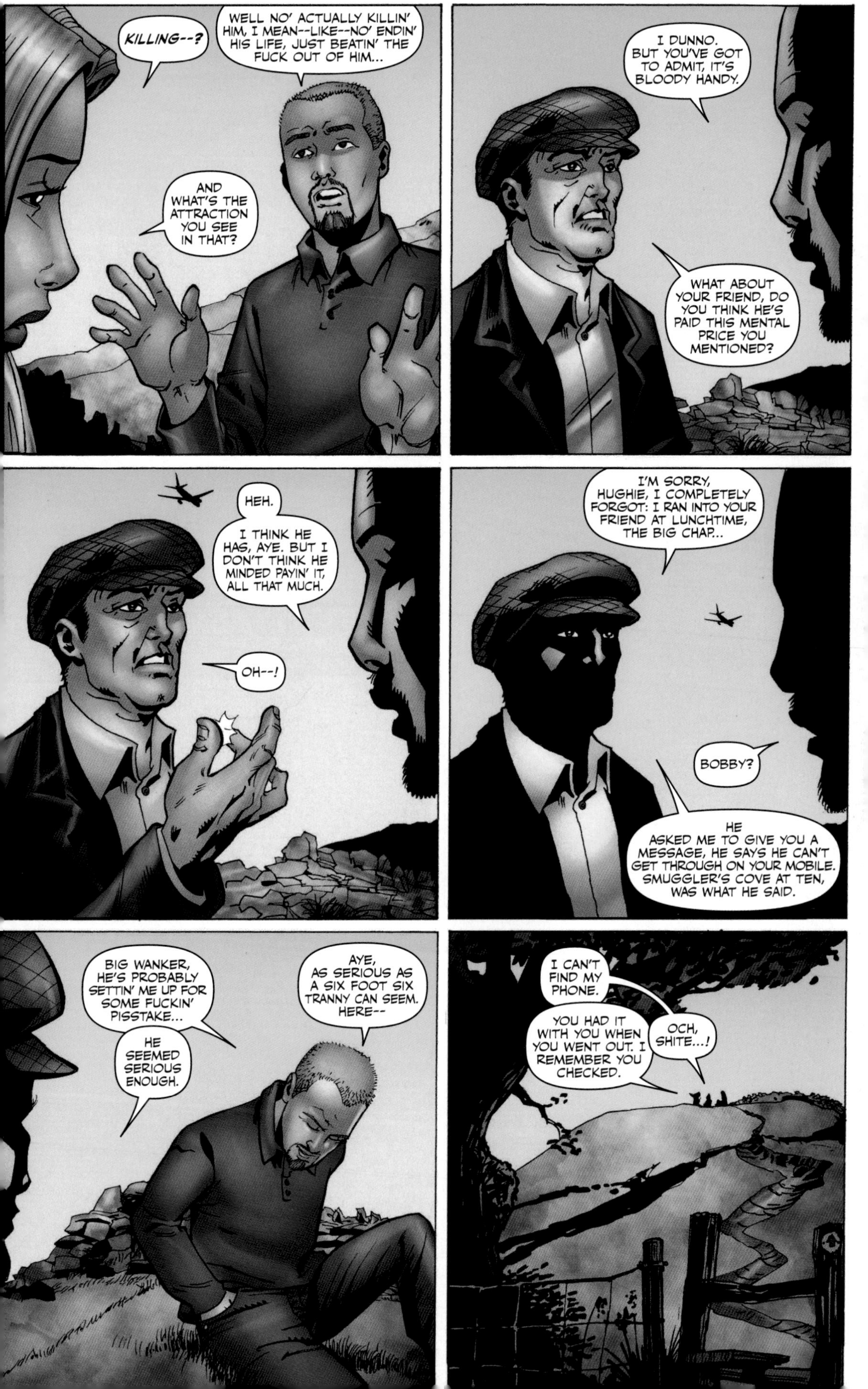
KILLING--?
WELL NO' ACTUALLY KILLIN' HIM, I MEAN--LIKE--NO' ENDIN' HIS LIFE, JUST BEATIN' THE FUCK OUT OF HIM...
AND WHAT'S THE ATTRACTION YOU SEE IN THAT?
I DUNNO. BUT YOU'VE GOT TO ADMIT, IT'S BLOODY HANDY.
WHAT ABOUT YOUR FRIEND, DO YOU THINK HE'S PAID THIS MENTAL PRICE YOU MENTIONED?
HEH.
I THINK HE HAS, AYE. BUT I DON'T THINK HE MINDED PAYIN' IT, ALL THAT MUCH.
OH--!
I'M SORRY, HUGHIE, I COMPLETELY FORGOT: I RAN INTO YOUR FRIEND AT LUNCHTIME, THE BIG CHAP...
BOBBY?
HE ASKED ME TO GIVE YOU A MESSAGE, HE SAYS HE CAN'T GET THROUGH ON YOUR MOBILE. SMUGGLER'S COVE AT TEN, WAS WHAT HE SAID.
BIG WANKER, HE'S PROBABLY SETTIN' ME UP FOR SOME FUCKIN' PISSTAKE...
HE SEEMED SERIOUS ENOUGH.
AYE, AS SERIOUS AS A SIX FOOT SIX TRANNY CAN SEEM. HERE--
I CAN'T FIND MY PHONE.
YOU HAD IT WITH YOU WHEN YOU WENT OUT. I REMEMBER YOU CHECKED.
OCH, SHITE...!

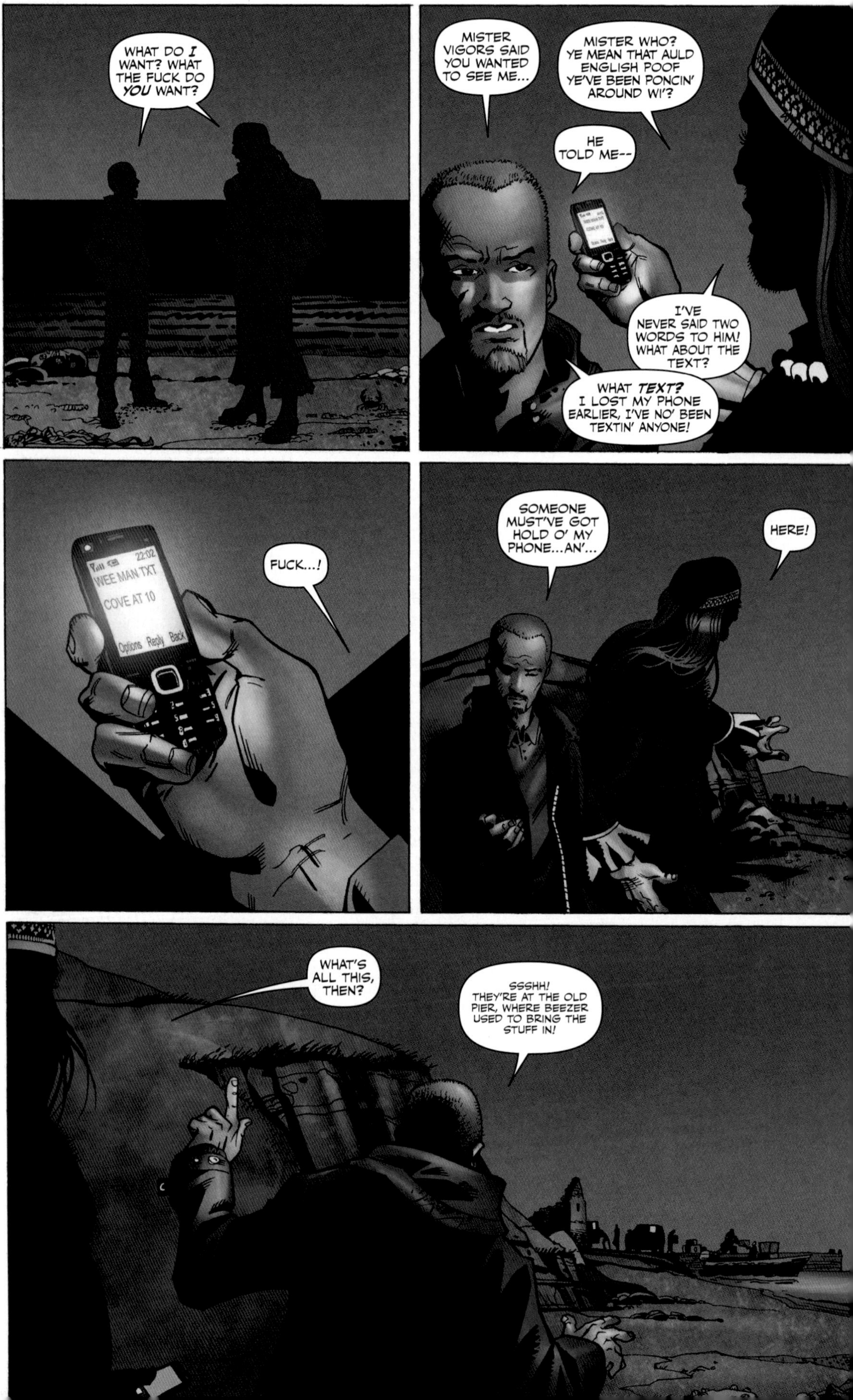
WHAT DO *I* WANT? WHAT THE FUCK DO *YOU* WANT?
MISTER VIGORS SAID YOU WANTED TO SEE ME...
MISTER WHO? YE MEAN THAT AULD ENGLISH POOF YE'VE BEEN PONCIN' AROUND WI'?
HE TOLD ME--
I'VE NEVER SAID TWO WORDS TO HIM! WHAT ABOUT THE TEXT?
WHAT *TEXT?* I LOST MY PHONE EARLIER, I'VE NO' BEEN TEXTIN' ANYONE!
22:02
WEE MAN TXT
COVE AT 10
Options Reply Back
FUCK...!
SOMEONE MUST'VE GOT HOLD O' MY PHONE...AN'...
HERE!
WHAT'S ALL THIS, THEN?
SSSHH! THEY'RE AT THE OLD PIER, WHERE BEEZER USED TO BRING THE STUFF IN!

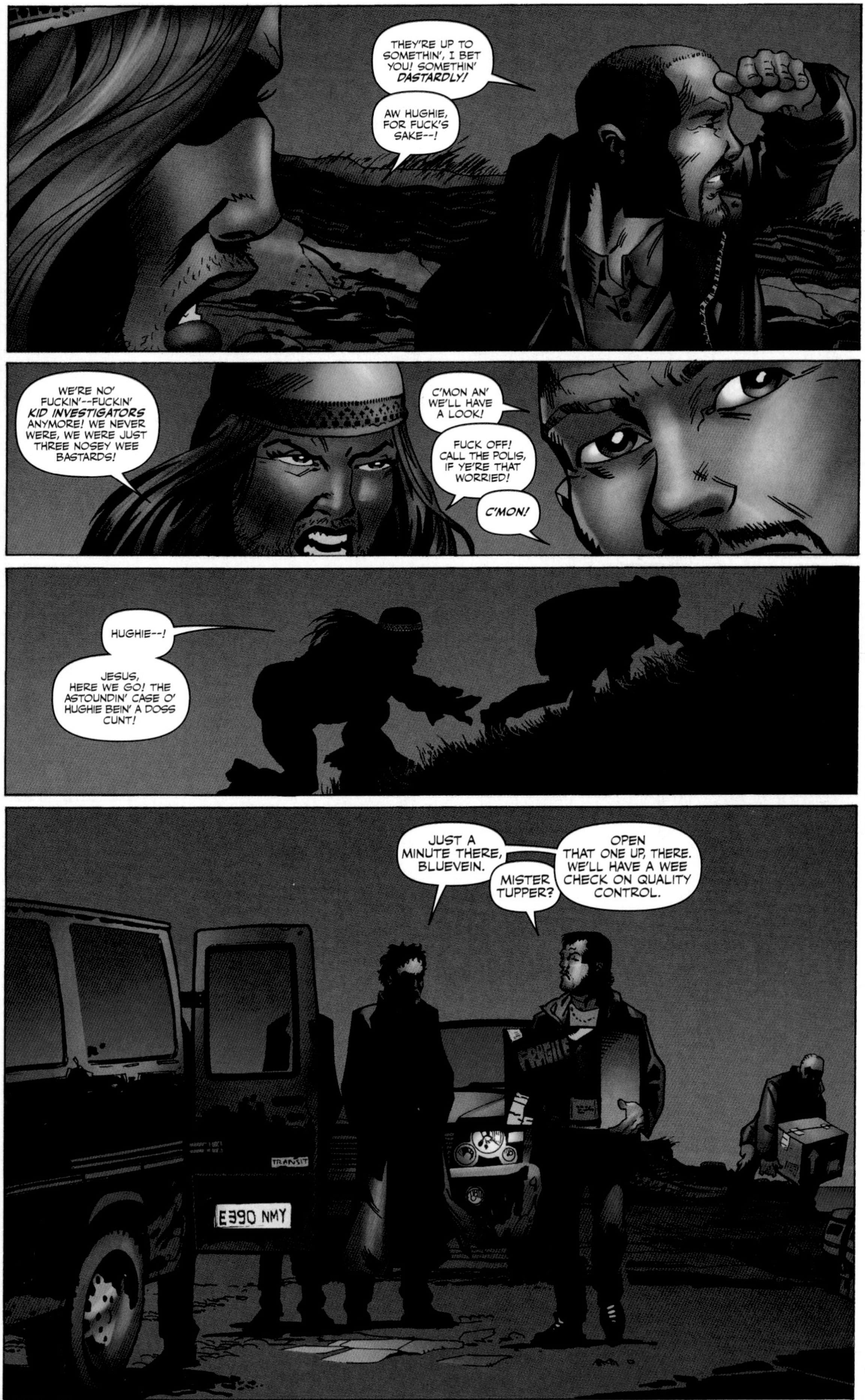

THEY'RE UP TO SOMETHIN', I BET YOU! SOMETHIN' *DASTARDLY!*
AW HUGHIE, FOR FUCK'S SAKE--!
WE'RE NO' FUCKIN'--FUCKIN' *KID INVESTIGATORS* ANYMORE! WE NEVER WERE, WE WERE JUST THREE NOSEY WEE BASTARDS!
C'MON AN' WE'LL HAVE A LOOK!
FUCK OFF! CALL THE POLIS, IF YE'RE THAT WORRIED!
C'MON!
HUGHIE--!
JESUS, HERE WE GO! THE ASTOUNDIN' CASE O' HUGHIE BEIN' A DOSS CUNT!
JUST A MINUTE THERE, BLUEVEIN.
MISTER TUPPER?
OPEN THAT ONE UP, THERE. WE'LL HAVE A WEE CHECK ON QUALITY CONTROL.
FRAGILE
TRANSIT
E390 NMY

ALL RIGHT, FAIR ENOUGH. GIVE US A SECOND AN' I'LL PHONE THE--

WAIT.

STILL YOU DO NOT TRUST US...?

RELAX, UPYERBUMOVICH. CALL IT A RANDOM TASTE-TEST, ALL RIGHT?

THERE YE GO, MCWANK. GET YER PROBOSCIS INTO THAT LOT.

WHAT D'YOU MEAN, WAIT--?

I THOUGHT I--I DUNNO--

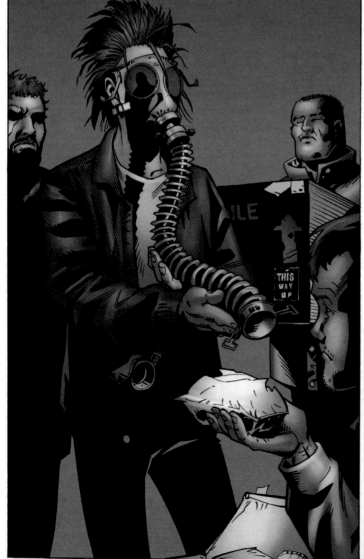

DET?!

FUCK--!

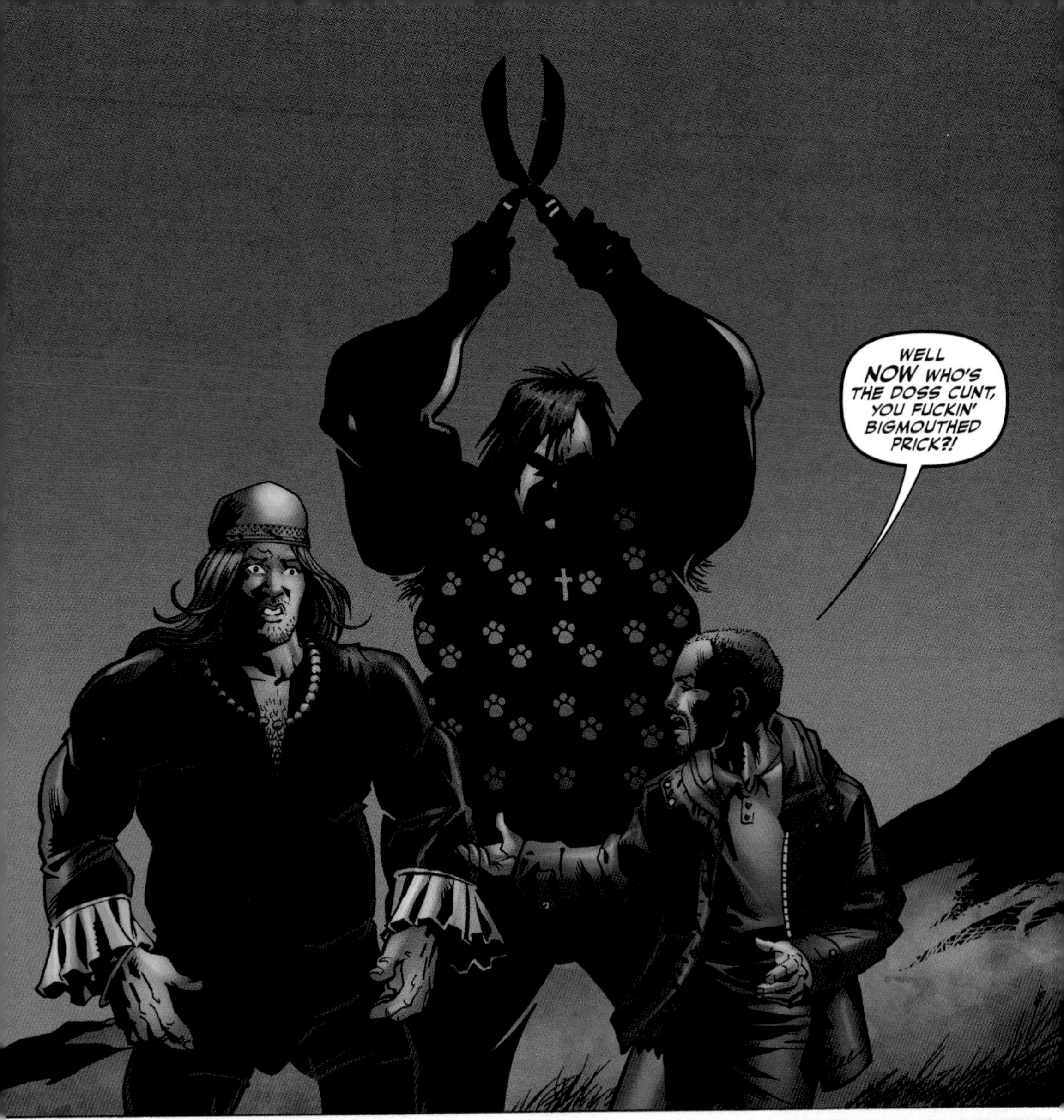
WELL NOW WHO'S THE DOSS CUNT, YOU FUCKIN' BIGMOUTHED PRICK?!

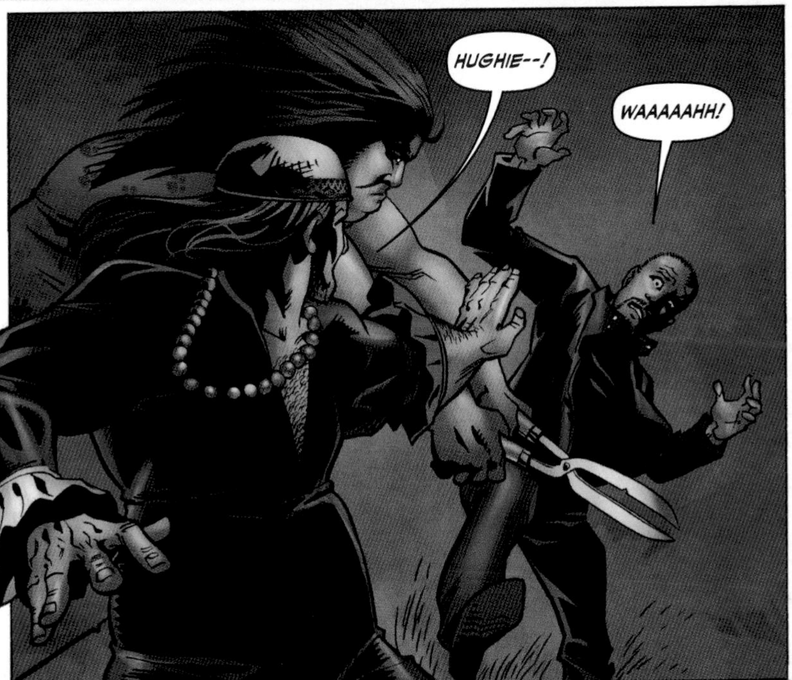
HUGHIE--!
WAAAAAHH!

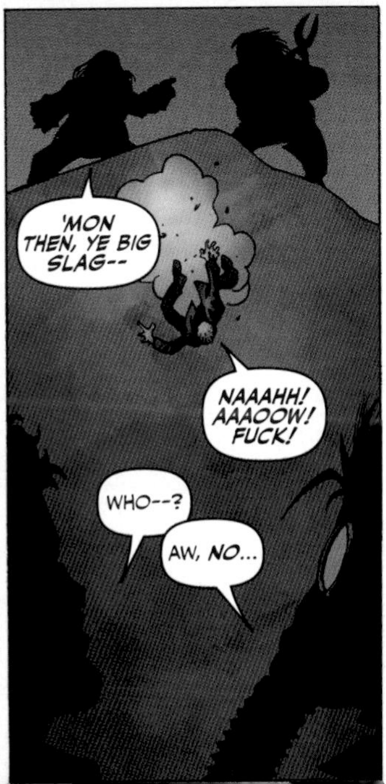
'MON THEN, YE BIG SLAG--
NAAAHH! AAAOOW! FUCK!
WHO--?
AW, NO...

GIRLFIGHT!!

EH?

DET, WHAT'RE YOU--

AW SHITE, HUGHIE, LISTEN--

WHAT'S THIS WEE BUFTY DOIN' HERE? WHAT'D YOU TELL HIM?

HOLY FUCK.

THERE'S V IN THAT.

HUGHIE...!

AAAAARRRRGGGGHH!!

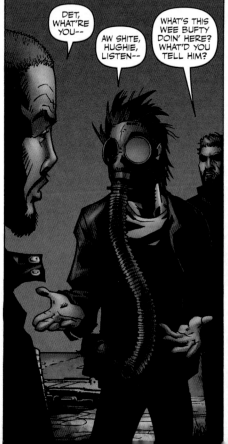

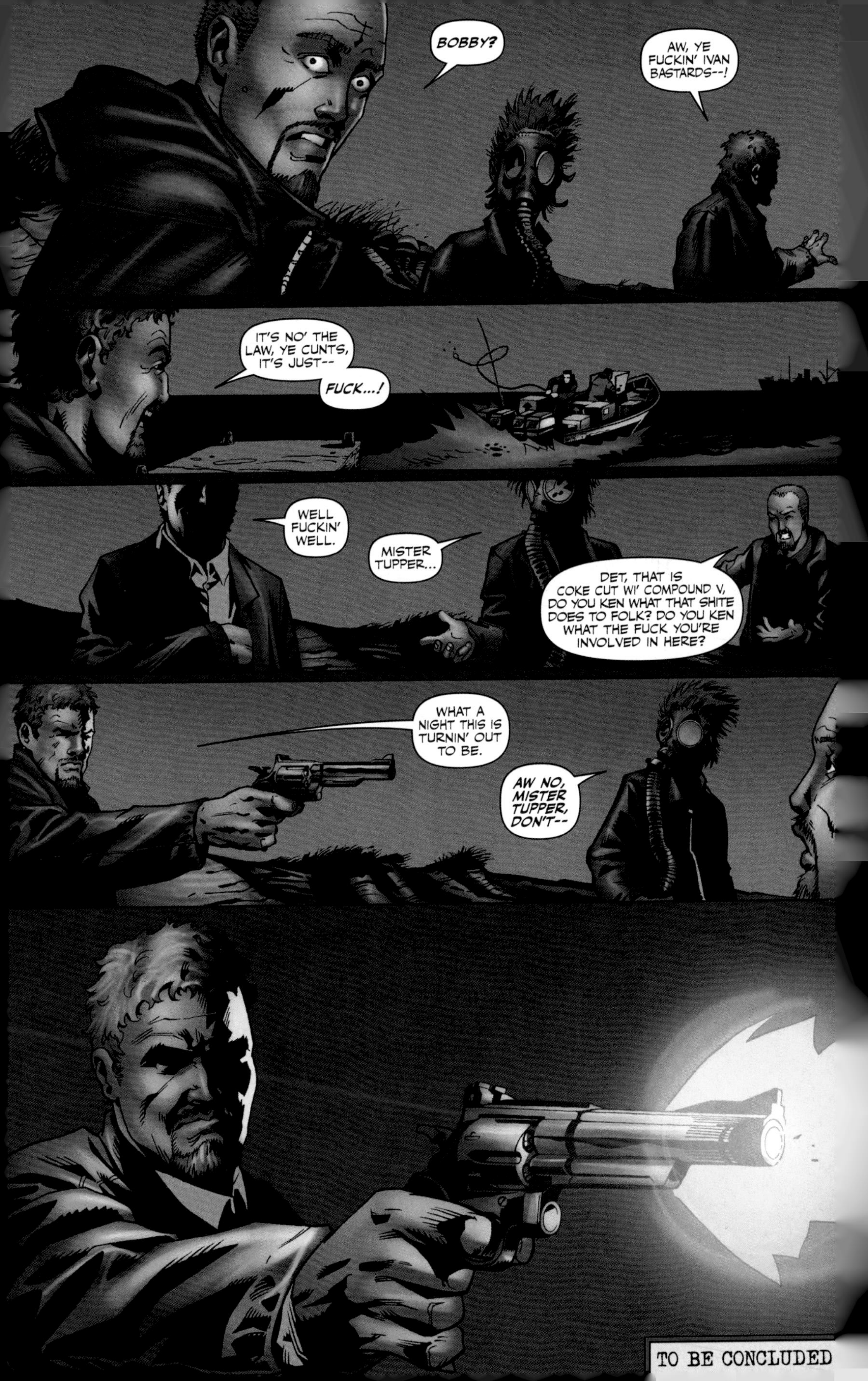
BOBBY?
AW, YE FUCKIN' IVAN BASTARDS--!
IT'S NO' THE LAW, YE CUNTS, IT'S JUST--
FUCK...!
WELL FUCKIN' WELL.
MISTER TUPPER...
DET, THAT IS COKE CUT WI' COMPOUND V, DO YOU KEN WHAT THAT SHITE DOES TO FOLK? DO YOU KEN WHAT THE FUCK YOU'RE INVOLVED IN HERE?
WHAT A NIGHT THIS IS TURNIN' OUT TO BE.
AW NO, MISTER TUPPER, DON'T--
TO BE CONCLUDED

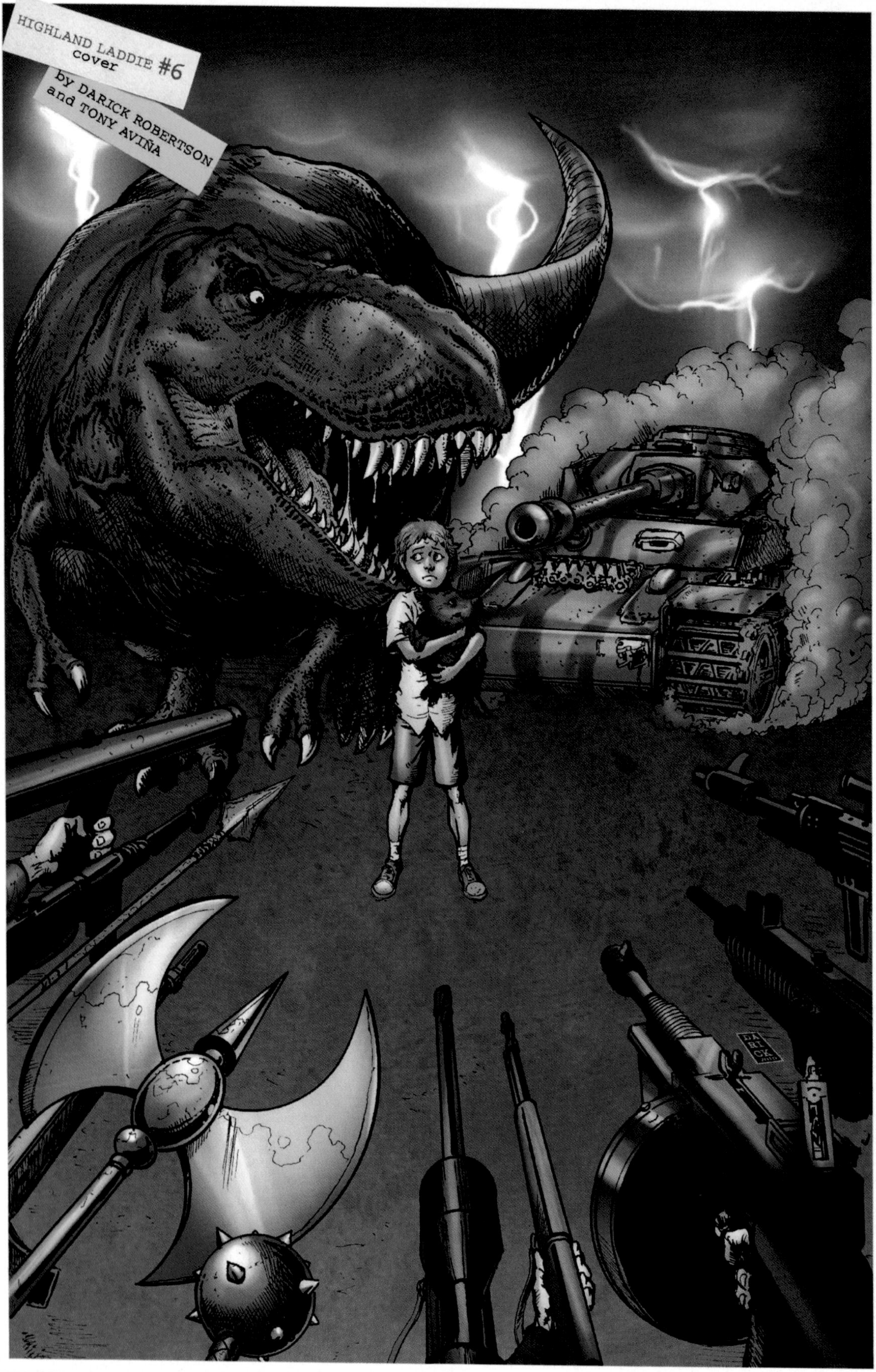
HIGHLAND LADDIE #6
cover
by DARICK ROBERTSON
and TONY AVIÑA

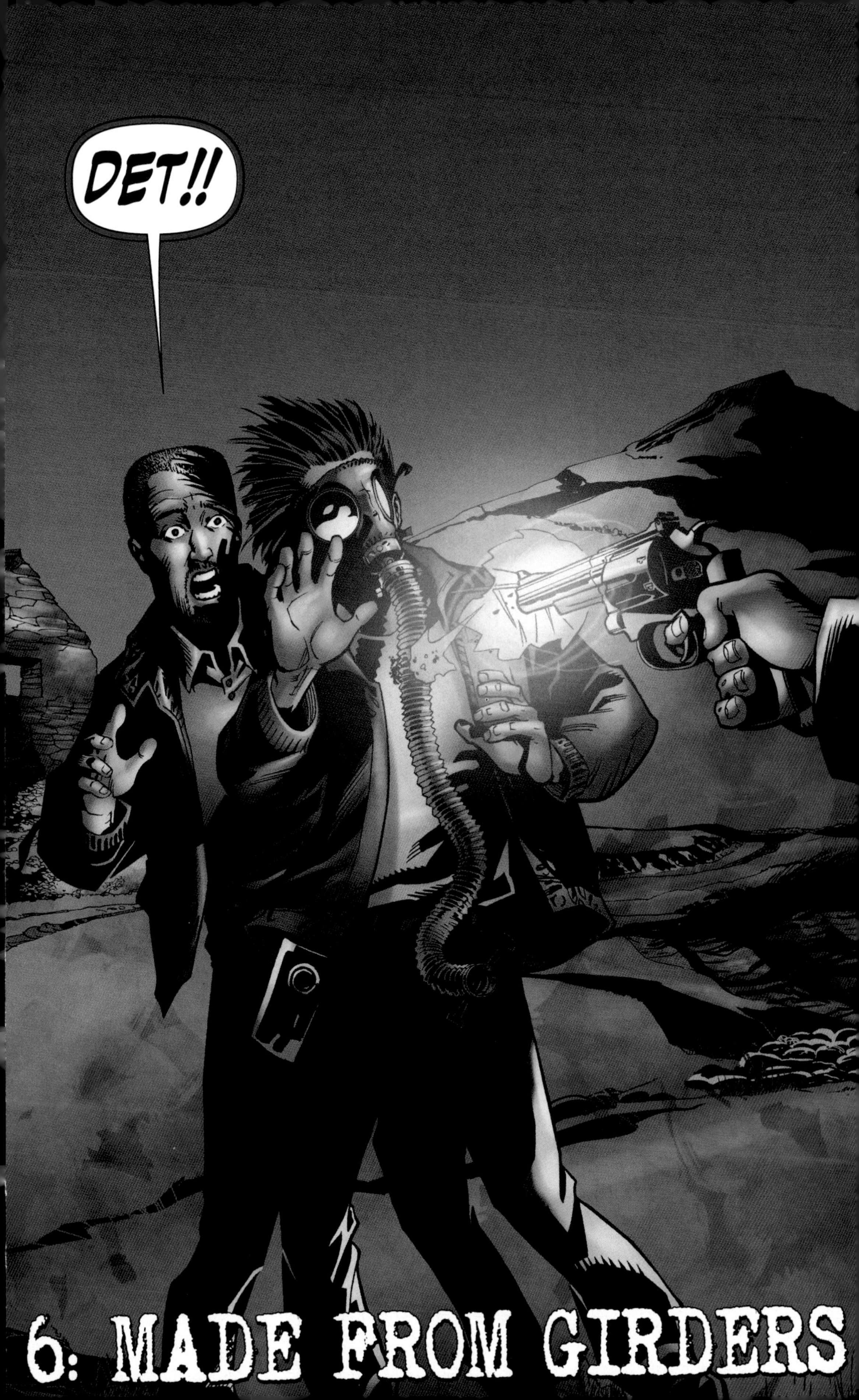
DET!!

6: MADE FROM GIRDERS

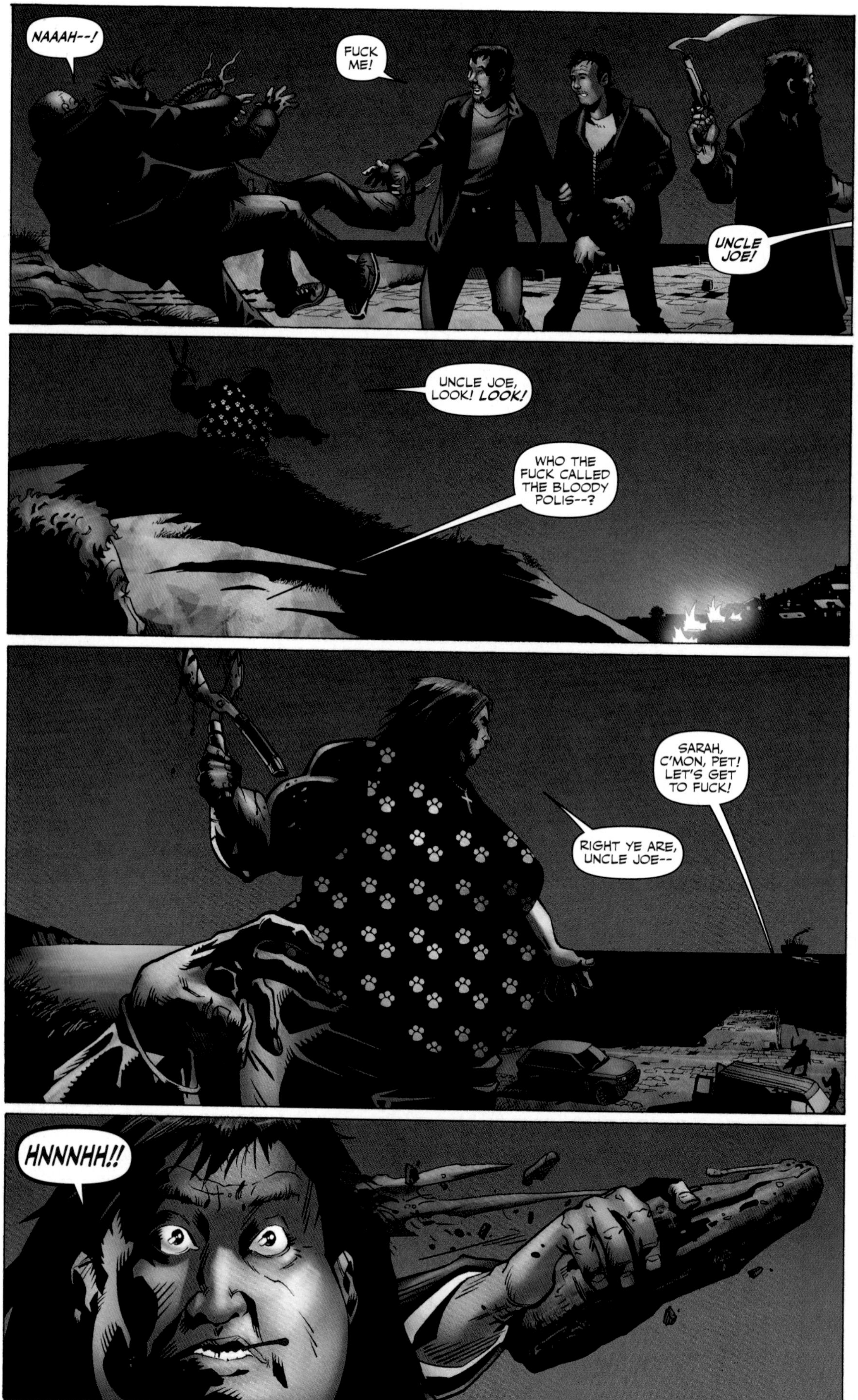
NAAAH--!
FUCK ME!
UNCLE JOE!
UNCLE JOE, LOOK! LOOK!
WHO THE FUCK CALLED THE BLOODY POLIS--?
SARAH, C'MON, PET! LET'S GET TO FUCK!
RIGHT YE ARE, UNCLE JOE--
HNNNHH!!

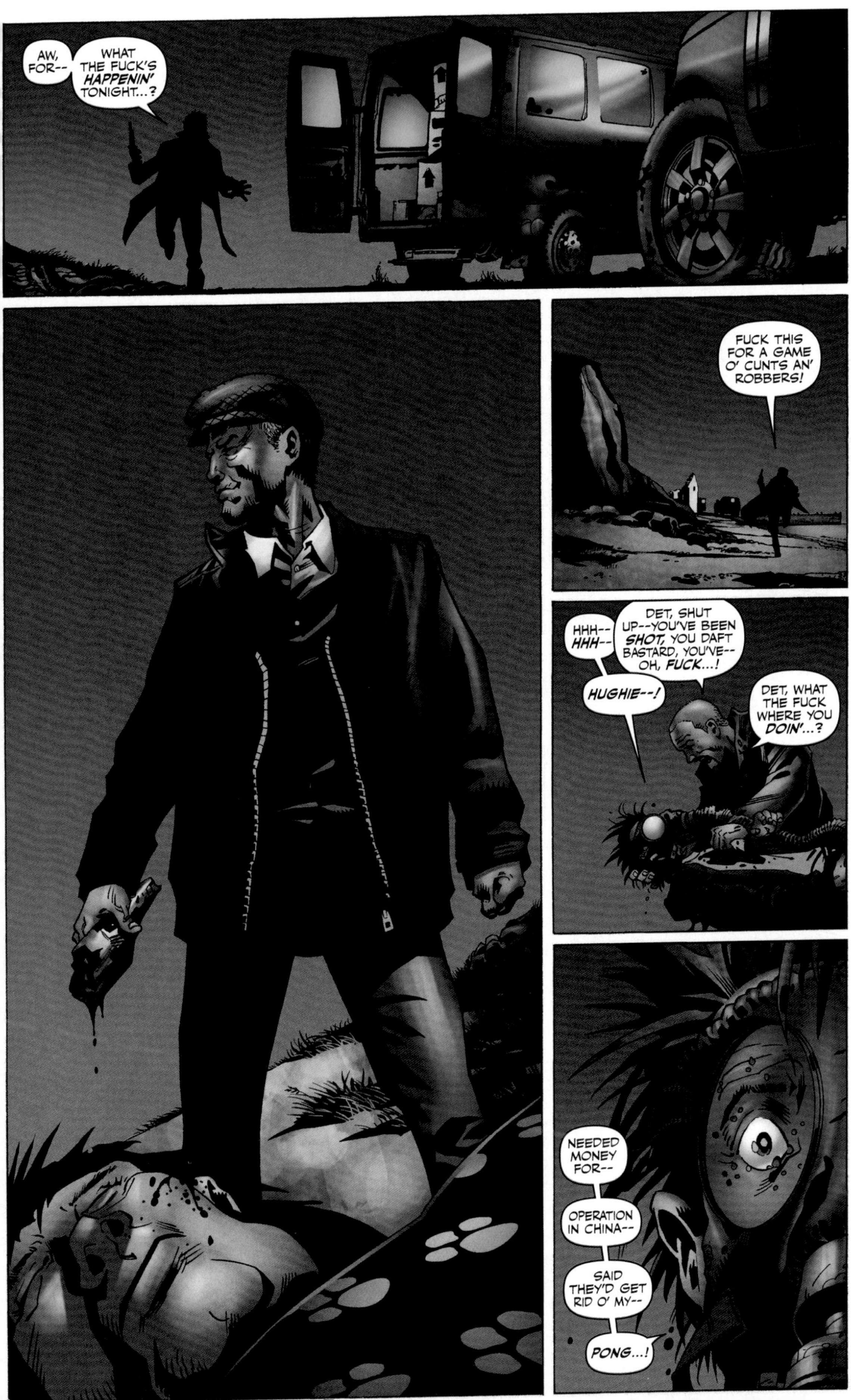
AW, FOR--
WHAT THE FUCK'S HAPPENIN' TONIGHT...?
FUCK THIS FOR A GAME O' CUNTS AN' ROBBERS!
HHH-- HHH--
DET, SHUT UP--YOU'VE BEEN SHOT, YOU DAFT BASTARD, YOU'VE-- OH, FUCK...!
HUGHIE--!
DET, WHAT THE FUCK WHERE YOU DOIN'...?
NEEDED MONEY FOR--
OPERATION IN CHINA--
SAID THEY'D GET RID O' MY--
PONG...!

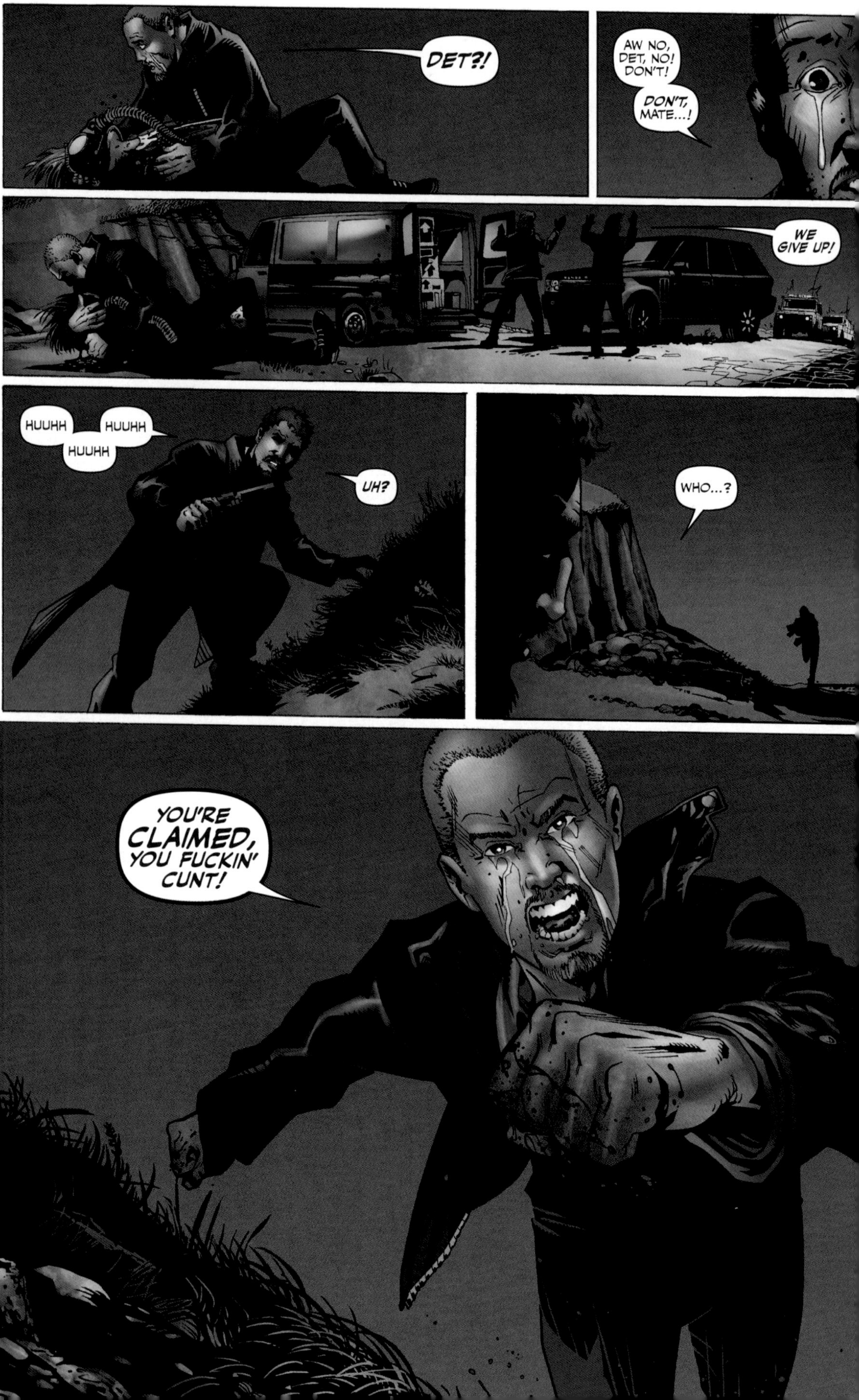
DET?!
AW NO, DET, NO! DON'T!
DON'T, MATE...!
WE GIVE UP!
HUUHH
HUUHH
HUUHH
UH?
WHO...?
YOU'RE CLAIMED, YOU FUCKIN' CUNT!

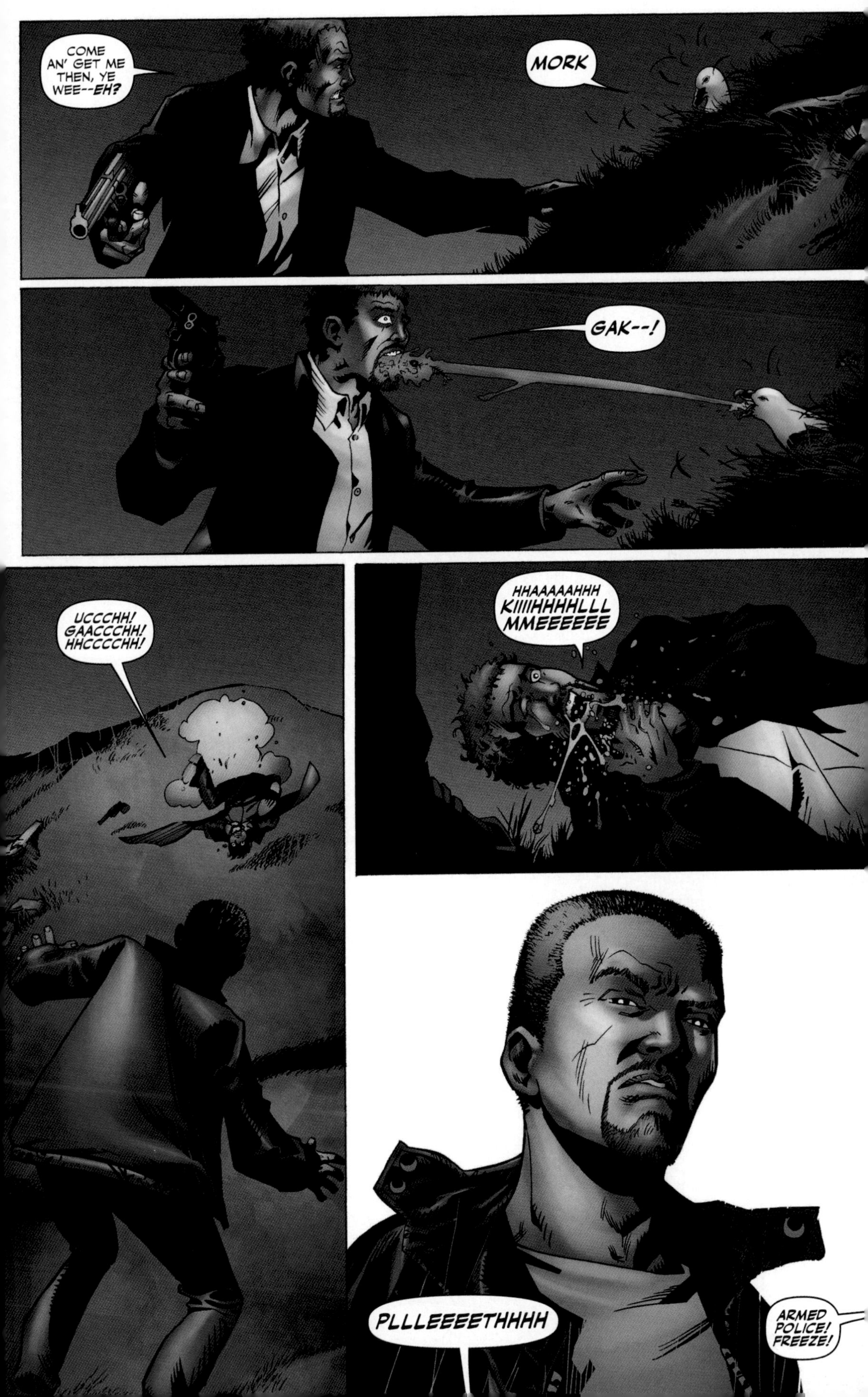
COME AN' GET ME THEN, YE WEE--EH?
MORK
GAK--!
UCCCHH! GAACCCHH! HHCCCCHH!
HHAAAAAAHHH KIIIIHHHHLLL MMEEEEEE
PLLLEEEETHHHH
ARMED POLICE! FREEZE!

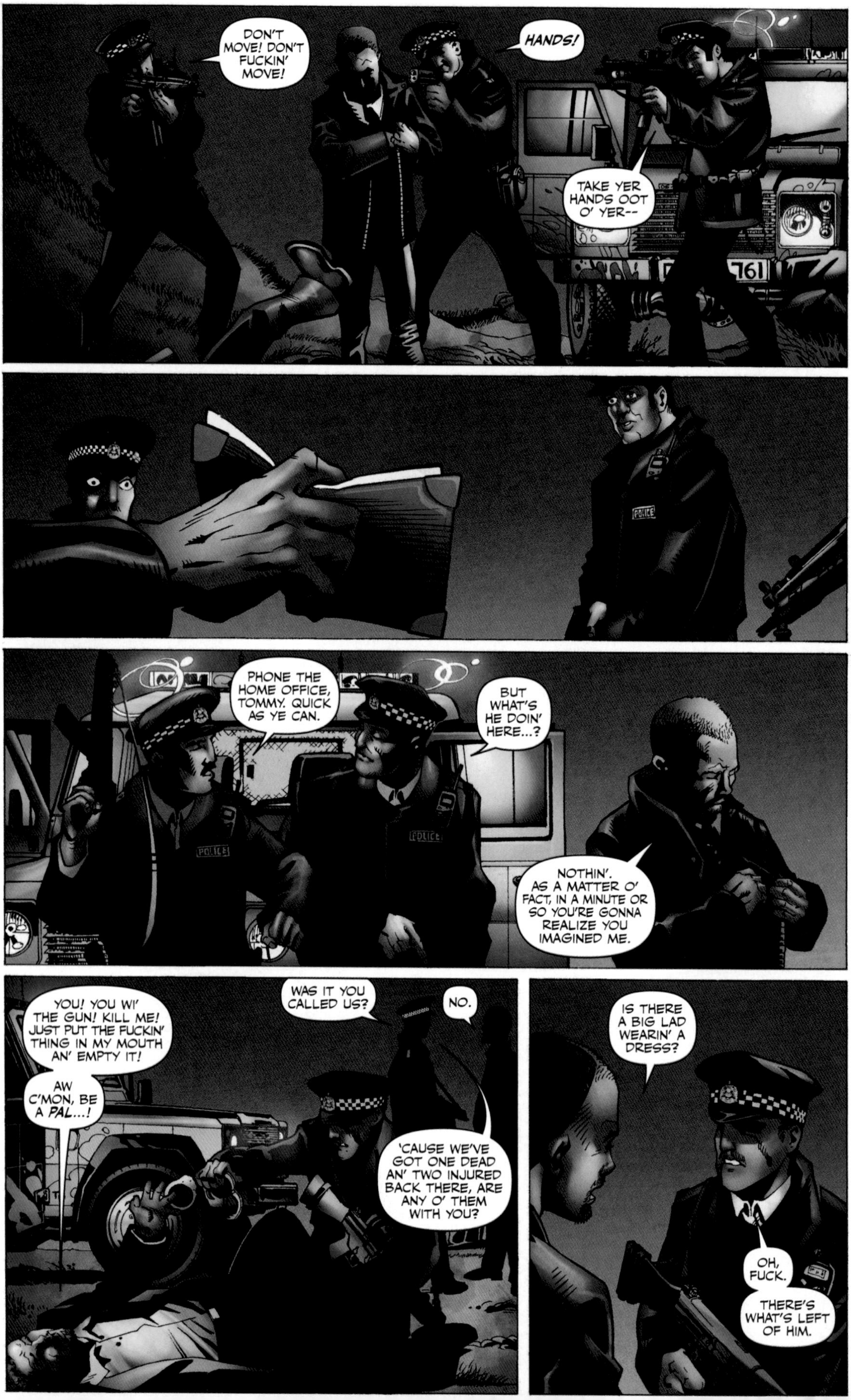
DON'T MOVE! DON'T FUCKIN' MOVE!
HANDS!
TAKE YER HANDS OOT O' YER--
POLICE
PHONE THE HOME OFFICE, TOMMY. QUICK AS YE CAN.
BUT WHAT'S HE DOIN' HERE...?
NOTHIN'. AS A MATTER O' FACT, IN A MINUTE OR SO YOU'RE GONNA REALIZE YOU IMAGINED ME.
YOU! YOU WI' THE GUN! KILL ME! JUST PUT THE FUCKIN' THING IN MY MOUTH AN' EMPTY IT!
AW C'MON, BE A *PAL*...!
WAS IT YOU CALLED US?
NO.
'CAUSE WE'VE GOT ONE DEAD AN' TWO INJURED BACK THERE, ARE ANY O' THEM WITH YOU?
IS THERE A BIG LAD WEARIN' A DRESS?
OH, FUCK.
THERE'S WHAT'S LEFT OF HIM.

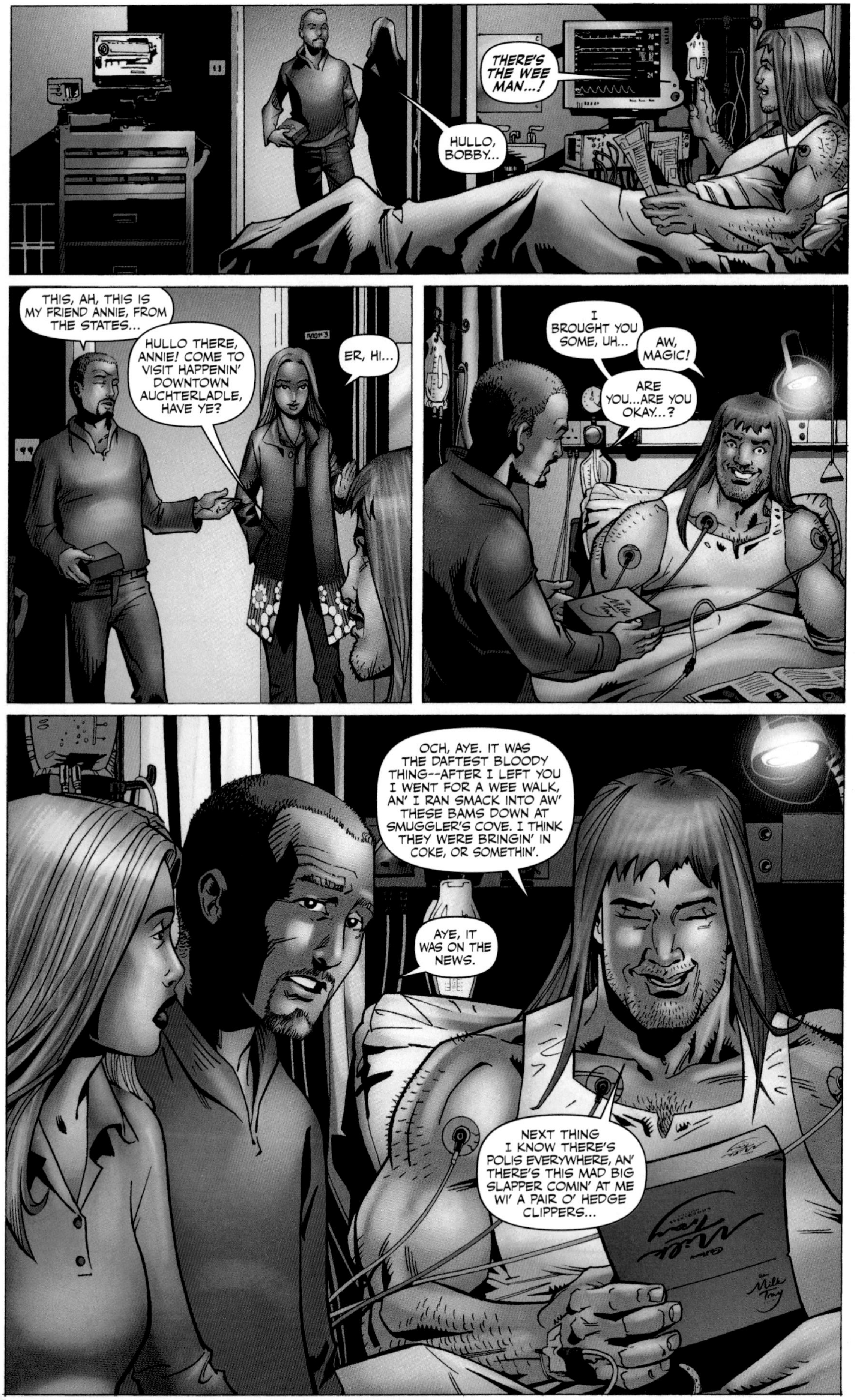
THERE'S THE WEE MAN...!
HULLO, BOBBY...
THIS, AH, THIS IS MY FRIEND ANNIE, FROM THE STATES...
HULLO THERE, ANNIE! COME TO VISIT HAPPENIN' DOWNTOWN AUCHTERLADLE, HAVE YE?
ER, HI...
I BROUGHT YOU SOME, UH...
AW, MAGIC!
ARE YOU...ARE YOU OKAY...?
OCH, AYE. IT WAS THE DAFTEST BLOODY THING--AFTER I LEFT YOU I WENT FOR A WEE WALK, AN' I RAN SMACK INTO AW' THESE BAMS DOWN AT SMUGGLER'S COVE. I THINK THEY WERE BRINGIN' IN COKE, OR SOMETHIN'.
AYE, IT WAS ON THE NEWS.
NEXT THING I KNOW THERE'S POLIS EVERYWHERE, AN' THERE'S THIS MAD BIG SLAPPER COMIN' AT ME WI' A PAIR O' HEDGE CLIPPERS...

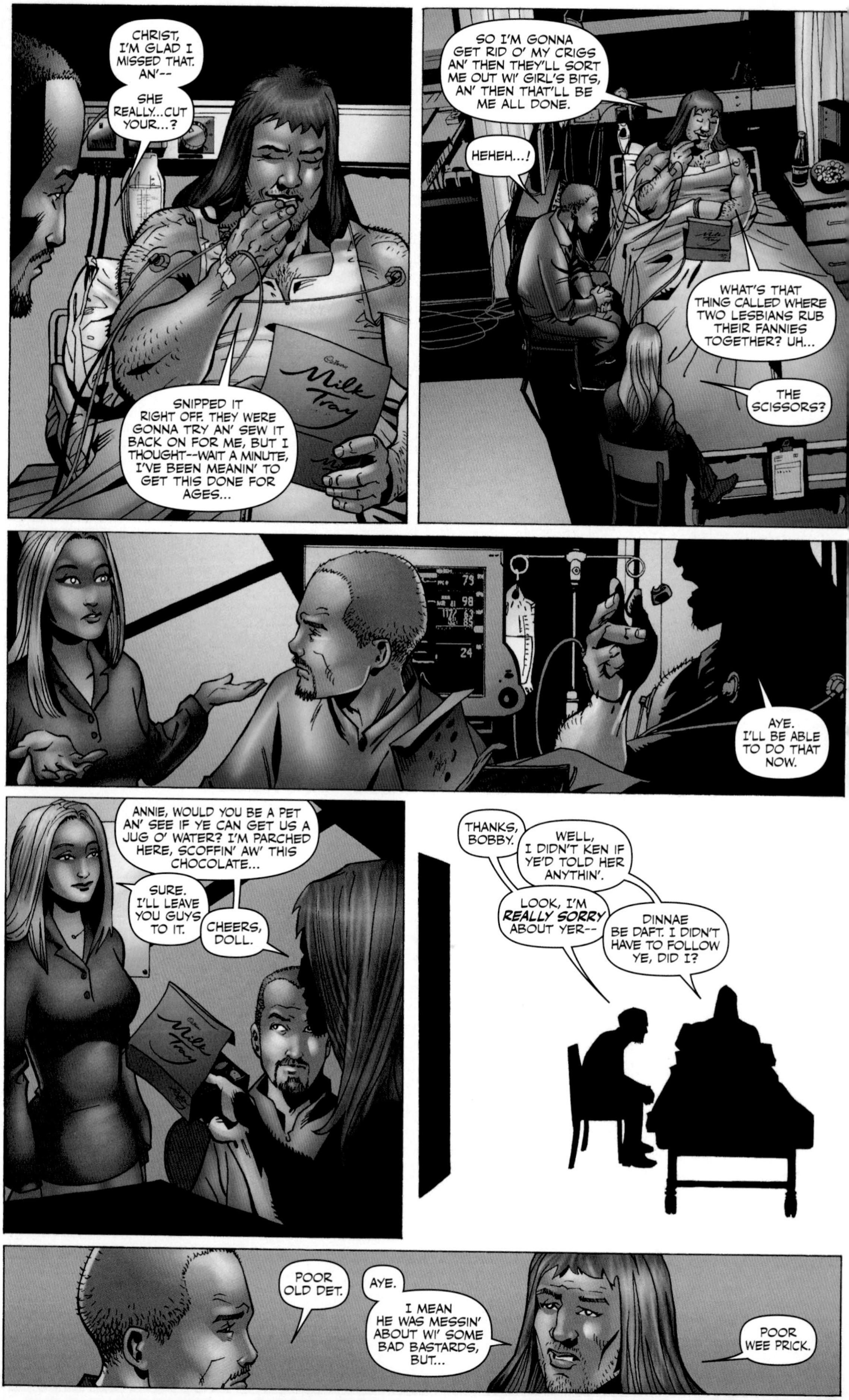
CHRIST, I'M GLAD I MISSED THAT. AN'--
SHE REALLY...CUT YOUR...?
SNIPPED IT RIGHT OFF. THEY WERE GONNA TRY AN' SEW IT BACK ON FOR ME, BUT I THOUGHT--WAIT A MINUTE, I'VE BEEN MEANIN' TO GET THIS DONE FOR AGES...
Milk Tray
SO I'M GONNA GET RID O' MY CRIGS AN' THEN THEY'LL SORT ME OUT WI' GIRL'S BITS, AN' THEN THAT'LL BE ME ALL DONE.
HEHEH...!
WHAT'S THAT THING CALLED WHERE TWO LESBIANS RUB THEIR FANNIES TOGETHER? UH...
THE SCISSORS?
AYE. I'LL BE ABLE TO DO THAT NOW.
ANNIE, WOULD YOU BE A PET AN' SEE IF YE CAN GET US A JUG O' WATER? I'M PARCHED HERE, SCOFFIN' AW' THIS CHOCOLATE...
SURE. I'LL LEAVE YOU GUYS TO IT.
CHEERS, DOLL.
THANKS, BOBBY.
WELL, I DIDN'T KEN IF YE'D TOLD HER ANYTHIN'.
LOOK, I'M *REALLY SORRY* ABOUT YER--
DINNAE BE DAFT. I DIDN'T HAVE TO FOLLOW YE, DID I?
POOR OLD DET.
AYE.
I MEAN HE WAS MESSIN' ABOUT WI' SOME BAD BASTARDS, BUT...
POOR WEE PRICK.

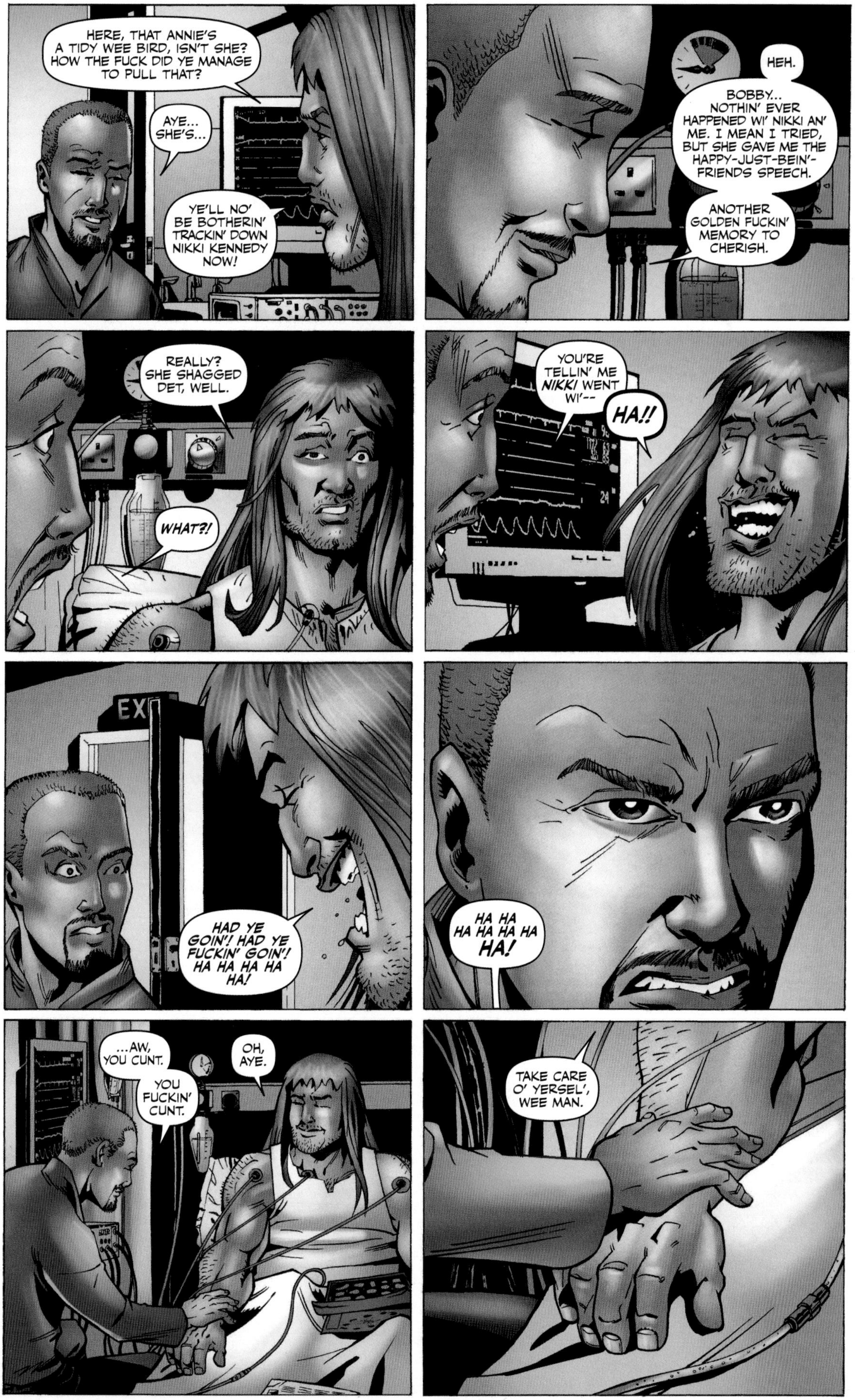
HERE, THAT ANNIE'S A TIDY WEE BIRD, ISN'T SHE? HOW THE FUCK DID YE MANAGE TO PULL THAT?
AYE... SHE'S...
YE'LL NO' BE BOTHERIN' TRACKIN' DOWN NIKKI KENNEDY NOW!
HEH.
BOBBY... NOTHIN' EVER HAPPENED WI' NIKKI AN' ME. I MEAN I TRIED, BUT SHE GAVE ME THE HAPPY-JUST-BEIN'-FRIENDS SPEECH.
ANOTHER GOLDEN FUCKIN' MEMORY TO CHERISH.
REALLY? SHE SHAGGED DET, WELL.
WHAT?!
YOU'RE TELLIN' ME NIKKI WENT WI'--
HA!!
HAD YE GOIN'! HAD YE FUCKIN' GOIN'! HA HA HA HA HA!
HA HA HA HA HA HA HA!
...AW, YOU CUNT.
YOU FUCKIN' CUNT.
OH, AYE.
TAKE CARE O' YERSEL', WEE MAN.

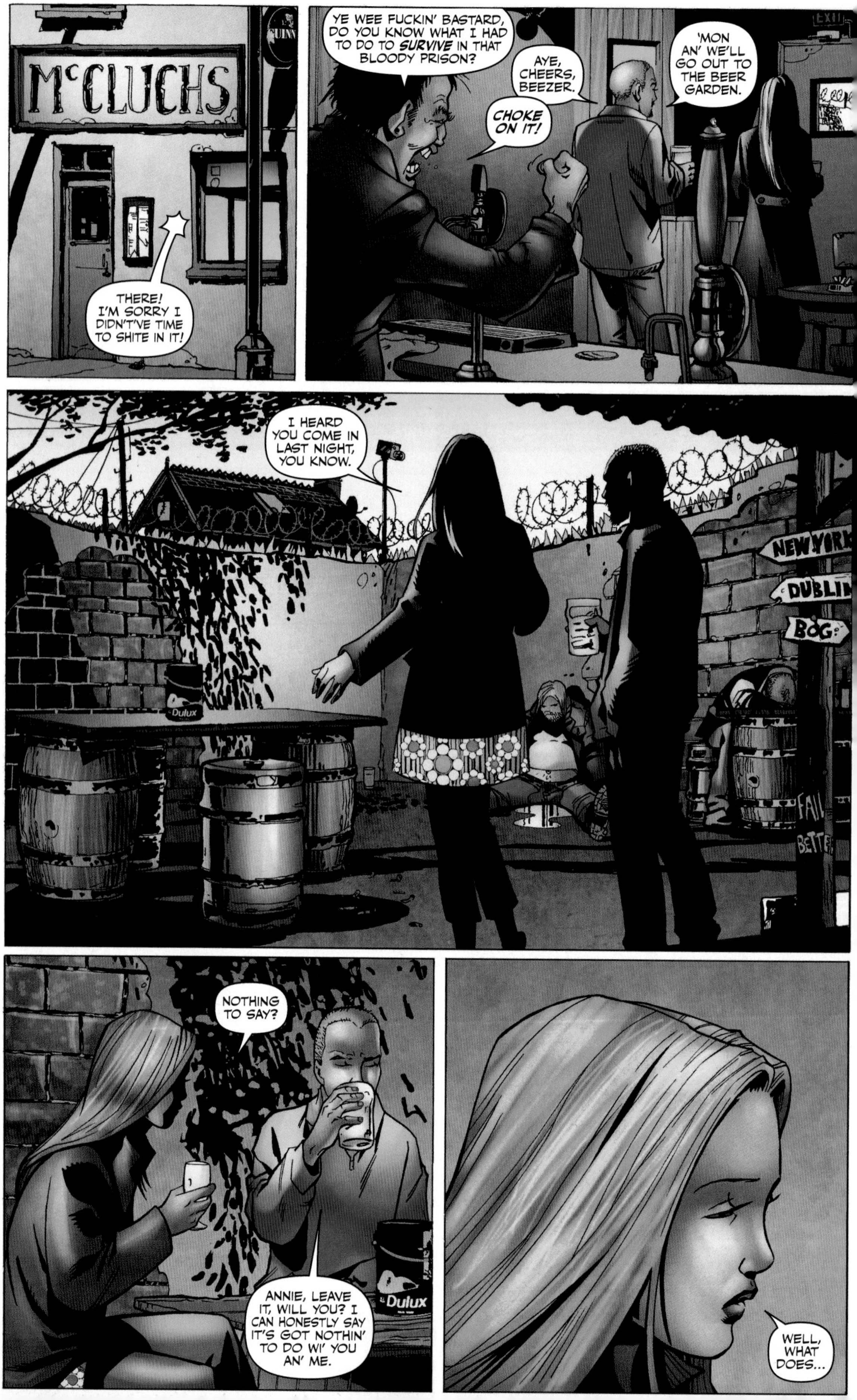
McCLUCHS
THERE! I'M SORRY I DIDN'T'VE TIME TO SHITE IN IT!
YE WEE FUCKIN' BASTARD, DO YOU KNOW WHAT I HAD TO DO TO *SURVIVE* IN THAT BLOODY PRISON?
AYE, CHEERS, BEEZER.
CHOKE ON IT!
'MON AN' WE'LL GO OUT TO THE BEER GARDEN.
EXIT
I HEARD YOU COME IN LAST NIGHT, YOU KNOW.
NEW YORK
DUBLIN
BOG
Dulux
NOTHING TO SAY?
ANNIE, LEAVE IT, WILL YOU? I CAN HONESTLY SAY IT'S GOT NOTHIN' TO DO WI' YOU AN' ME.
Dulux
WELL, WHAT DOES...

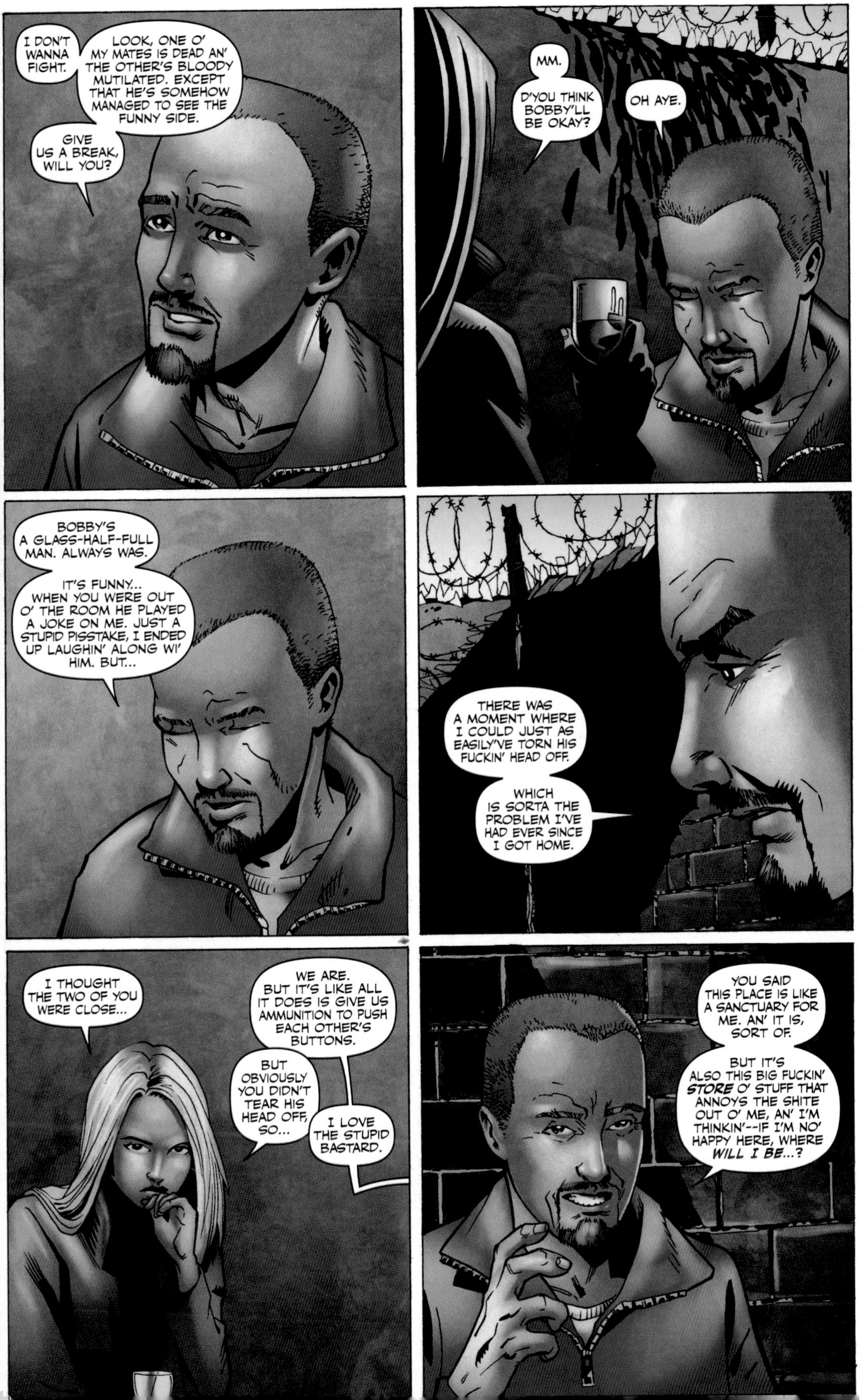
I DON'T WANNA FIGHT.
LOOK, ONE O' MY MATES IS DEAD AN' THE OTHER'S BLOODY MUTILATED. EXCEPT THAT HE'S SOMEHOW MANAGED TO SEE THE FUNNY SIDE.
GIVE US A BREAK, WILL YOU?
MM.
D'YOU THINK BOBBY'LL BE OKAY?
OH AYE.
BOBBY'S A GLASS-HALF-FULL MAN. ALWAYS WAS.
IT'S FUNNY... WHEN YOU WERE OUT O' THE ROOM HE PLAYED A JOKE ON ME. JUST A STUPID PISSTAKE, I ENDED UP LAUGHIN' ALONG WI' HIM. BUT...
THERE WAS A MOMENT WHERE I COULD JUST AS EASILY'VE TORN HIS FUCKIN' HEAD OFF.
WHICH IS SORTA THE PROBLEM I'VE HAD EVER SINCE I GOT HOME.
I THOUGHT THE TWO OF YOU WERE CLOSE...
WE ARE. BUT IT'S LIKE ALL IT DOES IS GIVE US AMMUNITION TO PUSH EACH OTHER'S BUTTONS.
BUT OBVIOUSLY YOU DIDN'T TEAR HIS HEAD OFF, SO...
I LOVE THE STUPID BASTARD.
YOU SAID THIS PLACE IS LIKE A SANCTUARY FOR ME. AN' IT IS, SORT OF.
BUT IT'S ALSO THIS BIG FUCKIN' *STORE* O' STUFF THAT ANNOYS THE SHITE OUT O' ME, AN' I'M THINKIN'--IF I'M NO' HAPPY HERE, WHERE *WILL I BE*...?

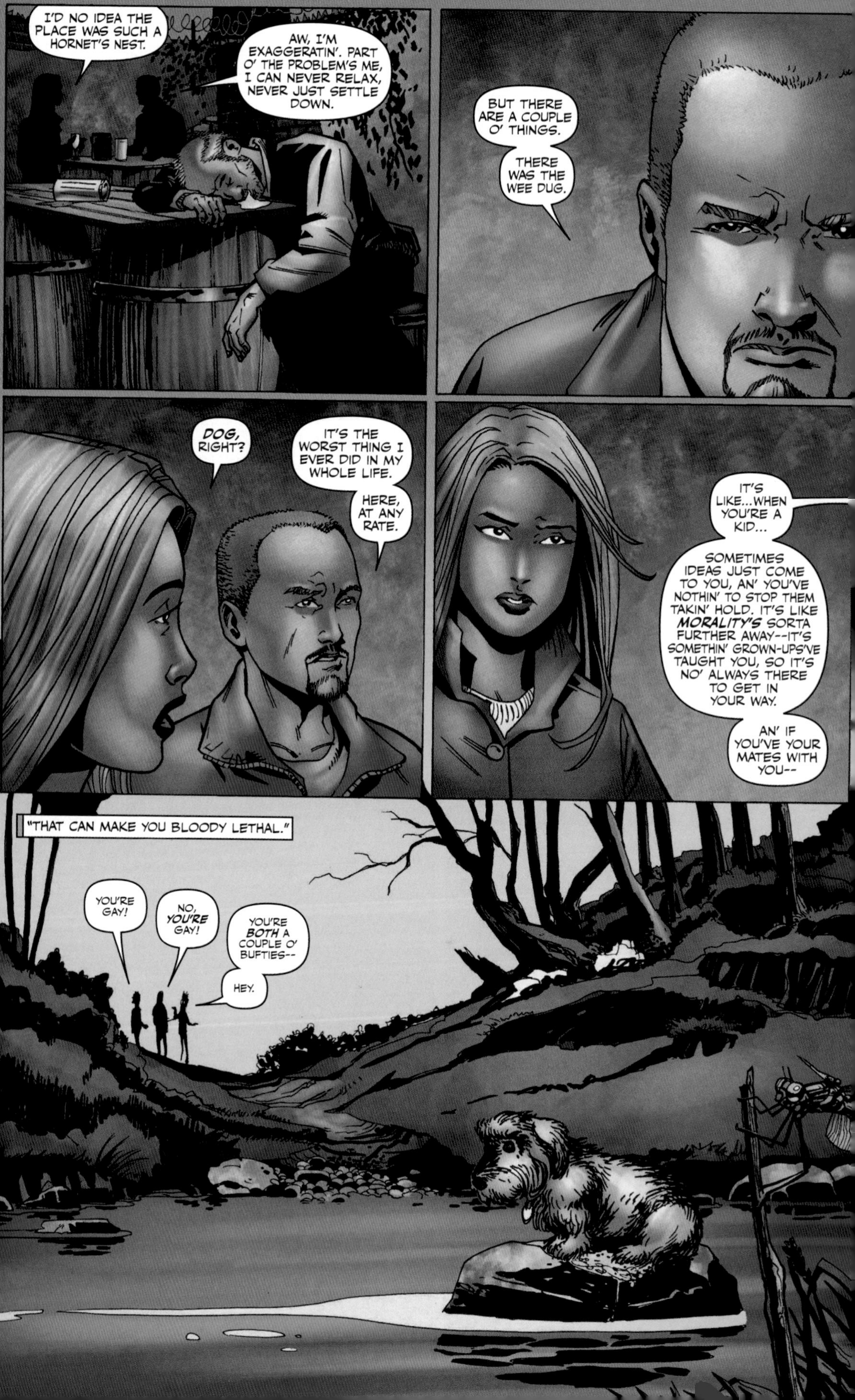
I'D NO IDEA THE PLACE WAS SUCH A HORNET'S NEST.
AW, I'M EXAGGERATIN'. PART O' THE PROBLEM'S ME, I CAN NEVER RELAX, NEVER JUST SETTLE DOWN.
BUT THERE ARE A COUPLE O' THINGS.
THERE WAS THE WEE DUG.
DOG, RIGHT?
IT'S THE WORST THING I EVER DID IN MY WHOLE LIFE.
HERE, AT ANY RATE.
IT'S LIKE...WHEN YOU'RE A KID...
SOMETIMES IDEAS JUST COME TO YOU, AN' YOU'VE NOTHIN' TO STOP THEM TAKIN' HOLD. IT'S LIKE *MORALITY'S* SORTA FURTHER AWAY--IT'S SOMETHIN' GROWN-UPS'VE TAUGHT YOU, SO IT'S NO' ALWAYS THERE TO GET IN YOUR WAY.
AN' IF YOU'VE YOUR MATES WITH YOU--
"THAT CAN MAKE YOU BLOODY LETHAL."
YOU'RE GAY!
NO, *YOU'RE* GAY!
YOU'RE *BOTH* A COUPLE O' BUFTIES--
HEY.

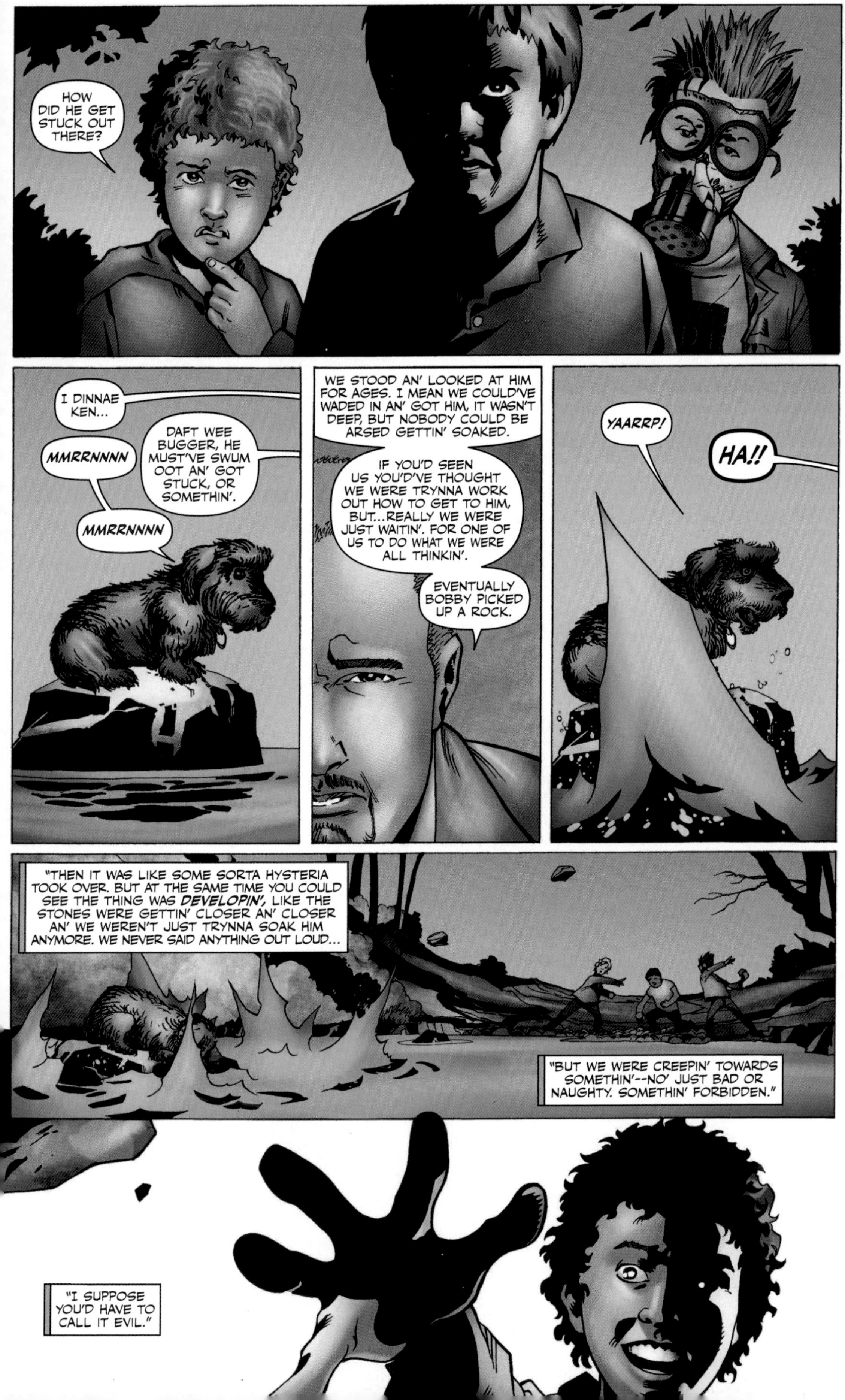
HOW DID HE GET STUCK OUT THERE?
I DINNAE KEN...
DAFT WEE BUGGER, HE MUST'VE SWUM OOT AN' GOT STUCK, OR SOMETHIN'.
MMRRNNNN
MMRRNNNN
WE STOOD AN' LOOKED AT HIM FOR AGES. I MEAN WE COULD'VE WADED IN AN' GOT HIM, IT WASN'T DEEP, BUT NOBODY COULD BE ARSED GETTIN' SOAKED.
IF YOU'D SEEN US YOU'D'VE THOUGHT WE WERE TRYNNA WORK OUT HOW TO GET TO HIM, BUT...REALLY WE WERE JUST WAITIN'. FOR ONE OF US TO DO WHAT WE WERE ALL THINKIN'.
EVENTUALLY BOBBY PICKED UP A ROCK.
YAARRP!
HA!!
"THEN IT WAS LIKE SOME SORTA HYSTERIA TOOK OVER. BUT AT THE SAME TIME YOU COULD SEE THE THING WAS DEVELOPIN', LIKE THE STONES WERE GETTIN' CLOSER AN' CLOSER AN' WE WEREN'T JUST TRYNNA SOAK HIM ANYMORE. WE NEVER SAID ANYTHING OUT LOUD...
"BUT WE WERE CREEPIN' TOWARDS SOMETHIN'--NO' JUST BAD OR NAUGHTY. SOMETHIN' FORBIDDEN."
"I SUPPOSE YOU'D HAVE TO CALL IT EVIL."

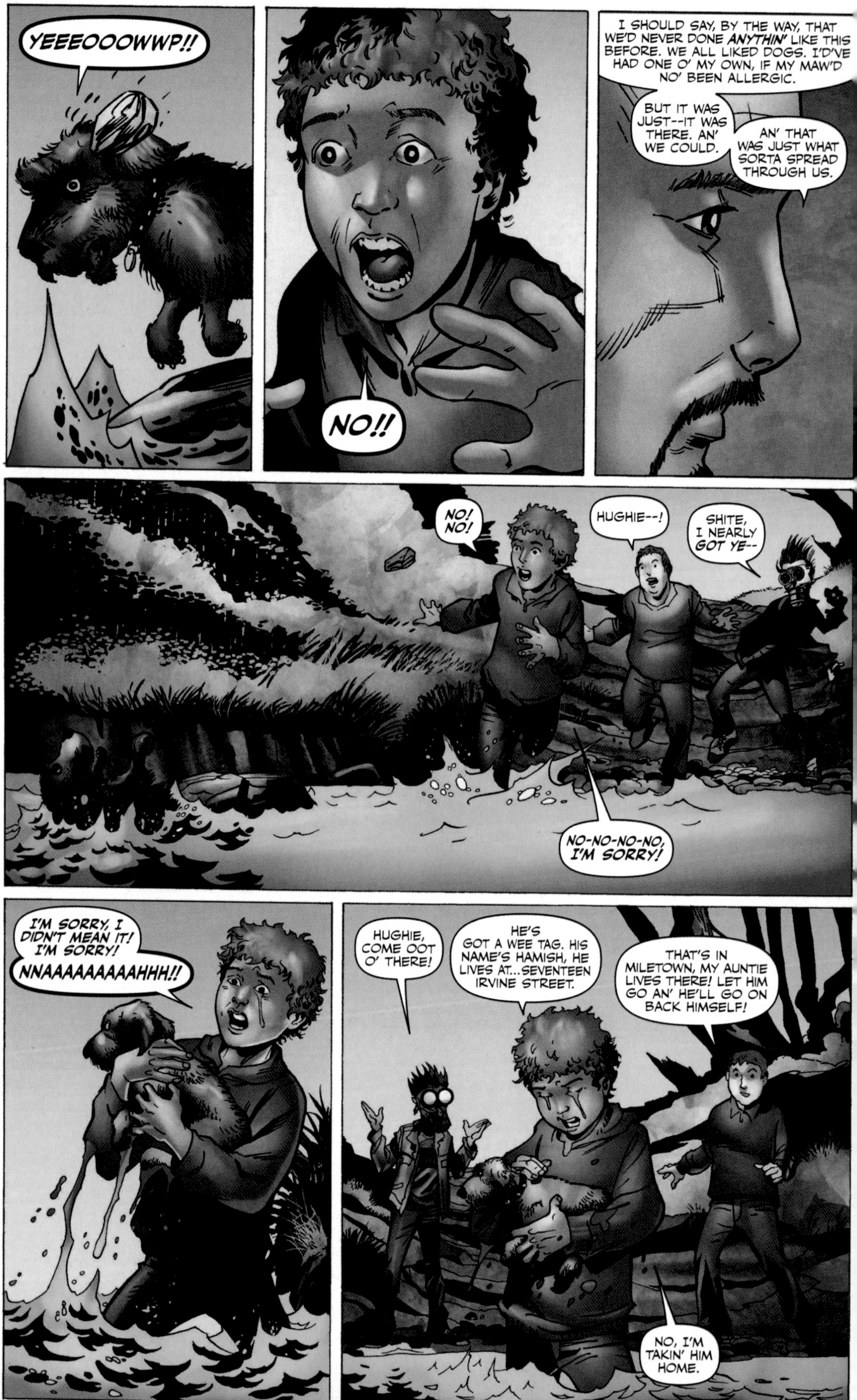
YEEEOOOWWP!!
NO!!
I SHOULD SAY, BY THE WAY, THAT WE'D NEVER DONE ANYTHIN' LIKE THIS BEFORE. WE ALL LIKED DOGS. I'D'VE HAD ONE O' MY OWN, IF MY MAW'D NO' BEEN ALLERGIC.
BUT IT WAS JUST--IT WAS THERE. AN' WE COULD.
AN' THAT WAS JUST WHAT SORTA SPREAD THROUGH US.
NO! NO!
HUGHIE--!
SHITE, I NEARLY GOT YE--
NO-NO-NO-NO, I'M SORRY!
I'M SORRY, I DIDN'T MEAN IT! I'M SORRY! NNAAAAAAAAAAHHH!!
HUGHIE, COME OOT O' THERE!
HE'S GOT A WEE TAG. HIS NAME'S HAMISH, HE LIVES AT...SEVENTEEN IRVINE STREET.
THAT'S IN MILETOWN, MY AUNTIE LIVES THERE! LET HIM GO AN' HE'LL GO ON BACK HIMSELF!
NO, I'M TAKIN' HIM HOME.

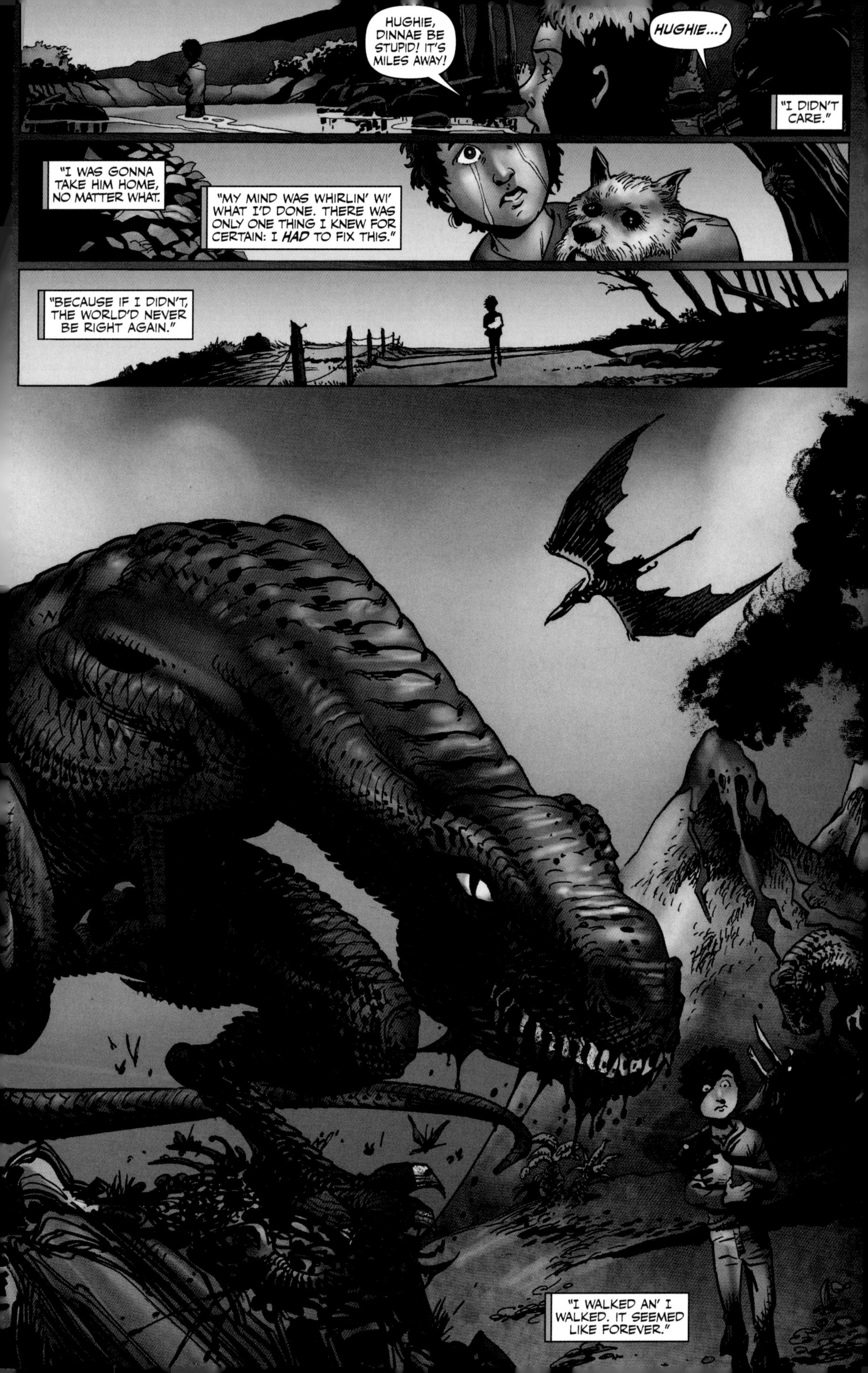
HUGHIE, DINNAE BE STUPID! IT'S MILES AWAY!
HUGHIE...!
"I DIDN'T CARE."
"I WAS GONNA TAKE HIM HOME, NO MATTER WHAT.
"MY MIND WAS WHIRLIN' WI' WHAT I'D DONE. THERE WAS ONLY ONE THING I KNEW FOR CERTAIN: I HAD TO FIX THIS."
"BECAUSE IF I DIDN'T, THE WORLD'D NEVER BE RIGHT AGAIN."
"I WALKED AN' I WALKED. IT SEEMED LIKE FOREVER."

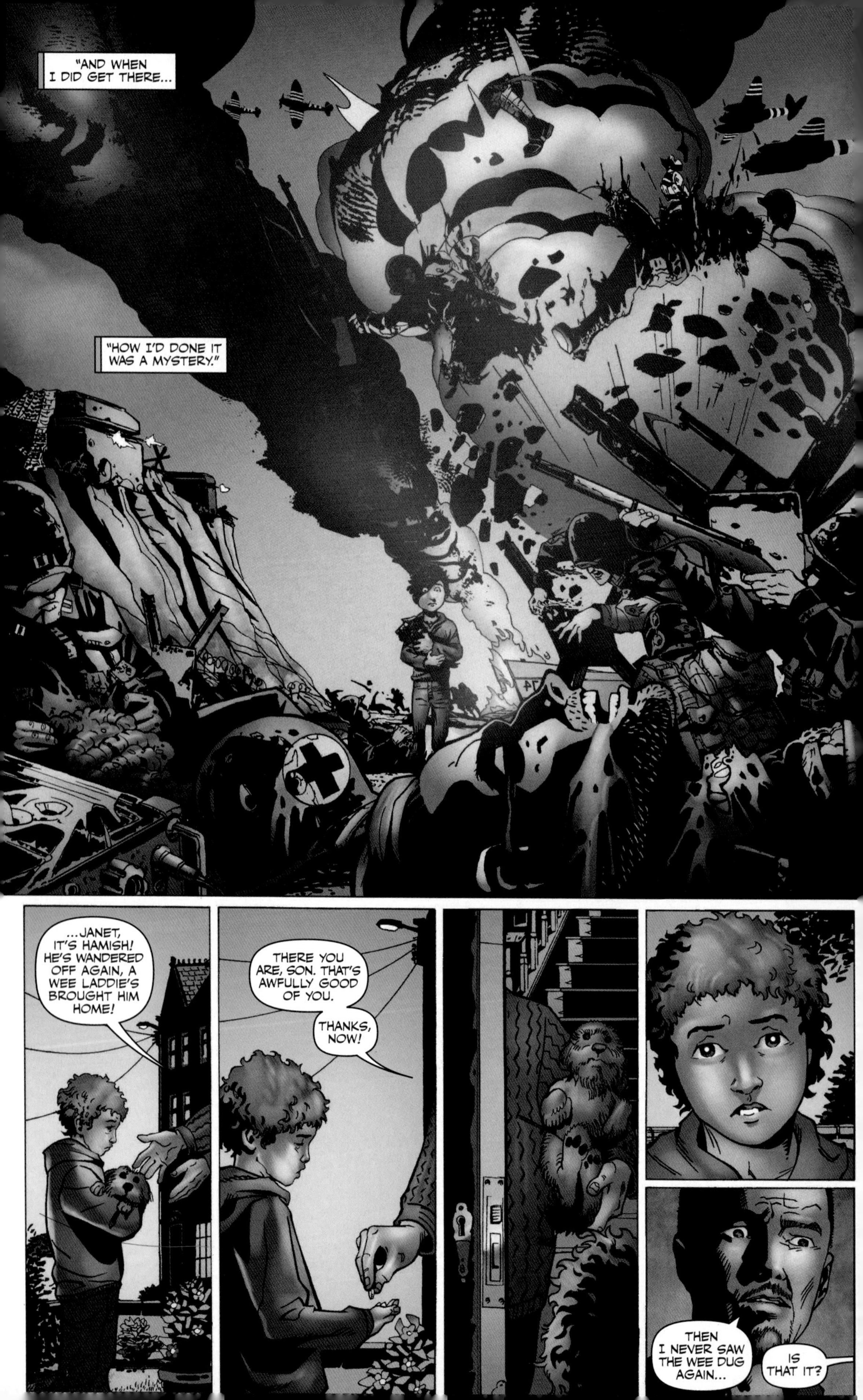
"AND WHEN I DID GET THERE...
"HOW I'D DONE IT WAS A MYSTERY."
...JANET, IT'S HAMISH! HE'S WANDERED OFF AGAIN, A WEE LADDIE'S BROUGHT HIM HOME!
THERE YOU ARE, SON. THAT'S AWFULLY GOOD OF YOU.
THANKS, NOW!
THEN I NEVER SAW THE WEE DUG AGAIN...
IS THAT IT?

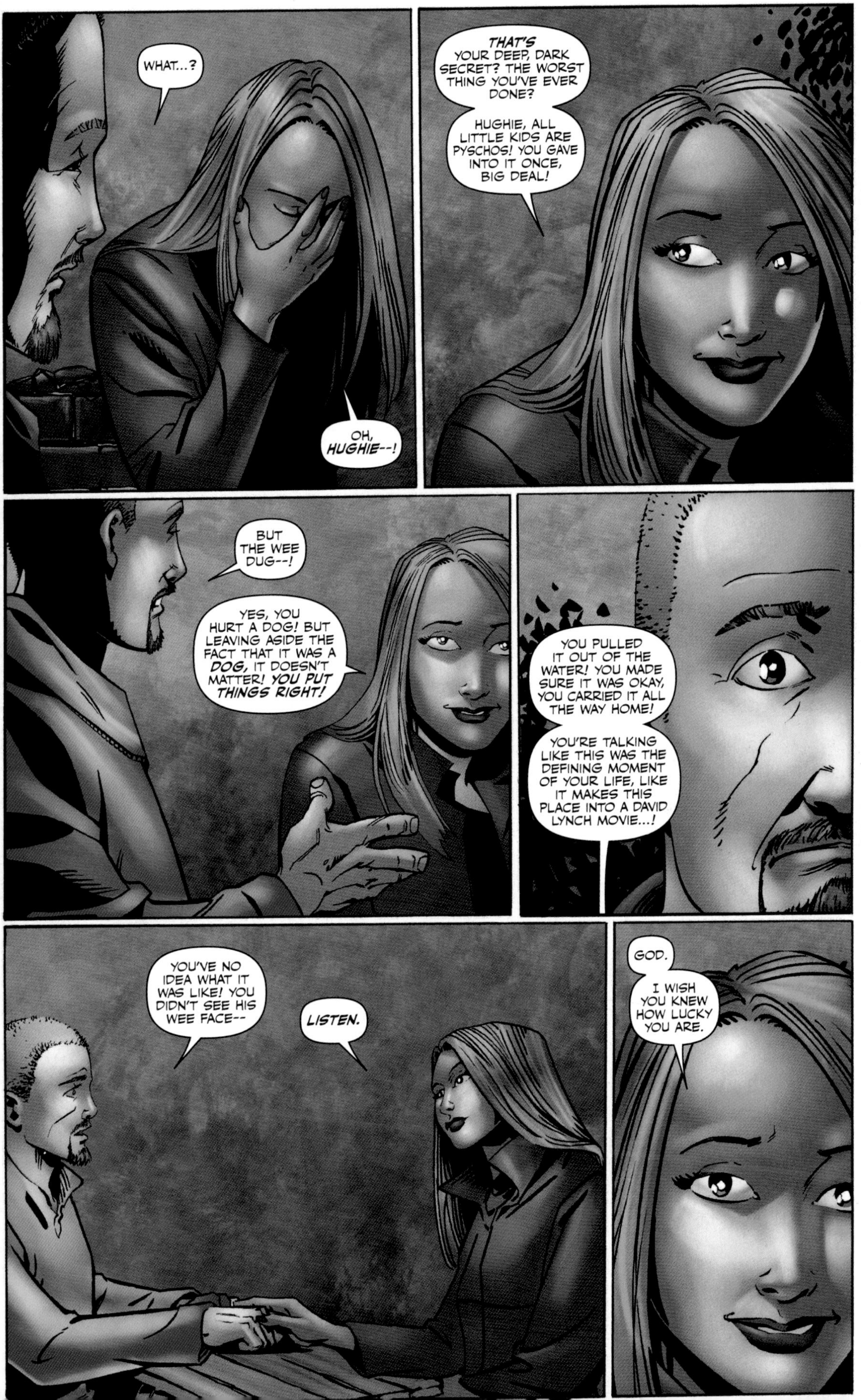
WHAT...?
OH, HUGHIE--!
THAT'S YOUR DEEP, DARK SECRET? THE WORST THING YOU'VE EVER DONE?
HUGHIE, ALL LITTLE KIDS ARE PYSCHOS! YOU GAVE INTO IT ONCE, BIG DEAL!
BUT THE WEE DUG--!
YES, YOU HURT A DOG! BUT LEAVING ASIDE THE FACT THAT IT WAS A DOG, IT DOESN'T MATTER! YOU PUT THINGS RIGHT!
YOU PULLED IT OUT OF THE WATER! YOU MADE SURE IT WAS OKAY, YOU CARRIED IT ALL THE WAY HOME!
YOU'RE TALKING LIKE THIS WAS THE DEFINING MOMENT OF YOUR LIFE, LIKE IT MAKES THIS PLACE INTO A DAVID LYNCH MOVIE...!
YOU'VE NO IDEA WHAT IT WAS LIKE! YOU DIDN'T SEE HIS WEE FACE--
LISTEN.
GOD.
I WISH YOU KNEW HOW LUCKY YOU ARE.

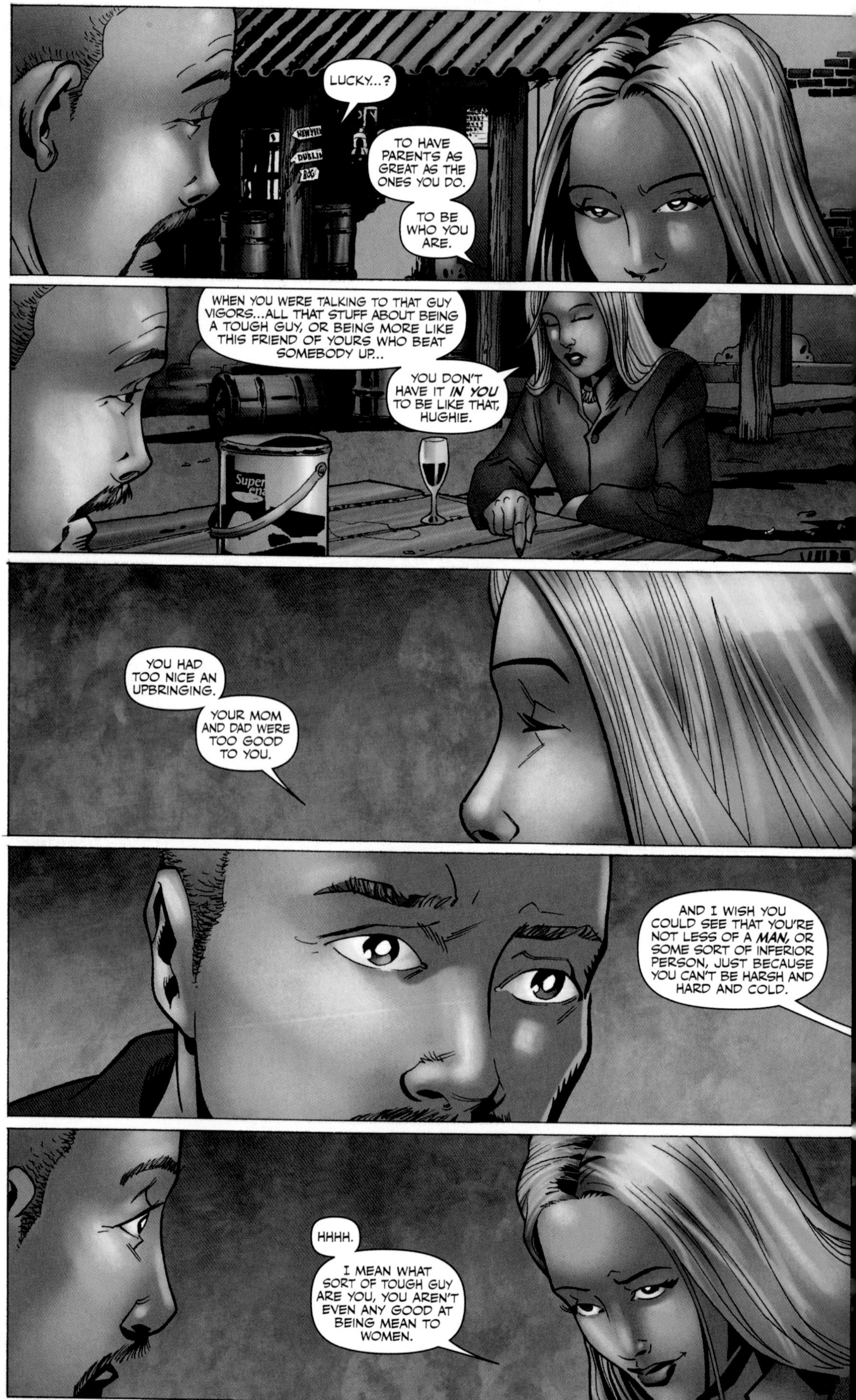

LUCKY...?
TO HAVE PARENTS AS GREAT AS THE ONES YOU DO.
TO BE WHO YOU ARE.
NEW YORK
DUBLIN
WHEN YOU WERE TALKING TO THAT GUY VIGORS...ALL THAT STUFF ABOUT BEING A TOUGH GUY, OR BEING MORE LIKE THIS FRIEND OF YOURS WHO BEAT SOMEBODY UP...
YOU DON'T HAVE IT *IN YOU* TO BE LIKE THAT, HUGHIE.
YOU HAD TOO NICE AN UPBRINGING.
YOUR MOM AND DAD WERE TOO GOOD TO YOU.
AND I WISH YOU COULD SEE THAT YOU'RE NOT LESS OF A *MAN,* OR SOME SORT OF INFERIOR PERSON, JUST BECAUSE YOU CAN'T BE HARSH AND HARD AND COLD.
HHHH.
I MEAN WHAT SORT OF TOUGH GUY ARE YOU, YOU AREN'T EVEN ANY GOOD AT BEING MEAN TO WOMEN.

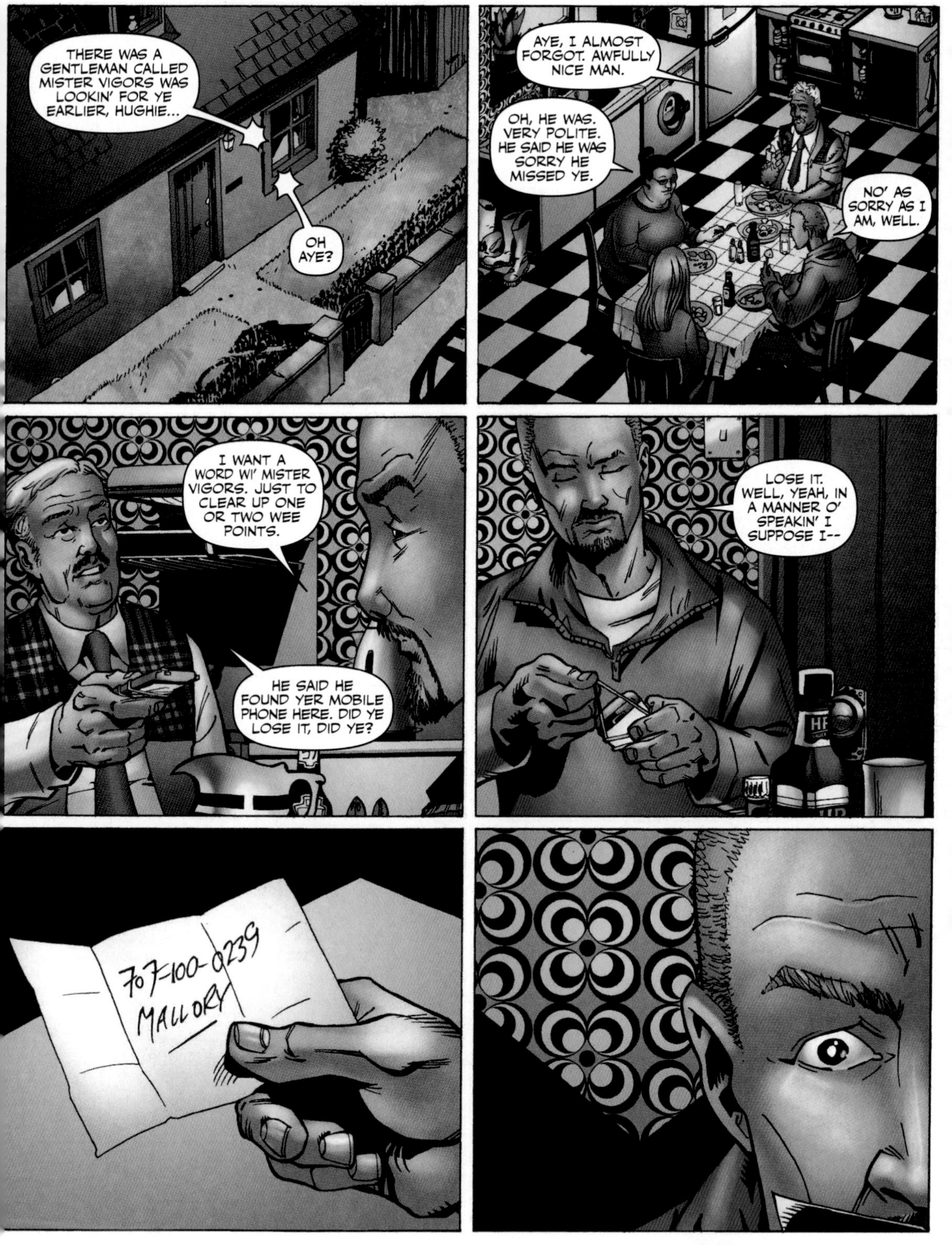
THERE WAS A GENTLEMAN CALLED MISTER VIGORS WAS LOOKIN' FOR YE EARLIER, HUGHIE...
OH AYE?
AYE, I ALMOST FORGOT. AWFULLY NICE MAN.
OH, HE WAS. VERY POLITE. HE SAID HE WAS SORRY HE MISSED YE.
NO' AS SORRY AS I AM, WELL.
I WANT A WORD WI' MISTER VIGORS. JUST TO CLEAR UP ONE OR TWO WEE POINTS.
HE SAID HE FOUND YER MOBILE PHONE HERE. DID YE LOSE IT, DID YE?
LOSE IT. WELL, YEAH, IN A MANNER O' SPEAKIN' I SUPPOSE I--
HP
707-100-0239
MALLORY

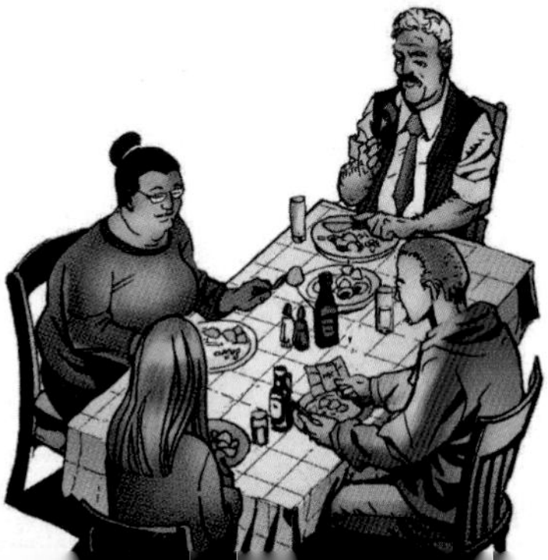

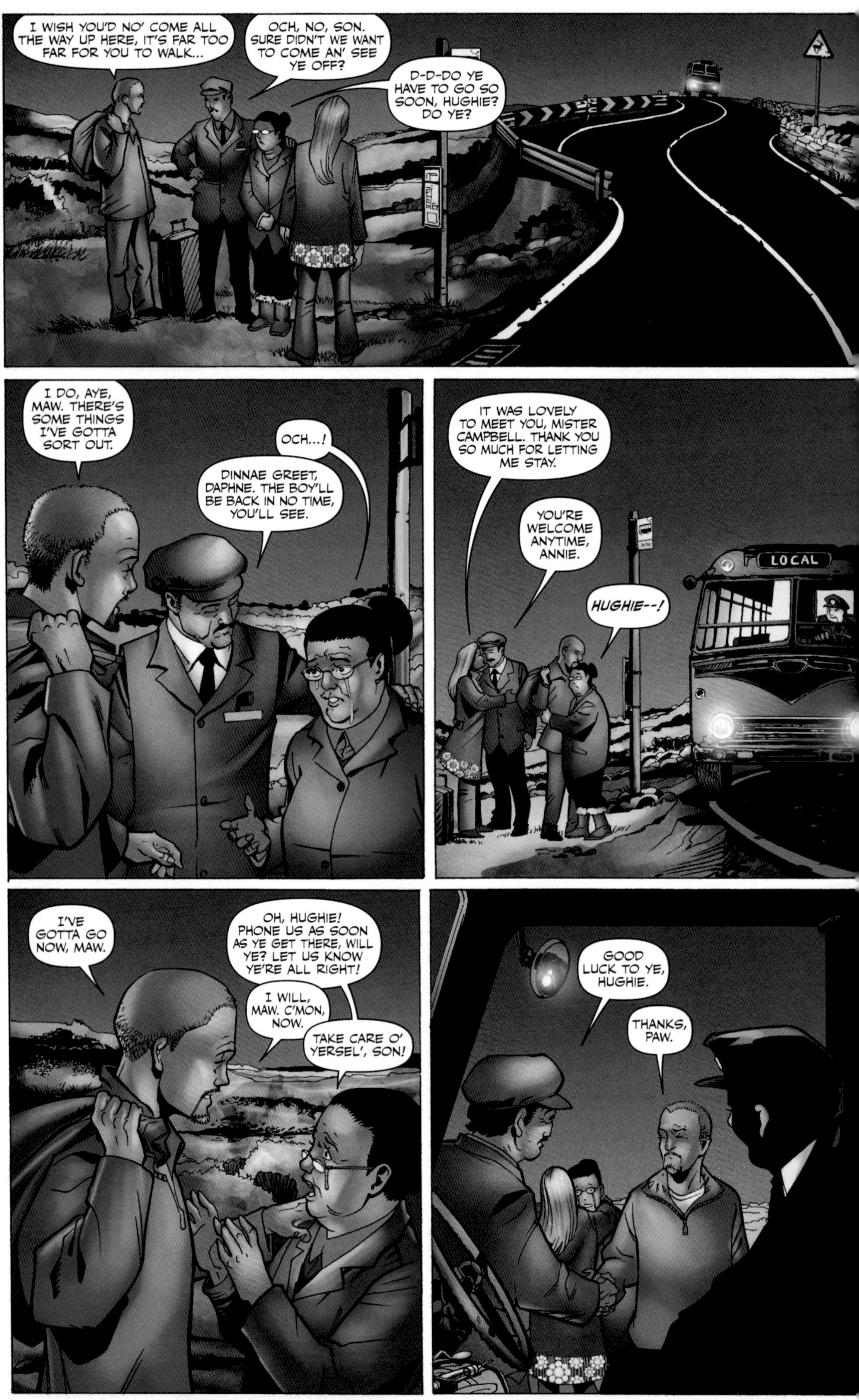
I WISH YOU'D NO' COME ALL THE WAY UP HERE, IT'S FAR TOO FAR FOR YOU TO WALK...
OCH, NO, SON. SURE DIDN'T WE WANT TO COME AN' SEE YE OFF?
D-D-DO YE HAVE TO GO SO SOON, HUGHIE? DO YE?
I DO, AYE, MAW. THERE'S SOME THINGS I'VE GOTTA SORT OUT.
OCH...!
DINNAE GREET, DAPHNE. THE BOY'LL BE BACK IN NO TIME, YOU'LL SEE.
IT WAS LOVELY TO MEET YOU, MISTER CAMPBELL. THANK YOU SO MUCH FOR LETTING ME STAY.
YOU'RE WELCOME ANYTIME, ANNIE.
HUGHIE--!
LOCAL
I'VE GOTTA GO NOW, MAW.
OH, HUGHIE! PHONE US AS SOON AS YE GET THERE, WILL YE? LET US KNOW YE'RE ALL RIGHT!
I WILL, MAW. C'MON, NOW.
TAKE CARE O' YERSEL', SON!
GOOD LUCK TO YE, HUGHIE.
THANKS, PAW.

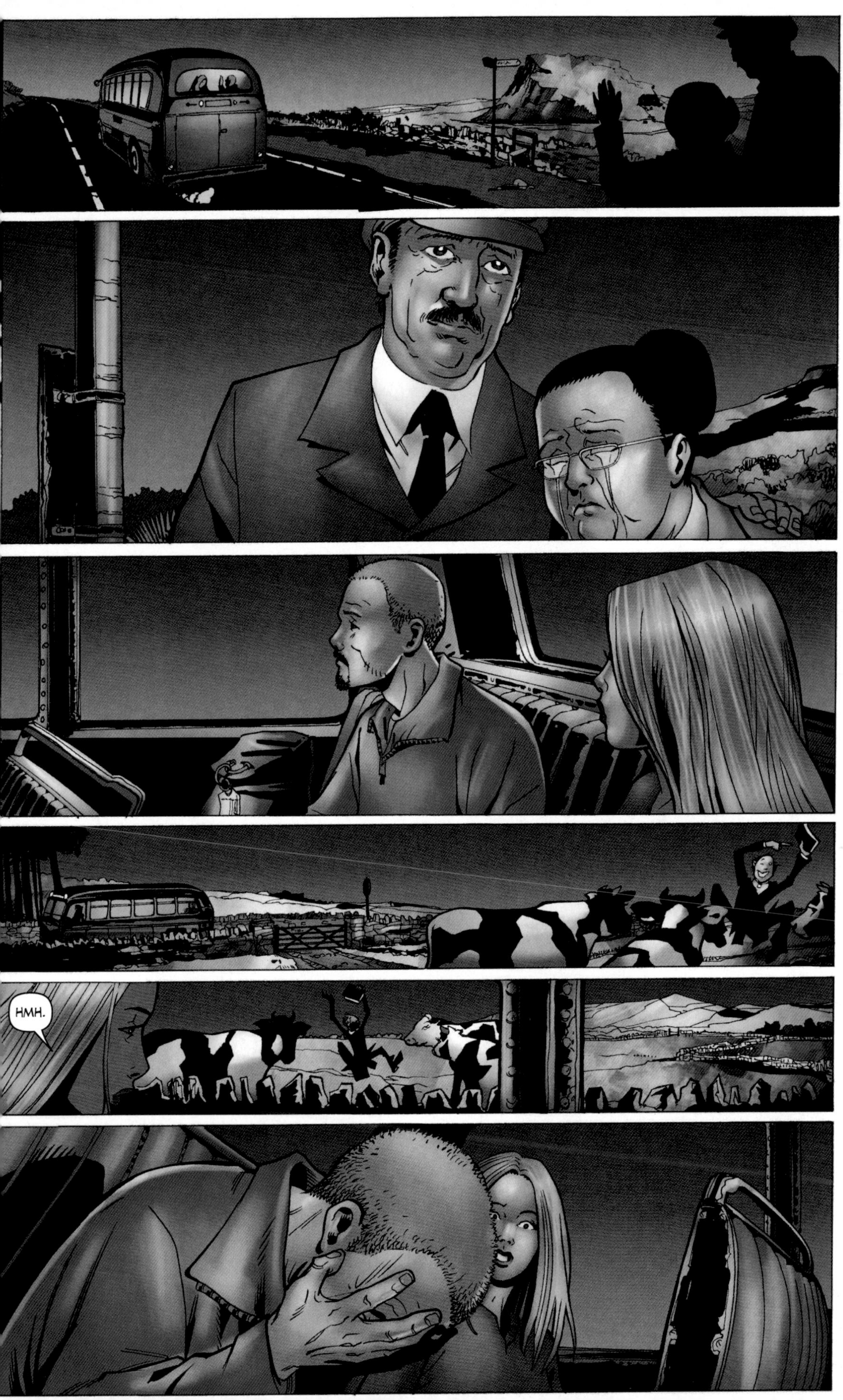
HMH.

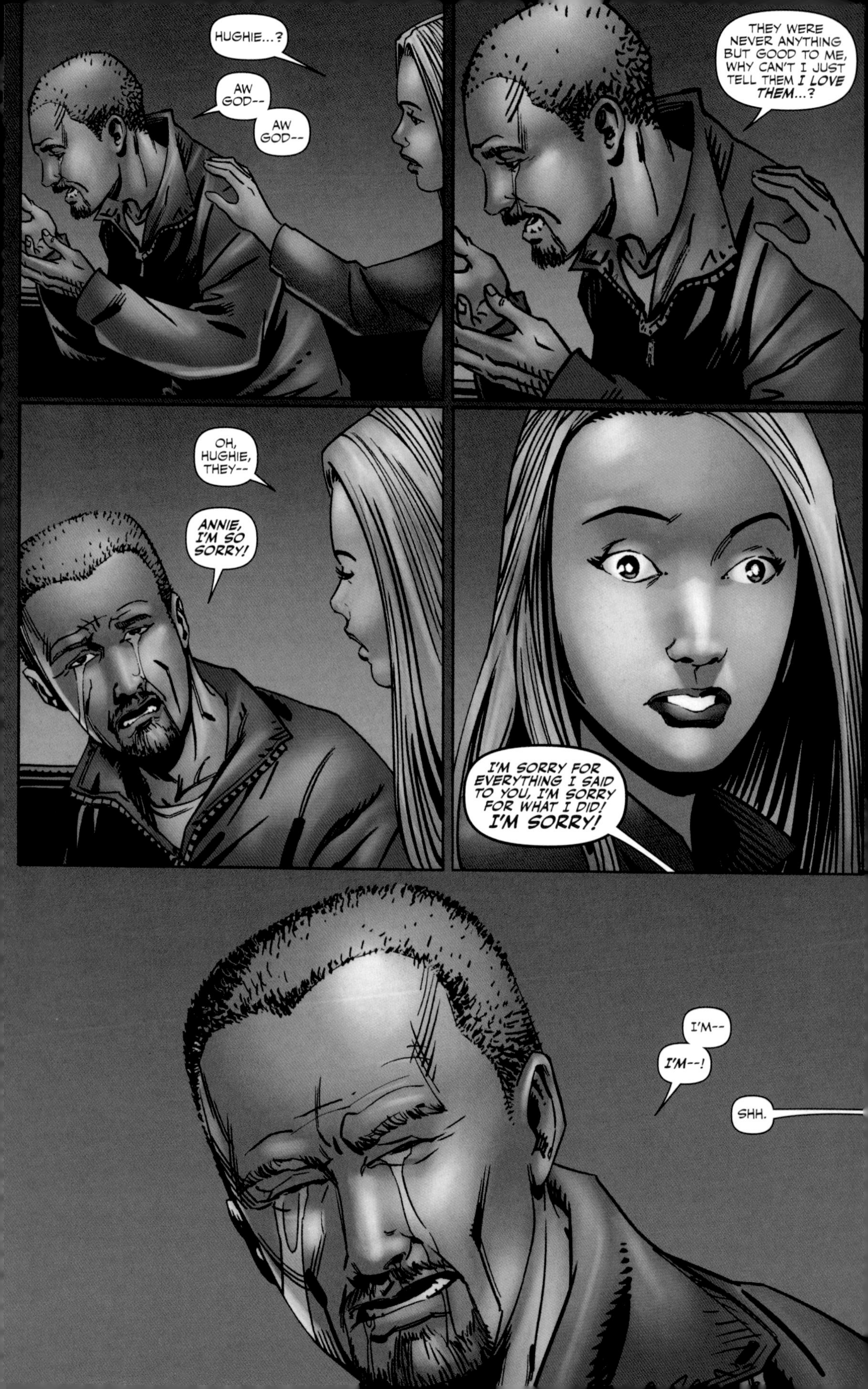
HUGHIE...?
AW GOD--
AW GOD--
THEY WERE NEVER ANYTHING BUT GOOD TO ME, WHY CAN'T I JUST TELL THEM *I LOVE THEM*...?
OH, HUGHIE, THEY--
ANNIE, I'M SO SORRY!
I'M SORRY FOR EVERYTHING I SAID TO YOU, I'M SORRY FOR WHAT I DID! ***I'M SORRY!***
I'M--
I'M--!
SHH.

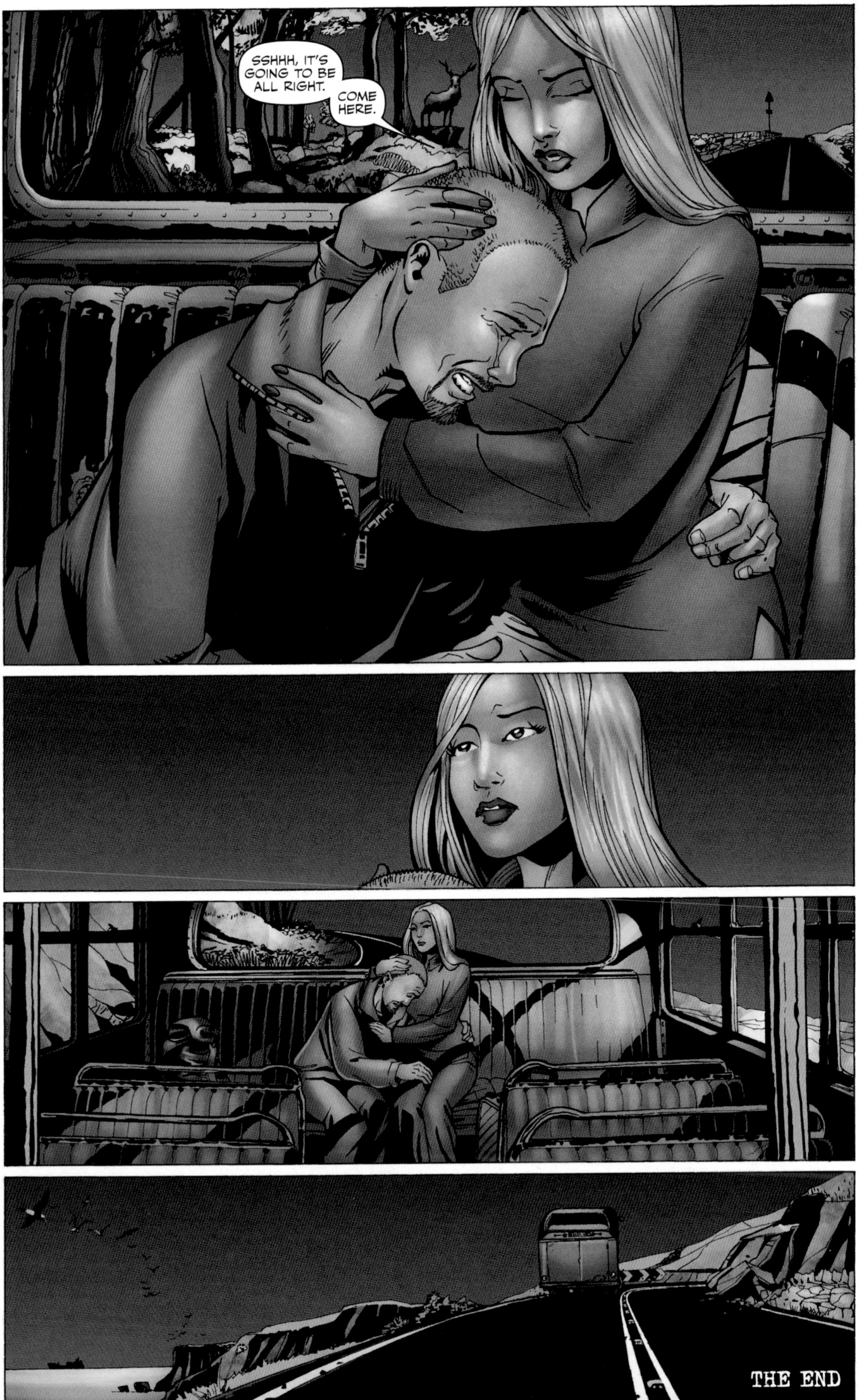
SSHHH, IT'S GOING TO BE ALL RIGHT.
COME HERE.
THE END

THE BOYS 41
GARTH ENNIS

PAGE ONE

1.

Day. Malchemical stands in Superduper's living room with a weary grimace and plastic cup of soda. The room has been decked out for a party- sans alcohol- with soda, pastries, cookies and a huge cake with WELCOME MALCHEMICAL spelt out in icing. A banner hanging from the ceiling repeats the sentiment. The seven members of Superduper stand behind their new leader, all with soda, all smiling expectantly- not at all put off by his wretched attitude, assuming they even notice. Good close up on him here- he wears trunks and boots, the rest of his body displays the same coloured striping as his face.

Malchem:　　　WHAT THE FUCK DID I DO TO DESERVE **THIS?**

Title:　　　　**THE INNOCENTS** part two

PAGE TWO

1.

Widen out. Auntie Sis and the others watch cheerfully as Malchemical wanders over to the cake.

Auntie:　　　INTRODUCTIONS! SO FROM THE LEFT—

Malchem:　　　YEAH, YEAH, I ALREADY READ ALL THE SHIT. BLACK HOLE
　　　　　　　AND BOBBY BUTTFUCK AND WHATEVER.

Bobby:　　　　**BOBBY BADOING!!**

2.

Bobby squeals with delight and bounces out of the room like a human space bouncer, little limbs flailing, his arse apparently having quite rubbery qualities. The others grin, happy for him. Malchemical doesn't bother to look.

Bobby:　　　　**BADOING-BADOING-**
　　　　　　　BADOING-BADOING-
　　　　　　　BADOING!

3.

Nearest us Malchemical digs a chunk of cake out with his fingers, not worried about plates or knives. He looks at it thoughtfully. The others are most expectant.

Black Hole:　　SO WHEN DO WE BEGIN
　　　　　　　OUR FIRST ADVENTURE,
　　　　　　　MALCHEMICAL?

Malchem:	HUH?
Auntie Sis:	HE'S ONLY JUST ARRIVED, GIVE HIM A CHANCE TO SETTLE IN!
" "	I THINK WHAT BLACK HOLE MEANS IS, WHAT ARE YOUR
	PLANS FOR SUPERDUPER NOW THAT YOU'RE TEAM LEADER?

4.

Malchemical starts eating cake off his fingers. Auntie Sis picks up a knife, Ladyfold starts handing out paper plates.

Malchem:	I DUNNO EXACTLY. WHAT'D THE LAST GUY DO?
" "	THIS ISN'T THAT BAD…
Auntie:	OKAY EVERYBODY, CAKE! LADYFOLD, COULD YOU—THANKS.
" "	WE DIDN'T EXACTLY HAVE A LEADER BEFORE. WE'VE BEEN SORT OF WAITING TO GO OUT ON, ON MISSIONS, I SUPPOSE.

PAGE THREE

1.

Malchemical frowns as Auntie Sis cuts the cake, the others waiting expectantly.

Malchem:	WAITING? YOU JUST SIT AROUND ALL DAY?
Auntie:	WELL, NO, WE GO OUT ON PATROL AND TAKE CARE OF ANY LOCAL STUFF, YOU KNOW. WE'RE GOING OUT LATER TODAY, IF YOU'D LIKE TO COME ALONG.
Malchem:	I'LL PASS…

2.

She turns to us as she passes out cake. Further back the Klanker suddenly jerks rigid.

Auntie:	ARE YOU SURE? GET TO KNOW THE—
Klanker:	**FUCKINGCUNT!!**

3.

Malchemical turns, sees them reassuring Klanker. Bobby bounces back in, delighted.

Malchem:	WHAT--?
Klanker:	I'M SORRY! I'M SORRY!
Auntie:	KLANKER, **IT'S OKAY**…
Bobby:	**BADOING-BADOING-BADOING- CAKE!**

4.

Malchemical points, smiling in disbelief. Auntie gets between him and the rest, anxious.

Malchem: WHAT'D HE SAY? DID HE SAY **FUCKING CUNT?**

Auntie: HE CAN'T HELP IT, SHHH, DON'T—

Malchem: CAN'T HELP IT, D'YOU MEAN—OH, THAT IS **BEAUTIFUL...!**

5.

Malchemical starts laughing his ass off, watched by the rather alarmed Auntie Sis. Further back the others comfort the Klanker, one of them handing him a slice of cake. Fortunately, none of them seem have noticed Malchemical carrying on.

Malchem: **HA HA HA HA HA, FUCKING GREAT! HA HA HA HA HA!!**

PAGE FOUR

1.

Wide. Nearest us Bobby has cut himself a gigantic slice of cake and is holding it with both hands wh munching greedily on it. Auntie Sis suddenly has too much to do- holding up a hand to reassure the puzzled Kid Camo, turning to admonish Bobby, anxious. Malchemical's laughing so hard he has to l himself up on the wall.

Malchem: **HA HA HA HA <u>HA</u>--!**

Kid Camo: WHAT'S SO FUNNY?

Auntie: IT'S NOTHING, KID CAMO, MALCHEMICAL'S JUST—OH,
                    BOBBY, USE A **PLATE...!**

2.

Malchemical giggles to himself nearest, wipes a tear from his eye. Auntie Sis watches him carefully concerned and slightly displeased- first hint that she doesn't like what she sees here, that she's dete danger for Superduper.

3.

Auntie Sis only, watching us intently. Eyes narrowed slightly. She's the only one smart enough to s Malchemical for what he is, and the implications have her worried.

Auntie: I THINK YOU SHOULD JOIN US ON PATROL.

"   "   I THINK IT MIGHT DO YOU SOME GOOD.

4.

Malchemical's too amused to worry, or even be mean at this point. Doesn't bother to look at her. S Shadow wanders up with the same slightly confused look as before, face still bruised and bandage

Malchem: WHATEVER YOU SAY, SWEETHEART. JESUS.

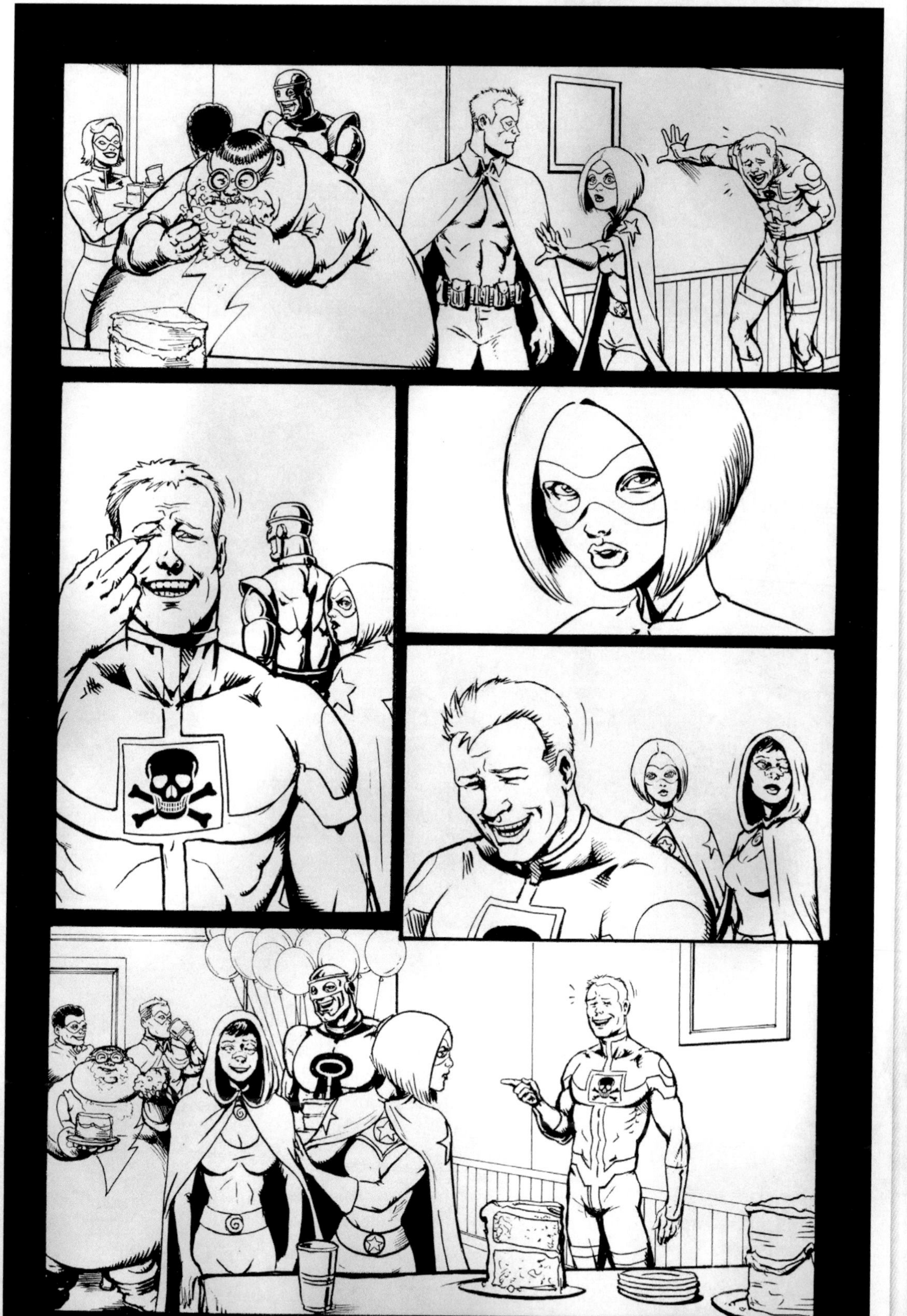

Stool: I DIDN'T GET ANY... ANY, UM...

5.

Auntie Sis leads her away, frowning at Malchemical, irritated. Piece of cake on a plate on the table nearest. Malchemic watches them go, grinning, bewildered.

Auntie: CAKE. YOU DID, STOOL SHADOW, YOU JUST PUT IT DOWN OVER HERE.

Stool: THANKS, AUNTIE SIS...

Malchem: WHAT THE FUCK DID YOU DO TO THIS ONE, **BEAT HER?**

PAGE FIVE

1.

Day. Through binocs shot of Superduper leaving their house, Malchemical bringing up the rear.

Jag: **KKRRRZZZZTT**

Jag 2:   KRRRCCCCHHH EYE OUT OF EVILDOERS! OH, **BOY!**

2.

Binocs again. They get closer, so we can see the Klanker smiling hopefully, then Auntie Sis looking irritated, then Malchemical smirking unpleasantly to himself. Note that they're not aware they're being observed.

Jag: YOU GOT IT, BOBBY BADOING! THE BAD GUYS AREN'T GONNA KNOW WHAT HIT THEM!

Jag 2:   YEAH, THE WORLD NEED FEAR NO FUCKING CUNT...

Jag 3:   MALCHEMICAL, WHY DON'T **KRRRCCCHHHHH**

3.

Close up on someone's hand as they slowly turn a dial on a little portable audio receiver.

Jag: **KRRRCCHHHH** OPPORTUNITY TO **KKRRRRRCCCCHH** OBSERVE? THAT WAY YOU CAN LEARN MORE ABOUT WHAT WE DO AND HOW WE OPERATE, DON'T YOU THINK?

4.

View past a hire car parked down the street from the house, someone sitting at the wheel with their back to us. Without the binocs the eight figures are really only identifiable by shape as they proceed down the street in a line.

Jag: SOUNDS GOOD TO ME, DOLLFACE.

Car: JESUS CHRIST...

5.

Hughie lowers the binocs, gazes offshot in pitying disbelief. The receiver's on the dashboard with a lead running up to Hughie's headphones, another lead running up to the directional mike he's hung on the open window nearest, pointed in Superduper's direction.

Hughie: WHERE THE FUCK TO BEGIN?

PAGE SIX

1.

A terrified kitten stuck on a tree branch, mewling pathetically.

Kitten: MRRRAAAAOOOOWWW

"   "   MRRRAAAAOOOOWWW

Down: SSSHHH, MINNIE…

Down 2: THERE'S A GOOD KITTY…

2.

Wide. In the front yard of a suburban bungalow, a little old couple watch nervously, Auntie Sis reassuring them. Malchemical and the Black Hole are also watching nearer us. Bobby Badoing lies on his back about twenty feet below the kitten, with Klanker, Ladyfold and Stool Shadow standing around him, waving reassuringly to the tiny animal.

l.o. lady: OH DEAR, WILL SHE BE ALL RIGHT--?

Auntie: OF COURSE SHE WILL, MA'AM. MINNIE'S IN VERY GOOD
                     HANDS.

Ladyfold: THERE, THERE, LITTLE PUSSY-CAT…

Klanker: PUSS-PUSS-PUSS-PUSS-PUSS…

Black Hole: SO WHAT YOU HAVE HERE IS A PRETTY TYPICAL OPERATION,
                     AH—

3.

Black Hole points offshot. Malchemical stares, can't quite believe he's here for this.

Black Hole: BOBBY BADOING'S STANDING BY IN CASE THE KITTEN FALLS,
                     AH, HE'S THERE AS A SORT OF SAFETY NET… LADYFOLD,
                     STOOL SHADOW AND THE KLANKER ARE DOING THEIR BEST
                     TO DISTRACT IT…

Off: MINNIE! LOOK! MINNIE!

4.

The kitten on the branch, still terrified. Behind it, part of the tree trunk seems to have come to life- a

pair of eyes peering intently at the kitten, an arm extending with a hand ready to grab it. The kitten hasn't seen this yet (Kid Camo can turn himself into a layer of protoplasm, able to slide over and assume the shape and colour of any object, effectively rendering himself invisible).

Down: THAT'S RIGHT, KITTY, YOU LOOK AT ME!

Minnie: MMRRRAAAAOOOOWWW

Off: AND IN THE MEANTIME, **KID CAMO** IS USING HIS **PROTO-POWER** TO GET WITHIN GRABBING DISTANCE!

PAGE SEVEN

1.

Kid Camo reaches for the kitten, misses, and falls off the trunk of the tree- a flat liquid creature with one arm and a pair of bulging eyes, same colour as the tree trunk. The kitten squeals and jumps for its life.

Kid: **WAAAH--!**

Minnie: **MMRRAAAOOW!**

Off: OH NO!

2.

Minnie lands on the surprised Bobby's gut and bounces twenty feet in the air. Ladyfold grabs for her, misses.

Bobby: **WUFF!**

Minnie: **MMMMMRRRRRAAAAOOOOOWWW!!**

Ladyfold: SOMEBODY CATCH HER--!

3.

Kid Camo lands in a heap, a pair of eyes in the middle of a big splat. Further back Klanker adopts his dramatic pose again, Auntie Sis running forward to stop him.

Kid: **UHHGGH!!**

Klanker: GOING FOR IT! **BODY OF IRON!**

Auntie: KLANKER, DON'T—

4.

Malchemical stares in total disbelief as Klanker's energy field flashes and replaces him with about a hundred pounds of anchor chain, which falls to the ground in an untidy heap.

5.

Bobby suddenly jams his hands down his pants, squeals in alarm.

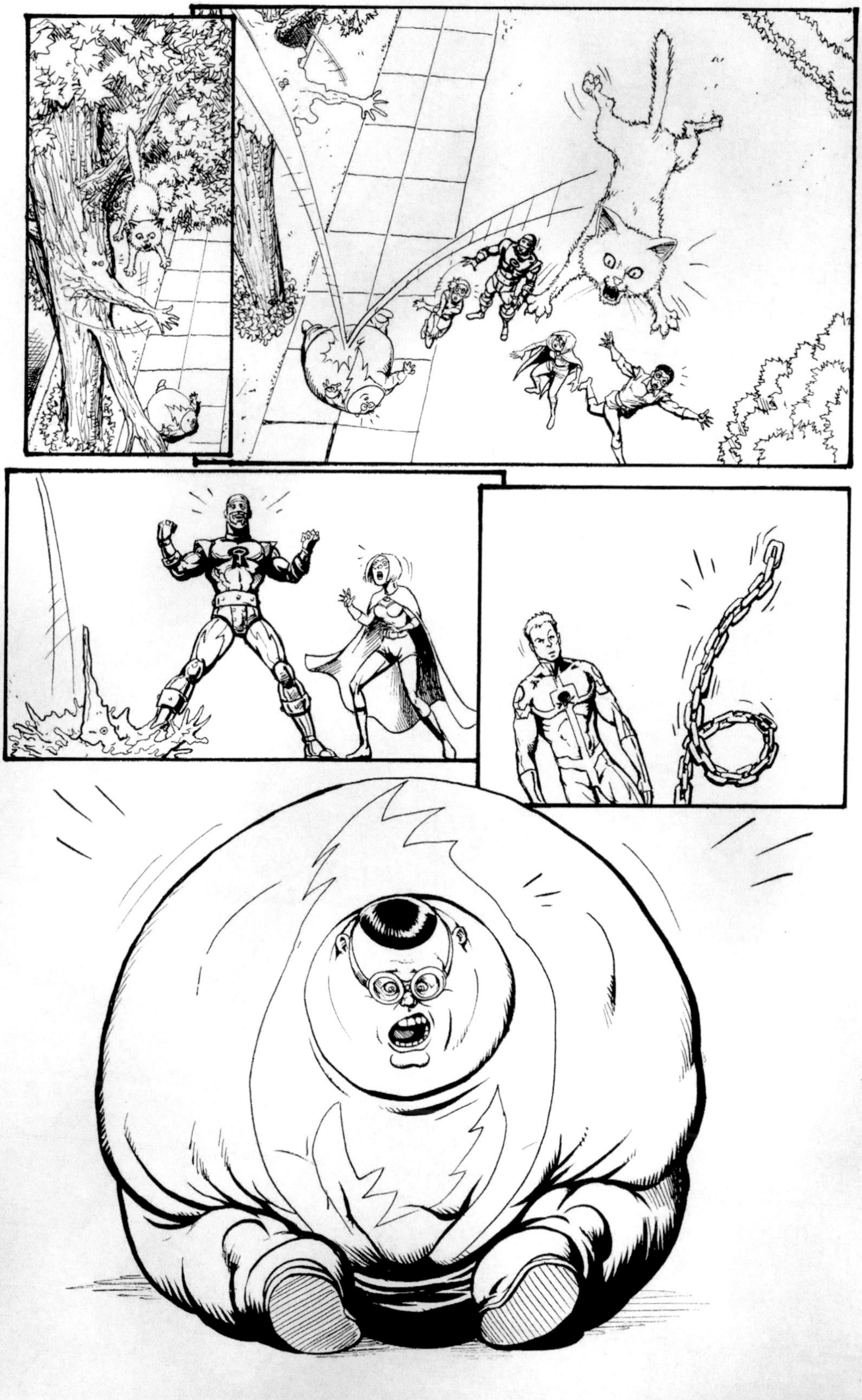

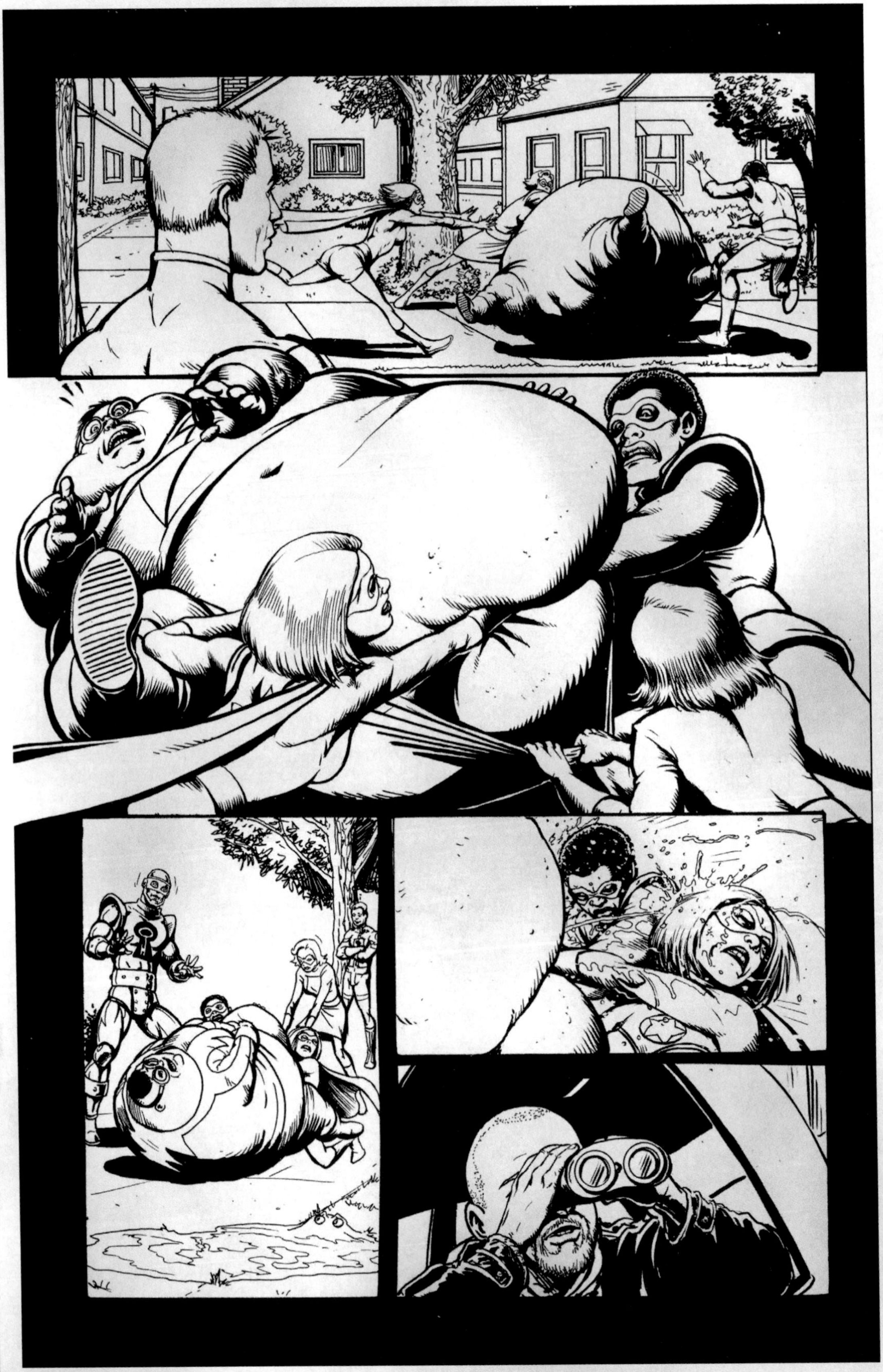

Off: OH, **KLANKER...!**

Off 2:   KID CAMO, ARE YOU—

Off 3:   WHAT ABOUT THE KITTEN, WHERE—

Bobby: **OOOOH! OOOOOOHH! I CAN'T FIND MY <u>WEE-WEE STICK!</u>**

<u>PAGE EIGHT</u>

1.

Malchemical stares as everyone rushes to help Bobby, who rolls around like an egg with tiny limbs, can't even stand up.

Bobby: **I CAN'T FIND MY WEE-WEE STICK! <u>I CAN'T FIND MY WEE-WEE STICK!</u>**

Auntie: **HELP HIM--!**

Malchem: HE CAN'T **WHAT....?**

2.

Ladyfold has yanked down the squealing Bobby's pants, revealing his huge gut and the huge folds of flab that fall away to his thighs, completely hiding his crotch. Auntie Sis and the Black Hole are groping desperately in the flab, arms sunk in to the elbows.

Auntie: BOBBY NEEDS HELP GOING TO THE BATHROOM, HE CAN'T REACH HIS—

Bobby: **WHERE IS IT? WHERE IS IT? HELP!**

Black Hole: I THINK I'VE GOT—**NO--!**

3.

Pull back as they struggle to help the floundering Bobby. Nearest us Kid Camo is just a trembling, grass-coloured puddle on the lawn, eyes bulging with terrible, straining effort.

Kid Camo: I CAN'T GET IT UP! I CAN'T GET IT UP!

Auntie: PULL THE FLAB ASIDE!

Black Hole: IT'S TOO DEEP UNDER—

Auntie: JUST GRAB A FOLD AND **PULL!**

4.

Close up. They yank up a big fold of flab and piss squirts out both sides of the fold below that one, catching Auntie Sis in the eyes and Black Hole in the mouth. Bobby squeals in torment. Note that we don't see genitalia, the piss simply comes out from under the fat.

Auntie: **NAAAH!**

Black Hole: **GUUUHH!**

Bobby: **MY WEE-WEE STIIIIICK...!**

5.

Hughie watching through the binocs, face twisting in weary disbelief.

Hughie: SERIOUS PLAYERS.

"   "   OH AYE.

PAGE NINE
1.

Auntie Sis wipes piss from her face, does her best to comfort the blubbering Bobby (who's back on his feet now). Black Hole spits and spits, disgusted. Malchemical watches them, thoughtful.

Auntie: IT'S ALL RIGHT, BOBBY, IT'S OKAY. IT WAS JUST THE KITTEN
                 LANDING ON YOUR TUMMY.

Black Hole: **TOOFF! TOOFF!**

Malchem: PRETTY TYPICAL OPERATION, HUH?

2.

Malchemical raises an eye, smiles, mildly amused. Can't even be bothered sneering.

Malchem: I BELIEVE YOU.

"   "   I GUESS THIS IS WHERE THEY SEND THE ABORTIONS THAT
                     LIVE.

3.

Binocs. Malchemical turns and strides towards us (unaware of Hughie), rolling his eyes in weary derision. Bobby, Black Hole, Ladyfold and Stool Shadow watch him go, stricken, but Auntie Sis shoots him a look of pure murder.

Off: MY, MY.

4.

Hughie lowers his binocs, little grim.

Hughie: YOU'RE A NICE BASTARD, AREN'T YOU, PAL?

5.

The others stare at Auntie Sis, confused and a little scared, but she just looks tired now.

Bobby: **AUNTIE SIS, WHAT DID HE—**

Auntie: NOTHING, BOBBY. HE DIDN'T MEAN ANYTHING.

"   "   YOU AND BLACK HOLE CAN CARRY THE KLANKER. GIRLS,
              FIND SOMETHING TO PUT KID CAMO IN.

6.

Long shot. Hughie's car is parked across the street, Malchemical strolling off in the distance, the little figures of Superduper standing next to the pile of chains and puddle of Kid Camo. Nearest us, the terrified kitten sits on the edge of the bungalow roof and trembles.

Auntie: LET'S GO HOME.

PAGE TEN

1.

MM peers at his computer screen, eyes narrowed. Frenchie sits nearest with his feet up, reading a magazine called FROMAGE. He doesn't look up. No one else around.

MM: FRENCHIE, AMM I GOIN' CRAZY HERE…?

Frenchie: IF YOU THINK I AM THE ONE TO ASK?

"   "   PEUT-ETRE.

2.

View past MM as he peers at the screen. Frenchie looks round now.

MM: LEGEND ACCESSES THE VOUGHT MAINFRAME WHENEVER HE
              WANTS, RIGHT? PUTS THE FILE TOGETHER FOR BUTCHER
              EVERY MONTH?

Frenchie: AH… NON.

"   "   IN POINT OF FACT, C'EST LES FRERES MCGUINEA WHO DO THE
              WORK. LA LEGENDE MERELY PASSES ON THE FILE.

3.

Frenchie looks thoughtful. MM still seems troubled.

Frenchie: AND DISCUSSES WITH M'SIEU CHARCUTER… WHATEVER
              HORRORS MIGHT BE ON HIS MIND…

MM: RIGHT, BUT THE POINT IS IT COMES FROM VOUGHT: LEGEND
              DON'T READ EVERY WORD, BUT IT STILL COMES STRAIGHT
              FROM THE ASSHOLE A' THE BEAST.

4.

MM only, frowning, concentrating hard.

Off: POURQUOI…?

MM: 'CAUSE I JUST HACKED THE MAINFRAME MYSELF.

"   "   AN' WHAT I'M SEEIN' DON'T ADD UP.

5.

Frenchie looks up, genuinely interested, magazine forgotten.

Frenchie: YOU DID WHAT?

Off: OLD PASSWORD. GOT ME A COUPLE MINUTES 'FORE THEY
                   SHUT ME OUT.

PAGE ELEVEN
1.

Frenchie comes over to look at the computer too. He isn't shocked here, but he's intrigued. MM is deep in thought.

MM: BUTCHER SENDS HUGHIE TO CHECK OUT SUPERDUPER — WHO
                   GOTTA BE THE MUTHAFUCKAS LEAST WORTH CHECKIN' OUT
                   IN RECORDED HISTORY, AM I RIGHT?

Frenchie: OUI. LA "LEAGUE OF DWEEBS", N'EST-CE PAS?

MM: OKAY.

2.

Close up on the screen, showing the same Vought logo we've seen before along with a flashing message: UNAUTHORISED LOG ON and DISCONTINUED

Off: REASON HE GIVES IS MALCHEMICAL, THE ASSHOLE FROM
                   TEAM TITANIC. BEEN SENT TO TAKE OVER SUPERDUPER, SO
                   NOW HUGHIE GOTTA GO SEE IF THAT MEANS THEY GETTING'
                   SERIOUS NOW…

Off 2:   OUI…?

Off: SOUNDED LIKE BULLSHIT TO ME, TOO.

3.

MM sits back, stares at the screen, bothered.

MM: WHY MALCHEMICAL GOT THE JOB AIN'T NOTHIN' TO **DO**
                   WITH SUPERDUPER. AIN'T EVEN PARTA THIS MAKIN'
                   -EVERYTHING-DARK SHIT.

"   "   REAL REASON'S IN THE TITANIC FILE, RIGHT NEXT TO
                   MALCHEMICAL'S GODDAMN AIRLINE TICKET. AIN'T NO WAY
                   THE MCGUINEAS COULDA MISSED IT.

4.

MM frowns. Frenchie's eyes narrow. Both looking at the screen here.

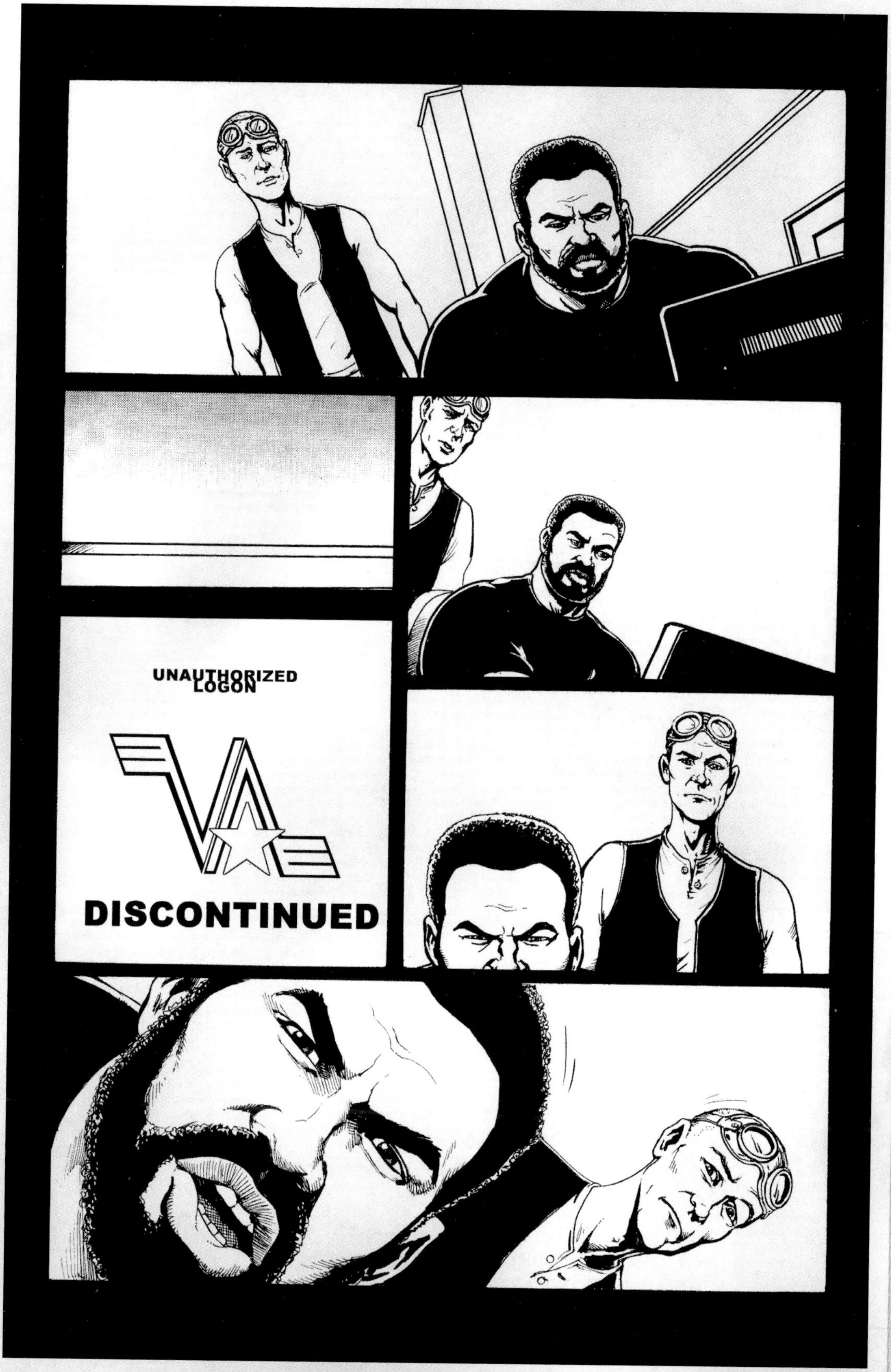
UNAUTHORIZED LOGON
DISCONTINUED

MM: SO IT HADDA BE IN THE SHIT THE LEGEND GAVE TO BUTCHER…

Frenchie: BUT NOT NECESSARILY IN LE SHIT **HE** GAVE TO HUGHIE, IS THAT WHAT YOU ARE SAYING?

5.

Closer. MM fumes, quietly but deeply annoyed. Frenchie glances at him, slightly taken aback.

MM: … MUTHA**FUCKA**.

"   " WHAT KINDA GODDAMN GAMES YOU PLAYIN' NOW?

PAGE TWELVE

1.

Malchemical has bought a case of Bud and is stocking the fridge with it. He turns, sees Auntie Sis in the doorway, watching him coolly. She's cleaned up, tied her hair back.

Auntie: SO WHAT DID YOU DO TO DESERVE THIS?

2.

Close in. Malchemical smiles, puzzled. She eyes him without relish.

Malchem; HUH?

Auntie: TO WHAT DO WE OWE THE PLEASURE OF YOUR COMPANY.

3.

He smiles wearily, goes back to the fridge. Auntie Sis watches him from further back.

Malchem: OH, FUCK… OKAY, YOU KNOW HOW I CAN CHANGE SHAPE?

Auintie: YES…

Malchem: SHAPE, FORM, CHEMICAL COMPOSITION, ALL THAT. KIND OF LIKE YOUR LITTLE PAL KID CAMO, ONLY NOT SO GODDAMN LAME.

4.

Close up on the fridge as his hand shoves another six in, ramming the remains of the cake aside and crushing it. He's also knocked over a container of jelly beans to make room for his beers. The fridge is full of soda, jello, candy, cookies, all manner of treats.

Off: WELL, I WANTED TO FUCK MY TEAM LEADER'S GIRLFRIEND— YOU KNOW, THE ORANGE BITCH? SO I MADE MYSELF LOOK LIKE HIM AND WENT TO SEE HER.

"   " TROUBLE WAS, SHE'D NEVER TRIED ANAL BEFORE. AND SHE ENDED UP LIKING IT QUITE A BIT. SO, THE NEXT TIME SHE'S

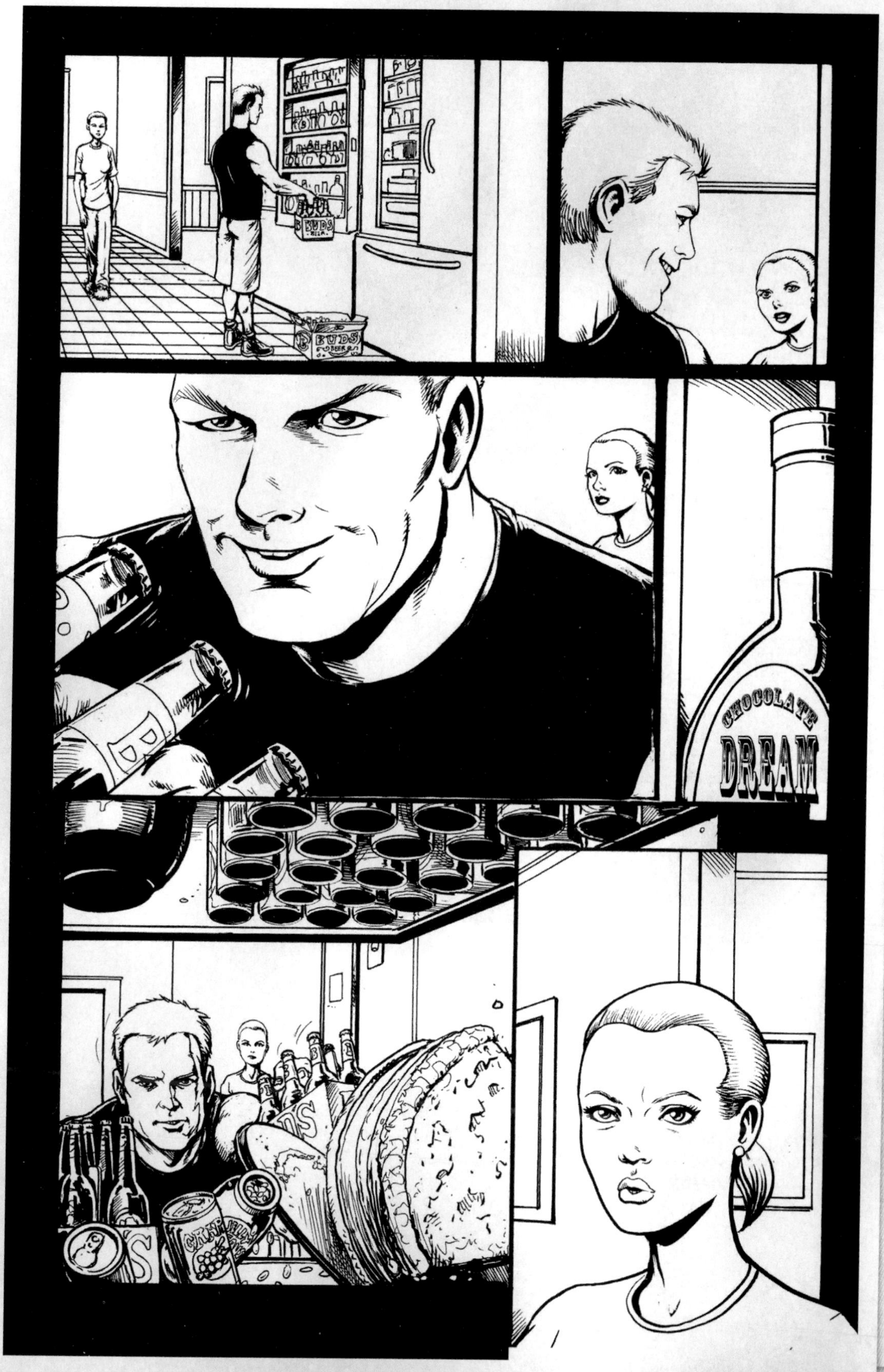
BUDS
BUDS
CHOCOLATE
DREAM

IN THE SACK WITH THE REAL HIM, IT'S "OOOH, DO ME LIKE
YOU DID LAST NIGHT"... AND...

5.

Auntie Sis only, deeply unimpressed.

Off: WELL.

" " ONE THING LED TO ANOTHER.

Auntie: THAT'S A LOVELY STORY.

PAGE THIRTEEN

1.

Malchemical closes the fridge, bottle of Bud in hand. Auntie Sis watches him coolly.

Auntie: THESE KIDS AREN'T LIKE THAT, YOU KNOW.

Malchem: NO SHIT...

Auntie: THEY AREN'T LIKE REGULAR SUPER-PEOPLE AT ALL. THEY
     DON'T NEED TO BE EXPOSED TO THAT KIND OF THING.

2.

Malchemical only, smiling to himself as he morphs the end of his thumb into a bottle opener, uses it to
flip the top off the bottle.

Malchem: WHAT KIND?

Off: YOURS.

" " LOOK, I'M NOT NAÏVE. I'VE BEEN TO SOME OF THE PARTIES
     AND SO ON, I'VE HEARD ALL ABOUT HEROGASM.

3.

Auntie Sis only, little grim.

Auntie: I KNOW THAT BOBBY AND LADYFOLD AND THE OTHERS ARE
     ABOUT AS FAR FROM ALL THAT STUFF AS IT'S POSSIBLE TO
     BE, BUT I FOR ONE THINK THAT'S A GOOD THING.

" " THEY GENUINELY WANT TO USE THE POWERS THEY HAVE TO
     DO GOOD. TO HELP PEOPLE, TO MAKE THE WORLD A BETTER
     PLACE.

" " THEY WANT TO BE SUPERHEROES.

4.

Malchemical swigs his beer, raises an eye. She gets a little awkward.

Malchem:　　　BY GETTING CATS OUT OF FUCKING TREES?

Auntie:　　　THEY DO WHAT THEY CAN. IT'S NOT EASY FOR THEM, THERE
　　　　　　　ARE SOME PRETTY OBVIOUS LIMITATIONS TO THEIR
　　　　　　　ABILITIES, AND THEIR OUTLOOK IS A LITTLE… SHELTERED…

5.

Closer. Malchemical smiles in slight disbelief. She locks eyes with him, quite venomous.

Malchem:　　　ARE YOU TELLING ME THEY'RE RETARDED…?

Auntie:　　　NO. THAT IS NOT THE WORD I USED.

"　　　"　　　I SAID SHELTERED, UNDERSTAND?

PAGE FOURTEEN
1.

Malchemical turns away, smiling to himself, highly amused. She glares at him.

Malchem:　　　OH-KAY…

Auntie:　　　WHAT I'M TRYING TO TELL YOU IS WE'RE PERFECTLY HAPPY
　　　　　　　THE WAY WE ARE. WE GET ON WITH DOING OUR OWN THING,
　　　　　　　AND WHEN WE'RE CALLED UPON WE MAKE WHATEVER
　　　　　　　PUBLIC APPEARANCES WE'RE SUPPOSED TO.

2.

Auntie Sis only, grim.

Auntie:　　　WE DIDN'T ASK TO BE **DARK**. WE CERTAINLY DIDN'T ASK FOR
　　　　　　　OUR NEW TEAM LEADER.

"　　　"　　　AS A MATTER OF FACT, WE'RE NOT ASKING
　　　　　　　VOUGHT-AMERICAN FOR ANYTHING BUT TO BE ALLOWED TO
　　　　　　　CONTINUE AS WE ALWAYS HAVE.

3.

Malchemical turns to smirk unpleasantly at us, quietly certain of himself.

Malchem:　　　AND WHO IS IT PAYS THE BILLS?

4.

He smiles and swigs his beer again. She wasn't ready for that one, can't think of anything to say,
awkward.

5.

Wide view. She watches him as he tosses his bottle in the sink, opens the fridge to get another. Nowhere near as confident as she was. He doesn't look at her.

Auntie: I'M TAKING THEM OUT FOR ICE CREAM.

"   "   I'D PREFER IT IF YOU DIDN'T COME.

Malchem: THEN THIS MUST BE YOUR LUCKY DAY…

PAGE FIFTEEN

1.

Hughie exits a nice little motel in the nice little Jersey town he's staying in, speaking on his cellphone, smiling.

Hughie: WHAT I KNOW?

"   "   AH, NO' VERY MUCH, I SOMETIMES THINK. THE MORE I
          LEARN, THE MORE CONFUSIN' THE WORLD SEEMS TO GET.

Jag: WHAT ABOUT IF WE NARROWED IT DOWN TO ME IN
          PARTICULAR?

2.

Annie's on the phone too, gazing out the window at a tree-lined street of brownstones, several floors up. Bit faraway here.

Jag: WELL, I KEN YOU'RE A WEE DARLIN'. ABSOLUTELY
          GORGEOUS. AN' NO' JUST THAT, YOU'RE ONE O' THE NICEST
          PEOPLE I EVER MET.

Annie: YEAH… I DIDN'T MEAN THAT SO MUCH. MORE WHAT DO YOU
          KNOW ABOUT ME?

3.

Hughie thinks about it, slightly puzzled but still pretty cheerful.

Hughie: UH… OKAY, YOUR NAME'S ANNIE JANUARY. YOU'RE
          TWENTY-FOUR. BLONDE HAIR, BLUE EYES, SMASHIN' FIGURE.
          YOU'RE FROM DES MOINES IN IOWA, BUT YOU DON'T LIKE IT
          VERY MUCH.

"   "   YOU WORK IN THE FASHION BUSINESS AS SOME SORT O'
          SALES REP, BUT I'M NO' TOO SURE O' THE DETAILS. AN'
          YOU'VE A WEAKNESS FOR SHORTARSED WEE SCOTSMEN OF
          DUBIOUS CHARACTER AN' APPEARANCE.

4.

Annie only, miles away, slight hint of anxiety.

Annie: I'M THINKING OF QUITTING MY JOB AND DOING SOMETHING
          DIFFERENT.

| " | " | I'VE GOT SOME MONEY SAVED UP, I'M LOOKING AT RENTALS IN THE WEST VILLAGE. |

5.

Pull back. Annie's standing at the window of a nice little one-bedroom apartment, pine floors, clean white walls, doors off the living room to bedroom and bog, kitchenette in one corner. A 30-something pregnant couple are also wandering around, a yuppie in a sharp suit studies a flyer as the real estate woman tries to sell him on the place.

| Jag: | JINGS…! |

| Annie: | I JUST— |

| " | " | YOU SAID YOU LOVED ME. WOULD YOU STILL LOVE ME IF YOU FOUND OUT SOMETHING YOU DIDN'T LIKE ABOUT ME? |

PAGE SIXTEEN
1.

Hughie's peering offshot, attention caught by something, intrigued.

| Hughie: | THE VILLAGE IS AWFULLY **EXPENSIVE**, ANNIE, HOW'RE YOU GONNA AFFORD TO LIVE THERE…? |

| Jag: | I DO PRETTY WELL WITH COMMISSIONS AND STUFF. I JUST CAN'T STAND THE JOB. |

| " | " | THAT ISN'T WHAT I ASKED YOU, HUGHIE. |

| Hughie: | HEY— |

2.

Annie only, listening carefully.

| Annie: | WHAT? |

| Jag: | NOTHIN'. SORRY, I THOUGHT I SAW SOMEONE I KNEW. |

| " | " | IF I FOUND OUT SOMETHIN' I DIDN'T LIKE—WHY, WHAT'VE YOU DONE? |

3.

Superduper proceed down the street towards us, smiling cheerfully, Auntie Sis (happier now) in the lead. A young mom smiles as her kid waves to them, Ladyfold waving back. Hughie's just across the street, hurrying to keep pace with them, watching them while speaking on the phone.

| Jag: | NOTHING. I MEAN THAT'S NOT THE POINT, I'M ASKING YOU WHAT IF. |

| Hughie: | BUT THAT'S DAFT, WHAT'S THE POINT O' THAT? |

| Jag: | HUMOR ME. |

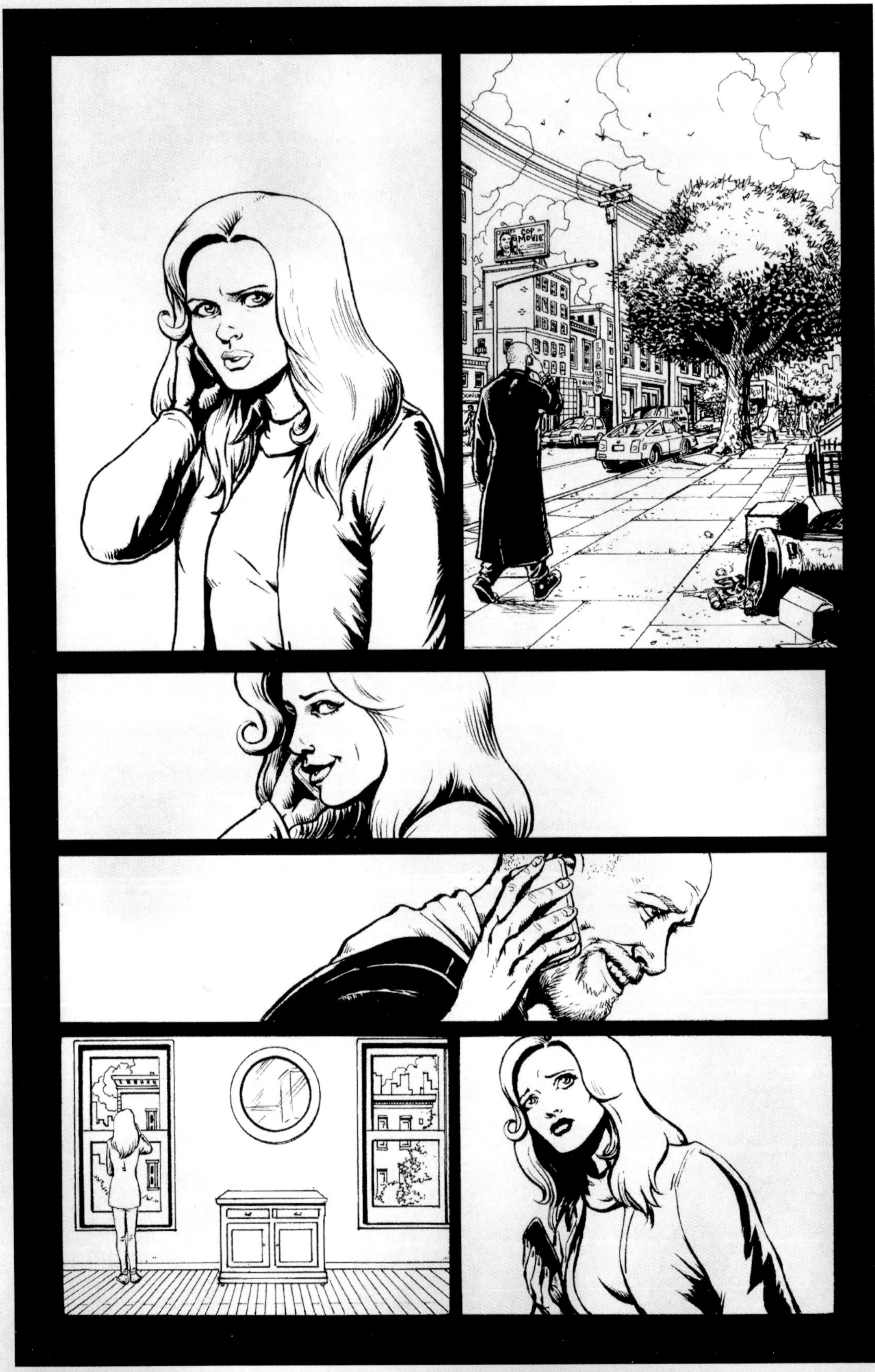

4.

Annie only, little awkward now.

Jag: BUT—

Annie: REMEMBER LAST NIGHT YOU SAID IT WAS DIFFICULT TO
                TRUST PEOPLE? AND WHEN WE TALKED IN THE PARK THAT
                TIME, I SAID HOW PRECIOUS IT CAN BE WHEN YOU FIND
                SOMEONE YOU DO TRUST?

"   "   ALL THIS STUFF I'M TALKING ABOUT DOING, IT'S A PRETTY
                MAJOR CHANGE FOR ME. I MIGHT KIND OF NEED YOU TO BE
                THERE FOR ME WHILE I'M DOING IT.

5.

Hughie hurries across the street, holds up a hand as a car stops to let him go.

Jag: I JUST—I GUESS I'M A LITTLE SCARED, IS ALL.

Hughie: AYE, OKAY. ALL RIGHT, THEN.

PAGE SEVENTEEN

1.

Annie's face twists, little bit frustrated.

Jag: HAVE YOU EVER MURDERED ANYONE?

Annie: HUGHIE--!

Jag: NO, I'M SERIOUS. HAVE YOU?

2.

Wide shot, Hughie following Superduper down the street.

Jag: … NO.

Hughie: SOLD ANYONE INTO SLAVERY?

Jag: NO.

Hughie: DONE ANYTHIN' TERRIBLE WI' KIDS?

Jag: NO.

Hughie: KICKED A WEE DUG?

Jag: UH…

3.

Annie smiles wearily. This isn't what she hoped for.

Jag: **DOG**. SORRY.

Annie: NO.

Jag: WELL THEN YOU'RE GOLDEN, HEN. 'CAUSE THOSE'RE THE
                  ONLY THINGS'D MAKE ME NOT WANNA BE WI' YOU.

4.

Hughie smiles, little bit perplexed.

Hughie: ANNIE, HONESTLY, I MEANT WHAT I SAID. I LOVE YOU.
                  NOTHIN'S GONNA CHANGE THAT.

"   "   IF YOU'RE GONNA STOP DOIN' A JOB THAT MAKES YOU
                  MISERABLE AN' GO ON AN' DO SOMETHIN' DIFFERENT, I'LL
                  BE BEHIND YOU A HUNDRED PERCENT—OKAY?

5.

View across the apartment at Annie gazing out the window, got her back to us.

Annie: OKAY.

Jag: ALL RIGHT, I'VE GOTTA GO NOW. I'LL CALL YOU LATER ON.

"   "   I LOVE YOU!

Annie: YOU TOO.

6.

Close up on Annie as she puts her phone away, gazing offshot, still faraway but with a hint of anxious foreboding.

PAGE EIGHTEEN
1.

Superduper have gotten themselves ice creams and are sitting around a table outside and ice cream parlor. The customers watch them, quite impressed, they seem pretty popular locally. Everyone has a cup with a couple of scoops, except Bobby, who's guzzling a fruit bowl-sized cup loaded with scoops of ice cream and sprinkles. All very happy. No one sees Hughie further back with a cone, watching them discretely.

Kid Camo: BUT IT REALLY SOUNDED LIKE HE—

Auntie: HONESTLY, KID CAMO, MALCHEMICAL'S FINE. HE JUST NEEDS
                  TO GET USED TO US.

"   "   GOSH, BOBBY, THAT'S A LOT OF ICE CREAM--!

Bobby: **GLOM GLOM GLOM GLOM**

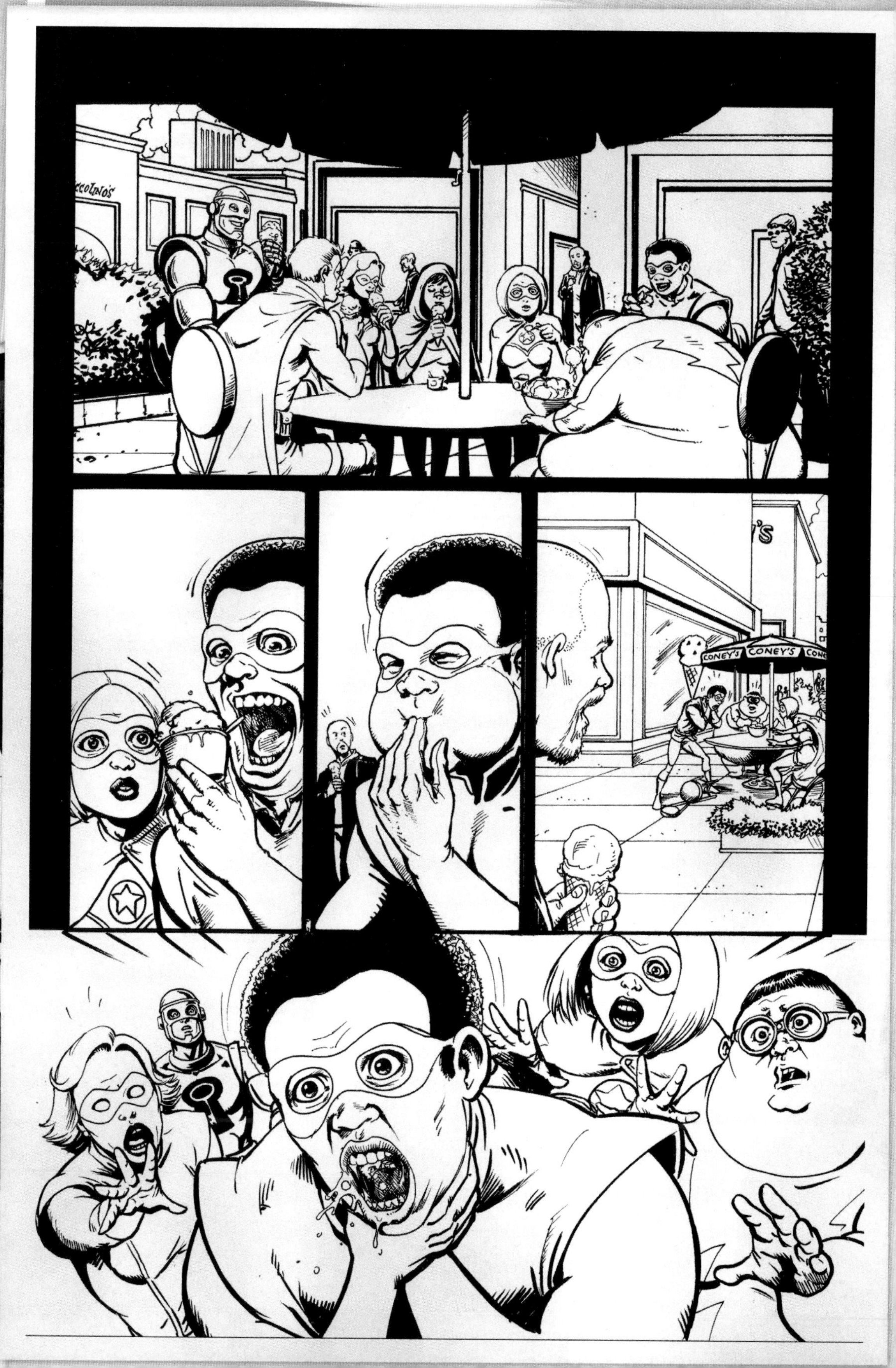
CONEY'S CONEY'S CONEY'S

Black Hole: HUH! I COULD EAT AS MUCH AS THAT IF I WANTED TO!

2.

Auntie Sis frowns as the Black Hole opens his mouth wide, lifts up his cup.

Black Hole: I'M THE BLACK HOLE, I CAN CONSUME ALL MATTER!

Auntie: I DON'T KNOW IF THAT'S SUCH A—

Black Hole: **WATCH!**

3.

He shoves the whole lot into his mouth, spoon and cup and all. Further back Hughie watches, slightly thrown.

Black Hole: **GALOMMP**

4.

View past Hughie. Black Hole suddenly leaps to his feet, slams his hands to his throat.

Black Hole: **GAKK--!**

Auntie: BLACK HOLE?

5.

Black Hole's choking. Ice cream flies from his mouth and he claws at his throat, eyes bulging in terror. The others are horrified. Auntie Sis leaps up in alarm.

Black Hole: **GAAAAHHHKK—**

Ladyfold: OH NO!

Klanker: IS HE--?

Auntie: **MOVE!**

PAGE NINETEEN

1.

The whole place is watching now as Auntie Sis desperately tries the Heimlich on the gasping, choking Black Hole. The others watch, helpless and scared. Even Bobby's stopped eating.

Auntie: BLACK HOLE, STAY STILL, I CAN'T—

Black Hole: **KKAAAAACCCCHHHH**

Klanker: IT ISN'T WORKING…!

2.

Hughie stares, stricken, realizing he's going to have to do something.

Off: THE SPOON'S BROKEN—IT'S IN HIS THROAT, I CAN'T REACH IT—

Off 2:   **SOMEONE CALL NINE ONE ONE!**

3.

Flashback. In a bare walled room in the Flatiron, Frenchie is teaching Hughie first aid- there's a first aid kit laid out on a table, and Frenchie is watching approvingly as Hughie performs the Heimlich on a demonstration dummy.

Frenchie: TRES BON, PETIT HUGHIE. MAIS WHAT DO WE DO IF THE
                  HEIMLICH MANOUVRE DOES NOT CLEAR THE OBSTRUCTION?

Hughie: UH… TRACHEOTOMY?

Frenchie: YOU HAVE BEEN PAYING ATTENTION, MON BRAVE. DESCRIBE
                  THE PROCESS, IF YOU PLEASE.

4.

Hughie shoves through the supes surrounding Auntie Sis and Black Hole, who's now writhing on the ground. Auntie Sis is helpless, and knows it. Hughie's unfolding a pen knife, which causes some alarm.

Auntie: BLACK HOLE! **BLACK HOLE, CAN YOU HEAR ME?**

Hughie: MOVE-MOVE-MOVE, LET US THROUGH!

Bobby: **WAAAAH, HE'S GOT A KNIFE!**

5.

Flashback. Hughie thinks about it, Frenchie is pleased. The dummy's on the floor nearest

Hughie: YOU… PUT THE VICTIM ON THEIR BACK… YOU FIND THE
                  STERNAL NOTCH… AN' YOU CUT INTO THE TRACHEA JUST
                  BELOW THE THYROID…

"   "   YOU MAKE A CROSS CUT TO ENLARGE THE INCISION AN' PUT
                  A TRACHEOTOMY TUBE IN, THEN YOU TAPE IT UP SO IT'S
                  AIRTIGHT. IF YOU'VE NO' GOT A TUBE YOU CAN USE A PEN
                  OR WHATEVER.

Frenchie: CORRECT.

"   "   NOW: DEMONSTRATE.

PAGE TWENTY

1.

Flashback. Hughie's kneeling over the dummy, about to start, when the Female appears nearest us. Rear view on her. Hughie stares at her, alarmed at whatever he's seeing.

Frenchie: BUT BEFORE YOU BEGIN.

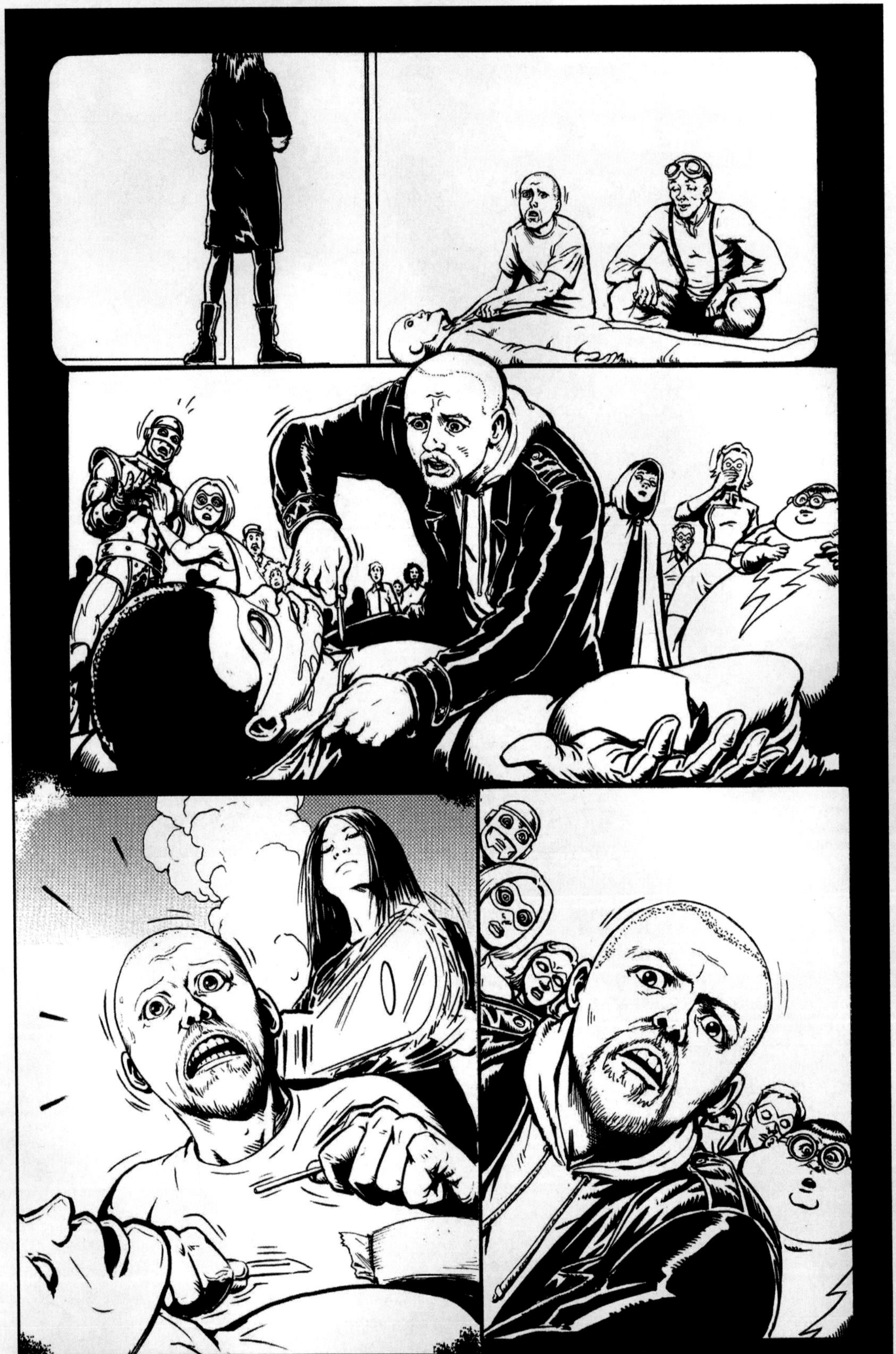

"   "   SUCH QUIET CONDITIONS ARE UNLIKELY IN REAL LIFE,
            PETIT HUGHIE. WE MUST INTRODUCE AN ELEMENT OF…

"   "   STRESS?

2.

Black Hole is unconscious. Hughie's nervously pulling his costume aside to get at his throat, knife in hand. The Klanker's appalled, but Auntie Sis grabs his hand before he can stop Hughie. Everyone's riveted.

Klanker: **NO--!**

Auntie: KLANKER, IT'S OKAY, IT'S OKAY! I KNOW WHAT HE'S DOING!

Hughie: CHRIST, THAT MAKES ON OF US…!

3.

The terrified Hughie's hands tremble like a drunk's as he prepares to cut the dummy's throat. Roll of tape and biro (ink tube pulled out of the plastic) to hand. Frenchie watches calmly, both of them shouting to be heard over the roaring, spinning chainsaw the Female's holding next to (not over) Hughie's head. She stares blankly at him.

Hughie: **FOR FUCK'S SAKE, FRENCHIE--!**

Frenchie: **COURAGE, PETIT HUGHIE! IF YOU ARE TO STAND BESIDE
              LES BOYS, YOU MUST DEVELOP SUCH SKILLS!**

4.

Black Hole's pov as Hughie nervously works on him, the horrified/fascinated members of Superduper peering down at him behind Hughie.

Hughie: CAN SOMEBODY GIVE US A PEN OR A STRAW? AN' I'M GONNA
              NEED A WEE BIT O' TAPE, TOO—

Bobby: **OOOOOOOHHH--!**

PAGE TWENTY-ONE

1.

The dummy's throat has been cut from ear to ear. The pen sticks out of the gap at a bad angle. The wretched, trembling Hughie has succeeded only in taping his fingers together. Only Frenchie's and the Female's legs are in shot- she's lowered the saw, switched it off.

Frenchie: HMMM.

"   "   MORE PRACTICE IS CALLED FOR.

2.

Hughie sits back and closes his eyes with enormous relief, holding up his bloody hands. Nearest us the Black Hole slowly opens his eyes, extremely woozy, breathing through the drinking straw taped neatly into the blood-smeared hole in his throat.

Black Hole: HHHHHHHH

"   "   HHHHHHHH

"   "   HHHHHHHH

Hughie: THANK FUCK.

3.

Pull back, wide view. Hughie stands, wipes his hands on a napkin. Auntie Sis kneels to cradle Black Hole's head but looks up at Hughie- as do the rest, all amazed and delighted. The crowd of bystanders are pretty impressed too.

Auntie: IT'S OKAY, BLACK HOLE, DON'T TRY AND MOVE YET…
           LISTEN, THANK YOU **SO MUCH…!**

Hughie: AYE, HE NEEDS A PROPER DOCTOR, BUT. THE AMBULANCE
           SHOULD BE HERE ANY MINUTE.

Klanker: YOU SAVED OUR FRIEND, MISTER! WHAT'S YOUR NAME?

4.

Hughie's caught a little off guard. Klanker turns to us, grins with delight.

Hughie: OH, IT'S H—

"   "   IT'S HUH, HUH, HUH, IT'S HAMISH…

Klanker: HEY, EVERY BODY, HAMISH SAVED THE BLACK HOLE'S LIFE!
           HE'S A **HERO!**

5.

Hughie can't believe it as Superduper crowd around him and the onlookers start applauding. Lots of pats on the back.

Crowd: YEAH! HAMISH!

Crowd 2:   **YEAH!**

Crowd 3:   **YOU ROCK, DUDE!**

Kid Camo: HE'D HAVE **DIED** IF IT WASN'T FOR YOU!

PAGE TWENTY-TWO
1.

Big. Hughie's completely freaked out as Ladyfold and Klanker both hug him tight and Bobby shrieks with joy. Everyone's grinning and applauding, everyone loves him.

Bobby: **YOU'RE OUR BESTEST PAL!**

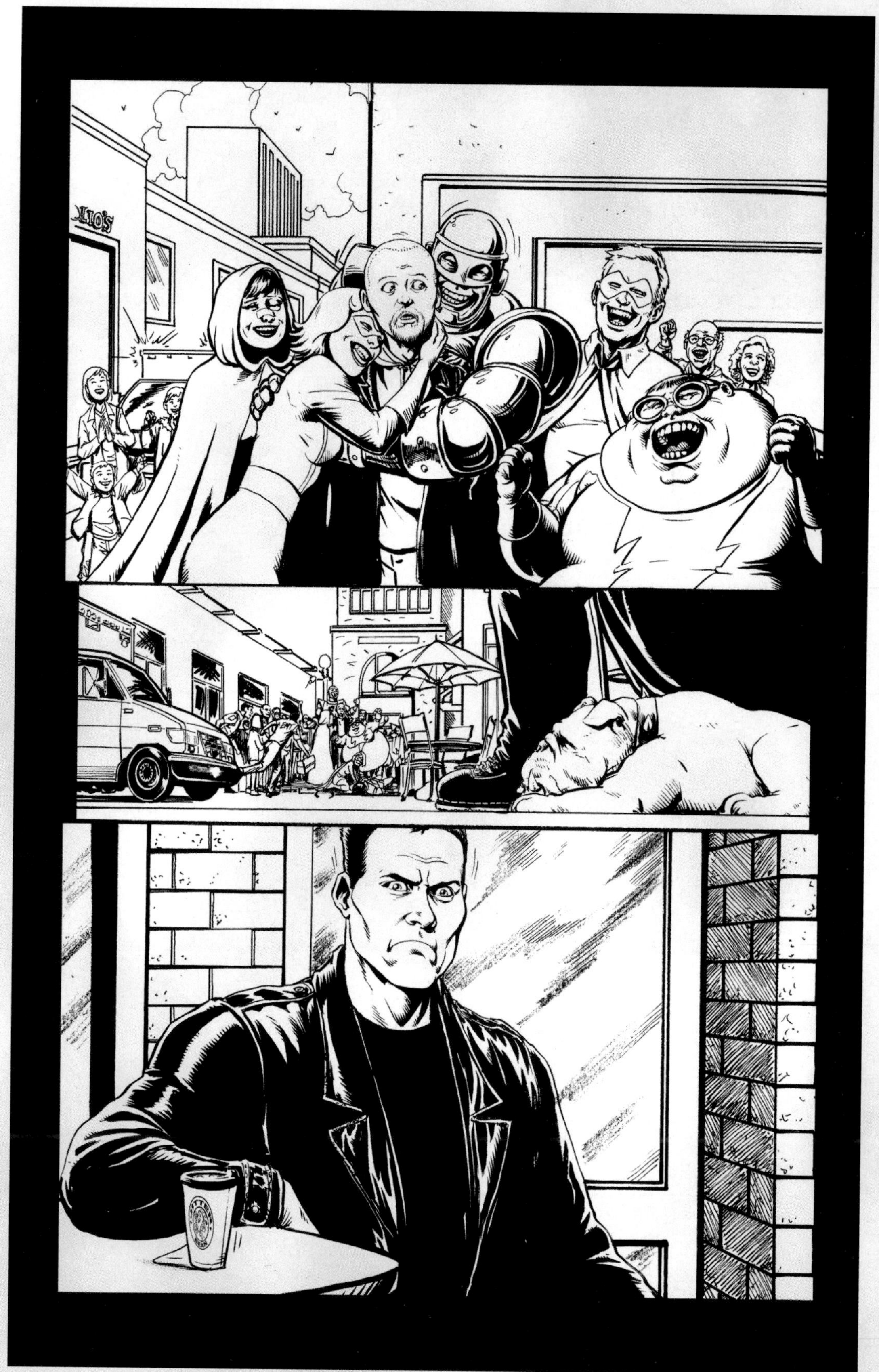

2.

View past someone standing outside a coffee shop across the street, watching as the ambulance pulls up next to Hughie and the others. Terror dozes at the observer's feet.

3.

Butcher stares past us, face rigid, eyes like saucers. Half astonishment, half slowly building fury. Coffee on the table forgotten.

NEXT: **FUCKINGCUNT!!** (SORRY…)

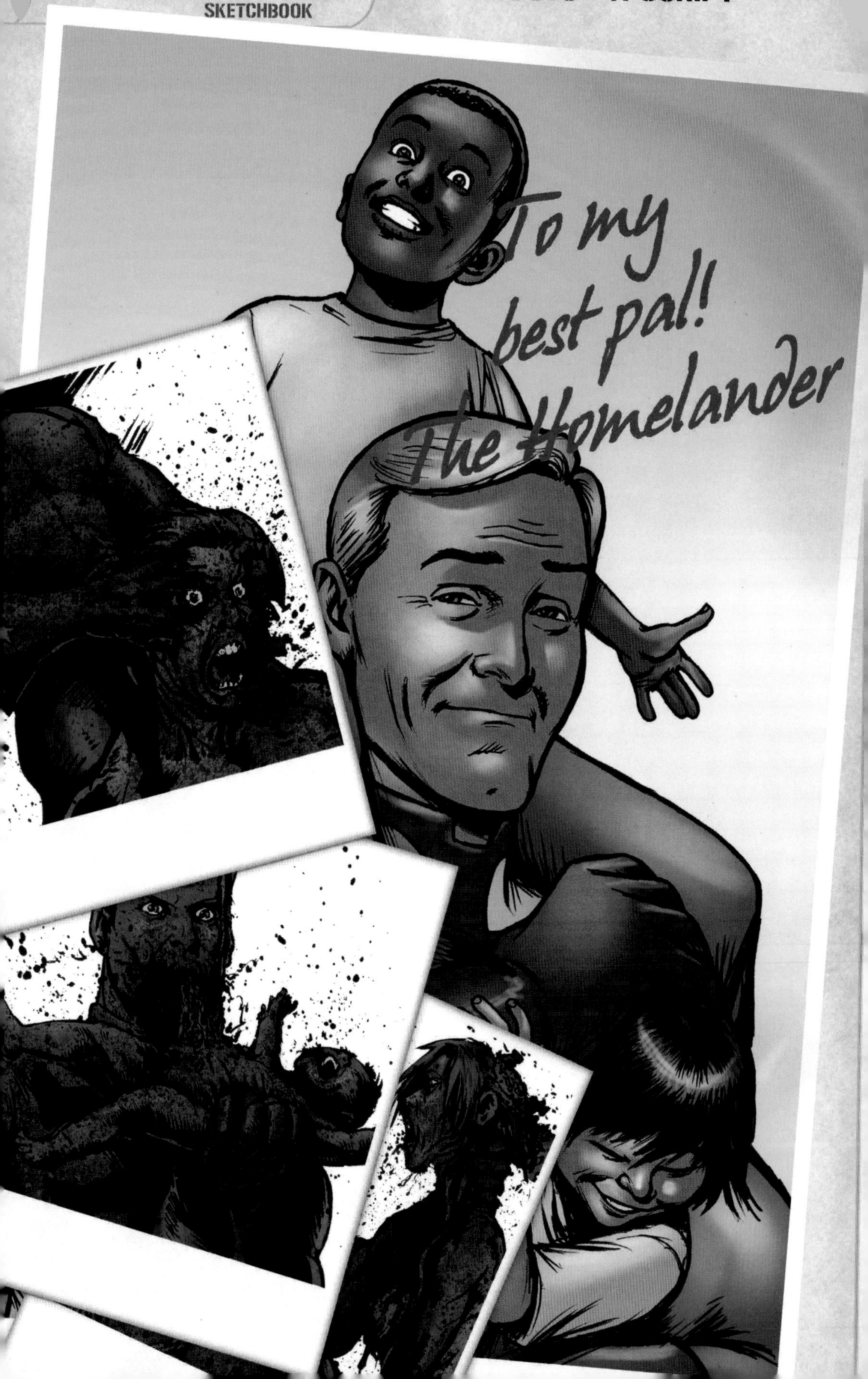
To my
best pal!
The Homelander

JOHN McCREA
SKETCHBOOK

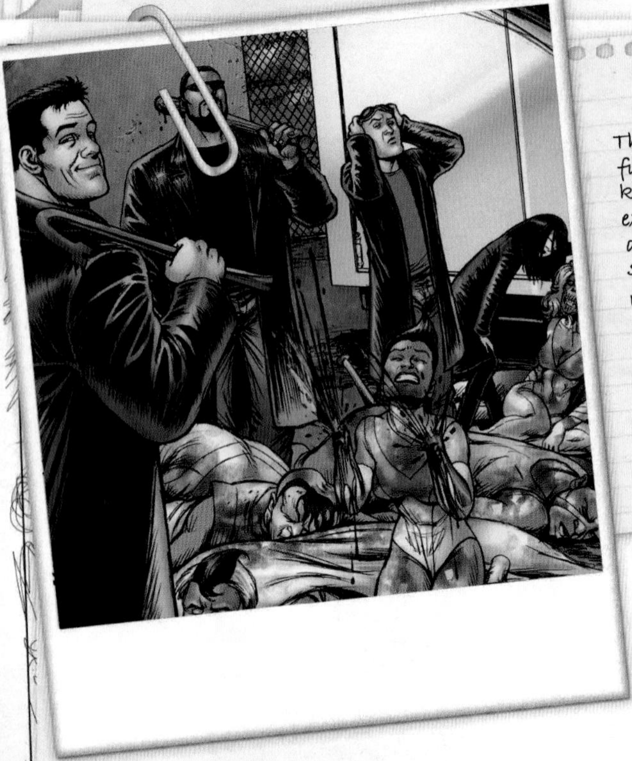

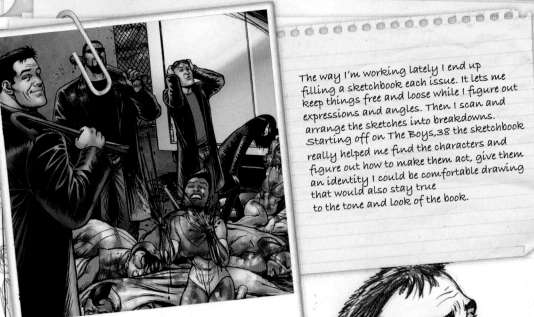

The way I'm working lately I end up filling a sketchbook each issue. It lets me keep things free and loose while I figure out expressions and angles. Then I scan and arrange the sketches into breakdowns. Starting off on The Boys,38 the sketchbook really helped me find the characters and figure out how to make them act, give them an identity I could be comfortable drawing that would also stay true to the tone and look of the book.

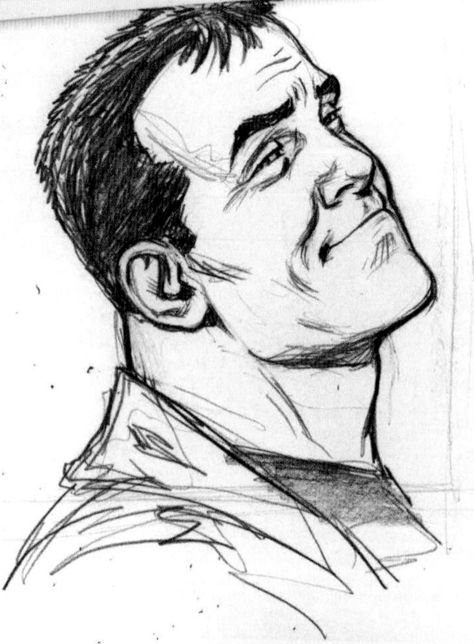

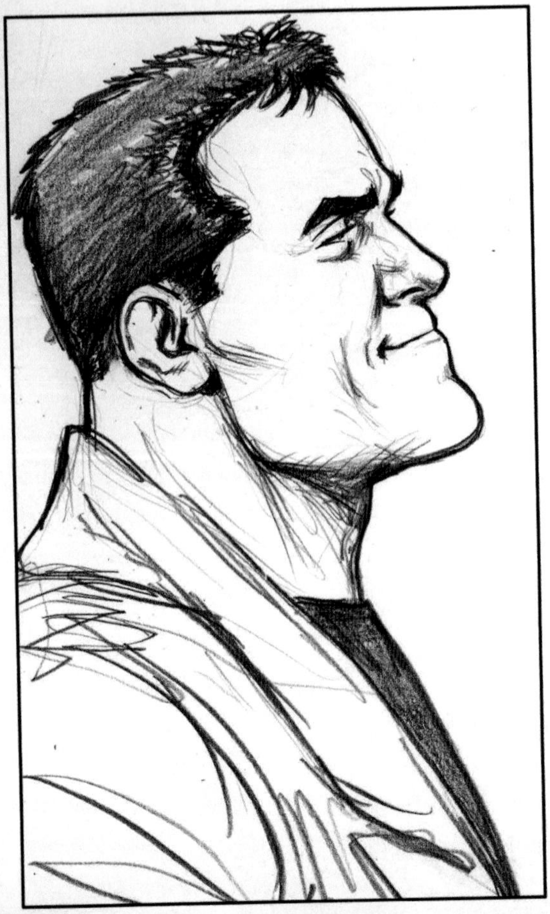

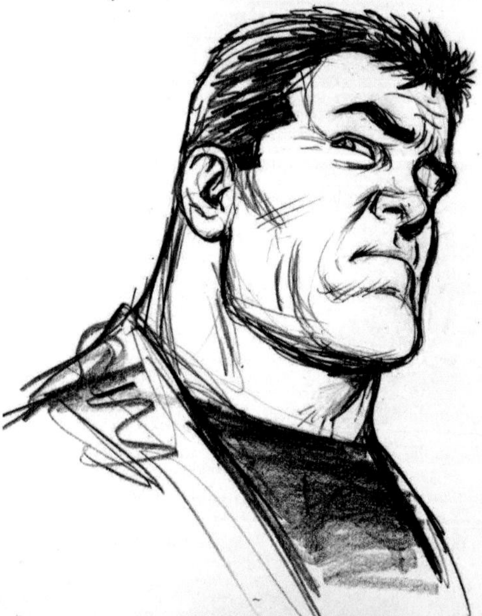

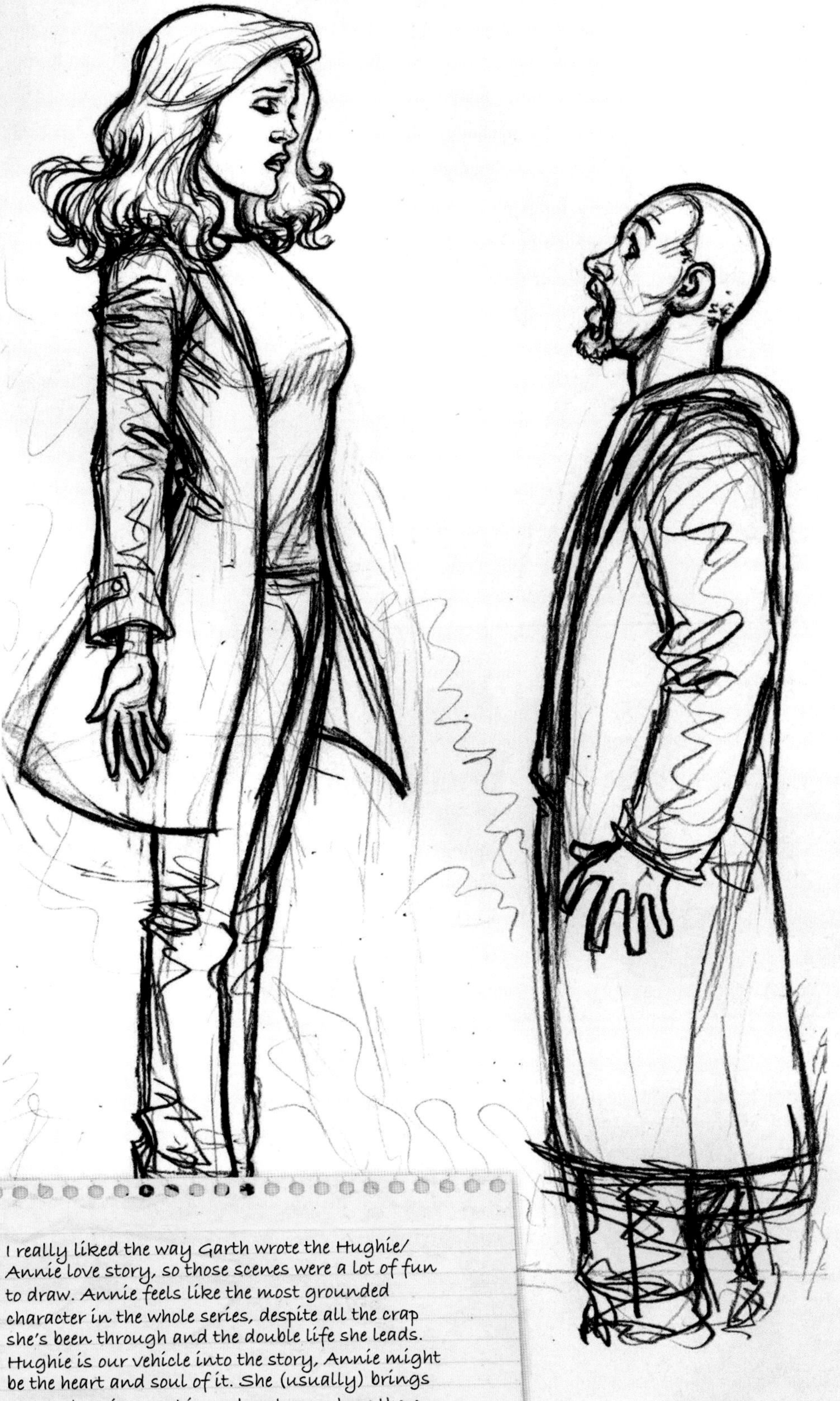

I really liked the way Garth wrote the Hughie/Annie love story, so those scenes were a lot of fun to draw. Annie feels like the most grounded character in the whole series, despite all the crap she's been through and the double life she leads. Hughie is our vehicle into the story, Annie might be the heart and soul of it. She (usually) brings out the best in Hughie and makes us hope there can be a happily ever after in a Garth Ennis story...

JOHN McCREA
SKETCHBOOK

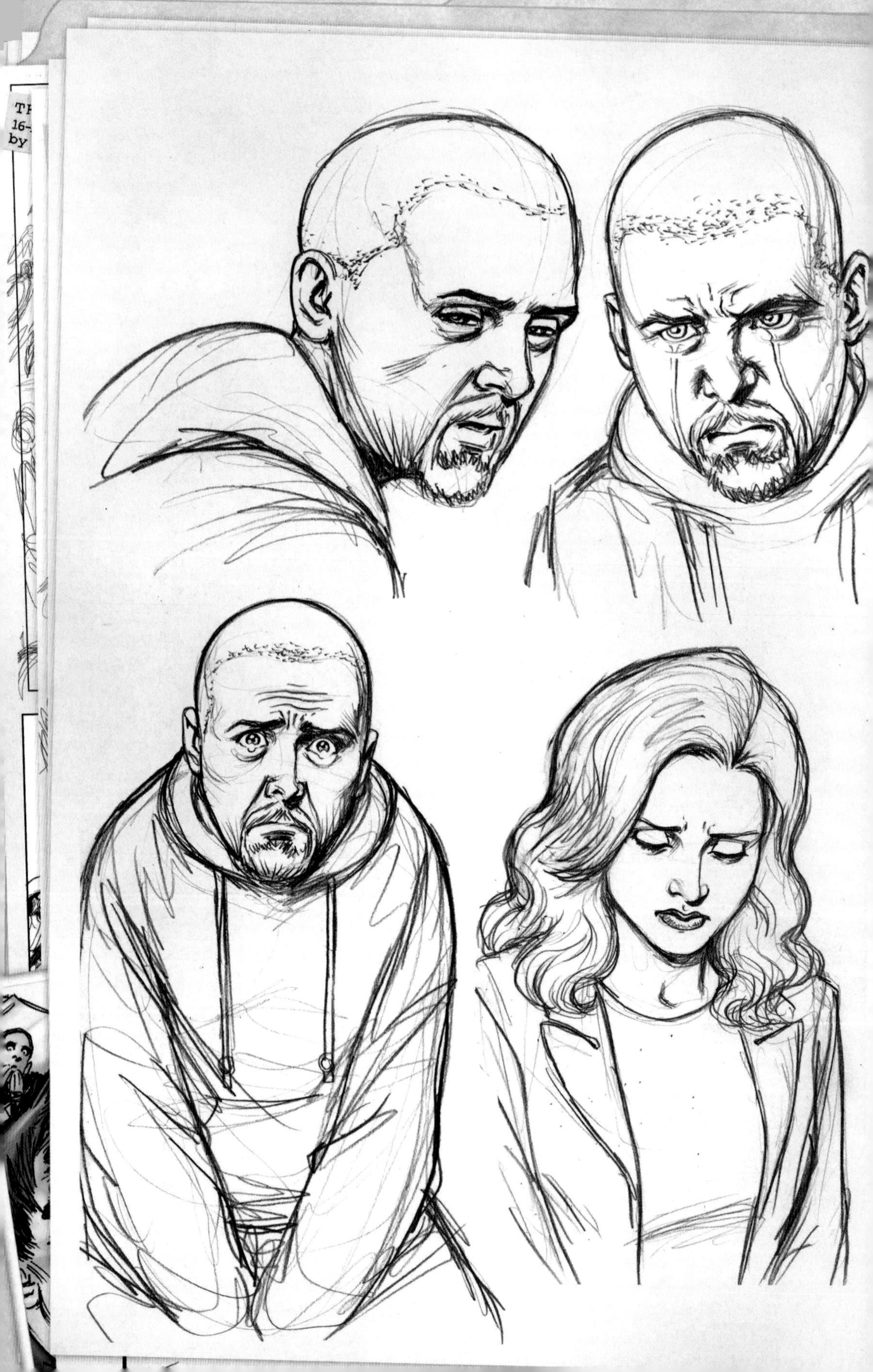

You'd think Hughie would be the easiest character to draw, having an obvious reference in real life and all, but... not so much. Got to walk a tightrope with Hughie, too much reference can stiffen things up. If one guy on the page looks photo realistic everyone else has to live up to that, live in that same world. So I started out using ref until I got the hang of the character and then I just started making Hughie up same as everybody else. Look in the mirror, make faces, try to get the acting right and make the characters tell the story.

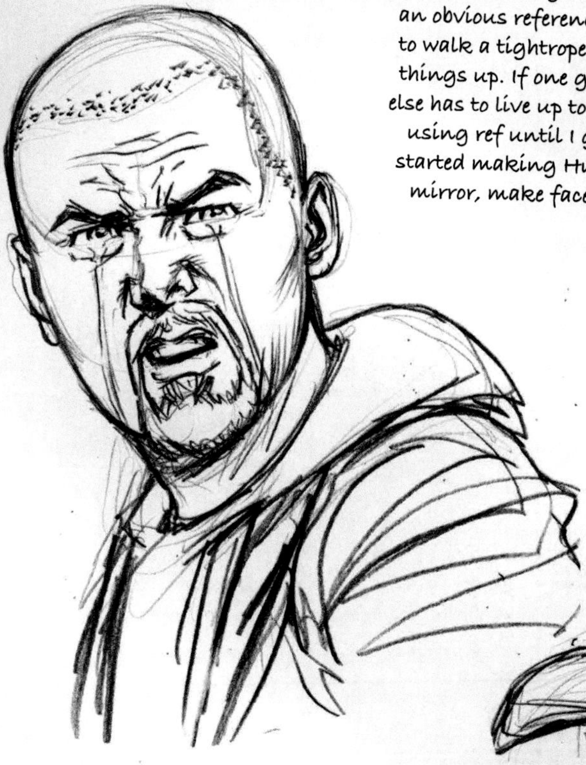

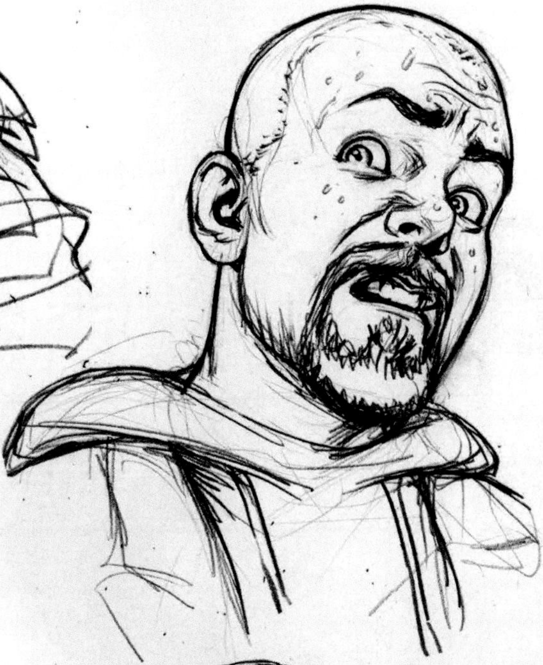

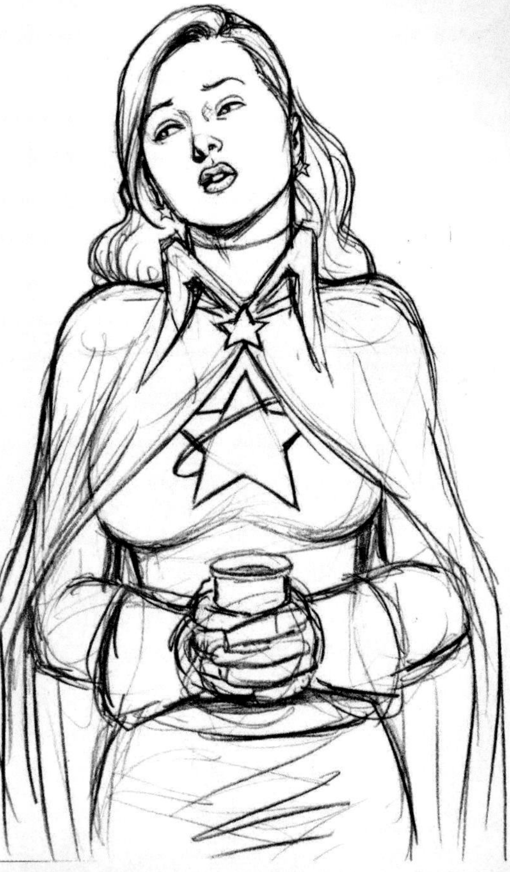

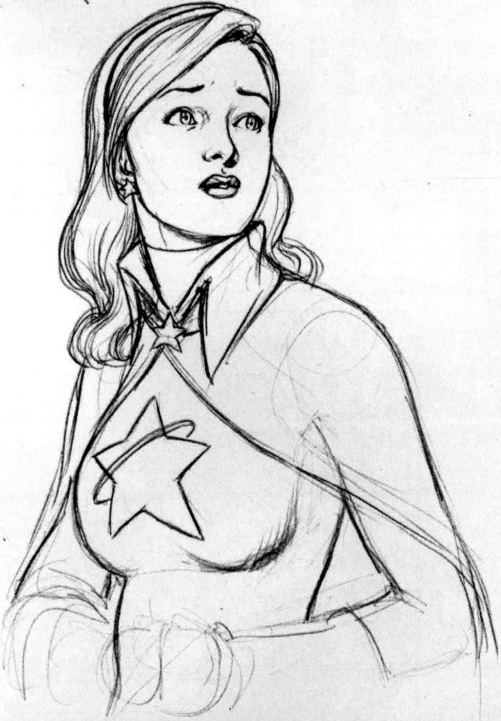

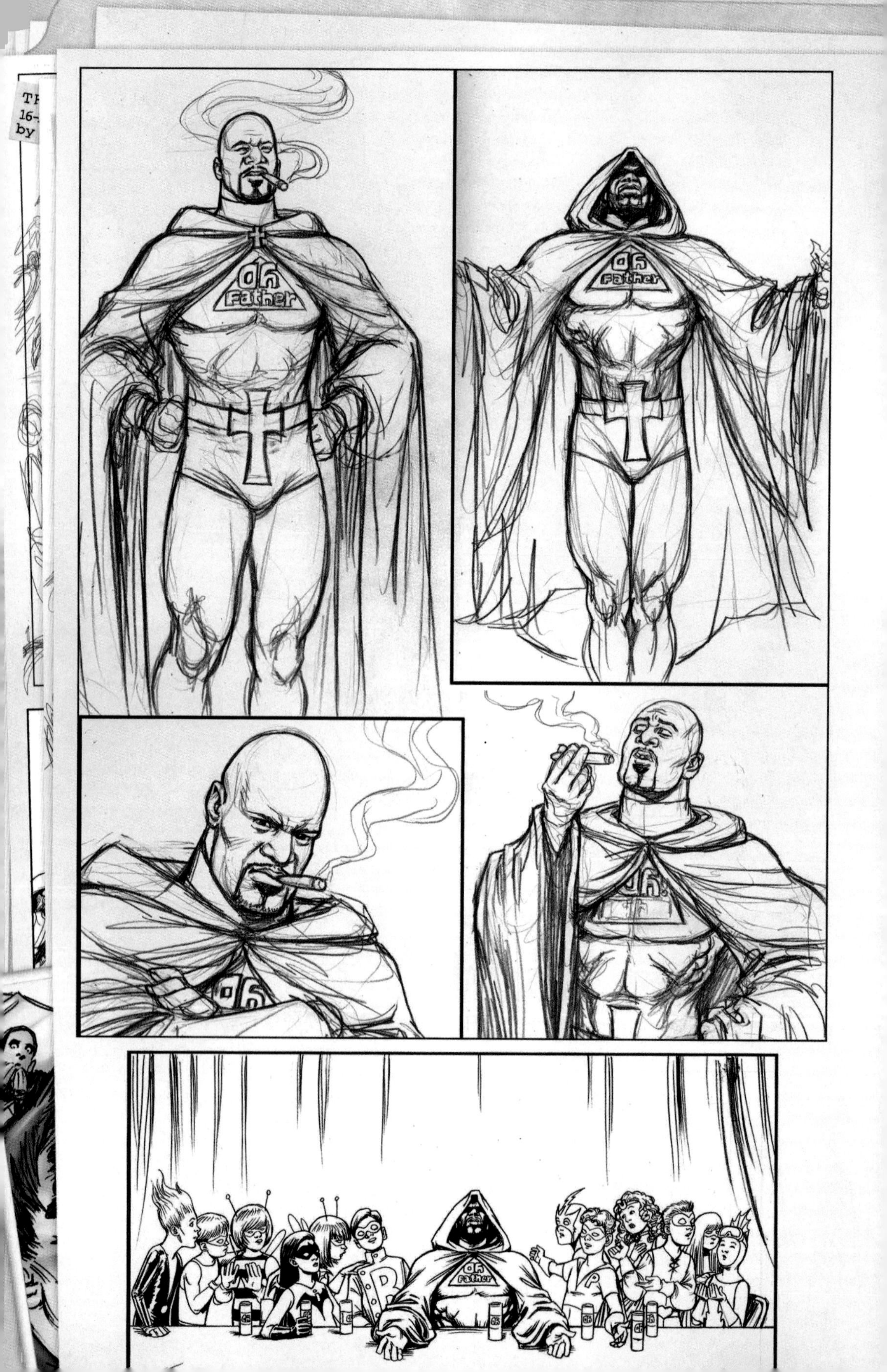

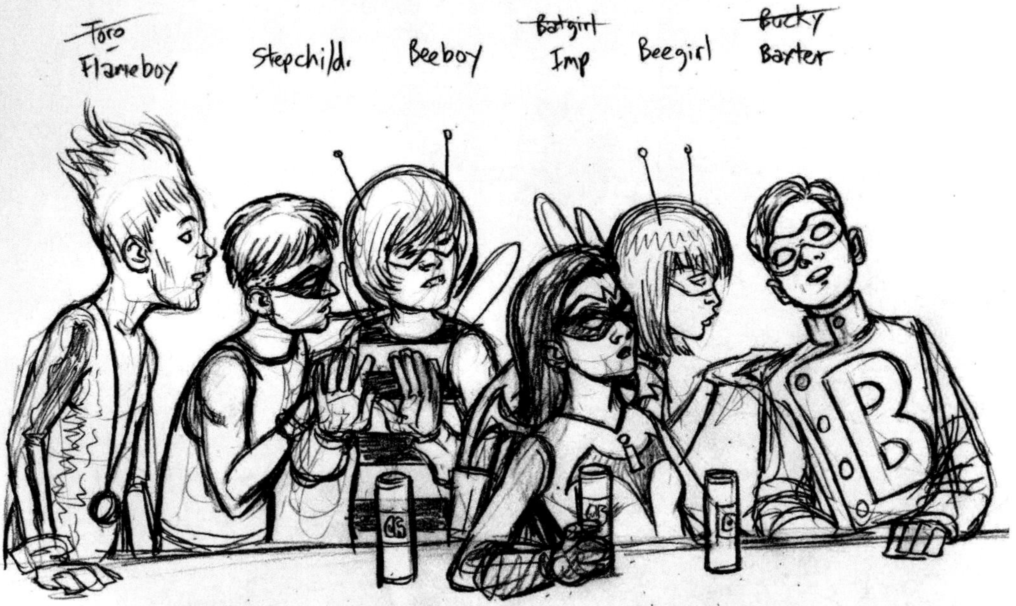
~~Toro~~ Flameboy
Stepchild.
Beeboy
~~Batgirl~~ Imp
Beegirl
~~Bucky~~ Barter

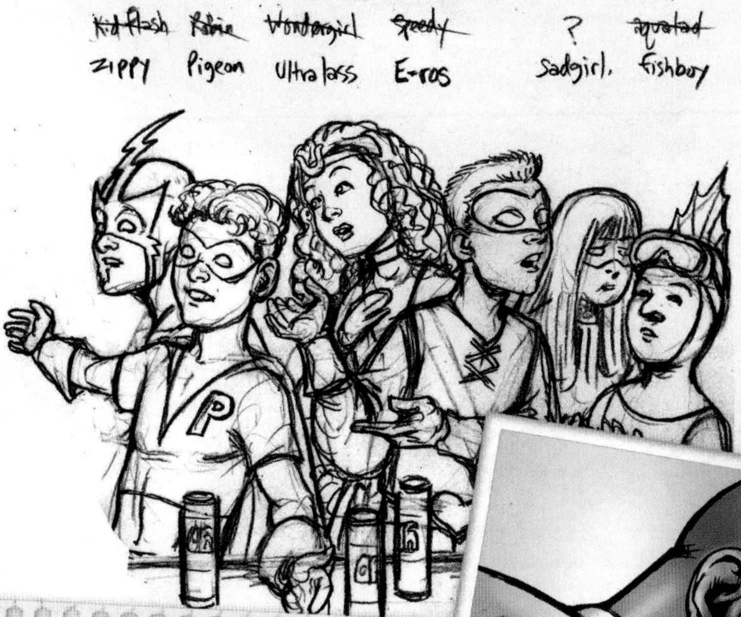
~~Kid Flash~~ ZIPPY
~~Robin~~ Pigeon
~~Wondergirl~~ Ultralass
~~Speedy~~ E-ros
? Sadgirl.
~~aqualad~~ fishboy

Oh Father and Sidekick Twelve were great. Posing them ala Da Vinci was a challenge, but good fun. Got to make the kids up from scratch, just based on whatever various teen sidekicks were out there. Sidekick Twelve don't really have official, individual names, I just made them up for myself. And yes, Stepchild is in there because I couldn't think of any other superkids and thought we could use a real whipping boy with no powers, as in "beat like a redheaded..." Couldn't call him Rented Mule.

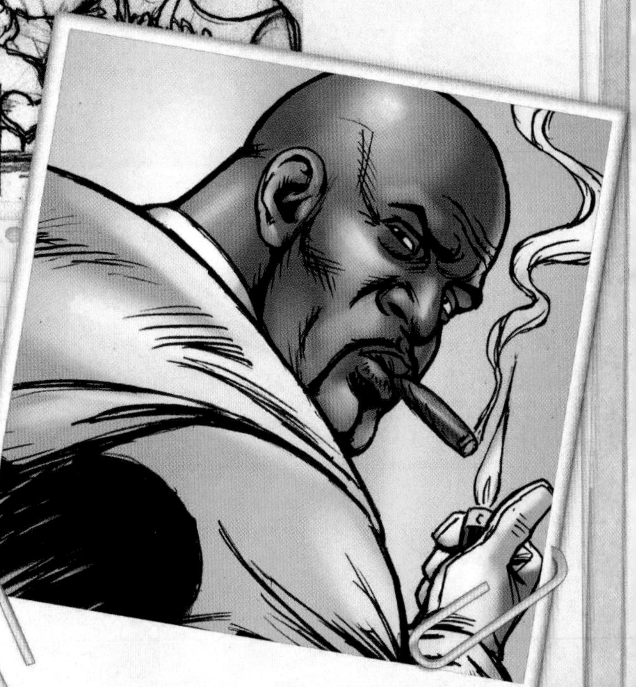

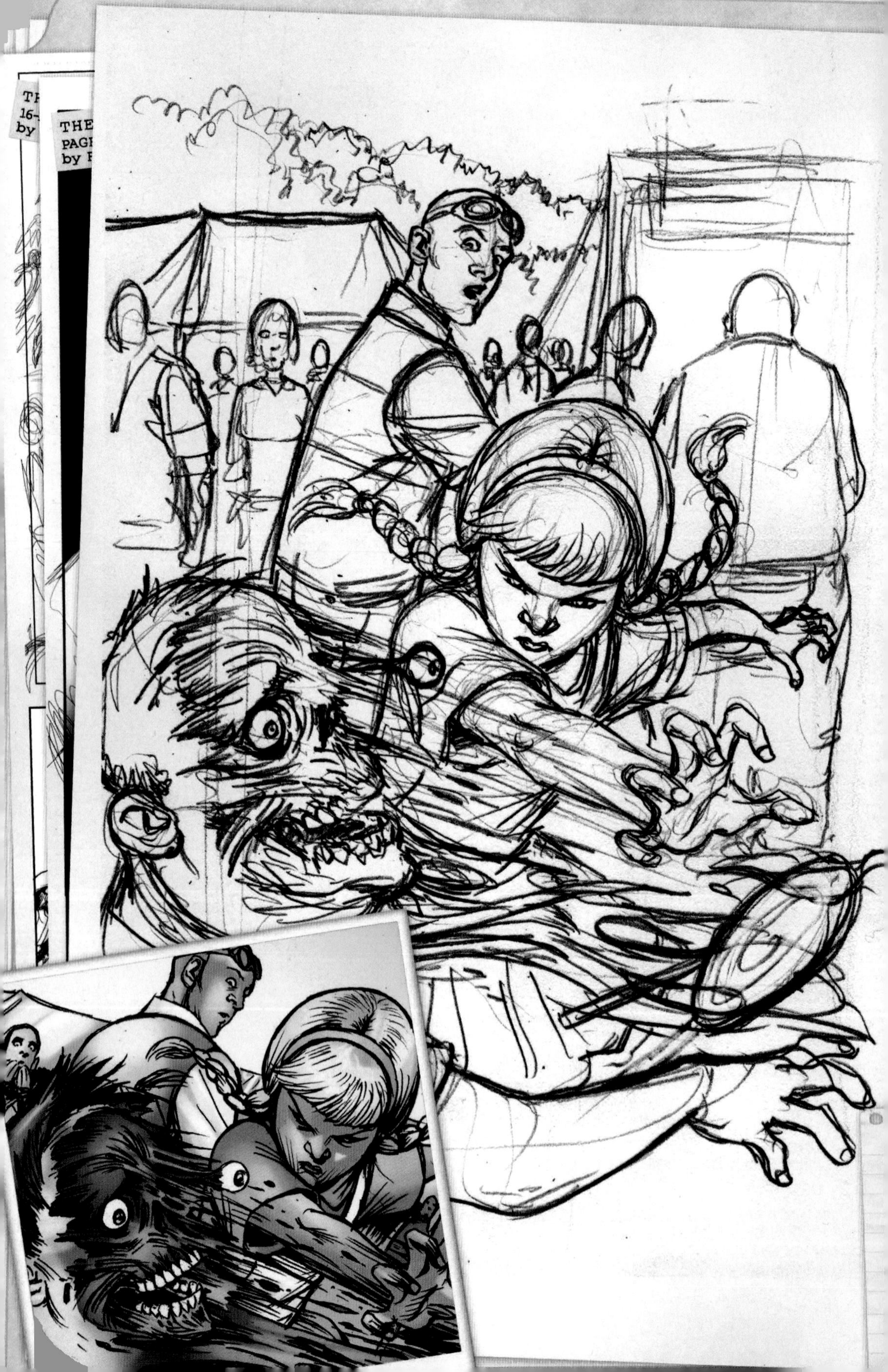

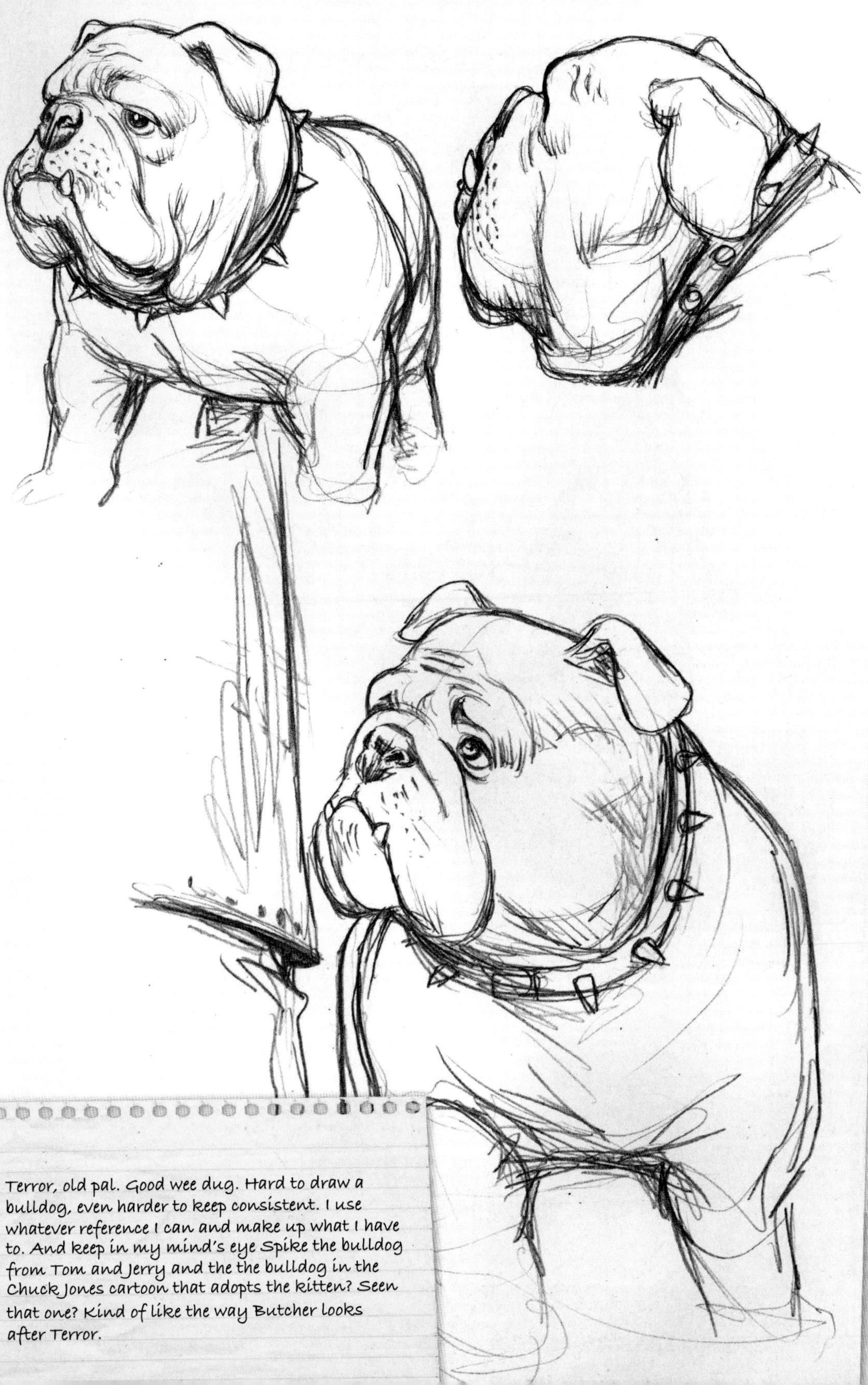

Terror, old pal. Good wee dug. Hard to draw a bulldog, even harder to keep consistent. I use whatever reference I can and make up what I have to. And keep in my mind's eye Spike the bulldog from Tom and Jerry and the the bulldog in the Chuck Jones cartoon that adopts the kitten? Seen that one? Kind of like the way Butcher looks after Terror.

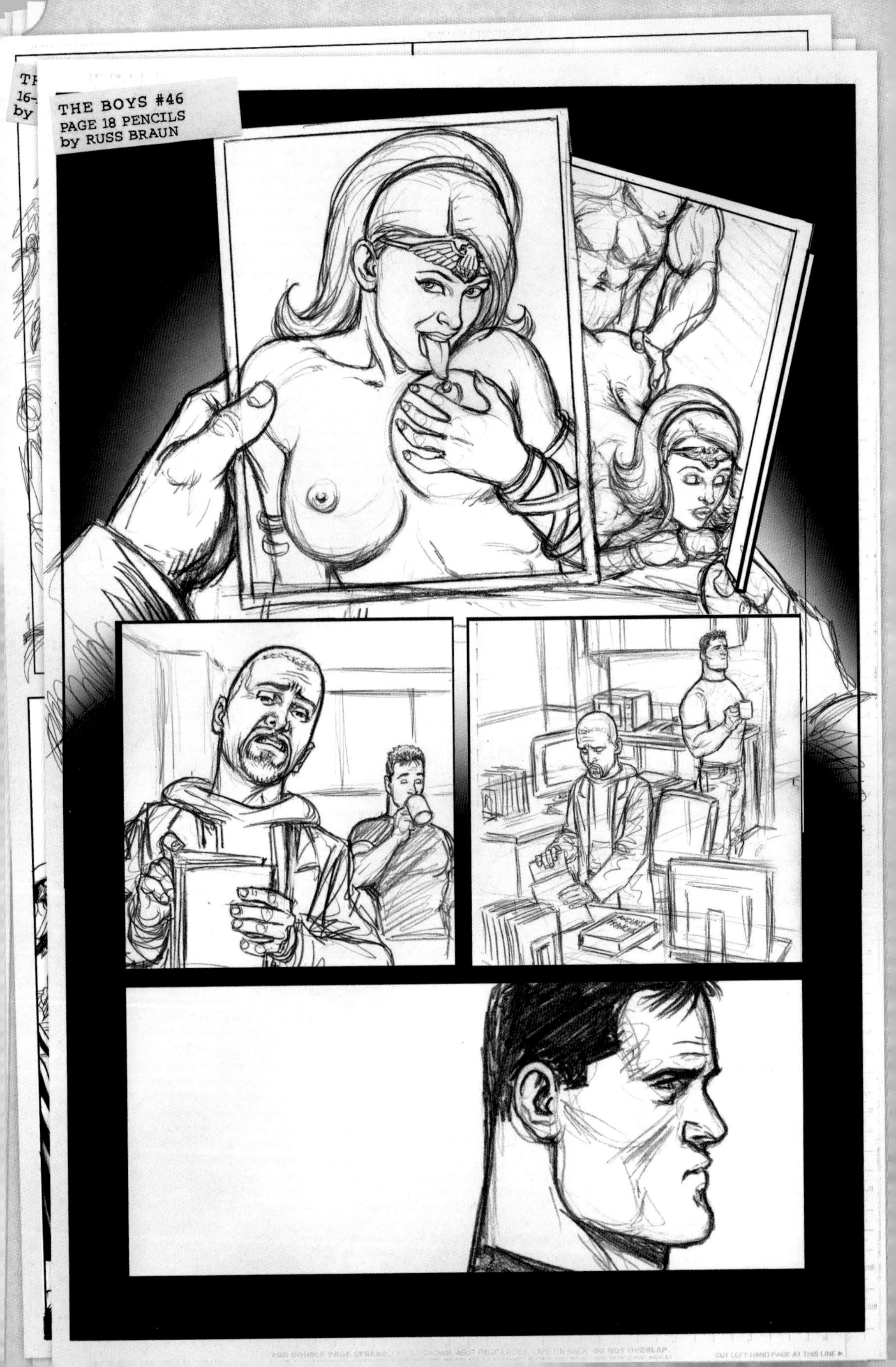

THE BOYS #46
PAGE 18 PENCILS
by RUSS BRAUN

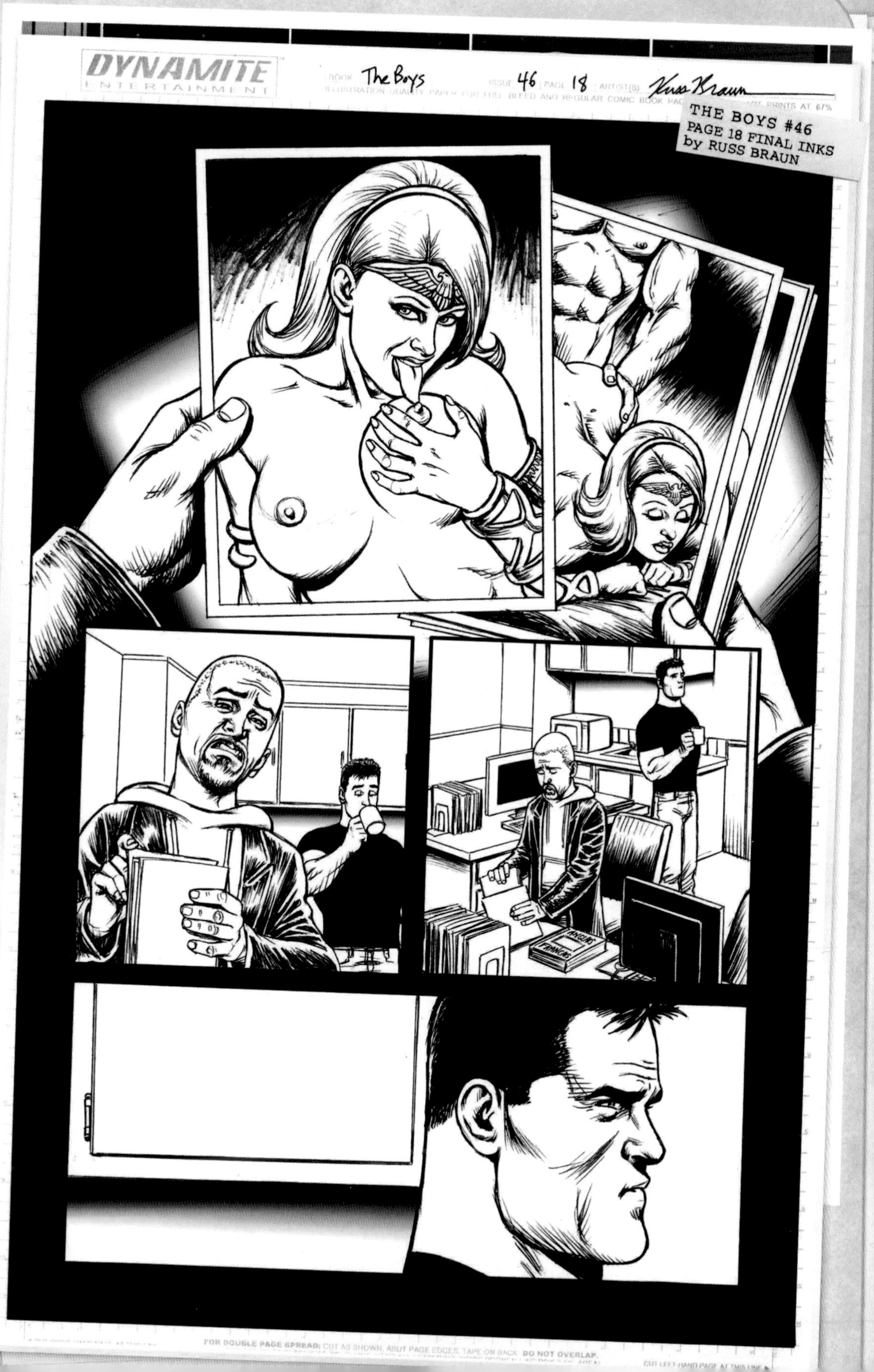
DYNAMITE ENTERTAINMENT
BOOK The Boys ISSUE 46 PAGE 18 ARTIST(S) Russ Braun
THE BOYS #46
PAGE 18 FINAL INKS
by RUSS BRAUN
FOR DOUBLE PAGE SPREAD: CUT AS SHOWN. ABUT PAGE EDGES. TAPE ON BACK. DO NOT OVERLAP.

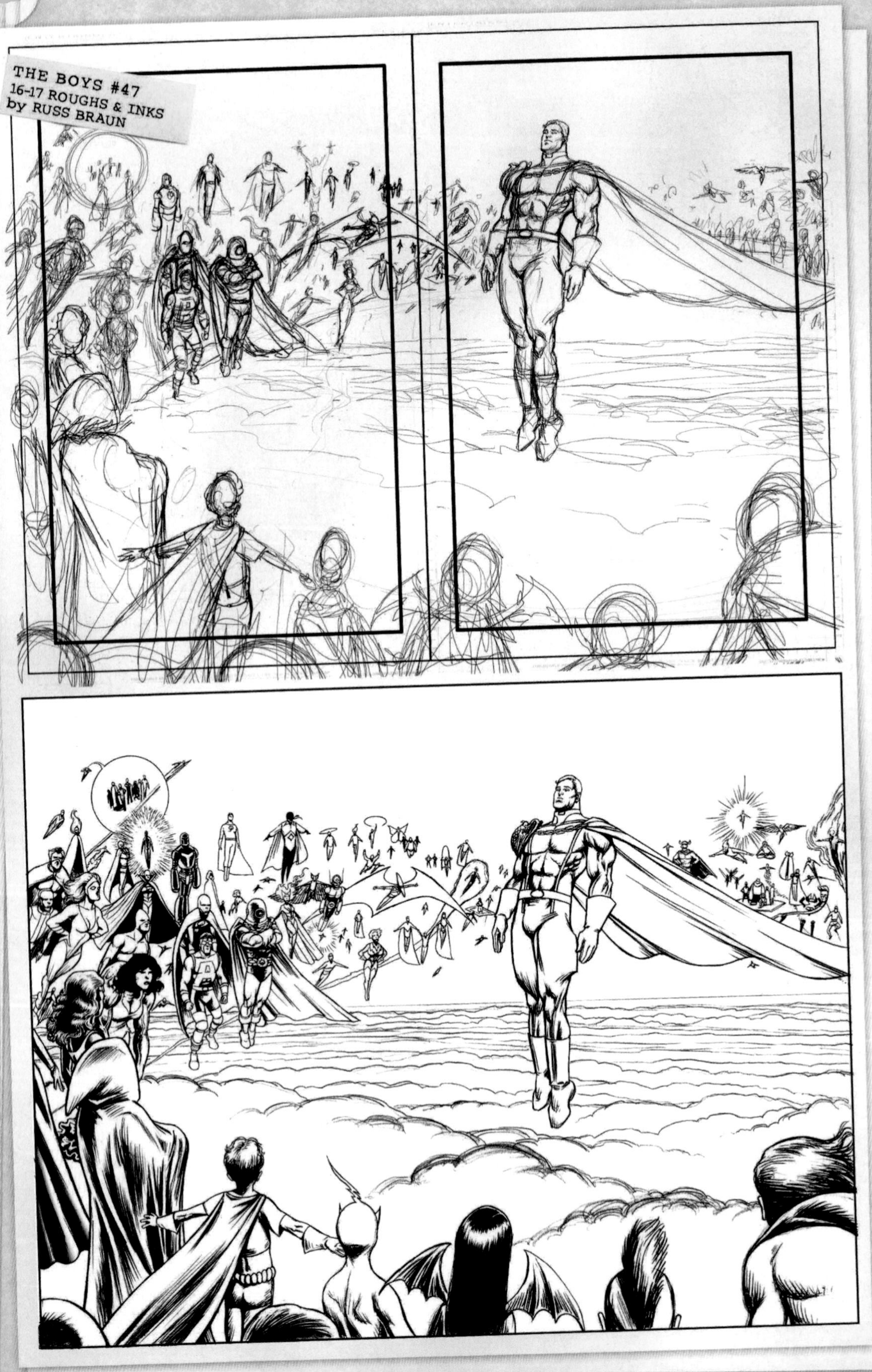
THE BOYS #47
16-17 ROUGHS & INKS
by RUSS BRAUN

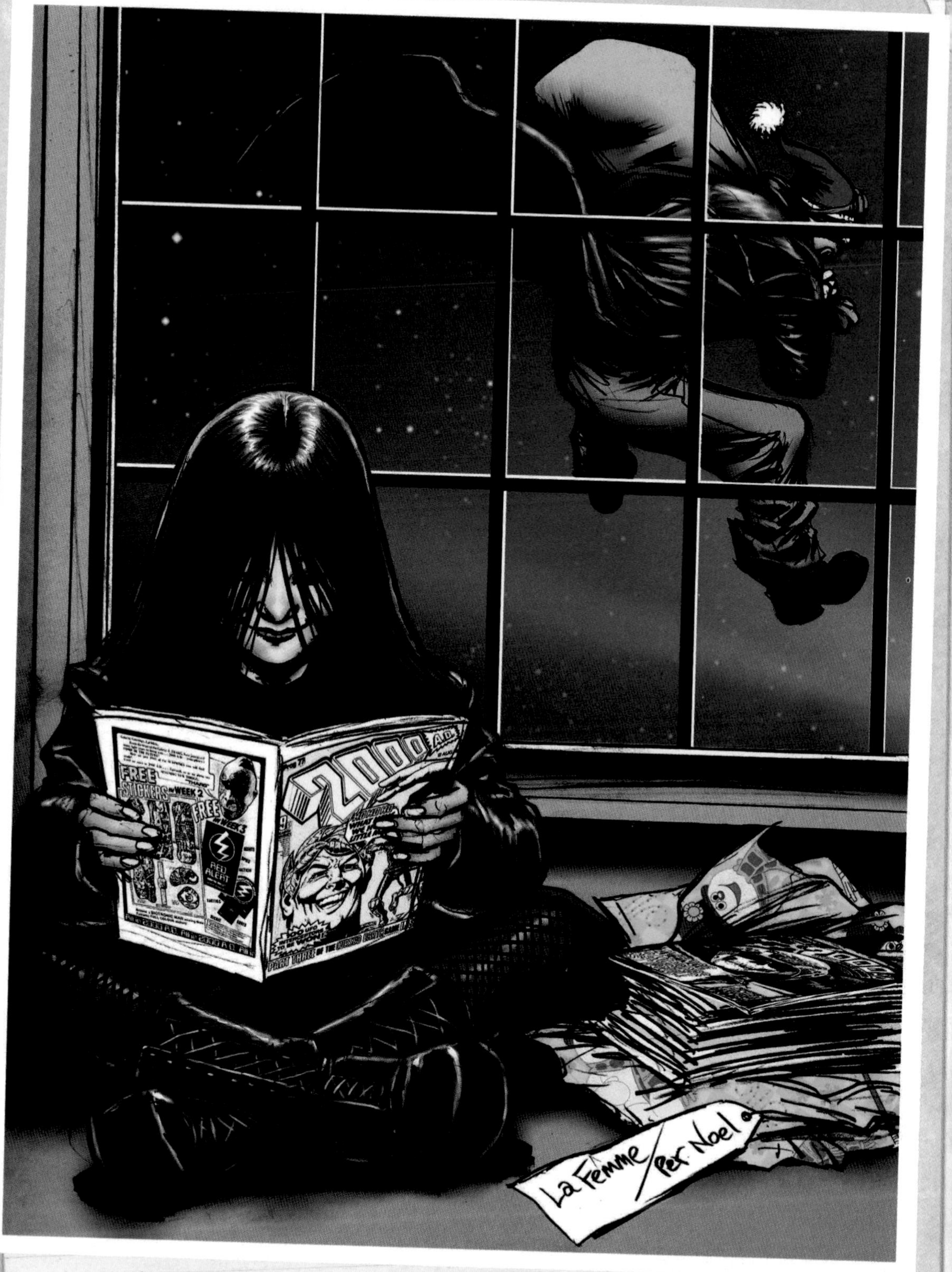
FREE STICKERS
2000 AD
RED ALERT
La Femme
Per Noel

Every year I try to come up with a Christmas card based on whatever book I'm working on. I've done Son of Satan as Son of Santa, even had the Night Witches flying their PO-2 next to Santa's sleigh. The Boys and Christmas are not a natural fit. But then I remembered the scene where Frenchie gave the Female a huge box of 2000ADs, combined that with a scene of him jumping out of the Flatiron Building in a Santa hat and... Voila! My favorite characters in the series. Got to love the crazy, touching relationship they have, adorable little psychopaths.

JOHN McCREA
SKETCHBOOK

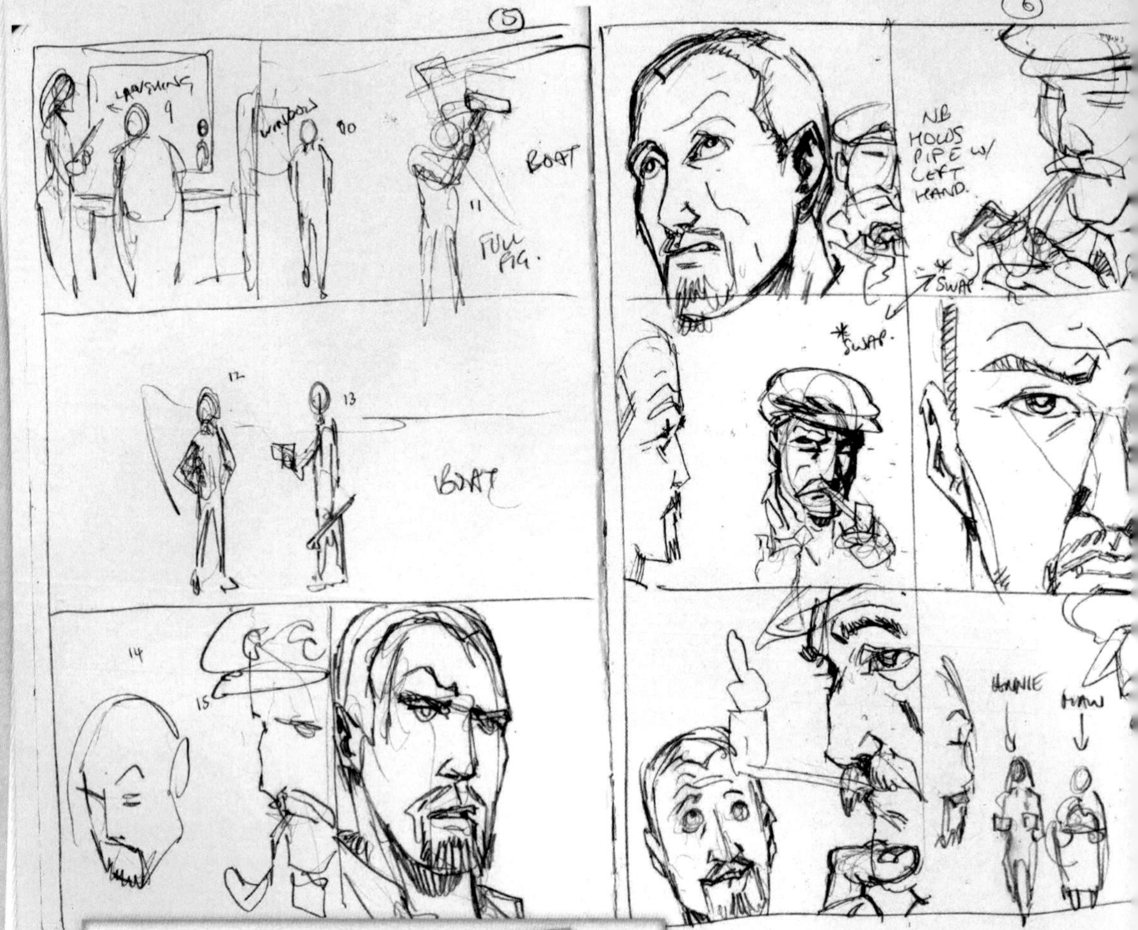

5
BOAT
FULL FIG.
BOAT
6
NB HOLDS PIPE W/ LEFT HAND.
SWAP
SWAP

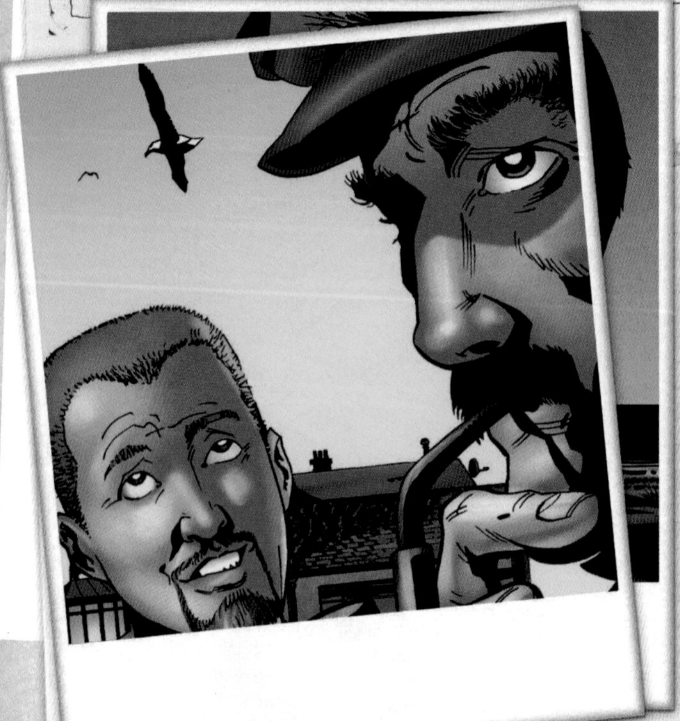

A couple of my thumbnails from my sketchbook-this is done to get an idea of pacing, placing the figures for word balloon flow and other arcane secrets privy only to the mind of the artist....

And opposite is the first finished page with Det (the smelly one)- Keith and I thought a good way to show how smelly he was would be to draw flies around him, but Garth nixed it- "Don't be a fuckin' cunt, McCrea. How many smelly bastards have you met that actually had flies buzzin' around them? You wanker."

But Keith and I put a lot of effort into those flies, so here they are in all their glory...

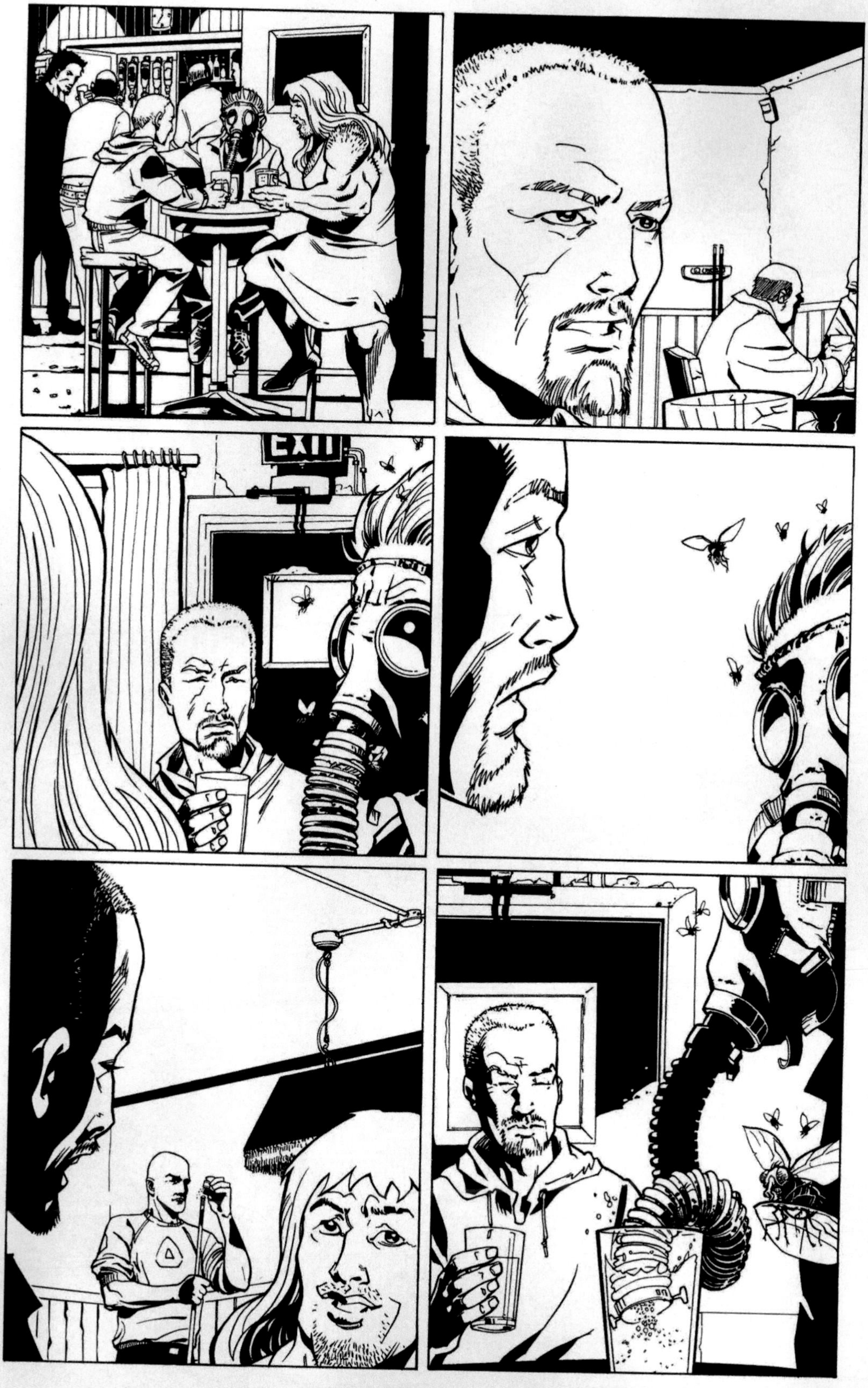
EXIT

This is a print Keith and I did to promote our working on the Boys-
obviously it hasn't been seen much outside the UK as we both hate travel.
This shows the stages the piece went through, from my demented first
scribblings to Keith's masterful colours-

bon voyage!

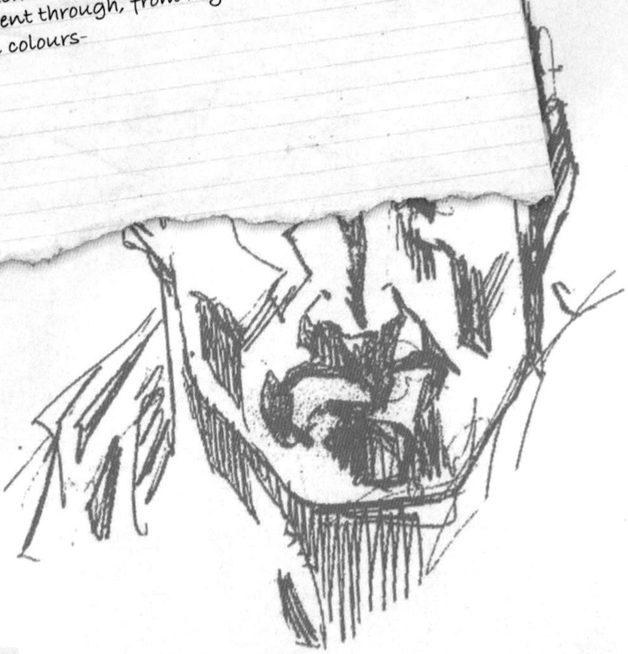

ROUGH PENCILS

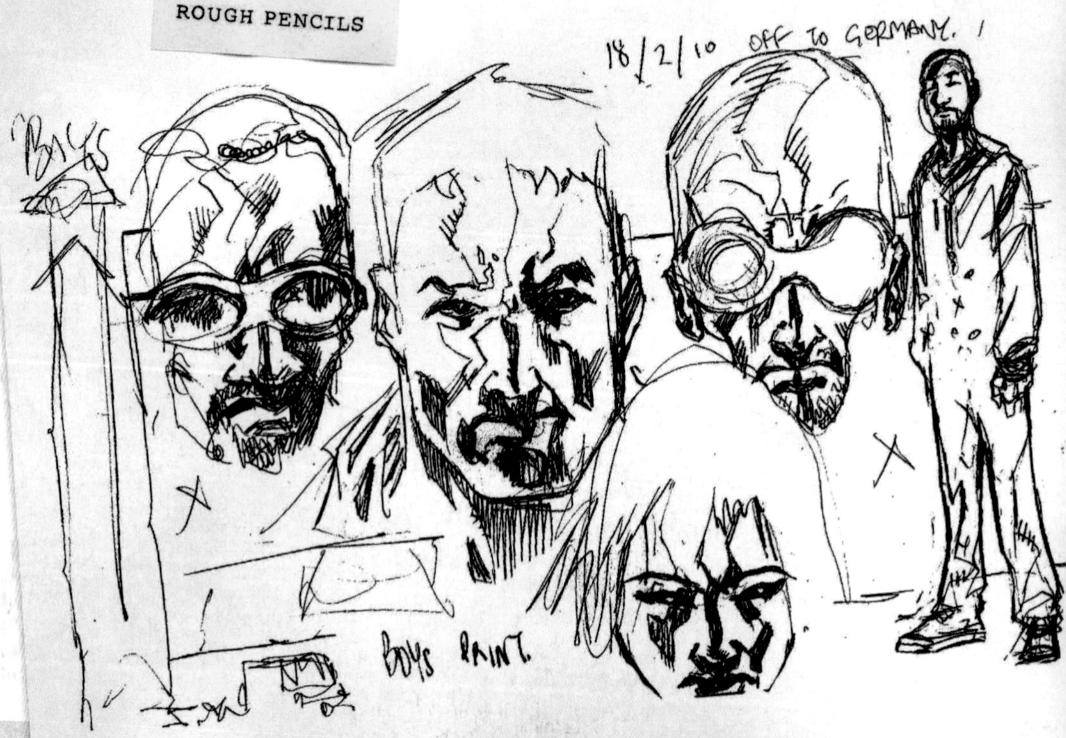
18/2/10 OFF TO GERMANY. !
BOYS
BOYS PRINT.

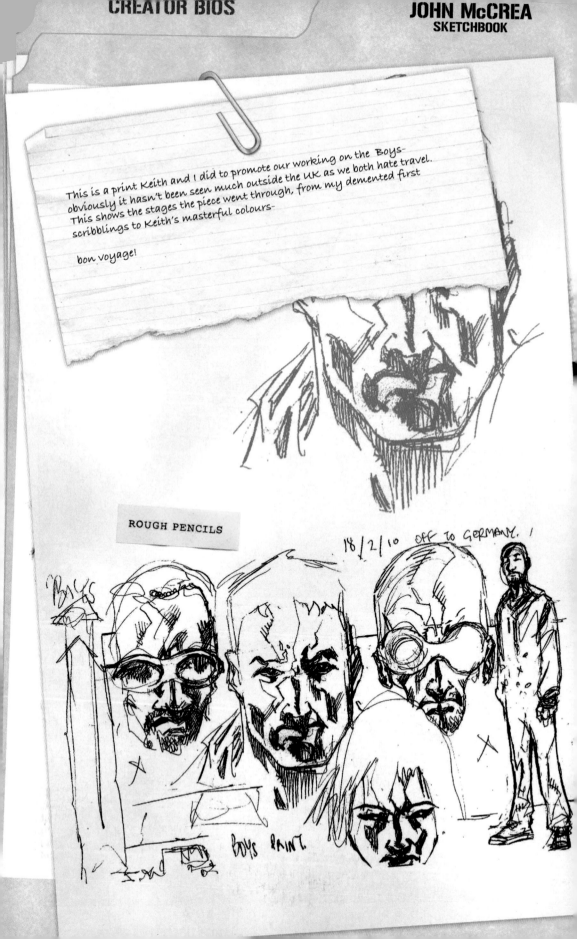

FINISHED PENCILS

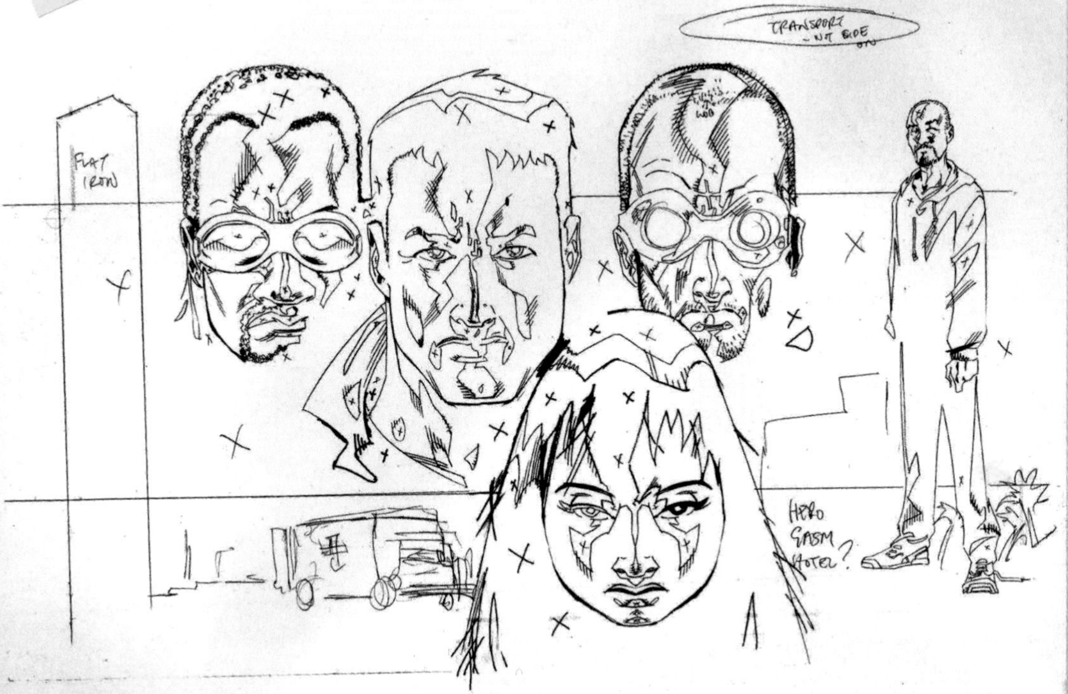
TRANSPORT - NOT RIDE
FLAT IRON
HERO GASM HOTEL?

FINISHED INKS

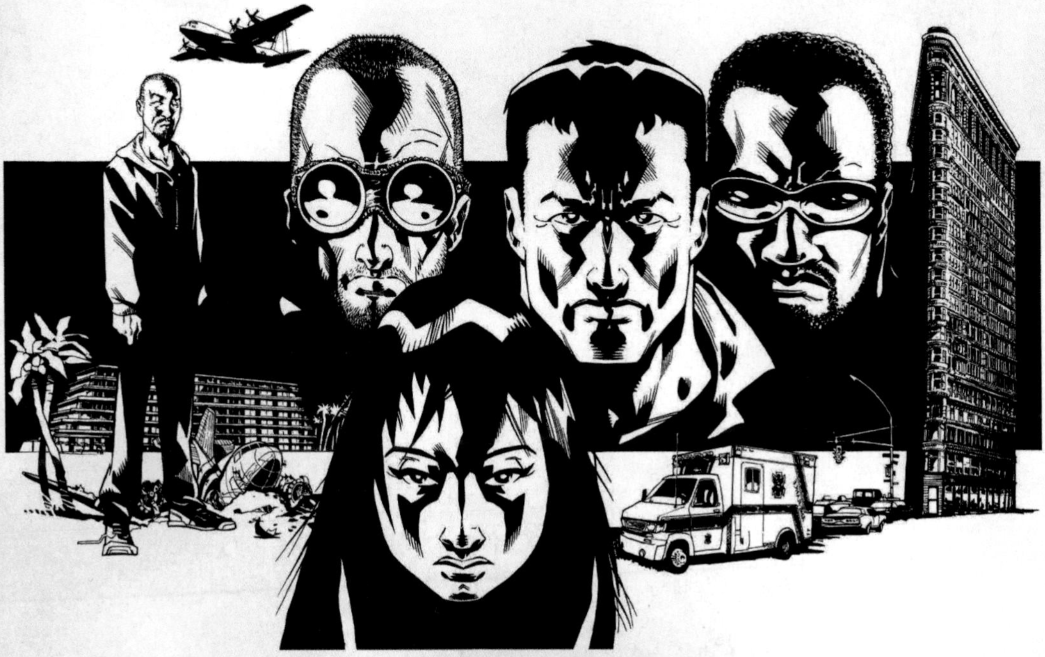

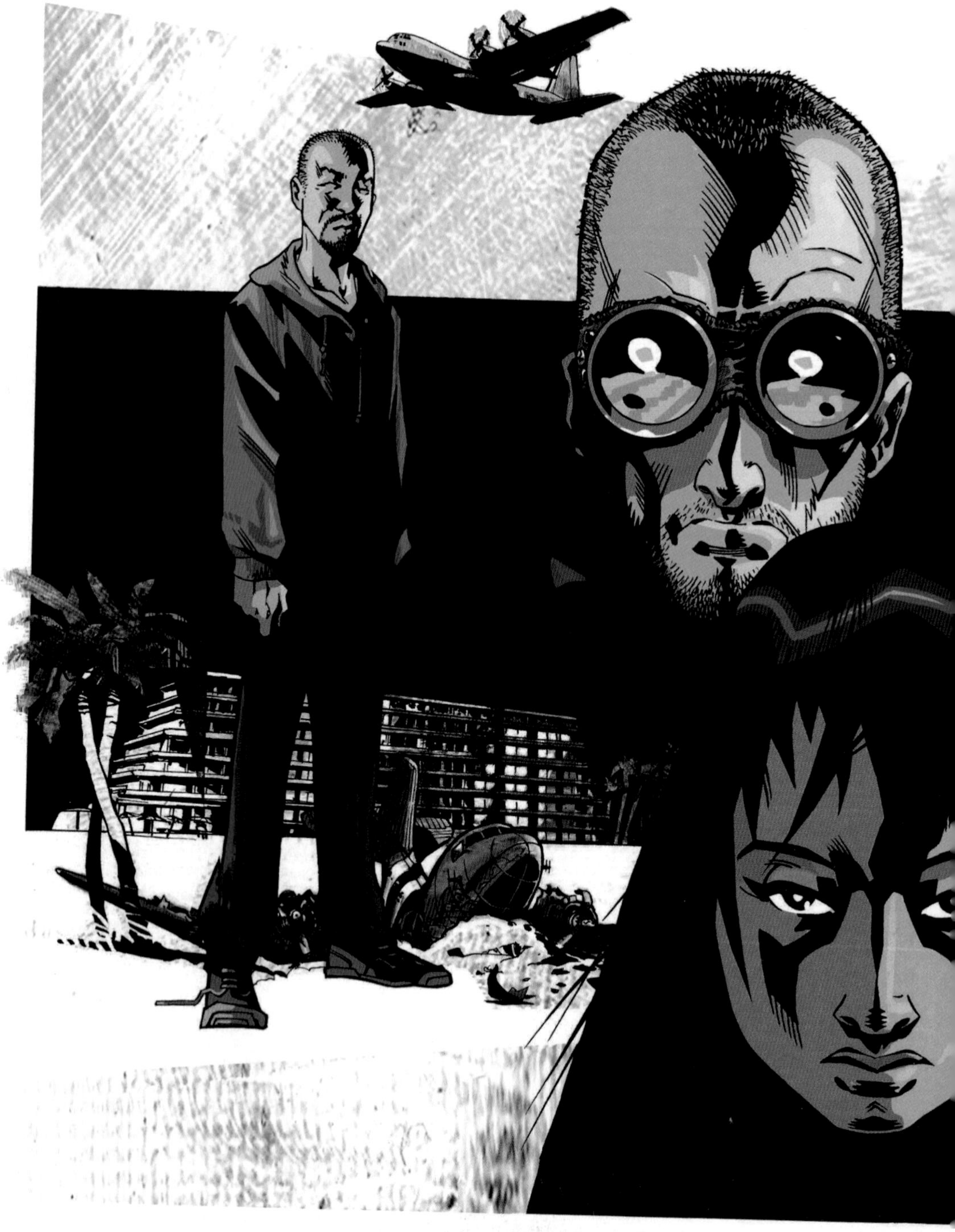

FINAL COLORED
PIECE

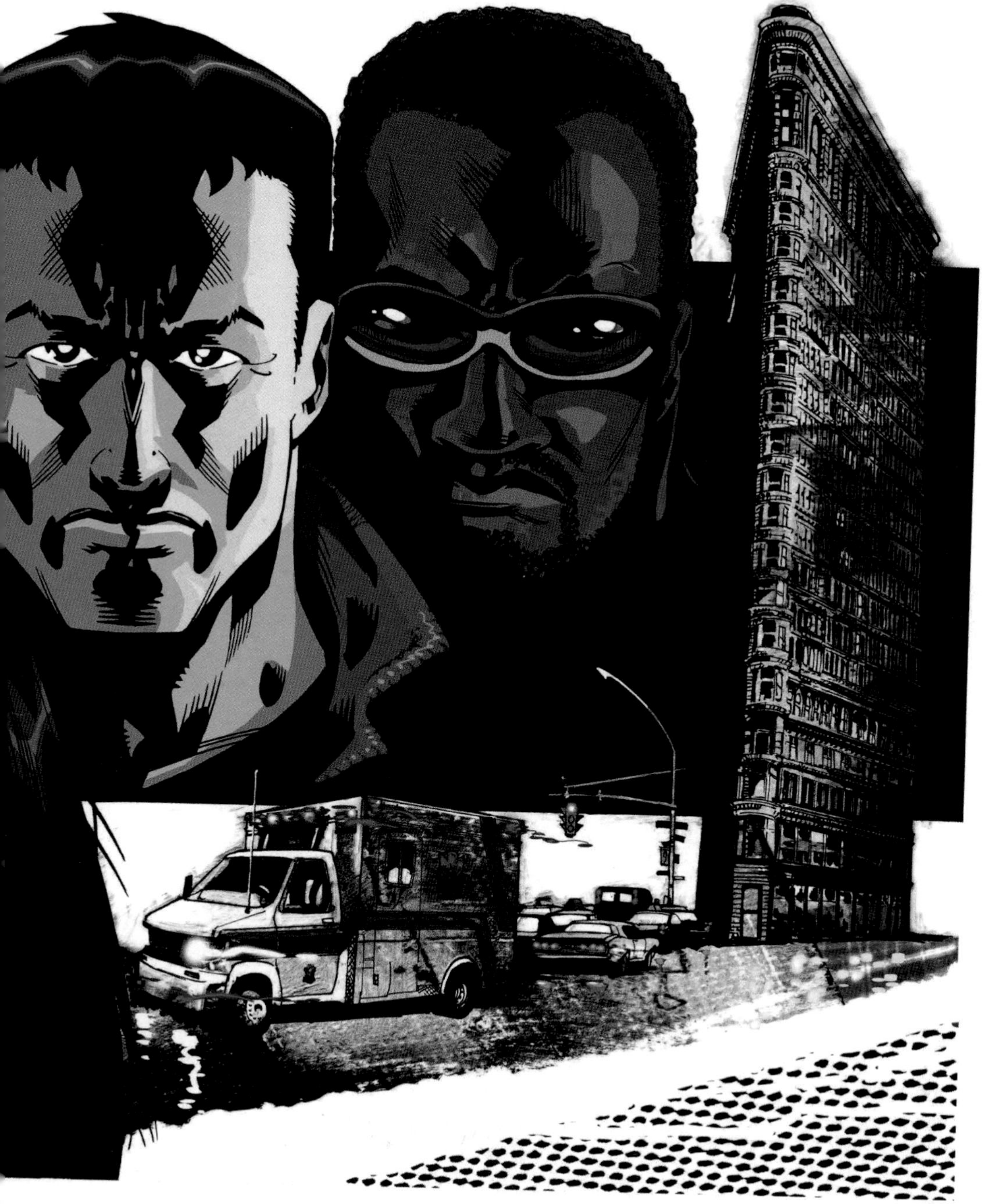

GARTH ENNIS

Garth Ennis has been writing comics since 1989. Credits include *Preacher*, *Hitman*, *Crossed*, *Rover Red Charlie*, *Code Pru*, *Caliban*, *War Stories*, *A Walk Through Hell* and *Sara*, and successful runs on *The Punisher* and *Fury* for Marvel Comics. Originally from Northern Ireland, Ennis now resides in New York City with his wife, Ruth.

DARICK ROBERTSON

Darick Robertson is an American comic book artist, writer and creator with a decades long career in the industry. Born and raised in the Northern California Bay Area and self trained as an artist, his notable works include co-creating the award winning *Transmetropolitan*, *The Boys*, *Happy!*, and *Oliver* with Gary Whitta for Image Comics, debuting in January 2019. Darick has illustrated for both Marvel and DC Comics on characters including Batman, The Justice League, Wolverine, The Punisher, and Spider-man.

JOHN McCREA

Artist John McCrea was born in Belfast, and has worked extensively in the British and American comic book industries. He previously worked with writer Garth Ennis on *Troubled Souls*, *For a Few Troubles More*, *Judge Dredd*, *The Demon*, *Hitman*, *Dicks*, *Chopper,* and *All Star Section Eight*. He can be found online at www.johnmccrea.com

KEITH BURNS

Keith Burns has drawn the war comics *Castles in the Sky* and *Out of the Blue*, as well as the successful revival of classic British character *Johnny Red*. He is a member of the Guild of Aviation Artists. Originally from Dublin, Ireland, Burns now resides in England.

RUSS BRAUN

New York native Russ Braun has been drawing comics for twenty-five years, with time out for a seven year stint at Disney Feature Animation. Mostly working for DC/Vertigo on everything from *Batman: Venom* to *Jack of Fables*, he also worked on *Hellstorm: Son of Satan* for Marvel Max, *Jimmy's Bastards* for Aftershock, *The Boys*, and three series of *Battlefields* with Garth Ennis for Dynamite.

TONY AVIÑA

Tony Aviña got his start as an in-house colorist at WIldwtorm. His credits include *Sleeper*, *Storm-watch: Team Achilles*, *Authority: Prime*, *Battlefields*, *The Boys*, *Sherlock Holmes*, *Green Lantern*, *Justice League*, *Batman '66*, *Wonder Woman '77*, and *Suicide Squad: Hell to Pay*. He currently lives in St. Louis, which, contrary to popular belief, isn't one big farm (it's actually three or four moderately sized farms).

SIMON BOWLAND

Simon Bowland has been lettering comics since 2004, and in that time has worked for all of the mainstream publishers. Born and bred in the UK, Simon still lives there today alongside Pippa, his partner, and Jess, their tabby cat.

COLLECT THE COMPLETE SERIES!

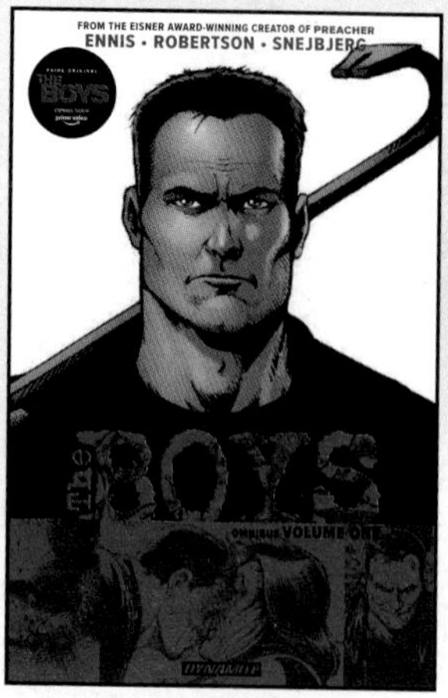
FROM THE EISNER AWARD-WINNING CREATOR OF PREACHER
ENNIS • ROBERTSON • SNEJBJERG
THE BOYS
OMNIBUS VOLUME ONE

THE BOYS
OMNIBUS VOL. 1 TP
978-1-5241-0859-5
Ennis, Robertson,
Snejbjerg

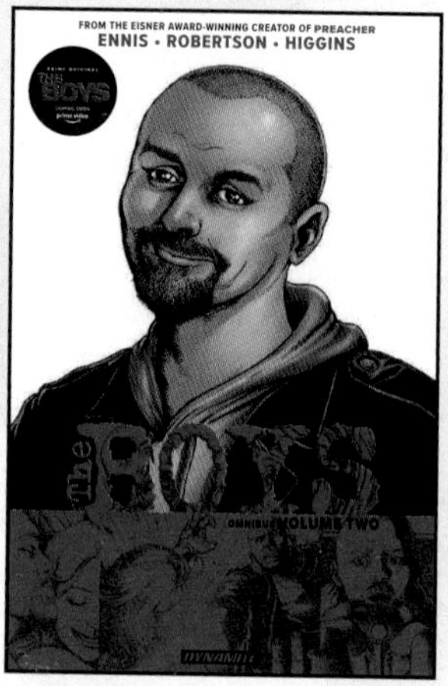
FROM THE EISNER AWARD-WINNING CREATOR OF PREACHER
ENNIS • ROBERTSON • HIGGINS
THE BOYS
OMNIBUS VOLUME TWO

THE BOYS
OMNIBUS VOL. 2 TP
978-1-5241-0970-7
Ennis, Robertson,
Higgins

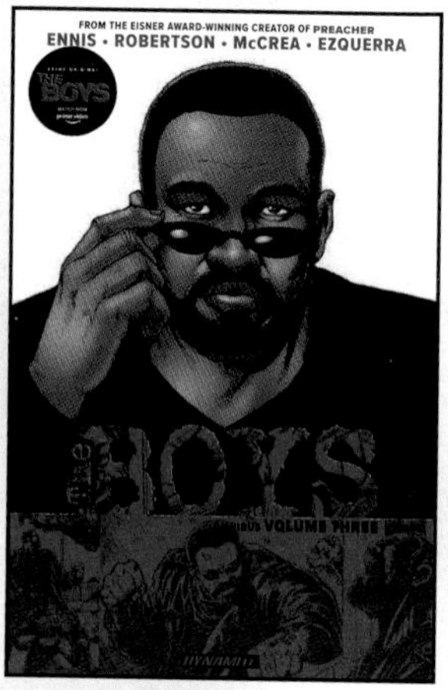
FROM THE EISNER AWARD-WINNING CREATOR OF PREACHER
ENNIS • ROBERTSON • McCREA • EZQUERRA
THE BOYS
OMNIBUS VOLUME THREE

THE BOYS
OMNIBUS VOL. 3 TP
978-1-5241-1003-1
Ennis, Robertson
McCrea, Ezquerra

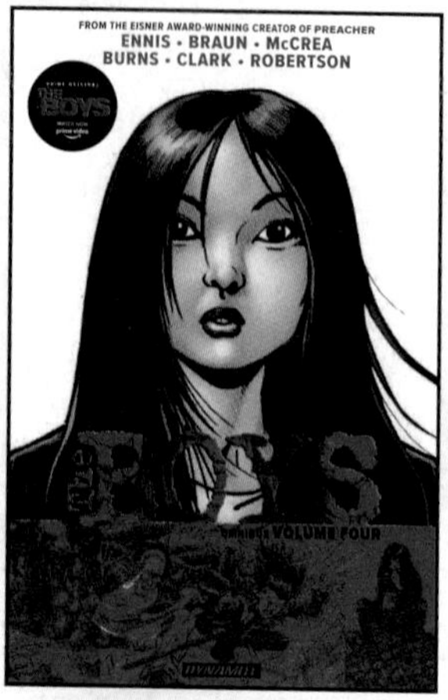
FROM THE EISNER AWARD-WINNING CREATOR OF PREACHER
ENNIS • BRAUN • McCREA
BURNS • CLARK • ROBERTSON
THE BOYS
OMNIBUS VOLUME FOUR

THE BOYS
OMNIBUS VOL. 4 TP
978-1-5241-1140-3
Ennis, Braun, McCrea,
Burns, Clark, Robertson

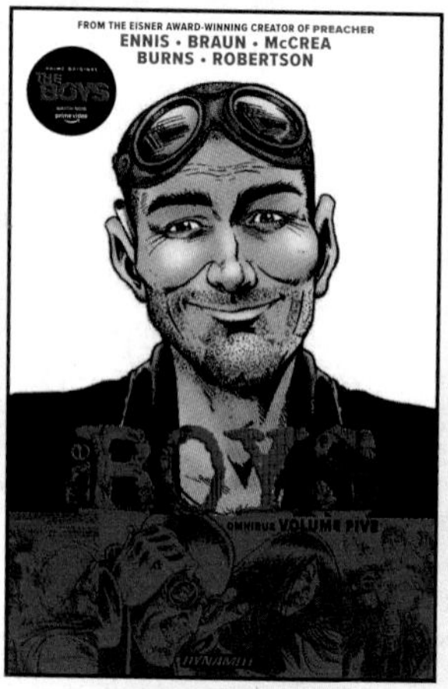
FROM THE EISNER AWARD-WINNING CREATOR OF PREACHER
ENNIS • BRAUN • McCREA
BURNS • ROBERTSON
THE BOYS
OMNIBUS VOLUME FIVE

THE BOYS
OMNIBUS VOL. 5 TP
978-1-5241-1334-6
Ennis. Braun, McCrea,
Burns, Robertson

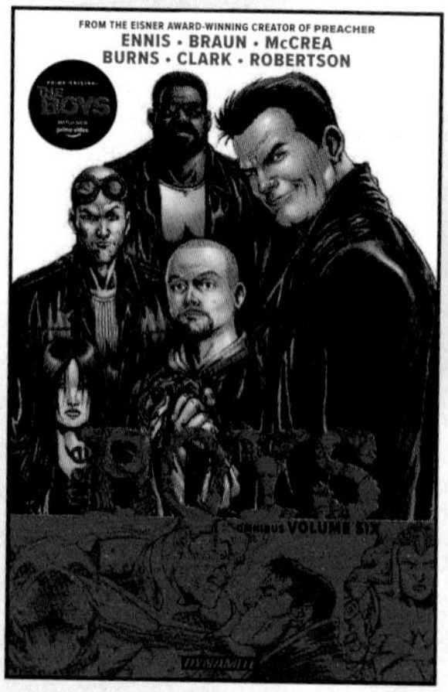
FROM THE EISNER AWARD-WINNING CREATOR OF PREACHER
ENNIS • BRAUN • McCREA
BURNS • CLARK • ROBERTSON
THE BOYS
OMNIBUS VOLUME SIX

THE BOYS
OMNIBUS VOL. 6 TP
978-1-5241-1337-7
Ennis, Braun, McCrea,
Burns, Clark, Robertson

ALSO AVAILABLE FROM GARTH ENNIS & DYNAMITE:

THE COMPLETE BATTLEFIELDS VOL. 1 TP 978-1-60690-0255-4
THE COMPLETE BATTLEFIELDS VOL. 2 TP 978-1-5241-0385-9
THE COMPLETE BATTLEFIELDS VOL. 3 TP 978-1-5241-0474-0

RED TEAM VOL. 1 TP 978-1-6069-0443-5
RED TEAM VOL. 2: DOUBLE TAP, CENTER MASS TP 978-1-5241-0395-8

A TRAIN CALLED LOVE TP 978-1-5241-0168-8
JENNIFER BLOOD VOL. 1: A WOMEN'S WORK IS NEVER DONE TP 978-1-6069-0261-5

VISIT WWW.DYNAMITE.COM FOR A FULL LIST!